T0397159

THE CAMBRIDGE COMPANION TO ROMAN COMEDY

EDITED BY

Martin T. Dinter

King's College London

CAMBRIDGE
UNIVERSITY PRESS

University Printing House, Cambridge CB2 8BS, United Kingdom

One Liberty Plaza, 20th Floor, New York, NY 10006, USA

477 Williamstown Road, Port Melbourne, VIC 3207, Australia

314–321, 3rd Floor, Plot 3, Splendor Forum, Jasola District Centre,
New Delhi – 110025, India

79 Anson Road, #06–04/06, Singapore 079906

Cambridge University Press is part of the University of Cambridge.

It furthers the University's mission by disseminating knowledge in the pursuit of
education, learning, and research at the highest international levels of excellence.

www.cambridge.org
Information on this title: www.cambridge.org/9781107002104
DOI: 10.1017/9780511740466

© Cambridge University Press 2019

This publication is in copyright. Subject to statutory exception
and to the provisions of relevant collective licensing agreements,
no reproduction of any part may take place without the written
permission of Cambridge University Press.

First published 2019

Printed in the United Kingdom by TJ International Ltd. Padstow Cornwall

A catalogue record for this publication is available from the British Library.

Library of Congress Cataloging-in-Publication Data
NAMES: Dinter, Martin T., editor.
TITLE: The Cambridge companion to Roman comedy / edited by Martin T. Dinter.
OTHER TITLES: Cambridge companions to literature.
DESCRIPTION: Cambridge : Cambridge University Press, 2019. | Series: Cambridge companions to literature
IDENTIFIERS: LCCN 2018029897 | ISBN 9781107002104
SUBJECTS: LCSH: Latin drama (Comedy) – History and criticism.
CLASSIFICATION: LCC PA6069 .C25 2019 | DDC 872/.0109–dc23
LC record available at https://lccn.loc.gov/2019029897

ISBN 978-1-107-00210-4 Hardback
ISBN 978-0-521-17388-9 Paperback

Cambridge University Press has no responsibility for the persistence or accuracy of
URLs for external or third-party internet websites referred to in this publication
and does not guarantee that any content on such websites is, or will remain,
accurate or appropriate.

To the memory of
Elaine Fantham
and
Robert Germany

CONTENTS

CONTENTS

ILLUSTRATIONS

CONTRIBUTORS

ANDREAS BARTHOLOMÄ read both Classics (Cambridge University) and Law (Ludwig-Maximilians-Universität, Munich). He is working at the Leopold-Wenger-Institut für Antike Rechtsgeschichte und Papyrusforschung, Munich. His research focuses on ancient law, especially law and comedy, and German civil law.

CÉLINE CANDIARD is lecturer in Theatrical Studies at the Université Lumière-Lyon 2 (France). Specialising in ancient comedy and its reception in the early modern period, she is the author of *Esclaves et valets vedettes dans les comédies de la Rome antique et la France d'Ancien Régime* (2017).

ISABELLA TARDIN CARDOSO is Professor of Classics at the University of Campinas (Unicamp) and visiting Professor at the University of Heidelberg. She is the co-editor of the journal *Phaos*. Previous publications include *Estico de Plauto* (2006) and 'Ilusão e engano em Plauto' (2010). On the topos of *theatrum mundi* and the epistemology of classical philology she has published 'Theatrum mundi: Philologie und Nachahmung' (2009) and *Trompe-l'oeil: Philologie und Illusion* (2011). An updated version of her study on Plautus' meta-language *Ars Plautina* (2005) will appear shortly along with some of her essays on the Brazilian reception of Roman comedy.

DAVID CHRISTENSON is Professor of Classics at the University of Arizona. He is the author of a Cambridge Greek and Latin Classics commentary on Plautus' *Amphitruo* (2000), a companion to Plautus' *Casina* (2019), a forthcoming CGLC commentary on Plautus' *Pseudolus*, and a monograph entitled *Roman Comedy*. He has published three volumes of translations: *Plautus: Casina, Amphitryon, Captiui, Pseudolus* (2008), *Roman Comedy: Five Plays by Plautus and Terence (Menaechmi, Rudens, Truculentus, Adelphoe, Eunuchus)* (2010), and *Hysterical Laughter: Four Ancient Comedies about Women* (2014).

ANNA CLARK is Associate Professor in Ancient History at Oxford University and Tutor in Roman History at Christ Church, Oxford. She is the author of *Divine Qualities: Cult and Community in Republican Rome* (2007) and is currently preparing a volume of case studies on Roman society which challenges existing political, religious, and cultural classifications. She has also published numerous articles on epistolography and historiography in both Republican and early Imperial Rome.

MARTIN T. DINTER is Senior Lecturer in Latin Literature and Language at King's College London. He is the author of *Anatomizing Civil War: Studies in Lucan's Epic Technique* (2012) as well as the co-editor of *A Companion to the Neronian Age* (2013). He has published articles on Virgil, Horace, Lucan, Seneca, and Flavian epic and is currently preparing a book-length study on Cato the Elder. He has also co-edited three volumes on Roman declamation: *Ps-Quintilian* (2016), *Calpurnius Flaccus* (2017), and *Seneca the Elder* (forthcoming).

DOROTA DUTSCH is Associate Professor of Classics at the University of California Santa Barbara. She is the author of *Female Discourse in Roman Comedy* (2008) and numerous articles and book chapters on gender, Roman comedy, and classical reception. She has co-edited *Women in Roman Republican Drama* (2015) with Sharon L. James and David Konstan; *Fall of Cities in the Mediterranean* (2015) with Mary Bachvarova and Ann Suter; *Ancient Obscenities* with Ann Suter; and *Blackwell Companion to Classical Reception in Eastern and Central Europe* (2017) with Zara M. Torlone and Dana Munteanu. Her current book project traces the history of the female Pythagorean in the Greek intellectual tradition. *The Blackwell Companion to Plautus*, co-edited with G. F. Franko, is forthcoming in 2019.

ELAINE FANTHAM was Giger Professor of Latin *emerita* at Princeton University. She is the author of commentaries on Seneca, Lucan, Ovid, and Cicero as well as numerous other books such as *Roman Literary Culture* (1996; expanded 2nd edn 2013), *The Roman World of Cicero's De Oratore* (2004), and *Julia Augusti: The Emperor's Daughter* (2006), as well as *Latin Poets and Italian Gods* (2009) among others. Her collected papers have appeared under the title *Roman Readings: Roman Response to Greek Literature from Plautus to Statius and Quintilian* (2011).

WILLIAM FITZGERALD is Professor of Latin at King's College London. His publications include *Catullan Provocations: Lyric Poetry and the Drama of Position* (1995), *Slavery and the Roman Literary Imagination* (2000), *Martial: the World of the Epigram* (2007), *How to Read a Latin Poem If You Can't Read Latin Yet* (2013), as well as *Variety – The Life of a Roman Concept* (2016).

ROBERT GERMANY was Assistant Professor of Classics at Haverford College. He is the author of *Mimetic Contagion: Art and Artifice in Terence's* Eunuchus (2016) and of chapters in *The Blackwell Companion to Terence* (2013) and *Menander in*

Contexts (2014). Up to his untimely death he was working on a monograph on the unity of time in ancient and modern theatre.

FLORIAN HURKA works at the University of Kiel in Germany. He studied Classics, History and Theology at Osnabrück, Bristol, and Freiburg im Breisgau. He received his PhD in Freiburg (2002) and completed his habilitation in Mainz (2007). He has published a monograph on textual criticism in Valerius Flaccus (2003) and is author of a commentary on Plautus' *Asinaria* (2010) as well as co-editor of volumes on Plautus' *Cistellaria* (2004, with Rolf Hartkamp) and Petrarch (2005, with Ulrike Auhagen and Stephan Faller). He has also published widely on neo-Latin literature.

EVANGELOS KARAKASIS studied Classics at the University of Ioannina, Greece (BA, 1995) and Pembroke College, University of Cambridge (MPhil, 1997; PhD, 2001); at present he is Associate Professor of Latin at the University of Ioannina. He is the author of *Terence and the Language of Roman Comedy* (2005), *Song-Exchange in Roman Pastoral* (2011), and of various papers on Roman comedy, elegy, pastoral, epic, and novel. He is also the editor of the *Trends in Classics* Special Issue (4.1), entitled *Singing in the Shadow ... Pastoral Encounters in Post–Vergilian Poetry*. He has recently co-edited the volume *Plautine Trends: Studies in Plautine Comedy and its Reception* (2014) and published the monograph *T. Calpurnius Siculus – A Pastoral Poet in Neronian Rome* (2016).

MAREK THUE KRETSCHMER is Professor of Medieval Latin Literature at the Norwegian University of Science and Technology. He is the author of *Rewriting Roman History in the Middle Ages* (2007) and *Latin Love Elegy and the Dawn of the Ovidian Age* (forthcoming). He has written several articles especially on the reception of the Latin Classics, among which is his contribution to *The Cambridge Companion to Latin Love Elegy* (2013).

GESINE MANUWALD is Professor of Latin at University College London. Her research interests cover Roman drama, Roman epic, Cicero's oratory, and the reception of classical literature, especially in Neo-Latin poetry. Her publications include a study of the Roman dramatic genre of *fabula praetexta* (2001), a monograph on the tragedian Pacuvius (2003), an anthology of texts from and about Roman drama (2010), a comprehensive treatment of Roman Republican theatre in English (2011) and in German (2016), and an edition of the fragments of Ennius' tragedies (2012) which have been reprinted as part of a Loeb edition (2018), as well as numerous articles and encyclopedia entries on Roman tragedy and comedy.

C. W. MARSHALL is Professor of Greek at the University of British Columbia in Vancouver, Canada. He has published widely on ancient theatre, including *The Stagecraft and Performance of Roman Comedy* (2006). His research has been generously supported by the Social Sciences and Humanities Research Council of Canada.

ROBERT S. MIOLA is the Gerard Manley Hopkins Professor of English and a lecturer in Classics at Loyola University in Maryland. He has published on Shakespeare, the Renaissance reception of classical texts, and early modern Catholicism. He has edited plays of Shakespeare and Jonson and is currently working on editions of *Macbeth* and of Chapman's Homer.

TIMOTHY J. MOORE is John and Penelope Biggs Distinguished Professor of Classics at Washington University in St Louis. He holds degrees from Millersville University and the University of North Carolina at Chapel Hill. He is the author of *Artistry and Ideology: Livy's Vocabulary of Virtue* (1989), *The Theater of Plautus: Playing to the Audience* (1998), as well as *Music in Roman Comedy* and *Roman Theatre* (both published in 2012). He also co-edited, along with Wolfgang Polleichtner, the volume *Form und Bedeutung im lateinischen Drama/Form and Meaning in Latin Drama* (2013). In addition, he has written numerous articles on ancient music and music archaeology, Latin literature, American musical theatre, and Japanese kyōgen comedy.

COSTAS PANAYOTAKIS is Professor of Latin at the University of Glasgow. He researches low Roman drama (mime and Atellane comedy) and Petronius' novel. He is the author of *Theatrum Arbitri: Theatrical Elements in the Satyrica of Petronius* (1995) and *Decimus Laberius: The Fragments* (2010). He has also published book-length annotated translations into Modern Greek of one play of Plautus and two of Terence. He is currently working towards an edition (with translation and commentary) of the fragments of all the Atellane playwrights and of the *sententiae* attributed to the mimographer Publilius.

BEATRICE RADDEN KEEFE received her PhD from the Courtauld Institute of Art in 2009 for a dissertation on the illustrated manuscripts of Terence's comedies. She has worked on the Roman de la Rose Digital Library project at Johns Hopkins University and at Princeton University's Index of Christian Art. She has published widely on manuscript studies and is currently writing a book entitled *The Illustrated Afterlife of Terence's Comedies*.

ALISON SHARROCK is Professor of Classics at the University of Manchester. After starting out with Ovid, elegy, and literary theory, she turned to Roman comedy and published *Reading Roman Comedy: Poetics and Playfulness in Plautus and Terence* (2009), as well as a number of articles on the comic playwrights. More recently, she has now returned to Ovid, this time to work on the *Metamorphoses* as an epic poem. She continues to be interested in literary theory, including feminism and the so-called cognitive approaches to literature.

MARIO TELÒ is Professor of Classics at Berkeley. He obtained his BA and his PhD at the Scuola Normale Superiore, Pisa (Italy), where from 2004 to 2007 he was Junior Research Fellow in Greek Literature. His research interests mainly comprise Greek and Roman drama, the Greek novel, thing and affect theory, and genre theory, but he has also published in other fields of Greek and Latin literature (Hellenistic poetry, the Greek novel, Roman tragedy and comedy, ecphrastic literature, the modern reception of Greek tragedy). In 2007 he published an extensive commentary on Eupolis' *Demoi*, the best preserved fragmentary play of Old Comedy. He has recently published *Aristophanes and the Cloak of Comedy: Affect, Aesthetics, and the Canon* (2016).

PROLOGUE
Martin T. Dinter

Prologues of Roman comedy occasionally drag the producer on stage. He then captures the goodwill of the audience and prepares the stage for the coming performance. He offers some details of the production history and instructs the audience to be quiet and pay attention, telling them how to enjoy the play. Other prologues simply give some idea of what is on offer, a guide for finding one's feet among all the cunning slaves, young men in love, old fathers, pimps, braggart soldiers, courtesans, virtuous maidens, parasites and well-meaning mothers that people Roman comedy. Unlike a handbook or introduction, this volume accompanies, rather than guides, those approaching Roman comedy. Thus, whilst the volume provides introductory material throughout, each chapter also aims to awaken the reader's curiosity and to be useful to 'think with' when pondering Roman comedy rather than to sound an authoritative and exhaustive voice on one particular subject. Nevertheless, readers completely new to Roman comedy will find that the chapters placed at the beginning of this volume such as Alison Sharrock's Introduction, Gesine Manuwald's 'Plautus and Terence in their Roman Contexts' and Costas Panayotakis' 'Roman Laughter: Native Italian Drama and its Influence on Plautus' provide a good entry point to Roman comedy. In addition, chapters with more technical content such as Toph Marshall's 'Stage Action in Roman Comedy' or Tim Moore's 'Music and Metre' will provide both introductory material and original research in order to showcase the depth and breadth of their respective fields. In the same vein, the chapters on reception alternate between broad overviews of what is out there and case studies with close readings, in the hope of whetting your appetite for more. À la comic prologue, I shall now briefly preview the comic reader's contents to provide orientation.

Sharrock first, then. Her introduction challenges the axiom that the primary purpose of comedy is the production of humour and the elicitation of laughter. Highlighting a number of possible ways to read Roman comedy today, she showcases different theories of laughter and provides a potted

xvii

history of scholarly approaches to the genre. Questioning a number of preconceptions about sundry supposedly near-universal motifs of Roman comedy, she points out that what we think we know about the genre must constantly be renegotiated and held up for comparison against what each instance actually provides.

Part I: The World of Roman Comedy

Manuwald provides valuable background and context for our exploration of Roman comedy by tracing the development of the genre of the *fabula palliata* (comedy in Greek dress). By tracing predecessors and contemporaries of Plautus and Terence, such as Livius Andronicus, Naevius, Ennius, Caecilius Statius and Luscius Lanuvinus, she reconstructs the emergence of generic conventions. Sextus Turpilius, who follows Terence's (and Caecilius') 'Hellenised' version of *fabula palliata* in titles, models and themes, but remains closer to Plautus (and Naevius) in style, language and scene structures, forms the endpoint of the genre as we know it. Manuwald supplements her diachronic analysis of a succession of *palliatae* with a synchronic sweep across contemporary dramatic genres in Rome: in addition to dramatic genres such as the *fabula Atellana* or *mimus*, there was a fourfold conspectus consisting of two Greek and two Roman versions or two serious and two light varieties of drama. What is more, prose genres, such as oratory and historiography, and the poetic genres epic and satire, which were emerging and developing in Rome at the same time as drama, provide further context for Roman comedy. In addition, references to Roman conventions and explanations of customs which were common in Greece but not in Rome show how contemporary historical and social conditions framed the genre. Finally, contexts of reception, from the immediate effect of performance on audiences to the formation of a canon, complete the discussion.

Panayotakis paints a picture of long-standing and non-Romanocentric theatrical traditions in Republican Italy which existed independently from, and perhaps even before, the advent of the *palliata* in Rome. Scholarship has highlighted the influence of unscripted forms of Italian popular entertainment on Plautus' adaptations of Greek comedies and made a case for the formative influence of South Italian and Sicilian drama, Oscan farce, and Italian mime. Panayotakis surveys and re-considers the evidence for non-literary low drama in the early Republic and relates this evidence to the *comoedia palliata*, especially Plautine theatre. Although details concerning the influence of native drama and the combination process remain opaque, and the pre-literary forms of Italian comedy still present themselves as shadowy and elusive, he nevertheless underlines that Plautus' scripts were the product of a dynamic and proud negotiation of living cultures. As such, they constitute the first literary specimen of a confidently emerging new civilisation.

Telò points to Roman comedy's acknowledged appropriation of the repertoire of Greek New Comedy, which transforms the stage into a site for meditation on literary inventiveness, repetition, and cultural transcoding, while also creating a field for self-reflexive narrative and theatrical practices. He investigates how the translation and adaptation of Greek comic models, so essential to the poetic workshop of the *palliata* and to the invention of Roman cultural identity, are manifested in the dramatic constructions of Plautus and Terence. Then he charts important ways in which the plots of Plautus and Terence provide commentary on the modes of literary transposition that shape their identities. In the process, he illuminates the distinctive strategies of authorial self-presentation that characterise Plautus' and Terence's positioning of their plays against Greek models.

Germany revisits the judgement that Plautus and Terence were notoriously 'apolitical', especially in comparison with Aristophanes. Today, however, we have grown accustomed to thinking of politics in more capacious terms, not simply as advocacy for or against specific public persons or programmes, but as a broader set of discourses pertaining to the mediation of power in society and to the very constitution of social life. Instances of political engagement can thus be plotted on a spectrum of abstraction, ranging from explicitly partisan activism to tacit and apparently unconscious implication in a system of values. Germany begins his study at the more concrete end of the spectrum, examining topical allusions (and their absence) in Roman comedy before venturing onto the more abstract terrain of cultural politics and the politics of everyday life. In the first section he offers a fresh reading of the famous allusion to Naevius in *Miles Gloriosus*, and in the second he extends the investigation of politics to embrace one of Roman comedy's most remarkable features: its propensity for metatheatrical play.

Part II: The Fabric of Roman Comedy

Marshall discusses the importance of stage action in Roman comedy. He emphasises that comedies were written to be performed, and so the physical dimension of a play is just as significant as its literary features. He supports his argument with examples from Plautus' *Mercator* and Terence's *Hecyra*. These plays reveal that stage sets often supplemented the urban landscape as backdrop. Meanwhile the soundtrack to each play was provided by a single *tibicen* (piper), who complemented and enhanced metrical verses and evoked appropriate emotions by modulating his tune. However, Marshall also examines offstage space and the fluidity of the Roman stage, which was not flatly delineated but instead negotiated through actors' cues. This flexibility meant that audiences watched multiple scenes at once; while they enjoyed the onstage action, they also imagined what was happening outside the performance space. This dramatic technique is applied perfectly in *Hec.* 314–19: Philumena loudly gives birth offstage while Pamphilus and Parmeno discuss unrelated matters onstage. Indeed, Marshall challenges the idea of a single and visible 'stage'; spectators, sounds, and costumes combined into a multisensory environment during performances of Roman comedy.

Moore zooms in on music and metre in Roman comedy. He discusses the *tibia* in detail, noting that the instrument had a wide dynamic range and a murmuring tone. As pipes were constructed with double reeds, two (or three) tunes could be played at once, allowing for contrapuntal arrangements. Pipers also practised circular breathing, which enabled them to produce sustained musical accompaniment. While the pipe hummed on, actors complemented the music by singing along and performing gestural dances. Besides shedding light on the soundtrack of Roman comedy, Moore also discusses its metrical patterns. He shows how metre was not only a stylistic choice, but also an opportunity for characterisation. Accordingly, powerful characters, such as Pardalisca in *Casina*, dictate the metre in which their interlocutors speak. Similarly, determined characters opt for bacchiacs, two long syllables after a short one, which convey persistence and even insistence. As Moore concludes, music, metre, and meaning cooperated in Roman comedy, culminating in a sophisticated theatrical experience for ancient spectators.

A main goal for both Plautus and Terence was to elicit laughter from the audience. **Cardoso** outlines how they achieved this aim by discussing the comic technique of Roman comedy. She analyses both verbal humour, from puns to hyperbole, and non-verbal humour which includes gestures, vocal modulations, and costumes. In some instances non-verbal and verbal humour combine into a coherent and amusing whole, as in the *seruus currens* (running slave) routine. Some character types were more prone to slapstick humour than others; most notably, pimps were often involved in onstage fights, in keeping with their lower social status. Indeed, as written sources rarely include stage directions, much of the performative element in Roman comedy must be inferred from dialogue, characterisation, and plot. These clues are crucial in reconstructing the Roman stage and recreating the physical humour of performances in antiquity.

Metatheatre serves to remind us that plays are fictional and theatrical constructs. The crafty slave Pseudolus provides a definitive example of this concept when he asserts that he will not give his plan away 'because plays are long enough as it is' (*Ps.* 388). **Christenson** explores instances of metatheatre in Roman comedy. On an individual level, each play employs metatheatre for a distinct purpose; while *Eunuchus* uses it to evoke discussions about masculinity and hierarchy, *Rudens* instead questions the role of morality in comedy and tragedy. More generally, however, metatheatre gained efficacy from the fact that Roman society was based upon festivals, pageants, and performances. Hence, by deconstructing theatrical spectacles, metatheatrical references encouraged the audience to reflect upon their own social lives. Indeed, metatheatre demolishes preconceptions about playwriting, smashes the invisible 'fourth wall' between the stage and spectator, and allows comedic messages to cross from fiction into reality.

Readers of Latin new to Plautus and Terence are often put off by their use of archaic language. **Karakasis'** chapter addresses this phenomenon by comparing the idiom of Roman comedy to the more standard forms of Classical Latin, as exemplified by the prose works of Caesar and Cicero. In doing so, he provides a full morphology of unusual word forms found in both Plautus and Terence. He argues that Early Latin was consciously channelled into Plautine comedy to create a colloquial tone, whereas Terentian verse was comparatively modern, in keeping with the playwright's taut style. He also demonstrates that Plautus and Terence did not reproduce real dialect, but instead created an artificial *Kunstsprache* for comic purposes. Finally, he provides a typology of linguistic characterisation, in which he differentiates between stock characters based on their speech patterns. In Roman comedy, speech indeed makes the man: while women use *amabo* for 'please', male characters tend to use the more forceful *quaeso*. These patterns recur throughout the Plautine and Terentian corpus with notable regularity, revealing that Roman comic diction was indeed meticulously planned and crafted.

Part III: The Sociology of Roman Comedy

Dinter discusses the morality of Roman comedy. He places special focus on moral relationships within families, and especially on interactions between fathers and sons. Often seen as the domain of the overly strict father who admonishes his wayward son, the household features other members, such as slaves and tutors, who participate in the wider struggle between what presents as Roman traditional morality and Hellenic *laissez-faire*. This chapter also draws upon *sententiae* – pithy maxims – as well as moralising passages, which regularly reveal the true values that motivate comic characters. These can, however, also be used rhetorically simply to win an argument or –

usually by slaves – as part of a play's comic technique. As postscript, the post-classical collection of *sententiae* 'Cato's *Disticha*' condenses the morality of Roman comedy for educational purposes.

Fitzgerald highlights the central role of slaves in Roman comedy. He notes that slaves were so closely linked to the genre that they constituted 'crucial ingredients' in Terence's recipe for laugher (Ter. *Eun.* 36). Accordingly, slaves feature in multiple ways for comedic effect: the *servus currens* ('running slave') contributed to slapstick humour, while the *servus callidus* ('cunning slave') advanced the plot by devising tricky schemes. Fitzgerald also outlines how slave characters interacted with other comic *personae*, such as the wayward son and disgruntled master, and highlights the metatheatricality of slave characters within Roman comedy. In addition, he asks how a free audience responded to running gags about beating, crucifixion, and torture, while examining the relationship between relatively mild onstage punishments and the grim reality that many Roman slaves endured.

At first sight, Roman comedy is bound by rigid sexual stereotypes. But **Dutsch** breaks new ground by comparing two antithetical character types – the mother (*mater*) and the whore (*meretrix*). She challenges this apparently direct polarity by observing that on the one hand mothers act as pimps, while on the other prostitutes proudly display strong maternal instincts. Indeed, while Roman playwrights were obliged to pay lip service to existing codes of female sexual behaviour, they often portrayed women in a sensitive and compassionate light. Plautus emphasised that women were forced into prostitution by financial pressures, and Terence's prostitutes are often upwardly mobile, ambitious workers looking to improve their social status. By portraying women with such profound nuance and ambiguity, Roman comedy invited its spectators to look beyond the inflexible social categories of 'mothers' and 'whores'.

Clark explores the intimate tie between gods and Roman comedy. Gods were celebrated during festivals, which doubled as performance opportunities for the plays of Plautus and Terence. Moreover, gods drive plot and action: at the end of Plautus' *Amphitruo* Alcmena gives birth to Jupiter's son, Hercules, along with her own mortal offspring. She thus attains the elevated status accorded to a god's companion, and averts her cuckolded husband's anger. Clark also compares Roman New Comedy with its Greek counterpart, concluding that Plautus and Terence reference the gods more often than Menander and Diphilus did. Furthermore, Clark relates intriguing patterns in divine invocations. Hercules is mentioned most often, and lovers naturally call upon Venus and Cupid, but even slave characters demonstrate a profound understanding of the full pantheon, including Jupiter, Minerva, and Ops.

Given the scarcity of extant sources on Republican Roman law, jurists have drawn heavily on fictional sources, such as the comedies of Plautus and Terence, for information on the pre-imperial legal system. **Bartholomä** assesses the extent to which Roman comedy constitutes a reliable source of information about Roman law. This question is complicated by the mixture of both Greek and Roman law codes in Roman comedy, which have been further contaminated by wholly imaginary 'stage laws'. These fictional legal concepts were concocted for entertainment purposes only, with no basis in reality. In the course of his analysis, Bartholomä summarises several key legal concepts, from the *mancipatio* (ownership transfer) to the *dos* (dowry). He concludes that there is no generic rule that governs whether a given comedic passage conformed to Greek or Roman law. Scholars must consider each passage on an individual basis in order to glean insights about classical jurisprudence.

According to Terence, 'old men become far too worried about money' (*Adel.* 955). **Fantham** reveals that this preoccupation was shared by young men, who sought funds with which to impress their love interests. She establishes that most adolescents in Greece and Rome depended on their fathers for money. If these fathers proved tight-fisted, the erstwhile lovers were obliged to earn their own allowance. This basic scenario, fuelled by financial tension, occurs in more than two-thirds of the Plautine and Terentian corpus. However, raising funds through legitimate means proves so difficult in Roman comedy that even married men resort to domestic embezzlement. Most notably, Chremes in Terence's *Phormio* steals from his wife's estates in order to support his mistress. Fantham concludes that financial and sexual misbehaviour are linked phenomena; comic denouements do not only ensure a happy ending for fictional lovers, but also include the fair restitution of ill-gotten gains. She ends her chapter with a glossary of financial and commercial terms, which helps readers to navigate the complex economics of Roman comedy.

Part IV: The Reception of Roman Comedy

Manuwald examines audience reactions to Roman comedy in antiquity. By drawing upon source material such as Cicero's *De Oratore* and Aulus Gellius' *Attic Nights*, she demonstrates that Roman audiences enthusiastically supported revivals of their favourite plays. Audience response was not, however, limited to passive spectatorship; it also entailed active engagement with comedic texts. From the first century AD onwards, grammarians such as Servius Clodius catalogued the plays of Plautus and Terence, whilst making an effort to distinguish between the authentic and the spurious. Scholars also responded to Roman comedy by creating canons of plays or rankings of playwrights. In the hands of grammarians and scholars, comedy then transcended its original performative role and attained literary status. The editions they produced did not only further the transmission of the plays of Plautus and Terence, but also contributed to the prominence of Roman comedy up to the early Christian era.

Radden Keefe surveys the illustrated manuscript tradition of Plautus' and Terence's plays. By exploring the palaeographical features of surviving manuscripts, she reconstructs how Roman comedies were edited from Late Antiquity onwards. In her survey of textual transmission, she also points out that some illuminators painted unique scenes in each manuscript based on what they deemed crucial, useful, or interesting. Moreover, they also transposed Roman comedy into medieval settings. Most notably, the Tours manuscript of Terence's works includes drawings of Chaerea – originally disguised as a eunuch – in a monk's habit. Nevertheless, Radden Keefe emphasises that not all depictions were unique; scribes often worked from a set of model illustrations. These 'copying relationships' explain the similarities between the illustrations of the Vatican, Paris, and Milan manuscripts of Terence. However, these manuscripts also show the efforts of several artists to improve upon or update whatever model they worked from.

Hrotsvit of Ganderheim was a learned Saxon noblewoman who took the veil in the tenth century. As a medieval female writer and a composer of Latin drama, she was doubly unique. **Kretschmer** pays homage to the work of this enigmatic figure by exploring the relationship between her plays and those of Terence. He outlines the influence of both Terentian and biblical imagery on Hrotsvit's corpus. Numerous character parallels exist, such as that between Terence's Chaerea (from *Eunuchus*) and Hrotsvit's Calimachus; both *personae* resolve to rape the girls for which they have fallen in a misguided attempt at love. Kretschmer also explores the social and personal aspects of Hrotsvit's writing. Hrotsvit uses Terentian motifs and phrases, but moulds them into a Christian context; hence, her work represents the 'Christianisation of Terence'. Hrotsvit was no mere hagiographer, but an eloquent and enthusiastic adaptor of Roman comedy.

Early modern England proved fertile ground for Roman comedy. Revival performances of Plautus and Terence were staged at the universities of Oxford and Cambridge, where classical playwrights were celebrated as both didactic tools and sources of entertainment. **Miola** outlines how Roman comedy flourished in this environment, though in a sanitised form that would appeal to Christian audiences. He reveals that the originals were often adapted for early modern versions with new characters and settings. Thomas Heywood's adaptation of *Rudens* featured innovations such as a monastic choir, offstage duets between heroines, and a ballad in praise of poverty. The resulting pastiche speaks volumes about the invasion of post-classical versions of Roman comedy by Christian themes. Miola also explores the close relationship between Shakespeare's Falstaff and the Roman stock character of the *miles gloriosus* (boastful soldier). Furthermore, he analyses *Hamlet* with reference to Roman New Comedy: Ophelia is the maiden, Hamlet the brash young man (*adulescens*), and Polonius the archetypal blocking father, a riled-up *senex iratus*. Early modern playwrights borrowed heavily from Roman comedy, which provided them with situations, characters, and dramatic codes.

Candiard discusses the reception of Roman comedy in early modern Italy and France. She focuses on the crucial role of schools and universities in disseminating ancient plays, and explores how educational systems encouraged the birth of national comedy. Indeed, Italian and French comedies, most famously those of Ludovico Dolce and Jean de Rotrou, were heavily influenced by Plautus and Terence. Nevertheless, it was not only *fabula palliata* (comedy in Greek dress) which provided inspiration for early modern poets. Atellan Farce, also spawned a key theatrical innovation in the form of the *commedia dell'arte*. Candiard outlines how Roman stock characters and scenes migrated into this new genre. Nevertheless, Roman comedy was not only adapted into French and Italian plays. It also stimulated the production of theoretical works and commentaries, used for teaching, translating, and interpreting ancient plays in an early modern context.

Following on from Candiard's chapter on Roman comedy in Italy and France, **Hurka** analyses the impact of Plautus and Terence in early modern Germany. In the Humanist era, plays were read for the purpose of moral instruction. It was not until the Enlightenment that an active reception occurred, and Roman comedies were adapted for the German stage. However, even as Latin comedies attained an apex of popularity, they were displaced in the intellectual climate by Greek texts. Gotthold Ephraim Lessing exemplifies this shift in attitudes. He began his career as an advocate for Plautine comedy, but later turned towards Greek literature. Indeed, by outlining the rise and fall of Roman comedy among German intellectuals, Hurka provides a comprehensive overview of early modern reactions – and rejections – of Roman comedy.

Recent scholarship has brought to the fore the performative aspect of Roman comedy. Plautus and Terence were not writing for readers, but for spectators. Comedic meaning is therefore not conveyed by the dialogue alone, but also through music, costumes, and sets. In her chapter, **Candiard** explores how auditory and visual effects help update Roman comedy for a modern audience. She explains how Amphitryon has been converted into musicals and films, and outlines the new subplots and special effects that were introduced in the transposition process. These radical revisions helped to create blockbusters like Jean-Luc Godard's 1993 film *Hélas pour moi (Alas For Me)*. In addition, Candiard emphasises the remarkable comedic continuity from Plautus and Terence to Jeeves and Wooster: modern sitcoms, films, and musicals retain strong echoes of their Roman originals.

ACKNOWLEDGEMENTS

It is my pleasure to thank the Vatican Library, the British Library, Antike Kunst, the Bibliothèque nationale de France, the Veneranda Biblioteca Ambrosiana, the Bodleian Library, the Leiden University Library, the Bibliothèque municipale de Tours, the Museo Archeologico Nazionale, Naples, and the Sovraintendenza di Roma Capitale for permission to reproduce images from their holdings in this volume.

Thanks are due to Michael Sharp and his team at Cambridge University Press, Elizabeth Hanlon above all, for their kind support in producing this companion and for allowing me to include so many illustrations. The anonymous readers for Cambridge University Press have made many a wise comment as has been acknowledged by contributors throughout and deserve our heartfelt thanks. I am moreover deeply grateful towards John Henderson for reading and commenting on the full manuscript. I also thank Mary Morton for copyediting this volume and Antonia Ruppel as well as Mauredson Lima Silva for their help with the formatting. Astrid Khoo has kindly compiled the *index locorum* and the *index rerum* and offered invaluable assistance with processing the proofs. One contributor has filled in for a sick colleague at a late stage in the editorial process and deserves my special thanks. Toph Marshall has kindly looked over the late Robert Germany's text before publication. Warm thanks are due to Charles Guèrin for his cultural diplomacy regarding image rights and to my students at King's College London, Universidad Nacional Autónoma de México (UNAM), Universidade de São Paulo (USP), Universidade Federal de Rio de Janeiro (UFRJ), and Universidade Estadual de Campinas (UNICAMP) as well as Universidade Federal de Juiz de Fora (UFJF) for their input and humour. Marcos Martinho, Paula Correa, Charlene Miotti, and Gerardo Ramirez have been the kindest of hosts on these occasions.

EXTANT PLAYS BY PLAUTUS AND TERENCE

Those coming to Roman comedy through translations occasionally face the problem that the Latin titles of Roman comedy translate in more than one way. To avoid confusion this volume will refer to the plays by their Latin titles either in full or abbreviated as listed below. In brackets I give the English titles as used in the most widely available translations as an aid to locating references.

1 Plautus

Translations are given in brackets; the plays for which no translation is given have been named after one of their characters.

Amph.   *Amphitruo* (Amphitryon)
As.   *Asinaria* (The Story About the Asses; The Comedy of Asses; The One About the Asses)
Aul.   *Aulularia* (The Pot of Gold; The Concealed Treasure)
Bacch.   *Bacchides* (The Bacchis Sisters; The Two Bacchises)
Capt.   *Captiui* (The Captives; The Prisoners)
Cas.   *Casina*
Cist.   *Cistellaria* (The Story About the Little Box; The Casket Comedy)
Curc.   *Curculio*
Ep.   *Epidicus*
Men.   *Menaechmi* (The Menaechmus Brothers; The Two Menaechmuses; The Brothers Menaechmus)
Merc.   *Mercator* (The Merchant)
Mil.   *Miles Gloriosus* (The Braggart Soldier; The Swaggering Soldier)
Most.   *Mostellaria* (The Little Ghost Story; The Ghost; The Haunted House)
Persa   *Persa* (The Persian)
Poen.   *Poenulus* (The Little Carthaginian)

Ps.   *Pseudolus*
Ru.   *Rudens* (The Rope)
St.   *Stichus*
Trin.   *Trinummus* (The Three Pennies; The Three Dollar Day)
Truc.   *Truculentus*
Vid.   *Vidularia* (The Story About the Suitcase; The Tale of a Travelling-Bag)

2 Terence

Ad.   *Adelphoe* (The Brothers)
And.   *Andria* (The Girl from Andros; The Woman of Andros)
Eun.   *Eunuchus* (The Eunuch)
Haut. *Heauton Timorumenos* (The Self-Tormentor)
Hec.   *Hecyra* (The Mother-in-Law; Her Husband's Mother)
Ph.   *Phormio*

ABBREVIATIONS USED FOR REFERENCES TO FRAGMENTS

Acc.	Accius
Afr.	Afranius
At.	Atta
Atell.	Atellana
D.	Dangel (Accius)
Enn.	Ennius
FPL³	*Fragmenta poetarum Latinorum*, third edition
Fr.	Fragment
Gram.	Grammatical works
Inc.	*incertum*
Lab.	Laberius
Liv. Andr.	Livius Andronicus
Mim.	mimus
Naev.	Naevius
Nov.	Novius
ORF	*Oratorum Romanorum Fragmenta* (Malcovati)
Pac.	Pacuvius
Pall.	*palliata*
Plaut.	Plautus
Pomp.	Pomponius
Praet.	*praetexta*
R.³	Ribbeck, third edition (dramatic fragments)
Sk.	Skutsch (Ennius' *Annales*)
Ter.	Terence
Tit.	Titinius
Tog.	*togata*
Trag.	*crepidata*
Turp.	Turpilius
V.²	Vahlen, second edition (Ennius)
W.	Warmington (fragments of early playwrights and Lucilius)

ALISON SHARROCK

Introduction: Roman Comedy

> quod si personis isdem huic uti non licet:
> qui mage licet currentem seruom scribere,
> bonas matronas facere, meretrices malas,
> parasitum edacem, gloriosum militem,
> puerum supponi, falli per seruom senem,
> amare odisse suspicari? denique
> nullumst iam dictum quod non dictum sit prius. (*Eun.* 35–41)

But if he is not allowed to use the same characters as others do, how is it more permissible to create a running slave, to make matrons good and prostitutes bad, a parasite greedy, a soldier boastful, to sneak in a baby, to have an old man deceived by a slave, to love, to hate and to suspect? In sum, nothing is now said which has not been said before.

> sed quasi poeta, tabulas quom cepit sibi,
> quaerit quod nusquam gentiumst, reperit tamen,
> facit illud ueri simile quod mendacium est,
> nunc ego poeta fiam: uiginti minas,
> quae nunc nusquam sunt gentium, inueniam tamen. (*Ps.* 401–5)

But just like a poet, when he picks up his writing-tablets, seeks something which exists nowhere in the world – and finds it, and makes what is false seem like truth, so now I shall become a poet: those twenty minae, which exist nowhere in the world, I shall nevertheless invent.

There's nothing new under the sun; I'll invent it out of nowhere. I offer these two quotations not to suggest 'Plautus against Terence', originality *against* tradition, but as a nutshell in which the paradoxical genius of Roman comedy may sit comfortably and laugh at our attempts to tie him down. For what is comedy? An art and a natural gift; artificial, yet basic to all human societies; all in the timing, dependent on the number of audiences, yet subjective and personal; dependent on recognition, yet cheating of expectation; subversive, and also reactionary; culture-specific, yet drawing on that most fundamental and fundamentally human of psychosomatic actions – laughter.

Critics down the ages have attempted to confine the comic spirit to a theoretical box by seeking to articulate its essence.[1] In the ancient world, much comic theorising was directed towards moral justification of comedy, unsurprisingly given comedy's rather obvious connections with naughtiness,[2] in which the reason we laugh is in order to correct the failings of others, and so too in society and even in ourselves. Such moralising sometimes (often) became itself the subject of comic playwrights' humour,[3] but such humour only works because everyone knows its basis: the notion that comedy is for the edification of society needs to be recognisable in order for it to be undermined.

The moralising tradition had extensive progeny in discussions of comedy throughout the medieval and early modern periods, but it was not the only ancient theoretical contribution to the nature of comedy. The lost second book of Aristotle's *Poetics* famously and enticingly theorised about comedy as the extant book does for tragedy, certainly including the moral argument but also exploring other aspects of laughter and how it may be elicited by literature. We can hear echoes of Aristotle's theories of comedy in the later ancient *Tractatus Coislinianus* which almost certainly derives from Aristotle, if at several removes, and from which scholars have partly reconstructed what Aristotle might have said.[4] The best bit of the *Tractatus* is a list of the causes of laughter, both in diction and in substance.[5] It includes such recognisable comic techniques as deception, illogicality, cheating of expectation, and vulgarity, in addition to various forms of word-play. What the author does not appear to do is to try to find some overarching scheme into which all these causes of laughter may be fitted, his centralising drive being more towards the purposes of comedy (a reflection of the Aristotelian cathartic effect of tragedy) rather than its causes.

---

[1] Purdie (1993) points out that any attempt to say 'what comedy is', while it may be both useful and perhaps inevitable, risks bringing the joke on itself – a common problem for the critic of comedy. As she says, 'even at its simplest, joking is always overdetermined' (13, see also 36). See also Hokenson (2006) and Olson (1968) on theories of comedy, plus, specifically with regard to Roman comedy, Duckworth (1994).

[2] Dover (1972); Anderson (1993) 92. Ancient critical and moral anxiety about comedy is in part an extension of ancient anxiety about representation in general, on which, with regard to comedy, see Sharrock (2009) 2–6.

[3] See Sharrock (2009) 258–60.

[4] See Cooper (1922) esp. 224–6; Janko (1984). Watson (2012) makes a strong case for the Aristotelian authenticity of the *Tractatus*, as well as offering extensive analysis of its contribution to the theory of comedy. Grube (1965) 144–9 is doubtful about the Aristotelian purity of the *Tractatus*, but for our purposes even some confused echoes of the classical Greek theorist, by way of versions and epitomes through different periods of antiquity and beyond, tell us something of what people have felt it appropriate to say about comedy over the centuries.

[5] Grube (1965) 141 gives a good brief account of the list.

Many later critics have had a go at the 'essence of comedy', including Bergson's notion of automation (something is comic when it displays a certain inelasticity and a kind of automatism, like a puppet or clockwork, but still keeping the pretence of life – bear in mind that he was writing at the time of the rise of the machine in Western culture), Baudelaire's absolute and reductive humour (this theory, with its roots in Romanticism, sought to distinguish between 'absolute' comedy which is creative, spontaneous, and life-affirming, and on the other hand 'significant' – in the sense of signifying – or 'reductive' comedy, which works by reference to, or even is parasitic on, social reality, so for example political satire would come into this category), and Freud's emphasis on the unconscious (Freud's famous *Jokes and Their Relation to the Unconscious*, first published in 1905, is the great-grandfather of all those 'Freudian slips' of language at which we laugh, but the theory goes much wider than that, with the idea that all joking activity works to persuade our inner policeman, and society, to let us do things that it thinks we should not, while providing safe release for pent-up emotions), to mention only those which arise from the late nineteenth and early twentieth centuries' anxious interaction with the development of modernity.[6] The drive for moral superiority and the correction of society has by no means disappeared, manifesting itself particularly in political satire, but it now sits alongside the potential of comedy to overturn society. Bakhtin's theory of Carnival has been highly influential in this mode, but it leaves a problem for critics of all comedy, not only Roman, as to the extent to which innovations such as the Roman Saturnalia and the medieval Feast of Fools serve as much to reinforce hierarchies as they do to question or undermine them.[7]

So far, I may seem to have played into the common notion that the primary purpose of comedy is the production of humour and the elicitation of laughter. One of the reasons for the relatively poor press gained by Roman comedy in the modern world (by which I mean, approximately, the Western world since the Second World War) is that many people have not found the plays particularly funny. There are two approaches that I suggest we take to addressing this problem: on the one hand, the plays of Plautus and Terence are funnier than is thought, while, on the other hand, humour is not their

---

[6] See Sharrock (2009) 166–7.

[7] See Germany's contribution to this volume. The classic work on the destabilising drive of Roman comedy is Segal (1968/1987). Bakhtin (1984) is one of the more readable works of this difficult but brilliant Russian critic. The role of his theories in understanding Roman comedy have been as yet little pursued, although there has been some work on Aristophanes, for example Platter (1993). The main Bakhtinian influence on classical scholarship has been in the field of the novel, on which see particularly Branham (2005).

only goal. As regards the second point, it is worth stressing that Roman comedy, as a genre, has dramatic entertainment as its primary goal, not laughter. The vein is light and the outcome positive – these are essentials of ancient comedy, more than the production of belly laughs. There are various reasons for our historic difficulties in appreciating the humour of Roman comedy: lack of familiarity and understanding; the perennial difficulty in treating a play-script as if it were the entire performance; a false and damagingly prejudiced (in its true sense: judged in advance of knowledge) desire for lost Greek originals, which have often been constructed precisely out of negative criticisms of Roman plays; and then all the usual difficulties of appreciating the humour of another culture.[8] Many people of my generation thus struggled through the difficult Latin of perhaps one or if they were (un)lucky two plays of Plautus, often chosen more for their perceived connection with something Greek than for their own sake, for example *Aulularia* or *Bacchides*, and then far too often the atypical *Adelphi* of Terence,[9] without any understanding of how it fits into and disturbs comic tradition, nor any sense that it might actually have something to say about Roman families.

Despite the challenge of translating laughter into different cultures, it is worth noting that Plautus and (yes, even) Terence provide us with easier access to Roman humour than pretty much any other Roman text. I would offer the following as a comparison. As an undergraduate, the second play that I read (after a disastrous interaction with *Bacchides* and Menander's *Dis Exapaton*, which I think has scarred me for life) was Plautus' *Rudens*. Despite no great enthusiasm for the task, I was pushed into laughing out loud – in the library – at the magnificent *licet* scene between the old man Daemones and the slave Trachalio (*Rud.* 1212).[10] The old man gives Trachalio a series of instructions, to which the slave replies each time *licet*. Since this word means something like 'okay', it is not of itself funny. What makes it funny is the repetition, and Trachalio's control in contrast with the old man's eagerness and excitement. At one point, Trachalio turns the interaction around, and he tricks Daemones into saying *licet* to a series of delights for himself. Finally, in comes the unknowing slave Gripus and asks '*Quam mox licet te compellare, Daemones?*' ('How soon will it be okay to talk to you, Daemones?', 1227). One can easily supply the stage direction 'Daemones jumps out of his skin'. Contrast the easy humour of that scene with my contemporaneous reading of the incomprehensible 'joke' in the interchange between Sarmentus and Messius at Hor. *Sat.* 1.5.56–61. To be fair, there are

---

[8] See Douglas (1999) ch. 10, first published in 1970, on the challenge of interpreting jokes of other cultures.

[9] For the argument that *Adelphi* is unusual within Roman comedy, see Sharrock (2009) 98.

[10] For discussion of the scene, see Sharrock (2009) 175–7.

plenty of jokes in Plautus and Terence that do take a bit of explanation in order to be appreciated by the modern reader, but perhaps the biggest hurdles to enjoyment are the prejudice about secondariness (on which see Telò in this volume) and the failure to perceive both the diversity of the corpus and, paradoxically, the role of repetition in the games comedy plays with itself, its tradition, and its audience.

A standard defence of the perceived unfunniness of Roman comedy is to say that the play-script is merely a shadowy reflection of the glorious visual extravaganza which would be the play in performance. This is a fair point, which can apply to the script of any performance genre. What is surprising, I suggest, is how little true it is that the experience of Roman comedy is irreparably damaged by treating it as a text. How is it that the supposedly so inadequate script of a genre which was meant to produce one-off entertainment for the masses could so quickly become a literary text, the subject of a huge scholarly industry within 100 years of its production, a school text (in the case of Terence) from which to learn good Latin, an intertext with other far more elevated genres (such as the oratory of Cicero), and be rediscovered to help form the dramatic tradition of modern Europe mostly not through continuous theatre history but through the reading of texts? The answer, I suggest, is word-play – this is a performance genre, yes, but one in which the words carry so much of the burden of production that they can transmit its spirit even in the absence of all that music, dancing, colour, and movement which would no doubt have enhanced the original performance.[11] In the contemporary world, most of us most of the time get our Plautus and Terence in the form of a text, whether Latin, English translation, or a mixture of the two. We may lose something by comparison with the experience of the original audience, but we also gain something: not only do we have the imaginative possibilities of constructing ourselves as audience, but we also have the opportunity for literary readings which allow us to break free of the real-time constraints of performance, to compare one play with another, one passage with another, to superimpose the first-time reader and the knowledgeable reader on top of each other and watch them both from the vantage point of a super-reader. It is also much easier for us to put the play in question into a literary historical context. In doing so, we are sharing in the experience of readers throughout most of antiquity and the Middle Ages, as well as the modern world, who have treated these texts, to a greater or lesser extent at different times, as works of literature in their own right.

---

[11] Beacham (1991) is a sustained effort to offer more than a textual reading of Roman comedy. Anxieties about reading play-texts as if they were plays is not confined to the ancient world. See Fortier (2002) 12.

In the nineteenth and early twentieth centuries, scholarship on Roman comedy was dominated by three areas: language, the establishment of a fixed text, and the question of the plays' relationship with their so-called Greek originals. It was mainly these three elements which made Plautus important enough to command the attention of great nineteenth-century scholars such as Friedrich Leo.[12] The work of Plautus in particular was of great linguistic interest for its contribution to the history of the Latin language, being the earliest extensive text and one which bears a closer relationship with colloquial language than most works of literature. The linguistic tradition has taken something of a new turn in recent years, with the focus changed from what Plautus and Terence can tell us about the language to what the language can tell us about Plautus and Terence.[13] Establishment of the text of Plautus is extraordinarily fraught (Terence is much easier): as Slater says: 'the texts themselves sometimes seem to be quicksand beneath our feet'.[14] In addition to the normal problems of textual transmission from antiquity, the plays of Plautus had to contend with a living theatrical tradition, with actors and producers who used and abused them both within and after Plautus' lifetime, leaving traces, visible and possibly invisible, of their handiwork in the play-texts that have reached us.[15] To a lesser extent the same is true of Terence, whose texts, despite their complete and, seemingly, relatively stable form, contain an alternative ending (*Andria*) and a highly complex alternative beginning (*Hecyra*), which may be the result of multiple performances.[16] Indeed, we might see the layering of the texts caused by their life in the living theatre as a continuation of that which derives from their origins as in some sense translations of Hellenistic Greek plays. As I suggest above, the search for originals was a dominant strand in scholarship on Roman comedy. This was *Quellenforschung* on steroids, for not only was it regularly directed at assessment (often negative) of the Roman achievement by comparison with the Greek, but it was also driven by a desire to unearth the lost glories of Greek originals by stripping away the covering of Roman dross. My characterisation of this scholarship is something of a straw man, and so hardly fair or representative of the best of such work, but neither is it entirely wrong to be concerned both at the circularity of some of the

---

[12] See Leo (1895–6) and (1895).   [13] Karakasis (2005); Fontaine (2010).

[14] Slater (2000) 3. This quotation is so good I have made it twice: Sharrock (2009) 18. On the problem of the text of Plautus, see especially Gratwick (1993) 3–4; Tarrant (1983) 302–3; on the textual transmission of Terence, see Reeve (1983).

[15] An extreme example of this mode of reading Plautus is the work of Zwierlein (1990–2).

[16] On which, see Sharrock (2009) 243–8.

arguments put forward by this 'analyst' school of reading Roman comedy and also at the resultant distraction from reading the plays in their own right.[17]

In the second half of the twentieth century, the reading of Roman comedy was enhanced by a number of developments, which in their different ways sought to explore the theatrical and social significance of the plays. Konstan's 1983 book, called simply *Roman Comedy*, provided a particularly sensitive analysis of the social meanings of the plays, and paved the way for more explicitly political readings such as those introduced in James (1998a). On the theatrical side, while Roman comedy has not enjoyed the spectacular modern success of Greek drama and remains very much the poor relation in the *Archive of Performances of Greek and Roman Drama*,[18] it had a long tradition of performance, both in Latin and, more often, in translation, in public schools such as Eton and the King's School, Canterbury, from as early as the sixteenth century, when Nicholas Udall, author of the Plautine inter-text *Ralph Roister-Doister* and producer of many Roman plays in closer translation, was headmaster of Eton. The baton has now been taken up most effectively, to my knowledge, by American institutions, such as the National Endowment for the Humanities summer school on Roman comedy and performance in 2012.[19] In Britain, Richard Beacham (also an American) has spearheaded work on Plautus as living theatre[20] and on the archaeology of the Roman stage.

The physical staging is not the only way of engaging with the text of Roman comedy as performance. Marshall (2006) is an outstanding example of the scholarly reading of the 'stagecraft and performance' of these plays, while my own 2009 book sought to approach the plays as a reader, but a reader who is always conscious of playing the imaginative role of audience. In recent years also, the so-called Freiburg school of Plautine scholarship has reacted to the analyst school of thought, and interacted interestingly with the performance-based and the social-embedded approaches, by stressing the contribution to Roman comedy from native Italian theatrical traditions, including those involving improvisation.[21] While apparent improvisation within a fixed text can only be a mimesis of making it up on the spot,[22] we can never know what role true improvisation might have played in

---

[17] A recent example of this mode of reading Plautus, and a good paper in its own terms, is Lowe (2007).

[18] www.apgrd.ox.ac.uk//.   [19] http://nehsummer2012romancomedy.web.unc.edu/.

[20] Beacham (1991) and (forthcoming).

[21] A representative example of the relationship between the improvisatory reading and the analyst tradition would be Stärk (1989).

[22] Arnott (2001).

performance and indeed in the rather fluid development of these texts. A 'mimesis of making it up' might be one way to characterise metatheatre, that great explosion of critical engagement with the plays of Plautus, which began with Slater (1985). While not everyone appreciates the virtues of this approach,[23] its staying power is considerable and a sign of its success is the way the metatheatrical approaches have now been taken up by scholars of Greek literature also, just as happened with intertextuality which was also pioneered for classical literature by Latinists.

So what exactly are they saying about Roman comedy? If I were, most unfairly, to pick two strands in the history of recent criticism on Plautus and Terence and to characterise one as negative and the other as positive, then the first would be the search for Greek originals and the second the celebration of metatheatre. The question of the relationship between the plays of Plautus and Terence and those of Greek New Comedy thankfully features relatively little in this volume, while the analysis of Roman comedy as a site of complex interaction with earlier theatrical and comic traditions both Greek and Roman has instead been highlighted (Telò and Panayotakis). Much earlier criticism has tended towards the circular, reconstructing Greek plays on the basis of Roman difference and then analysing the Roman as different. Even when it has been directed towards celebrating Roman originality, such as in the groundbreaking work of Fraenkel, it often falls into the trap of assuming or excusing Roman inferiority.[24] For a truly powerful intertextual reading of Roman comedy against Greek, we really need more texts of Greek comedy than currently exist, but it is good to see the tide turning in this direction.[25] It does so alongside the great development in, originally, Plautine studies which is metatheatrical reading, in which the great game of the play is reference to itself as play.[26] Terentian studies have been slower to gain admittance to the metatheatrical party, but it is becoming acknowledged that he deserves to sit at the head of the table.[27]

Terence says of two plays of Menander, the *Perinthia* and the *Andria*, that *qui utramvis recte norit ambas noverit* ('whoever knows the one, knows

---

[23] Rosenmeyer (2002).

[24] Fraenkel (2007) is the English translation of the magisterial 1922 book, the aim of which was undoubtedly to celebrate Plautine brilliance, but which did so in ways that could be taken, and were often taken, as disparagement of Roman contribution. See Halporn (1993) for an account of the literary history of what he nicely calls the 'Homeric Question of Latin Studies'.

[25] It is worth remembering just how little we know for sure about Greek New Comedy. Handley (2011) 146, for example, estimates that we have just about 5 per cent of Menander – and that mostly in tiny snippets.

[26] Slater (2000, originally 1985); Moore (1998b); and very many readings thereafter.

[27] See Christenson in this volume.

them both', Ter. *And.* 10). Many people would take this as the pot calling the kettle black, but it is important to realise that he is *only joking*. One of the common complaints against Roman comedy is that it is 'all the same'. This, I suggest, is doubly wrong: first, because the games with stock characters, theatrical conventions, repeated scenes, stock plots, and so on which drive so much of the humour of Roman comedy depend on those elements being recognisable, which can only be the case if they exist elsewhere; and, second, because in fact the plays are considerably less similar to each other than is generally thought. To illustrate this point, let us take a few examples of what would generally be thought of as standard elements in Roman comedy, and see how common they actually are. What we will find is that they do indeed keep popping up often enough for us to recognise and enjoy them, but, in Plautus especially, rather less often than we might expect. As regards Terence, we will find that certain leitmotifs do indeed have a high degree of prevalence within his corpus, sometimes to the extent that they have entered the popular imagination as parts of 'Roman comedy' without actually being at all common in Plautus. I have tried elsewhere to argue that Terence is 'self-consciously aware of his place in an established literary tradition. He is, I suggest, more artful, more artificial, more farcical than is generally assumed, as well as being (even) more literary.'[28] He is both more and less like Plautus than is often thought: less like, in that many of his plot elements are relatively rare in Plautus, but more like in his metatheatrical artistry, his obsession with plotting, and his skirting with the absurd.

Let us take first that most Plautine of characters, the controlling slave, who drives the action of the play and plots against the anti-comic forces of authority such as the stern father in order to promote the interests of the young lover. This *architectus*, as Palaestrio is cleverly called at *Mil.* 901, is often seen as some sort of reflection of the playwright himself. Ten or so years ago, I tried the experiment of asking a random group of Classicists, not comedy specialists, how many plays of Plautus they thought contained a character of this nature, to which the answer was all or nearly all of them. I asked how many plays of Terence contained this character, to which the answer was none of them. I would say that the answer is something more along the following lines.[29] The classic examples in Plautus are Pseudolus and Epidicus in their own plays, Palaestrio in *Miles Gloriosus*, Tranio in *Mostellaria*, and Chrysalus in *Bacchides*. A further group of plays, including *Persa*, *Amphitruo* (where the god Mercury is only pretending to be a comic slave), and *Asinaria*, give some role to a character of this nature, while in *Poenulus* and *Curculio* aspects of the role are shared between the

---

[28] Sharrock (2009) 20–1.   [29] See Sharrock (2009) 116–17 and 131–40.

active parasite who directs the action and the ironic slave who directs the audience's view of the play. Many other plays contain controlling characters who draw on the metatheatrical role of the slave-*architectus* (for example, the *matrona* in *Casina*, the prostitute Phronesium in *Truculentus*, and the group of old men in *Trinummus*), but they are not slaves. The slave-*architectus* Toxilus in *Persa* performs his role conventionally, with one very major exception – he is working for himself as lover. In all, I would suggest that just under half of the plays of Plautus contain a clever slave who controls the action. On the other hand, all of Terence's plays, except the extremely unusual *Adelphi*, contain a character who either plays the role as if he were in competition with Pseudolus (Davos in *Andria*, Syrus in *Heauton Timorumenos*) or plays around with the edges of the role (*Hecyra*, *Phormio*, where again the role is shared with someone who also plays around with the role of parasite[30]), or try to resist the role (*Eunuchus*).[31]

What about the topos of recognition? The paradigm is that of the baby, usually a girl, usually exposed at birth but sometimes lost in other ways, who is brought up as a slave, usually with a view to prostitution, but conveniently develops a relationship only with one lover, whom she will marry when she is recognised as a citizen. To pull out all the stops, the recognition should take place by means of some physical tokens, such as a ring, a bracelet, or some other trinket. Is this almost universal? No. Less than half of the extant plays of Plautus contain an explicit example of someone turning out to be someone else and thus enabling (or, in the case of *Epidicus*, obstructing) a marriage, but of those perhaps only three, *Cistellaria*, *Curculio*, and *Rudens*, can be described as full-blown classic examples of the motif. Several others play with the idea in a variety of ways. There is, for example, the way that a recognition-plot hovers around the edges of Plautus' *Casina*, although neither of the young couple ever appears, because this is a play about a *senex amator* and his conflict with his magnificent wife, who herself controls the action. With delightful disregard for propriety and comic convention, the prologue nonchalantly informs us that the nubile supposed slave girl Casina who is the bone of contention between father and mother/son will turn out to be freeborn and able to marry the son, but that the son will not appear in the play, because 'Plautus did not want him [to get back in time] and so demolished a bridge on his way' (*Cas.* 64).[32] *Poenulus* also contains the recognition of lost daughters by their father, but in this case the father in

---

[30] See Frangoulidis (1995); Sharrock (2014); and further bibliography mentioned there.
[31] See Sharrock (2009) 140–62.
[32] Many critics have traditionally suggested that Plautus has gone further in many of his plays and removed recognition plots where they would have existed in the Greek originals. See for example Auhagen (2009).

question is the Carthaginian Hanno, who will also recognise the lover of one of the daughters as his nephew, in a play replete with complexities of ethnicity, kinship, and acting which can hardly be called conventional. In *Captiui*, a citizen child has been sold into slavery and brought up as such until he is recognised and so can regain his rightful place in the family and society, but this is the one play with no women, and the child is a boy who, as the close companion of his master, was taken prisoner of war and swapped identities with his master in order to enable the latter's escape. Although there is indeed a recognition scene here, it does not enable marriage but sonship, although not until after the son-slave in question, Tyndarus, has been the only slave in Roman comedy actually to suffer the punishments which are so often threatened but never otherwise imposed, no doubt because he is not really a slave.[33]

If the plays of Plautus give surprisingly little space to the recognition plot, Terence is full of it. Apart from *Adelphi*, only *Hecyra* does not have a conventional recognition which enables a marriage. *Hecyra*, the only play of Terence also not straightforwardly to have a double plot, does in fact feature both doubling and recognition, but the same characters play both parts, and the recognition scene comes when this fact itself is recognised: the premarital rapist who had fathered the child which is now destroying the young marriage turns out to be the husband himself and all is, in a sense, well.[34] Does this mean that, while Plautus' plays are clearly not 'all the same', the accusation does stick to Terence? It perhaps would not be entirely unfair to describe four of the six plays of Terence, *And.*, *Haut.*, *Euch.*, and *Phorm.*, as variations on a theme, just as Terence's highly original prologues are seven such variations (seven, because there are two extant prologues to *Hecyra*). The remaining two also play with many similar motifs and character types and this degree of similarity is precisely what allows the extraordinarily sensitive (if by no means always comfortable) development of plot and character offered by Terence's corpus. Not only does it contain some daringly original moves, such as a rape which takes place within the play (*Eun.*), and a parasite who invites others to a party at his house (*Phorm.*), but also it changes the European dramatic tradition by its remarkable innovation of leaving the audience in a state of uncertainty over the progress of the plot (especially *Hec.*, but throughout).[35]

---

[33] See Fitzgerald in this volume.   [34] See Sharrock (2009) 233–49.
[35] To be fair, considerably fewer plays of Plautus than is generally thought tell us at the beginning how they are going to turn out, for many Terentian innovations actually have Plautine seeds, but Terence's development must nonetheless stand as a significant move away from irony and towards surprise in the manipulation of the reader.

Premarital rape as a forerunner to the immediate context of the plot occurs only in Plautus' *Aulularia*, Terence's *Andria*, *Hecyra*, and *Adelphi*, with the action moved to the middle of the play in *Eunuchus*. Another interesting variant is in Plautus' *Epidicus*. Here, the premarital rape has taken place in the older generation: the young man's father, Periphanes, now a widower, wants to find and marry the woman he wronged years previously. Her daughter, the result of the rape/previous relationship, is the beloved of the young man Stratippocles, which means that, for Roman society at least, the recognition obstructs any possible marriage, rather than allowing it. Terence's *Phormio* also uses the motif of a previous relationship among the older generation, in this case presented as full-blown bigamy.[36] And that is all. Any familiarity with the plays just mentioned will show how extremely different they all are. What a skilled reader of Roman comedy can, at least usually, rely on, however, is that the nature of a previous relationship will be dictated by the original and eventual social situation of the woman. What this means is that if a woman is known to be a citizen and potentially marriageable, the 'relationship' is presented as rape, although the degree of force relative to persuasion/real relationship varies from the extreme of *Hecyra* (a chance, almost absurd, meeting in the street provoking the rape) to the less irresponsible but still cowardly behaviour of the young man in *Aulularia*, *Andria*, and *Adelphi*. Terence makes explicit in his *Phormio* example what is also implicit in Plautus' *Epidicus*, namely that 'rape' is more like a euphemism (if that is not too paradoxical a description) for an ongoing relationship. Those ongoing relationships with apparently unmarriageable girls, but who will be recognised and thus married, generally have not produced offspring: *Cistellaria* and *Rudens* are the only straightforward examples. In *Phormio*, Terence provides variation insofar as to have the young couple properly married, but recognition is still needed in order to gain the father's acceptance of the situation.

What about some of the other supposedly near-universal motifs? Although tension between the generations is common,[37] rivalry between father and son for the same erotic object occurs only in three plays of Plautus (*Casina*, *Asinaria*, and *Mercator*) and none of Terence. Getting money out of the old man in order to allow the young man to pursue his amatory adventures is another comic topos which might seem to be excessively common in Plautus and Terence. There are indeed some magnificent examples of the phenomenon: Pseudolus creating his *minae* out of nowhere by tricking the old man Simo into promising them himself; Chrysalus, similarly, using a double bluff of trust and mistrust to get money out of his old man Nicobulus; Epidicus

---

[36] See Sharrock (2014).   [37] See Dinter and Fantham in this volume.

developing a series of fiendishly complicated tricks in order to keep up with his young master's changing demands for erotic support. Nor is the motif confined to the simple tricking of fathers: the titular asses of *Asinaria* provide some money which should be going to the rich wife Artemona, but which is appropriated by the disreputable old man Demaenetus in order to allow his son to hire a prostitute for a year, on the condition that he, Demaenetus, gets the first turn; the old men in *Trinummus*, a play where everything is backwards, set up a perhaps unnecessarily complicated trick to provide the dowry to enable the marriage of a young girl, despite her brother's profligacy. But again there are many plays which do not really feature the extortion of money in the standard way at all: examples would be *Aulularia, Captiui, Cistellaria, Menaechmi, Stichus*, and Terence's *Adelphi*.

The last of these is a magnificent example because it appears at first glance to conform to many of the topoi of the genre, but ends up refusing most of the conventional mechanisms for addressing those topoi. *Adelphi* takes Terentian doubling to excess: two brothers are between them the fathers of two sons who are also brothers, in that the older of the older brothers had two sons, one of whom was adopted by his uncle, who had never married – so the younger men are brothers and cousins at the same time. Two love plots are intertwined through the play, as in most plays of Terence, one being a prostitute-affair and the other a citizen-affair, leading of course to marriage. There is even a slave who does an ordinary 'running slave' routine, apparently without irony. This, after the many playful and self-conscious pseudo-running slaves which the genre has produced through the past 50 or so years, cannot be other than double bluff. Moreover, despite the existence of two love affairs of different natures, the play involves neither the extortion of money nor a recognition scene. Instead of the conventional trick to get hold of money in order to buy the prostitute-beloved, the dynamic young man (not her lover, but his cousin-brother, who apparently does not have sufficient dynamism to admit to his own fathering a child on a poor citizen) simply cuts to the quick and steals the girl from the pimp. In this, the last extant play of Roman comedy as we know it, it seems as though Terence is playing a particularly complicated game with tradition. For that reason, I would strongly recommend that *Adelphi* should be a play read not as an introduction to Roman comedy, but by those who have already gained extensive experience and understanding of this complex and highly sophisticated genre. Indeed, it is hard to find a play which is not better read with a knowledge of other plays, but, since one must start somewhere, I would suggest that a good starting place would be either of the two plays with which I began this discussion: Plautus' comic masterpiece *Pseudolus*, or Terence's *Eunuchus*, for its magnificent mixing of rumbustious humour and complex human interaction. For comedy is a genre in which, as Terence says, we know that prostitutes are meant to be bad and old men are meant to be tricked, but we also need to learn that what we think we know about the genre must be constantly renegotiated and held up for comparison against what each instantiation of it actually provides. In its own time and in its long afterlife, Roman comedy is like spring, always old and always new.

Further Reading

The best further reading in order to appreciate some of the issues which I have been trying to explore in this chapter would be the plays themselves. They gain a great deal by greater familiarity. A good test would be to watch *A Funny Thing Happened on the Way to the Forum*, which is easiest to do in the film version directed by Richard Lester (1966), and to see how many references to different plays one can identify. It is a fine example of inter-textual *contaminatio*, that is, the mixing of elements from different plays, which shows that the value of this practice was appreciated by the performance culture of the 1960s, when classical literary criticism was still lagging behind and failing to understand that when Terence defended himself from the accusation in the prologue to *Eunuchus* he was actually making an important point about the nature of literature.[38]

---

[38] See Sharrock (2009) 91–3.

PART I

The World of Roman Comedy

I

GESINE MANUWALD

Plautus and Terence in Their Roman Contexts

Introduction

Scenic productions formed a significant element of Roman festival culture from its inception. Literary versions of such performances came into being with the adoption of the dramatic genres of tragedy and comedy from Greece; soon, further dramatic genres established themselves. Out of the great number of plays written over the centuries only a few have been preserved in full: from the Republican period there are comedies by Plautus and Terence; from imperial times there are tragedies and one *fabula prae-texta* transmitted under Seneca's name. It is no surprise then that works by Plautus, Terence, and Seneca have received the greatest attention; but their historical, social, and literary contexts have not always been adequately taken into account.

Even though modern recipients will never be able to approach Roman dramas in the same way as original audiences did, attempts at appreciating these plays within their historical framework are possible. With regard to the comedies of Plautus and Terence from the Republican period, this means that they have to be placed within the context of their dramatic genre, which covers, beyond the two well-known playwrights, a large number of poets over an extended period of time. These dramas should also be seen within the context of other dramatic genres and of Republican literature more generally, of their historical and social settings, and of the performance conditions as determined by organisational structures and audience reception. This chapter will look at these framing contexts, which mutually condition each other (on Roman vs. Greek comedy, see Telò in this volume).

Context 1: The Dramatic Genre of *Fabula Palliata*

The emergence of literary Roman drama is conventionally dated to 240 BC. In this year Rome's first poet Livius Andronicus brought Latin drama(s) based on existing Greek models on stage; his plays were shown at a festival organised by Roman magistrates right after the conclusion of the First Punic War (264–241 BC).[1] Discrepancies in the sources leave it unclear whether Livius Andronicus produced one or two dramas on this occasion and whether these were a tragedy and/or comedy; at any rate the poet established Greek-style tragedy (*fabula crepidata* = tragedy in Greek dress) and Greek-style comedy (*fabula palliata* = comedy in Greek dress) in Rome. By the time Plautus (*c.* 250–184 BC) started producing Greek-style comedies towards the end of the third century BC, this type of drama had already been composed and watched at Rome for a few decades. In addition to Livius Andronicus (*c.* 280/70–200 BC), poets active in the area of comedy before Plautus or contemporary with him include Naevius (*c.* 280/60–200 BC) and Ennius (239–169 BC).

Hence Plautus could build on established dramatic conventions and rely on the audience's familiarity with them. The increasing sophistication of dramatic genres is probably the reason why Plautus is the first known Roman dramatist to have concentrated on one dramatic genre only (*fabula palliata*). In this area he seems to have been prolific: twenty-one (almost complete) plays are extant, and many more titles and fragments survive under his name, some of which, however, are likely to be spurious. Many plays came to be attributed to this successful playwright; 130 plays circulated under his name at some point, according to ancient evidence (Gell. *NA* 3.3). This situation served as an incentive for early scholars to look at Plautus' output and try to separate genuine from spurious works.[2]

While the surviving fragments of comedies by Livius Andronicus and Ennius are meagre and do not allow a valid assessment of their specific characteristics, the extant remains of Naevius' comedies (titles of about 35 comedies and about 140, partly incomplete, comic verses) are more substantial; in fact, Naevius was mainly regarded as a writer of comedies in antiquity.[3] On the basis of the available titles and fragments it seems that his comedies exhibited typical motifs and plot structures of (Greek and Roman) New Comedy: there are figures such as parasites, braggart soldiers, rivals, prostitutes, twins, and even quadruplets; plots feature love affairs, conflicts between fathers and sons because of love relationships or the need for money, as well as slaves directing the course of action. Some comedies were apparently made more complex by 'double' plots, i.e. featuring two fathers and two sons with similar problems, by issues around mistaken

---

[1] Cf. Cic. *Brut.* 72; *Tusc.* 1.3; *Sen.* 50; Liv. 7.2.8; Val. Max. 2.4.4; Gell. *NA* 17.21.42; Cass. *Chron.*, p. 128 *MGH* AA 11.2 (on 239 BC).
[2] Cf. Manuwald's chapter on reception in this volume.
[3] Cf. Gell. *NA* 15.24; Hieron. *Ab Abr.* 1816, 201 BC (p. 135g Helm).

‍

identity or by metatheatrical statements, some of which seem to come from prologues.[4]

The prologue to Terence's *Andria* claims that Naevius was one of the Roman comic poets who used *contaminatio*, i.e. who combined elements from several Greek models into one Latin play (Ter. *An.* 15–21). On the whole Naevius kept the Greek setting and the Greek point of view of his models, while at the same time including allusions to Roman reality as well as references to Roman virtues and socially and politically relevant values.[5] Equally, Naevius enhanced the Roman element in other literary genres, composing dramas and an epic on topics from Roman history. All this points to creative adaptation and poetic originality in Naevius' output.

As has been recognised, there are similarities in diction and individual motifs between Naevius and Plautus,[6] and a few titles are assigned to both poets in the textual tradition (*Carbonaria, Colax, Nervolaria*).[7] Plautus is said to have revised and updated plays of older poets, which thereby gained characteristic features of his style and were ascribed to him (Gell. *NA* 3.3.13). This relationship to predecessors and the fact that some traits commonly associated with Plautus are already present in the works of his older contemporary indicate that Plautus worked in an emerging comic tradition and developed existing elements further.

The dramas by Plautus and those by Terence (*c.* 195/4–159 BC) are separated by several decades, during which the poet Caecilius Statius (*c.* 230/20–168/7 BC) was active. Owing to this chronological position, modern scholars often regard Caecilius as an intermediary or transitional figure.[8] As his dramatic output only survives in fragments (42 titles of comedies and almost 300, partly incomplete, lines), it is difficult to get a proper idea of his plays. But Caecilius' comedies must have been impressive: Cicero says that

---

[4] Cf. e.g. parasites (Naev. *Colax* [cf. Ter. *Eun.* 23–34]; *Pall.* 60 R.³ = 57 W.); braggart soldiers (Naev. *Colax* [cf. Ter. *Eun.* 23–34]); rivals (Naev. *Pall.* 41–2 R.³ = 42–3 W.); prostitutes (Naev. *Pall.* 75–9 R.³ = 74–9 W.); conflicts between fathers and sons on account of love relationships and money (Naev. *Pall.* 95; 96–8 R.³ = 105; 94–6 W.); twins and even quadruplets (Naev. *Pall.* 2–3 R.³ = 2–3 W.; *Quadrigemini*); love affairs (Naev. *Pall.* 55; 90–1; 96–8 R.³ = 60; 88–9; 94–6 W.); banquets (Naev. *Pall.* 81 R.³ = 72 W.); important role of slaves (names of slaves as titles); double plots (Naev. *Pall.* 83–4; 86 R.³ = 80–1; 82 W.); confusions between characters (Naev. *Pall.* 2–3 R.³ = 2–3 W.); metatheatrical statements (Naev. *Pall.* 1; 17; 72–4 R.³ = 1; 15; 69–71 W.).

[5] Cf. e.g. Naev. *Pall.* 69; 83–4; 92–3; 108–10 R.³ = 67; 80–1; 90–1; *Inc.* 1–3 W.

[6] Cf. e.g. Naev. *Pall.* 53 R.³ = 58 W.: Plaut. *St.* 118–19 – Naev. *Pall.* 82 R.³ = 84–5 W.: Plaut. *Most.* 323–4 – Naev. *Pall.* 95 R.³ = 105 W.: Plaut. *Most.* 233–4.

[7] In the case of *Nervolaria* this depends on an emendation of the title for Naevius' play as transmitted in Nonius Marcellus (Non., p. 151.2 M. = 220 L.: Nervularia *Ritschl*: herularia *codd.*).

[8] On the position of Plautus, Caecilius Statius, and Terence within the *palliata* tradition cf. esp. Wright (1974); Franko (2013).

Caecilius may 'perhaps' (*fortasse*) be called the greatest comic writer (Cic. *Opt. gen.* 2); Volcacius Sedigitus' canon (*c.* 100 BC) of the ten best writers of comedy is headed by Caecilius (cf. Gell. *NA* 15.24); Quintilian reports that the ancients extolled Caecilius (Quint. *Inst.* 10.1.99); and (on one occasion) Gellius refers to him as 'that famous writer of comedies' (Gell. *NA* 4.20.13: *ille comoediarum poeta inclutus*).[9]

Caecilius' impact may have been based on stunning scenes as well as on sophisticated and dramatically effective plot construction (cf. Varro, *Sat. Men.* 399 B.) In addition, he is mentioned as one of those poets who easily moved the emotions (cf. Varro, fr. 40 Funaioli). In terms of content he seems to have used stock comic plots, but to have varied them significantly in some of his plays and included metatheatrical statements on typical features of *fabulae palliatae* (e.g. Caec. *Pall.* 243–4 R.³ = 236–7 W.). His father figures were apparently known to be harsh (cf. Cic. *Cael.* 37–8; Quint. *Inst.* 11.1.39). Questions of social interaction and reputation, problems concerning the legitimacy and education of children, other issues of family relationships, the portrayal of human conditions, such as poverty or old age, appear to have been prominent in his plots (e.g. Caec. *Hypobolimaeus, Plocium*, and *Synephebi*; Cic. *Sen.* 24–6).

The prologue to Terence's *Hecyra* reveals (Ter. *Hec.* 1–57) that Caecilius worked with the same producer as Terence, Ambivius Turpio. According to Terence's text, Ambivius Turpio was interested in both poets and supported them through the difficult early stages of their careers. Both dramatists were apparently confronted by opponents and initially driven off the stage; hence both are likely to have written plays that had the potential for success and therefore annoyed rivals.[10] The two dramatists might therefore share characteristics, even if other sources testify to differences in specific areas such as language or character portrayal. The story, though chronologically problematic, that Caecilius enjoyed *Andria* when the young Terence read this play to him[11] also indicates that some affinity was perceived between the two.

Caecilius' dramas are likely to have discussed serious topics, but also to have included impressive stage effects. Issues and values featuring in his plays, as can be inferred from the fragments, are mostly concerned with

---

[9] Elsewhere Caecilius is criticised for ruining Menander's *Plokion* (Gell. *NA* 2.23).

[10] The interpretation of the prologues to Terence's *Hecyra* has been controversial, and the two unsuccessful performances of the play have often been seen as a sign of Terence's failure to produce plays of sufficient interest to Roman audiences. However, the text of the prologue suggests that the performances were interrupted not by the original audience leaving, but by other people entering the venue; these disturbances might have been arranged by Terence's opponents. On the *Hecyra* prologues, cf. esp. Gilula (1978); (1981); Sandbach (1982); Parker (1996) 592–601.

[11] Cf. Suet./Donat. *Vita Ter.* 3; Hieron. *Ab Abr.* 1859, 158 BC (p. 142a Helm).

family life, the corresponding relationships, and the impact on one's position in society, which looks forward to Terence, just as the more limited range of models and the use of Greek titles. By contrast, Caecilius' predecessors Naevius and Plautus not only drew on a wider variety of models and plot variations, but also touched on a broader range of socially and politically relevant values. Hence, with regard to themes, elements of dramatic technique, and contributions to literary discussions, Caecilius' plays indicate a development towards Terence, while they seem to have continued the Plautine tradition in areas such as metre, style, language, and comic effects.

Connections between all these poets and the emergence of generic conventions, including modifications within this framework, are further indicated by the fact that Terence refers to the practice of Ennius, Naevius, and Plautus as a precedent and distances himself from his contemporary opponent Luscius Lanuvinus, who seems to have followed different poetic principles (Ter. *An.* 6–7; 18–21; *Haut.* 22; *Eun.* 6–26; *Ph.* 1).

Terence does not mark the end of the history of *fabula palliata*: in the second half of the second century there was Sex. Turpilius (d. 104/3 BC). Turpilius' works, of which thirteen titles and just over 200, partly incomplete, lines survive, show the continuation of characteristics of Terentian comedy in titles and themes, but also feature innovations in the comic plot, determined partly by the dramatic conventions of his time.

In addition to the standard characters and situations of New Comedy,[12] Turpilius' dramas include attention to everyday occupations, such as sailors, fishermen, and conditions at sea.[13] Some fragments have the character of sayings, sometimes combined with a (popular-)philosophical connotation (e.g. Turp. *Pall.* 9–10; 28; 40; 142–4; 213 R.^{3}). Additionally, the possible appropriation of plays from Greek Middle Comedy and a play entitled *Leucadia*, with its reference to the story of Sappho and Phaon, indicate that Turpilius might have pursued the development of *fabula palliata* towards the presentation of more serious topics and introduced 'supernatural' or 'mythical' aspects.

This suggests that Turpilius continued the tendency towards a more refined, 'Hellenic' style of drama and made his plays attractive by including reminiscences of Plautine comedy, at a time when audiences could be said to prefer revivals of Plautine comedy to productions of new plays (cf. Plaut.

---

[12] Cf. e.g. love affairs (Turp. *Pall.* 37–9 R.^{3}); marriages (Turp. *Pall.* 3; 41; 163; 164; 166 R.^{3}); evil pimps (Turp. *Pall.* 133–5 R.^{3}); (greedy) courtesans (Turp. *Pall.* 33; 42; 160–2; 185–8 R.^{3}); slaves (Turp. *Pall.* 69–70 R.^{3}); strict old men/fathers (Turp. *Pall.* 35–6 R.^{3}); tricks/intrigues of scheming slaves against old men (Turp. *Pall.* 136–8; 205–6 R.^{3}).

[13] Cf. e.g. Turp. *Pall.* 21–2; 23; 48–9; 139–41; 214–16 R.^{3}; *Leucadia*.

Cas. 5–20). Thus it may be concluded that Turpilius combined characteristics of both Plautus/Naevius and Terence/Caecilius: he followed Terence's (and Caecilius') 'Hellenised' version of *fabula palliata* in titles, models, and themes, but remained closer to Plautus (and Naevius) in style, language, and scene structures. This adaptation of standard comic techniques was presumably also a reaction to the tastes of contemporary audiences, since additional features such as turbulent and sophisticated incidents on stage or a higher frequency of low-life figures can also be observed in works of other dramatic genres produced in this period.

For the period after Turpilius' death there is no record of new *fabulae palliatae* written for the Roman stage. Yet, revival performances of comedies (like those of works of other dramatic genres) continued until the end of the Republic (cf. e.g. Cic. *Rosc. Am.* 47; *Sest.* 118–23; *Fam.* 9.22.1; *Sen.* 65). Eventually, however, alternative forms of comic entertainment and contests for actors and poets (cf. e.g. Macr. *Sat.* 2.7.2–9) became more and more prominent. In contrast to tragedy, comedy was not taken up as literary drama in imperial times, presumably since it was less effective without a performance dimension and did not lend itself equally readily to discussions of general questions of a more explicit ethical or philosophical nature.

Overall, the characteristics of the major writers of *fabula palliata* during the Republican period, in connection with their chronological position, indicate that there was a continuous evolution of this dramatic genre from the exuberant to the more refined and serious, while dramatic effects were kept for the benefit of audiences; these elements were altered and adapted in response to general changes in the evolution of dramatic performances. Beyond their individual poetic characteristics, the two comic playwrights of whom entire plays are extant, Plautus and Terence, can therefore be placed within such developments.

Context 2: Republican Drama

In order to establish the place of Greek-style comedy within the framework of Republican drama more precisely, the diachronic analysis of a succession of *palliata* poets must be supplemented by a synchronic look at contemporary dramatic genres in Rome, since *fabula palliata* developed within this broader dramatic context.

Looking in hindsight at the genres of Roman drama, ancient scholars, in particular the late-Republican polymath Varro, established a coherent system of Greek and Roman varieties, their characteristics, and their mutual relationship, which was taken up by late-antique commentators and grammarians.[14] In addition to dramatic genres such as *fabula Atellana* or *mimus*, which were regarded as low and relatively insignificant, there was a fourfold arrangement of two Greek and two Roman versions or two serious and two light varieties of drama: i.e. Greek-style serious drama (*fabula crepidata*/tragedy) based on Greek myth; Roman-style serious drama (*fabula praetexta*) based on events from Roman history; Greek-style comedy (*fabula palliata*/comedy) representing everyday events of ordinary people set in Greece; and Roman-style comedy (*fabula togata*) representing everyday events of ordinary people set in Rome. *Fabula palliata* is distinguished from its Roman comic counterpart by its setting and characters, but also by its more fanciful character and greater freedom from the conventions of Roman life, since the action takes place in a foreign country. It differs from serious forms of drama by its personnel, consisting of ordinary human beings including slaves, as well as by the atmosphere of its plots.

This arrangement of dramatic genres is a neat, academic system, which holds true for the most part, but there are also overlaps and mutual influences that cross generic boundaries. The most obvious instance is Plautus' *Amphitruo*, which the poet defines as a 'tragicomedy', using a term that seems to have been coined for the occasion (Plaut. *Amph.* 50–63). The play exhibits a mixture of dramatic genres, since both gods and slaves take part in the action, as outlined in the prologue. However, the 'combination' can be regarded as going beyond that because the piece includes scenes of a more serious and elevated nature set in a comic context. Plautus comes back to generic questions in prologues to other dramas (esp. Plaut. *Capt.* 55–62), but nowhere else does he explicitly transgress generic boundaries, even though plays such as *Captiui* or *Rudens* also include scenes and motifs reminiscent of tragedy (see Telò in this volume).[15] In addition to these straightforward and rather serious uses of 'tragic' elements, Plautus exploits typical structures and diction found in tragedies in his own plots for comic or parodic effects (e.g. Plaut. *Merc.* 195–7; *Most.* 496b–504; *Pseud.* 702–7). He even refers to particular tragedies and tragic scenes, presumably Roman adaptations (Plaut. *Amph.* 41–5; *Poen.* 1–15; *Ru.* 86).

In Terence the impact of tragedy is not primarily felt by explicit allusions (but cf. Ter. *Eun.* 590 with Donat. ad loc.) or generic discussions; his works rather exemplify an increasing convergence of serious and light dramatic genres towards the end of the Republic, as his plays have a noticeably serious

---

[14] Cf. e.g. Diom. *Ars* 3, *Gramm. Lat.* 1.482–91 Keil; Euanth. *Fab.* 4.1–3; Donat. *Com.* 6. 1–2; on Ter. *Ad.* 7; Lydus, *Mag.* 1.40; *Lib. gloss.* 1.2–8; 2.9–11.

[15] *Captiui* with its warlike theme has been compared to contemporary *fabulae praetextae* and interpreted as a comic version of a *fabula praetexta*, possibly performed in connection with Flamininus' return to Rome in 194 BC; cf. Lefèvre (1998).

dimension and take up themes such as family relationships and problems of education, which could equally feature in tragedy. Even if Terence builds on themes in Greek models, his choices and the way of presentation could be influenced by developments in contemporary tragedy.[16]

The reduced role of the clever slave and the less exuberant action in later *fabulae palliatae* could also have been shaped in response to the conventions and tone of the emerging *fabula togata*. This dramatic genre of comedy set in Rome seems to have been developed on the model of *fabula palliata* as an instance of differentiation, when the latter was becoming more restrained and Hellenic,[17] in order to provide a Roman counterpart: while the subject matter and plot outlines of *fabulae togatae* and *palliatae* were similar, the character of *fabulae togatae* was more serious (Sen. *Ep.* 8.8; 89.7) and the atmosphere was more sober and closer to Roman reality, so that, for instance, slaves were not normally allowed to be cleverer than their masters (Donat. on Ter. *Eun.* 57).[18] At the same time, Roman tragedy (just as Greek models by Euripides, for example) seems to have increasingly employed successful comic techniques (such as false identity) over the course of the Republican period.

Such connections and similarities point to mutual interdependence and influences among all forms of Roman Republican drama, which will have had an impact on the development of the *fabula palliata* and perhaps also on its eventual decline.

Context 3: Republican Literary Texts

Although the framework of Roman drama is most important for the development of Roman comedy, a public genre such as drama cannot be separated from other areas of formalised speech or writing. Prose genres such as oratory and historiography as well as the poetic genres of epic or satire were emerging and developing in Rome at the same time as drama; while in

---

[16] On Terence and tragedy, cf. Sharrock (2009) 219–32; (2013) 55–61. On the relation of *fabula palliata* to tragedy, see Telò in this volume.

[17] Sheets (1983) has suggested that in Plautus' time the *fabula palliata* was still in the process of acquiring its characteristic form, distinct from tragedy. Although the fluidity of generic boundaries in this period may be one of the explanations for the experimental character of his plays, there is already a clear awareness of the components of a standard comedy in Plautus.

[18] Since there is no unambiguous evidence on the emergence of the *fabula togata*, different views have been put forward. All things considered, *fabulae togatae* are most likely to have appeared in the early second century BC, when *fabulae palliatae* were still being written, and therefore to be a further variant rather than a replacement. Cf. e.g. Duckworth (1952) 68–9; Beare (1964) 129.

this period epic poetry was produced by writers who were also dramatists, oratory and historiography were the domain of Roman politicians and noblemen from the start.

A link to epic and historiography may be noticed in humorous (real or fictitious) battle narratives, but otherwise a significant impact of these literary genres is not particularly noticeable in Greek-style Roman comedy. To oratory, however, there are closer correspondences, especially as it was becoming more sophisticated in this period and speeches started to get published (cf. also Cic. *Brut.* 65), which indicates their recognition as pieces of formal writing. A relationship to oratory is most obvious in Terence's metaliterary prologues, which acquire the status of defence speeches and in some of which the speaker explicitly defines himself as 'orator' in the double sense of the word (Ter. *Haut.* 11; *Hec.* 9; *Ad.* 1–5).[19] In the body of a play characters' speeches may show signs of the conventions of rhetoric, such as *captatio benevolentiae*, ring-composition or rhetorical figures, or include parody of elaborate rhetoric (cf. e.g. Plaut. *Most.* 84–156; *Ps.* 394–414; Caec. *Pall.* 142–57 R.³ = 136–50 W.). Whether at this point in time both comedy and oratory, which developed in tandem, were influenced by Greek models and rhetorical theory or developed and formalised elements of a 'native Latin tradition of rhetoric' or a combination of both, close connections between the two genres are obvious.[20]

Further (less literary) forms of formal speech, such as prayers, legal language, battle reports or other technical business, have also left their mark as formalised statements in the respective styles have been incorporated or parodied, particularly by Plautus (e.g. Plaut. *Amph.* 203–61; *Mil.* 200–34).[21]

References of this kind, as well as rhetorical construction of speeches, will have linked *fabulae palliatae* to real-life experiences of Roman audiences.

Context 4: Historical and Social Background

While the contexts surveyed so far are 'literary' (in a broad sense of the term), the genre of drama, being performed to mixed audiences, is rooted within contemporary historical and social conditions. In Rome, even plays developed from earlier Greek dramas were selected and adapted to fit a Roman framework. On a more superficial level such an adjustment is clear from the replacement of Greek terms and customs by the corresponding Roman versions, by the inclusion of allusions to Roman institutions and to Roman

---

[19] Cf. esp. Goldberg (1983) (with references).   [20] See Barsby (2007).
[21] On passages with military allusions, cf. Gaiser (1972) 1,089–93.

or Italian localities and towns (e.g. Plaut. *Capt.* 90; 489; 877b–885a; Ter. *Eun.* 255–9), by references to Roman conventions such as praetorian edicts (e.g. Plaut. *Curc.* 280–98), and by the explanation of customs common in Greece, but not in Rome (e.g. Plaut. *Cas.* 68–78; *St.* 446–8).[22] Above all, the adaptation is obvious from the choice of plots that showcase problems of relevance to all humans or the aftermath of a war, with both issues relevant to contemporary Roman audiences.

Although Plautus and Terence are frequently considered together, they are separated by several decades during which historical circumstances changed. Almost all of Plautus' plays were written during the Second Punic War (218–201 BC) or shortly afterwards, when Rome dealt with the threat of a foreign enemy and asserted the position of the emerging Roman empire, developing the Romans' view of themselves in the process. In Terence's time no major war was under way, but as a result of preceding conflicts in the East there had been a huge influx of Greek learning and culture, and Rome had to position itself in relation to this. Therefore it is not surprising that wars and their consequences play a significant role in Plautine comedy (e.g. Plaut. *Amph.*; *Capt.*; *Ep.*; *Mil.*) while more 'humane' and 'philosophical' topics or questions concerning the internal organisation of communities are prominent in Terence's works.

More generally, during the third and second centuries BC Roman society was subject to an increasing exposure to Greek culture.[23] In the age of Plautus, in the wake of the Punic Wars, the Romans adapted and adopted elements of Greek culture, then the leading cultural force, to demonstrate their growing standing. On the basis of a highly sophisticated model, the Romans began to shape their own literature in Latin. In Terence's time, after the Third Macedonian War (171–168 BC), the exchange intensified, when important Greek philosophers and other scholars spent time in Rome and interacted with the Roman cultural elite. Against this background it is not a surprise that Plautus and Terence, like contemporary dramatists, looked to Greek comedies as models: while this provided them with a paradigm for plot and themes, they were confident enough to adapt the dramas to the Roman context.

The incoming riches from Rome's conquests and the increased cultural interaction with the areas brought under Rome's control had an impact on Roman society and the attitude to Greek customs. Still, the world depicted in *fabulae palliatae* was a foreign world, where different conventions with

---

[22] On references to the Roman world, cf. also Gaiser (1972) 1,088–95; for a study of some of the comic themes in a Roman context, see Leigh (2004); on allusions to the contemporary situation in Terence, cf. also Starks (2013).

[23] On this aspect, cf. e.g. Gruen (1990).

respect to the role of prostitutes, marriage conventions or the relationship between masters and slaves or the members of different generations operated, as the poets sometimes indicate (e.g. Plaut. *Cas.* 68–78; *St.* 446–8). Accordingly, lascivious and debauched behaviour can be defined as 'behaving like a Greek' (*pergraecari*: e.g. Plaut. *Bacch.* 813; *Most.* 22; 64; 960; *Poen.* 603). This contrast between societies does not mean, however, that the topics presented in the plays are irrelevant for Roman audiences: what these dramas say about inter-human relationships is transferable.

As regards the poets' own social and cultural position, Plautus and Terence, like all early 'Roman' poets, did not come from the city of Rome: Plautus hailed from Umbrian Sarsina,[24] and Terence was a native of North Africa.[25] While these dramatists eventually moved to Rome and started writing in Latin for Roman audiences, because of their background, they will have been familiar with the literature and culture of peoples in the Mediterranean by the time they came to Rome. The poets' movement between cultures is illustrated by the famous statement of Plautus' contemporary Ennius, who said that he had three hearts, referring to his command of Oscan, Greek, and Latin (cf. Gell. *NA* 17.17.1).

Further information about the poets' lives is mainly anecdotal. A report in Gellius (Gell. *NA* 3.3.14) suggests that Plautus may have had previous experience in theatre business before he started writing comedies, which could explain his familiarity with dramatic technique and the use of slapstick elements. Terence not only was not a Roman, but was also originally a slave of the senator Terentius Lucanus, who supported him because of his intelligence and later freed him; Terence thus enjoyed a good education (Suet./ Donat. *Vita Ter.* 1), which may have been an important basis for his literary activity. Various bits of evidence, such as information in the ancient *Vita* (Suet./Donat. *Vita Ter.* 2), allegations that noble friends had actually written his plays or at least had aided him in their composition, which are refuted in Terence's prologues (Ter. *Haut.* 22–4; *Ad.* 15–21), as well as the performance contexts of some comedies (at funeral games for L. Aemilius Paulus), suggest that Terence was in touch with prominent noblemen such as P. Cornelius Scipio Aemilianus Africanus and C. Laelius Sapiens. Therefore Terence is likely to have had first-hand knowledge of intellectual and cultural movements and of political developments in his time. Terence died young, and according to one version this happened on his way back from a voyage to Greece, which he had undertaken to find more Greek plays (Suet./Donat.

[24] Cf. Fest., p. 274.12–14 L.; Hieron. *Ab Abr.* 1817, 200 BC (p. 135h Helm); Plaut. *Most.* 770.
[25] Cf. Suet./Donat. *Vita Ter.* 1.

Vita Ter. 7); this might indicate that he was dissatisfied with what was currently available at Rome, either because the supply of as yet untouched dramas (which seem to have been the models required) was exhausted or because he was looking for particular types of pieces.

Context 5: Organisation and Audience Reception

While the literary surroundings will have shaped the content, style, and structure of individual dramas, the physical circumstances of a drama's production influence the immediate effect of a performance on audiences and are therefore relevant for the context of reception.[26]

Originally, comedies, like works of other dramatic genres in Rome, were written for a single performance at a public festival.[27] Because dramatic performances only took place at festivals, which were organised by the authorities (or individual noblemen) and were established typically in honour of a god (with the appropriate rituals), they were placed within a broad religious and political framework. Initially, the only way to approach a Roman comedy was to watch a production in the theatre. Only later did scripts of plays become more widely available, so that by the first century BC dramas could be both watched and read, as Cicero testifies (Cic. *Rab. Post.* 29); this triggered the first scholarly activities in the late Republic.[28]

Since dramatic performances, like races in the circus, belonged to the festival entertainment provided by the organiser, there was no entrance fee. Performances were in principle open to everybody. Audiences therefore are likely to have been mixed as to background, social class, age, sex, and occupation, consisting of locals and visitors from elsewhere. Free citizens, slaves, married ladies, nurses with infants, prostitutes, attendants on magistrates, and ushers are mentioned as among the members of the audience in comic prologues (esp. Plaut. *Poen.* 5–35; Ter. *Hec.* 28–48). Dramatic poets seem to have taken the variety of social and intellectual backgrounds into account: they conveyed essential information in a straightforward format and produced scripts that could be received by different members of the audience on different levels, as the plays included both impressive stage action and discussions of complex topics. At the same time Plautus and Terence play with and talk about standard comic conventions (e.g. in prologues); this implies that they expected a significant portion of audiences to be familiar with these and thus able to appreciate such metatheatrical elements.

---

[26] For more details on setting and staging, cf. Marshall (2006) and his chapter in this volume.
[27] On Republican festivals, cf. Bernstein (1998).
[28] On the importance of scholarly activities in the late Republic for establishing 'dramatic literature', cf. Goldberg (2005).

As regards the venue for performances, poets writing plays for particular festivals will have been aware of the location and the arrangements for stage and auditorium; however, it is not known whether they took this into account when composing their plays. At any rate the particular character of the various festivals hardly seems to have affected the contents of dramas. For audiences, however, the venue contributed to shaping their overall experience. Since Rome did not have a permanent stone theatre until the dedication of Pompey's theatre in 55 BC,[29] all stages were wooden and temporary, although they had reached a remarkable degree of sophistication by the end of the Republican period.[30] Initially, temporary stages were erected in the Forum, the Circus Maximus or in front of the temple of the deity honoured by the festival. This means that many of the original venues were rather cramped spaces, where the audience used seating created *ad hoc* close to the stage.[31] In the early days there was no stratified seating according to social class, which later brought senators and equestrians to the front. Close interaction with the audience in the early days is indicated in Plautine comedies by the fact that they have characters address audiences or adopt the viewpoint of audiences (e.g. Plaut. *Merc.* 160; *Ru.* 1249–53; *Truc.* 931–2).

After the structure of the Roman theatre had developed into the form that is known from preserved stone theatres and from the description by the Augustan architect Vitruvius (Vitr. 5.6), stage and auditorium each filled about a half-circle opposite each other, and all action took place on stage.[32] Since there was no view into the distance as the stage bordered on a high stage wall (elaborately decorated in later periods) and Roman theatres tended to be erected on flat ground, audiences were turned into onlookers watching events in an enclosed space. The creation of such an illusion might have been appropriate for dramas such as *fabulae palliatae* set in a foreign country.

There is little evidence on the immediate impact of Roman plays. Terence's *Eunuchus* is known to have been the most successful Republican comedy in financial terms, as it earned the poet an unprecedented high sum, which was recorded on the title page of the script (Suet./Donat. *Vita Ter.* 3; Donat. on Ter. *Eun., praef.* 1.6*). Clearly, one of Terence's comedies was a success. The problems arising at the first performances of some of his plays, which

---

[29] On the building and the inaugural ceremonies, cf. e.g. Cic. *Fam.* 7.1–4; *Off.* 2.57; *Pis.* 65; Asc. on Cic. *Pis.*; *Pis.* 65 (p. 1; 15–16 C.); Tac. *Ann.* 14.20.2; Plin. *HN* 7.158; 8.20; Tert. *De spect.* 10.5; Cass. Dio 39.38.1–3; Plut. *Pomp.* 52.5.

[30] Cf. esp. Plin. *HN* 34.36; 36.5–6; 36.113–15 on the *scaena* of the curule aedile M. Aemilius Scaurus in 58 BC.

[31] On the layout and size of the early performance spaces, cf. Goldberg (1998) (on the Palatine).

[32] On the architecture of Roman theatres, cf. Sear (2006).

Terence only overcame thanks to the persistence and support of his impresario Ambivius Turpio, seem to have been caused by the envy and malice of opponents rather than by faults of his plays; that such steps were taken suggests that Terence's dramas were rather successful with audiences. Equally, revivals of Plautine plays were demanded by audiences in about the middle of the second century BC according to the prologue to Plautus' *Casina*, added for a revival performance about a generation after the first performance, since people enjoyed Plautus' plays and preferred them to worthless new ones (Plaut. *Cas.* 5–20).

Hence it seems that both comic playwrights whose complete plays are extant, Plautus as well as Terence, were successful in the Republican period, though presumably their plays made an impact in different ways due to their specific character.[33] Other *palliata* writers, such as Naevius and Caecilius, are likely to have enjoyed some success, at least initially, as ancient comments indicate. However, it was Plautus and Terence who soon developed into 'classics': the numerous plays that circulated under Plautus' name show his standing as a writer of comedies, while Terence was praised as a literary model and became a school author.

Conclusion

Since *fabulae palliatae* from the Republican period contain almost no specific references to contemporary events or individuals (as this seems to have been discouraged at Rome and is in line with the nature of the genre anyway), they may be studied on their own as entertaining pieces of literature. However, for an attempt at appreciating these plays in their historical setting and at explaining their characteristics and peculiarities, a range of contexts in which they were composed and transmitted has to be taken into account. These suggest a productive interaction with literary developments at Rome as well as the historical and social conditions at the time: obviously, despite being based on Greek models, these *fabulae palliatae* were an active element in Roman life, changing with the times, which may explain their popularity with contemporary audiences.

Further Reading

The surviving fragments of Livius Andronicus, Naevius, Ennius, Pacuvius, Accius, and Caecilius Statius are most conveniently accessible in E. H. Warmington's *Remains of Old Latin* (1935–6), including an English

---

[33] Cf. also Parker (1996).

translation and a brief commentary. The remains of the works of all fragmentary dramatic poets (with full critical apparatus) are assembled in O. Ribbeck's *Scaenicae Romanorum poesis fragmenta* (2nd edn, 1871/1873 and 3rd edn, 1897/1898). The fragments of Caecilius Statius, the *palliata* poet of whom the largest amount of text is extant (after Plautus and Terence), have been edited by T. Guardì (1974).

Essential information, *testimonia*, and bibliography on all Republican writers are provided in W. Suerbaum (2002, in German).

A. J. Boyle (2006) is a recent introduction to the contemporary genre of tragedy; G. Manuwald (2001, in German) offers information on the contemporary genre of *fabula praetexta*. There is no general treatment of *fabula togata*, but the introductions to editions of the fragments, e.g. A. Daviault (1981, in French) and T. Guardì (1985, in Italian), provide overviews, although the editions themselves have not met with universal approval.

Most works on Roman comedy focus on the plays of Plautus and Terence. J. Wright (1974) is a notable exception as his study includes poets whose dramas only survive in fragments; his analysis is designed to prove that Terence is the exception to an otherwise coherent *palliata* tradition. More general works on Republican drama such as W. Beare (1964) and G. Manuwald (2011) or on Roman comedy such as G. E. Duckworth (1952/1994) discuss details of context, setting, and generic conventions that apply to all Roman comic poets. N. J. Lowe (2008) surveys the development and the main features of both Greek and Roman comedy. For more details on stagecraft, see C. W. Marshall (2006); on Roman theatre architecture, see F. Sear (2006); and on festivals, see F. Bernstein (1998, in German).

Information on the historical, social, and cultural conditions in the Roman Republic can be found in H. I. Flower (2004) and in N. Rosenstein–R. Morstein-Marx (2006). E. S. Gruen (1990) discusses the period of interaction between Hellenic culture and Roman values, with particular reference to the mutual relationship between cultural activity and politics. M. Leigh (2004) is one of the few works that bridges the gap between cultural studies and analyses of Roman comedy by looking at the links between comedy and the contemporary historical situation.

2

COSTAS PANAYOTAKIS

Native Italian Drama and Its Influence on Plautus

The popularity throughout antiquity of the pioneering playwrights Plautus and Terence, who composed Latin adaptations of Greek comedies (*comoediae palliatae* 'comedies in Greek dress'), and the fact that they are the only Roman comic dramatists of whom we currently have complete scripts, have often created a misleading impression about the significance of other, equally important, Italian forms of entertainment, which may well have been in existence long before 240, the date at which the 'half-Greek' freedman Livius Andronicus from Tarentum in South Italy is said to have presented the first-ever *comoedia palliata* in front of an audience at a public festival.[1] These Italian spectacles were presumably improvised in their early stages, but acquired literary form (that is, became verse scripts) by the first century BC in the hands of innovative dramatists (such as Novius and Pomponius, who composed *fabulae Atellanae* 'Atellane comedies', and Decimus Laberius, who wrote mime plays) and actors (such as Publilius, who both composed mime plays and acted in them). The aim of this chapter is not to rehearse the features of Atellane comedy and mime as types of literary drama, but to consider the evidence for non-literary low drama in the early Republic and to relate this evidence to the *comoedia palliata*, especially Plautine theatre. How and why does our knowledge of native Italian drama enhance our appreciation of Plautus' dramatic techniques? To what extent and why was Plautus influenced by contemporary unscripted theatre?

The Greek and the Italian Backgrounds to the *Comoedia Palliata*

Livy's celebrated but partly problematic account of the origins of theatrical shows (*ludi scaenici*) in Rome connects the roots of Roman drama with neighbouring Etruria, and with the introduction in 364 (for religious purposes) of an elegant, native Etruscan, dance form which seems to have taken

---

[1] All dates are BC unless otherwise stated.

32

Roman youth by storm.[2] This does not mean that there was no theatrical life elsewhere in Italy at the time: mythological burlesque and farce had flourished in the hands of the Sicilian (Doric) comic playwrights Sophron, Xenarchus, and Epicharmus (fifth century BC), and continued to do so in the 'burlesque tragedy' (*hilarotragōidia* is the term used in the lexicon *Suda* ρ 171) of Rhinthon from Tarentum (third century BC).[3] Their works, which were composed long before – or, in Rhinthon's case, at the time when – the travelling troupes of actors known as the 'Artists of Dionysus' took on tour to Greek-speaking Italy and Sicily the plays of Euripides Menander, and other playwrights associated mainly with Greek New Comedy (about 290), would not have gone unnoticed by the rest of Italy. It is thus unsurprising to find influences from Greek myth and tragedy in Etruscan theatre-related language, material culture, and literature.[4] But Livy mentions neither the Greek playwrights writing in Sicily before 364, nor the activities of the 'Artists of Dionysus', nor the fact that Latin comedy and tragedy, at their earliest stage, were essentially creative adaptations of Greek comedy and tragedy. He may have followed his sources (Varro?) in omitting all this, or he may have wished (for patriotic reasons?) to dissociate Roman drama from Greek influences; but he was not entirely wrong or misleading in doing so.

For the picture of a purely, or even predominantly, Hellenic theatrical culture in the early and mid-Republican Roman periods is greatly complicated by the undeniable presence in Italy of strong traditions of indigenous types of comic activity. They began life outside Rome – or, even, outside Italy – as oral and unscripted spectacles, and they included the low comic dramas that Livy (7.2) calls 'Atellane', ribald verses known as 'Fescennine', and mime shows which used verbal humour and gestures to provoke laughter.[5] A shared feature of these jocular modes of entertainment was their non-Roman character. Atellane drama was comedy in the Oscan dialect associated with the town Atella in Campania. 'Fescennine verses' seem to have been songs of an indecent or satirical nature circulating in oral or written form; they were embedded in various cultural and literary contexts (harvest festivals, weddings or wedding poems, and soldiers' songs at military processions and triumphs), and were called 'Fescennine' most probably because of

---

[2] Livy 7.2.1–13; cf. Val. Max. 2.4.4. Oakley (1998) 40–55, 58–72, and 776–8 is essential reading alongside Livy's text.

[3] Sophron (and Xenarchus): Hordern (2004) and Olson (2007) 38, 63–7; Epicharmus: Olson (2007) 33–7, 40–60, and Denard (2007) 143–5; Rhinthon: Olivieri (1946) 7–24 and Gigante (1971).

[4] For the relevant evidence, see Oakley (1998) 52.

[5] Good general overviews on these popular types of entertainment are in Griffith (2007) and Denard (2007). More detailed works are mentioned in the section on 'Further Reading'.

their origin from the town Fescennium in Etruria.[6] Mime actors appear to have been improvising not only in Rome but also elsewhere in Italy or on non-Italian soil such as Macedon, Syria, and Egypt. Performances of mimes, like those of Atellane drama, eventually reached the Roman stage in the form of plays with fixed scripts in literary verse. But this seems to have happened no earlier than the beginning of the first century BC, that is, a century after Plautus' death.

The multicultural, even cosmopolitan, character of the backgrounds and experiences of the people involved in putting on such spectacles renders misleading any attempt at arguing that the plays produced were genuinely Roman cultural works. So when it is said that Latin mime plays or Atellane comedies composed in Latin or in Oscan were produced on the *Roman* stage (that is, in Rome and for an audience that was predominantly Roman), we should not forget that mimographers and Atellane playwrights would have been consciously and deliberately working not only to please Roman audiences but also to adhere, more or less faithfully, to long-established, *non-Roman* theatrical traditions, which had their own conventions and recognisable features; the audience would have been familiar with these features and would have expected to see them on the stage. Audience expectations would also have had an impact on the ways in which playwrights adapted Greek plays of New Comedy for Latin-speaking audiences at festivals held in Rome.[7] It is hardly original or surprising to observe that playwrights of the *comoedia palliata* would occasionally have looked outside the dramatic framework within which they were working, with a view to incorporating into their scripts allusions to Roman law, social life, religion, the army, the Senate, and native Italian forms of entertainment.[8] Dramatists who composed *comoediae palliatae* did not do so for themselves, but had their sponsors, agents, and audience to think about (whether they also had financial or career concerns I cannot say); and they neither lived in a cultural vacuum nor seem to have resisted being influenced by theatre other than Greek New Comedy.[9] It is this tension, then, between following a non-Roman (for example Greek or Sicilian or Oscan or Etruscan or Syrian) theatrical tradition and modifying it by mixing and matching elements

---

[6] Space constraints do not allow me to elaborate here on the origins and use of Fescennine verses in Roman culture and society; interested readers may profitably consult the excellent article on *Fescennini (versus)* by L. Holford-Strevens in *OCD*[3], Oakley (1998) 59–60 (with further bibliography); Denard (2007) 142–3; Ruffell (2003).

[7] See Manuwald 261–75 in this volume.

[8] See the chapters by Clark and Bartholomä in this volume.

[9] Gellius (2.23.12) believed that Caecilius Statius, the famous composer of *comoediae palliatae* after Plautus and before Terence, had 'inculcated' into his plays comic elements associated with mime drama.

from different dramatic categories that makes the scripts of the *comoedia palliata*, the *fabula Atellana*, and the literary *mimus* interesting, exciting, and good to think with. The theatrical conventions within which playwrights were working were not straitjackets, and the intense cultural cross-pollination which took place in Rome and the rest of Italy in the early Republic makes it absolutely essential that, if we wish to understand and appreciate how authors such as Plautus appropriated Greek culture, we would need to take into account other theatrical activities in Italy at that time.

Opportunities to Watch Latin Mime and Atellane Comedy

Mime in Roman theatrical culture is best understood as a general term that signified a wide range of spectacles that did not belong to masked comic and tragic drama. The term itself (*mimus*) betrays Greek origins. There is fairly good evidence showing that some Romans would have witnessed performances of mimes of some sort probably long before 240, the year when *comoediae palliatae* were supposed to have been introduced to Roman culture. Athenaeus talks about an actor, dated to the fourth century BC, by the name of Kleōn, who apparently was *autoprosōpos* 'maskless' and had the nickname *mimaulos* 'mime actor accompanied on the flute'; he seems to have been the best performer of 'Italian mimes', and it is tempting to interpret the adjective *Italikōn* as a reference to mime plays which were Italian in source and content, and were originally performed on Italian soil.[10] Furthermore, literary sources and inscriptional evidence refer to two other mime actors who (if the dates are correct) were active long before the end of the third century BC. One is C. Pomponius, an aged mime actor who performed at the festival in honour of Apollo in Rome in 212, and appears to be connected with the origins of the proverb 'all's well: the old man is dancing'.[11] The other is the mime actor Protogenes, who was buried at Amiternum (a Sabine town) at some point between *c.* 200 and 150 (these dates were suggested to me by M. Crawford). The epitaph on his *stēlē* says the following:

> Here lies the charming mime actor (*mimus*) Protogenes, slave of Cloulius, who gave much delight to people with his frivolities.[12]

The term *mimus*, with which the crowd-pleasing Protogenes was defined in the *stēlē*, indicates that mime had probably been largely integrated within

[10] See Athen. 10.452f–453a and *RE* XI.I 719 s.v. Kleon 10.
[11] For the date, see Beare (1964³) 151 and Cicu (1988) 23–4, and for the incident in which C. Pomponius was involved, Panayotakis (2010) 23–4.
[12] For bibliography on this actor and his dates, the Latin text on his *stēlē* (*CIL* 1.1297 = *CIL* 12.1861 = *CIL* 9.4463 = *ILS* 5221), and a discussion, see Panayotakis (2010) 23–5.

Italian theatrical culture by the second half of the third century BC. During the same period (241, according to Velleius Paterculus (1.14.8), or 238, in line with Pliny the Elder (*NH* 18.286)) the festival in honour of Flora, goddess of vegetation, fertility, and sensualism was established. Originally a festival without a fixed date, it was held annually from 173, and its 'shows at the *circus*' (*ludi circenses*) were joined by 'theatrical shows' (*ludi scaenici*), comprising perhaps only mime plays, and lasting from 28 April to 2 May. It is conceivable that mime plays had also been performed at this festival before 173 and with great success, hence the decision to devote the programme to mime repertory.[13] If so, the Romans from at least the late third century BC might have had more opportunities to watch mimes than our current evidence explicitly suggests.

Similar uncertainty surrounds the evidence regarding the early stages of Atellane comedy. The adjective *Atellanus* 'Atellane' is shown to be linked with theatre not before the early first century BC (Varro *Men.* 189), and its feminine form (*Atellana*) is first attested as a technical term only in Cicero's time (*Fam.* 9.16.7, written in 46) with reference to the noun *fabula* 'play'; with the phrase, Cicero seems to indicate a category of Italian comedy which was named, we believe, after the town Atella in west central Italy. In Varro's mind (and in the mind of his source?) Atella must have been the place in Campania where this type of popular entertainment originated or at least became prominent. The inhabitants of Rome might have come to know about Oscan jokes and Campanian theatrical traditions perhaps from the time of the First Samnite War in 343, when the populations of Rome and Capua first seem to have come into direct contact, and very probably after 312, when the Appian Way was opened.

To sum up, I list below in chronological order what I consider to be milestones in the process of familiarisation of the Romans with native Italian shows (such as Etruscan dancing, mime, and Campanian comedy), the roots of which are traced outside Rome (or even, in the case of mime, outside Italy), but which flourished in Italy and are at least of comparable antiquity with (if not older than) the *comoedia palliata*. It is reasonable, therefore, to assume that many of the Italian comic playwrights of the early Republic, who 'translated' into Latin the scripts of Greek New Comedy, would have been brought up in, and influenced by, this Italian theatrical background; naturally they may have wished to exploit, selectively and for various reasons, features of that background. The audience who watched the

---

[13] On the *Floralia* and its content, see Cicu (1988) 25–31; Wiseman (1999); Panayotakis (2010) 25–6.

Latin adaptations would have been expected to identify these features and be entertained by them.

364	Plague in Rome; Etruscan dancers are invited to perform.
343	Oscan invaders from Samnium attack Capua, which seeks Rome's assistance.
343–341	First Samnite War.
338	As a result of the settlement after the Latin War Atella becomes a Roman ally.
312	The link between Capua and Rome is strengthened because of the construction of the Appian Way.
241 or 238	The festival in honour of Flora (*Floralia*) is established.
240	Livius Andronicus turns from the composition of 'musical medleys' (*saturae*) to the composition of 'plays' (*fabulae*) with 'plot' (*argumentum*). He puts on the first production of what would later be known as *comoedia palliata*.
216	Atella changes sides and supports Hannibal (Livy 22.61.11).
212	The aged mime actor C. Pomponius performs at Rome during the festival in honour of Apollo.
211	Rome punishes Atella by confiscating its territory (Livy 26.16.5; Pol. 9.45).
c. 205–*c.* 184	Plautus composes comedies.
200	Plautus' *Stichus* is produced at the Plebeian Games.
c. 200–150	During this period the mime actor Protogenes (of Greek origin?) dies, and his *stēlē*, found in Samnium, records his life and achievements.
191	Plautus' *Pseudolus* is produced at the Megalesian Games.
173	The festival of the *Floralia* (with mime plays in its programme?) becomes annual.

In addition to the events above, it is significant that the ancient biographical tradition for Latin playwrights, which goes back to literary scholars such as Accius and Varro, presents Livius Andronicus, the 'founder' of *comoedia palliata*, and Naevius, who composed at least 30 *comoediae palliatae* between 235 and 204, as provincial Italians. Livius originated probably from Tarentum in Magna Graecia and Naevius from Capua in Campania, areas in which theatre as a cultural institution was vibrant and long-standing.[14] A generation after Naevius the population in Capua and elsewhere in Italy outside Rome would have been able to watch plays in permanent stone theatres, which began to be built at least from the second century BC, long before 55, when the Romans themselves got the chance to sit in the first stone theatre in Rome.[15]

But demonstrating that there were opportunities for some Romans to witness Oscan humour or mime wit does not help us much to visualise clearly what exactly happened at these performances. As far as pre-literary mime shows are concerned, there would certainly have been dancing and low (visual and oral) jokes (this much we can safely assume on the basis of the evidence discussed above). There might also have been a representation of indelicate scenes (or of serious stories in an unseemly fashion) related to Roman legend, but the exact format and content of the shows remain far from clear.

In relation to pre-literary Atellane plays, we are told by Livy (and I have found no cogent reason to doubt his testimony at this point) that amateur (masked) actors enacted farcical situations, which, initially, were probably improvised and delivered in Oscan language (Livy 7.2.12, Val. Max. 2.4.4, Paul.-Fest. 238L). Very little else may be said with certainty about the early stages of Atellane drama and its development into a fully fledged staged spectacle in the early first century BC. In spite (or, perhaps, because) of the lack of evidence, some scholars have sought to infer and reconstruct the content and nature of the pre-literary *Atellana* on the basis of its literary version. The approach is not unreasonable methodologically, because the target audience for the literary plays of Pomponius, Novius, Mummius, Aprissius, and other Atellane playwrights, would presumably have been Romans – not Campanians – expecting to see farce in what they would have perceived as the traditional Oscan fashion; but it is a hazardous approach. From 115 titles and (approximately) 320 lines it is possible for us to identify in the scripts a fondness (but perhaps no more than that) for playful obscenity, exemplified in imaginatively crude language and low subject matter (both of these features appear also in the literary mimes of Decimus Laberius), and the presence of what *may have been* stock characters with 'speaking' names that betray Greek, Latin, or Etruscan influence in their morphology: *Maccus* 'Fool' is probably related to the Greek verb *makkoan* 'to be

---

[14] Evidence in Livingstone (2004) xi–xiii (for Livius) and in Marmorale (1950) 15–21 (for Naevius). For the *testimonia* and further bibliography on these two playwrights, see also Schauer (2012) 21–7 and 67–70. For their fragments, see Livingstone (2004) 47–82; Paponi (2005); Spaltenstein (2008).

[15] Evidence for stone theatres built outside Rome before 55 in Rawson (1991) 471–3.

stupid'; *Pappus* 'Old Man' originates from the Greek *pappos* 'grand-father'; on *Bucco* 'Fathead', see below; *Manducus* or *Manduco* 'Glutton' is derived from the verb *manducare* 'to chew'; *Dossennus* '(?)Hunchback' is apparently formed from the root of the Latin noun *dorsum* 'back' and the Etruscan suffix *–ennus*.[16] These characters seem to have been involved in typically comic situations, if the titles of the fragmentary plays are anything to go by (*The Adopted Bucco, Pappus' Jug, The Maccus Twins, Maccus the Soldier, Maccus the Trustee, Maccus the Maiden, Pappus the Farmer, Pappus Past and Gone, Pappus' Spouse, The Two Dossenni, Maccus the Innkeeper, Maccus in Exile*). It is unclear whether these situations would have applied also to the early, pre-literary, stages of the *Atellana*. In any case, neither the obscenity nor the existence of specifically named stock characters squares with the general comic ethos of Plautus (let alone Terence), although it is true that the words *maccus, manducus*, and *bucco* are used by Plautus as nouns or as proper names; the word *Dossennus* was employed by Horace to characterise Plautus himself (more about these words later). Mythological scenes (known from tragedy) seem to have featured frequently (and perhaps satirically?) in the repertory of the literary *Atellana*, but only in the absence, it seems, of the above-named characters; this *may* mean that mythological burlesque did not appear in the pre-literary version of Oscan farce.

Plautine *Palliata* and Unscripted Low Drama

Early scholarly discussions of the influence unscripted forms of Italian popular entertainment exerted on Plautus' adaptations of Greek comedies make a case for the formative influence of South Italian and Sicilian drama, Oscan farce, and Italian mime.[17] The conclusions are only partly persuasive, mainly because the arguments were based on evidence that was often vague and impressionistic. In the 1950s Paolo Frassinetti, who would go on to edit the fragments of the literary *Atellana*, re-examined the evidence for

---

[16] See Blänsdorf (2003) 225–6; Adams (2003) 164–5; Debouy (2010) 167–8.

[17] See Beare (1930) – his views, focusing on *fabula Atellana*, were developed in Beare (1964[3]) 137–42 – and Little (1938). Neither of them considers the South Italian/Sicilian words in Plautus discussed by Adams (2003) 251–2 n. 100. The issue of the connection between Atellane comedy and the Greek comedy of Epicharmus, Sophron, Rhinthon, Sopater, and the so-called 'Phlyax vases' has now been comprehensively discussed by Brown (2013) (with earlier bibliography). The best assessment of the evidence, drawn from literary sources, on the so-called 'pre-literary stage' of Atellane comedy is in Monda (2013). I read Brown (2013) and Monda (2013) long after I finished writing this chapter, and I was pleased with the scepticism and caution in the approach and conclusions of both of these scholars.

the link between pre-literary Atellane comedy and Plautus, but he was doubtful about the existence (let alone strength) of such a link, and concluded his discussion much more sceptically than his predecessors.[18] His reservations are possibly reinforced by the fact that there are hardly any Oscanisms in the extant scripts attributed to Plautus.[19] But it is possible to argue that we should not expect to find many Oscan linguistic borrowings in Plautus, possibly because he addressed his plays to Roman audiences, not all of whom would have understood Oscan, or because he may have deliberately wished to suppress, for his own reasons, the presence of the Oscan dialect in his scripts.[20] Although Plautus' Latinity does not appear to be Oscanised, his dramaturgy may well have been indebted to Oscan farce in non-linguistic ways. This possibility would not have found favour with Frassinetti, but his scepticism has not been shared by Eckard Lefèvre and the 'Freiburg-school' of Plautine scholarship, according to which Plautus greatly favoured (oral and improvised) popular farce both in his character portrayal and in his plot construction, and was only minimally influenced by Greek comedy in these areas.[21] What evidence is there in the scripts for this thesis?

(1) One of the scenes in the *Rudens*, a play of uncertain date, is the conversation between the ruthless villain Labrax and his unfortunate comrade Charmides (485–552). The pimp and his friend survive shipwreck, and when they first appear they give the impression that they are two jesters on stage exchanging jokes that could have been made outside the context of the play. Their dialogue is fast-paced, witty, and filled with puns; it does very little to advance the plot, and contains the sort of jokes which Cicero will associate with mime (*De Or.* 2.259, 2.274). One of Labrax's jokes is particularly pertinent to my discussion:

---

[18] Frassinetti (1953) 84–93.

[19] Plautus' few Oscanisms are discussed in Adams (2003) 122–3. Likewise, scholars tend to stress the linguistic, metrical, and thematic similarities between the *comoedia palliata* and the scripted *fabula Atellana* of Novius and Pomponius of the early first century BC (see, for example, Beare (1964³) 143–8; Karakasis (2005) 234–46; Lefèvre (2010) 23–34) – and some of them are undeniable – but the differences (outlined by de Melo (2010)) are equally (if not more) revealing about the predominant comic register in each of these theatrical categories.

[20] The evidence for Oscan bilingualism in the early Republic and for the influence of Oscan on early Latin literary authors is cited and discussed in Adams (2003) 112–55.

[21] See, for instance, the six essays on Plautus' originality, exemplified through six of his plays, in Lefèvre–Stärk–Vogt-Spira (1991), the nineteen essays by a host of Anglophone, Italian, and German scholars, which Benz–Stärk–Vogt-Spira (1995) edited and divided into four sections ('Improvisation', 'Farce', 'Mime elements', and 'Extemporisation'), as well as Blänsdorf (2003) 225 and Lefèvre (2010) 15–22. See also Cardoso's chapter in this volume.

LABRAX: Do you think I should hire out my services to a show as a Manducus?
CHARMIDES: Why?
LABRAX: Because my teeth are constantly clattering.

(Plautus Ru. 535–6)

For the joke to make sense we need to assume that the audience was familiar with a (cultic?) figure with clattering teeth; we know that an effigy of a figure called Manducus was included in festive processions amongst other effigies which provoked fear and laughter (Paul.-Fest. 115L). Varro (LL 7.95), without mentioning Plautus' passage, explicitly relates this Manducus to Atellane comedy, and identifies him with Dosennus, another character associated with Atellane comedy who seems to have been fond of food (more about him later).

(2) In the Asinaria, the production of which cannot be firmly dated, the prologue speaker says that:

> in Greek this comedy is entitled Ass-driver;   10
> Demophilus was its author, but Maccus turned it into a foreign language.

(Plautus As. 10–11)

Although the word Maccus, here clearly used as a proper name cited in juxtaposition to the name Demophilus, betrays Greek influence in its etymology (see above and Ar. Eq. 396), it has long been recognised that it is identical to the name of one of the characters connected with scripted Atellane comedy (Apul. Apol. 81). Maccus as a proper name will also recur (but with spelling variations and rarely in the nominative case) in the manuscripts of late-antique grammarians (Diom. GL 1.490.20 K) and lexicographers, such as Nonius Marcellus, who cite the fragments of the literary Atellana. Moreover, the connection between 'Maccus' the author of the Asinaria and 'Maccus' the Atellane character makes sense in the context of the Plautine passage, because it creates the contrasting pairs 'Greek language vs. "foreign" (that is, Latin) language' and 'Greek high culture vs. Italian popular culture'.[22] Elsewhere in the manuscripts of the Plautine corpus Plautus' name has been transmitted as Plautus, Plauti ('of Plautus' but also 'of Plautius'), Macci Titi ('of Maccus Titus' but also 'of Maccius Titus'), and T. Macci Plauti. A person called 'Titus Maccius Plautus' would have a family name (Maccius) that associates him with 'The Fool' of literary Atellane comedy (Maccus), and his third name or cognomen (Plautus 'flat-footed') would recall actors in mime plays (planipedes; plautus is a synonym for planipes) who did not wear shoes when performing on stage. On the basis of the above evidence a persuasive argument has been formulated, interpreting Plautus' full name as a cleverly

---

[22] On this passage, see also Telò in this volume.

conceived string of nicknames which acknowledge his debt to Italian farce and mime and perhaps even indicate a professional connection with the low stage: *T. Maccius Plautus* 'Dickie Clownson Tumbler, Esq.', in Gratwick's words.[23]

(3) In the *Bacchides*, about the production date of which we can say only that it followed the production date of the Plautine *Epidicus*, the old man Nicobulus curses himself for being so foolish as to be deceived by the cunning slave Chrysalus. The passage is sung and abounds in synonyms and alliteration; one of its lines should here be cited in Latin:

> stulti, stolidi, fatui, fungi, bardi, blenni, buccones 1088
>
> of the fatheads, the fools, the dullards, the dolts, the babblers, the blundering blockheads, the mushrooms ... (Plautus *Bacch.* 1088)

The word I am interested in is the disparaging term *buccones*, attested in inscriptions and explained by Isidore (10.30) as a derivative of *bucca* 'the lower part of the cheek(s)'.[24] So a *bucco* may well have been a term of abuse referring to people who puff their cheeks out or have their mouth open all the time (see *OLD* s.v. *bucca* 1c). The same word (*bucco*) appears also in the fragments of the Atellane playwrights Pomponius and Aprissius, and all the modern editors of the literary *Atellana* print it with a capital *B*, thus making it a term of reference to a stock character. Barsby, whose translation I cite above, rightly implies that the term *bucco* in Plautus' passage denotes a 'gaping idiot';[25] there is no cogent reason for us to print the word with a capital *B* and so suggest that Nicobulus (or Plautus) had a specific character in mind ('*The* Gaping Idiot' as opposed to '*a* gaping idiot') who would come to be associated with the literary Atellane comedy of Pomponius and Aprissius. Likewise, even a cursory look at the texts of Varro (*LL* 6.68) and Nonius Marcellus, who cite the Atellane titles and fragments of Pomponius and Aprissius, demonstrates that *bucco* should not always be interpreted as *Bucco*. To complicate matters further, even if we were absolutely certain that all the attestations of *maccus*, *bucco*, and *manducus* in the titles and fragments of the literary *Atellana*, and in the testimonies of non-dramatic authors such as Apuleius,[26] referred to specific characters associated with fixed masks and a set of defined characteristics,[27] we cannot rule out the possibility that it was Plautus (rather than the oral and improvised

---

[23] Although this view was, as far as I know, originally put forth by F. Leo, it was Gratwick (1973) who articulated it in persuasive detail. His arguments have not been superseded.

[24] To the inscriptional evidence mentioned in *TLL* II 2229.26–7 add *ILS* 5219 Dessau.

[25] Barsby (1986) 183.   [26] Apuleius links *macci* 'fools' with *buccones* 'idiots' (*Apol.* 81).

[27] Here I have in mind the mask of a person with a large, open mouth bearing the inscription BVCO; it dates to the first century AD and was found in Pompeii (now in the National

Oscan farce) who inspired Pomponius, Novius, and the other playwrights of the literary *Atellana* in the first century BC or slightly earlier to turn these imaginative terms of abuse into recognisable stage figures.

(4) The strong likelihood that Plautus' theatre was influential in the shaping of the literary *fabula Atellana* militates against tracing evidence for preliterary Atellane comedy and its influence on Plautus in a difficult passage of Horace (*Epist.* 2.1.170–3), in which he rebukes Plautus for his unrefined portrayal of parasites:[28]

> quantus sit [*scil.* Plautus] Dossennus edacibus in parasitis   173
>
> what a great Dossennus Plautus is in the midst of his greedy parasites

Varro states that 'in the Atellane comedies they call Dossennus Manducus' (*LL* 7.95); on the basis of Varro's statement some scholars have viewed Dosennus as the type of the gluttonous, greedy, and vulgar parasite, and have taken Horace's passage as yet another indication that Plautus was influenced by Atellane comedy. Leaving aside the uncertainty which surrounds the correct spelling of the word *Dossennus* in the manuscripts of the ancient authors who are supposed to refer to it,[29] it is crucial to bear in mind that Horace's view of what constitutes 'primitive' or 'Atellane' treatment of comic parasites (and perhaps of character portrayal in comedy as a whole?) in Plautus' plays was defined and influenced not by Horace's experience of pre-literary Oscan farce but by the *literary* scripts of the *fabula Atellana* which Horace read, and by the Atellane plays which he may have seen performed (perhaps even in Oscan dialect) in Rome.[30] Understanding the perspective from which Horace evaluated Plautus in relation to Atellane

---

Archaeological Museum in Naples, Inv. 322286). It is reproduced clearly on the cover of Raffaelli and Tontini (2010).

[28] The meaning of the line is not clear; Lefèvre (2010) 19–20 gathers most of the modern scholarly interpretations, including the influential view of Lowe (1989): 'In identifying Plautus with Dossennus Horace ... implies that Plautus' comedy approximates to popular farce' (169). Lefèvre does not cite Jocelyn (1995) 236–7: 'The accusation levelled against Plautus in line 173 must be, therefore, that when he wrote a part for the *parasitus edax* the result was something more appropriate to the well-known Atellane personage than to an Athenian gentleman down on his luck. ... I should prefer, however, to relate the accusation to gross and vulgar language thought inappropriate to the parasite in particular and to comedy in general.'

[29] In Varro *LL* 7.95 the word *Dossennum* is K. O. Müller's emendation for the nonsensical manuscript reading *ad obsenum*; however, it is not an implausible emendation, because there is no accusative in the transmitted text to function as the object of the verb: *Dossennum* fills that gap. There are serious textual problems in all the instances in which the name *Dossennus* appears in the early manuscripts of Nonius Marcellus (who cites the Atellane fragments of Pomponius).

[30] See Strabo 5.3.6; Cic. *Ad Fam.* 7.1.3; Suet. *Iul.* 39.1 and *Aug.* 43.1; Adams (2003) 117–18.

comedy opens up a big can of worms: what is the exact relationship between the scripted *fabula Atellana* and the pre-literary Atellane comedy? I do not have the space to deal with this controversial topic here;[31] but it is one thing to say that Horace found Plautus' parasites to be 'Atellane' in some way, and another to assert that Plautus was inspired by pre-literary Atellane shows in his portrayal of comic parasites. The latter does not necessarily follow from the former, mainly because Horace's perception of Plautine dramaturgy was coloured by, and filtered through, the scripts of the literary *fabula Atellana*, which may well have had very little similarity with the pre-literary forms of entertainment taking place in Campania centuries before Horace's time.

This leaves us with very little to go on: a general atmosphere of farce, some jokes, and a couple of comic terms of abuse. And yet some scholars have wished to find traces of Atellane influence on Plautus even in the technique of improvisation, in which memorable Plautine slaves such as Pseudolus, Chrysalus, and Tranio appear to be experts, or in Plautus' fondness for creating prolonged scenes in which two characters exchange silly jokes and witty puns in a competitive, almost agonistic, fashion.[32] But the amusingly improvised lies of cunning slaves such as Tranio in the *Mostellaria* are embedded within a carefully constructed literary play that is far from improvised, although it deliberately gives such an impression so as to extol the genius of the heroic slave (and of the playwright himself). How close would this scenario have been to the pre-literary mime or the pre-literary *Atellana*, both of which would presumably have been artless forms of drama? Consider, also, the following statement:

> The influence of the AF [= *fabula Atellana*] on the comedies of Plautus is evident from his joy in rough comedy, in word-play and alternating sarcastic speeches, in the motif of the greedy parasite, in the mockery of the besotted old man and in the connection of his [that is, Plautus'] own name with the AF role of Maccus (*As.* prol. 11).[33]

The problem here is that comic techniques such as word-play and rough visual humour seem to have been stock ingredients also in unscripted Italian mime, whose impact on Plautine drama, like the impact of pre-literary Atellane comedy, seems to me to be, at best, nebulous and indefinable, in

---

[31] A useful overview is given by Lefèvre (2010), but see above, n. 17.
[32] See the articles in Benz–Stärk–Vogt-Spira (1995), as well as Petersmann (1989) and Lefèvre (2010) 21–2.
[33] Blänsdorf (2003) 225 with references to Lowe (1989) and Höttemann (1993).

spite of confident assertions to the contrary.[34] It might even be wiser to relate such features to popular culture as a whole without any affiliation to specific literary or pre-literary modes of stage entertainment.

Conclusions

I started my discussion on a positive note presenting a lively picture of long-standing and non-Romanocentric theatrical traditions in Republican Italy which existed independently from, and perhaps even before, the advent of the *comoedia palliata* in Rome. I wish to retain this impression but also qualify it somewhat by stressing that the ways in which the interaction between theatrical cultures took place was far from straightforward. I do not wish to deny that Plautus was influenced by 'Italian' (= South Italian, Sicilian, Oscan, Etruscan, perhaps Umbrian, if it is true that he came from Sarsina in Umbria) or even non-Italian (in the case of mime) low drama, when translating Greek New Comedy into Latin. There is some evidence to support this view and, in any case, we have seen that Plautus does not seem to have been the only playwright to combine dramatic traditions.[35] However, the details of the influence and of the combination process are unclear, while the pre-literary forms of Italian comedy with no fixed script in literary verse seem to be shadowy and elusive, almost 'ghost-like', categories for us. On the other hand, the exciting consequence of our inability to specify the features of indigenous Italian theatrical forms and to relate them explicitly to Plautine points of reference (such as character portrayal, visual humour, word-play or storylines) is our appreciation that Plautus' scripts were the product of a dynamic and proud negotiation of living cultures and the first literary specimen of a confidently emerging new civilisation.

Further Reading

General monographs on Roman drama tend to focus on the *literary* versions of popular low theatre, including mime and Campanian comedy. The roots,

---

[34] See, for example, the views of Benz (1995) 149–52; Petrone (1995) 171–83; Lefèvre (2010) 36. As far as the literary mime is concerned, I have no doubt that the mimographer Laberius, in the mid-first century BC, was to an extent inspired by the *comoedia palliata* and particularly by Plautus in forming some of his characters and comic neologisms, but the picture is greatly complicated by Pomponius, Laberius' comic predecessor, and his fondness for puns (see Seneca Rhetor, *Contr.* 7.3.9 Winterbottom), and by the striking dissimilarities which exist between the linguistic register and prosody of the extant Laberius and the vocabulary and versification of Plautus and Terence (Panayotakis (2010) 57–76).

[35] Above, n. 7.

development, and importance of Latin mime and Atellane comedy *in their pre-literary form* are rarely discussed in detail. I recommend (for mime) Wüst (1932), Beare (1964³) 149–58, Cicu (1988), Fantham (1988), and Panayotakis (2010) 1–32; and (for Atellane comedy) Frassinetti (1953), Beare (1964³) 137–48, Petersmann (1989), Lefèvre (2010), and the articles in the recently published edited volume on the pre-literary Atellana: see Raffaelli and Tontini (2013).

3

MARIO TELÒ*

Roman Comedy and the Poetics of Adaptation

Every act of literary creation endeavours to bridge the gap between fiction and reality by transplanting a textually constructed subjective experience into the cultural realm of its audience. When a play announces itself as a deliberate remake of a prior work, the process of cultural adaptation is programmatically disclosed and converted into a subject of theatrical discourse. This is especially true in the case of the *comoediae palliatae* ('comedies in Greek dress') of the archaic Roman dramatists, which present themselves as revisitations of works originally conceived in and for a different cultural context.

All the plays of Roman comedy are overt adaptations of originals of Greek 'New Comedy' (*nea*), so called to distinguish the Hellenistic evolution of the comic genre from its fifth-century manifestations, grouped under the label of 'Old Comedy' (*archaia*). The transition from the *archaia* to the *nea* marks an apparently radical thematic and tonal shift: from political topicality to familial domesticity, from vitriolic, 'iambic' abuse to psychological humour, from rampant obscenity to restrained laughter.[1] It is from the main representatives of New Comedy (Menander, Diphilus, Philemon), whose works became known to Roman culture in the middle of the third century BC, that the Latin comedians drew their plots with stock characters, bourgeois atmospheres, and Greek settings.[2] Roman comedy thus was born and developed as a genre of remakes.

Roman comedy's acknowledged appropriation of the repertoire of Greek New Comedy, then, transforms the stage into a site for meditating upon

---

* Many thanks are due to M. T. Dinter, E. Gowers, A. Press, and A. Richlin as well as the Cambridge University Press anonymous readers for commenting on previous drafts of this chapter. This chapter was submitted in 2014. The updating of the bibliography has been limited to a few references.

[1] In Old Comedy, an escapist, non-political dimension coexisted alongside the topical one: cf. Csapo (2000). New Comedy elevates such a dimension to dominant status.

[2] On laughter in New Comedy, see Halliwell (2008) 388–428. On the cultural dissemination of New Comedy, especially Menander, in antiquity, see Nervegna (2013) and Le Guen (2014); on the beginnings of Roman comedy, see most recently Manuwald (2011), ch. 1, and Brown (2014). For a synchronic treatment of Greek New Comedy and Roman comedy, see Hunter (1985).

literary inventiveness, repetition, and cultural transcoding, and creates a field for self-reflexive narrative and theatrical practices. The intrigues and the pyrotechnic manoeuvres that, more than any other character, the scheming slave of Roman, especially Plautine, comedy orchestrates, have been proved to evoke plot-making and role-playing.[3] This all-pervasive theatrical self-awareness, which blurs the boundaries between fiction and reality, constitutes one of the signature features of the Roman re-interpretation and re-invention of Greek Hellenistic comedy.

In this chapter I will investigate how the practices of translation and adaptation of Greek comic models essential to the poetic workshop of the *palliata* and to the invention of Roman cultural identity are manifested in the dramatic constructions of Plautus and Terence.[4] I will not pursue the model-hunting and traditional comparative criticism that have occupied classical philology for so long. Except for the fortunate case of Plautus' *Bacchides* and Menander's *The Double Deceiver* (*Dis Exapaton*), the possibility of setting the Roman plays alongside their Greek originals is hindered by the dearth of textual evidence.[5] Instead I will chart some of the ways in which the plots of Plautus and Terence comment upon the modes of literary transposition that shape their identities. In so doing, I hope to get at some of the distinctive strategies of authorial self-presentation that underlie Plautus' and Terence's positioning of their plays against the Greek models. What emerges from these strategies, their negotiation of closeness and distance, fidelity to and subversion of an original, is the unified notion of translation as a troubled form of textual survival.

In the first section I explore the connection between the practice of translation as defined by the Latin verb *uortere* ('change, modify, translate') and the Plautine figure of the resourceful slave. In the second section I use this connection to consider how the process of adaptation is reflected in the plot of *Bacchides*. In the last section I examine the paradigms of literary and cultural appropriation that are at work in Terence's first play, *Andria*, ultimately teasing out the ways in which Plautus, the 'destroyer' of Greek models, and Terence, the 'saviour', come together, enmeshed in the same dynamic of translation as appropriation without possession.

---

[3] Cf. Barchiesi (1970); Slater (1985); Moore (1998b); McCarthy (2000); Jenkins (2005); Sharrock (2009) 96–162; on Terentian slaves as plot-makers, see Moodie (2009). Cf. also Christenson and Fitzgerald in this volume.

[4] I am not concerned here with the ways in which Plautus' and Terence's adaptations shed light on the Hellenism of archaic Roman literature. For a new assessment of this topic, see Feeney (2016), who, however, devotes limited attention to comedy.

[5] On Aulus Gellius' comparison of Caecilius Statius' *Necklace (Plocium)* and its Menandrian original, see below. For a survey of the available comparisons, see Fontaine (2014d) 409–14.

Greek Models and the Art of Versatility in Plautus

Huic nomen Graece Onago est fabulae;
Demophilus scripsit, Maccus uortit barbare;
Asinariam uolt esse, si per uos licet.

The name of this play is *Onagos* ('Donkey-Driver') in Greek. Demophilus wrote it and Maccus translated it into barbarian language. He wants it to be *The Comedy of Donkeys*, if that is all right by you. (Plautus, *As.* 10–12[6])

In this prologue and that of *Trinummus* Plautus introduces his *fabula* as a translation of a play written by an author of Greek New Comedy (in this case, Demophilus) into Latin. Both the terms *uortit* and *barbare* are marked and have generated different readings of this statement, which pairs the invention of comedy with the discovery and the 'irruption of (cultural) otherness'.[7] In presenting his play as a barbaric version of a Greek original, is Plautus looking down upon his adaptation as a 'reverse alchemy which transmutes the gold of Athens into Roman dross' or is he indulging in a 'self-deprecating joke'?[8] If as seems likely the latter interpretation hits the mark, how shall we unpack this claim?

In the same play the adjective *uorsutus* ('wily'), which is etymologically connected with the verb *uortere*, is used twice (*As.* 119, 255) to represent the versatile intellectual ability (*As.* 255 *ingenium … uorsutum*) of Libanus, the *seruus callidus* ('cunning slave'), who is invested with the customary task of weaving (and unweaving) all the plot's intrigues. Here as in other plays this intratextual connection between prologue and plot leads to an explicit identification of the comic poet's persona as a 'barbaric' adapter with the figure of the cunning slave.[9]

In the prologue of *Amphitryo* Mercury comes on stage dressed up as Sosia, the slave of Amphitryo, to guard the door of the house in which Jupiter is acting out the role of Alcmena's husband:

---

[6] Here and elsewhere I reproduce, with slight adjustments, the translations of de Melo (2011b and c).

[7] Henderson (2006) 128. On the use of the adjective *barbarus* and the thematisation of the Greece vs. Rome opposition in Plautus, cf. Moore (1998b) 50–66; Leigh (2004) 4–12; Goldberg (2007a) 131–5.

[8] The quotations are taken from Segal (1987) 6 and Sharrock (2009) 28 respectively. Translating *Trinummus* as the 'Über-Coin', Fontaine (2014a) 531–2 reads in the prologue of *Trinummus* a triumphant statement of adherence to the Greek model, Philemon's Θησαυρός ('The Treasure').

[9] Cf. Slater (1985) 51 n. 15 and Gowers (1993) 89 n. 151. In *The Swaggering Soldier (Miles Gloriosus)*, ll. 209–13 the slave Palaestrio's incarnation of the comic spirit is associated with a figure of *poeta barbarus* ('foreign poet'), probably Naevius: cf. Richlin (2014) 186.
On Plautus as a slave name, see Richlin (2017a) 136. For the sake of convenience, I will use the well-documented phrase *seruus callidus*, even if, with Richlin (2017a) 25, I acknowledge its patronising dimension.

nunc ne hunc ornatum uos meum admiremini,
quod ego huc processi sic cum seruili schema:
ueterem atque antiquam rem nouam ad uos proferam,
propterea ornatus in nouom incessi modum.
nam meus pater intus nunc est eccum Iuppiter;   120
in Amphitruonis uortit sese imaginem
omnesque eum esse censent serui qui uident:
ita uorsipellem se facit quando lubet.

Now don't be surprised about this outfit of mine, since I've come here like this
in slave's dress: I'll bring to you an old and ancient tale anew, hence I've come
here clothed in a new way. Well, you see, my father Jupiter is inside now, he's
turned himself into Amphitryo's image, and all the slaves who see him believe
that he's the real thing. He changes his skin like that whenever he wants.

(Plautus, *Amph.* 116–23)

In l. 118 the expression *ueterem atque antiquam rem* is charged with a double
valence, denoting the mythical story of Jupiter's encounter *en travesti* with
Alcmena, which the present play turns into a dramatic subject, as well as the
Greek original on which Plautus' *fabula* is based.[10] The process of adaptation is clearly mapped onto the language of theatrical disguise, as the occurrence of *uortit* in l. 121 indicates with utmost clarity.[11] Thus, the transition
from Greek to Roman comedy takes the figurative shape of a degrading
metamorphosis of gods into men and, to be more precise, slaves.[12]
Mercury's *seruili schema* consists not only in donning Sosia's mask, but
also in appropriating disguise and deception as behavioural codes that, in
the world of Plautine comedy, pertain first and foremost to slaves.[13]
As a result of his impersonation of Amphitryo, Jupiter, too, intrudes into
the sphere of action of a *seruus callidus*. It is no coincidence that the epithet
uorsipellis ('skin-changing'), which Mercury assigns to his father in l. 123, is
accorded special emphasis within the lyric self-portrayal of Chrysalus, a slave
who dominates the scene in *Bacchides*:[14]

non mihi isti placent Parmenones, Syri,
qui duas aut tris minas auferunt eris.   650
nequius nil est quam egens

[10] On *Amphitryo*'s original, cf. Hunter (1987); Christenson (2000) 53–5; Oniga (2002).
[11] On the play's thematisation of disguise and role-playing, see Slater (1990) and Moore
(1998b) 108–25.
[12] On *uertere* as metamorphosis, see Bettini (2012) 37.
[13] Cf. e.g. *Epidicus*, 189 *iam ego me conuortam in hirudinem* ('I will turn myself into
a leech'), spoken by the title character, a slave. Cf. Wright (1975) and Muecke (1986).
[14] On these lines, cf. Slater (1985) 103–4; Damen (1995); Goldberg (2007a) 134; Sharrock
(2009) 203.

> consili seruos, nisi habet
> multipotens pectus:
> ubiquomque usus siet, pectore expromat suo.
> ...
>
> uorsipellem frugi conuenit esse hominem,
> pectus quoi sapit,
> bonus sit bonis, malus sit malis;   660
> utquomque res sit, ita animum habeat.

I don't like those Parmenos and Syruses, who take two or three minas away from their masters. Nothing is more worthless than a slave who lacks intelligence, if he doesn't have a powerful mind; whenever necessary, he should draw a plan from his own mind ... a man who has cleverness in his heart should be able to change his skin. Let him be good to the good, let him be bad to the bad. Whatever the situation is like, he should adapt to it.   (Plautus, *Bacch.* 649–61)

In this blatantly metatheatrical moment, Chrysalus sets himself against his Greek predecessors – Syrus was the name of his Menandrian alter ego, as we know from the surviving fragments of *The Double Deceiver* – and contrasts their limited resourcefulness with his formidable *adapting* ability. It is precisely his chameleonic talent, evoked through the adjective *uorsipellis*, that ensures his practical success and marks his superiority over his Greek counterparts. The secret of Chrysalus' art of deception resides, in other words, in the symbolic kinship with Ulysses (Odysseus) – the archetypal *uorsutus* and chameleonic hero – that he claims for himself in his virtuoso Trojan monody (*Bacch.* 940 *ego sum Ulixes* 'I am Ulysses').[15] In this context, he likens his deceitful defeat of his master, who had attempted to keep Chrysalus' manipulations under control by tying him up, to Ulysses' success in saving his life after he had been caught making his way into Troy disguised as a beggar (*Bacch.* 948–52). Chrysalus is a twin brother of Pseudolus, the quintessential trickster and slave-as-poet, who according to one of his victims even surpasses Ulysses in acting as a *uorsutus seruus*:[16]

> nimis illic mortalis doctus, nimis uorsutus, nimis malus;
> superauit dolum Troianum atque Ulixem Pseudolus.

[15] On the monody of Chrysalus as a Plautine invention, cf. Fraenkel (2007) 46–53 [= (1960) 61–72]; Slater (1985) 109–12; Barsby (1986) 170–1.
[16] On Pseudolus as a metatheatrical figure, cf. Stehle (1984); Slater (1985) 118–46; Sharrock (1996) and (2009) 117; Moore (1998b) 92–107; Hunter (2006) 81–3; Feeney (2010). It is worth recalling that Livius Andronicus translated the Odyssean epithet πολύτροπος ('versatile') with *uorsutus*: cf. Hinds (1998) 61–2 (with n. 20), who connects *uorsutus* with *Plautus uortit barbare*.

He's a very smart, very clever, very wicked fellow; Pseudolus has surpassed the
Trojan trick and Ulysses.   (Plautus, *Ps.* 1243–4)

It is thus evident that Plautus' thematic concern with the ethical and social
adaptability of his slaves calls attention to his plays' nature as adapted texts.
Plautus uses Ulysses' polytropic identity to assimilate slaves' overturning of
social hierarchies to the imaginative re-creation and subversion of the Greek
models that lie at the core of his dramatic production.[17] The analogy between
the practice of adaptation and Ulysses' behavioural (and narrative) versatility enables Plautus to flip the terms of the oppositions 'original/copy',
'Greek/barbaric' and to recast his condition of secondariness as an expression of intellectual supremacy or to turn a 'minor' position into a power of
disruption.[18] In this light, it is easy to perceive an echo of the poet's voice and
his role as an Ulyssean adapter in the following exchange between the slave
Epidicus – 'more versatile than a potter's wheel' (*Ep.* 371 *uorsutior ... quam
rota figularis*) – and two old men (Periphanes and Apoecides), the first of
whom is his master:[19]

EP. si aequom siet
me plus sapere quam uos, dederim uobis consilium catum
quod laudetis, ut ego opino, uterque –
PER. ergo ubi id est, Epidice?
EP. –atque ad eam rem conducibile.
AP. quid istuc dubitas dicere?   260
EP. *uos priores esse oportet, nos posterius dicere,
qui plus sapitis.*
PER. heia uero! age dice.
EP. at deridebitis.

EP: If it were proper for me to be wiser than you, I'd give you a smart plan you'd
both praise, as I think –
PER: Then where is it, Epidicus?
EP: –and expedient for this matter.
AP: Why are you hesitating to tell us about it?

---

[17] In *Most.* 1149–51, the slave Tranio pairs his old master, whom he has just defeated, with
Diphilus and Philemon. Anderson (1993) 33 notes that, in this passage, 'speaking through
the mouth of the triumphant slave ... Plautus offers to give "lessons" to his dead
predecessors'.
[18] My use of the term 'minor' is indebted to Deleuze and Guattari (1986), who expand on
Kafka's idea of 'minor literature' as a destabilisation (or 'deterritorialisation') of major
literatures. As a deterritorialised form of German, Yiddish is a primary example of 'minor
literature'. On the 'inferiority complex' in Latin literature, see Matzner and Harrison
(2018), especially Fitzgerald's chapter.
[19] On Epidicus as a plot-crafter and dramatic architect, cf. Slater (1985) 19–34 and Sharrock
(2009) 121–30.

EP: *You ought to come first, we ought to speak later. You are wiser.*

PER: Come off it! Go on, tell us.

EP: But you'll laugh at me.

(Plautus, *Ep.* 257–62)

The self-effacing gesture that Epidicus adopts in this dialogue establishes another connective thread between the figure of Ulysses and Plautus' poetics of adaptation. In the several contests in which he takes part throughout the *Odyssey*, Odysseus (Ulysses) repeatedly proves his cunning versatility through 'the ploy of winning by coming last'.[20] This technique finds its most eloquent manifestation in the athletic games of Book 8, where the contrast between his unremarkable physical appearance and his victorious mental agility places Odysseus in the role of the satiric underdog. The Odyssean incarnation of this role holds a central position within the modes of self-representation of the interrelated genres of iambic poetry and Old Comedy, which combined invective and mockery with the distinctive postures of comic abjection and self-abasement;[21] in particular, it informs the stance that Aristophanes assumes in relation to tragedy. By defining his comic persona through the neologism τρυγῳδός ('trugedian, comic poet'), which puns on and distorts τραγῳδός ('tragic poet'), Aristophanes purports to construe comedy as a barbaric version of tragedy, but when he parodically adapts tragic scenes into the utopian plots of his rascal heroes, the intergeneric battle thus staged resolves itself in a tongue-in-cheek display of comedy's power to outdo its sister genre.[22] If understood against this background, the self-deprecating joke of the prologue of *Asinaria* evinces a similar gesture of self-positioning: parading his power of destabilisation of the Greek master signifier, his ability to open up Odyssean lines of flight through self-abjection, the Plautine adapter can exclaim, like Deleuze and Guattari, 'there is nothing that is major … except the minor.'[23] Coupled with the Ulyssean

---

[20] Purves (2011) 541. See also Pucci (1982) and Detienne-Vernant (1991) 11–26. Both Odysseus and Plautus' clever slaves operate through *tactics*, i.e., 'procedures that gain validity in relation to the pertinence they lend to time – to the circumstances which the precise instant of an intervention transforms into a favorable situation' [de Certeau (1984) 38]. As de Certeau (1984) 37 observes, a tactic 'is the space of the other' and 'an art of the weak'.

[21] Cf. Rosen (1990) and (2007) *passim*; on Odysseus as an archetype of iambic values, cf. also Worman (2008) 37–9; Steiner (2009); on this role in Roman satire, cf. Richlin (1992) 172. On Plautine comedy's intersections with satire, cf. Dessen (1977).

[22] For this view of the intergeneric battle of comedy and tragedy, cf. Dobrov (2001) 89–156 and Wright (2013); on τρυγῳδία, see esp. Platter (2007) 158.

[23] Deleuze and Guattari (1986) 26. See also Gunderson (2015) 46: 'Forget authenticity, authority, and authorship, says Plautus.'

manoeuvring that his resourceful slaves deploy against their old masters, Plautus' appropriation of New Comedy amounts to an enactment of iambic poetics.

This reading is borne out by another prologic statement, which describes the kinship between Plautus' *Casina* and Diphilus' *Allotment*:

> Κληρούμενοι uocatur haec comoedia
> graece, latine Sortientes. Diphilus
> hanc graece scripsit, postid rursum denuo
> latine Plautus cum latranti nomine.

This comedy is called *Kleroumenoi* ('Allotment') in Greek, in Latin 'Men Casting Lots.' Diphilus wrote it in Greek, and after that Plautus with the barking name wrote it again in Latin.   (Plautus, *Cas.* 31–4)

In this case, Plautus claims to have produced not just an adaptation, but a complete rewriting of the Greek original.[24] In fact, as hinted in *Cas.* 64–6, Plautus' play transmutes Diphilus' plot of Oedipal rivalry into a drama of gender conflict revolving around Cleostrata's discovery and denunciation of her husband's sordid plan to seize upon the maid loved by his son.[25] In this play, which does not feature any *seruus callidus*, the conjugal tension between Cleostrata and Lysidamus takes the metatheatrical form of a struggle over the role of plot-crafter.[26] When Cleostrata and her allies finally force Lysidamus to capitulate, such a victory is fancifully figured as the triumph of a group of predatory animals (wolves and dogs) over a castrated ram or a domesticated goat.[27] At *Cas.* 969–70 ('Here's my wife facing me! Wolves on one side, dogs on the other') the disparaging canine assimilation that his ally Olympio had previously reserved for Cleostrata (*Cas.* 320 *dies atque noctes cum cane aetatem exigis*, 'you spend your days and nights with a bitch!') turns, as it were, against Lysidamus and marks his defeat. The emphasis that, in the prologue, Plautus lays on the canine resonances of his name (meaning 'flat-eared dog') seems, thus, to forge a connection between his Latin transposition of Diphilus' original and the

---

[24] Differently from ll. 5–22, which were probably added for a revival of the play, these lines are generally considered Plautine: cf. MacCary-Willcock (1976) 97. On the relationship with Diphilus' original, see O' Bryhim (1989); Anderson (1993) 53–9; Arnott (2003); Lowe (2003).

[25] Cf. Moore (1998b) 167 and Sharrock (2009) 37.

[26] Cf. Slater (1985) 70–93; Moore (1998b) 158–80; Franko (1999); McCarthy (2000) 109–12; Sharrock (2009) 134–5. At *Casina*, 489–90 Chalinus, Cleostrata's chief ally, forecasts the defeat of Lysidamus' 'troops' as follows: *age modo, fabricamini, / malo hercle uostro tam uorsuti uiuitis* ('just go on, you two, make your plots, you'll pay a high price for being such tricksters').

[27] Cf. Franko (1999).

effective scheming of his female mouthpiece within the plot.[28] As a result, the Plautine transcoding of the Greek play proves to be not only interwoven with the gender reversal triggered by Cleostrata, but also anchored in the discursive territory of mockery and invective. In fact, in both the Greek and Roman tradition the dog customarily conjures the image of the attack-poet.[29] The result is a multiplicity of subversive metamorphoses or 'becomings': from man to woman, from human to non-human animal, from language to the intensity of sound.

The intersections between prologues and plots that I have teased out here suggest that Plautus positions the models of Greek New Comedy alongside the figures of social authority outsmarted by his tricksters as interchangeable iambic targets. This means that the deceptive intrigues of Plautine drama are figured as narratives of comic invective, which, as we shall see in the next section, can also intimate transgressive manipulations of, even aggression against, the Greek originals.

Gained in Translation: Gluing Together and Dismantling in Plautus' *Two Sisters Named Bacchis*

In his comparison of Caecilius Statius' *Necklace* (*Plocium*) and its Menandrian original, Aulus Gellius assigns the palm of superiority to the Greek play, justifying this verdict as follows:

> Quae Menander praeclare et apposite et facete scripsit, ea Caecilius, ne qua potuit quidem, conatus est enarrare, sed quasi minime probanda praetermisit et alia nescio quae mimica inculcauit et illud Menandri de uita hominum media sumptum, simplex et uerum et delectabile, nescio quo pacto omisit.

> Some of Menander's lines, brilliant, apt and witty, Cecilius has not attempted to reproduce, even where he might have done so; but he has passed them by as if they were of no value, and has dragged in some other farcical stuff; and what Menander took from actual life, simple, realistic and delightful, this for some reason or other Caecilius has missed. (*Attic Nights* 2.23.11; transl. Rolfe).

Foreshadowing the value judgements of many modern critics, Gellius views the process of adaptation as an unsuccessful experiment in textual engineering or surgical art that, by imposing clumsy omissions, replacements, and

---

[28] On Plautus' name, cf. MacCary-Willcock (1976) 102; Richlin (2017a) 136. Connors (2004) 182 observes that 'the echo of *latine* in the sound of the word for barking (*latranti*) seems to suggest that Latin itself might be a kind of barbarous barking'. On Cleostrata's assimilation to a dog, see Dutsch (2008) 81–5.

[29] On invective poets' self-assimilation to dogs, see Dickie (1981); Oliensis (1998) 69–70; Steiner (2001); Barchiesi (2002) 65–6; Worman (2008) 34–5; Telò (2014).

additions upon the original, compromises dramatic realism, psychological propriety, and literary refinement.[30] The discovery in 1968 of a substantial fragment of Menander's *The Double Deceiver* – the Greek play that F. Ritschl had already identified as the original of Plautus' *Bacchides* – has allowed critics, following in the footsteps of Gellius, to map out the intertextual procedures that shape the Roman remake.[31]

The plot of the two plays is centred upon the attempts that a resourceful slave (Syrus/Chrysalus) makes at bringing together his young master (Sostratus/Mnesilochus) and the courtesan Bacchis by tricking the money necessary to buy her contract out of his master's old father (Nicobulus). The two deceptions that give the Greek play its name are converted, in the Plautine version, into three cash transactions masterfully devised by Chrysalus. The surviving fragment of Menander's *The Double Deceiver* roughly overlaps with Plautus *Bacch.* 486–560 and corresponds to the moment of transition from the first to the second deception. Misled by the suspicion that Bacchis is two-timing him with his friend (Moschus/Pistoclerus), who is actually having an affair with her twin sister, Sostratus/Mnesilochus decides to return to his father the money that Chrysalus had earlier finagled from him. After the discovery of the truth, the *seruus uorsutus* has to think up another plan to recover the cash.

What emerges from the intricate re-arrangement of incidents, dialogues, and monologues, and entries and exits that Plautus crafted to adjust the act-based structure of the Greek original to the Roman stage is 'a shift from the illusion of casualness to a deliberate formality', from hard-won naturalism 'to more artificial and humorous conventions' and the transformation of bourgeois drama into a stylised and melodramatic 'comic fantasy' stage-managed by Chrysalus.[32] Thanks to the metatheatrical genius of this *seruus uorsutus*, self-reflexive signposting of the process of adaptation is also gained in translation.

The monody in which Chrysalus voices his dissatisfaction with the techniques of deception used by his Menandrian predecessors, Parmenon and Syrus (*Bacch.* 649) starts out as a celebration of his own double trickery (*Bacch.* 641): *nam duplex hodie facinus feci, duplicibus spoliis sum adfectus*

---

[30] On Gellius' judgement, cf. Vardi (1996) 507–8; Jenson (1997); Gunderson (2009) 142–3. According to Leo (1912) 87, the Greek plays adapted by Plautus 'were finer and better before Plautus laid his hands on them'; cf. also Holford-Strevens (2003) 199: 'the contrast bears out Gellius' comment: it is truly bronze for gold'.

[31] Cf. Handley (1968); Lefèvre (1978a); Bain (1979); Goldberg (1990); Damen (1992) and (1995); Anderson (1993) 1–29; Halporn (1993) 201–4; Owens (1994); Gratwick (1995); Handley (1997), (2001), and (2002a) 182–4; Lefèvre (2001); Jacques (2004); Fontaine (2014a) 520–6.

[32] Goldberg (1990) 200–1.

('I did a double deed today, I'm carrying off double spoils'). At this point, Chrysalus has replayed only one of the two deceits plotted by Syrus in the original, but, according to the Roman slave, having managed to extort a much larger sum of money from his old master represents in itself a redoubling of his Greek forebear's trickery. The repetition of *duplex* in *Bacch.* 641 puns on the title of the Menandrian play (Δὶς ἐξαπατῶν, *The Double Deceiver*), throwing into relief Plautus' agonistic stance toward his model through a sort of preview of the third deception, which will bring the plot to an end.[33] If we compare the Plautine play with the extant fragment of *The Double Deceiver*, we can unravel other layers of this stance.

Let us consider these two passages:

CH.	quid uis curem?	692
MN.	ut ad senem etiam alteram facias uiam.	
	compara, fabricare, finge quod lubet, conglutina,	
	ut senem hodie doctum docte fallas aurumque auferas.	
	. . .	
	immo si audias quae dicta dixit me aduorsum tibi . . .	
CH.	quid dixit?	
MN.	si tu illum solem sibi solem esse diceres,	
	se illum lunam credere esse et noctem qui nunc est dies.	700
	. . .	
	de ducentis nummis primum intendam ballistam in senem:	
	ea ballista si peruortam turrim et propugnacula,	710
	recta porta inuadam extemplo in oppidum antiquom et uetus.	

CH: What do you want me to take care of?

MN: That you have a second go yet at the old man. Plan, devise, invent whatever you like, glue together a plot so that you deceive the clever man cleverly today and take away the gold . . . Well, if you were to hear the things he said to me about you . . .

CH: What did he say?

MN: *That if you told him that the sun up there is the sun, he'd believe that it's the moon and that what's now day is the night. [. . .]*

CH: First I'll point my catapult toward the old man for the two hundred minas. If I knock down the tower and ramparts with that catapult, I'll instantly storm into the old and ancient town right through the gate. (Plautus, *Bacch.* 692–711)

(B) ἦ [γ]ὰ[ρ Ϲ]ύροϲ τὸν ἥλιόν μ[οι] το[υ]τονὶ
εἰ] νῦν πα[ρ]αϲτὰϲ ἐξέχ[ει]ν φάϲκοι, ϲκότον   85

---

[33] Cf. Damen (1995). On the third deception as Plautine innovation, cf. Fraenkel (2007) 46–7 [=(1960) 62–3] and Owens (1994).

νομίcαιμ' ἂν εἶναι, νύκτα γεγονέναι· γόης
ἀ]κ[ό]λ[α]cτος.
(c.) οὔκουν ἔcτι τοῦτό μ[οι], πάτερ,
'οὐ]θὲν ἀποτεύξει τοῦ πατρὸ[c] cὺ χρηcτὸc ὤν';

(B) For sure, if Syrus were standing by me and said the sun was shining here, I'd think it was dark, that night had come – an incorrigible trickster.

(SO) So I can depend on this, then, father: 'As a good son, your father won't deny you'?

(Menander, *The Double Deceiver*, 84–8, ed. and transl. Handley)

Bacch. 699–700 look like a 'faithful' rendition of ll. 84–5 of the Greek original – probably faithful enough to satisfy Gellius' obsession with fidelity in translation. Nevertheless, the Menandrian lines appear in the 'wrong' place. Plautus suppresses the paternal–filial reconciliation during which Sostratus returned the cash stolen by Syrus to his father (the anonymous B of the Greek text), but conflates some of the textual material of this dialogue in the following scene between Mnesilochus and Chrysalus, which moves the plot forward to the orchestration of the second deceit. The reported speech that, in *Bacch.* 699–700, frames the direct quotation from Menander mimics, as it were, the citational nature of its content and turns the Greek model into an imaginary offstage space. What is more significant is that the language of adaptation is jokingly encoded within the thematic texture of the Plautine scene.

The sequence of imperatives through which, in *Bacch.* 693, Mnesilochus prods Chrysalus to contrive another deception against his father is closed by the form *conglutina*. This verb indicates an assemblage of parts similar, as the poetological usage of the Greek equivalent (συγ)κολλάω ('glue together') suggests, to the process of textual conflation that lurks behind this dialogue.[34] In other words, the occurrence of the marked verb *conglutina* suggests a relation of contiguity between Chrysalus' piecing together of his new intrigue and Plautus' re-arrangement of the Greek original.[35] The resonance of *peruortam* with *uortere* confirms that Chrysalus' military attack against *oppidum antiquom et uetus*, which he

[34] For (συγ)κολλάω as designating the act of literary composition: cf. Pindar, *Nemean Odes* 7. 77–9; Plato, *Menexenus* 236b and *Phaedrus* 278e. On this metaphor, see Nünlist (1998) 124–5 and Porter (2010) 270. In Aristophanes, *Knights* 463 and *Wasps* 1041, the verb indicates the construction of a plot or a conspiracy: cf. Brotherton (1926) 42. *Conglutino*, which is not attested before Plautus, could be a calque of the Greek verb, expressing Mnesilochus' homage to Chrysalus' inventiveness: for similar examples, cf. Adams (2003) 352; see also Fontaine (2010) 168–74.

[35] It is significant that Chrysalus' bad influence on Mnesilochus is labelled as *congraecari* (l. 743) and *pergraecari* (l. 813), both meaning 'to (mis)behave like a Greek'. On the Plautine slaves' code-switching from Latin to Greek, cf. Adams (2003) 351–2.

announces later (*Bacch.* 710–1), anticipating his Trojan monody, is directed not only at Mnesilochus' old father, but also at the Menandrian subtext
of the slave's action.[36] At *Bacch.* 711, *inuadam* epitomises Chrysalus'
farcical or, in Gellius' words, mimic reconfiguration of the Greek model
in the form of an aggressive stage movement comparable to the intemperate
running of slave characters that ancient critics deem emblematic of Plautus'
dramatic style.[37] In other words, the same violent and deceptive practice of
textual recasting (*inculcauit*, from *inculco*, i.e., *in* + *calco*, 'to tread upon')
that Gellius laments in Cecilius is self-consciously inscribed within the
planning of Chrysalus' plot. Gluing together is a subversive, aggressive
kind of textual assemblage that disorganises the original. But rather than
amounting to an aesthetic disfiguration, as ancient and some modern critics
hold, it turns translation into a politically charged 'dismantling' of the
master signifier,[38] that is to say, an operation that disrupts the unity and
autonomy of the textual *archê*, opening it up to anti-hierarchical, nomadic
pressure. At the same time, as we will see in the next section, there may also
be a sense in which this dismantling is a constructive act, a form of nomadic
preservation.

Families and Shipwrecks: Archive and Adaptation in Terence

Terence 'places his prologues squarely into the tradition of "comic agon-
ism"' by harnessing fictional autobiography and interpoetic rivalry as
rhetorical instruments of authorial and generic self-projection.[39] Within
his prologic literary polemics, Terence's use (or abuse) of the Greek models
figures as a privileged terrain of apparent contention with his alleged
detractors, in particular the mysterious (and made up?) *maleuolus uetus
poeta* ('malignant old poet'), identified by Donatus with Luscius
Lanuvinus. This theme is accorded special prominence in the prologue of
the *Andria*, which provides the first and crucial chapter of the story of
Terence and his critics:

---

[36] On the expression *ueterem atque antiquam rem* as an allusion to the model of *Amphitryo*,
see above. Jenkins (2005) 383–90 explores the connection between Chrysalus' Trojan
expedition against Nicobulus and his role as a 'semiotic manipulator'.
[37] On Horace's and later critics' use of the *seruus currens* ('running slave') as a symbol of
Plautine farce, cf. Jocelyn (1995); Hunter (2002) 192–6 and (2009) 89–99.
The metatheatrical reading of *Poen.* 522–3 proposed by Hunter (2002) 192 demonstrates
that this identification is suggested by Plautus himself.
[38] 'Dismantling' is the term that Deleuze and Guattari (1986) 56 employ to qualify the
operations of 'minor' literature: see above n. 18.
[39] Sharrock (2009) 75. Cf. also Goldberg (1986) 31–60; Habinek (1998) 56–7; Gowers
(2004); Lada-Richards (2004); Christenson in this volume.

Menander fecit Andriam et Perinthiam.
Qui utramuis recte norit ambas nouerit,   10
non ita dissimili sunt argumento, et tamen
dissimili oratione sunt factae ac stilo.
quae conuenere in Andriam ex Perinthia
fatetur *transtulisse* atque usum pro suis.
Id isti uituperant factum atque in eo disputant   15
contaminari non decere fabulas.

Menander wrote *The Girl from Andros* and *The Girl from Perinthos*. If you know one, you know them both, since the plots are not very different, though they are written in a different language and style. Our author confesses that he has transferred anything suitable from *The Girl from Perinthos* to *The Girl from Andros* and made free use of it. His critics abuse him for doing this, arguing that it is not right to contaminate plays in this way.

(*And.* 9–16, transl. Barsby, adapted)

What, according to this account, Terence's detractors object to in his techniques of adaptation is the practice of *contaminatio* ('contamination') – an illegitimate crossbreeding of Greek models that spoils texts otherwise available for translation and disrupts the purist mirage of unidirectional intertextuality.[40]

The narrative of these lines bears striking similarities to the plot of the play. The interweaving of sibling comedies devised by Terence recalls the familial reunion that takes place at the end of the piece: Glycerium, the attractive Andrian courtesan of the title, is recognised as the sister of her young lover's betrothed, Philumena. In addition, the courtesan also stands for 'Terence's new, beautifully made drama ... which he fights to make ... regarded as fresh, not contaminated'.[41] In particular, marked as it is by the verb *transfero* (*And.* 952 *quor non illam huc transferri iubes?* 'why don't you have her brought over here?'), Glycerium's final acceptance into the family of Pamphilus (her lover and future husband) directly intersects with the contents of the prologue (*And.* 14 *fatetur transtulisse*), offering Terence's audience and critics 'an inviting model for his own charitable reception'.[42] The girl–play equivalence is a cliché of comic self-criticism that dates back

---

[40] The classic discussion of *contaminatio* is in Fraenkel (2007) 173–218 [= (1960) 252–320]; on the connection with the idea of spoiling, see Goldberg (1986) 91–122. Cf. also Guastella (1988) 11–72; Habinek (1998) 56; Barsby (2002); Lowe (2008) 122–4; Sharrock (2009) 86–7 and 91. For attempts to reconstruct the relationship between Terence's *Andria* and its Menandrian models, cf. most recently Lefèvre (2008).

[41] Gowers (2004) 154. For other connections of prologue and plot in the play, see Moodie (2009) and Germany (2013).

[42] Gowers (2004) 154.

to Aristophanes and re-appears in Plautus' prologues;[43] if we look at the key moments of the plot of *Andria* with this equivalence in mind, we can recognise the elements of Terence's self-representation as an adapter of Greek texts.

The dramatic movement of the plot unfolds in parallel with the gradual disclosure of the circumstances of Glycerium's migrations from Athens, where she was born, to the island of Andros and from Andros to Athens again. We discover that her paternal uncle left Athens on a ship to avoid war (*And.* 935) and brought along Glycerium, still a small girl (*And.* 924 *parua uirgo*); during the journey he was shipwrecked on the coast of Andros (*And.* 222, 923 *naue fracta ad Andrum eiectus est*) and lost everything (*And.* 924 *egens*), but before dying (*And.* 223) he handed over the little child to the father of Chrysis, the prostitute who, at the beginning of the play, is wrongly thought to be Glycerium's sister (*And.* 223–4, 924–5). To escape poverty and the indifference of her relatives (*And.* 71), Chrysis departed from Andros together with Glycerium and moved to Athens. Two details of this narrative – foster parenthood and shipwreck – support the possibility of a mutual assimilation between Glycerium and Terence's play. In the parabasis of *Clouds*, which is a pervasive presence of Terence's prologues, Aristophanes describes the performative conditions of his first comedies in the terms of a typical plot of New Comedy;[44] given his inexperience as a 'mother' of plays, he brought himself to expose his 'children' and let somebody else 'raise' them (i.e., put them on):[45]

κἀγώ, παρθένος γὰρ ἔτ' ἦ κοὐκ ἐξῆν πώ μοι τεκεῖν,
ἐξέθηκα, παῖς δ' ἑτέρα τις λαβοῦσ' ἀνείλετο,
ὑμεῖς δ' ἐξεθρέψατε γενναίως κἀπαιδεύσατε.

and I, being a maiden still unmarried and not yet allowed to be a mother, exposed my child and another maiden took it up, and you nobly raised and educated it.   (Aristophanes, *Clouds* 530–2; transl. J. Henderson)

The combination of exposure (ἐξέθηκα) and adoptive upbringing undergone by Aristophanes' plays accords well with the destiny of Glycerium after her uncle's death (*And.* 223–4 *hanc eiectam Chrysidis / patrem recepisse orbam paruam*, 'the father of Chrysis took this small orphan who had been abandoned').[46]

[43] In Aristophanes, *Clouds* 534–9, Aristophanes claims that his play is as σώφρων ('chaste') as Electra. In *Capt.* 1029 Plautus makes a similar statement, which resonates with the description of Casina's chastity in *Cas.* 81–3: cf. Hunter (1985) 30–1.
[44] Cf. Arnott (1985); Ehrman (1985); Hunter (1985) 30–3; Sharrock (2009) 76–8, 244.
[45] Cf. Telò (2010) 287–96 and (2016) 128–30; Leitao (2012) 124–34.
[46] On these lines, cf. Gowers (2004) 153–4; Moodie (2009) 152–3; Sharrock (2009) 145.

Significantly, the shipwreck motif permeates the anecdotes regarding Terence's death that are preserved by Suetonius in his *Life of Terence*:[47]

> Q. Cosconius redeuntem e Graecia perisse in mari dicit cum C et VIII fabulis conuersis a Menandro. Ceteri mortuum esse in Arcadia Stymphali siue Leucadiae tradunt, Cn. Cornelio Dolabella M. Fulvio Nobiliore consulibus, morbo aut implicitum ex dolore ac taedio amissarum sarcinarum, quas in naue praemiserat, ac simul fabularum quas nouas fecerat.

> Quintus Cosconius says that Terence died in the sea while coming back from Greece, with 108 plays translated from Menander. Others report that he died at Stymphalus in Arcadia or on the island of Leucadia – when Gnaeus Cornelius Dolabella and Marcus Fulvius Nobilior were consuls – because of illness or because he was beset with sorrow and discomfort for the loss of both the belongings that he had stored in the ship and the new plays that he had composed. (Suetonius, *The Life of Terence* 90–5)

No other play of Terence features a shipwreck.[48] It is, thus, quite easy to infer that Suetonius' sources reconfigure the plot of the *Andria* as a biographical narrative. The fatal shipwreck of Glycerium's uncle on a sea journey is taken as a cue for concocting the story of Terence's dying on the job. This biographical (mis)reading is particularly revealing, insofar as it implicitly suggests that, in the prologue of the play, the technique of *translatio* that Terence defends against his critics (*And.* 14 *fatetur transtulisse*) is literalised as a spatial transition and merged with the perilous *translationes* of Glycerium from place to place.[49] If understood against the charge of *contaminatio* – which implies the disfiguring and spoiling of the Greek models – the salvation of Glycerium after her uncle's shipwreck can be regarded as an image of the hard-won preservation of the originals' textual integrity that Terence claims for his comedies.[50] In a similar fashion, in the prologue of his last comedy, *Adelphoe*, he claims to have 'rescued' (*Ad.* 14 *reprehensum*) a scene of Diphilus' *Those Who Die Together (Synapothnescontes)* that, in his version, Plautus had left out.[51] The use of the verb *reprehendere* ('to rescue', but also 'to reprove') in this passage assimilates Terence's protection

---

[47] Cf. Rostagni (1944) 39–40.

[48] The only other extant Roman comedy that dramatises a story of shipwreck is *Rudens*. On the contrast of land/sea in Roman comedy, cf. Leigh (2004) 118–48.

[49] For a similar phenomenon in Virgil's *Aeneid*, cf. Barchiesi (2009) 100–1.

[50] Cf. *Haut.* 4–5 *ex integra Graeca integram comoediam / hodie sum acturus* ('I am about to perform an uncontaminated comedy from an uncontaminated Greek play'), where Terence presents his play as 'a virgin piece in transit' (Henderson [2004] 56): on these lines, cf. also Goldberg (1986) 135; Slater (1992) 90–1; McElduff (2004) 123–4; Sharrock (2009) 73–4.

[51] Cf. Goldberg (1986) 93–4; Henderson (1999) 46; Barsby (2002) 252; Gowers (2004) 161–3.

of the Greek play to the benevolent paternal and didactic role that Demea, the Terentian father par excellence, offers to his sons in the finale (*Ad.* 994): *reprehendere et corrigere me et secundare in loco* ('reproofing, correcting and supporting [you] from time to time').[52] In the same finale Demea also fosters a joining of families through marriage in the terms of a conciliatory *translatio* that will bring his son's beloved girl into his house (*Ad.* 909–10): *hac transfer, unam fac domum. / transduce et matrem et familiam omnem ad nos* ('fetch [her] across this way, unite the two families, bring the mother and the whole household over to us').

While the plot of *Andria* may have provided the basis of Suetonius' biographical narrative, the play's overarching, obsessive concern with the themes of survival, protection, and integrity[53] seems at odds with the story of Terence's failure and death. But Suetonius' narrative of destruction exposes the limits and contradictions of Terence's (defensive) self-presentation as 'saviour', which emerges from the play, showing its self-ironical, self-undermining potential. One is struck by the image of Terence dying under the burden of more than a hundred plays collected – archived – in his ship.[54] Terence's death by drowning or from deadly melancholy for the lost plays – a longing similar to the agony of *Andria*'s young lover – can be interpreted in the light of what Derrida calls *archive fever*, the illusory desire to reproduce a self-identical past by gathering all remains into the same space, producing a consignation.[55] In a sense, Terence's fatal shipwreck fulfills the death drive that, in Derrida's view, is the psychic engine of *archive fever*.[56] In other words, the obsession with preserving, saving the 'original' – assimilated to the integrity of the *puella*[57] – is not just doomed to fail, but is the cause of the failure, embedding within itself the destruction it compulsively seeks to avoid. The effort to save and preserve is emblematic of a desire for possession – epitomised by the young lover's passionate address to the *puella* (**mea Glycerium** 133) – which is antithetical to translation, a practice where the 'original' has 'refugee status, as language in a state of perpetual transit,

---

[52] On this passage and its connections with the prologue, cf. Gowers (2004) 162–3. On the thematisation of paternity in *Adelphoe*, cf., in particular, Henderson (1999) 40–1 and Leigh (2004) 158–91.

[53] See, e.g., 141 (*seruaui*); 288 (*tutandam*); 295 (*tutorem*); 319, 482 (*salutem*); 480 (*ego in portu nauigo*); 487 (*superstes*); 611 (*incolumem*), etc.

[54] Richlin (2017b) 170 interprets the episode as a metaphor of Rome's 'cargo' literature, reliant not just on textual commodities, but also human ones – like Terence himself as a slave.

[55] Derrida (1996). The title, *Archive fever*, is the translation of the French *mal d'archive*.

[56] The preservation and reproduction pursued by the archive are, in Derrida's view, forms of repetition, and, as he puts it, 'the logic of repetition . . . remains, according to Freud, indissociable from the death drive' (1996) 11.

[57] In l. 72, the phrase *aetate integra* is used of Chrysis. Cf. n. 50.

retreat, and referential infinitude'.[58] The apparent conformity of Terence the slave to the (external) imperative of archival, possessive consignation, the counterpart to 'faithful', preservative translation,[59] is undermined by translation's intrinsic similarity to a fugitive slave, its 'dispossessive' nature.[60] Paradoxically, Terence and the plays could be more readily saved if set 'free', dispersed, albeit exposed to potential destruction. His death is that of a literary legacy when it is handed over to a preservative, reproductive, reparative enterprise, to a power destined for failure in its hunger for possession.

When, in *Andria*, the truth surfaces – that Glycerium is a free girl – the young lover's father responds to the bearer of news with outrage, 'Do you intend to glue together marriage and affairs with prostitutes (*meretricios amores nuptiis conglutinas* (913))?' In these words we can see the horror of *contaminatio*, the practice of programmatic, subversive 'mixing', that we read into Plautus' use of the same verb *conglutino* in *Bacchides*. The juxtaposition, mutual '*con*tamination', and alteration of apparent opposites (affairs and marriage, slave and free, Roman and Greek) challenge the self-defeating archival *con*glomeration, with its pursuit of preservation, sameness, and integrity, that we see dramatised in Suetonius' account. The anarchical or 'an-archivic'[61] destruction that Plautus boldly embraces and Terence seems (forced) to disown, may be the only possible form of survival. *Vertere* troubles *vert*icality – it is always haunted by its compound, *subuertere*, that is, literally 'to cause to topple over', to destabilise an upright position.[62] *Vertere*, as expressed by the vertiginous turns of the *seruus callidus*, is itself an act of spinning, losing 'rectitude' – and sinking. The practice of adaptation occurs on the edge of a reciprocal 'becoming'[63] – for both the translating subject and the translated object. 'Dismantling', i.e., refusing to possess (and

---

[58] The citation is from Apter (2013) 240, referring to de Man's commentary on Walter Benjamin's essay 'The Task of the Translator' (1985).

[59] In *Eunuchus*, the most Plautine of his plays, Terence uses transvestitism and rape as figurative tools for advertising a different, more violent model of adaptation based on the interplay between assimilation and domination: cf. Dessen (1995) 137; Gowers (2004) 157–8; Sharrock (2009) 90–2; Gunderson (2015) 28–32. On this play's strategies of literary self-positioning, see also Fontaine (2014c) and Caston (2014).

[60] On the 'dispossessive' nature of translation – 'sundered filiation' or 'orphaned ... literary propert[y]' – see Apter (2013) 298–334. I owe to Apter the equivalence between translation and the 'fugitive slave', a concept she borrows from Best (2004), a theorisation of the relation between ideas of possession and American racist discourse on slavery. On the poetics of property in Plautus, see Dressler (2016).

[61] 'Anarchivic' is the neologism used by Derrida (1996) 10 to qualify the death drive that energises *archive fever*.

[62] For a feminist critique of 'rectitude' and 'verticality', see Cavarero (2016).

[63] *Vertere* is etymologically connected with the German *werden*.

be possessed), to reproduce and stabilise, and thus accepting the 'untranslatable'[64] is a paradoxical means of granting survival to an inherited literary tradition. This survival by translation may be better described as *sur*vivance – not just living on, but a survival that exceeds itself, that is, a preservation that thrives on dismantling itself, on the very act of spinning, of toppling over.[65]

Further Reading

Fantham (1978), Gilula (1989), Halporn (1993), Barsby (2002), Danese (2002), and Fontaine (2014d) offer helpful overviews of the relation of Roman comedy to its Greek originals. Following in the footsteps of Leo (1912) and Fraenkel (1960/2007), most of the studies on this topic have shown a prevailing interest in identifying *Plautinisches im Plautus* and *Terentianisches im Terenz*, sometimes arriving at problematic results because of the uncertainties in the reconstruction of the Greek models. For a useful appraisal of this methodology, see Lowe (1992) 152–7. Important and fruitful applications of this approach can be found, among others, in Anderson (1993), Arnott (1964b), (2001), Auhagen (2004), Barsby (1993), (2004a), Fantham (1965), (1968a), (1968b), Grant (1975), Handley (2002b), Hunter (1980), (1981), (1987), Lefèvre (1978b), (1995), (1999), (2008), Lowe (2001), (2003), O'Bryhim (1989). On Menander's *The Double Deceiver* and Plautus' *Two Sisters Named Bacchis*, see the bibliographical references listed above, n. 31; on Caecilius Statius' *Necklace* and its Menandrian model, cf. Traina (1974) 41–53, Riedweg (1993), and Fontaine (2014d) 412–14. Sharrock (2009) 163–249 and Fontaine (2014b), (2014c) approach Roman comedy's engagement with Greek models within the framework of intertextuality and repetition. McElduff (2004) supplies a refreshing assessment of the problem of translation in Terence; Brown (2013) surveys the prologic accounts of Terence's self-styled relationship with New Comedy.

---

[64] On the 'untranslatable', see Apter (2013); on 'dismantling', see above n. 38.
[65] On the term '*sur*vivance' as a description of translation – a survival that is '*plus de vie* and *plus que vie*' – see Derrida (1985) 25.

4

ROBERT GERMANY

The Politics of Roman Comedy

> sed sumne ego stultus, qui rem curo publicam,
> ubi sint magistratus, quos curare oporteat?
>
> I must be crazy, getting worked up about politics.
> We've got politicians for that![1]
>
> (Plautus, *Persa* 75–6)

If this book had been written a couple of generations ago, every chapter would have been substantially different in content, methodology, and emphasis, but this chapter would not have existed at all. Plautus and Terence were notoriously 'apolitical', especially by comparison with Aristophanes, and it would almost certainly have been taken for granted that there was not much to say about the politics of Roman comedy beyond pointing out its absence. Today the situation is different, but not because we have discovered some previously unnoticed fund of political jokes in these plays. Rather, we have grown accustomed to thinking of politics in more capacious terms, not simply as advocacy for or against specific public persons or programmes, but as a broader set of discourses pertaining to the mediation of power in society and to the very constitution of social life.[2] Indeed, even apoliticism, the studied refusal to address overtly political themes, presupposes an implicit definition of politics, as opposed to the rest of life, and an intensely political commitment to policing the boundary between the two. Instances of political engagement could thus be plotted on a spectrum of abstraction, ranging from explicitly partisan activism to tacit and apparently unconscious implication in a system of values. I begin this study at the more concrete end of the spectrum, examining topical allusions (and their absence) in Roman comedy and move on from there to consider the more abstract rubric of

---

[1] All translations are my own.

[2] The history of the term 'politics' in the twentieth century is immensely complex, and the bibliography on this issue is vast. For a brief but excellent survey of the various relevant modes of thinking about politics, specifically in their application to antiquity, see Hammer (2009).

cultural politics and the politics of everyday life. In the first section I offer a fresh reading of the famous allusion to Naevius in *Miles Gloriosus*, and in the second I extend the investigation of politics to embrace one of Roman comedy's most remarkable features, its propensity for metatheatrical play.

These comedies were produced in the context of state-funded *ludi* under the management of a junior magistrate whose future political career may have been affected by their success or failure, so it is implicitly unlikely that Roman comedy could be devoid of political import. It would be true – but only trivially so – simply to insist that everything public is political. I hope to go beyond such banality here and show how Roman comedy is richly imbedded in concerns that must legitimately count as political. Our central contention is that comedy is not just political in the sense that it touches on politics, but that it also has a political function, that comedy is, to misquote Clausewitz, the continuation of politics by other means.

The Politics of Topical Allusion

sed in uitium libertas excidit et uim
dignam lege regi; lex est accepta chorusque
turpiter obticuit sublato iure nocendi.

But freedom transgressed into licence and into aggression
Deserving law's bit. A law was passed and the chorus
Was silenced in shame when the right to offend was annulled.[3]

One of the most mysterious differences between Attic Old Comedy and New Comedy is the disappearance of the overt political engagement so abundant in Cratinus, Eupolis, and Aristophanes. Horace's rapid survey of the history of Greek drama at *Ars* 275–84 gives canonical formulation to the most enduring account of this shift: once poetic freedom could be cast as offensive attack, legal measures effectively curbed the playwrights' *parrhesia* (candidness). The choruses of Old Comedy were the locus of the plays' most concentrated political bombast as we know from the Aristophanic parabases (the moments in which the chorus is left to address the audience directly). Choruses were diminished in New Comedy to (apparently) non-verbal placeholders in between acts, so that the silence of the Menandrian chorus would become proverbial in antiquity.[4] Horace thus explains the single

---

[3] Hor. *Ars* 282–4.
[4] On the proverbial silence of Menander's chorus, well into the Byzantine period, see Burkert (2000). Of course, the New Comic chorus was not actually silent; they generally represented a band of revellers, and can thus be assumed to have made a good deal of noise! The papyri simply indicate where the chorus fit into the play with the word XOPOY, but transmit no text. Whether the chorus provided an interlude of music and dance without

most striking formal change from Old Comedy to New as a reflex of a political development, and the suppression of the chorus becomes legible as an act of erasure.

It has been difficult to pinpoint what specific law, if any, Horace had in mind; we have a few similar hints in the scholia to Aristophanes, but there is no clear evidence of long-term legal sanctions limiting comic licence.[5] Nevertheless, most scholars in the past have followed Horace in attributing New Comedy's near silence on public issues and persons to a changed political climate in which the poets could fear reprisals against more out-spoken engagement.[6] Under Macedonian rule, it is often assumed, the great age of Athenian democracy was at an end, and the citizen audience could hardly have taken much interest anyway in so depressing and futile a subject as politics had become. More recent scholarship, however, has tended to emphasise the robust continuity of democratic institutions and ideals right through the fourth century BC and the ways in which New Comedy may have been embedded in contemporary political discourses, if only covertly or allegorically.[7]

If Greek New Comedy has thus been somewhat rehabilitated for the history of political thought, the problem of Roman comedy's evident apoliti-cism becomes all the more interesting. The third- and second-century BC playwrights working in Latin took their models for nascent Roman tragedy from the fifth-century Athenian 'classics', especially Euripides, but when it

---

song or whether they also sang songs that were not transmitted, we can only guess. In either case, Menander's chorus is only 'silent' for cultures (such as Horace's and our own) in which Menander is typically read, rather than watched.

[5] The testimony pertaining to Athenian legal regulation of comic speech is most fully treated at Pauly-Wissowa's *Realencyclopedia* (1921) vol. xi 1233–6, but a convenient evaluation of the evidence (in English) may be found in Maidment (1935) 9–11. Horace also mentions the outspokenness of Old Comedy at *S.* 1.4.1–5 and makes a similar point about the legal restriction of early Roman *libertas* (freedom (of speech)) at *Ep.* 2.1.152–5. On Horace, slander, and the law, see most recently Lowrie (2005).

[6] Sandbach (1977) 69 on Athenian politics in this period: 'They were bitter and sometimes deadly. They were not a suitable subject for entertainment on a holiday. Even Aristophanes had shut his eyes to many unpleasant political facts; the authors of New Comedy shut their eyes, generally speaking, to politics as a whole.' More recently in the same vein, see Patterson (1998) 186–91. Some scholars have been less inclined to accept such excuses on behalf of New Comedy's apoliticism and have expressed a harsh verdict on its 'escapism'. See, for example, Green (1993) 74.

[7] More often now the dispute is between those who would read Menander as a Macedonian sympathiser (Major (1997)), and those who read him as a voice of democratic resistance (Lape (2004b)). More globally, Csapo (2000) makes a strong case that the sharp line we perceive between Old Comic political engagement and New Comic reticence is itself an artefact of critical history under the dominant (and falsifying) influence of Aristotle's theory of comedy.

came to comedy they ignored Aristophanes and the other fifth-century poets and drew their inspiration from New Comedy instead. This choice is easy enough to explain in terms of intelligibility: the dense topical allusions of Old Comedy would have been totally opaque to all but the most learned Romans in the third century, just as they often are for us, whereas the New Comic world of Hellenistic stock types in a reliably non-specific historical environment was readily learnable or already recognisable from daily life in Rome. Greek New Comedy's investment in Athenian democratic culture, subtle enough to escape scholarly attention until recently and still ambiguous in its import, would have been just the kind of feature that could be left out of a Roman version without causing structural problems or could even be retained and go unnoticed. The last-minute revelation of the ingénue's citizen status, for example, which makes possible so many happy endings in Menander, might also have democratic overtones for an Athenian audience still steeped in the myth of autochthony and laws stipulating citizenship only in cases of bilateral Athenian descent.[8] In Rome, however, where the franchise was less stringently mythologised, the marriage laws different, and there was no democratic tradition being threatened by Macedonian overlords, the discovery of the girlfriend's Athenian parentage could hardly have so much political resonance.

The problem of intelligibility could have been solved, of course, by finding local substitutes for many of the Athenian topical references. Just as Livius Andronicus could replace the Homeric *Mousa* with a Latin *Camena* (*Odissia*, fr. 1), surely there must have been a home-grown scoundrel who could have stood in for Aristophanes' vilified Cleon. But apart from intelligibility there may have been other reasons for the poets of Roman comedy to avoid the kind of personal invective characteristic of Old Comedy. Early Roman culture seems to have been significantly less tolerant of comic lampoon, beginning at least with the Twelve Tables (fifth century BC), which prescribed the death penalty for very few crimes, but among them: 'if anyone committed slander or composed a poem to bring ill repute or disgrace on someone else' (Cic. *Rep.* 4.12). We cannot know how consistently this law was ever enforced or what statutory analogue there may have been in the middle Republic, but it is interesting that the text comes to us in the mouth of Cicero's Scipio (dramatic date, 129 BC) as part of his critique of early Greek poetic licence and its contrast with Roman practice. 'But really,' Scipio asserts in the same passage, 'it was no more decent to attack Pericles with poetry and perform it onstage, than it would have been if our Plautus or Naevius had spoken ill of P. and Cn. Scipio or Caecilius of Marcus Cato.'

---

[8] See Lape (2004b) 68–109 and *passim*.

The odd thing about this unreal hypothetical is that the comic poet Naevius apparently did mock P. Cornelius Scipio for a youthful peccadillo, a humiliating moment involving a girl and the great commander dragged home by his own father half dressed.[9] The only thing we know of Naevius suffering from Scipio, perhaps by way of payback, was a witty insult punning on Naevius' name: *quid hoc Naeuio ignauius?* (What could be more knavish than this Naevius? (quoted in Cicero's *De. Or* 2.249)). This was not the only time Naevius tangled with a public figure, however, and he is said to have found himself incarcerated at Rome 'because of his constant slander and abuse of prominent members of the community, after the fashion of the Greek poets' (Aulus Gellius *NA* 3.3.15). Though it is impossible to be sure about the boundary between history and legend, Naevius' run-in with the Metelli is one of the better-attested literary events of the late third century.[10] Probably in 206 BC, when Q. Caecilius Metellus was consul, Naevius insulted the powerful family with an ambiguous line: *fato Metelli Romae fiunt consules* ('By fate the Metelli are made consuls at Rome' or 'To the misfortune of Rome the Metelli are made consuls'). The double meaning rests in the word *fato*, which might mean 'by chance' or, more darkly, 'to (Rome's) misfortune', *Romae* being construed as a locative in the first instance and as a dative in the second. The line is an iambic senarius and is generally assumed to have been spoken in a comedy.[11] But the Metelli were not amused; they fired back the pasquinade: *dabunt malum Metelli Naeuio poetae* ('The Metelli will give the poet Naevius a thrashing').

As grisly as this response sounds, scholars may have erred in reading it as altogether unsporting.[12] The threat is metrical, after all, and there are obviously less playful ways the Metelli could have responded than with a poetic riposte. In fact, the first-century AD grammarian Q. Asconius Pedianus in his commentary to one of Cicero's speeches (*ad Cic. Ver.* 1.29) refers to it as a *parodia* (parody), and this may be exactly right. The word *poetae* should certainly be construed primarily with *Naeuio* (dative), but by

---

[9] Aulus Gellius (*NA* 7.8.5–6) tells the story and gives the offending iambic septenarii.

[10] For a survey of all the ancient testimony pertaining to both this controversy and the one involving P. Cornelius Scipio, see Jocelyn (1969). Gruen (1990) 96–106 rejects the historicity of this story, but see also Sánchez Vendramini (2009).

[11] Mattingly (1960) 415.

[12] Not all modern readers have failed to detect the possibility of wit in Metellus' reply. Goldberg (1989) 254–5 and Gruen (1990) 100, independently of each other, note that *malum dare* is the standard comic formula for threatened punishment, and they argue that this repartee was only mistakenly interpreted by later generations as a serious political quarrel. As I make clear below, I agree with Goldberg and Gruen on the comic valence of *malum dare*, but I do not believe that playfulness should be confused with benign intention.

form it could also be read with *Metelli* (nominative). This syntactical equivocation would echo Naevius' case-play on *Romae*, and it would make the Metelli the poets in the same emphatic final line position as they were made consuls in Naevius' line. The first word of Naevius' attack, *fato*, fronted the poet's game of semantic instability, and the Metelli answer by inverting the structure and revealing in the last word of their reply that they can play the poet's game too. If the Metelli are hinting at appropriation of Naevius' role of comic poet, what role are they giving Naevius? The comic convention of *malum* = 'the punishment threatened for a slave' may indicate how they mean to cast him.

How long Naevius was imprisoned we can only guess, but there seems to be a reference in Plautus' *Miles Gloriosus* to his incarceration as a current fact. The tricky slave Palaestrio is wracking his brains to think up a plan to save the day, and the genial old man Periplectomenus gives a running commentary on the slave's dumb-show. At one point in his cogitations Palaestrio strikes a pose like Rodin's *Thinker* and Periplectomenus remarks:

> ecce autem aedificat: columnam mento suffigit suo.
> apage, non placet profecto mihi illaec aedificatio;
> nam os columnatum poetae esse indaudiui barbaro,
> quoi bini custodes semper totis horis occubant.
>
> Hey look, he's building! He's got a column propped beneath his chin.
> No thanks! I don't care for that type of building too much.
> For I've heard there's a barbarian poet with a columned mouth
> And two guards watching him all the time.　　　　　(*Mil.* 209–12)

Plautus usually refers to Romans as *barbari*, and the interpretation of this *poeta barbarus* as a reference to Naevius may be traced back to antiquity and has been accepted by almost all modern scholars.[13]

If the biographical tradition about Naevius is even roughly correct, it was bound to be an effective cautionary tale for other comic poets of that period who may have wished to call out prominent political figures from the stage, and it probably goes a long way towards explaining why there is not more direct topical reference of any kind in Plautus and Terence. Any allusion to controversial current events in Roman comedy would have to be vague

---

[13] Paulus' *Fest.* 32 seems to make this identification, and if his epitome of an epitome of Verrius Flaccus can be trusted, then the reading is traceable back to the Augustan period. Gruen (1990) 104 doubts all the biographical traditions about Naevius, including even this identification, but most scholars have not been persuaded to such radical scepticism. See, for example, Moore (1998b) 73 and Rochette (1998). In the context of a general dismissal of topicality in comedy, Leigh (2004) 20, n. 95 remarks, 'It is, however, hard to believe that Plaut. *Mil.* 210–12 is not an allusion to the imprisonment of Naevius.'

enough to provide a cover of plausible deniability, but this vagueness may also make the reference unintelligible for us. For example, assuming this passage in *Miles Gloriosus* is a reference to Naevius, what precisely is being said about him? What could possibly be meant by *os columnatum* ('columned mouth')?[14] Whatever the details of the punishment hinted at here, it would be fanciful to read Periplectomenus' negative reaction (*non placet profecto mihi*) as an indication of Plautus' sympathetic solidarity with his fellow playwright. But then what is Plautus' point in alluding to Naevius at all?

Naevius and his troubles are introduced into a passage that is already richly complex in its associative significance. Both within *Miles Gloriosus* and elsewhere, Plautus loves to describe the tricky slave who authors a comic subplot as an *architectus*, a word that will be applied to Palaestrio no less than six times by the end of the play.[15] By describing Palaestrio as a builder (*aedificat*) in the moment that he is crafting his intrigue, this passage introduces one of the play's most important unifying themes and analogises Palaestrio's role to that of the comic poet.[16] But Palaestrio's contorted thinking pose reminds Periplectomenus of the tortured posture of another comic poet now languishing in prison, and Palaestrio finds himself sliding within the metaphor from builder to part of the building. Periplectomenus' fear is that the architect becomes trapped by his own creation (*aedificat ... os columnatum*), just as Naevius became tangled in the unintended effects of his poem. Palaestrio's creation, his play-within-the-play, should make a comic butt of Pyrgopolinices, the eponymous *miles gloriosus* ('braggart soldier'), but if he fails and gets caught out by his opponent, he will be treated to a slave's punishment. Thus the analogy between Palaestrio and Naevius requires an obvious extension to their adversaries, Pyrgopolinices and Metellus. In this connection, since Pyrgopolinices is explicitly a soldier of fortune (*Mil.* 72–7; 948–50), I note that in addition to being a family name, *metellus* is also a common noun, attested in Accius, meaning 'mercenary'.[17]

[14] Suggestions have ranged from metaphorically forcible silencing (as we might say a 'gag order') to some kind of stockade or even irrumation. See Jocelyn (1969) 36; Killeen (1973).
[15] *Mil.* 901, 902, 915, 919, and 1139 (2x). Cf. *Poen.* 1110. See Maurice (2007) 423.
[16] On the theme of building in *Mil.*, see Forehand (1973) 10–11; on the metatheatrical valence of this passage, see Frangoulidis (1994), who does see Palaestrio as playwright, and Sharrock as well as Christenson in this volume.
[17] Paul. *Fest.* p. 146 M: *metelli dicuntur in lege militari quasi mercenarii. Accius Annali XXVII: calones famulique metellique caculaeque; a quo genere hominum Caeciliae familiae cognomen putatur ductum*, ('*Metellus* is a military term, roughly mercenary. Accius *Annals* 27: "porters, attendants, *metelli*, and stewards". The cognomen of the Caecilian family is thought to derive from this type of person.') Scholars have argued that Naevius actually used the common noun *metelli* in his attack on Metellus, hoping

If Palaestrio is too much like Naevius then Pyrgopolinices may turn out to be another Metellus, so Periplectomenus rejects this identification scheme (*non placet profecto mihi*) and casts about for another public figure to serve as Palaestrio's model. In the six lines immediately following the passage quoted above, he continues to praise Palaestrio's resourceful diligence, rallying him to banish delay and spring into action. He demands to know whether his words are getting through, and Palaestrio acknowledges that he is listening (*audio*, *Mil.* 218). The audience's attention also thus dramatically focused, Periplectomenus launches into an elaborate address as to a military leader (*Mil.* 219–30), figuring Palaestrio as a general and his foe as a public enemy (*hostis, perduellis*). The speech is too lengthy to be quoted in its entirety here, but in a long-neglected essay A. F. West argued that many details of the exhortation only make full sense if the speech is understood as an apostrophe to Scipio Africanus.[18] On the basis of the timing of Naevius' troubles with the Metelli and the available *ludi scaenici* soon after, West argues fairly convincingly for a production date of *Miles Gloriosus* in mid-205 BC, when Scipio was consul, fresh from victories in Spain and preparing for the campaign that would finally turn the tide against Hannibal.

If West is even roughly right on the production date (and his estimation is perfectly in line with the consensus of other scholars who hazard guesses on this issue), it is hard to see how this speech could not be heard in reference to current events, particularly given the admonition to surround and besiege the enemy, the strategy which had nearly defeated Hannibal in 212 BC at the Battle of Capua, the rejection of the Fabian policy of delay in favour of Scipio's policy of immediate action (*propere hoc, non placide decet*, 'this has got to go fast, not slow', *Mil.* 220), and the hints at a Scipionic personality cult of the general (*tute unus ... confidentiast ...*, 'you alone ... I have faith ... ' *Mil.* 229). But the point of the passage is not so much to ride the popular wave of patriotic hope for Scipio's success, as West assumes. Rather, if read in tension with the immediately preceding Naevius reference, it becomes clear what Periplectomenus is doing: Palaestrio as Naevius implies Pyrgopolinices as Metellus and portends failure for the good guys, so Periplectomenus suggests Palaestrio as Scipio, recasting the 'braggart soldier' as Hannibal.[19]

homonymy would be enough to save him, but the relevance of this word for Pyrgopolinices has not been noted. See Sánchez Vendramini (2009) 473.

[18] West (1887).

[19] The first thing Palaestrio says about Pyrgopolinices after this scene is that he is 'wrapped in elephant skin rather than his own and no smarter than a rock' (*Mil.* 235–6). Whichever real-life figure Pyrgopolinices is aligned with in the audience's mind, the elephant presents interesting resonances. The beast's associative possibilities with Hannibal are obvious enough, and it was the perennial emblem of the Metelli after 251 BC and L. Caecilius

This assumed identity is not only more propitious for Palaestrio, it also gives a promising part to everyone else. Periplectomenus repeatedly mentions the general's troops (*arripe opem auxiliumque*, 'marshal your supplies and forces', *Mil.* 220; *legiones tuas*, 'your legions', *Mil.* 224; *res subitaria est*, 'it's a job that will need volunteers', *Mil.* 225). West points out that the adjective *subitarius* in a military context is used only for volunteer forces, which fits perfectly with Scipio's situation in the summer of 205 training an army of fresh volunteers in Sicily in preparation to invade Africa.[20] Livy tells the story (29.1) of Scipio masterfully delegating the training of these Roman volunteers to more experienced Sicilian forces on an individual basis, thus getting his army ready with minimal trouble and expense. But this language also fits perfectly with the image that will be repeated throughout the play of Palaestrio as the master instructor of his troupe of volunteers and specifically as a commander able to delegate training.[21] Periplectomenus has landed on a public paradigm that will be auspicious for Palaestrio and his friends and that will cast Pyrgopolinices not as an ascendant Metellus, but as a Hannibal on the run.

We have tarried so long with these topical allusions in *Miles Gloriosus* for three reasons. First, the Naevius affair may well explain why we see so little direct political reference in Plautus and Terence, so it is worth taking the fullest possible stock of Plautus' reaction to it. Second, these allusions have been noted but never interpreted. They have a point in the play, namely to establish a paradigm for Palaestrio's struggle with Pyrgopolinices, and because the one model is meant to replace the other, they must be understood together. Third, the reference to Naevius in *Miles Gloriosus*, though it has sometimes been disputed, is perhaps the most generally recognised topical allusion in extant Roman comedy.[22] Of course many passages have been suggested over the years as possible topical references, some more plausibly than others, but all must be acknowledged as speculative. Apart from *Stichus* (200 BC) and *Pseudolus* (191 BC) none of Plautus' plays come with *didascalia* ('theatre notices') giving the original production date. Heavily veiled and only subjectively legible allusions thus become the basis for dating most of

---

Metellus' defeat of Hasdrubal at Panormus. One wonders, also, whether the infamous stupidity of the Metelli was a trope that went back this far. Many years later Scipio Aemilianus would mock the Metelli for their stupidity, saying of C. Caecilius Metellus Caprarius, *si quintum pareret mater eius, asinum fuisse parituram*, ('If his mother had given birth to a fifth child, it would have been a donkey.' Cic. *De Or.* 2.267).

[20] West (1887) 31.

[21] For Palaestrio as both direct trainer and as overseer relying on troops who are already up to speed to teach the newcomers, see *Mil.* 247, 256, 354, 793, 795, 812, 903, 905, 1035, and 1173.

[22] See above, n. 16.

the comedies, by matching them to historical events attested in Livy or Polybius.[23]

There is an obvious circularity in the attempt to read Plautus' plays for their allusions to current events, while simultaneously figuring out which events are current by dating the plays on the basis of these allusions. But there is a further problem in the evident assumption that topical references must be contemporaneous with specific legislative or military events. For instance, in *Aulularia* Megadorus twice complains of the luxurious ways of women (*Aul.* 167–9, 475–535), and these denunciations have sometimes been taken as evidence that the play should be dated to around 195 BC when the *lex Oppia*, a sumptuary law regulating feminine adornment, was debated and repealed.[24] But the *lex Oppia* had been in place since 215 BC and there is no reason to assume that cavils about women and their finery could only come up because of its repeal. Indeed, purple and gold are everywhere associated with women in comedy, including, by chance, one of the two securely dated Plautine plays, *Stichus*, five years before the repeal of the *lex Oppia*.[25] Other attempts to detect topical allusions in Plautus run into similar problems. *Stichus* and *Pseudolus* and the plays of Terence, because they can be dated with some confidence by production notes, ought to furnish a more solid basis for reading topical allusions (assuming they are there to be read), but strangely here too most suggestions have met with only mixed assent.[26]

Cultural Politics and the Politics of Everyday Life

Most recent scholarship has avoided this morass of speculation by moving away from the search for allusions to specific persons and events, focusing instead on the presence of themes of more general or typological political significance in Roman comedy.[27] In this vein, returning to the issue of feminine luxury in *Aulularia*, we might note that although there is nothing

[23] The two grandest attempts to establish a chronology for Plautus' plays are still Buck (1940) and Schutter (1952). The tide seems to have turned decisively against such studies after Harvey (1986).

[24] See, for example, Buck (1940) 37; Haury (1976); Moore (1998b) 162.

[25] Harvey (1986) 300–1.

[26] For recent work on topical allusions in *Stichus* and *Pseudolus*, see Owens (2000) and Augoustakis (2007), respectively. It may be that the difficulty of finding such references in Terence is due to his closer adherence to his Greek models. The most obvious contender, though much disputed, is the case for some connection between L. Aemilius Paullus and the bifurcated models of paternity in *Adelphi*. On the complex problem of this identification, see Leigh (2004) 158–91.

[27] Exemplary in this regard are Galinsky (1966), Gruen (1990) 124–57, and Leigh (2004).

in Megadorus' remarks to connect them specifically to the repeal of the *lex Oppia*, they can certainly be associated with the persistent Plautine trope of the perils of prodigality, a theme of some prominence in Roman political discourse of the late third and early second centuries BC.[28] The *lex Orchia* (182 BC) and the *lex Fannia* (161 BC), laws restricting libertine expenditure at meals, were both passed after Plautus' death but before the death of Terence. Plautus' outrageous catalogues of gourmandising excess thus cannot be allusions to these laws, but the moral convictions and patterns of thought that gave rise to these restrictions, with their explicit lists of forbidden fancy foodstuffs and prescribed quantities, can hardly be irrelevant to the impulse that generated the comic poet's luridly fantastic banquets.[29] In 184 BC, the traditional year of Plautus' death, Cato delivered a speech on dowries (*de dote*) and another on women's clothing and transportation (*de uestitu et uehiculis*).[30] Megadorus' criticism of spendthrift dowered wives with ivory chariots and purple clothes may not be a comment on the *lex Oppia*, but it shares with the *lex Oppia* and with Cato's speeches a common genealogy in Roman public discourses weaving together gender, display, domestic authority, imported luxuries, and the imperilled social order. In other words, whatever his complaints' precise relationship to the *lex Oppia*, they are indisputably political.[31] Such oblique political engagement as this, however, hardly makes Megadorus a partisan, still less does it make Plautus one. Are we meant to take Megadorus' protestation seriously, perhaps even hear it as an indication of the playwright's cultural sympathies, or is this a parody of such moralistic harangues, spoken by a hypocritical old fool? Critics are divided on this question.[32] The apparent difficulty of parsing the playwright's own political sentiments is hardly unique to this case; there

---

[28] See, for example, the prologue of *Trinummus*, where a personified Luxuria introduces her daughter, Inopia, into the home where she has been helping a young man destroy his inheritance.

[29] On Plautus' complex love affair with food and the cook's role in metaphorical spicing and cultural mixture, see Gowers (1993) 50–108.

[30] Malcovati (1953) *ORF* 158 and 93, respectively; cf. Liv. 39.44.

[31] Megadorus' horror of rich wives is explicitly framed as public prescription. If everyone accepted his views, 'society would be happier' (*fiat ciuitas concordior, Aul.* 481), and Euclio agrees that Megadorus should be made 'commissar of ladylike behaviour' (*moribus praefectum mulierum hunc factum uelim, Aul.* 504). For a reading of Megadorus' programme within *Aulularia*'s larger moralistic theme of the danger of wealth, see Kruschwitz (2002) 151–6.

[32] Most scholars seem to incline to the latter view, pointing out that, for all his austerity, Megadorus is a *senex amator* who will be soundly tweaked by the play's events. See Gruen (1990) 146; Moore (1998b) 163–4. The fact that Megadorus will be one of the play's butts, however, does not necessarily make him wrong here. For a more sympathetic view of his complaints as valid social criticism, see Konstan (1983) 44–5.

seems to be no political issue where we can speak conclusively of Plautus or Terence having a legible partisan position.

The most extensively studied cultural political issue in Roman comedy is surely Hellenism, and here perhaps more than anywhere else there is deep ambivalence, reflective no doubt of the combined attraction and suspicion with which many Romans in this period regarded Greek culture.[33] Roman comedy itself is – paradoxically enough – Greek, both because it is an adaptation of a Greek form of entertainment and more importantly because it remembers this fact constantly, reinscribing Greekness into its own text by naming the Greek source in the prologue, retaining Greek character names, locations, and civic institutions, and even calling itself *fabula palliata*. Romans, when they are mentioned at all, are *barbari* in every instance but one, and that one exception only proves the rule: it is a complaint about the stench of Roman oarsmen.[34] The plays thus pretend to look out at the world from an emphatically Greek perspective, and their characters' charm and comic heroism seem partially attributable to this performance of Greekness.[35] But the characters are not only charming, they are also often devious and dissolute, and references to 'Greek trustworthiness' (*Graeca fides*) and 'Greeking it up' (*pergraecari*) at luxurious feasts make it clear that these moral shortcomings too are integral to the Hellenic ethnicity as constructed in Roman comedy.[36] Across the long history of the Roman importation and adaptation of Greek culture, few periods were as decisive as the late third and early second centuries BC, but it would be a mistake to think of this process as 'Hellenisation' if only because the Romans had been absorbing Greek cultural practices for centuries. Rather, we may perhaps more accurately think of it as a period of Romanisation, in the sense that the accelerating pace of assimilation of Greek cultural forms, along with other shifts in the experience of Roman *imperium*, was

---

[33] See Moore (1998b) 50–66. For the Roman cultural engagement with Greece more generally in this period, see Gruen (1990) and (1992).

[34] For *barbarus* (or *barbaricus*) = Roman or Italian, see *As.* 11, *Trin.* 19, *St.* 193, *Capt.* 492 and Telò in this volume; on *Mil.* 211, see pp. 71–2 above. For the stinky *Romani remiges*, see *Poen.* 1314.

[35] Donatus, *ad Eu.* 57: *concessum est in palliata poetis comicis seruos dominis sapentiores fingere, quod idem in togata non fere licet* ('In *fabula palliata* the comic poets are allowed to make slaves smarter than their masters, which is pretty much not permitted in *fabula togata*'). In *Stichus* the eponymous hero invites the audience to see his bad behaviour in its cultural context: *atque id ne uos miremini, hominis seruolos / potare, amare atque ad cenam condicere: / licet haec Athenis nobis* ('And don't be surprised to see us slaves drinking, making love, throwing parties: that's how we roll in Athens', *St.* 446–8).

[36] For *graeca fides*, see *As.* 199; for *pergraecari*, see *Most.* 22, 64 and 960.

prompting the Romans to articulate a distinctively non-Greek cultural space for themselves, even in the most overtly 'Greek' practices.[37] For all these reasons, when it comes to thinking about Greece, we should not expect Roman comedy to be ideologically tidy. These plays do not represent a philhellenic programme foisted on the masses by a cultural elite, nor are they a form of xenophobic popular resistance. But they are no less political for being politically complex.

These cultural issues – luxury and Hellenism – concern the behaviour of the rich and the public construction of Romanness vis-à-vis a cultural other. But Roman comedy also engages with the politics of everyday life, as encountered by all social levels, in the privacy of their most intimate experiences of power. Most cultures could fairly be described as male-dominated, but Roman society was patriarchal in the proper sense of the word: the metaphor of paternity was everywhere inscribed in relations of hegemony.[38] The Senate was a body of 'fathers' (*patres*), consisting largely of the traditional aristocratic class, the Patricians (*patricii*). Its control was not, at least notionally, in the nature of raw power or command (*potestas* or *imperium*), which was vested in the magistrates and people, but rather *auctoritas*, a vaguely defined cache of social esteem, explicitly on the model of a Roman father's advisory influence within his family.[39] Roman society itself was expansive and diverse but internally organised into subsidiary networks of patrons (*patroni*) and their clients, bound together with ties of mutual obligation defined more by custom than statute. This patronage system might nest to several levels, so a given individual could be one man's patron and another man's client, and it could also extend beyond individuals to corporate bodies, such as guilds, religious associations, and even foreign cities. When we speak of the organisation of power in the household as a form of politics we may be inclined to assume that we are applying a public metaphor to a private affair and that the metaphor works only because domestic experience has been so thoroughly infiltrated by the public discourse of power.[40] But to a Roman this essentially Gramscian formulation would probably have seemed backwards, since the political organisation of Roman society at all levels and even the Senate's relationship to foreign cities was understood as a form of paternal authority. Rome's

---

[37] See Habinek (1998) 34–68.   [38] See Dinter in this volume.

[39] *cum potestas in populo, auctoritas in senatu sit* ('While power resides in the people, authority rests in the Senate', Cic. *Leg.* 3.28). For a nuanced treatment of the distinction between *auctoritas* and *potestas*, see Hellegouarc'h (1963) 299–307. Though primarily focused on a later period, Galinsky (1996) 10–41 is useful.

[40] Connolly (2007) 42 (my emphasis): 'Taken as a collection of individuals, "the people" incorporate ruling practices in their own lives, especially in the household, where the treatment of slaves and women *enacts the polity in miniature*.'

politics begins at home, and her comedy's almost exclusively domestic interest, far from rendering it politically irrelevant, makes it an invaluable source for understanding the strategies that governed the generation and management of *auctoritas*.

Comedy's inversion of domestic authority is, of course, one of its primary sources of appeal.[41] Forty years ago Erich Segal popularised the idea that the evident ascendency of clever slaves, impecunious lovers, and other comic underdogs was a mark of the genre's Saturnalian inversion of Roman norms, offering the pleasure of Oedipal fantasy to slaves and sons in the audience, while reassuring any bourgeois old men in attendance that all such shenanigans were strictly holiday fantasy played out in the Never Never Land of an obviously imaginary Greece.[42] Scholars have since extended this Freudian approach to provide more sophisticated accounts of how various segments of the audience may have found pleasure watching the ceaseless bidding for control within these comedies and may have been able to identify with the success of either of these parties or even of both simultaneously.[43] If such 'cross-identification' was part of the aesthetic experience of Roman comedy, it would be extremely fanciful to take the preponderance of slaves smarter than their masters as evidence that the Roman comic playwrights resented the institution of slavery and intended to subvert or even substantially critique it. Bakhtin's concept of carnival may be apt for describing the inversion of social norms in Roman comedy, especially given the festival context of production, but the holiday was never supposed to last forever, and the question remains whether the political point of carnival is the subversion of norms or the final containment of disruptive forces.[44] Most scholars would incline strongly to the latter view of Roman comedy, as a periodic 'safety valve' of discontent rather than as a hotbed of revolution, but there may be richer ways of understanding carnival than with this sterile dichotomy, for the two alternatives are neither mutually exclusive nor fully coherent without each other. On any of these three general models of carnival – as bitter critique, as pointedly temporary folly, or as some eternally unstable and permanently renegotiable combination of the two – the carnivalesque aspects of Roman comedy are inevitably political, though in different senses for each model.

---

[41] See Fantham in this volume.   [42] Segal (1968).

[43] See Parker (1989); McCarthy (2000) 17–29; Fitzgerald (2000) 36–47. See also Fitzgerald in this volume.

[44] For carnival, see Bakhtin (1984). Bakhtin clearly believed in the liberatory potential of carnival; for the 'pessimistic' perspective, consider Eagleton (1981) 148: 'Carnival, after all, is a *licensed* affair in every sense, a permissible rupture of hegemony, a contained popular blow-off as disturbing and relatively ineffectual as a revolutionary work of art. As Shakespeare's Ophelia remarks, there is no slander in an allowed fool.'

Alongside the charismatic tricky slaves, comedy also occasionally presents virtuous but less successful slaves complaining of the injustice of their lot in quite pathetic terms.[45] These rants generally lead nowhere, dramatically, unless perhaps they help characterise the slave's master as unlovable even to his own household. But the master's nastiness is usually already sufficiently clear, so the very gratuitousness of these scenes invites interpretation. Similarly, women in Roman comedy, for all their typical petulance, occasionally give voice to complaints about men that are undeniably accurate and fair, and it is hard to imagine playing the scene entirely for laughs.[46] Carnival is probably not an apposite category for explaining the social function or the appeal of such scenes, but like the carnivalesque motif of authority inversion, these articulate protests against the injustice of masters preying on their slaves and husbands cheating on their wives would probably have evoked different responses from different segments of the audience and maybe complex responses within the same viewer.

As a rule, the women in Roman comedy are not simply passive victims of men, and their combination of vulnerability to and power over elite males is in many ways analogous to the tricky slave's. The successful female comic character, whether matron, madam, or mistress, may exercise nearly absolute control over money, sex, and the play's resolution, and this power can even be expressed as patronal authority. So, for example, in *Eunuchus* when the prostitute Thais magnanimously forgives Chaerea for raping her adopted sister, he pleads with her to help him in his suit to marry the girl. He hopes that *magna familiaritas* ('a great friendship', *Eun.* 874) will arise between himself and Thais, and now he clarifies how their relationship will be structured: *ego me tuae commendo et committo fide[i] / te mihi patronam capio, Thai'* ('I do hereby entrust myself to your good faith / I take you as my patroness, Thais', *Eun.* 886–7). The play of dominance and submission between the rape and this scene is inescapably political in that it turns on the complex dynamics of power between man and woman, guardian and protégé, citizen and alien, and these dichotomies are built into the ideological structures that organise Roman society, but the negotiation for authority becomes more pointedly mapped onto the Roman political landscape when it ends in what amounts to a *deditio in fidem* (surrendering oneself).[47]

---

[45] For example, *Poen.* 823–44, on which see Slater (2004), and *Ps.* 767–89, on which see Jocelyn (2000). *Captiui* is a special case, both because of the intensity with which it considers the slave's perspective and because it is, in some sense, *not* a slave's perspective. See Konstan (1983) 57–72 and Thalmann (1996) and Fitzgerald in this volume.

[46] For example, *Merc.* 817–29. See Dutsch in this volume.

[47] For a survey of *deditio in fidem* in Roman political practice of this period, see Dahlheim (1968) 5–82.

Comedy thus elevates slaves to triumphing generals and prostitutes to patrons, but these are not simply promotions, they are new roles, and recognisably Roman ones at that. In adopting these roles, however briefly, the characters simultaneously rupture the theatrical illusion of Greekness and hint at their own artefactual status as roles played in a play. This metatheatrical aspect of Roman comedy is one of its most distinguishing features, but it has typically been associated with only the most primly formalist modes of reading.[48] I believe we are now in a position to consider the relationship between self-conscious, variable role-playing and the nego-tiation of *auctoritas* – in short, the politics of metatheatricality in Roman comedy.

Moderns, especially 'late' moderns, tend to assume a sharp dichotomy between identity and performance: playing is so totally antithetical to being oneself that the presence of one implies the absence or impairment of the other. This divide has been problematised in recent years by theorists such as Judith Butler, and Romanists, armed with performance theory, have discov-ered the remarkable extent to which the ancient Romans understood identity to be necessarily inflected by performance, if not indeed performative to the core.[49] This awareness is perhaps nowhere so evident as in the Roman theorisation of rhetoric, a discipline that came into its own and was first formalised in handbooks during the floruit of Roman comedy.[50] Rhetoric and comedy were thus historically parallel performance arts and reflect overlapping modes of thinking about the intense interpenetration of ethical and acted selves.[51] Rhetorical theory's relationship to the irreducible

---

[48] On metatheatricality, see Christensen in this volume. For criticism of metatheatricality studies as a kind of hyper-formalism, see Rosenmeyer (2002) 93–4. Moore (1998b) 67–90 argues that Plautine metatheatricality is consistently connected to the deflation of moralistic pomposity. His conclusion fits well with my claim here about what metatheatricality 'means'.

[49] Butler's theory of performance is anchored in her proposal of the radical performativity of gender, on which see Butler (1990) and (1993); on the political ramifications of performance more generally, see Butler (1997). For examples of the application of performance theory to Roman culture, see Gunderson (2000) and Wray (2001).

[50] See Quint. *Inst.* 3.1.19–20 and Dinter in this volume.

[51] The similarity between rhetoric and comedy may also be described as institutional homology. The principal occasion for Republican oratory was the *contio*, an open-air assembly where a magistrate would address a crowd on some political issue and petition them for support. Some scholars, following Syme (1939), doubt the real importance of popular opinion in Roman politics, where others, especially Millar (1984), have seen the *contiones* as a democratic element in Rome's governance structure. Even if the people's assent was not strictly necessary, *contiones* were never framed as mere proclamations or top-down assertions of senatorial control. Rather, the orator would address the crowd as 'the People' and solicitously bid for their sovereign favour. Recently scholars have focused on this illocutionary function of the *contio* and theorised that the *contio*'s real significance lay in its performative authorisation of the people as a constitutive partner in the Roman

performativity of selfhood, the lability of identity in play, is at times remarkably candid and at others ambivalent, but rhetoric's problem is comedy's proper domain. The one prevaricates where the other gleefully embraces, but the consistent 'lesson' of both comedy and rhetoric is that *auctoritas* is radically inseparable from the performance of a role.[52] This role is encoded in relatively fixed and legible features, such as dress, comportment, and voice, but an actor/orator can change roles between performances and even slide from role to role within a single performance, and such changes may naturally entail expansion or diminution of power, since power is always mediated through a contextually located persona.

Ulrich Gotter has posited a fundamental difference between Greek and Roman formulations of power precisely here. The Greeks generally conceived of power as an impersonal abstraction, whereas 'the exercise of influence in Rome, whether on the basis of *potestas* or *auctoritas*, was highly context-specific. All forms of legitimate power that the Romans lexically defined were inextricably linked to certain roles and positions within Roman society. Hence one and the same person could embody them at various moments to varying degrees of intensity.'[53] There is something distinctively Roman, then, in Roman comedy's insistence that the contest for control plays out in the field of stock character types and in variable role-playing within and between those types. Stock characters construct a world in which there is a shockingly small number of generic human forms interacting with each other according to a fixed economy of complementarity. They also imply that moral character, at least in its rudiments and in most cases in its entirety, is fully legible from appearance and behaviour. Finally, they remind us that there is a radical fungibility built into all such systems of social roles, such that for most practical purposes we are interchangeable with any other specimen of our type.

The Romans of later generations, no less than those of the middle Republic, found themselves reflected in and formed by the theory of human nature implicit in this type system, and comedy continued to provide the Romans with a grammar for articulating differential constraints on freedom of action.

---

state: SPQR. See esp. Morstein-Marx (2004). Comedy's open-air performance venue, its framing appeals to the audience for attention and applause, and most importantly – if my argument in this chapter is right – its implicit role in situating audience members within a social regime all make it similar to the *contio*.

[52] Connolly (2007) 204: 'Comedy helps teach citizens how to behave in the community, especially when the competitive negotiations of social status cause pain.'

[53] Gotter (2008) 201. Gotter cites two remarkable stories in Aulus Gellius (2.2.1–13) showing elite Roman fascination with their own practice of navigating simultaneous, overlapping roles and the requisite shifts in decorum depending on which role is dominant at a given moment.

For example, when Roscius of Ameria is accused of murdering his father, the prosecutor, Erucius, posits that he must have been motivated by hatred and resentment after the father expressed a clear preference for his other son by keeping him in the city, while he left Roscius in the country to manage the estates. When Cicero comes to this point in the prosecution's narrative he would like to forgive poor Erucius for having so little idea how things work in the father–son relationship, after all Erucius probably doesn't even know who his own father is, but still he might have learned how these things work from literature: 'Look at comedy, do you think that old man in Caecilius loved Eutychus, the country son, more than the other one, Chaerestratus? ... You think he kept the one in the city to honour him and left the other in the country to punish him?' (*Pro Sexto Roscio Amerino*. 46–7). Cicero explains that he could just as easily point to family and friends who kept their sons on the farm precisely because they loved them so much, but he is not sure they would like to be named in a trial. 'Besides nobody is going to be more recognisable for you than this Eutychus, and it makes no difference whether I name this comic youth or someone from the country near Veii. In fact, I think the poets construct these things just so we can see our own characters represented in other persons, an exact likeness of everyday life.'

The political impact of Roman comedy is revealed here not only because comedy furnishes Cicero with a locus of authoritative appeal in a legal speech rife with political import, but more significantly because it establishes a code of ethical predictability.[54] Roscius' character is interchangeable with Caecilius' Eutychus, just as Eutychus is essentially the same as all the other country sons of Roman comedy. He is also like all the Italian country sons Cicero could cite, but, in a move reminiscent of the dynamics we saw in the first half of this chapter, the locals' names are suppressed and a (Greek) comic character is used as a cover for them. Thus the comic 'good son' type must serve both as an index for Roscius and the Italian boys and as a screen, effectively obscuring further inquiry into their real characters. Roman comedy's claim to verisimilitude becomes its profoundly political justification as an authoritative construction of the roles by which Romans live and understand each other.

Further Reading

The most ambitious chronological schemes for Plautus' plays, and thus also the best compendia of older scholarship on topicality, are still Buck (1940) and Schutter (1952), although such projects are now almost universally

---

[54] See Vasaly (1993) 157–72 and Harries (2007) 134–6.

dismissed as hopeless. In the more plausible effort to elucidate general cultural politics (including nasty Carthaginian stereotypes, repatriated Roman prisoners of war, suspicious maritime trade, and whether fathers should be stern or lenient), Leigh (2004) is excellent. On Roman culture and Hellenism, not just in comedy, but in the middle Republic more generally, Gruen (1990) and (1992) are indispensable, as is ch. 2 of Habinek (1998). On slavery, McCarthy (2000) and Fitzgerald (2000) should be read together. For rhetoric and theatricality, see Connolly (2007), esp. ch. 1 and 5.

PART II

The Fabric of Roman Comedy

5

C. W. MARSHALL

Stage Action in Roman Comedy

Theatre takes place on a stage, creating fictional worlds that are revealed to spectators in the course of a performance. The audience is always aware of the physical realities of the performance (in Rome, the actors are wearing masks, are dressed in costumes, and deliver verse after a period of rehearsal), but it is simultaneously drawn into the fictional world created. The theatrical reality (actors) and the dramatic world created (characters) superimpose themselves, and the audience is continually encouraged to perceive both realities simultaneously. This can be done through metatheatre, the explicit recognition of the dramatic frame by the actors, but there are also other techniques available to create and foster this dual awareness.[1] This chapter describes some of these techniques as they apply to two plays in particular: *Mercator* ('The Merchant') by Plautus, based on a Greek original by Philemon, and *Hecyra* ('The Mother-in-Law') by Terence, based on a Greek original by Apollodorus of Carystus (neither of the Greek plays survives). From the examples in these two plays, a general picture applicable to the rest of Roman comedy emerges.

Roman comedy was performed at festivals (*ludi*), and there were a limited number of opportunities to see a play during the year. Though the precise number of performance days in Rome varied (somewhere between twenty-five and thirty seems likely), it would seem that there were three or four regular opportunities for a troupe to be hired annually, and this might be supplemented with funeral or votive games.[2] Troupes of four to nine performers would be hired on contract to perform a play at a given festival (*Ps.* 1334–5 suggest that the same play would be performed each day). It is possible that three or four actors formed the core of the troupe, with additional performers being hired as required for particular plays.[3] Depending on the festival, any of a number of venues throughout the city may have been

---

[1] Slater (1985) offers an important foundational statement for metatheatre in Plautus, and see Christenson in this volume. Revermann (2006) 107–45 provides a theoretic framework for the interpretation of theatrical space that is relevant to the present discussion.

[2] Duckworth (1952) 73–9; Beare (1964) 162–3; Marshall (2006) 16–20; Manuwald (2011) 41–55; Franko (2014).

[3] Marshall (2006) 114–20, and see Manuwald (2011) 80–90.

used. An area in front of a temple might be designated, allowing spectators to sit on the temple steps, or a section of the forum might be assigned by the festival organisers.[4] A play had to be flexible enough to accommodate any available venue.

The set was for the most part conventional, defined in the course of performance by the characters' words and the exigencies of plot. Following a practice also found on the Aristophanic stage, the house doors serve 'as a thematically charged boundary between private and public spaces', and the two side entrances 'as a route into the wider world outside'.[5] Unlike the Aristophanic stage, the stage of New Comedy (both the Greek plays from the fourth and third centuries and their adaptations into Latin from the third and second centuries) regularly depicted an ordinary street in a Greek city, in front of two or three houses.[6] The cities of ancient comedy did not have strict zoning regulations: sometimes one of the visible doorways leads to a temple (with a stage altar placed in front to mark its identity for the audience), and sometimes one house is a brothel. Indeed, the conventions of the stage are so regular that there is no need for a naturalistic set of any kind. Wherever the venue was established, the generic stage space probably remained uncharacterised beyond a generic stage building that could be adapted to almost any play. Terence mentions that his theatrical venue could in the same day also be used by gladiators or possibly boxers, with tightrope walkers performing nearby (*Hec.* 33–41); some audience members might not even have intended to see a play.

Roman comedies were presented without interruption or interval, with music provided by a single *tibicen* (piper) that stops and starts, shaping the play into discrete units (in Terence, surviving didascalic notices indicate that the *tibicen* was a slave). These units do not always correspond with the act-breaks that are marked in the manuscripts; the five-act structure is an artificial way of thinking about Roman comedy, even though it was a feature of the Greek source plays (though with breaks at different points). Performance was continuous, with musical and non-musical sections alternating. The plays were entirely in verse, and various metres were employed to lend variety and tone to the scenes. Unaccompanied passages were spoken, and accompanied passages chanted in a form of recitative or sung, with the metrical form ever shifting (*cantica mixtis modis*).[7] While such sung passages

---

[4] Duckworth (1952) 79–85; Beare (1964) 164–83; Moore (1991); Goldberg (1998); Marshall (2006) 31–48; Manuwald (2011) 55–68.

[5] Lowe (2006) 51–2.

[6] Beare (1964) 275–302; Marshall (2006) 49–56; Manuwald (2011) 68–80.

[7] Duckworth (1952) 361–83; Beare (1964) 219–32; Moore (1998b) and (1999); and in this volume, Marshall (2006) 203–44; Manuwald (2011) 325–30.

are very rare in Terence, they represent a significant part of Plautus' dramatic technique. The musical and metrical variation established a pulse for the play, which the playwright and actors could modulate to create dramatic effect. The points of juncture (when music starts or stops) are always important in performance, and at such points one often finds the entries of significant characters, or an empty stage, as one set of characters leaves and another enters.[8] Such moments also allow the audience to assume that an hour or so passes, but even this should not be pushed too strictly. Time on the Roman comic stage is as elastic as is space, and if the plot requires a character to go to the forum, hire a cook, and return within the passage of only five minutes' time, then that is acceptable within the dramatic world.

The name Romans gave to their versions of Greek New Comedy was *fabulae palliatae* ('comedies in Greek dress'). The genre was therefore defined by its costume, as were *fabulae togatae* ('comedies in togas'), another comic genre that happens not to survive. Actors wore masks that drew on the conventions of the Hellenistic Greek masking tradition, from which the genre also borrowed its plots, but the masks also found inspiration in native improvisational comedy, the *fabulae Atellanae* ('Atellan farces').[9] While old men (*senes*) and young men (*adulescentes*), women and slaves could have a generic appearance (individuated by costume, props, gesture, voice, etc.), Roman comedy could equally create unique faces for dominant characters. The use of 'stock characters' therefore is not a limitation, but an opportunity to present characters whose inner nature does not reflect their apparent (presumed) outward appearance, and to present new characters whose wild appearance challenges any expectations of their behaviour.

The action of Roman comedy is also flexible, shifting constantly, with familiar comic routines being strung together around the frame of a Greek plot. Not everyone in Rome was literate, and the demands placed upon actors do not necessarily involve the delivery of memorised lines. There was probably a considerable amount of improvisation in performance, with the extant texts representing transcripts assembled after a successful run, complete with variant forms of some jokes.[10] These routines (like Italian *lazzi*) were not tied to particular words, but to performance situations that tended to recur. All of this gave a rough, almost raw, feel to the experience of watching Roman comedy. Plays were part of the entertainment available at

---

[8] Only one passage (*Ps.* 573a) suggests that the *tibicen* could conceivably offer musical interludes at these points.

[9] Duckworth (1952) 88–94; Beare (1964) 184–95; Marshall (2006) 56–66 and 126–58; Manuwald (2011) 169–77; and see Panayotakis in this volume.

[10] Goldberg (1995) and (2004); Marshall (2006) 245–79; Petrides (2014); and see Cardoso in this volume.

a festival, but it was the city that was celebrating, and actors had to work to convert the energy and enthusiasm of the Roman spectators in the audience into a supportive performance environment that conjures up a remote Greek world.

Two extraordinary scenes in Plautus' *Mercator* reveal the rich flexibility of the Roman comic stage. In *Mercator*, Charinus has returned from an extended sea voyage with Pasicompsa, a female sex slave from Rhodes, whom he hopes to introduce to his house as his mother's maid, so that he may have ongoing sexual access to her. His father Demipho has seen her and become infatuated as well. Not knowing the nature of his son's relationship with her, he hopes to buy Pasicompsa for himself, to keep in his neighbour's house, so that he may have ongoing sexual access to her.

The humour of the first scene emerges in part from the parallelism of the situation of father and son, neither of whom will admit to his true motives, and in part from the remarkable use of stage space, as the play seems to direct itself, virtually providing instructions for the play's blocking – the relative positions of actors and their movements on stage during a scene. Demipho sees his son coming from the harbour. When Charinus arrives on stage, the *tibicen* begins to play and Charinus sings a *canticum* (*Merc.* 335–63), unaware that his father is onstage with him. This is a typical stage arrangement – one character eavesdropping on another – and exemplifies how a coherent and interpretable dramatic meaning is created on stage during the performance of a Roman comedy: Charinus' delivery is out, to the audience, while the characters can share the stage and not be seen by each other. As the metre shifts, Demipho indicates that he has heard his son only indistinctly, and the two become aware of each other through a patterned routine (*Merc.* 364–7).[11] They converse, but can break into asides (*Merc.* 379–84), passages in which characters reveal information to the audience aloud that cannot be thought to have been overheard by their interlocutors.[12] Not every line spoken to the audience is an aside, however. Employing non-naturalistic delivery and acting styles, the plays create a continuum between the stage world and the world of the audience that is almost seamless, somehow both Roman and Greek, both contemporary and set a century before in a fictional world created by one of the Greek playwrights of New Comedy. When Demipho offers to buy a (less attractive) Syrian or Egyptian as a slave for his wife and to sell Pasicompsa, Charinus becomes desperate. Both are ashamed of their lust for her, and both want to own her in secret from the

---

[11] See Marshall (1999) for how these mutual recognitions may be performed.

[12] For this strict definition of an aside, see Bain (1977) 13–19. Asides can even finish a verse line (as in *Merc.* 401) or begin one (as in *Merc.* 402), as the metre exerts a force greater than the regular pattern of the spoken dialogue.

other. Their rivalry increases until each claims to represent another man (Demipho an unnamed *senex*; Charinus an unnamed *adulescens*) who has asked him to buy them a slave girl (*Merc.* 426–8).

In this auction scene, *Mercator* begins to break new ground dramaturgically. While there are frequently characters that exist only within the dramatic world and are never realised on stage, here each character invents a *doppelgänger* for himself that could not possibly appear onstage. The artificiality of the stage world in *Mercator* is reinforced as the dialogue proceeds. Demipho claims his buyer will pay 20 minas, Charinus raises to 27, and Demipho to 30; each onstage character is peering in different directions offstage, towards his fictional buyer, as the bids keep rising to 35, 37, and 40 minas (*Merc.* 429–47). Neither can see the other's buyer in the liminal offstage space, but each accepts that the other's buyer is there, signalling them for some reason at a distance, as the fraudulent auction continues, escalating the price of a sale that cannot take place. Further, at this point, the audience has not yet seen Pasicompsa: she too only exists in the unrealised offstage space, and (as far as the audience knows) may not ever appear on stage (in Plautus' *Casina*, for example, the audience never sees the title character). The audience is therefore invited to focus on the clash of male egos rather than the sufferings of the sex slave Pasicompsa. The fictional bidders evaporate as quickly as they appeared, as tactics shift: Demipho exerts paternal authority; Charinus counters that he lacks full ownership; Demipho insists that he will go to the harbour alone to sell her (*Merc.* 448–65). As father and son separate, the engagement that they have with each other dissolves as well. Demipho exits, addressing the audience and remaining unheard by Charinus (another aside, *Merc.* 466–8), and Charinus falls into paratragic paroxysms of grief (*Merc.* 468–73). He is interrupted by his friend Eutychus, who promises help. Eutychus usurps the role of the *seruus callidus*, offering assistance that the audience might reasonably have expected from the slave Acanthio, who had appeared earlier.[13] If the audience feels any disappointment in this substitution, it is countered by the fact that here is an *adulescens* who will work with Charinus to help him keep Pasicompsa; in the same way, Demipho has already signalled that he will ask Eutychus' father Lysimachus to work on his behalf. The imagined bidders from fifty lines earlier have manifested as a *senex/adulescens* pair of next-door neighbours.

It is legitimate to ask what, if anything, is real in the stage world of Roman comedy. *Mercator* imagines a fictional Athens that extends beyond the limited space defined by the two visible households, but the offstage space remains less real than that before the audience. Even for the characters within

---

[13] Marshall (2010) 74–8.

the dramatic world, offstage locations are less imminent than the spectators, who can be addressed and recognised by characters and eavesdrop on events in the way that the stage characters themselves often do. The nebulous off-stage space is defined with a conventional binary distinction – harbour one way, forum the other – that exists if the play requires it, but can also be ignored (as happens in *Rudens*). It can present whatever the plot might require, even a doctor to provide poison (a possibility raised and discarded at *Merc.* 472). *Mercator* presses this on/offstage division more starkly than other plays, as imagined characters first occupy the offstage space exclusively, only to become real (within the dramatic world) later through the process of coming onstage. Indeed, at *Merc.* 499 (as the metre shifts again), Demipho's agent Lysimachus returns bringing Pasicompsa with him, making her tangible to both characters and audience. In doing so Plautus evokes a genuine sympathy for her from the audience as she is trafficked from one owner to another.[14]

For the actors playing scenes like this, much of the blocking emerges from the dialogue itself: characters tell the audience whether they are eavesdrop-ping, whether they can see other characters, and in which direction they are leaving; this in turn reinforces the reality of the dramatic world. But the reality is limited: it is shaped by the few buildings and characters that the audience sees standing in a line, from stage left to stage right. The masks, which define characters by status (slave or free) and by generational age categories (e.g. *adulescens, senex*), encourage the audience to perceive the dramatic world in these two dimensions. The actual blocking does not need to be this limited in practice, of course. Yet this possible framing means that there always exists a natural stage picture onto which the actors can fall back. This points to another feature of Roman comic performance: plays are not written for particular festivals (and therefore particular venues), but can be offered for multiple *ludi*, conceivably in multiple cities. This flexibility and the verbalisation of stage directions in performance probably indicates another feature of Roman comedy: troupes would have limited opportunity (if any) to rehearse in the actual performance space. Plays reveal elements not only of their production, but also of their preparation: the least flexible Roman comedy (Plautus' *Amphitruo*, which uniquely requires a roof for actors to stand on and only a single door) is also the only mythological comedy, and this would seem to suggest that the context of its original performance was not a standard festival.

A later scene in *Mercator* continues the play's aggressive testing of the limits of the dramatic world created in performance. Charinus emerges from

[14] James (2010).

92

his house and prepares to take himself into exile, in search of either Pasicompsa or death; at the same time Eutychus appears from his house cataloguing his sources of happiness (*Merc.* 830–63). The irony of the two young men not seeing each other, one elated and one desperate, is regularly reinforced for the audience: e.g. *cogito quonam ego illum curram quaeritatum* (*Merc.* 857: 'I wonder where I should run in search for him', Eutychus asks the audience, as he stands in plain sight and within – at most – a few metres of Charinus). Yet neither sees the other until they perform the recognition routine Demipho and Charinus had performed earlier (*Merc.* 864–83). This time, the exchange is protracted, as the two address the audience for some time before they face each other. As with most comic routines, this allows expansion or contraction depending on audience response or other environmental conditions. It also allows the characters to shape their own stage-worlds. When Charinus declares '*sol abit*' (*Merc.* 873: 'The sun is setting'), it is not clear that the Roman stage allows a spectator to distinguish between his description of the dramatic reality and a character's metaphorical outburst. Eutychus extends the metaphor as the pathetic fallacy takes hold: he has a clear sky and a cool breeze while that of Charinus is stormy and dark (*Merc.* 874–80). The absence of visual contact between the characters (and, because of the implicit blocking, between the actors) keeps the two realities separate for as long as possible. Until the characters actually look at each other, both worlds exist, sharing the same stage and even the same dramatic space.

The demands on the spectator from this scene are extreme, but they are possible precisely because Roman comedy is performed in an outdoor space, in the natural light, with almost no environmental features provided by the troupe to establish the scene. Everything is accomplished with words, with the actor's use of the assigned stage space, and with the audience's imagination. When the two characters finally make contact, shaking hands at *Merc.* 883, the doubling collapses, but a sense of spatial instability remains. Charinus was dressed as a traveller (*Merc.* 851), but on hearing that Pasicompsa is within Eutychus' house, he summons a slave from his own house, and undergoes a transformation of costume: he removes his *chlamys*, a travelling cloak and puts on a *pallium*, the ordinary Greek outdoor wear (*Merc.* 910–12). When Eutychus does not let Charinus inside his house immediately, Charinus removes the *pallium* and again dons the *chlamys*, along with his belt, sword, and flask (*Merc.* 921–7). The comic business as the character readies himself for exile perhaps recalls tragic arming scenes, but it also marks Charinus' willingness to distance himself from the single stage reality established at *Merc.* 883.

Whereas the earlier auction scene demonstrated that offstage space in Roman comedy could possess elements of both the real and the imaginary, Charinus demonstrates that the same flexibility exists even on stage, as he appears to enter a completely new geographical space. Whether it is a sign of tragic madness or melancholic delusion, or if he somehow redefines the stage to conform to his will, *Mercator* allows Charinus to disentangle himself from the transient reality of the stage world and from the specificity of a generic street. His dialogue with Eutychus continues, but while Eutychus remains in Athens, Charinus mounts a chariot and travels to Cyprus and then Chalcis, where he meets a Zacynthian who tells him his woman is in Athens, to which he returns by ship, ending his exile (*Merc.* 931–47). The stage has no chariot or ship – these will have been mimed by the actor – and so Eutychus' interpretation, that Charinus is mad or dreaming (*Merc.* 932, 950–1), is a plausible way to frame what the audience has witnessed. It is not the only way, however, because the play has been so concerned to emphasise how malleable Roman stage space can be: the location does not refocus completely (Eutychus is still in Athens), but two geographical spaces are superimposed. The destinations are among those Charinus had considered as places of exile at *Merc.* 646–7, and the audience has seen Charinus move around the performance area, albeit in comically inappropriate ways (taking a chariot to an island, for instance). Space and time conflate, and what would normally be a lengthy journey is accomplished in minutes. Further, Eutychus perceives things have changed: at *Merc.* 918 he was unwilling to let Charinus inside his house, but he admits him at *Merc.* 956. Charinus never returns to the stage nor is the audience ever provided with a clear explanation of the nature of this exile, but it has shared the experience with him. As the spectators' perceptions are insufficient to interpret what is being depicted since they are so dependent on cues from the actors for what the stage space represents, in the end they must share Eutychus' uncertainty as well.

The flexibility and imprecision of the Plautine stage can be helpfully compared to the practice of Terence. In one sense, all of Terence's plays mark themselves as existing in a specifically fictional world by their prologues: one of the actors, sometimes L. Ambivius Turpio, *dominus gregis* (troupe leader; lit. 'master of the flock') and actor in Terence's plays, would speak in his own, unmasked identity.[15] Terentian prologues do not deal with the plot directly, but instead discuss the practicalities of staging

[15] Gowers (2004) and see Christenson in this volume. The closest parallel for unmasked delivery is *Curc.* 462–86, where the Roman *choragus* ('costume-renter') speaks directly to the audience. This is the most explicit intrusion of the Roman reality into the fictional Greek world created in Roman comedy. The role is apparently played by an actor dressed as backstage personnel and is not masked (see Moore (1991) and Marshall (2006) 197).

a play at the *ludi* and the competitive rivalry between poets; fully scripted and in verse, the prologues serve to mediate the transition into the dramatic world in a very specific way for the spectators, framing the rest of the play in a way that might encourage a more distanced (theatrically aware) view.[16]

An overview of Terence's *Hecyra* demonstrates a complementary use of the stage space to that seen in Plautus. Turpio's troupe performed *Hecyra* at least three times, first in 165, and twice in 160. Different prologues were written for each performance, and elements survive from the two prologues of 160. Such changes are obvious, but other changes to the overall text might also have been made. The plot concerns the young man Pamphilus, who has raped and impregnated Philumena at a festival and, not knowing it was the same woman, married her two months later. Because of his relationship with the prostitute Bacchis, the marriage was not consummated for some time. As the play begins, Philumena is nine months pregnant, Pamphilus has been away and has returned home to find her in the process of giving birth, and now everybody – Pamphilus, Philumena, and their parents – is about to discover the details of Pamphilus' premarital sex life.

In *Hecyra* the offstage world blends more fully with the onstage world than it did in *Mercator*, and there is a stronger sense of continuity between onstage and offstage spaces. This effect is created in a number of ways. The coordinated timing of entrances and exits can lead to a dizzying effect, providing a momentum to the play that can go unnoticed when simply reading the script. After a gentle introduction, the comings and goings increase, which has the effect of shortening the time available to establish characters. Three entries and six exits occur in a busy passage of 108 lines (*Hec.* 415–522). This increases the sense of direct continuity with the offstage world. Parmeno arrives, leading a train of baggage carriers (one of whom speaks at *Hec.* 416–25) and notices his master standing on stage (*Hec.* 430). This is not the recognition *lazzo* seen in *Mercator*; Pamphilus is not eavesdropping but is awaiting Parmeno so that he can send him on a fictional errand to keep him away (a compressed version of the recognition *lazzo* is found at *Hec.* 727–31, however). When the two old men (*senes*) enter (*Hec.* 451), the audience naturally extends the dramatic world to include the offstage locations, and it accepts that the characters had passed the slave Parmeno a few hundred metres down the road. The separate departures of these characters – through Laches' door, Phidippus' door, and then Laches' door again as simultaneously Myrrina enters the stage through Phidippus'

---

[16] In contrast, Plautine prologues are typically spoken, as they had been in Greek New Comedy, within the same dramatic frame as the rest of the action, often by one of the characters or by an overseeing divinity.

door – provide a back-and-forth that demonstrates stage busy-ness while at the same time calling attention to the lack of traffic at Bacchis' door, which has remained unused since the play's initial entrance at *Hec.* 58. On a flexible stage with a default three-door set, it might simply be that the closed door of the brothel is not going to be used again, but some in the audience might see it as promising resolution to the predicament between Pamphilus and Philumena (which it eventually will provide).

The Terentian stage world is still not naturalistic, but it is more substantial than what was seen in Plautus. Characters continue to address the audience directly: these speeches can be proper asides (not heard by other characters on stage) or simply delivered out, extending the stage world to the audience. A nuanced effect is seen for example when characters speak to each other but are not heard by other interlocutors:

> LAC. heri Philumenam ad se accersi hic iussit. dic iussisse te.
> PHI. noli fodere. iussi. . . .

> LAC: (to Pamphilus) Yesterday this guy [Phidippus] ordered Philumena to be
> brought to him. (to Phidippus, *sotto voce*) Say that you ordered it.
> PHI: (to Laches, *sotto voce*) Don't bug me. (aloud) I ordered it.

(Terence, Hec. 466–7)

The shifting positions of the masks allow characters to stage-whisper: of course, '*sotto voce*' in the stage direction is not correct, since the actors must project loud enough to be heard in the outdoor festival performance space; nevertheless, the words *dic iussisse te* and *noli fodere* remain unheard by the character Pamphilus.

Audience expectations of how the stage space works are manipulated elsewhere in the play as well. At *Hec.* 607, Laches addresses his wife and son, who had come on stage at *Hec.* 577. It is clear that he has heard some of their conversation (*Hec.* 607–9), but he came onstage after them. The fact that all three characters have emerged from the same doorway suggests that Sostrata and Pamphilus had simply left the door open (there is no creak, as there had been at the neighbour's house at line *Hec.* 521). Laches follows them and is able to eavesdrop on part of their conversation, but exactly when he arrives is not determinable from the text of the play. Such unannounced entries are rare in New Comedy, but have the effect of increasing the permeability between the onstage and offstage worlds. Compare Pamphilus' long soliloquy earlier in the play (*Hec.* 361–414). Pamphilus relates to the audience the events that have happened inside Phidippus' house, as Philumena gives birth and her mother supplicates him, begging to keep Philumena's pregnancy secret from her father. The speech shares some features of a Greek tragic messenger speech, and, since it is all focalised through a single dramatic character, the audience is enlisted on

Pamphilus' side. It differs from a messenger speech in important ways, how-ever: the absence of any internal audiences (onstage) means that the Pamphilus actor addresses only the spectators. Terence seems almost to apologise that the traditional stage space depicts the street in front of the houses, rather than the (much more interesting) interior, where the real action is taking place.

This dramatic texturing is reinforced by Terence's use of unspeaking and offstage characters. At *Hec.* 726, Phidippus goes to the forum to find a wet nurse for Philumena and her baby. He returns at *Hec.* 767 with a nurse, and she immediately goes into his house (*Hec.* 770). Giving the nurse physical instantia-tion on stage makes demands on the troupe – an actor is assigned the role, a costume is decided, and a mask selected. Even if every choice is completely conventional, the appearance of this character for only three lines adds substance to the entire stage world. Some characters remain in the offstage world (a demanding soldier in Corinth is described at *Hec.* 85–6) but also contribute to the richness of the dramatic texture. Earlier in the play, Pamphilus had sent Parmeno to the acropolis in search of someone he has never seen before, Callidemides from Myconos (*Hec.* 431–3). It is not clear whether Callidemides actually exists or whether Pamphilus has invented him (a conclusion Parmeno reaches at *Hec.* 799–806); whatever the case, his master expects Parmeno to fail to find him. Callidemides is described, however, in detail: *magnus, rubicundus, crispus, crassus, caesius,* | *cadauerosa facie* (*Hec.* 440–1: 'he's a big guy, ruddy, curly-haired, fat, grey eyed, with the face of a corpse'). This is an unusually specific description, and would seem to offer the same guidance for an audience as the rich character descriptions sometimes found in Plautus (e.g. *Ps.* 1218–20, *As.* 400–1, *Ru.* 317–19). In those cases, the verbal description corresponds to a character mask; not so here, where there is promise of an equally detailed world just beyond the audience's view. Finally, as characters emerge from one of the houses, they are sometimes speaking to characters still within: Parmeno addresses a slave named Scirtus who remains inside (*Hec.* 76–80), and Phidippus speaks to Philumena as he comes onstage twice (*Hec.* 243–5, 623–6). This technique can be compared to Phidippus yelling at Pamphilus at *Hec.* 504, when Pamphilus is inside his house, or Laches going to his door at *Hec.* 719–20, calling for a slave to go to Bacchis' house.[17] When the unnamed, unspeaking slave appears, goes next door, and is admitted, it is the first use of the third doorway since line 58, and this too reinforces the tangibility of offstage space.

---

[17] At *Merc.* 800–2, the management of the performance space is accomplished in character, as Lysimachus goes to his door and calls his wife to remove props left by the cook earlier in the scene.

The use of offstage characters to create verisimilitude is crucial in *Hecyra* because of Terence's decision not to bring Philumena or her child onstage. This is not the result of a limited troupe size (the appearance of the slave and the nurse demonstrates that there are actors backstage), nor is it necessarily a legacy of the Greek original: in *Adelphoe*, Terence reworks his model by introducing a scene from a different play, by a different playwright, in order to bring an unspeaking sex slave, also named Bacchis, on stage for lines *Hec.* 155–75 of that play.[18] In a play that is about secrets being made public and about what information stays within one's own walls, the physical absence of Philumena is a crucial part of how Terence supports his theme. The child's birth becomes everyone's business, and reinforces the physical separation of Philumena from her husband. *Hecyra* keeps Pamphilus' wife secluded in her father's house, as a flurry of entrances and exits occur around her. The means of the couple's reconciliation is a ring Pamphilus stole the night he raped the woman he later wed, but which he subsequently gave to Bacchis. The lack of activity at Bacchis' house delays the recognition of the token that can only take place once she is involved. Indeed, Terence even acknowledges earlier in the play the existence of the ring and its potential to accomplish a generically conventional reconciliation (*Hec.* 572–4).

As Philumena is giving birth, the backstage world threatens to burst onto the performance area. While Pamphilus and Parmeno prepare to go inside, noise from the neighbour's house interrupts them:

> PAM. abi, Parmeno, intro ac me uenisse nuntia.
> PAR. hem! quid hoc est?
> PAM. tace!
> trepidari sentio et cursari rursum prorsum.
> PAR. agedum, ad fores!
> accedo propius. em, sensistin?
> PAM. noli fabularier.
> pro Iuppiter, clamorem audiui.
> PAR. tute loqueris, me uetas.
> MYR. (intus) tace, obsecro, mea gnata!
> PAM. matris uox uisast Philumenae.
> nullus sum! ...

> PAM: Go inside and say I have returned, Parmeno.
> *Loud noises associated with childbirth are heard inside Phidippus' house.*
> PAR: Hey! What's that?
> PAM: Quiet! I hear a commotion, and people running back and forth.

---

[18] Frauenfelder (1996) discusses the performance implications of this example of *contaminatio*.

PAR: Come on, I'm going closer to the doors. (Philumena, within, screams in pain) There! Did you hear that?

PAM: Don't speak. (another scream) By Jupiter, I heard a scream!

PAR: You're talking, but you told me not to.

MYR: (within) My daughter, I beg you, be quiet!

PAM: The voice seems to be Philumena's mother! I'm done for!

(Terence, Hec. 314–19)

Offstage actors are required to make the commotion that is heard here (including the actor playing Myrrina, a character that has not yet appeared on stage), and someone has to give Philumena a voice. Her two inarticulate screams in line *Hec.* 316 interrupt the verse of the men speaking on stage. Although a woman would not normally appear in public so soon after giving birth, the audience cannot know yet that this is all the substance Philumena is given in the play. This momentary auditory incursion into the stage environment again demonstrates that significant events are taking place in private, out of sight of the audience.

Roman comedy shapes the transient performance spaces erected for the *ludi* into a site that recreates the world of a Greek play from more than a century before. It is a vision of the Greek world, but it is not an unproblematic one, nor is it concerned with the faithful representation of a bygone play. The performance of Roman comedy offered spontaneous jokes, improvised comic routines, elaborate songs, exaggerated costumes and masks, and ridiculous characters in a festive atmosphere. The stories it told, however, typically concerned realistic relationships, as young men fell in love with slaves, non-citizen prostitutes, or their next-door neighbours. It is challenging for modern readers to integrate a world of slapstick comedy with stories of rape and slave-beating, but this is the world that the *fabula palliata* presents. Like all good theatre, genuine problems are raised and the audience is left to disentangle and interpret what it has seen. There is no single 'right' way to interpret Roman comedy. Through the consideration of how the stage is used, however, it is possible to see how the playwright has shaped the narrative, and how he draws his audience into becoming an extension of the exciting fictional world created by the stage action in Roman comedy.

Further Reading

For a long time, Duckworth (1952) and Beare (1964) provided the only overviews of Roman comic stagecraft. Since Slater (1985) and the new vocabulary for discussing stage action that book provided, new approaches have yielded rich results, none more than Goldberg (1998). Moore (1998b) helpfully explores the interaction between the Roman actor and the audience. I have tried to synthesise these advances in Marshall (2006). Manuwald (2011) 41–125 and 301–25 provides the best available overview on production practices in the Roman Republic, and see now Petrides (2014) and Bexley (2014). Goldberg (2018) explores possible sites of performance within the forum at Rome, using computer-generated models. His stage design is based on South Italian vase illustrations, and differs from what is suggested here.

6

TIMOTHY J. MOORE

Music and Metre

Late in Plautus' *Stichus*, the title character, his fellow slave Sangarinus, and their girlfriend, the slave-woman Stephanium, are having a party. Stichus and Sangarinus ask Stephanium to dance (755–75):

STI. age, mulsa mea suauitudo, salta: saltabo ego simul.	TR7
SA. numquam edepol med istoc uinces, quin ego ibidem	
pruriam.	
STE. siquidem mihi saltandum est, tum uos date bibat tibicini.	
STI. et quidem nobis. SA. tene, tibicen, primum; postidea loci	
si hoc eduxeris, proinde ut consuetu's antehac, celeriter	
lepidam et suauem cantionem aliquam occupito cinaedicam,	
ubi perpruriscamus usque ex unguiculis. inde huc aquam.	
SA. tene tu hoc, educe. dudum placuit potio:	IA6
nunc minus grauate iam accipit. tene tu. interim,	
meus oculus, da mihi sauium, dum illic bibit.	
STI. prostibilest tandem? stantem stanti sauium	
dare amicum amicae? euge euge, sic furi datur!	
SA. age, iam infla buccas, nunciam aliquid suauiter.	
redde cantionem ueteri pro uino nouam.	
SA. qui Ionicus aut cinaedicust, qui hoc tale facere possiet?	IA8
STI. si istoc me uorsu uiceris, alio me prouocato:	IA7
SA. fac tu hoc modo. STI. at tu hoc modo. SA. babae! STI. tatae!	
SA. papae! STI. pax!	
SA. nunc pariter ambo. omnis uoco cinaedos contra.	versreiz
satis esse nobis non magis potis quam fungo imber.	
STI. intro hinc abeamus nunciam: saltatum satis pro uinost.	IA7
uos, spectatores, plaudite atque ite ad uos commissatum.	

STI: Come on, my honeyed sweetness, dance: I'll dance	(TR7)
at the same time.	
SA: By god, you'll never beat me in that, so that I don't	
itch [with desire] at the same time.	

STE: Well, if I am to dance, then you two give the *tibicen* a drink.

STI: And we'll give ourselves a drink, too.

SA: First you take it, *tibicen*; then, if you drink this down, just as
you used to do before, quickly take up some sweet effeminate song,
with which we can itch through right up from our toenails. Let's have
some water here.

Grab on to this, drink it down. A bit ago he liked his drink. Now he   (IA6)
takes it with less reluctance. Take it. Meanwhile, my sweet, give me a
kiss, while he drinks.

STI: What, is she a streetwalker? For a boyfriend to give his girlfriend
a kiss standing in the street! (Stephanium slaps Sangarinus or makes
a similar gesture of rejection) Alright! That's what a thief gets!

SA: Come on, now puff up your cheeks, now play something sweetly.
Give us a new song in return for old wine.

(dancing)

What Ionian or *cinaedus* is there, who can do things like this?   (IA8)

STI: If you beat me with that turning, challenge me with another.   (IA7)

SA: You do it this way.

STI: Then you do it this way.

SA: Babae!

STI: Tatae!

SA: Papae!

STI: Enough!

SA: Now both of us together. I challenge all *cinaedi* to try to   (versreiz)
dance like us. We can't get enough, any more than a
mushroom can get enough rain.

STI: OK, let's go away from here now; we've danced enough for our wine.   (IA7)
You, spectators, applaud and go to your own parties.

This passage reveals the essential elements of Roman comedy's musical side:
actors singing and dancing to the accompaniment of an instrument called the
tibia, responding to metrical patterns produced by the playwright. In what
follows I will review each of these elements and then examine Roman
comedy's most musically exuberant play, Plautus' *Casina*.

Tibicen and Actors

Sangarinus gives a drink to the *tibicen*, a player of the *tibia*, a two-piped
instrument with double reeds (called *aulos* in Greek), which accompanied
almost all theatrical performances in the ancient world (see Figure 6.1).
Noted for its buzz-like tone, the *tibia* could be loud and strident or more
subdued. The two pipes could play divergent tunes, together reinforcing the
pitch and rhythm of the actors. Sangarinus' 'puff up your cheeks' refers to the

Figure 6.1 Roman mosaic showing a *tibia* and two comic masks. Musei Capitolini, Rome
© Photo Scala, Florence - courtesy of Sovraintendenza di Roma Capitale

standard practice of *tibicines*, evident in many visual portrayals, of playing with inflated cheeks. This practice may reflect the use of circular breathing, which allows players to play for long periods without pausing to take a breath. The easy interaction between *tibicen* and actors suggests that the *tibicen* was conspicuous visually as well as aurally, standing on or right in front of the stage. Though no visual portrayals of the original performances of Roman comedy survive, Figure 6.2, showing a performance in Southern Italy a century before Plautus' day, gives a sense of what the *Stichus* scene may have looked like. The *tibicen* may also have sometimes stood on the stage with the actors, as in Figure 6.3, a relief showing a comic performance of the first century CE. The production notices preserved in the manuscripts of the plays give the names of two of Roman comedy's *tibicines*: Marcipor, slave of Oppius, accompanied *Stichus*, and Flaccus, Claudius' slave, accompanied all the plays of Terence.

The actors sang while the *tibicen* played. At least on occasion they also danced. This passage is one of only three explicit references to dancing by actors in Roman comedy. Each describes dancing similar to what Sangarinus

Figure 6.2 Bell krater (Campanian red-figure ware) attributed to the Libation Painter, showing a scene from a comic performance. An actor appears to chastise a *tibicina* (a female player of the *tibia*), who accompanies the production.
Late Classical/Hellenistic Period, 350–325 BC
© National Gallery of Victoria, Melbourne,
Felton Bequest, 1973 (D14-1973)

and Stichus do here: dance done in imitation of *cinaedi*, who were professional performers known for their lewd movements (cf. Pl. *Per.* 801a–26, *Ps.* 1273–80a). Actors may also have danced with their feet in other scenes; and we are justified in assuming extensive gestural dance, for Roman comedy had an elaborate system of gestures, probably done in time with the music in the accompanied parts of the plays.

Figure 6.3 Roman bas-relief showing a scene from a comic performance.
A father is held back by his friend as he prepares to accost his son, who is returning home drunk
from a party with his slave and a *tibicina*. Museo Archeologico Nazionale, Naples, Italy
© Scala Archives/Art Resource, NY

Metre

Much remains uncertain about Roman comedy's music. No melodies have
survived, and the degree to which ancient actors' singing would have corre-
sponded to what we consider 'song' is not clear (for a review of evidence on
these matters, see Moore (2012) *passim*). Of one thing, however, we can be
sure: there was a close correspondence between Roman comedy's music and
the metres Plautus and Terence used.

The abbreviations on the right of the Latin verses and in parentheses in the
translation above refer to various types of metre. Like almost all Greek and
Latin verse forms, the metres of Roman comedy were based on patterns of
long and short syllables. Because a long syllable takes about twice as long to
say or sing as a short syllable, we can consider a short syllable one time-unit
(equivalent to an eighth note when sung), a long syllable two time-units
(equivalent to a quarter note).

The first of the abbreviations, 'tr7', stands for trochaic septenarius, the most common metre of Roman comedy (about 41% of the entire corpus, 46% of Plautus, and 25% of Terence). It belongs to a group of metres known as iambo-trochaics, which consist of alternations between elements (groups of one or two syllables) that must be two time-units (i.e., they must consist of either one long or two short syllables) and elements that may or must be one time-unit. In the trochaic septenarius, as in all trochaic verses, the element that must be two time-units comes first. In iambic verses the element that can be one time-unit comes first. In the following chart (Table 6.1) of the first verse quoted above:

L represents an element of two time-units,

s an element of one time-unit,

X an element that can be either one or two time-units, and

q an element that can be either one or two time-units, but must be only one syllable.

/ represents the caesura, a place where in most verses a word ends.

Parentheses surround a letter that is eliminated through a process called elision.

A trochaic septenarius thus consists of six repetitions of LX followed by Lsq. The *tibicen* reinforced this rhythmic pattern, perhaps by giving extra emphasis to the elements that had to be two time-units (L in the chart above).

Succeeding the trochaic septenarii in our passage are iambic senarii (ia6), which consist of five repetitions of XL plus sq. Sangarinus switches the metre to iambic senarii when the *tibicen* has stopped playing to take a drink, and the iambic senarii end when the *tibicen* has finished drinking. This reflects what other evidence tells us is the standard practice in Roman comedy: iambic senarii were with very few exceptions spoken without accompani-ment, while all other metres were nearly always sung to accompaniment. Scenes in iambic senarii are called *deuerbia*, scenes in other metres, *cantica*. The dichotomy between *cantica* and *deuerbia* is the most conspicuous fea-ture of Roman comedy's music. It is arguably the genre's most important determinant of tone, as more excited scenes are usually accompanied and scenes of calm, suspense, and the presentation of important information tend to be unaccompanied. It contributes significantly to characterisation: more serious and unsympathetic characters tend to deliver more iambic senarii than others, except for characters like clever slaves, whose ability to com-municate directly with the audience without the distraction of music con-tributes to the sense that they control what happens on stage. It is the most important factor in Roman comedy's structure, as plots progress through alternating musical and non-musical moments. It also means that most of Roman comedy was sung rather than delivered without accompaniment:

TABLE 6.1: Metrical chart of *Stichus* 755 (trochaic septenarius)

Element	1	2	3	4	5	6	7	8	9	10	11	12	13	14	15
Allowable time-units	L	X	L	X	L	X	L	X /	L	X	L	X	L	s	q
Syllable lengths	∪∪	—	—	∪∪	—	∪	—	—	—	—	—	—	∪∪	∪	—
Note value of syllables	♪♪	♩	♩	♪♪	♩	♪	♩	♩	♩	♩	♩	♩	♪♪	♪	♩
Words	a ge	mul	sa[1]	me a	sua	vi	tu	do	sal	ta	sal	ta	b(o)e go	si	mul

[1] The short syllable *sa* fills a long position through a licence known as the *locus Jacobsohnianus*.

iambic senarii make up less than 37% of Roman comedy as a whole, less than 34% of Plautus and about 48% of Terence.

Roman comedy also includes a number of other metres besides trochaic septenarii that were sung to accompaniment. The most common such metres are other iambo-trochaic verse forms. Among the verses following the iambic senarii in the passage above are one iambic octonarius (ia8: seven repetitions of XL plus sq) and four iambic septenarii (ia7: seven repetitions of XL plus q). Iambo-trochaic metres, including trochaic septenarii and iambic senarii, make up over 93% of Roman comedy, nearly 92% of Plautus and nearly 100% of Terence. Plautus regularly, however, and Terence in three brief passages, uses metres that employ patterns other than the standard alternation of L and X found in the iambo-trochaics. Two of the verses in our passage, for example, are *versus reiziani* (versreiz), which begin like iambic verses but end in five elements with their own patterns of long and short syllables. Most of the non-iambo-trochaic metres of Roman comedy fall into one of three categories: anapaestic metres (combinations of ∪∪—, —∪∪, and — —), cretics (based on the pattern —∪—), and bacchiacs (based on the pattern ∪— —). Passages such as this one, which include metres other than iambic senarii and trochaic septenarii and where the metre changes frequently, are known as polymetric passages.

Because there was a close connection between metrical patterns and musical rhythm in ancient vocal music, the accompanied metres give us a good sense of the rhythmic patterns sung and played. In producing these patterns the playwrights responded to a set of conventions, which in turn produced certain expectations in their audience. Playwrights contributed to the pleasure and meaning of their plays by fulfilling and disappointing these expectations. Because all Roman comedies end in metres other than iambic senarii, for example, the audience of *Stichus* experienced the pleasure of an expectation fulfilled as the *tibicen* played and the actors sang the final verses. All plays but two, however, end in trochaic septenarii, so by ending this play in iambic metres Plautus treated the audience to something special. In addition, individual metres could be associated with certain characters or effects. Old men are more likely than younger male characters, for example, to deliver unaccompanied iambic senarii; and cretics, with their one short syllable in between two long syllables, instill a sense of 'bounce' that lends itself both to playfulness and self-conscious performance.

Casina

In *Casina* Plautus produced Roman comedy's greatest musical *tour de force*: one-third of the play consists of polymetric passages. It will be impossible in this brief essay to describe all that happens musically in *Casina*, but by reviewing the play's overall musical structure and one of its polymetric moments we can get a good sense of the kinds of things Plautus and Terence could accomplish musically. In the discussion that follows all references are to *Casina* unless stated otherwise.

Musical Structure

In *Casina*'s unaccompanied prologue and another scene in iambic senarii featuring the slaves Olympio and Chalinus, spectators learn that an old man (the *Senex*) wants Casina, the slave-woman of his wife Cleostrata, to marry Olympio so that he himself can have sex with her. Cleostrata seeks to win the girl for her son by marrying her to Chalinus. Cleostrata brings the play's first music as she enters with her slave-woman Pardalisca (144). The music underlines Cleostrata's role as an ally of the young lover (lovers or their allies start the music in almost all Roman comedies), and it is the first clue that she will win the battle between husband and wife for the sympathy of the audience. Cleostrata, Pardalisca, and her neighbour Myrrhina, who argues that Cleostrata should yield to her husband, sing a long polymetric *canticum* (144–216), which continues as the *Senex* enters and argues with his wife (217–51). The metre changes to trochaic septenarii when the *Senex* turns the conversation to the subject of Casina's wedding (252).

In its opening scenes *Casina* follows the pattern typical of Roman comedy: the first scenes, unaccompanied, serve primarily as exposition. A character of special interest brings the first music, in metres other than trochaic septenarii. Trochaic septenarii begin when the plot gets moving in earnest. The *Senex* is at this point in control of the plot, so he begins the trochaic septenarii, during which he proposes that he and Cleostrata try to persuade each opposing slave to give up his claim to Casina (252–78).

The trochaic septenarii continue as the *Senex* fails to persuade Chalinus and proposes a lottery (279–308). When Chalinus has left and Olympio enters, the music stops, another musical pulling of the audience's sympathy away from the *Senex*'s cause (309–52). Cleostrata then brings music for the second time, as she returns with Chalinus (353). This time, however, there are no polymetrics, but the characters sing trochaic septenarii throughout the ensuing scene, during which Olympio and Chalinus draw lots for Casina, and Olympio wins (353–423). Although the presence of music responds to Cleostrata, the metre is the one the *Senex* started, as he continues to control the plot.

When all have left the stage except Chalinus, the music stops. The break in music here underlines Chalinus' despondency as he expresses his disappointment in a brief monologue (424–33). Early in the scene Olympio and the *Senex* re-enter, so the break also continues the dissociation of Olympio from music (434); and it removes distractions as important information is revealed, for the eavesdropping Chalinus learns that the *Senex* is using Olympio to get Casina for himself (437–503).

The next *canticum* also consists entirely of trochaic septenarii. Like the first two long passages of trochaic septenarii, it begins as a plan of the *Senex* is put into action, but this time the *Senex*'s plan is undone in the midst of the *canticum*. The trochaic septenarii last through two juxtaposed scenes: in the first the *Senex* plots with his neighbour Alcesimus to empty Alcesimus' house for his tryst with Casina by sending his wife Myrrhina to Cleostrata (515–30). In the second, Cleostrata undoes the plot by telling Alcesimus that she does not require Myrrhina (531–62). The juxtaposition of the opposing scenes without metrical change underlines the degree to which the *Senex*'s control of the plot is derailed during this *canticum*.

The musical downgrading of the *Senex* continues in the ensuing *deuerbium*. It begins when the *Senex* returns from the forum, exasperated that he has been kept away from Casina by a relative who needed his legal help (563). The passage makes a conspicuous contrast with the *Senex*'s previous return from the forum, when he sang the praises of love in anapaests (217). The musical contrast helps draw attention to the *Senex*'s changed status. Earlier he had determined the course of action in the battle for Casina, but now Cleostrata has temporarily foiled his plan and has taken charge of the plot: after the monologue Cleostrata tells the *Senex* that Alcesimus has refused to send Myrrhina to her house (576–90), and the plan for a rendezvous barely survives a scene of carping between the two old men (591–620).

Next Plautus marks a new initiative of Cleostrata by having her agent, Pardalisca, introduce one of the most elaborate *cantica* of Roman comedy, as she persuades the *Senex* that Casina rages inside with a sword, threatening to kill her would-be husband and his master. The polymetrics last through the deception and Olympio's return with the cook hired for his wedding (621–758).

Pardalisca then returns to the stage and, in iambic senarii, reports what has happened indoors: the women and cooks have kept the *Senex* and Olympio from eating their wedding meal (759–79). At the opening of the previous *canticum*, Pardalisca feigned panic to music as part of her ruse: here she calmly shares the truth with the spectators unaccompanied: the women's control of the plot is complete, as is their alignment with the audience. The iambic senarii continue as the *Senex* returns unfed from the house (780–97).

The play's next *canticum* begins as Olympio enters, commanding in trochaic septenarii that the *tibicen* play for his wedding procession (798). Aside from two iambic quaternarii as Olympio and the *Senex* sing the wedding hymn (800, 808), the trochaic septenarii continue as the two men prepare for the arrival of Casina (798–814): Plautus continues the pattern of having trochaic septenarii begin in response to the *Senex*'s wishes. In this passage he and Olympio think they have finally won, and they are ready to enjoy their prize.

Pardalisca, however, continuing the delaying tactics that have exasperated the two men offstage, switches to polymetrics as she presents the 'bride': the women have disguised Chalinus as Casina (815). This is the only time in the play that a long series of trochaic septenarii leads to any metre other than iambic senarii: again Plautus underlines musically an important moment in the women's progress towards victory. The polymetrics continue until immediately after 'Casina' has stomped on Olympio's foot, when the metre switches to iambic senarii (847–54). The sudden silence from the *tibicen* helps to indicate that all is not well for Olympio and the *Senex*, who are again dissociated from music.

The break in the music also allows the final *canticum* to begin with the ensuing entrance of Myrrhina with Pardalisca and Cleostrata, singing bacchiacs (855). Plautus thus creates, here at the beginning of the play's last musical section, an echo of the play's opening music, in which Cleostrata, like Myrrhina here, entered from Cleostrata's house accompanied by Pardalisca singing bacchiac quaternarii. The bacchiac echo brings several layers of meaning. First, it underlines the contrast in Cleostrata's position: she began the play's music with bacchiacs, at a loss as to how to combat her husband's desires, but when these bacchiacs are sung she has succeeded in besting him. Second, the bacchiacs underline the degree to which Myrrhina has come around to Cleostrata's side. She had opposed her neighbour in her only previous appearance and had delivered many anapaestic verses, the metre later used by the *Senex* at his entrance. Now she has joined Cleostrata in metre just as she has joined her in attitude. Third, this passage continues an association between bacchiacs and the play's women. Besides the bacchiacs in Cleostrata's first scene (144–6, 152–5, 160–1, 184/85), Pardalisca sang bacchiacs as she told the false story of Casina and the sword (647–59a, 663–76, 681–705), and bacchiacs were the dominant metre when 'Casina' was handed over to Olympio (828–42).

After more primarily bacchiac verses from the women, Olympio enters with anapaests (875–82). Anapaests have been associated with the *Senex* throughout the play. The first anapaests occurred at the first entrance of Myrrhina, who, as we have seen, began the play as the *Senex*'s ally (163–6, 171, 178). Anapaests returned as Myrrhina admonished Cleostrata to obey her husband (204–11) and when Cleostrata saw the *Senex* entering (212–13). The *Senex*'s first monody was entirely in anapaestic verses (217–28), and anapaests returned when he defended himself against his wife's accusations (239–42, 250). Pairs of anapaestic verses occurred as the *Senex* threatened Pardalisca (646–46a) and responded to the news that Casina had a sword (660–1). Anapaests next appeared when Olympio entered with the cook, and master and slave prepared to enjoy the wedding festivities (719–28, 735, 742–6, 748). Pardalisca hinted at the degree to which the tables had turned when she used anapaests while giving advice to the pretend Casina (818–20) and then handing 'her' over (829), but the *Senex* sang a final anapaestic verse as he thanked Venus for his success (841).

Olympio here provides ironic echoes of many of the earlier anapaests. Like Myrrhina, he enters from Alcesimus' house with anapaests, another ally of the *Senex*, this time in a much worse position. As the *Senex* made his first entrance with anapaests, joyfully singing of his love for Casina, Olympio's anapaests show us where that love has led. In his own last anapaests, Olympio was at his moment of greatest glory, lording it over his master as he prepared for a feast: he never got his feast, and now he has reached his nadir. The humiliation hinted at in Pardalisca's anapaests has now reached fulfillment.

Olympio's monody and his ensuing dialogue with the women offer a wide variety of metres (875–936), and the polymetrics continue as the *Senex*, like Olympio before him, flees from Alcesimus' house (937–62). The play's final trochaic septenarii start as Chalinus enters from Alcesimus' house seeking the *Senex* (963). The *Senex*'s humiliation is complete: as often happens in Roman comedy, the final switch to trochaic septenarii marks the moment at which the plot is largely completed and the characters can begin wrapping things up. The switch provides the final musical reinforcement of the play's reversal, for this is the first extended passage of trochaic septenarii that does not respond to the words or desires of the *Senex*.

We can thus chart the musical structure of *Casina* as follows (Table 6.2):

TABLE 6.2: Chart of the musical structure of Plautus' *Casina*

Unit of action	Iambic senarii	Trochaic septenarii	Other metres[1]	Parallel musical moments
Preliminaries				
	1–143: Prologue; Olympio and Chalinus			A1: No music for Olympio (89–131)
i. The Battle Lines are Drawn				
			144–251: Cleostrata and Pardalisca; Cleostrata and Myrrhina; *Senex* monody; *Senex* and Cleostrata	B1: Cleostrata bacchiacs (144ff.); C1: Myrrhina anapaests (163ff.); C2: *Senex* anapaests (212ff.)
		252–308: *Senex* and Cleostrata; Chalinus and *Senex*		D1: *Senex*'s wish starts tr7
	309–52: Olympio and *Senex*			A2: No music for Olympio and *Senex*
ii. Drawing Lots				
		353–423: Lot scene		D2: *Senex*'s wish starts tr7
	424–514: Chalinus monologue; *Senex* and Olympio with Chalinus aside; Chalinus monologue			A3: No music for Olympio and *Senex* (437–503)
iii. Alcesimus Plan and Disruption				
		515–62: *Senex* and Alcesimus; Cleostrata and Alcesimus		D3: *Senex*'s wish starts tr7
	563–620: *Senex* monologue; *Senex* and Cleostrata; *Senex* and Alcesimus			A4: No music for *Senex*

[1] Including very small groups of trochaic septenarii and iambic senarii.

TABLE 6.2: Continued

Unit of action	Iambic senarii	Trochaic septenarii	Other metres	Parallel musical moments
iv. Keeping Senex and Olympio from Eating				
			621–758: Pardalisca and Senex; Senex, Olympio and Cook	C3: Senex anapaests (646–46a, 660–1) B2: Pardalisca bacchiacs (647ff.) C4: Senex and Olympio anapaests (719ff.) A4: No music for Senex (780–97)
	759–97: Pardalisca monologue; Senex and Pardalisca			
v. Handing over the Bride				
		798–814 (with 2 ia4): Olympio and Senex		D3: Senex's wish starts tr7
			815–46: Pardalisca, Senex, Olympio, and 'bride'	C5: Pardalisca anapaests (818–20, 828) B3: Bacchiacs for transfer of 'bride' (828ff.) C6: Senex anapaests (841) A5: No music for Olympio and Senex
	847–54: Senex, Olympio and 'bride': Foot stomping and exit			
vi. Humiliation				
			855–962 : Women; Olympio and women; Senex, Olympio and women	B4: Women bacchiacs (855ff.) C7: Olympio anapaests (875ff.) D4: Senex's defeat starts tr7
	963–1018: Chalinus, Senex, Olympio, and women			

Polymetrics

It will be evident from the above that structural considerations helped to determine which metres occurred in Roman comedy's polymetric sections. Other factors, however, played a more important role there. The opening of *Casina*'s second polymetric section will give us a good example of the kinds of things Roman comedy's polymetrics could do.

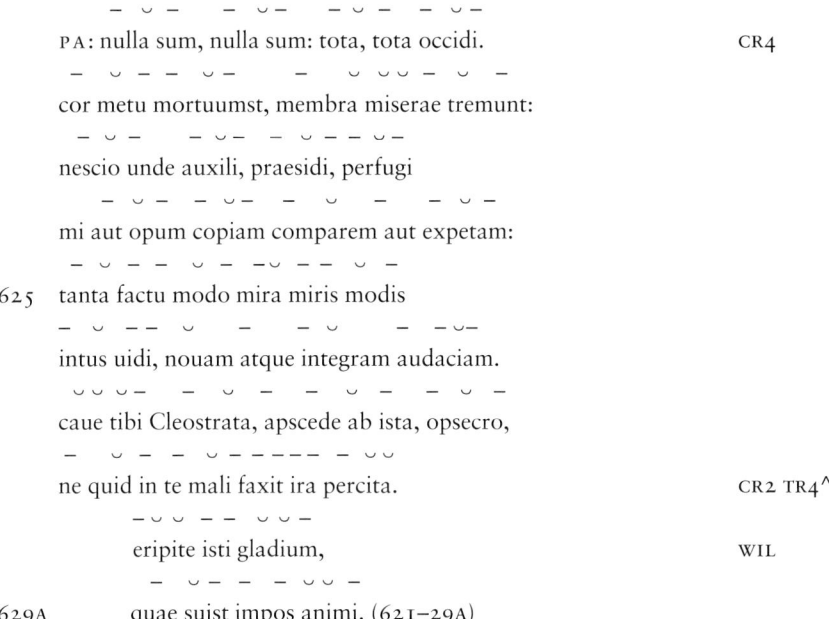

PA: nulla sum, nulla sum: tota, tota occidi.   CR4

cor metu mortuumst, membra miserae tremunt:

nescio unde auxili, praesidi, perfugi

mi aut opum copiam comparem aut expetam:

625   tanta factu modo mira miris modis

intus uidi, nouam atque integram audaciam.

caue tibi Cleostrata, apscede ab ista, opsecro,

ne quid in te mali faxit ira percita.   CR2 TR4^

eripite isti gladium,   WIL

629A   quae suist impos animi. (621–29A)

PA: I'm finished! I'm finished! Totally, totally dead! My heart has perished from fear, my limbs – poor me! – are shaking. I don't know where I can get any help, protection, escape, or aid, or where I should look for them. Such things I saw inside just now, astonishing deeds done in astonishing ways, a new and fresh kind of boldness. Watch out, Cleostrata! Get away from her, please, so she doesn't do you some harm, stirred up by her anger. Grab the sword away from her! She's not in control of her mind.

Plautus has not told the audience that Pardalisca's tale about Casina's madness is a ruse, but the metre hints that she is performing. She begins with cretic quaternarii (cr4), employing a metre used by the heroines of Roman tragedy (e.g., Enn. 81–6 Jocelyn). Characters overcome by panic usually fail to maintain the regularity of their metre, but Pardalisca's quaternarii are completely regular except for two resolutions. Only at the end of the cretics does her regularity break down with a string of long syllables (628: a cretic binarius (cr2) followed by a trochaic quaternarius catalectic (tr4)). When

Pardalisca reveals the reason for her terror and exhorts those indoors to snatch the sword from Casina, she switches to more exotic metres: 'cho2' is a pair of choriambs (—∪∪—), 'wil' a wilamowitzianus, four unpredictable elements followed by a choriamb. Both belong to a category known as aeolics, of which there are only about 100 examples in Roman comedy.

The *Senex* picks up Pardalisca's aeolics as he responds aside, hinting metrically at the power she has over him.

630   SE. nam quid est quod haec huc timida at-   WIL

630A   que exanimata exsiluit?   CHO2

     Pardalisca! PA. perii! | unde meae | usurpant aures sonitum?   TR8

     SE. respice modo ad me. |PA. o | ere mi … SE. quid tibi est?

            quid timida es? PA. perii!

     SE. quid, periisti? PA. perii, | et tu periisti. |SE. a, perii? quid ita?

634   PA. uae tibi! SE. immo uae tibi sit.   WIL

634A   PA. ne cadam, amabo, tene me.   CHO2

635/36   SE. quicquid est eloquere mi cito. PA. contine pectus: IA4 CRCOL

         face uentum, amabo, pallio.   IA4

         SE. timeo hoc negoti quid siet,

         nisi haec meraclo se uspiam

640   percussit flore Liberi. (630–40)

SE: What's this? Why'd she jump out here so frightened and half dead?
     Pardalisca!
PA: Oh no! From where did my ears catch a sound?
SE: Look at me.
PA: Oh! Master!
SE: What's the matter with you? Why are you so frightened?
PA: I'm finished!
SE: What do you mean, you're finished?
PA: I'm finished, and you're finished. SE: What? I'm finished? Why? PA:
     Woe to you!

SE: No, woe to you.
PA: Hold on to me, so I don't fall.
SE: Whatever it is, tell me quickly.
PA: Hold my chest. Please, make a breeze with your cloak.
SE: I'm worried about what this is, unless she's clobbered herself
    with some undiluted wine someplace.

The metre switches to trochaic octonarii (tr8) as the *Senex* addresses Pardalisca directly: he wants information, and he tries to bring her back from her exotic metre to something more prosaic and, with its trochaic rhythm, inclined towards progress. Pardalisca accedes to his trochaic metre, but in such a way that it is clear she is far from coming 'down to earth' or moving forward. After the two trochees of his *Pardalisca*, she almost loses the metre completely with unusual hiatuses (lack of elision, marked | above) and shortening of long syllables. Finally the *Senex*, caught up in her terror, uses a hiatus himself. Then the aeolics return as Pardalisca continues to resist the *Senex*'s attempt to get information.

Next the *Senex* tries a new tack: iambic quaternarii (ia4). Pardalisca at first ignores him, responding with a type of cretic verse known as a cretic colon (crcol). When she does pick up his metre, Plautus demonstrates her power again by having the *Senex*'s next verse echo hers metrically. The rest of his iambic quaternarii have no elements consisting of two short syllables, as he slows down and tries to distance himself from her panic.

Pardalisca returns to her original cretics as she reaches a climax of absurdity:

	— ⏑ — — — ⏑ — ⏑⏑ ⏑ — — — ⏑ —	
	PA. optine auris, amabo. SE. i in malam a me crucem,	CR4
	— ⏑ — — — ⏑ — — ⏑ —	
	pectus auris caput teque di perduint:	
	— — — — ⏑ — — — — — ⏑ —	
	nam nisi ex te scio quicquid hoc est, cito, hoc	
	— ⏑ ⏑ — — ⏑⏑ — — — ⏑⏑ — ⏑ ⏑ —	
	iam tibi istuc cerebrum dispercutiam, excetra tu,	DIPH
	— ⏑⏑ — — ⏑ ⏑ ⏑ — ⏑ ⏑ — —	
645	ludibrio, pessuma, adhuc quae me habuisti.	CHO2 ADON
	⏑⏑ — — — — — ⏑	
646	PA. ere mi ... SE. quid uis mea me ancilla?	AN4
	⏑ ⏑ — — — ⏑ ⏑ — — —	
646A	PA. nimium saeuis. SE. numero dicis.	
	⏑ — — ⏑ — — ⏑ ⏑ — — ⏑ — —	
	sed hoc quicquid est eloquere, in pauca confer:	BA4
	⏑ — — — ⏑ — — ⏑— — ⏑ — —	
	quid intus tumulti fuit? PA. scibis, audi. (641–8)	

PA: Please, grab a hold of my ears.

SE: Go to hell! The gods damn your chest, your ears, your head and you! If I don't find out immediately what this is all about, I'll smash your head open with this, you viper, you bitch who keep ridiculing me.

PA: Master!

SE: What is it, slave?

PA: You're too fierce.

SE: I can be a lot fiercer. But tell me what this is all about, and make it brief. What's all the confusion inside?

PA: You'll know. I'll tell you.

The *Senex* gives up on changing his metre and continues the cretics. As he gets to the core of his threats, though, his cretics break down into a pair of very irregular aeolic verses: a diphilean (diph) and a pair of choriambs followed by an adonic (adon). Repeated pairs of short syllables thus replace the single short syllable that marks the cretics, underlining his greater excitement. In response to the threat, Pardalisca initiates a pair of anapaestic quaternarii (an4), so the pairs of short syllables continue. Still struggling to get some information out of Pardalisca, the *Senex* tries yet another tactic, introducing bacchiac quaternarii (ba4). Bacchiacs, with their two long syllables following a single short syllable in each foot, are the slowest of Roman comedy's metres: they suit well the *Senex*'s determined attempt to get information. Pardalisca picks up the bacchiacs, appearing to acquiesce in the *Senex*'s demand. For her, however, the slow bacchiacs contribute to the delay with which she frustrates her master: only after another ten verses will she begin to reveal what is actually happening inside the house (658ff.).

Such cooperation between metre and meaning occurs throughout the polymetric sections of Roman comedy. Through this cooperation and the larger structural patterns, Plautus and Terence made each of their plays sophisticated works of musical theatre.

Further Reading

Moore (2012) is a thorough discussion of music in Roman comedy. For musical structure, see also Moore (1998a) and Marshall (2006). Gratwick (1982a) and Moore (1999) review the connections between music and character. Moore (2007) discusses music in Terence. For the connection between metre and musical accompaniment, see Moore (2008). Questa (2007) is the best introduction to Roman comedy's metres. Those with no Italian will do best to start with the sections on metre in Gratwick (1993) and (1999) and Barsby (1999). Questa (1995) has scanned, and Braun (1970) has analysed,

Plautus' polymetric songs. For identification of metres in the rest of Roman comedy, the *schemata metrorum* in the texts of Lindsay (1904–5) and Kauer and Lindsay (1958) are invaluable. Lindsay (1922), though dated, is still useful, as is the chapter on music in Beare (1964). For singing in the ancient theatre, see Hall (2002). Wille (1967) is an encyclopedic compilation of evidence for music in the Roman world. Moore (2016) is an online database of all the metrical changes in the extant plays of Plautus and Terence.

7

ISABELLA TARDIN CARDOSO*

Comic Technique

The film *City Lights* (1931), which is considered to showcase Charlie Chaplin's resistance to the talking movies of his time, is often remembered for an impressive detail which exemplifies its dramatic technique, namely its brilliant solution to the problem of how to communicate the reason why a blind flower girl takes the tramp for a millionaire. In order to narrate such a comic mistake without speech, there is a famous scene in which the tramp is buying a flower from the florist: the mistaken identity, as only the facial expressions of the actors convey, results from the closing thud of the door of a limousine. In fact, Chaplin includes some music and sound effects as a 'compromise solution to the challenge of sound' but totally rejects spoken language in this film.[1] By bringing sound into his *City Lights* the author is thus able to realise his plot and exemplify his sense of humour, while keeping his work within the boundaries and conventions that define the silent movie as a dramatic genre.

It goes without saying that there are huge differences in, for instance, epoch, medium, and genre that separate the movies produced at the beginning of the twentieth century from the *fabula palliata*, the comedy 'dressed à la Grecque' performed seasonally at the festivals (*ludi scaenici*) in ancient Rome – from which almost no contemporary material or textual evidence other than the texts of the plays themselves has been transmitted. However, once this distance is recognised, this starting point may prove useful for my brief consideration of the challenges and limitations that Plautus and Terence encountered when developing their comic technique.

For the authors of the *fabula palliata*, a great challenge was how to elicit laughter with plays which would follow a stereotypical pattern. Indeed, their repetitiveness (inherited from their Greek models) has been compared to that of contemporary forms of popular drama, such as soap operas or westerns.[2]

* I would like to thank my students and colleagues of the University of Campinas (Brazil), NY University, and the University of Heidelberg, as well as the editor and anonymous readers of this volume for helpful comments, suggestions, and assistance with the English version of this text.
[1] Maland (2007) 29.
[2] See Candiard on twentieth and twenty-first century reception in this volume.

120

Roman comedies were far from silent shows: their humour is sometimes generated by verbal means, like jokes, word-plays, puns, ambiguities, antithesis, hyperbolical comparisons, metaphors, and irony. But at times the main source is non-verbal, such as knockabout buffoonery or wild gesticulation. In this case, performance tends to be heavily dependent on physical behaviour (such as gestures, entrances, exits, and other movements on the stage) or vocal communication (sounds, modulations of the voice), as well as on matters of production and staging (costumes, elements of scenery, or stage properties in general). More often than not, both verbal and non-verbal elements are combined, to the point that they become inseparable in stock scenes such as the entrance of the *seruus currens* ('running slave') or the door-knocking routine.[3]

In this chapter, while discussing the non-verbal aspects of comic technique, I shall focus on the physical expression (movements of the body or its postures) and also facial expression of the actors. Thus, I will only occasionally refer to production and other issues of staging.[4] With this I hope to illustrate the sheer variety of verbal and non-verbal theatrical techniques that were employed by Roman authors via a selection of passages from the plays themselves, mainly from Plautus' *Stichus*, *Amphitruo*, *Miles Gloriosus* and Terence's *Phormio* and *Adelphoe*. As my focus will be on illustrating what verbal and non-verbal resources were available to Plautus and Terence from the repertory of the *fabula palliata*, conjectures about how the comic technique of their lost Greek models would have differed – frequent in studies of the texts discussed here – will not be considered.

Sadly no manual of Roman theatrical acting – such as the one Quintus Roscius, the praised comic actor with whom Cicero is said to have honed his performance skills (Plut. *Cic.* 5), reportedly wrote (Macr. 3. 14. 12) – is extant. But vocal expression (*uox*), physical expression and movement (*gestus*) as well as the facial expression (*uultus*) of actors' theatrical performance (*imitatio*) are discussed in Roman texts concerned with oratorical delivery (*actio* or *pronuntiatio*) dating from the first century BC onwards (e.g. Cicero *De Or.* 3. 213–27 and Quintilian *Inst.* 11. 3). In modern appreciation of Roman theatre some terminology concerning actor's performance has thus been borrowed from rhetoric – although it mentions theatrical *gestus* usually as something to be avoided for the sake of an orator's professional reputation.

---

[3] See also Fitzgerald in this volume.
[4] On the latter, see the further reading section of this chapter and Marshall in this volume.

Imagining Plays

Roman comedy provides entertainment that relies fundamentally upon words, or, to be more precise, provides plays that feature poetical and elaborate verbal language. As scholarship on popular drama and, more recently, on performance suggests, understanding the text itself depends on imagining how it could be staged.[5]

Up to a certain point extant manuscripts can be regarded as transmitting a sort of 'script', which presents versified speeches (in the form of dialogues, monologues, asides) written to be staged before a live audience.[6] This view – inspired by the performance criticism of Shakespeare – normally sets aside philological concerns for establishing the text in order to showcase the performability of the edited texts of Plautus.[7] However, attention to staging practices may in turn influence the understanding of passages of Roman comedy that have traditionally been suspected to be deviant, redundant, or incomplete by classical scholars. Instead of being regarded as flaws (generated by the playwrights, or by later interventions of actors, stage-managers, or copyists), many of them may be rehabilitated as artful devices that achieve a lively imitation of orality and improvisation in a comic play. For instance, as I suggested elsewere, from this perspective sometimes ellipsis and lack of syntactic parallelism (e.g. *St.* 233), as well as digressions (*Mil.* 1150–4), redundance (*St.* 75–9), and interruption of one's own speech (*St.* 484–5), can be considered as part of comic techniques which give the impression of a spontaneous elaboration of plans by a character, while certain contradictions may help to represent a character's shaping of an idea on the stage (e.g. *Ep.* 500–1; *St.* 176–8).[8]

Readers of Roman comedy become acquainted with certain stereotypical situations, which can serve as cross-references among the extant plays. Thus, although no stage directions as such survive in the texts, they can frequently be inferred from either such cross-references or the utterances of the characters.[9] A notorious example is the humorous depiction of the gesture of throwing on a cloak as typical for the running slave character in *Capt.* 778–80 (see also *Ep.* 194–5; *Ph.* 844–5). On the basis of this, the audience may expect the staging of such movement whenever this stock character appears. The following verses from the Terentian comedy *Phormio*, however, illustrate the limits of this approach. A witty, and (as the stichometry conveys) rapid rehearsal of facial

---

[5] Taladoire (1951) and (1956); Marshall in this volume.   [6] Slater (1985) 6.
[7] Styan (1975); see Slater (1985) 3–18; Christenson (2000) 18, 28, 165.
[8] On the verses of *Stichus*, see Petersmann (1973) and Cardoso (2006); on those of *Miles Gloriosus*, see Vogt-Spira (1998) 122–3; on those of *Epidicus*, see Slater (2000) 25; (2001) 121.
[9] See Warnecke (1910); Panayotakis (2005).

expressions is presented in a dialogue between a young man in love, the *adulescens* Antipho, and his old slave Geta who is trying to convince Antipho to show his father a fake facial expression of innocence:[10]

ANT: (...) Suppose I pretend. Would that do?
GET: (*scornfully*) You are joking!
ANT: (*putting on a brave face*) Look at my expression. There you are, is this all right?
GET: No.
ANT: (*trying again*) How about this?
GET: Nearly.
ANT: (*trying again*) Or this?
GET: Very well, keep that one. And make sure you answer him word for word, tit for tat, or he'll rout you with raging words. He's in an angry mood.
ANT: I know. (*Ph.* 210–13)

The transmitted text shows a character instructing another how he should employ facial and verbal expression to perform before a third person.[11] Indications concerning the staging of the scene are often added in brackets or in notes by translators (derived from their interpretation of the characters' speeches in the text itself). To make sense of this particular scene, such directions regarding non-vocal elements are essential, specifically concerning the facial expressions (*uultus*) mentioned (cf. *uoltum*, 210). Would, however, 'a brave face' be exactly the visual translation for 'this' (*sic*, 211)? What grimaces would successfully suggest the subsequent instances of 'this' (*sic ... sic*, 211)? This is just one of many examples of the way 'stage-directions' can be sourced in the transmitted texts by Plautus and Terence.

Imaginative reconstruction is our principal resource here; as the ancient grammarian Aelius Donatus remarks: 'here there is a passage which is more convenient to actors than to readers'.[12] Perhaps such 'imagination (...), aided by gestures of the actor' was even required from the theatregoers at the time of Plautus and Terence.[13] For it is not certain to what extent facial expressions could be perceived at all by members of a large theatrical audience, nor were such shifting expressions feasible on the stage if, as scholars nowadays tend to suppose, actors performed wearing masks.[14]

---

[10] Transl. (and stage directions) by Barsby (2001). Unless otherwise indicated, for Plautus' and Terence's plays I follow the Latin text of the OCT, respectively the volumes edited by Lindsay (1955) and (1956); and by Kauer and Lindsay (1958 and 1961).

[11] See Frangoulidis (1996); (2013) 284, and Christenson's chapter in this volume on metatheatre.

[12] Wessner (1963) 404.   [13] Beare (1955) 181.

[14] For a discussion of the use of masks in this particular scene, see Beare (1955) 296–7; Duckworth (1952) 93–4; Barsby (2001) 34–5, n. 26; Marshall (2006) 155–7.

Changes in facial expressions on stage, such as crying (e.g. *Amph.* 529; *As.* 620; *St.* 20; *Ad.* 679), blushing (*Ad.* 643), becoming 'green' or pale (*Men.* 829–30), or showing repugnance (*Cas.* 727; 730–2a) are borderline cases which remind us that, in many scenes, the gap between what is being said and what can be actually seen must still be filled by the audiences' imagination. Thus, determining when Plautus and Terence write 'stage directions' into the Latin text and what sort of 'actions' they suggest is not always a simple affair. Whether it is reading Donatus, commenting on Terentian texts for his school pupils in the fourth century AD, or whether it is through the illustrator or copyist of a medieval manuscript or even a modern reader (scholar or not): to a certain extent the manner in which we fill this gap is based on information (about dramatic literature, stage practice, and theory) that does not necessarily correspond to the theatrical context of Plautus' or Terence's times. Hence, avoiding setting up 'an opposition between performance criticism and literary criticism' can be beneficial.[15] Antipho's rehearsal showcases how Latin text and performance interact in order to represent verbal and non-verbal aspects of a comic situation.[16]

Gelasimus' Verbal Acrobatics

Explicit reference to verbal means as a source of humour is found in the speech of the parasite Gelasimus (Greek for 'Ridiculous') from Plautus' *Stichus* (*St.* 155–273).[17] Here, the character not only advertises his sale of 'funny words' (*logos ridiculos*, *St.* 221), but gives free samples of his wares. Among them, there are the usual ingredients of Plautine laughter: odd personification (hunger *St.* 155–70, food and drink *St.* 211–14, verbal expression *St.* 191), antithetic sequences of diminutives and superlatives ('very small', *paruolum, St.* 161; 'tiny' *pausillulam, St.* 163; 'too enormous and the most heavy', *multo maximam et grauissimam St.* 164), likely neologisms ('pieces-of-flatteries' and 'petty perjuries', *adsentatiunculas St.* 228; *perieratiunculas St.* 229, cf. *OLD*), pleonastic frequentatives (167) and word-play on Gelasimus' own name (*St.* 174–7; 240–2).[18] As a result, the audience encounters grotesque images, such as hunger as mother of the parasite (*St.* 155–9), and moreover an 'acrobatic'[19] inversion: the parasite pregnant with his own mother … from the semen of an elephant (*St.*

---

[15] Sharrock (2009) 20. [16] See Marshall's chapter on stagecraft in this volume.

[17] For this play, I follow the edition by Petersmann (1973). Details of the following discussion of Gelasimus' monologue are presented in Cardoso (2006) 32–5, 46–50, and 114–26.

[18] On the language of Plautus and Terence, see Karakasis in this volume.

[19] An expression coined by Bettini (2002) 240.

160–70)! Gelasimus hyperbolically yet tragicomically complains of his hunger and offers rich merchandise in an auction of his jokes and of himself.[20] The parasite acknowledges his own 'barbarian procedures' (*mores barbaros*, *St.* 193); after all, an auction (*St.* 195, 201, 207) is a Roman practice in a Greek setting.[21] But since 'barbarian' is also how Plautus calls his literary project when adapting Greek models, this speech with its Plautine exuberance could certainly count as a 'barbarism' as well.[22] The same applies to the loose syntax in which the double explanation of Gelasimus' name is presented (*St.* 174–8): his father called him 'ridiculous' because he was funny since childhood; but, he adds, poverty, too, made him 'ridiculous'.[23] The audience is left with the impression of continuous improvisation which, in turn, serves to portray the desperation of the character and the situation.[24]

Despite its slipshod appearance, a close reading shows that the humour which Gelasimus tries to sell is nevertheless carefully constructed: the whole scene is rooted in the verbal and performative technique of the *fabula palliata*. For instance, the parasite's speech recalls entrance monologues that this stock character of Greek and Roman comedy tends to make, showcasing techniques of improvisation.[25] Moreover, much of the laughter would stem from his addresses to the public (*St.* 220–34) and the funny asides of an eavesdropping woman slave (*St.* 196–7, 217, 235–7). Depending on how his self-deprecating jokes are interpreted by the actor, Gelasimus may remind us of a modern clown, someone like the hungry Charlie, but one whose loquaciousness steals the show, not only in this scene, but also in the rest of the play.[26]

Phormio's Poses

Comparing Gelasimus' speech with the monologue of Phormio, a parasite in the homonymous play by Terence (*Ph.* 884–93) already mentioned above, can help in the appreciation of Terentian verbal technique. Soon after discovering the terrible secret of his adversaries the parasite speaks to himself: 'now I must get new gestures and a new face' (*nunc gestus mihi uoltusque est*

---

[20] Arnott (1972) 64–74.   [21] Fraenkel (1960) 281.

[22] See e.g. *As.* 11; *Trin.* 19, Moore (1998b) 54–6, and Telò in this volume.

[23] See Fraenkel (1960) 280–1; Ernout (1957); Petersmann (1973), and Vogt-Spira (1991); epistemological aspects of these studies are discussed by Guastella (2002).

[24] Gaiser (1972) 1085 n. 274.

[25] See n. 21 above; esp. Fraenkel (1960) 273 and 277. See Vogt-Spira (1991) and Benz (2000) for the possible influence of oral Italic spectacles.

[26] See Fontaine (2010) 180–3. See also Fraenkel (1960) 268–81; Arnott (1972) 65–6 and 72, evoking Charlie Chaplin; Damon (2000) 65–75; Cardoso (2006) 46–9.

capiundus nouos, 890).[27] *Vultus* (the importance of which for deception was already highlighted in Antipho's rehearsal earlier in the play, see *Ph.* 210–13 quoted above) and *gestus* are explicit references to elements of theatrical and rhetorical performance. These terms, however, are used by Phormio in a metaphorical sense. They do not refer to the use of new masks, grimaces, or mimicry but rather to the new attitude to be adopted by the parasite, which is marked from the beginning to the end of the monologue as an improvised and deceptive pose (*de improuiso*, *Ph.* 884; *assimularam*, *Ph.* 893). This is Terence at his most metatheatrical, whose play with sounds, words, and theatrical illusion is more discrete in comparison to Plautus.[28]

At first glance that short monologue of *Phormio*'s parasite also pales in contrast with the exuberant speech of Gelasimus, the parasite of the Plautine play *Stichus*, and even with the vivid imagetic expression by Phormio elsewhere in his play (e.g. *Ph.* 315–45).[29] But its lack of morphological and syntactic distortion makes the diction of Phormio in this scene representative of the verbal mastery of Terence. Here symmetrical repetition expresses the tricky reasoning: 'The same money that has been given (*datumst*), will be given (*datum erit*) to them even if they do not want it' (*Ph.* 888–9). Accordingly, the actions which are verbalised in this concise and balanced monologue are not necessarily performed as such in a play-within-a-play by the character: at the end of the play it is funny to realise that they are just a pose, a vain promise of a comic deception to which Phormio's reference to face and gesture alludes.

What About Knockabout?

The opening scene of *Amphitruo* is uniquely representative of the way Plautus exploits gesturing on stage.[30] In this, the longest scene in all of Plautus' oeuvre (*Amph.* 153–462),[31] its dramatic setting is a uniquely long night during which the god Mercury stands guard in front of the house of the general Amphitruo. Disguised as a human (namely as Sosia, a slave of

---

[27] Latin text by Barsby (2001).
[28] Cf. Barsby's (2001) transl.: 'Now I must put on a new face *and change my role*' (*Ph.* 890, my italics); Damon (2000) 92. For sound effects in Plautus, see Taladoire (1956) 173–5; for Terence, see discussion in Vincent (2013) 71–7. On deception presented as theatre in Plautus, see Petrone (1983); on life as theatre and the play with illusion, see Duckworth (1952) 132–6; Cardoso (2010); (2011) 66–70. On metatheatre, see Christenson in this volume.
[29] See Arnott (1970) 33–8.
[30] On typically Plautine elements in this scene, see Fraenkel (1960) 21, 98, and 172–5; Lefèvre (1982) 8–13; Christenson (2000) 25–6 and 167–223; Costa (2013) 35–73, 79–88, and 112–57.
[31] See Christenson (2000) 165, whose Latin edition I follow.

Amphitruo), Mercury has the job of standing watch over the prolonged love encounter between the wife of Amphitruo and none other than Jupiter himself, disguised as her husband. Meanwhile the real Sosia, afraid of robbers in the dark streets (*Amph.* 153–74), approaches the house without noticing the presence of the deity. The encounter between Sosia and Mercury is delayed as long as possible: it takes more than a 100 verses before Mercury addresses the slave (*Amph.* 341). And only after a series of harsh questions and sharp answers from both sides does Mercury threaten Sosia directly (*Amph.* 348). However, it is only when Sosia stubbornly insists that he is indeed himself that he receives what the audience expects him to get – a beating: 'take that' (*uapula, Amph.* 370), says the god; 'easy, easy for heaven's sake!'[32] (*tuam fidem obsecro, Amph.* 373), 'I am done!' (*perii, Amph.* 374) shouts the slave, reacting to the pain of the blows; and once more Mercury assaults the slave – and again ('you'll take that', *uapulabis Amph.* 379) and again (*uapula, Amph.* 395).

Comic tradition itself exempts Plautine plays from apologising for deriving humour from physical violence.[33] Indeed, vigorous blows against slaves or other characters (e.g. *Mil.* 1394–425) and sharp threats (e.g. *St.* 62–3) are supposed to arouse laughter.[34] However, in this scene of *Amphitruo* the blows are not supposed to be funny for their own sake but instead derive their humour from the scene's composition as a whole. For instance, the threats that precede the fight are presented in an exaggerated, farcical fashion which keeps us from sympathising with the character who receives a beating. The contrast between high and low registers of speech and the amusing eavesdropping by Mercury provide ironic distance from the victim.[35] In addition, the outburst of physical violence does not come unexpectedly: we are prepared for it from the start of the scene.

A close reading of the speeches of Mercury and Sosia reveals that Sosia's very first utterance already signals the possible occurrence of violence, in that he declares his fear of being attacked in the streets. Aware of Sosia's presence, Mercury speaks in asides which generate striking dramatic irony as he comments on what he hears in the slave's speech. Still more striking is the fact that Sosia himself echoes, although unknowingly at first, Mercury's expressions (e.g. 'household slave', *uerna, Amph.* 179–80). This verbal 'ping-pong' creates a delightful sense of continuity between utterances by different characters, and highlights Sosia's premonition of his (comically) unhappy destiny (*Amph.* 180–5, 287–90, 295–9, 335–40).

---

[32] Transl. Nixon (1997).   [33] See Fitzgerald in this volume on whipping jokes.
[34] Fraenkel (1960) 235–6 and 155–7; Konstan and Raval (2018).
[35] Moore (1998b) 117–18; Christenson (2000) 26 n. 81.

When the slave finally sees someone in front of his master's house (*Amph.* 292) Mercury gets a chance to play with Sosia's fears before both characters eventually meet. Pretending that he cannot see the frightened slave, Mercury intentionally speaks out loud, and prepares the transformation of the stage into a boxing-ring.

When Mercury, conscious that he is not alone, fakes a monologue we witness a 'typical situation of Roman comedy'.[36] But how can we stage this passage? We could suppose that the god starts off by shadow-boxing and Sosia oddly replies that he is afraid of being 'welcomed with fists' (*hospitio pugneo*, *Amph.* 296). Alternatively, as there is no direct mention of fists before Sosia's remark, we can speculate that, only after hearing the odd expression of the slave, the god, as 'an exceptionally versatile player', takes up the hint and, by staging a lively personification (*agite, pugni*, *Amph.* 302), starts talking to his fists and imitates the sparring of a boxer.[37] Mercury then lets Sosia 'eavesdrop' (*Amph.* 300); the latter then addresses the public in humorous asides, vocally mimicking his own 'ppppanic': *perii pugnos ponderat* (*Amph.* 312) 'I am finished, he's a-weighting his fists!'.) Repetition of such menacing gestures (*Amph.* 323; 328) and reactions with slight variations ensure turbulent fun under the 'direction' of Mercury.[38]

Verbal and non-verbal means work together in this passage to sculpt the performance of the scene. That words related to *pugnus* ('fist') pervade the whole scene (25 of 28 instances in the whole play) is no coincidence: this feature provides an underlying theme for this particular scene. Plautus here makes his point verbally; the culmination, however, is physical, in that the sparring of voices ends in a boxing match on stage. A further recurrent comic technique is Sosia's tendency to misinterpret idiomatic expressions used by Mercury (e.g. *Amph.* 309–10; 327–8; 366–75). Sosia takes them in a much more literal and often 'physical' sense than they were intended. Among these 'errors' are many references to the body: ears (*Amph.* 325–6), tongue (*Amph.* 348), and olfactory allusions to flatulence (*Amph.* 321) are mentioned. This occurs in swift and smart jokes with light touches of the vulgar (*Amph.* 321) and obscene connotation (*Amph.* 348–9).[39]

Verbal arguments eventually convince Sosia that, not being himself, he should go away (*argumentis uicit*, *Amph.* 423; 430). The power of these very arguments is partially corroborated by the astonished slave's description of the visual aspects of the scene that is presented to the audience: identical costume, identical body, and therefore identical personality (*Amph.* 441–5).

---

[36] Bain (1977) 171. [37] Christenson (2000) 26. [38] Moore (1998b) 119.
[39] For Plautus' exploration of the olfactory sense for humorous purposes, see e.g. *Cas.* 236–40; MacCary and Willcock (1976) 95–6; Chiarini (1992) 26–8; Rocha (2013) 17–22.

However, the fact that Sosia leaves the stage only after a final threat – of a 'wreck of loins' (*lumbifragium, Amph.* 454, another likely neologism), demonstrates that, integrated into the plot and the tenor of the scene, Mercury's blows carry a decisive power of persuasion. Mercury's impersonation convinces as long as rough gesticulation – signalled and thematised by the text – joins forces with the play on words typical of Plautus' smart slaves.[40] Verbal and non-verbal means combine to affirm the ironic superiority of Mercury and lead the shocked Sosia into a tangible albeit comic identity crisis.

Terence's Stage Action

According to the prologues of *Hecyra*, earlier audiences had spurned the play to watch more exciting shows, such as the performance of a tightrope walker (*Hec.* 4, 34) or a boxing-match (*Hec.* 33), or to elbow their way to a seat at the gladiators' spectacles (*Hec.* 39–42). Similar metapoetical self-deprecating jokes can be found in other Roman comedies (for instance when the parasite in Plautus' *Stichus* (497–504) fails to sell his 'funny words'). Whether we believe this account or not it gives the impression that Terentian stagecraft uses vigorous knockabout moments rather sparingly.[41] Indeed, only two scenes, one in *Eunuchus* (771–816) and the other in *Adelphoe* (155–96), suggest that Terence exploits a repertoire of physical humour in his *fabulae palliatae*.[42]

In *Eunuchus*, props, clumsy actions, and amusingly embarrassing events occur in a very crowded scene (five speaking characters): on the one side, there are the *miles gloriosus* ('glorious soldier') Thraso, his ever-flattering parasite Gnatho, and 'a motley group of servants',[43] including Sanga; on the other side, there are the young man Chremes and his beloved *meretrix* (prostitute). Insulted, the foolish soldier enters the stage making threats: he proposes to 'take the house by storm' and 'carry off the girl' (*Eun.* 771–3). The military language employed here underlines the soldier's ridiculous behaviour: when Thraso 'strategically' positions his lame troop on stage in order to recover his *meretrix* from the young man, he explicitly mentions military formations such as columns (*Eun.* 774–5) and commands (*signum dabo, Eun.* 781). Such parody employs not only stage props (such as a 'sponge' as armament, *Eun.* 776–7), but also capitalises on the triviality

---

[40] Moore (1998b) 116; Christenson (2000) 27.
[41] On the prologue's veracity, see discussion in Parker (1996); Goldberg (2013) 86.
[42] Hunter (1985) 55–6.
[43] Brothers (2000) 194, whose Latin text and translations are here adopted. See also Goldberg (1986) 112 and Barsby (2001) 403.

of the domestic situation. Much of the humour arises from the ironic ambiguity of the speeches and frank asides of Gnatho, the flattering parasite, who
reveals the soldier's cowardice and the emptiness of the threats (*Eun.* 782,
786–7). After all, Thraso makes a hasty withdrawal – like a 'wind-bag'
(*nebulo, Eun.* 785) – without a single blow being struck (*Eun.* 814–16): no
real knockabout happens on stage. Despite the toying with props and stirring
of expectations, there is only 'a victory of words', of verbal humour, that
makes 'the soldier's retreat pathetic and ridiculous.'[44]

When another young man, however, fights for his beloved *meretrix* in
Terence's *Adelphoe* (155–96), physical aggression is used as a means of
persuasion.[45] It occurs in a scene that, as the prologue announces (*Ad.*
6–11), Terence borrowed from a play by the Greek poet Diphilus
(*Synapothnescontes*, 'Companions in death') and inserted into the
Adelphoe (which the Roman poet adapted from the homonymous play of
Menander). In explaining the elliptical sparseness of the scene's text at *Ad.*
158, the ancient commentator Donatus alleges that: 'no one expresses himself completely when he fights.'[46] However, for Donatus and for modern
readers, the very omissions that suggest vigorous gestures sometimes complicate the interpretation of the text, particularly when ascribing lines to
speakers and detailing stage directions.[47] Leaving aside these controversial
details, let us observe how the verbal and non-verbal interact in this scene.

It all begins with a desperate call for help from someone who affirms his
innocence (*Ad.* 155–6). But shortly afterwards Sannio, the victim, reveals
that he is a pimp (*Ad.* 160–1) and thereby gives the audience every reason to
dismiss his insistence on innocence and defencelessness. Overexposure of
legal terminology (*iniuriam, Ad.* 162, *ius* 164, *iusiurandum* 165, *iniuria* 166)
in Sannio's speech certainly helps him to lose the audience's sympathy, since
it is incongruous with the perjurious stock character of the pimp in New
Comedy (*Ad.* 188–9; cf. Plautus' *Capt.* 57; *Ps.* 363, 1081–4).[48] Given such
stereotyping, Aeschinus, the bold young man, does not really need to justify
the tough measures he takes to kidnap the *meretrix* he loves (and for whose
services he cannot pay). Aeschinus threatens Sannio once verbally, with an
expression that Terence uses sparingly 'he will take a blow' (*uapulet, Ad.*
159; cf. eight occurrences in the scene of *Amphitruo* analysed above).[49]
In what follows, the slave Parmeno is used as a sort of weapon against

---

[44] Goldberg (1986) 113.   [45] I follow the Latin text by Martin (1976).
[46] Wessner (1963) 37.   [47] See e.g. Fantham (1968a) and Frauenfelder (1996).
[48] Hartkamp (2004) 144–55 considers Sannio a grotesque character; for a different view, see
Gratwick (1982b) 120, who does not read the pimp as represented in a 'farcical Plautine
manner'.
[49] Martin (1976) 127.

Sannio, to be activated by the young master, with whom the slave should keep constant visual contact (*Ad.* 170): 'If I nod, don't wait', instructs the young man, 'plant your fist on his jaw instantly' (*Ad.* 171).[50] Often deixis is used to signal displacements (*Ad.* 156, 167–9) and gesticulation ('of this' *huius* in *Ad.* 163 probably indicates as a snap of fingers).

Regardless of who says what to whom in the disputed lines *Ad.* 172–3, Aeschinus must have nodded at least once, as the pimp screams (*o facinus indignum!*, *Ad.* 174), but … when the victim is struck again, the reader is misled for a minute into thinking that the master had signalled again: the slave has in fact struck of his own accord, whether having misinterpreted words or visual signs, or just on impulse. The beaten pimp, however, is not even spared the opponent's irony. For the *adulescens* comments sarcastically: 'I didn't nod. But it's a fault in the right direction' (*Ad.* 174).[51]

The confrontation between the laconic young man and the lamenting pimp, as well as the complex stage directions and the battering itself not only provoke laughter, but also seem to be carefully choreographed so as to smoothe the way for the scene's sarcastic and hilarious climax. Neither threats nor physical abuse are taken seriously by the greedy pimp: after much bashing, he accepts the insults as part of his job (*Ad.* 206–7), and does not even consider the possibility of letting the girl go, until financial questions are taken into consideration.

Recourse to aggressive measures against pimps are also found elsewhere in New Comedy. Sometimes merely verbal means are employed to portray the conflict, as in an impressive scene involving insults against a pimp in Plautus' *Pseudolus* (357–70). In *Adelphoe*, another option would have been to keep the knockabout scene offstage since the kidnapping of the girl was already divulged by Aeschinus' biological father in the previous part of the play (*Ad.* 88–93), an overlap that has given rise to claims of dramatic inconsistency.[52] Instead of merely narrating the deeds, Terence goes for a lively scene (adapted from another Greek model) that certainly provokes the immediate laughter of his spectators. However, together with metrical shifts that are introduced here, the striking stage action also performs an important function in a comedy that focuses on the conflict of generations of brothers: it introduces younger characters and contrasts them with the old men who held the stage earlier in the play.[53] The spectators may condemn Aeschinus' performance as too wild and let it reflect badly on the attitudes of his lenient father, or rather they may laugh at his witty sternness against the pimp.[54]

---

[50] Transl. by Barsby (2001) here and verse 174 below.
[51] Marti (1959) 98; Martin (1976) 130.
[52] Gratwick (1982b) 120; see the discussion in Traill (2013) 321. [53] Martin (1976) 126.
[54] Goldberg (1986) 104–5; Hunter (1985) 72.

In any case Terence's non-verbal comic technique assists with the character portrayal and helps to refine the play's engagement with ancient educational models.

A Comic Battle of Techniques

My final example, from Plautus' *Miles Gloriosus* (200–16), contains the most extensive depiction of a slave's gesticulation of Roman comedy.[55] The old man (*senex*) Periplectomenus observes and comments on the slave Palaestrio, who hatches a plan against a soldier. The slave beats his chest (*Mil.* 202), moves around to rest his left hand on his right thigh (*Mil.* 203), counts the fingers of the right hand, slaps his leg energetically (*Mil.* 204), shakes his head (*Mil.* 207) and so on. After such frantic gesticulation, he finally freezes in a pose said to be typical 'of a slave and of comedy' (*et dulice et comoedice, Mil.* 213). The old man could have said more directly 'of a comic slave', but the term *dulice* (a word that only occurs once, meaning 'in a slavelike manner') and the hendiadys reveal the scene's special character. For this remarkable description makes it clear that we are not meant to imagine the subservient posture of a hasty, breathless, disorderly cloaked *seruus currens* – the comic 'running slave', already mentioned above. Palaestrio poses as a *seruus callidus*, as a petulant and self-confident slave; a character whose posturing can also be observed in other Roman comedies (*Ps.* 459, *Capt.* 664) but whose gesticulation is nowhere else described in such detail.

Periplectomenus' description has been considered as a source that allows us a glimpse into what types of gesticulation were in use in the *fabula palliata*. In addition, when comparing these verses to passages in Quintilian (*Inst. Or.* 11.3) that recommend modes of delivery for respectable orators, a stock of gestures common to both oratory and comedy is revealed.[56] It is difficult to ascertain the extent to which the speech of Periplectomenus corresponds to actual postures of tricking slaves or other characters of Roman comedy, and we cannot tell whether or not they can be linked to the conventions of pantomime in ancient Rome.[57]

In fact, Periplectomenus' speech is more than a mere description of movements: the text enables the spectators to enjoy a delightful competition between the two characters and also between the non-verbal and the verbal on stage. The unusual wording of the verses describing the slave's gestures

---

[55] I follow the Latin text by Lindsay (1956). See Cardoso (2005) 127–266 and (2009) 94–109 on *Mil.* 200–16 in more detail.

[56] Graf (1992) 49–51.   [57] Zimmermann (1995); Hofmann (1995).

has prompted discussions about its authenticity;[58] yet its poetic effects form an essential part of that competition. For instance, in the expression (*pectus digitis pultat*, 'he beats his chest with his fingers', *Mil.* 202), the verb *pultare* ('to pound', 'to beat') normally refers to doors (e. g. *Mil.* 1254, 1297, 1298) and 'suggests the simile here of knocking at a door to call out his heart'.[59] Palaestrio is thus knocking on his 'heart's door' (*cor credo euocaturust foras, Mil.* 202) as powerfully as in the door-battering scenes typical of comedy. Remarkably, through this verbal allusion, stock comic scenes are evoked in a metaphor that recalls gestures in a comic drama.

Moreover, Periplectomenus does not necessarily refer to gestures, but rather to various *topoi* of the conventional portrayal of the stock character of the 'cunning slave', the *seruus callidus*, such as the solitude necessary to conceive a plan (*Mil.* 200, cf. *Ep.* 81; *Ps.* 394); the deep worry of those who urgently need a plan ('with a concerned face', *Mil.* 201; cf. *Epid.* 608–9); indecision (*Mil.* 203–8; cf. *Epid.* 81–102, 257–60); and finally, the slave – embodying his own aspirations to glory – posing as a statue of himself (*Mil.* 209), a homage that Chrysalus, the cunning slave of the play *Bacchides*, also proclaims to deserve (*Bacch.* 640–2).

Accordingly, the verbal ecphrasis ('description') of scenic performance in the character portrayal of Palaestrio may indicate important aspects of the comedy in which it occurs, for instance concerning the roles of the characters in the play's structure. Yet, hyperbolic (epic or mythological) comparison – a comic routine nowadays described as 'glorification' – is alluded to by the poetic description of a gesture on stage, in anticipation of the future deeds of Palaestrio. The depiction of the pose underlines that both Palaestrio and the soldier are boasters of their talents; both characters, concerned with their desire for *gloria*, are the main antagonists of Plautus' longest play.[60]

Conclusion: Text and Improvisation

As far as we can tell, on the Roman comic stage the body and facial expression of an actor – verbalised or inferred from the text – could function either to underline words or to elicit a verbal response. However, the non-verbal can also rebut utterances, as does the static pose of the slave Palaestrio just after the old man prophesies that the slave would never rest before he could fulfill his goal (*Mil.* 214–15). Such instances make us especially aware of gestures on stage that, although not written into the actual texts, will have been employed in comic routines. While reading the plays, one can imagine

---

[58] Zwierlein (1991) 236–7. [59] Hammond, Mack, Moskalew (1963) 95.
[60] Hanson (1965) 64–5.

that non-verbal means were used to undermine serious passages via amusing contrast, as may have happened, for instance, in Alcmena's aria in *Amphitruo* (633–53) or the conversation between the wives in *Stichus* (1–57). On these occasions gestures might even pair up with other comic devices – such as self-glorification and verbal redundancy as well as dissonant metre to produce thematic incongruence and comic effects that bear consequences for the appreciation of the structure of the whole play.[61]

Considering the pervasiveness of *gestus* – which is just one of many non-verbal modes involved in a theatrical production – acknowledges the importance of performance for the success of a comedy: a bad actor could spoil a good play (*Bacch.* 213–15), while a bad play could be saved by a good one (*Hec.* 16–23).[62] We cannot factor in how far a performance (such as that of the knockabout scene in *Adelphoe*) would depend on impromptu decisions by the members of the theatrical company (*grex*), or on their knowledge of a repertoire of conventional gestures of the *fabula palliata*.[63] But, from the many plays staged within the plays in metatheatrical moments, it is tempting to suppose that actual productions of Roman comedy would also count on the actors' improvisation skills.

For the majority of modern readers, the gap between what is read and what could be seen in Roman comic texts has been partially filled by scholars. As we saw in some of the scenes analysed, editors and translators, having taken on the task of 'transmitting' as far as possible the meaning of the text they publish, often try to visualise its staging and to put themselves in the place of a stage director.[64] Many insights also come from studying the remaining evidence for the material conditions of the performance: Beacham (1995) constructs a hypothetical full-scale replica of the Roman stage; and frequently scholars are engaged in productions of Roman comedy. Nevertheless our perception of Plautus' and Terence's comedies is influenced by non-contemporary evidence of their plays. This includes our acquaintance (performative or literary) with modern theatre and its theory and with other forms of entertainment such as Shakespearean drama, silent movies, Westerns, soap operas, and stand-up comedians. Acknowledging our aesthetic and epistemological distance from the original context of ancient spectacle means recognising that Roman comic technique is both resistant and open to new forms of reading, imagining, and performing.

---

[61] Cardoso (2001). [62] Barsby (1986) 115–16.
[63] Panayotakis (2005) 180 calls the rigidity of such conventions and repertoire into question; see also Marshall (2006) 168.
[64] Christenson (2000) 19.

Further Reading

A comprehensive appreciation of non-verbal language in Roman comedy is still a *desideratum*. For a helpful, if brief, account of the non-verbal in Roman comic texts, see Panayotakis (2005), who succinctly touches on many of the following items. For the study of the interplay between verbal and non-verbal in Roman comedy and its imitation of improvisation, see the influential approach of Slater (1985) (reprinted with additions in 2000), which is mostly focused on metatheatre (see the further reading section of Christenson in this volume).

For links between performative features of Roman comedy and the italic oral theatrical tradition, see Lèfevre, Stärk, Vogt-Spira (1991); Vogt-Spira (1993); Benz, Stärk, Vogt-Spira (1995) (with contributions in English), and Panayotakis in this volume. On eavesdropping and other stage conventions, see Bain (1977, on Roman comedy, see esp. ch. 10); on the door-knocking routine in Roman comedy and its antecedents, see Brown (1995) and (2000) and Traill (2001).

On Roman actors' gestures (compared to orators' gestures), see Graf (1992); Dutsch (2002); Fantham (2002); Fögen (2009). For lucid discussions of Plautus' and Terence's verbal humour, see respectively Fontaine (2010) and Vincent (2013).

8

DAVID CHRISTENSON

Metatheatre

In recent decades, the notion of metatheatre has gained considerable purchase in studies of Roman comedy, especial those of Plautus.[1] A critical
terminology to describe the tendency of Plautine comedy to broadcast its
status as *theatre-in-the-process-of-being-performed* seems warranted, as
characters in Plautus often refer to the stock roles they are playing (e.g.
Amph. 265–9, *As.* 174–5, *Ps.* 1081–3), comment on the audiences' reception
of the play (e.g. *Cas.* 1005–6, *Merc.* 160, *Poen.* 1224), refer to details of
theatrical production (e.g. *Curc.* 462–6, *Persa* 159–60, *Poen.* 597), and the
like. The term metatheatre[2] has evolved in theatrical studies to generally
describe the moves playwrights make to draw attention to their play's status
as a theatrical construct, regardless of whatever other motives might accom-
pany these moves (e.g. promoting audience participation in the spectacle,
reminding an audience that a play represents its own social experience, etc.).
Within the field of Classics of late, however, metatheatre has met with some
resistance on the grounds that it is over-used and too inclusive to be
meaningful;[3] that it has morphed into a fixed concept that fails to 'do justice
to the fluidity and liminality which are inherent in the theatrical experience';[4]
or even that 'metatheatre' is a superfluous tag in that all theatre is to some
extent self-reflexive and audiences are always aware that they are watching
a play.

   While the scepticism of classicists regarding the uncritical adoption of
new approaches and vocabularies is laudable, in the present case there
seems to be no advantage in jettisoning the term metatheatre altogether.
In response to this current scrutiny, however, I will apply the terms
'metatheatre' and 'metatheatrical' here in a limited sense (and scope) to
explicate an important aspect of early Roman comedy: Plautus' and
Terence's playful reflections on the genre of New Comedy, especially its

---

[1] E.g. Slater (1985) and Moore (1998b).   [2] Coined by Abel (1963).
[3] Thus Rosenmeyer (2002).   [4] Thumiger (2009) 53.

plots, characters, and conventions. This is not to imply the existence of a universal, theatrical sub-genre of metatheatre, into which plays of Plautus and Terence can indiscriminately be lumped together with, for instance, those of Brecht and Artaud. Instead, the aim of this chapter is to illuminate some of the more provocative effects that Roman comedy exerted on its original audiences in its particular historical and cultural setting(s). The degree to which each playwright strives for metatheatrical effect is significant, as is the specific nature of the metatheatrical strategies employed. These strategies and effects further allow us to identify differences between Plautus' and Terence's relationships with their audiences. Within the bodies of plays (formal prologues and epilogues are not treated here), Plautine characters tend to reveal their theatrical underpinnings more frequently and explicitly than those of Terence, while Terence's use of metatheatre is usually more subtle. I focus here on distinct examples of sustained metatheatre in three plays: Plautus' *Pseudolus* and *Rudens*, and Terence's *Eunuchus*.

Pseudolus

Pseudolus, which falls late in Plautus' career (191 BC) and so also when the *palliata* was well-established in Rome, is Plautus' most aggressively metatheatrical play. Its plot is a stereotypical one in New Comedy: a young lover (Calidorus) can no longer afford his liaison with a *meretrix* (Phoenicium), whose pimp (Ballio) has initiated the sale of her to a soldier. In the opening scene, Calidorus' family's crafty slave Pseudolus promises his maudlin younger master that he will procure Phoenicium. In a mock proclamation (*Ps.* 125–8), Pseudolus boldly exhorts the entire populace (the spectators obviously included) and all who know him personally (the play's other characters obviously included) to be wary of his forthcoming schemes. After two scenes featuring the super-pimp Ballio, Pseudolus employs the language of military siege (*Ps.* 384), a standard appropriation of clever slaves, to confidently assure Calidorus of Ballio's defeat. He sends Calidorus off to secure the services of someone as stereotypically clever as himself (*homine astuto, docto, cauto et callido*, *Ps.* 385), but in a familiar metatheatrical move refuses to divulge further details of his plot because 'plays are long enough as it is' (*Ps.* 388).

A seasoned *palliata* audience at this point assumes that Pseudolus has a foolproof plan and eagerly awaits its deft execution. But Pseudolus' bluster is entirely empty: he has merely been playing the role of *seruus callidus*. Left alone on stage, Pseudolus delivers the first in a series of monologues in which he confides to the audience that he is clueless:

> Where to start weaving your web of deceit,
> Or how to bring that design to completion?
> But I'll have to be just like a poet:
> He takes up his tablet and though he searches for
> What doesn't exist at all, he still finds it, and
> Makes complete fiction seem like the truth.
> That's it! I'll become a poet and find
> The twenty *minae* which are nowhere!   (*Ps.* 399–405)[5]

Pseudolus' confessed absence of a plan here immediately raises the prospect of his ability (as an actor) to improvise as well as to follow a premeditated script. But his comparison of himself to a *poeta* (*Ps.* 401, 404) – both a generic word for 'poet' and 'playwright'[6] in particular – also points to a larger theatrical role. Pseudolus overstates his predicament here in that an abundance of New Comedy plots are available to him, as he wishes to stress the need for novelty and freshness, both for actors and playwrights. Pseudolus' emphasis on innovation perhaps eliminates the possibility of his obtaining the funds for Phoenicium through a usual method in Roman comedy such as a scheme to dupe the *paterfamilias*. Immediately following Pseudolus' monologue here, Calidorus' father Simo enters and informs his friend Callipho that he is on the lookout for his son's schemes (*Ps.* 418–22). Pseudolus confronts the old men and confidently assures Simo that he will extract cash from him (*Ps.* 508–9), though, as Simo's money will not be needed to purchase Phoenicium, this exchange will take the form of a wager on whether or not the slave will cheat Ballio out of her. The affable old Callipho speaks for the audience when he declares to Pseudolus: 'It's a pleasure to be a spectator at your games' (*Ps.* 552; *ludos* indicates both a Roman comic festival and plays performed at it).

After the old men depart, Pseudolus delivers a monologue in which he again promises to deliver a plot with novelty:

> I have a sneaking suspicion that you all suspect
> I've only promised to do these daring deeds
> In order to entertain you during this play,
> And there's little chance I'll do what I promised.
> I'll keep my word. To the best of my knowledge,
> I don't know exactly how I'll do it, but I do know
> That I will. Now, it's the duty of every actor to be original

---

[5] All translations of *Pseudolus* are from Christenson (2008).

[6] That Pseudolus is thinking of comic playwrights in particular is supported by a fragment (probably from a prologue) of a Middle Comedy by Antiphanes (KA 189) in which the speaker asserts that whereas tragic poets inherit developed myths, comic poets must invent all plot details themselves.

> Enough to bring something original on stage:
> If he can't, let him step aside for someone who can.
> I'd like to slip inside for a while,
> To privately muster my army of tricks.
> I'll be right back after just a short delay.   (*Ps.* 562–73a)

A short musical interlude follows, and Pseudolus bursts upon the stage to announce that he at last has successfully mustered his army of tricks. His announcement comes with the typical fanfare of the self-congratulatory Plautine slave: (1) he scurrilously vaunts his 'distinguished' ancestry (*maiorum meum fretus uirtute, Ps.* 581; cf. 589–91); (2) he revels in his capacity for chicanery (*mea industria et malitia fraudulenta, Ps.* 582); and (3) he bombastically appropriates the grandiose language of military siege and triumph (*Ps.* 583–8).[7] If he in fact had a plan – and so all this bluster was not merely a kind of self-parody of the bravado of the *seruus callidus* – the audience never learns of it. *Opportunitas* (*Ps.* 669), for Pseudolus the personified goddess of dumb luck and improvisation, at this point intervenes, as the soldier's man Harpax fortuitously arrives. Pseudolus exclaims:

> This new and sudden situation calls for a new and sudden solution.
> First order of business: all my previous plans just flew out the window!
> Now I'll launch a full-scale assault against this military messenger.
>   (*Ps.* 601–3)

As if entirely improvising, Pseudolus now launches a new plan by pretending that he is Ballio's slave, and manages to obtain the all-important letter from the soldier, complete with the soldier's personal seal, that ultimately will allow him to secure Phoenicium for Calidorus.

The scheme thus quickly takes the form of a play-within-the-play or *mise-en-abyme*. Pseudolus informs Calidorus of this latest development, but again refuses to provide him with the details for the sake of the potentially bored audience: 'Need I remind you this play is being performed for the spectators? / They saw exactly what happened. I'll bring *you* up to speed later' (*Ps.* 720–1). At last apparently in possession of a workable plot, Pseudolus confidently sets about directing it to completion.

He instructs Calidorus' friend Charinus to hire an actor to play Harpax:

> Someone unscrupulous,
> Clever, devious and smart, a quick study
> Who has the natural talent to finish what he's started. (*Ps.* 724–6)

---

[7] For the slave as *triumphator*, see Fraenkel (2007) 159–72.

The stock epithets here – *malum, / callidum, doctum* – describe an actor cut from the same cloth as Pseudolus himself, who adds that he prefers a slave to a free man (*Ps.* 728). Pseudolus' casting call operates on two metatheatrical levels. First, he is seeking a mirror image of himself, namely the *seruus callidus* familiar from various Plautine comedies, to impersonate Harpax. And his specific request for a slave reflects the fact that the Roman acting troupe was (mostly) comprised of slaves. Pseudolus adds that he needs someone capable of improvising on the spot (*Ps.* 745), that he will costume this person in appropriate military garb (*Ps.* 734–5, 751–2), and, finally, personally train him for his role (764–6). Pseudolus next appears admiring the craft of his new charge Simia as he prepares to put the 'Monkeyman'[8] through his final paces (*Ps.* 905–55). Simia is indeed a quick study, already in character (*Ps.* 916–19), and, in pledging to steal Harpax's identity if necessary, he is as brash as any *seruus callidus*:

> I hope to god that the soldier's man,
> Shows up exactly at the same time I do.
> You can be damn sure I'll be a better Harpax than he is! So stay calm!
> I'll work all the kinks out of this plan for you nicely.
> My tricks and lies will so terrify our visiting soldier
> That he himself will deny that he is who he is,
> And solemnly swear that I'm him!   (*Ps.* 924–30)

Simia subsequently plays the part of Harpax with seamless perfection, even when he is forced to improvise because he doesn't know the soldier's name (*Ps.* 983–91), and Ballio leads him into his house to complete the transaction. In a monologue intervening before Simia's return with Phoenicium, Pseudolus expresses apprehension that he may have hired a better trickster than himself:

> Never, ever have I seen a worse human being,
> A more deviously wicked fellow than this Simia!
> He's so awfully damn good he scares me!
> What if, just when things are going well,
> He turns his wily weapons against me
> As soon as he gets the chance?   (*Ps.* 1017–22)

In positing the existence of a theatrical figure more competent than himself and so capable of launching another play-within-the-play (i.e. against him-

---

[8] For the broader associations of monkeys with play-making and creative adaptation in Plautus, see Connors (2004).

self), Pseudolus foregrounds one of the essential features of Plautine comedy: the seemingly endless expandability of duplicity in a duplicitous world, i.e. precisely as is implied in Gide's infinitely framed *mise-en-abyme*. The deception of Ballio proceeds without a hitch, and Phoenicium is swiftly recovered from the pimp.

Because *Pseudolus* appears to be a play about virtually nothing, and instead a play about the *creation* of a Plautine comedy, some critics have gone so far as to identify the character of Pseudolus with Plautus himself.[9] Whether or not one accepts this identification, *Pseudolus*, in its uncanny ability to lay bare convention, improvise, and complexly frame its theatricalised world, deserves its traditional place among Plautus' most delightful and playful comedies.

Rudens

Rudens is a comedy that engages in byplay with tragedy from the start. Recent scholarship on Greek comedy has adopted the musical term 'contrafact' in preference to 'paratragedy' to describe this phenomenon, as the former 'suggests the programmatic refashioning of a model into a new composition and offers the dramatic critic a refreshing alternative to the more limited "parody" with its ineluctable connotations of mockery and distortion in the service of humor'.[10] The opening scene of *Rudens* in fact leads us to suppose that the primary tragic model that is being subjected to 'contrafaction' by Plautus, or Diphilus, or both playwrights[11] is Euripides' lost *Alkmene* or a Roman adaptation of that play.[12] There the gruff country slave Sceparnio, while assessing the damage from the previous night's storm to his master's cottage, initiates the interplay between comedy and tragedy with an incongruously learned metaphor:

> The wind unroofed the cottage! Did I say 'wind'?
> Hardly a wind, but it must have been an *Alkmene* of Euripides
> That blew every last tile off the roof
> And created all new light and windows for us!   (*Ru.* 85–8)[13]

[9] Wright (1975); Hallett (1993); Hunter (2006) 81–3; more cautiously, Slater (1985) 143–6.
[10] Dobrov (2001) 16.
[11] Without Diphilus' play, it is impossible to sort out what is or is not Plautine in this regard. Plautus presumably did not leave in allusions to Greek tragedy (or Roman adaptations of it) that at least part of his audience would not catch. Cf. Sharrock (2009) 205, and, for a new appreciation of the bilingualism and biculturalism of Plautus' audience, Fontaine (2010).
[12] Skutsch (1968) 177–81 argues that the opening line of *Rudens* alludes to Ennius' *Alcumena*.
[13] All translations of *Rudens* are from Christenson (2010).

Unfortunately, the scant remains of Euripides' play, as supplemented by vase evidence, allow for only this broad outline: Alkmene is pursued by her husband Amphitryon, who mistakenly believes that she has committed adultery, and seeks sanctuary at an altar. There Amphitryon builds a pyre around her and is about to ignite it when a rainstorm is sent to prevent the conflagration. Zeus appears as *deus ex machina* and explains how he has had sex with Alkmene in the guise of Amphitryon, and the couple is reconciled.[14] This sketchy plot of *Alkmene* nonetheless suggests some tantalising connections with *Rudens*. In Plautus' play a pimp (Labrax) absconds with Palaestra, whom he had promised to sell to a young Athenian smitten with her (Plesidippus), and attempts to take her to Sicily where he hopes to fetch a higher price for her. A powerful rainstorm frustrates Labrax's plan, and Palaestra, along with her fellow slave Ampelisca, are saved when they wash up on the North African shore near the cottage of Daemones. Palaestra is a uniquely serious character in Plautine comedy, who in powerful song reflects on her unjust fate and even wishes for death (*Ru.* 185–219, 664–76).[15] Twice in the play, Palaestra (with Ampelisca) seeks refuge at an altar in the seashore temple of Venus (*Ru.* 559–61, 707). On the latter occasion, Labrax, angry at the apparent loss of his property, pledges to '[bring] in Vulcan' (*Ru.* 761) and 'burn these two women alive at the altar' (*Ru.* 768).[16] The rainstorm and concomitant shipwreck ultimately lead to Palaestra's rescue from a life of prostitution, as well as to her reunion with her parents (i.e. Daemones and his wife) and marriage with Plesidippus. The fateful storm, far from being a random occurrence, has been deliberately caused by Arcturus to punish the pimp (*Ru.* 67–9); in the prologue, the star represents himself as Jupiter's agent in meting out just deserts to human beings (*Ru.* 1–30).

While these broad motifs shared by *Rudens* and *Alkmene* probably do not allow us to confidently assume that Euripides' play (or Ennius' *Alcumena*) is a specifically targeted tragic text/contrafact, they go far to demonstrate how tragic byplay is at the root of what makes *Rudens* such an unusual comedy. The same is true of the plot, which is bifurcated in that it combines distinct elements, some typical of New Comedy, others of serious drama. On the comic side, there is a typical plot built around a lovesick young man, his beloved, and a pimp who stands in the way of their relationship. Plesidippus

---

[14] See further Christenson (2000) 48–9.
[15] Ampelisca serves as a kind of double to Palaestra in this regard (*Ru.* 220–8), though her personal circumstances are less compellingly developed.
[16] Marx (1928) 155 compares, in addition to the reconstructed *Alkmene* scene, Eur. *HF.* 243 and *And.* 257.

is aided by his trusty subaltern Trachalio, whose actions *vis-à-vis* the trunk fished out of the sea by Gripus directly lead to the discovery of Palaestra's true identity (*Ru.* 1052–190). Much of the usual comic fare is provided by the presence of Daemones' two rustic slaves, Sceparnio and Gripus (esp. *Ru.* 414–57, 906–1044). But within this comic construct lies the matter of Daemones' exile. Daemones is an Athenian who has been banished to the wilds of the North African coast for an unstated, but unjust cause. According to Arcturus, Daemones 'tripped himself up while trying to help others' (*Ru.* 37), and suffered the loss of both his daughter and his fortune as a result. The possibility for a further tragic error is hinted at in the play, when Daemones, still unaware that Palaestra is his daughter, betrays erotic feelings for her and Ampelisca (*Ru.* 892–6, 1045–8). Daemones reports having had a dream about a monkey in pursuit of swallows (*Ru.* 593–62) that turns out to portend Labrax's attempt to retrieve Palaestra and Ampelisca. He begins the dream narrative by likening dreams to plays sent to us by the gods (thus subtly suggesting a *mise-en-abyme* effect): *miris modis di ludos faciunt hominibus* (*Ru.* 593). In the dream, Daemones informs the monkey that 'swallows are descended from Philomela and Procne' (*Ru.* 604) – and so are his Athenian compatriots – and thereby calls to mind one of tragedy's most gruesome myths. And finally, there is the mysterious 'chorus' of fishermen, who appear briefly (*Ru.* 290–324) to complain of their hard fate as scavengers of the seashore and destitution that excludes them from elite urban culture (*Ru.* 296).

This tension between comic and serious elements in *Rudens* is increased through frequent appropriations of tragic language at surprising moments. When Sceparnio first spots Palaestra and Ampelisca struggling to reach the shore, he apostrophises Palaemon (*Ru.* 160), a relatively obscure figure of Greek myth originally named Melicertes who is renamed Palaemon after his rescue at sea by a dolphin and rebirth as a hero of the Isthmian Games.[17] Venus' pious and dignified priestess Ptolemocratia, upon first meeting the shipwrecked and suppliant girls, assumes that they have arrived by ship (in song): *equo ligneo per uias caerulas*, ('Over greenish-blue paths on a wooden steed', *Ru.* 268). Similarly, when Trachalio first spots Ampelisca emerging from the temple in conversation with the priestess inside, he asks *cuia ad aures / uox mihi aduoluit* ('Whose voice / hath winged its way to my ears', *Ru.* 332–3).[18] Even the angry exchange between the loathsome pimp and his friend Charmides (*Ru.* 485–558) after they wash up on the North African shore is full of

---

[17] For the recurrent theme of (re)birth via water in *Rudens*, see Leach (1974) and Christenson (2010) 16–17.
[18] See Marx (1928) 113 for parallels, both tragic and comic.

tragic resonances. As the two mutually assign moral blame for the ship-wreck to each other, Charmides likens his fateful decision to accept Labrax's hospitality to the tragically cannibalistic meals served up to Thyestes and Tereus (*Ru.* 509). In the lofty, alliterative style of early Roman tragedy, Charmides answers Labrax's apostrophe to Palaestra and Ampelisca thus: *piscibus in alto, credo, praebent pabulum* ('I believe they're providing piscine provisions in the deep', *Ru.* 513). Shortly there-after, the soaking wet Labrax apostrophises the nearby bulrush: O *scirpe, scripe,*[19] *laudo fortunas tuas, / qui semper seruas gloriam aritudinis* ('Oh sedge-grass, oh sedge-grass, how glorious is your fate, / To forever sustain the splendor of your aridity', *Ru.* 523-4). As his teeth continue to clatter, Labrax jokes that he could find employment at a festival as Manducus (*Ru.* 535) or 'Chomper-Man', thereby referring to Atellan farce and a 'low' form of native Italian comedy at the opposite end of the dramatic spectrum from Greek tragedy. Gripus describes his failed fishing expedition as one *sine squamoso pecu* ('devoid of the scaly flock', *Ru.* 942). Many more examples can be adduced to demonstrate the pointed frequency of heightened language and thought throughout *Rudens*.[20]

To what end can a Plautine comedy such as *Rudens* absorb serious themes, highly poetic language, and grand moral reflections (especially those on the justice of the universe) that more properly belong to tragedy? Can comedy be didactic? Near the end of the play, the ever-scrupulous Daemones rejects Gripus' suggestion that his master keep the trunk he has fished out of the sea:

> O Gripus, Gripus![21] The human condition is fraught
> With so many traps to fool and out-fox us,
> And more often than not these traps are baited.
> If we greedily grasp at that bait,
> We're grabbed, trapped, and ensnared by our very own greed.
> But if a person's careful and cautious, cagey and wary,
> He harvests long-lasting gain from what he's honestly obtained.
> To my way of thinking, lucre such as yours is never lucrative:
> It leaves a marriage with a larger dowry than it brought.
> You really think I'd knowingly accept and conceal plunder taken from another?
> That's absolutely not the way of this Daemones! Masters who are smart are wise to take the utmost caution
> Against becoming willful accomplices to the crimes of their slaves.
> When I've acted in a play, I don't care about my own profit.   (*Ru.* 1235-48)

---

[19] The anadiplosis here is a mannerism of Euripides: Mastronarde (2002) 184.

[20] E.g., the god Neptune figures prominently throughout the play, in both metonymy and metaphor: examples in Sharrock (2009) 217-18.

[21] For the anadiplosis here, see n. 19 above.

The actor playing Daemones thus closes his speech with a startling claim about his own moral probity: 'Daemones' speech is among the most ardently moralistic in Plautus. It is also one of the most conspicuously metatheatrical.'[22] In reply, the cynical Gripus, as if speaking on behalf of comedy in general, voices his doubt about the didacticism of comic actors having any lasting effect on audiences:

> I've seen comic actors speak words of wisdom like that
> And win all sorts of applause for
> Enlightening the folks in the crowd.
> But when the show was over and people made their way home,
> To judge by their behaviour anyway, they all forgot those lines. (*Ru.* 1249–53)

Rudens offers only an ambiguous response to the issue of comedy's moral import. Following a dialectical approach, Plautus leaves it to his audience to decide whether or not comedy can be morally enlightening or instructive. Daemones in the end is rewarded for his virtuousness and honesty, but Labrax is barely punished, and we hear nothing of the fate of other characters such as the pious Ptolemacratia and the chorus of fishermen. The persistent conflation of genres in *Rudens* contributes much to this closing sense of moral ambiguity, and is what sets this play distinctly apart from the rest of the Plautine corpus.

Eunuchus

Eunuchus takes its name from the two eunuchs – one real, one suppositious – featured in the play, which debuted at the festival of the Magna Mater (161 BC), a goddess known in Rome for her ecstatic cult and castrated priests. Phaedria, who as the play begins is engaged in competitive gift-exchange with the soldier Thraso, purchases an elderly eunuch named Dorus for Thais, a prostitute who maintains longstanding relationships with both men. Phaedria's brother Chaerea has become enamoured of Pamphila, an attractive sixteen-year-old girl who has just been delivered to Thais as a gift from Thraso. Chaerea and his slave Parmeno (*Eun.* 292–390) contemplate how the *adulescens* can gain access to Pamphila, and seize upon a plan for Chaerea to impersonate Dorus the eunuch. Their plot is articulated in markedly theatrical terms and hinges on the appropriation of the eunuch's 'flashy costume' (*uaria ueste, Eun.* 683; cf. 369–75). The precise manner in which this play-within-the-play is to be carried out contributes much to the delineation of Chaerea's character.

---

[22] Moore (1998b) 80. For a defence of the transmitted text in 1248, see Marx (1928) 213.

After agreeing to the plan, Chaerea tells Parmeno to take him offstage and 'dress him up' (*Eun. orna*, 377, a technical theatrical term) for his role. Parmeno briefly hesitates, but Chaerea then counters that their planned deception of Thais will constitute revenge against all prostitutes on behalf of their clients, a rivalry he frames in terms of comic stereotypes: *domum meritriciam* (*Eun.* 382) ~ *nos nostramque adulescentiam* (*Eun.* 383). Continuing in this theatricalising vein, Chaerea quips: *an potius haec patri aequomst fieri ut a me ludatur dolis*, ('Or do you think the thing to do is pull off some scheme at my father's expense?', *Eun.* 386).[23] Chaerea of course refers to the stock New Comedy plot whereby an *adulescens* schemes to fleece his father (*senex*) to finance his affair with a prostitute (*meretrix*). Such a conventional scheme could redound against himself on moral grounds, Chaerea argues, whereas revenge against greedy prostitutes would only be viewed as just (*Eun.* 387). The audience knows that Chaerea's sweeping assault on Thais is misdirected here, as she has genuine affection for Phaedria (*Eun.* 197–206) and plans to act in Pamphila's (and her own) best interests by establishing the girl's freebirth (cf. *Eun.* 144–9). The plot to punish Thais as an example for all prostitutes is thus deeply flawed from the start.

Chaerea's zeal to assume the role of Dorus the eunuch would have had special resonance with Terence's audience. The morally conservative Roman tradition branded actors with *infamia* for making spectacles of themselves on stage, and this censure took the form of public disgrace and forfeiture of certain citizen's rights.[24] To this way of thinking, Chaerea, who is an ephebe (an Athenian citizen-soldier in training), appears far too ready to swap his soldier's costume for the eunuch's flashy and effeminising outfit. Furthermore, a deceptive assault such as that planned by Parmeno and Chaerea against Thais and her household is almost always carried out by slaves in Roman comedy, not citizens of high status such as Chaerea.[25]

Chaerea initially believes that his *fabula* (so Phaedria dubs Chaerea's impersonation of Dorus, *Eun.* 689) is an enormous success, and the scene of self-congratulation in which he celebrates his rape of Pamphila is notorious (*Eun.* 549–614).[26] Parmeno similarly lauds himself for his direction of the plot against Thais, and even figures it as a kind of morality play:

> Parmeno is in for some much deserved glory!
> To downplay the fact that without any fuss or financial

---

[23] All translations of *Eunuchus* are from Christenson (2010).
[24] Edwards (1993) 98–136.   [25] Cf. Duckworth (1952) 160–75.
[26] For an assessment of an original audience's possible reactions to the rape, see Christenson (2013) 263–9.

Outlay I made possible what's usually
A very difficult and expensive affair
(seeing as the girl belongs to a greedy prostitute)—
There is this additional achievement I think I especially deserve a prize for:
I found a way for a young man to learn
All about the character and customs of prostitutes at an early age,
So that this newfound knowledge might inspire his eternal hatred of them!

                                                                    (*Eun.* 925–33)

Parmeno's brash assumption that he deserves a prize (*id uerost quod ego mi puto palmarium*, 930) recalls the *palma* of victory awarded in Roman dramatic contests,[27] and is characteristic of the bombast of the *seruus callidus* in Roman comedy, as it is best known from examples such as Pseudolus in Plautus. But Parmeno's exultation is far off the mark, given the real situation. Chaerea's father is about to enter and express his disapproval that his son knows anything at all about prostitutes at his young age (*Eun.* 986). Thais is no typically greedy comic prostitute, and, far from having learned to hate her, Chaerea has just exuberantly declared his affection for her (*Eun.* 882) and deemed her his 'patron' (*Eun.* 887) in aiding him in his desire to be with Pamphila again!

Parmeno gets his comeuppance for his mismanagement of the show in metatheatrical terms. Just before Parmeno's triumphant monologue, Thais' maid Pythias, still fuming over the brutal rape of Pamphila, had informed the audience of her intent to exact vengeance from him (*Eun.* 918–22). Pythias' revenge plot takes the well-known comic form of a false messenger's speech delivered by a distraught female who describes shocking (fictional) events taking place inside (*Eun.* 943–70; cf. *Cas.* 621–719). She convinces Parmeno that his master (*Eun.* 949) is being tortured inside for his sexual transgression against a free citizen of a distinguished Athenian family, though she pretends not to know that the young man is Chaerea, in order to force Parmeno to violate the clever slave's code by giving up his young master. He readily obliges her (*Eun.* 962) and, even worse, betrays his young master to Chaerea's father, who learns of the entire faux-eunuch plot from Parmeno (*Eun.* 982–96). Terence further emphasises Parmeno's utter failure as a *seruus callidus* by having him claim to Chaerea's father that he was *not* the instigator of the plot: *me impulsore haec non facit* (*Eun.* 988), an admission which flies in the face of the clever slave's characteristic pride in his roguery and defiance against his master's authority. Pythias returns from Thais' house to inform Parmeno that Chaerea has suffered the ultimate indignity of being seen in the eunuch's costume by his father (*Eun.*

---

[27] Barsby (1999) 258.

1015–16), and that Parmeno has been made a laughing stock inside, or as she expresses it in terms of comic stereotype: *at etiam primo callidum et disertum credidi hominem* ('I actually used to think you were a very clever fellow', *Eun.* 1011).

Eunuchus closes with one last metatheatrical flourish. After the parasite Gnatho strikes a compromise with Phaedria and Chaerea on Thraso's behalf that will allow the soldier to continue to enjoy Thais' company (*Eun.* 1083), he asks the brothers if he can join their clique: *unum etiam hoc uos oro, ut in uostrum gregem / recipiatis* (*Eun.* 1084–5). On one level, Gnatho is asking to be included in the group of characters centred around Thais' house. But the word *grex* is also the technical term for a troupe of actors. On a metatheatrical level then, Gnatho highlights the tendency of comedy to include – and critics have long found the inclusion of the defeated Thraso and his parasite Gnatho quite jarring here – all members of its cast in the final comic society projected at the play's end.[28] *Eunuchus* thus ends abruptly and arbitrarily, an effect which perhaps left at least some audience members wondering how this awkward entourage will coexist in their post-comic world, and about the prospects for the marriage forecast between Pamphila and her impetuous rapist. Terence's relatively subtle use of metatheatre in *Eunuchus* thus plays an important part in guiding the audience to assess the play's characters and situations.

The Appeal of Metatheatre in Plautus' and Terence's Rome

Ancient Roman society was deeply theatrical. Rome's religious cults featured officials in costume, who might chant, dance, or dramatically interpret the flight of birds as ritual required. Victorious generals celebrated important victories in an elaborate triumphal pageant featuring musicians, banners, sacrificial animals, spoils of war, and foreign captives, in which the commanders themselves came close to impersonating Jupiter in his four-horse chariot. Elite families staged elaborate and very public funeral processions, for which masked actors were hired to play the roles of distinguished ancestors. The social structure of daily life in Rome was extremely complex, both vertically and horizontally, and, for example, clients were obliged to perform a formal salute to their patrons each morning. All these activities enacted an often elaborate social script, firmly grounded in rules and conventions meant to establish and reaffirm social hierarchies and relationships of power.

---

[28] Cf. Aristotle, *Poetics* 1453a36.

A Roman who had seen any form of drama in the theatre would easily have grasped the meaning of the dictum 'all the world's a stage'.

Persistent metatheatre, as we have seen it employed by both Plautus and Terence, exposes the underpinnings of theatre – conventions, diction, tropes, genres, role-playing, plotting – for what they are: constructions that can be undermined, torn apart, reframed, or reoriented. This largely deconstructive approach to drama readily suggests to theatregoers a model for evaluating their own social lives. It is impossible to know, however, what form such 'self-analysis' or social critique might have taken for individual theatregoers in the two decades following the defeat of the Carthaginians in the Second Punic War in 201 BC, and the decade in which the final defeat of the Greeks took place at Pydna in 168 BC. For the Romans, this was a period of unprecedented military expansion and hegemony. It seems no accident then, that, in this age of fierce competition among the elite for the right to celebrate a triumph, so many Plautine and Terentian comedies feature a braggart soldier, for example, and that this stock figure is drawn to absurdly egotistical extremes. Chrysalus, one of Plautus' most flamboyant clever slaves, instructs the audience to stop wondering why he is not celebrating a triumph: 'I don't care for that – it's so common' (*Bacch.* 1072–3). This was also a socially dynamic period in Rome in which new wealth, foreigners, and alien customs were streaming into the city. Among the many hardships and upheavals of war was the possibility that conquerors might be conquered, kings might be taken as captives, and free persons might become slaves (*Captiui* focuses on this particular social paradox). Questions of identity figure prominently in the comedies of this period: three extant plays of Plautus are built on the ontological confusions that arise from the presence of doubles (*Amph.*, *Bacch.*, *Men.*); various other plays (e.g. *Ps.* and *Eun.*) feature characters whose seemingly unique identity is usurped by another character. It is mistaken, therefore, to assert that 'there is absolutely nothing unsettling or unsure for the audience's sense of reality in [Plautus'] comedies'.[29]

A clever slave such as Pseudolus, an outsider who shares his every metatheatrical move with the audience as he creatively triumphs over present circumstances while weaving his own social fabric, perhaps emblematises, if only fantastically, the possibilities for a more fluid society. *Eunuchus* employs metatheatre to elicit serious questions about morality, to provoke scepticism about status symbols (esp. costume as social integument), gender and sexuality, so that the play can interrogate what it means to be a 'real

---

[29] Anderson (1993) 139; critiqued by Batstone (2005) 29–30. For the confusion of sleep/ dreams with reality in *Amph.*, see Christenson (2000) 31.

man'. *Rudens* is more sharply focused on the constructs of language and literature (i.e. drama): can events bear different moral import, depending on whether they are viewed through the lens of comedy or tragedy? To what extent are comedy and tragedy not only distinct performative idioms but also distinct ways of processing human experience? It is not far-fetched to presume that such questions interested at least some second-century Roman theatregoers. Much more can be said about the effects of metatheatre in early Roman comedy and within the broader context of contemporary society, and it is my hope that discussion is still only starting.

Further Reading

The term 'metatheatre' was coined by Abel (1963) to describe what he saw as a new mode of drama (beginning in the Renaissance) that was centred on the concepts 'all the world's a stage' and 'life is a dream'. Barchiesi (1970) first applied Abel's notion of metatheatre to Plautine comedy. Slater's (1985) seminal study of Plautine performance elucidates metatheatrical strategies employed in several plays, but Slater is generally reluctant to explore connections between Plautus' use of metatheatre and Roman society (cf. Slater 1990). Moore (1998b) includes an excellent chapter entitled 'Metatheater and Morality' (67–90). Sharrock (2009) is keenly sensitive to the metatheatrical features of Roman comedy. See also Gowers (1993) 50–108 (*passim*). Other brief treatments of metatheatrical topics in Plautus include Muecke (1986) and Hardy (2005). Rosenmeyer (2000) and Thumiger (2009), though highly critical of the application of metatheatre to ancient drama, provide insights into the important issues (and disputes) associated with the concept. Batstone (2005) defends the utility of metatheatre for Plautine studies and advances the case for an ancient Roman audience's ability to perceive relationships between theatre and their own lives. Frangoulidis (1994), Knorr (2007), and Moodie (2009) treat aspects of Terence's use of metatheatre. Among the many works on metatheatre outside the field of Roman comedy, Hornby (1986), Maquerlot (1992), Nellhaus (2000), and Dobrov (2001) are particularly insightful.

9

EVANGELOS KARAKASIS

The Language of Roman Comedy

Introduction

Plautus (*c.* 254–184 BC) and Terence (*c.* 195–159 BC) make use of a Latin idiom older than the standardised Roman *sermo* of the classical period, mainly evidenced by the prose production (chiefly of Cicero and Caesar) of classical Latin (CL hereafter, *c.* 87 BC–AD 17). Therefore, their language differs from CL in terms of phonology, morphology, syntax, and lexicon. The aim of this chapter is to give a concise account of the major differences between the diction of the Roman dramatists and CL speech and secondly to assess the way Terentian language differs from Plautine speech, thus foreshadowing trends and directions of CL diction. The linguistic-stylistic unity of Roman comedy, from which Terence significantly distances himself, and the instances where Terentian diction appropriates Plautine linguistic features and techniques also form part of the analysis to follow. I will also address issues concerning the way Plautus and Terence make use of language as a means of characterisation, as well as the manner in which Plautine and Terentian comic diction interact with other literary *genera*, and the elevated diction of both literature and the official bureaucracy of the period.[1]

Archaisms – Plautus and Terence

Plautus and Terence make use of several archaic linguistic features, which may either be attributed to the historical evolution of Latin or may be viewed as part of their archaic stylistic register;[2] in other words, these features are felt to be archaic by the Roman playwrights themselves and thus appear to be

---

[1] Unless otherwise stated the following editions are followed. For Plautus and Terence, the Oxford Classical Texts by Lindsay (1905–6) and Kauer and Lindsay (1926, repr. 1958 and 1961); for Caecilius and Naevius (comic fragments), Warmington (1935–6); for Turpilius, Rychlewska (1971); for Titinius, Guardì (1985); for Afranius, Novius, and Pomponius, Ribbeck (1898).

[2] Cf. Smith (1890); Neue and Wagener (1892–5); Lindsay (1907); Bennett (1910–14); Allardice (1929); Harsh (1940); Bléry (1965); Hofmann and Szantyr (1965); Ernout and Thomas (1972); Barsby (1999); Rosén (1999); Karakasis (2005) 44–61; de Melo (2007).

used for specific stylistic effects. These Early Latin (EL hereafter) features are 'conscious archaisms' and are chiefly found in specific metrical positions, namely at the caesura and at the end of the line, as, e.g., in the case of the termination *-ier* for medio-passive infinitives in place of the CL *-i*, e.g. *amari* = *amarier*, archaic subjunctives (*siem, fuam*), and optatives, perfect endings in *-ēre*.

In particular, within the Plautine and the Terentian comic corpus one comes across the following most common, archaic linguistic phenomena, although in many instances Terence is more reserved than his predecessor in their use (e.g. metaplastic verbal forms, *tetuli* perfects and archaic optatives), probably due to the historical evolution of Latin.[3]

1 Phonology

In several cases, in both Plautus and Terence, one encounters various archaic spellings, common in EL: namely, the terminations *-os* and *-om* after *u*, with either vowel or consonant value, instead of the common *-us* and *-um* endings, cf. *saluom*, Plaut. *Aul.* 677, *seruos*, Ter. *Ph.* 295; superlative forms in *-umus* for *-imus*, cf. *plurumus*, Plaut. *Bacch.* 505, Ter. *Eun.* 2; root vowel *u* for *i*, cf. *existumat*, Plaut. *As.* 149, *existumavit*, Ter. *Eun.* 5; root vowel *o* instead of *e*, cf. *uortere* for *uertere*, Ter. *Eun.* 390; see also Plaut. *Men.* 134; *-ont* ending instead of *-unt* in case *u/v* precedes the vowel of the termination, cf. *instruontur* for *instruuntur*, Plaut. *Men.* 107, *uiuont* instead of *uiuunt*, Ter. *Ph.* 853; gerunds and gerundives in *-und-* instead of *-end-*, cf. *faciundum*, Plaut. *Amph.* 891, *faciundo*, Plaut. *Bacch.* 402, *recipiundum*, Ter. *Eun.* 1072; *c* is spelt as *qu*, thus *quor* vs. *cur*, *quoius* vs. *cuius*, *quoi* vs. *cui*, *quom* vs. *cum*, cf. Plaut. *Amph.* 581, *Men.* 221, 929, *Amph.* 441, Ter. *Eun.* 87, *And.* 336, *Eun.* 547, 77; adverbial spellings like *hoc* for *huc*, Plaut. *Amph.* 747, Ter. *Eun.* 394, *illoc* for *illuc*, Plaut. *Truc.* 647, Ter. *Eun.* 572. Plautine and Terentian manuscripts also offer archaic spellings of a range of individual lexemes, e.g. *nanctus* for *nactus*, cf. Plaut. *Bacch.* 217, Ter. *Eun.* 556.

2 Morphology/Derivation

2.1 Nouns, Adjectives, and Pronouns

2.1.1 Nominal endings: first-declension genitive singular in *-ai* instead of *-ae*, cf. *magnai rei publicai*, Plaut. *Mil.* 103, *hospitai*, Ter. *And.* 439; genitive plural in *-um* instead of *-orum* for second declension

---

[3] Cf. Palmer (1954) 89.

nouns/adjectives, apart from those denoting coins or measures (and a few standardised words like *deum* for *deorum*, where the substitution of the longer termination by its shorter version is regular in CL as well), cf. *nostrum . . . socium*, Plaut. *Men.* 134, *amicum, iniquom*, Ter. *Haut.* 24, 27; vocative ending in -*e* for syncopated nouns of the second declension, cf. *puere* at Plaut. *Bacch.* 577, Ter. *Eun.* 624; retention of older nominative forms, cf. *lacte* for *lac* at Plaut. *Men.* 1089, *alacris* for *alacer* at Ter. *Eun.* 304; locative singular in -*i* instead of -*e*, cf. *luci* at Plaut. *Amph.* 165, Ter. *Ad.* 841; ending -*uis* or -*i* for the genitive singular of fourth-declension nouns, cf. *gemiti*, Plaut. *Aul.* 722, *adventi*, Ter. *Ph.* 154, *anuis*, Ter. *Haut.* 287.

2.1.2 Archaic pronominal forms: e.g. first-declension forms for CL pronoun adjectives in -*ius*, -*i*, like *solus*, cf. *solae* as a feminine dative at Plaut. *Mil.* 1019, Ter. *Eun.* 1004, *alterae*, Ter. *Ph.* 928; EL *nostro(a)rum* for *nostrum*, cf. Plaut. *Amph.* fr. xix, Ter. *Eun.* 678, and *uostro(a)rum* in lieu of the CL *vestrum*, cf. Plaut. *Men.* 1085, Ter. *Hec.* 216; nominative singular of the masculine gender *ipsus* vs. CL *ipse*, Plaut. *Amph.* 415, Ter. *Ph.* 215; an old ablative form of the relative/interrogative *qui* in place of singular CL forms, Plaut. *Men.* 337, Ter. *Eun.* 273, 488; use of pronominal affixes like -*pte*, -*met*, -*te* (*mepte, egomet, tute*) with greater frequency than in CL, Plaut. *Amph.* 416, Ter. *Eun.* 252; addition of the affix *ce/c* at the end of several demonstrative pronouns, cf. *hisce* either for the nominative *hi*, Plaut. *Men.* 958, Ter. *Eun.* 249, or instead of *his*, Plaut. *Men.* 1012, Ter. *Ph.* 442, *istic* for *iste*, Plaut. *Men.* 146, Ter. *Eun.* 953, *illic* for *ille*, Plaut. *Men.* 98, Ter. *Eun.* 12. However, Terence seems to favour the normal CL equivalents of the following pronoun forms: *ille* vs. *illic, illa* vs. *illaec, illud* vs. *illuc, illo* vs. *illoc, iste* vs. *istic, istum* vs. *istunc, istam* vs. *istanc*.[4]

2.1.3 *Ecce* is a further common EL form, probably derived from *ed/id* and the demonstrative affix -*ce*, cf. Plaut. *Men.* 784, Ter. *Eun.* 297; see also *eccum*, from *ecce* + *eum/hum* (*hunc*), Plaut. *Men.* 109, Ter. *Haut.* 241; *eccam*, from *ecce* + *eam/ham* (*hanc*), Plaut. *Men.* 565, Ter. *Hec.* 854; *eccos* for *ecce* + *eos*, Plaut. *Men.* 219, Ter. *Haut.* 256.

2.2 Verbal Forms

2.2.1 Sigmatic forms: sigmatic futures and subjunctives, apart from the *faxo/faxim* forms which are common in all periods of Latin, cf.

---

[4] Cf. Barsby (1999) 26–7 and n. 88.

capso, Plaut. *Bacch.* 712, *locassim*, *Aul.* 228, *appellassis*, Ter. *Ph.* 742.

2.2.2 EL subjunctive and optative formations: archaic subjunctive forms (not present stem subjunctive ending in *-ās*, cf. *creduas*, Plaut. *Trin.* 606, Ter. *Ph.* 993, subjunctive of *esse* in *siem, fuam, forem*, cf. Plaut. *Amph.* 57, *Bacch.* 156, *Amph.* 21, Ter. *Hec.* 637, 610, 601), traces of old subjunctive-optative forms in *-im*, like *duim* or *perduim*, Plaut. *Poen.* 884, Ter. *Haut.* 811.

2.2.3 EL imperatives: second singular active present imperatives of *facere, dicere, ducere* without deletion of the final *-e*, Plaut. *Cas.* 353, *Ep.* 399, *Aul.* 787, Ter. *And.* 680; the imperative *cedo* ('give it', 'bring it', plural *cette*), cf. Plaut. *Men.* 197, Ter. *Eun.* 162.

2.2.4 EL change of conjugation: *-ibam, -ibo* (imperfect/future) forms for verbs of the fourth conjugation, cf. *scibat* for *sciebat*, Plaut. *Amph.* 22, Ter. *Ph.* 529, *scibo* for *sciam*, Plaut. *Men.* 386, Ter. *Eun.* 726; fourth-conjugation forms for verbs belonging to the third conjugation, cf. *(e)moriri* for *(e)mori*, Plaut. *As.* 121, Ter. *Eun.* 432.

2.2.5 Archaic endings: perfect indicative endings of the third plural in *-ēre* for *-ērunt* (*pertulere*, Plaut. *Amph.* 216, *dedere*, Ter. *Eun.* 544) and passive forms in *-re* for *-ris* for the second singular (*irascere*, Plaut. *Curc.* 186; *patiare*, Ter. *Eun.* 212); the latter is more common in Terence than in Plautus.[5]

2.2.6 Archaic reduplicated forms, cf. *tetuli*, Plaut. *Bacch.* 811, Ter. *And.* 808, EL present deponent/passive infinitive forms in *-ier*, cf. *uiderier*, Plaut. *Curc.* 260; *laudarier*, Ter. *Ad.* 535.

2.2.7 Various EL stems and verbal forms: present stems of *coepi*, cf. *coepere*, Plaut. *Persa* 121; *coeperet*, Ter. *Ad.* 397; a range of *potis* forms in place of *posse*, Ter. *Eun.* 101; as for *potesse* for *posse*, cf. Plaut. *Bacch.* 559, Ter. *Eun.* 666.

3 Syntax

3.1 Use of the oblique cases: extended use of the partitive genitive (with neuter forms), cf. Plaut. *Amph.* 580, Ter. *And.* 338; blurred case usage, cf. *careo* + accusative in place of the regular CL ablative, Plaut. *Curc.* 136, Ter. *Eun.* 223; various prepositional syntagms such as *clanculum* + accusative, Plaut. *Men.* 605, Ter. *Ad.* 52–3.

3.2 EL circumstantial complements: forms of the verb *ire* + supine in the function of a weak future, Plaut. *Cas.* 977, Ter. *Haut.* 655; dative

---

[5] Cf. Palmer (1954) 89; Barsby (1999) 122.

gerundive expressions denoting purpose, Plaut. *Persa* 428, Ter. *Ad.* 545, *Hec.* 821.

3.3 Subordinate clauses: loose use of the indicative (free use of temporal clauses introduced by *antequam* and *priusquam* and construed with the present indicative, for future actions, Plaut. *As.* 232, Ter. *Ph.* 719; *nunc cum* and *ut* causal clauses construed with the indicative, Plaut. *Mil.* 1045, *Ps.* 278, Ter. *Ad.* 737–8, *Haut.* 649; use of the indicative in indirect questions, Plaut. *Men.* 207, Ter. *Eun.* 100), EL individual subordinate clauses and complements (*ut* + perfect tense clauses in the sense of 'since', 'now that', Plaut. *Bacch.* 374, Ter. *Hec.* 751–2; *usus est* + *ut* subject clause as a complement, Plaut. *Mil.* 1132, Ter. *Haut.* 81).

3.4 EL infinitive and imperative constructions: *scilicet* + infinitive, Plaut. *Curc.* 263, Ter. *Haut.* 892; *ne* + present imperatives with the inhibitive function, Plaut. *Poen.* 1191a, Ter. *Haut.* 83–4.

4 *Lexicon*

Miscellaneous isolated examples of individual lexemes and composite phrases complement the overall EL linguistic picture of Plautine and Terentian diction, namely the use of: i) nouns and adjectives such as *famelicus, ganeum, partio* for *partus, satias* in place of *satietas*; ii) verbs like *occipere* in the sense of 'to begin' instead of *incipere* or *coepisse, percipere* in the sense of 'to take hold of', *praestolo/or, se capessere* for *abire*, the imperative form *inque*, cf. Plaut. *Ps.* 538, Ter. *Ph.* 919; iii) indeclinable forms such as *praeut* in the sense of 'in comparison to', *eccere*, a common EL interjection probably derived from *ecce* + *rem*, cf. Plaut. *Men.* 401, Ter. *Ph.* 319; and iv) various EL syntagms like the collocations *minime gentium, absente nobis*.

Several EL features of Plautus' language completely disappear from Terentian diction, e.g. the sigmatic infinitives, cf. *oppugnassere*, Plaut. *Amph.* 210, along with the archaic nominal forms, cf. the ablative *gnatabus* for *gnatis*, Plaut. *fr. inc.* 174, and pronominal forms, e.g. *tis* for *tui*, Plaut. *Ps.* 6.[6]

The Linguistic Unity of Roman Comedy – the Case of Terence

Archaisms; Plautus, the Comic Tradition vs. Terence

What is more, in Terentian diction, several archaic linguistic features, common in Plautus and in one or in several other authors of the *palliata*, the *togata*, and the *atellana*, are also eliminated. Terence in general seems to

---

[6] Cf. also Section 3a below.

anticipate later CL linguistic developments and thus, in several instances, distances himself, on a linguistic level as well, from the rest of the Roman comic tradition.[7] EL features avoided in the Terentian corpus include the following:

1 Morphology/Derivation

1.1 Pronouns: accusative/ablative of the personal pronouns in *-d, med, ted,* (Plaut. *As.* 632, Caec. *com.* 8), *eumpse* for *ipsum* (Plaut. *Most.* 346, Caec. *com.* 26), i.e., the accusative of the demonstrative *ipse* is thus considered, in terms of declension, as a compound word, unlike the practice of both Terence and CL; the EL form *ibus* for *eis* of the demonstrative *is* (Plaut. *Mil.* 74, Tit. *tog.* 48, Pomp. *atel.* 104).

1.2 Adjectives: EL/archaising derivative adjectives in *-arius* instead of *-aris* forms, cf. *singularius* for *singularis, uulgarius* for *uulgaris,* Turp. *com.* 29 and 206–7, Afr. *tog.* 263, Nov. *atel.* 99; Plautus often makes use of EL/archaising derivatives of this kind; see e.g. Plaut. *Most.* 361 (*praesentarius*), *Trin.* 895 (*manifestarius*), in opposition to Terence who restricts himself to CL and Post Classical (PC hereafter, AD 17 – sixth century AD) *-arius* formations (*temerarius, iocularius*).

1.3 Verbs: EL verbal by-forms such as *danunt* for *dant* (Plaut. *Capt.* 819, Caec. *com.* 170, probably conscious archaisms in view of their position either just before the caesura or at line endings, but not included by Terence in his archaising register), non-periphrastic forms of *nolo* (like *noltis* for *non uultis*), see Caec. *com.* 4; cf. also Plaut. *Curc.* 82, Tit. *tog.* 108; a further conscious archaising feature, old optatives of the verb *edo, edim, -is, -e* (Plaut. *Aul.* 430, Caec. *com.* 14, Naev. *com.* 27, Nov. *atel.* 6, Pomp. *atel.* 34), active EL for CL deponent forms, cf. *opino* for *opinor* (Plaut. *Bacch.* 487, Caec. *com.* 15).

1.4 Prepositions: use, in compound forms, of the old preposition *endo*, later appearing as *indo* or *indu*, cf. *indaudio* for *inaudio*, Plaut. *Capt.* 30, Afr. *tog.* 68.

2 Syntax

Accusative as the object of a periphrasis consisting of an adjective + *esse*, of the type *inscius fui = non sciui* (Plaut. *Most.* 100, Turp. *com.* 67), various

---

[7] Cf. Karakasis (2005) 145–246; for the language of Roman comedy, see also Fraenkel (1935); Vereecke (1971); Pasquazi Bagnolini (1977); Guardì (1981); Mandolfo (2004); Livan (2005); de Melo (2010).

instances of blurred case usage, cf. *fastidire* with the genitive instead of the accusative (Plaut. *Aul.* 245, Turp. *com.* 104, Tit. *tog.* 94; the verb seems to acquire a genitive complement in analogy with adjectival forms of the same stem (*fastidiosus*) and is construed with the genitive, a phenomenon common in the comic tradition (e.g. with *cupio, studeo*), but absent in Terence).

3 *Lexicon*

Various individual EL/archaising lexemes and syntagms further complement Terence's standing out from the rest of the comic tradition: i) nouns: *mihi diuidiae est* combinations in place of *taedet, aegre est* constructions (Plaut. *Bacch.* 770, Turp. *com.* 60); ii) verbs: *bitere* for *uadere, proficisci* (Plaut. *Ps.* 254, Pomp. *atel.* 150), *deliquare/delicare* in the sense of 'to explain' (Plaut. *Mil.* 844, Caec. *com.* 123, Tit. *tog.* 80–1, 103, a further conscious archaism found at the end of the verse), *perbitere* for *perire* (Plaut. *Ps.* 778, Tit. *tog.* 19); iii) adverbs: *cordate* for *prudenter* (Plaut. *Mil.* 1088, Afr. *tog.* 220), *efflictim* for *uehementer* (Plaut. *Cas.* 49, Naev. *com.* 37–8, Pomp. *atel.* 42); iv) several particles: *nec* or *noenu* in place of *non* (Plaut. *As.* 471, Turp. *com.* 25/Plaut. *Aul.* 67, Caec. *com.* 204), *tandem* as equivalent to *tamen* (Plaut. *Aul.* 371, Tit. *tog.* 46).

Unclassical Linguistic Options. Plautus, the Comic Tradition and Terence: a Distinction

Terence is considered a *puri sermonis amator* (lover of natural and unaffected speech, Suet. *Vita Ter.* 7, 9ff. (Wessner)) and this characterisation seems to be because he foreshadows, in many ways, later CL trends; several linguistic features which are shunned by CL standardised speech are also absent from Terence. On the contrary, they occur in Plautus and several other authors not only of the *palliata*, but also of the *togata* and the *Atellana*. Thus Terence once again, in direct opposition to the rest of the comic writers, avoids those features that appear in EL, are avoided in CL, and resurface in literature in the less strict – as far as 'linguistic purity' is concerned – PC Latin texts. Features of this kind include the following:[8]

1 *Morphology/Derivation*

1.1 Noun formations: namely, nouns in *-tas* for CL *-tudo, -tia, -edo* and equivalent formations; *pulchritas* for *pulcritudo*, *dulcitas* for *dulcedo*,

---

[8] Cf. Karakasis (2005) 145–246.

cf. Caec. *com.* 50, 207; see also Plaut. *Mil.* 1171. Terence either adopts similar formations which have the sanction of CL (cf. *largitas, Ad.* 985) or, in the case of unclassical *-tas* derivatives, opts for the CL equivalent (cf. *pulchritudo, Ph.*105); nouns in *-ntia,* e.g. *ualentia,* cf. Tit. *tog.* 124; see also Plaut. *Trin.* 222, Nov. *atel.* 38; nouns in *-mentum,* e.g. *peniculamentum,* Caec. *com.* 118; see also Plaut. *Amph.* 696, Afr. *tog.* 378; nouns in *-bulum,* e.g. *rutabulum,* Naev. *ex inc.* 8; see also Plaut. *Bacch.* 596; nouns in *-o, -onis,* e.g. *lustro,* Naev. *ex inc.* 20, see also Plaut. *Bacch.* 1089; derivative compounds in *-ium,* e.g. *tentipellium,* Afr. *tog.* 281; see also Plaut. *Bacch.* 720, Tit. *tog.* 171.

1.2 Adjectival forms: adjectives in *-bundus,* e.g. *cassabundus,* Naev. *ex inc.* 22, see also Plaut. *St.* 444; adjectives in *-lentus,* e.g. *lotiolentus,* Tit. *tog.* 138; see also Plaut. *Merc.* 639; adjectives, formed on the model of participles, from denominative verbs in *-are,* e.g. *fimbriatus,* Tit. *tog.* 115; see also Plaut. *Mil.* 768.

1.3 Verbal by-forms: first-declension by-forms for nouns regularly declined according to the fifth declension, cf. *effigia* for *effigies,* Plaut. *Ru.* 420, Afr. *tog.* 364; third-conjugation forms for first- and second-conjugation verbs, cf. *lavere,* Plaut. *Amph.* 1102, Afr. *tog.* 186, *olĕre,* Plaut. *Most.* 268, Afr. *tog.* 177; second-conjugation by-forms for third-conjugation verbs, cf. *dicebo* for *dicam,* Nov. *atel.* 8; see also Plaut. *Epid.* 188.

1.4 Adverbial formations: adverbs in *-e* in place of *-ter,* derived from third-declension adjectives, cf. *perspicace* for *perspicaciter,* Afr. *tog.* 59; see also Plaut. *Capt.* 439, Pomp. *atel.* 109; adverbs in *-o* for CL *-e* equivalents, cf. *occulto* for *occulte,* Afr. *tog.* 295; see also Plaut. *Truc.* 61.

2 Stylistic Options

Unclassical alliterative combination of a simple verb and an adverb of the same root, e.g. *curre cursim,* Afr. *tog.* 295; see also Plaut. *Ps.* 358, Pomp. *atel.* 109.

3 Lexicon

The linguistic unity of the comic tradition from which Terence distances himself is further evidenced, on the level of the lexicon, by miscellaneous isolated lexemes and syntagms: i) nouns: e.g. *labea* for *labrum* (Plaut. *St.* 723a, Pomp. *atel.* 144, Tit. *tog.* 172); ii) verbs: e.g. *extundere* with the meaning of *extorquere, inuenire,* Plaut. *Most.* 220–1, Afr. *tog.* 110); iii) adverbs: e.g. *peregri* for *peregre* (Plaut. *Amph.* 5, Naev. *com.* 91), *publicitus* in the sense of 'publicly' (Plaut. *Persa* 509, Caec. *com.* 175).

Colloquialism

It is true that Terence does not avail himself of the distinct colloquialism of Plautine diction.[9] Instead he tries to render in Latin the milder idiom of Menandrean language as well as to imitate the refined everyday Roman colloquial/spoken idiom (parataxis and asyndeton for hypotaxis, juxtaposition for coordination, parenthesis, anacolutha, pleonasm and repetition, frequent abuse and interjections, various formulaic phrases (e.g. set questions, answers, and imperatives), lengthened and contracted, 'allegro' forms.[10] Therefore he constantly uses, with a greater frequency than Plautus, elliptical constructions and rapid dialogue, interruption patterns and broken sentences, which textually mark the spontaneous character of everyday diction (*Ph.* 935ff.).[11]

'Colloquial' is a term which covers a wide range of styles from everyday spoken language to the vulgar diction of lower classes.[12] The term colloquial as used in this chapter refers, however, to those linguistic features of a lower social register that are common in comedy, in opposition to higher genres of the early Republican period (tragedy, epic). They disappear from the classical purist *sermo* with the exception of lighter genres (such as epistolography or satire) only to reappear in Late Latin texts, like the Christian authors of the first period, in technical treatises often drawing on the colloquial register, as well as in Romance languages deriving from the vernacular and not from CL.[13] The only low-level colloquial formations that appear in the Terentian corpus are the following, and, what is more, they are used chiefly with a specific stylistic effect, that is in the speech of lower-level characters, as will be elaborated later.[14]

Lower-Level Colloquialisms Which Do Appear in Terence but in the Mouths of Lower-Level Characters

1 Derivation

1.1 Substantives and adjectives: substantives in -*arius, palmarium, cetarius, Eun.* 930, 257; substantives in -*tor,* -*trix, extortor, aduorsatrix, Ph.* 374, *Haut.* 1007; adjectives in -*inus, mustelinus, Eun.* 689; adjectives in -*osus, cadauerosus, Hec.* 441; diminutives, *cistella, tardiusculus, grandiusculus, Eun.* 753, *Haut.* 515, *And.* 814.

---

[9] Cf. also Baldi (2002) 228–31.
[10] Clackson and Horrocks (2007), 176, 179, cf. Papadimitriou (1998); see also Hofmann (1951); Barsby (1999) 20–3; Bagordo (2001).
[11] Cf. Hough (1970).
[12] Cf. Karakasis (2005) 22–3; see also Dickey and Chahoud (2010).
[13] Cf. Karakasis (2005) 26–8.
[14] Cf. Karakasis (2005) 21–43; see also Wahrmann (1908).

1.2 Verbal forms: diminutive derivative verbs, *sorbillare, Ad.* 591; verbs in *-issare, patrissare, Ad.* 564; frequentatives, *commetare, Haut.* 444; verbs compounded with *ad, apposcere, Haut.* 838, and *cum, commitigare, collocupletare, Eun.* 1028, *Haut.* 258.

1.3 Adverbs: adverbs in *-im, unciatim, Ph.* 43.

2 Syntax

Colloquial syntax, as in the case of the autonomous partitive genitive, cf. *Ph.* 709–10: *ante brumam autem noui negoti incipere* (cf. Löfstedt (1911) 108–9).

3 Lexicon

Various low-level lexemes and phrases: i) nouns and adjectives: cf. *lapis* in the sense of *stultus* (*Hec.* 214), *mastigia* for *homo nequam* (*Ad.* 781); ii) pronouns: cf. *quidam* referring with contempt to a particular person (*Eun.* 483), *ipsus/ipse* with the meaning of *dominus* (*And.* 265); iii) verbs: cf. *crepare* with the meaning of 'to knock on the door' (*Haut.* 173), *emungere*, construed with the ablative of separation, in the sense of 'to cheat' (*Ph.* 682), *enicare* for *uexando molestias praebere* (*And.* 660), *flocci facere* (*Eun.* 303), *posse* in the sense of 'to be capable of sexual intercourse' (*Eun.* 666), *scortari* in the meaning of 'to consort with prostitutes' (*Haut.* 206).

Lower-Level Colloquialisms Which Do Not Appear in Terence But Which Plautus Shares with the Rest of Roman Comedy

Thus in the Terentian corpus one does not come across distinct colloquial linguistic markers which Plautus shares with the rest of the comic playwrights, namely:[15]

1 Various colloquial derivatives: substantives in *-bulum, -mentum*, verbal nouns in *-tio; nomina personalia* in *-o, -onis*; adjectives in *-arius, -atus, -lentus* (see also above on unclassical features).

2 Colloquial syntax: cf. *utor* with an accusative complement (Plaut. *Poen.* 1088, Turp. *com.* 166, Tit. *tog.* 99, Nov. *atel.* 99); temporal *quando* (Naev. *com.* 27, Plaut. *Amph.* 123, Tit. *tog.* 125).

3 Colloquial stylistic options: addition of diminutive suffixes to both nouns and their modifying adjectives, cf. *papilla bellula* (Plaut. *Cas.* 848; see also Naev. *com. ex inc.* 7, Caec. *com.* 71 (Rib.), Afr. *tog.* 224–5, Tit. *tog.* 142);

---

[15] Cf. Karakasis (2005) 145–246.

alliterative combination of an adjective and of an adverb of the same root, cf. *bella belle* (Plaut. *Curc.* 521; see also Afr. *tog.* 38).

4 Various individual colloquial lexemes: i) nouns and adjectives: e.g. *spurcus* for *obscenus, impurus* (Plaut. *As.* 807, Pomp. *atel.* 155), *tricae* for *impedimenta, implicationes* (Plaut. *Curc.* 613, Turpil. *com.* 47); ii) verbs: e.g. *frunisci* for *frui* (Plaut. *Ru.* 1012, Nov. *atel.* 77–8); iii) adverbs: e.g. *repentino* in the sense of 'at once' (Plaut. *Ps.* 39, Afr. *tog.* 82).

Consequently Terence earned the positive evaluative remarks of both Cicero and Caesar for his refined diction (cf. Suet. *Vit. Ter.* 7; cf. also Cic. *Att.* 7.3.10: *elegantiam sermonis*, Hor. *Epist.* 2.1.59, and Quint. 10.1.99) in opposition to Caecilius for example, clearly in the linguistic line of Plautus, whom Cicero considers as writing in a bad Latin style (*malus auctor Latinitatis, Att.* 7.3.10). This refined Terentian diction may also be associated with his alleged membership in the 'sophisticated' so-called Scipionic circle.[16]

This unity of the Roman comic tradition and Terence's separation from it, long established on the stylistic level (cf. Wright (1974)), is further evidenced by several other linguistic features without any particular archaic, colloquial, or unclassical character that other comic poets share with Plautus but not with Terence, e.g. the use of an accusative instead of a genitive complement with verbs of remembering and forgetting (Plaut. *Cist.* 381, *Trin.* 1013–14, Caec. *com.* 56, Turp. *com.* 158, 173); *numero* for *cito* (Plaut. *Amph.* 180, Caec. *com.* 5, Turp. *com.* 35, Afr. *tog.* 270); cf. Karakasis (2005) 150–246, *passim*.

Markers of Elevated Language

However, the language of both Plautus and Terence is also a literary construction, a *Kunstsprache*, and, therefore, it can by no means be considered as a pure reflection of everyday colloquialism;[17] Plautine and Terentian diction is, in many instances, a rhetorically embellished *sermo*, often stylised and made up (fraught with 'inflated/padded' style[18] (cf. Plaut. *Curc.* 148, Ter. *Ph.* 563)), a wide range of figures of speech and word-play (cf. Plaut. *Capt.* 439, Ter. *Ph.* 59–61), which, what is more, occasionally also makes use of various additional means to distance itself from common linguistic habits. In this endeavour the comic dramatists draw not only on their archaising register but also on the diction of higher poetic registers (epic, tragedy) as

[16] Cf. especially Comerci (1994); Beacham (1991) 46–8 vs. Strasburger (1966); Astin (1967) 294–306; Zetzel (1972); Parker (1996) 604–7.
[17] Cf. Happ (1967).   [18] A term coined by Palmer (1954) 86.

Plautus does mainly in his recitative lines and *cantica*.[19] They also employ specialised registers such as sacral language as well as legal and formal-official *sermo* in general.[20] This practice may thus involve mock epic and tragic speech, or parody of ritual and official diction (e.g. parody of a praetor's edict as in Plaut. *Capt.* 814). The means by which this mock solemnity is achieved are chiefly the following:[21]

1 Lexicon

1.1 Various individual lexemes: e.g. *atrox* (a tragic word occurring in the paratragic context of Plaut. *Capt.* 539, cf. also Ter. *Hec.* 377 in Pamphilus' passionate monologue),[22] *limen* of the threshold (a word of tragic associations, cf. Acc. *trag.* 531, also exploited in Pardalisca's monody at Plaut. *Cas.* 815, i.e. in a passage parodying once again ritual, official, and tragic language; see also Ter. *Hec.* 378 in Pamphilus' monologue).[23] There are also additional instances of lexical items employed in mock official/elevated instances of chiefly Plautine comedy, e.g. *satias* vs. *satietas, uspiam, gradus, quadrupes*.[24]

1.2 Various individual syntagms: e.g. *pedem efferre* (a combination occurring in both tragedy, Enn. *trag.* 215, and formal, highly stylised comic instances, cf. Plaut. *Bacch.* 423; see also Ter. *And.* 808 in the speech of the high-status character Crito, where the equally archaic and elevated *tetulissem* also appears) vs. the less elevated *domo abire, ferre opem* vs. *ferre auxilium, paucis* vs. *ad pauca*.[25]

2 Morphology/Derivation

2.1 Various morphological options as compounds in *-dicus, -ficus, -gerus* cherished by the *genus grande* of the early Republic, used by Plautus in mock-elevated lines and as a means to characterise the diction of his gods, his old men, and his *adulescentes in amore* as well as by Terence in very formal, well stylised contexts, as is the case of Pamphilus' imitating Chrysis' speech, before she passes away at *And.* 294.[26]

---

[19] Cf. Haffter (1934); see also Happ (1967).
[20] Cf. Thierfelder (1939); Hoffmann (1980–1); Danese (1985); Hunter (1985) 114–36; Piccaluga (1991); Blänsdorf (1996).
[21] Cf. also Karakasis (2005) 90–100; for a comparative analysis of EL comic, tragic, and epic diction, cf. Ploen (1882); see also Jocelyn (1967).
[22] Cf. Lindsay (1900) 259.   [23] Cf. Fraenkel (1960) 432.
[24] Cf. Karakasis (2005) 93–4.   [25] Cf. Karakasis (2005) 95–6.
[26] Cf. Maltby (1976) 207–8.

3 *Stylistic Options*

3.1 Perfect or present + future of the same verb in a paratactic construction in the same line (cf. Enn. *trag.* 270, Plaut. *Bacch.* 1087, i.e. in a passage full of highly stylised paratragic diction);[27] the combination also occurs mainly in the diction of high-status characters of Terentian comedy, e.g. in the speech of the old man Phidippus at *Hec.* 722. Further elevated stylistic options include the disjunction of *per* from its object, *dicam* + accusative + infinitive syntagms in direct/indirect questions, the accumulation of synonymous expressions in bi-membered combinations where the second element repeats the first in a longer form (cf. *Ad.* 145–6: *uerum si augeam aut etiam adiutor siem eius iracundiae*), triple anaphora of *o* + vocative combinations, relative clauses repeating the noun to which they refer, in imitation of legal texts, see *Ad.* 854: *i ergo intro, et quoi reist, ei rei [hilarum] hunc sumamus diem.*[28]

Plautus in Terence

One should, however, take into account that Terentian diction is not homogeneous, presenting instead a certain evolution, as far as archaisms are concerned, for example, from an overall EL *Andria* to the *Adelphoe*, where most of the archaisms appear for stylistic effect, namely for imparting an obsolete linguistic colouring to the diction of old people. As previously remarked, Terence is known for his linguistic and stylistic alienation from a stylistic consensus exhibited by the whole of the Roman comic tradition, thus anticipating, in several cases, later CL options. However, his Latin is not always so 'refined'; after the failure of the *Hecyra*, and especially in the *Eunuchus*, where the traditional farcical comic pair of the soldier and the flatterer/parasite is put on stage, Terence tries both thematically and linguistically to adhere to an established Roman comic generic code, and to Plautine diction in particular.[29] The younger comic playwright's diction thus becomes more Plautine/traditional, as is evidenced by the use of the following common Plautine linguistic features and stylistic options:

---

[27] Cf. Barsby (1986) 183. [28] Cf. Kroll (1910–12) 8–10; Karakasis (2005) 92–9.
[29] Cf. Karakasis (2005) 121–43; for an account of the differences between the two main comic playwrights, which *Eunuchus* seems to eliminate, cf. also Müller (1913); Hofmann (1951) 9–39; Duckworth (1952) 331–60; Miniconi (1958); Palmer (1954) 74–94; Lilja (1965) 78–85; Fantham (1972); Barsby (1999) 19–27.

Plautus in Terence's Eunuchus

1 Unclassical formations by means of colloquial affixes; as previously claimed, Terence, against the Plautine tradition, as a rule avoids derivation by means of affixes productive in colloquial texts, and regularly restricts himself to formations accepted by CL. Yet the *Eunuchus* seems to constitute a clear exception. Thus one comes across the following non-classical forms by means of colloquial affixes: *curatura* instead of *cura* or *curatio, Eun.* 316; *habitudo, Eun.* 242; *palmarium, Eun.* 930; *mustelinus, Eun.* 689. One should pay attention to the fact that the non-CL forms occurring in Terentian comedy do not show an even distribution in all his plays or do not appear more frequently in his earlier plays; thus the higher concentration of such non-CL words and expressions in Terence's fourth play, i.e. the *Eunuchus*, should in all probability be read as a conscious stylistic choice of the poet himself, thus standing closer to the diction of the comic tradition from which in general he stands apart.[30]

2 Individual terms of abuse commonly found in Plautus, namely *fur* (*Eun.* 23, 776), *scelestus* (*Eun.* 71, 668, 709, 817, 832, 944), *pessumus* (*Eun.* 152, 1017); common Plautine abuse techniques also appear in concentration in the *Eunuchus*, e.g. animal terms such as *canis* (*Eun.* 803; see also vv. 426, 598, 704); combinations of a noun + a definitive genitive (*genetiuus definitiuus*), of the type *monstrum hominis* (*Eun.* 696). The percentage of abuse in *Eunuchus* approximates ratios occurring in Plautine comedy, 5.9 per cent;[31] what is more, the piling up of terms of abuse (cf. *Eun.* 668–70) also brings Terence closer to Plautus in this comedy.

3 Interjections common in Plautus, especially Greek ones, *papae* (*Eun.* 229, 279, 317, 416), *apage* (*Eun.* 756, 904), avoided in Terence with the exception of primary interjectional forms (*ah, au*), which are three times more common in the Terentian corpus than in Plautine comedy.[32]

4 Greek words; the ratio of the presence of Greek words in the *Eunuchus*, as in the case of non-CL formations, once again approximates Plautine percentages.[33]

5 Plautine figurative usage and metaphorical techniques, namely agricultural imagery (*Eun.* 79, 236, 381) and noun metaphors (*Eun.* 85), whereas Terence normally prefers simple verb metaphors, lengthy comparisons, and prolonged images (*Eun.* 103–5, 121) as well as syntagms comprising the so-called genitive of definition; cf. *festus dies hominis* (*Eun.* 560).

---

[30] Cf. also Maltby (1976) 213.   [31] Cf. Karakasis (2005) 129.
[32] Cf. Barsby (1999) 21–2.   [33] Cf. Maltby (1985) 120; Karakasis (2005) 142.

6 Plautine formulaic expressions: e.g. conventional greeting formulas such as *unde is* (*Eun.* 305) and entrance formulas such as *eccum Parmenonem incedere uideo* (*Eun.* 918–19).

7 Individual lexical options like *amabo* as a modifier of a request in the imperative (*Eun.* 130, 150, 534, 663, 838) and *poste* for *post* (*Eun.* 493).

8 Individual syntactical options also having the sanction of Plautine diction, such as perfect forms of *esse* with the perfect participle in place of present/imperfect forms of *esse* (*Eun.* 280: *profectus fueras* vs. *profectus eras*, 569); *quid si* conditional clauses with the perfect indicative (*Eun.* 875); *nisi quia* with the meaning of 'except for the fact that' introducing substantive causal clauses (*Eun.* 736); the construction of *equidem* with the third singular (*Eun.* 956).

9 Individual familiar Plautine stylistic options, as the *figura etymologica facinus facere* (*Eun.* 644); *di immortales* syntagms without a preceding contact-morpheme (e.g. *pro*, *Eun.* 232); questions of the type: *quid + tibi + abstract noun in -tio + <est>*, cf. *Eun.* 671: *quid huc tidi reditiost? quid uestis mutatio?*

This linguistic adhesion of the *Eunuchus* to the comic tradition is obvious from the very first lines of the drama, where, according to Hellenistic practices, the playwright seeks to reveal his stylistic programmatic intentions; thus in vv. 47–8: *ita me comparem non perpeti meretricum contumelias?*, *ita* foreshadows a following *ut* clause. However, what follows instead is a colloquial infinitive construction, of the type also found in instances like Turp. *com.* 100 and Tit. *tog.* 57.[34] Thus Terence makes his stylistic orientation towards a traditional comic colloquialism clear.

Plautus in Terence's Heauton Timorumenos *and* Adelphoe

Such a linguistic movement towards Plautine diction is also evident in individual scenes of other dramas, where Terence deviates from his original, evidently reworking his material in a Plautine/traditionally comic direction. This seems to be especially the case with the last scene of Terence's *Heauton Timorumenos* and the Sannio scene in the *Adelphoe*.[35] Here Terence contaminates his principal model, Menander's *Adelphoi B*, with a scene from Diphilus' *Synapothnescontes* (cf. again the Plautine terms of abuse *periurus, pestis, scelestus, stultus* (*Ad.* 189, 159, 218); *quamquam* introducing an adversative clause, yet without a correlative particle in the main clause,

---

[34] Cf. Barsby (1999) 92.   [35] Cf. Maltby (1983).

which is a common construction in Plautine drama (159); *promerere* in the sense of 'to do somebody a good/bad turn' (201)).

Language as a Means for Character Differentiation

Roman comedy occasionally focuses on issues of linguistic interest; in Plautus' *Truculentus*, for example, Astaphium is presented as censuring Truculentus' *rabo* instead of *arrabo*, a linguistic usage the rustic character ironically defends on the analogy of a Praenestine pronunciation of *ciconia* as *conea* (*Truc.* 688–91). What is more, Plautus and Terence appear to be making use of linguistic and stylistic means for the linguistic individualisation of various characters and character types.[36] It has long been observed for both Plautus and Terence that they often put Greek words in the mouths of slaves and characters of a lower social status in general (pimps, parasites). Rustic/vulgar spellings have also been claimed in several Plautine instances as a means of linguistic characterisation (cf. *billam* at *Truc.* 648 by the rustic Strabax of the Palatine manuscripts).[37] What is more, misspellings of *b* as *v* at Plaut. *Mil.* 832–60 seem to be a further conscious authorial choice to depict the slave's intoxicated state.[38] In the *Menaechmi* there is evidence that the twin brothers are differentiated by contrasting vocabulary, in *Stichus* the linguistic individualisation of the leading sister comes from her penchant for moral language, whereas in the *Aulularia* Euclio's concise asyndetic style contrasts with Staphyla's fondness for periphrasis as well as with Megadorus' 'stylish speech'.[39] However, in the case of Terentian comedy, linguistic characterisation seems to be more refined and developed as a system throughout the Terentian corpus. Earlier views claim that all Terentian characters use the same refined Latin idiom.[40] They, however, ignore Donatus' convincing individual remarks arguing the opposite.[41] There is now compelling evidence that, within the Terentian comic corpus, the following linguistic characterisation patterns occur:

1 Colloquialisms (in the sense described above) are largely found in the diction of low-status characters (i.e., slaves, parasites, prostitutes) or rustic figures, i.e. characters living in the country (like Demea in the

---

[36] For Plautine linguistic characterisation techniques in particular, cf. Karakasis (2005), 6–7 and n. 12. See also Nicolson (1893); Tschernjaew (1900); Hough (1947); Shipp (1953); Carney (1964); Salat (1967); Arnott (1970); Gilleland (1979); Adams (1984); Nuñez (1995); Martin (1995); Müller (1997); Maltby (1976, 1979, 1985, 1995); Papadimitriou (1998); Barsby (2004); Dutsch (2008).

[37] Cf. Petersmann (1996–7); Danese (2006); Fontaine (2010) 29–30.

[38] Cf. Stadter (1968).   [39] Cf. Leach (1969); Arnott (1972); Stockert (1982).

[40] Cf. Marouzeau (1947) 47; Shipp (1960) 55.   [41] Cf. Reich (1933).

Adelphoe). The basic dichotomy *urbs* vs. *rus*, on which Roman comedy frequently capitalises, is thus evidenced on the stylistic/linguistic level as well. Colloquialisms appearing in the diction of other character types do not occur in concentration in their speech, but only as random instances, when their interlocutor is either a low-status or a rustic character.

2 With the exception of the *Eunuchus*, most EL/archaic linguistic features appear in the diction of old people; as far as archaising diction is concerned, a binary linguistic opposition is developed between Chremes and Menedemus in *Heauton Timorumenos* as well as between Demea and Micio in the *Adelphoe*. *Senes* residing in the country, namely Chremes and Demea, resort to archaism more often than their 'urban doubles'.

3 Long-winded expressions (combinations of synonyms, e.g. *petere et poscere*, as well as pleonastic expressions, e.g. *at tamen, quisquam homo*) are a characteristic linguistic habit of 'senile speech'; such a linguistic differentiation takes place in the Terentian prologues as well. Pleonastic expressions of the kind described above characterise the diction of the old actor L. Ambivius Turpio in the prologue of both the *Heauton Timorumenos* and the *Hecyra*. Such techniques of linguistic differentiation are particularly evident in senarii, which approximate everyday common speech. Linguistic characterisation by means of long-winded diction is absent from the *Andria* and the *Eunuchus*. It appears for the first time in the *Heauton Timorumenos* and is perfected in Terence's last drama, the *Adelphoe*. Occasional instances of padded style in the diction of other characters chiefly occur, only as random cases, when their addressee is an old person.

4 Low and rustic characters occasionally resort to syntactical Hellenisms as well, as is the case in the use of an adverb in an adjectival function (*And.* 175–6: *eri semper lenitas uerebar quorsum euaderet*), and the gnomic perfect (*Ad.* 855). The Roman nobility's tendency to avoid Hellenisms as a rule may account for this allocation of Greek words and syntactic options in both Plautus and Terence.

5 Features belonging to a higher stylistic register (drawn from tragedy and epic, ritual and legal diction, as well as the language of the official administration) are common in the speech of the so-called higher characters (i.e, *senes, matronae, adulescentes*). As in the case of EL/archaising and colloquial features, a binary linguistic opposition is developed between the urban Micio, who makes use of several features of elevated colouring, and the rustic Demea in the *Adelphoe*. A similar opposition, as far as markers of elevated language are concerned, is not developed in the pair of *senes* in the earlier *Heauton Timorumenos*. This fact could be seen as

indicating an advancement of Terentian linguistic characterisation techniques in the playwright's last play.

6 Idiolectal features without any particular archaic or colloquial colouring, on the level of both vocabulary and syntax, characterise the speech of individual characters and character types. Old people, for example, make use of the noun *homo* in the sense of *quis, quiuis, aliquis* and, from a syntactical point of view, *si* in the sense of *etsi, etiamsi, quamuis*, whereas low-status characters use *noster/nostra* in the sense of *dominus/domina* and *quod* clauses of general reference in the subjunctive with the meaning of 'as to the fact that'. Similarly, individual characters also have a penchant for specific lexemes and syntactical options; thus Demea in the *Adelphoe* often uses rustic imagery closely connected to his identity as a *senex rusticus* and frequently appeals to Jupiter, whereas Simo in the *Andria* has a penchant for using *praeter* in the sense of *prae* or *magis quam*, that is, in a comparative function. In the case of idiolects, once again, the use of a particular linguistic option is conditioned not only by the speaker but also by the addressee; thus a linguistic option favoured in the speech of a particular character or character type, as evidenced by the ratio of its appearance in his/her diction, occasionally may appear in the speech of another character, when functioning as the interlocutor of the comic figure associated with this particular linguistic option. Thus *recte* in the sense of *iuste, iure, merito* favoured by old people is at *Eun.* 981 spoken by the slave Parmeno to the *senex* Chremes/Laches.

What is more, individual characters occasionally do not exhibit the same linguistic behaviour as the one shown by the rest of the characters belonging to the same social/linguistic category. Thus, the *meretrix* Bacchis in the *Hecyra* often adopts linguistic favourites of old people's diction (e.g. *recte* in the sense of *iuste, iure, merito* (*Hec.* 862), *reor* at the expense of *puto* (819)). Her being a *bona meretrix* may account for the decorum of her language. The *adulescens* Chaerea in the *Eunuchus*, on the other hand, although belonging to the high characters, often intersperses his diction with linguistics options preferred by low characters (cf. *quod* in the sense of 'as to the fact that', introducing clauses of general reference in the subjunctive, *Eun.* 1064). In Chaerea's case the fact that he is at the moment an ephebe, i.e. he is doing his military service, may explain this tendency of his to make use of features belonging to a lower linguistic register (cf. also the colloquialism *flocci facere* at 303). Last but not least, in cases of reported speech, the linguistic habits of the initial speaker are often kept; thus when Pamphilus reports his mother-in-law's speech at *Hec.* 382ff., he makes use of several features associated with the diction of old persons, e.g. *uolo ut* constructions.

There is also a crucial distinction between male and female speech in both Plautus and Terence. Female linguistic markers include particular oaths (*ecastor, mecastor*), interjections (*au*), and politeness modifiers (*amabo*), while men respectively use *hercle, mehercle*,[42] *ei*, and the parenthetic *quaeso*. Although not found exclusively in the language of female characters, the oath *pol*, the modifier *obsecro*, self-pitying *misera* forms as well as endearments of the type *mi/mea* + vocative are more common in female diction. Such distinctions are less clear-cut in Plautus than in Terence, who, in addition, has the penchant of using female markers in concentration/ clusters, cf. *Eun.* 663–7.

Several parallel patterns of linguistic characterisation appear in Menandrean diction as well and the Roman playwright seems to be following here the stylistic techniques of his Greek predecessor.[43]

Further Reading

Palmer (1954) is a good introduction to the archaic and colloquial character of Plautine and Terentian diction as well as their rather artificial and stylised character; for EL features, apart from the various individual comments in commentaries of individual plays, a very good, concise discussion appears in Raios (1998) 120–6, while de Melo (2007) is a recent study of the archaic verbal forms in the comic corpus. Wright (1974) constitutes a classic discussion of the stylistic unity of the Roman *palliata*, while linguistic evidence for this unity from which Terence stands apart comes from Karakasis (2005), also dealing with instances of Terentian appropriation of Plautine language as well as the means employed by Terence in order to distinguish his characters from a linguistic point of view. A further very good discussion of colloquialism/spoken Latin in Terence appears in Bagordo (2001) and Papadimitriou (1998). A very good account of the use of Greek words in Plautus and Terence is offered by Maltby (1995) and (1985) respectively, whereas Maltby (1979) and (1983) have also become standard reference works for the linguistic characterisation of old men in Terence and the Plautine linguistic colouring of the *Heauton Timorumenos'* last scene, respectively. What is more, Maltby (1976) is still the best comparative analysis of the language of Plautus and Terence. Last, Adams (1984) and Dutsch (2008) are two further excellent discussions of female diction in

---

[42] Along with Plautus' assertive women, cf. Stockert (2004).
[43] On Menandrean diction, cf. especially Zini (1938); Arnott (1964, 1995); Sandbach (1970); Webster (1974) 99–110; Del Corno (1975); Katsouris (1975) 101–83; Bain (1984); Brenk (1987); Kriter Spiro (1997) 201–53.

Roman comedy. Issues of figurative diction/imagery and abuse are aptly discussed in Fantham (1972), Maltby (2007), and Lilja (1965), respectively. For a persuasive approach to Plautine metrics through Latin linguistics, one should consult Fortson (2008), for Plautine nominal declension Gerschner (2002) is invaluable, whereas Plautine word-play is the focus of Fontaine's (2010) serious philological work. De Melo (2011) is a further recent, compelling and systematic account of the language of Roman comedy, whereas the sub-chapter on Plautine language in the introduction of de Melo (2011b) offers a further concise but thorough overview and analysis of Plautine diction. Last but not least, Karakasis (2014) constitutes a further, up-to-date account of the language of the *palliata* with an emphasis on the EL/archaic, the colloquial, the elevated, and the unclassical features of comic diction, as well as on issues of linguistic characterisation.

PART III

The Sociology of Roman Comedy

10

MARTIN T. DINTER

Fathers and Sons

Comedy and *Paideia*

Ancient drama is often said to have played an important civic function as a 'didactic' medium. Roman comedy presents explicit references to teaching, besides featuring scenarios where protreptic, lecturing, pontificating, and sententiousness are acted out between the players, whether for their benefit and our edification or for their bamboozlement and our merriment. The scripts also deploy various 'direct to camera/audience' set-pieces and metatheatric interruptions where the play 'teaches' the audience. One play, Plautus' *Bacchides* is built round the institutions of school and pedagogue for sons, and in the figure of Lydus supplements *and* challenges paternal responsibility for educating boys. Schooling is bound to provoke funny feelings when the Roman theatre hosts issues opening onto cultural anxieties involved in attuning to Hellenisation. When zooming in on *sententiae* in comedy, however, we will unearth the morals this genre projects.

The comedies of Plautus offer a number of passages in which characters outline conservative moral positions. We would expect the stern fathers of Roman comedy to extol their equally stern morals but instead we frequently find slaves, women, or outsiders – sometimes even pimps cheated of their money – reciting Roman morals (*mores*) in the Romanised Greek world of Roman comedy.

One of Roman comedy's most downright moralising passages is not heard from the mouth of a complaining parent but rather from a pontificating elder on his way to admonish one of his peers. Megaronides at the beginning of Plautus' *Trinummus* gives us his impression of the current state of moral affairs. The play starts programmatically with a prologue spoken by Luxury personified, accompanied by her daughter Poverty, two characters who embody every father's fear that the overspending son will ruin his household.[1] Megaronides' moralising outlook and reproachful mission

---

[1] On this prologue as a Plautine addition to Philemon's original, see Hunter (1980) and Lefevre (1995).

make Cato the Elder, the (self-appointed) apostle of morals and Plautus' contemporary, a possible model for this character. Some scholars have even suggested a politicised reading of this play (and others) as a showcase of the conflict between the morally conservative forces in Rome and the philhellenists. The former were embodied by Cato the Elder, who agitated against excessive philhellenism and those parts of Greek culture which he saw as undermining Roman character; the latter faction was led by Scipio Africanus and his brother Lucius.[2] As the foremost supporters of philhellenism in Rome, they were associated by Cato and his ilk with the negative, morally corrupting aspects of Greek influence upon Rome.[3] Megaronides complains as follows:

> Amicum castigare ob meritam noxiam
> immoene est facinus, uerum in aetate utile
> et conducibile [...]
> nam hic nimium morbus mores inuasit bonos;
> ita plerique omnes iam sunt intermortui.
> sed dum illi aegrotant, interim mores mali
> quasi herba inrigua succreuere uberrime:
> eorum licet iam metere messem maxumam,
> neque quicquam hic nunc est uile nisi mores mali.
> nimioque hic pluris pauciorum gratiam
> faciunt pars hominum quam id quod prosint pluribus.
> ita uincunt illud conducibile gratiae,
> quae in rebus multis opstant odiosaeque sunt
> remoramque faciunt rei priuatae et publicae.

> It's a very disagreeable thing to have to castigate a friend whose faults deserve it [...] There is a plague of wickedness rife in this city, destroying all the laws of morality; indeed most of them are by now a dead letter, while morality withers wickedness flourishes like a well watered plant. Wickedness is the cheapest thing you can find around here; you can pick a peck for nothing; there are far too many people who think more of pleasing a few friends than of what is best

---

[2] We should note that the negative reaction of Cato and his contemporaries to the incorporation of Greek learning into Roman education has often been overstated and in recent scholarship the image of Cato's conservatism in relation to education has been revised: see Astin (1978) 157–81; Gruen (1992) 52–83; Staden (1996); Stroup (2007); Bloomer (2011) 9–36. Cato's name, however, continues – and rightly so – to be associated with a conservative moral position.

[3] Benz (1990) 58 points to Meganorides' use of an initial *sententia* and Lefevre (1990) 50–1 to the character's use of *castigare* as possible links to Cato's persona. See Leigh (2004) 14–19 for further possible allusions to Cato in Plautine comedy and 160 for a revisionist approach to Cato's opposition towards Greek education. Leigh (2004) 161–2 and 172–3 also opposes a simple identification of *Adelphoe*'s Demea with Cato and Micio with M. Aemilius Paullus as suggested by MacKendrick (1954). Echoes, however, remain.

for the majority. Thus what is desirable takes second place to interest, and interest is everywhere a confounded plague, and an obstacle to private and public good. (Plautus *Trin.* 23–38, transl. Waitling)

While few scholars nowadays would subscribe to any overt representation of contemporaneous political figures in Roman comedy it is nevertheless clear that the comic genre parades its concern with public morals.[4] *Trinummus* is particularly rich in moralising passages – see *Trin.* 1032–9 where the slave (!) Stasimus echoes Megaronides' moral concerns and coins the apt phrase: 'Law has about as much control over morals as parents have over their children!' – and has been mined for its (occasional irreverent or absurd) representation of Roman morals (Stein (1970), Anderson (1979), and Braun (2000)). In addition, throughout the plays we find a prominent discourse on how to incorporate wayward sons into society and guarantee that they become mature and suitably married adults that will perpetuate the family line.[5] This 'reintegration of the lover into the traditional community' (Konstan (1983) 159) through marriage is complemented by scenes of fathers fondly remembering those (presumably) happy days of their wild youth before they took on the responsibilities of adulthood (Hunter (1985) 97–8). In Plautus' *Bacchides* the pedagogue Lydus delivers a tragicomic monologue (*Bacch.* 375–81) just before he discovers the young man Pistoclerus' escapades. Lydus compares the entrance to the house of the two Bacchis-sisters to the entry of the underworld – definitively the tutor's protégé is on the wrong path here – and links the sisters' name Bacchis in an etymological word-play (*Bacchides* = *Bacchae*) with the out-of-bounds religious festival *Bacchanalia* (for the god of wine Bacchus). We thus hardly dare to imagine what might be going on inside that house... In addition, Lydus spells out how the actions of the wayward son Pistoclerus are going to expose family and friends (including his tutor) to disgrace, shame, ruin, and destruction (*ad probrum, damnum, flagitium appellere una et perdere*, *Bacch.* 378). Plautus has transposed the traditionally paternal worries that the offspring is going to ruin the household onto the family tutor. This allows him to characterise Pistoclerus' father Philoxenus as lenient (and possibly forward-looking) in his educational attitudes. Lydus on the other hand continuously voices his conservative values firmly. Soon afterwards he even challenges Philoxenus' sense of paternal responsibility when blaming the father for being a corrupting influence on his son (*Bacch.* 408–15, note the strong demarcation of *te* (you, the

---

[4] See Germany in this volume. Lentano (1993) argues that a juncture from a speech of Cato (frg. 128 M (*parsimonia/duritia*)) has had an impact on *And.* 74–5 as well as *Most.* 149–55 and *Truc.* 309–11 or at least had become part of public discourse on morals at the time.

[5] James (1998b) 31 n. 5 points out how even transgressions such as rape invariably lead to a citizen marriage.

father) and *ego* (I, the tutor) in this passage). The verses that follow provide a unique assessment – from a tutor's perspective – of the good old values in the educational trade. Lydus reminds Philoxenus of the stern education he has 'enjoyed' in his youth. Certainly no fun and frolics feature here but rather an education centred on physical activity and reading practice with an occasional beating thrown in for good measure.[6]

> LYD. Non sino, neque equidem illum me uiuo corrumpi sinam.
> sed tu, qui pro tam corrupto dicis causam filio,
> eademne erat haec disciplina tibi, cum tu adulescens eras?
> nego tibi hoc annis uiginti fuisse primis copiae,
> digitum longe a paedagogo pedem ut efferres aedibus.
> ante solem exorientem nisi in palaestram ueneras,
> gymnasi praefecto haud mediocris poenas penderes.
> id quom optigerat, hoc etiam ad malum accersebatur malum:
> et discipulus et magister perhibebantur improbi.
> ibi cursu luctando hasta disco pugilatu pila
> saliendo sese exercebant magis quam scorto aut sauiis:
> ibi suam aetatem extendebant, non in latebrosis locis.
> inde de hippodromo et palaestra ubi reuenisses domum,
> cincticulo praecinctus in sella apud magistrum adsideres
> cum libro: cum legeres, si unam peccauisses syllabam,
> fieret corium tam maculosum quam est nutricis pallium.
> [...]
> PHIL. Alii, Lyde, nunc sunt mores.

LYD: No, I will not be, and I will not let him be corrupted while I am alive. But for you, who defends such a corrupt son, when you were a teenager was there the same sort of education? I doubt it. In your first twenty years you didn't have the chance to put your foot out of the house more than one finger's breadth away from your tutor. If you didn't turn up at the sports ground before sunrise, you'd pay quite a price to the head of the gymnasium. If this happened to anyone, this trouble would be added to the other trouble: both pupil and tutor would be considered worthless. They'd train themselves there by running, wrestling, throwing the spear and the discus, boxing, playing ball, and jumping, rather than by cavorting with a prostitute and stealing kisses. There they'd spend their lives, not in dark dens. When you came home from there, the race court and the sports ground, you'd sit down on a chair by your teacher, clad in a loincloth; when you were reading your book, if you got a single syllable wrong, your skin would become as spotted as a nurse's shawl. [...]

---

[6] Barsby (1986) 133–5 traces the ascendency of this speech to Aristophanes' *Clouds* (961–1023). Cf. Bonner (1977) on the actual Roman educational system. For a full account of ancient education, see Marrou (1975) with Pailler and Payen (2004) and also the essays in Too (2001).

PHIL: Lydus, things are different now.

(Plautus *Bacch.* 419–37, transl. adapted from de Melo (2011))

Despite this austere regime, Philoxenus – like most fathers in Roman comedy – has managed to sneak away and to do 'some of those things [i.e. fun] . . . in his youth (*Bacch.* 410)' against which the tutor Lydus is raging. In this context it seems significant that Philoxenus uses the keyword *mores* (customs/morals) not to join the tutor and defend (old) Roman morals but instead to note (and approve of) changes in morality. This certainly helps to put the tutor's outburst into perspective and reveals that he looks at the past through rose-tinted glasses. What is more in Roman comedy, masters usually whip slaves, not slaves masters, and the shift of power from father to slave tutor could scarcely sit comfortably with the Roman elite.[7] If we turn once again to Cato the Elder as model for Roman *mores* a detail from Plutarch's *Life of Cato the Elder* (47.5–7) reveals that he took personal interest in the education of his son (as Augustus would later in that of his grandchildren) and disapproved of investing a slave pedagogue with too much authority.

The *Bacchides* also demonstrates how this educational shift – from the Roman *mos maiorum* (the stern tradition of the Elders) to a more *laissez faire* attitude (Philoxenus' *mores alii*), which its critics attributed to moral decline brought on by Rome's Hellenisation – plays out for the tutor himself in a passage where Lydus laments his loss of authority:

> Id equidem ego certo scio.
> nam olim populi prius honorem capiebat suffragio,
> quam magistro desinebat esse dicto oboediens;
> at nunc, prius quam septuennis est, si attingas eum manu,
> extemplo puer paédagogo tabula disrumpit caput.

> That I know for sure. In the olden days a man would hold an office by popular vote before ceasing to obey his tutor. Now, however, before a boy is seven years old, if you lay a hand on him, he immediately cracks the tutor's head with his tablet.
> (Plautus *Bacch.* 438–42, transl. adapted from de Melo (2011))

The fathers' behaviour at the end of the *Bacchides*, however, endorses Lydus' point that not all is well with Roman morals and education.[8] While the

---

[7] Cf. Fitzgerald in this volume on the recurrence of whipping jokes in Roman comedy and Young (1987) on the social status of the pedagogue, his role, attitudes toward him, and the temporary nature of his role.

[8] We should not forget that Roman comedy also projects an alternative ideal of Roman education, that of the country man – a Cincinnatus-like figure – such as the grandfather of young Charinus in *Merc.* 64–72, who (mercilessly) prepared Charinus' father when a

Bacchis sisters through recurrent imagery and word-play portray the fathers as sheep that can be fleeced (*Bacch.* 1120–206), the fathers themselves are only too happy to join the flock of suitors. Indeed, the end of the play explicitly states that these fathers are becoming rivals of their sons for the favour of the courtesans and thereby undermines any moralising attitudes the fathers have displayed previously.[9]

This particular comic situation involving fathers and sons, however, does make an impact on education: it penetrates the world of Roman declamation by providing food for thought for rhetorical exercise and debate in the declamation schools that served to train future lawyers.[10] The early second century AD rhetorician Calpurnius Flaccus' collection of declamatory cases contains the following example:

filius meretricis suae redemptor

diuersas meretrices amabant pater et filius. pater filio pecuniam dedit, ut amatam patris redimeret. ille suam redemit. abdicatur.

The son who bought the freedom of his mistress

The Situation: A father and a son were conducting love affairs with different mistresses. The father gave his son money to buy the release of the one loved by his father. The son bought the release of his own mistress. He is disinherited.

(Calpurnius Flaccus 37, transl. adapted from Sussman (1994))

Similarly Quintilian's *Minor Declamations* 14 and 15, in which a prostitute gives her poor lover an anti-love potion that actually works but is then accused of poisoning him, provide scenarios that seem to take their inspiration from the world of Roman comedy.[11] They spell out in terms of rhetorical exercise, couched in the guise of court speeches, the projected social

---

young man to be a farmer and run the family estate. See Grilli (1979) and Leigh (2004) 98–157. The latter traces Roman comedy's dichotomy of morally corrupting sea/city with morally sound countryside to the Catonian *De agricultura*. Gratwick (1987) 244–5 illuminates the stern character of Demea in the *Adelphoe*: 'Demea has his own role-model and guru in Hegio, the idealised peasant-farmer, of whom precious few still walk the earth [...] it is ironic that Demea's hard work has lifted him out of the very class he admires.'

[9] Cf. Barsby (1986) 184. 'In terms of the plot, the obligatory happy ending of comedy has been achieved [...]. It is true that the *menage à six* is not likely to be a very permanent arrangement.'

[10] Batstone (2009) 213–17 traces echoes of court speeches in *Miles Gloriosus* and *Rudens*. Sussman (1994) 200 on Calpurnius Flaccus 37 lists further examples of declamations inspired by comedy.

[11] In addition Gunderson (2017) 271 describes the pair as 'a rhetorical fugue on an elegiac theme set by Catullus, *odi et amo*, "I hate and I love." The melody's bass notes are provided by the *Lex Cornelia de sicariis et veneficiis*, the law against poisoners.'

repercussions of the behaviour of Roman comedy's young male protagonists, which in some cases take effect many generations down the line.[12]

In my analysis so far, I have bought into a narrative of moral decline, but that has led to a simplistic view of good (old) Roman versus corrupting (new) Greek and has left out of account the benefits of Rome's Hellenisation, a cultural revolution that forced the Roman educational system to react to the Greek ideal of *paideia*.[13] This idea of rearing, educating, and socialising the ideal citizen through a combination of (what we call today) liberal arts, science, and physical education will ultimately lead Cicero in his *Tusculan Disputations* to propose a system of education that would regenerate the morals of the younger generation of aristocrats and lead them back to the standards of their ancestors while incorporating Greek philosophy.[14] Even before that, the adoption (or at least recognition) of this ideal which encourages critical thinking will have provided potential for conflict with the absolute powers of the stern Roman *paterfamilias*, whose ideal was to produce a new head of family in his image. The omnipotence of the male head of a Roman family over all members of his household including adult sons is a much-noted feature in scholarship discussing father–son relations in Roman comedy.[15] For, how can a son possibly dare to scheme against his father if the latter can have him put to death without trial for disobedience (in reality admittedly a rare event)? One comedy in particular, Terence's *Adelphoe*, plays out contrasting paternal approaches to bringing up sons.[16] One father, Micio, is overly forgiving towards his adopted son, while his brother Demea, the biological father of the two sons featuring in this play, is overly strict towards his. Leaving aside for the most part the play's fascinating discourse on nature versus nurture, and indulgence versus moral stricture, or as Lape (2004a) puts it 'natural kinship' versus 'social kinship', and jumping straight to its end, the play offers a remarkable reconciliation of the 'absolute' authority figure of the *paterfamilias* with some of the more liberal educational tendencies of Micio. Nevertheless, the impression remains that

---

[12] See van Mal-Maeder (2007) 10–17 for comedy's influence on declamation. Further examples include Calpurnius Flaccus 5 (brothel-keeper kills customers), 30 (grandson from a liaison with a prostitute acknowledged as legitimate), 51 (the rapist of two women who brings up his son), and 53 (the sons adopted in each other's place).

[13] On the Greek ideal of *paideia*, see Jaeger (1945). See also Hadot (1997) for an account of *enkuklios paideia* and the liberal arts as they relate to the Romans.

[14] Gildenhard (2007) 89–206 mines the prefaces of the five books of the *Tusculan Disputations* for the political and didactic intent of Cicero's *paideia Romana*.

[15] Wlosok (1990) 48 and Lape (2004a) 35. On the *patria potestas* of the paterfamilias, cf. Crook (1967); Saller (1986), (1991), and (1999); Dixon (2001).

[16] Henderson (1999) 38–68 highlights the pitfalls of any educational philosophy on display in the *Adelphoe*.

the overindulgent Micio is somehow punished by being made to end his bachelor life, marry, and take on responsibility. In Lape's view this 'union of opposites' (Lape (2004a) 49) re-asserts Demea's authority over his son(s) but it also imbues his at times farcically stern character with a sense of humanity.[17]

> DE. nunc adeo si ob eam rem uobis mea uita inuisa, Aeschine, est,
> quia non iusta iniusta prorsus omnia omnino obsequor,
> missam facio: ecfundite, emite, facite quod uobis lubet.
> sed si id uoltis potius, quae uos propter adulescentiam
> minus uidetis, magis inpense cupitis, consulitis parum,
> haec reprehendere et corrigere quem, obsecundare in loco:
> ecce me qui id faciam uobis. AE. Tibi, pater, permittimus:
> plus scis quod opus factost.

> DE: Now Aeschinus if you two don't like my ways because I won't go along with everything you do indiscriminately right or wrong, I wash my hands of you. Spend, squander, do what you want. If, on the other hand, where your youth makes you shortsighted, hotheaded or reckless, you need reproof, correction, and support from time to time, here I am at your service. AE: We put it into your hand father. You know better what ought to be done.
>
> (Terence *Ad.* 989–96, transl. Barsby (2001))

Wlosok has highlighted the reaction of the son to his (biological) father's offer as a seal of approval for Demea's change in character as he moves – still warning of the fallacies of moral corruption – towards a less tyrannical and more advisory paternal role. She even suggests that Terence's last comedy provides a model for a more humane father–son relationship that is not characterised by excessive leniency towards sons but cultivates and gently modernises elements of the traditional Roman role of the *paterfamilias*.[18]

---

[17] The end of *Adelphoe* has been discussed from a variety of viewpoints, cf. Arnott (1963); Johnson (1968); Grant (1975); Greenberg (1979–80); Damen (1990). Gratwick (1987) 260–1 casts doubt on Demea's 'genuine change of heart' as proposed by Martin (1976) and sees an unacceptable change in character 'in Demea's suddenly acquiring a wise head and consequent moral weight' (257).

[18] Wlosok (1990) 59. Henderson (2004) points out that the supposed 'humanism' the fathers of Roman comedy put on stage has frequently been over-interpreted. Jocelyn (1973) showcases impressively how the *sententia* '*homo sum: humani nil a me alienum puto*' has been misread as an expression of Terentian *humanitas* whilst it serves in its original context to justify a neighbour's nosiness. See also Hermand (2011) on Cicero's use of this *sententia*.

Comedy's Moral

Roman comedy on the whole tends to employ *sententiae* in the format of
gnomic generalisations, akin to proverbs, that can be made to serve as all-
convincing moral argument and to construct moral authority for the speaker.
It is hard to argue against their universal appeal. When concentrating on this
stylistic feature of Roman comedy we will find that the use of *sententiae* often
economises on argumentation and cuts short debate. At the same time
sententiae showcase the morals of Roman comedy.

Unsurprisingly, the literary technique of *Adelphoe* relies heavily on *sententiae*. The stern father Demea learns from his slave Syrus that his son
Ctesipho (supposedly) criticised his brother Aeschinus' lewd behaviour
with the words *non tu hoc argumentum perdis sed uitam tuam* ('It's not
the money that you are squandering, it's your life', *Ad.* 410). This prompts
him to outline the basics of moral instruction, handed down from father
to son.

DE. Saluos sit spero: est similis maiorum suom. SY. Hui!
DE. Syre, praeceptorum plenust istorum ille. SY. Phy!
domi habuit unde disceret. DE. Fit sedulo:
nil praetermitto: consuefacio: denique
inspicere tamquam in speculum in uitas omnium
iubeo atque ex aliis sumere exemplum sibi.
hoc facito. SY. Recte sane. DE. Hoc fugito. SY. Callide.
DE. Hoc laudist. SY. Istaec res est. DE. Hoc uitio datur.
SY. Probissume. DE. Porro autem SY. Non hercle otiumst
nunc mi auscultandi. piscis ex sententia
nanctus sum: ei mihi ne corrumpantur cautiost:
nam id nobis tam flagitiumst quam illa, Demea,
non facere uobis, quae modo dixti et quod queo
conseruis ad eundem istunc praecipio modum:
hoc salsumst, hoc adustumst, hoc lautumst parum:
illud recte: iterum sic memento. sedulo
moneo, quae possum pro mea sapientia:
postremo tamquam in speculum in patinas, Demea,
inspicere iubeo et moneo quid facto usus sit.

DE: Bless him! He gives me hope. He is a chip off the old block. SY:
(pretending to be impressed) Wow! DE: Syrus, he is full of these maxims.
SY: (slyly) He had someone to learn from at home. DE: One does one's best.
I never turn a blind eye. I teach him good habits. Above all I tell him to look
into the lives of others as if into a mirror and to take from them an example

for himself. 'Do this,' I say. s y: Quite right. d e: 'Avoid that.' s y: Splendid. d e: 'This is praiseworthy.' s y: Just the thing. d e: 'This is wrong.' s y: Excellent. d e: Then again ... [...] s y: As far as I can, I instruct my fellow slaves on the same principles as yours. 'Too salty.' I say. 'A bit burnt. Not clean enough. Just right: be sure to do the same next time.' I do my best to advise them with such wisdom as I have. Above all I tell them to look into the saucepan as if into a mirror, Demea, and I advise them what lessons to learn.

(Terence *Ad.* 411–29, transl. Barsby (2011))

Demea in his speech provides the linguistic backbones of any good morally instructive *sententia*.[19] The slave Syrus then comically fills the generic pontificating of 'Father Demea' with situational instructions from his life in the kitchens where the saucepan must service as the poor man's mirror of life. Initially Syrus, however, has prompted Demea to enter 'pontification mode' by bringing up (or should we say making up) the *sententia* quoted above (*Ad.* 410).

In addition, *sententiae* play a central role in staging and settling the conflict between the two brothers in *Adelphoe* (the older pair, that is). Micio confronts Demea with a maxim to justify having meddled with both sons' affairs: *Nam uetus uerbum hoc quidemst, communia esse amicorum inter se omnia* 'There is an old saying that friends share everything in common', *Ad.* 803; cf. also Plato *Laws* 739c, *Phaedrus* 279c, and Aristotle *Ethics* 8.9.1), which Demea dismisses harshly (and almost uniquely – for maxims are usually well-received) as 'coming too late'. However, just a few verses later it becomes clear that Demea was actually paying attention to his brother's strategy of argumentation. For Demea is quoting back at Micio a maxim previously employed by his brother.[20] Let us look at Micio's version first:

> Solum unum hoc uitium affert senectus hominibus:
> attentiores sumus ad rem omnes quam sat est,
> quod illos sat aetas acuet.

---

[19] Gratwick (1987) 244–5 points out the limitations of Demea's instructions as he provides linguistic backbones only without achieving the level of abstraction that would create a moralising *sententia*: 'Demea's method is to go on applying an approach which might suit young children as yet incapable of appreciating general principles at an age when the subject ought to be asking, "Yes, but what is it that is common to and behind your praise of ABC and blame of XYZ?" Demea does not in fact have a criterion of right and wrong derived from principles, only an excessive awe of what most people think, leading him near to hypocrisy (734).'

[20] See also *Merc.* 374–5 where the son quotes back one of his father's favourite maxims to escape further paternal attention.

But there is one fault which old age brings to us. We all become far too worried about money, on which time will sharpen *their* (the sons') attitudes soon enough. (Terence *Ad.* 833–5)

And then consider Demea's version:

> postremo nunc meum illud uerbum facio, quod tu, Micio,
> bene et sapienter dixti dudum: 'uitium commune omniumst,
> quod nimium ad rem in senecta attenti sumus'.

When all is said and done, can't I adopt for myself the remark which you made just now, Micio, so wisely and so well? 'It's a common fault of all of us that in old age we are too worried about money.' (Terence *Ad.* 952–4)

With this example of comic intratextuality Demea adopts and adapts the argumentative technique his brother has employed previously. In this case the *sententia*'s persuasive force succeeds, for Micio cannot easily undermine a *sententia* he has just employed himself without sabotaging his own moral standing. At the play's very end Demea thus forces Micio into giving away a larg(ish) plot of land.

We should remember, however, that maxims are often ironically used in Roman comedy by characters whose moral high ground leaves much to be desired or who occasionally abuse their sententious force to justify inappropriate actions (often this forms part of a play's comic technique).[21] Nevertheless, in all cases these maxims showcase the morals deemed acceptable in the world of comedy. Sometimes a character quotes a *sententia* like a proverb in conversation usually clearly marked with a preamble such as 'there is an old saying' or similar. These are obvious instances of sententiousness that can be easily recognised and which signal that comedy is already looking back onto a gnomic tradition. Other less overt instances occur unmarked but have identical nomothetic qualities as their marked counterparts; they are helping to lay down the moral laws of Roman comedy. To exemplify this let me place together those *sententiae* from Terence's *Adelphoe* that deal with one of Roman comedy's pre-eminent concerns: interpersonal relationships and how to deal with the vagaries of life:

> Accipiunda et mussitanda iniuria adulescentiumst.

You have to accept the misbehaviour of young men and grit your teeth.
(Terence *Ad.* 207)

[21] See n. 18 above.

> Ut homost, ita morem geras.

You have to take people as you find them. (Terence *Ad.* 431)

> Re ipsa repperi
> facilitate nil esse homini melius atque clementia.

I've discovered that in reality nothing is better for a man than to be generous and easygoing. (Terence *Ad.* 860–1)

> Ita uiast hominum quasi quom ludas tesseris.
> Si illus quod maxume opus est iactu non cadit,
> illus quod cecidit forte, id arte ut corrigas.

Life is like a game of dice. If you don't get the exact throw you want, you have to use your skill and make the best of the one you do get. (Terence *Ad.* 739–41)

> Numquam ita quisquam bene subdacta ratione ad uitam fuit
> quin res, aetas, usus semper aliquid apportet noui,
> aliquid moneat, ut illa quae te scisse credas nescias,
> et quae tibi putaris prima, in experiundo ut repudies.

Nobody has ever had such a well worked-out plan of life that circumstances, age, and experience don't introduce some new factor, teach some new lesson, so that you no longer know what you thought you knew and you reject in practice what you had reckoned to be of prime importance. (Terence *Ad.* 855–8)

Despite constituting a random sample from but one of Terence's plays these *sententiae* provide us with a good idea about the attitude displayed in this Roman comedy. If we were to extend my reading practice to all of Terence's extant plays (and those of Plautus too) we would face the 'morals' of comedy expressed through its sententiousness. In addition – at least according to ancient thought that links an author's *persona* to the *sententiae* in that author's oeuvre – we gain a reflection of Plautus and Terence themselves.[22] While the Renaissance uses collections of *sententiae* from Roman comedy for teaching Latin through sound bites and paratactic *sententiae*, these collections simultaneously unearth and showcase the morals of Roman comedy, linking back to the (not always so) stern fathers, the tutors, and the elderly that are voicing their moral

---

[22] Already Anaximenes' *Ars Rhetorica ad Alexandrum* 11.1 defines *gnomai* as expressions of an author's opinion. See also the etymology provided by Quintilian: *Sententiam ueteres quod animo sensissent uocauerant*. ('The ancients used the word *sententia* to mean what they felt in their minds', Quint. *Inst.* 8.5.1).

opinion, as well as the contemporaneous moral discourse in Republican Rome.

An egregious example of *sententiae* being recycled in a post-classical context would be Cato's *Disticha*. A spurious collection of 144 hexametric *disticha* called the *Dicta/Disticha Catonis*, the authorship of which was traditionally ascribed to Cato the Elder, was in quasi universal use for basic grammar and reading instruction in Late Antiquity and throughout the Middle Ages.[23] This collection frequently offers moral sayings, the gist of which comes very close to both the moral opinions expressed and the proverbs used by the characters of Roman comedy. Below I have selected but two of 'Cato's' sayings that reflect concerns also found in comedy.

> 16. Multorum cum facta senex et dicta recenses,
> Fac tibi succurrant, iuuenis quae feceris ipse.

> 16. When you as an old man reprimand another's faults,
> recall that when young you too gave cause for blame.

> 29. Quod uile est, carum, quod carum, uile putato:
> Sic tu nec cupidus nec auarus nosceris ulli.

> 29. Despise the dear and value the mean thing;
> So no harm can come to anyone through your greed or lust.

To Roman schoolboys reading Plautus and Terence, the *Disticha Catonis* must thus have often seemed like a condensed version of comic morale that casts the shadow of Cato the Elder over Roman comedy.[24]

Unlike tragedy, however, comedy seems to harbour few illusions as to the effectiveness of its moral teachings. For in the *Adelphoe* Micio suggests that it's not morals but lack of money that kept both him and Demea from 'having fun' when they were young.

> MI. haec si ne, que ego neque tu fecimus,
>   non siit egestas facere nos: tu nunc tibi
>   id laudi ducis, quod tunc fecisti inopia.
>   iniuriumst: nam si esset unde id fieret,

[23] Boas (1952) for a critical text and Duff (1961) for an English translation as well as Wayland Johnson Chase (1922). For the history and transmission of the *Disticha*, see Boas (1914) and Sallmann (1997). Bloomer (2011) 139–69 traces the *Disticha*'s use as school text.
[24] Grimal (1986) 392 poses the question of which ethical positions displayed in the *Trinummus* would have met with Cato's approval.

faceremus. et tu illum tuom, si esses homo
sineres nunc facere, dum per aetatem licet,
potius quam, ubi te exspectatum eiecisset foras,
alieniore aetate post faceret tamen.

MI: If you and I didn't do these things, it was because we could not afford them. Are you now claiming credit for behaviour forced on you by poverty? That's not reasonable. If we'd had the means to do these things, we would have done them. And, if you had any humanity, you would allow that son of yours to do them while he has the excuse of youth, rather than have him do them at a less appropriate age when he has at long last seen you to the grave. (Terence *Ad.* 103–10)

Even Syrus, the household slave, seems to have internalised that all that sententiousness on display has little educational effect. We ought to recall the position of Syrus' remark as it forms the conclusion/culminaton of his exchange about *sententiae* with his master that I have cited previously. Does he, we wonder, offer us instructions on how to read the *Adelphoe* as a whole?[25]

SY. quid tu hic agas? ubi siquid bene praecipias, nemo optemperet.

SY: Well, you won't achieve much here. If you give any good advice nobody takes any notice.

(Terence *Ad.* 433–4)

According to this reading of Roman comedy all moral content showcased in the plays is presented in vain. The genre does thus not provide the cathartic edification that tragedy offers. That might well be a realistic assessment of primary audiences but one should not forget Plautus and Terence's long career as school texts with their plays mined explicitly for grammatical instructions and moral guidance.[26]

Further Reading

James (1998b), Lape (2004a), Henderson (2004), Fantham (2004d) as well as the relevant sections of Konstan (1983) and Hunter (1985) provide good points of entry into father and son relationships in Roman comedy.

Gruen (1992) showcases how Roman identity developed *vis-à-vis* Hellenism. See Jaeger (1945) on *paideia*, Bonner (1977) on Roman education

---

[25] See also the slave Gripus in *Ru.* 1249–53 quoted by Christenson in this volume.
[26] See Müller (2013) 363–79, Cain (2013) 380–96 in Augoustakis and Traill (2013) as well as Manuwald on reception in this volume.

in general, and Gildenhard (2007) on Cicero's attempts to incorporate the Greek concept of *paideia* into the Roman educational ideal. Bloomer (2011) traces the Roman school curriculum and the use of the *Disticha Catonis* in schools. Jocelyn (1973) unearths the history of one famous Terentian *sententia*.

11

WILLIAM FITZGERALD

Slaves and Roman Comedy

The topic of slavery in Roman comedy might belong either in a study of ancient slavery or of ancient comedy. Comedy was the pre-eminent place in Roman culture where the experience and interaction of masters and slaves was stylised, and it is partly through stylisations of one kind or another that citizens lived with slavery. At the same time there is a close relation in the Roman mind between the genre of comedy and slaves. In the prologue to the *Eunuchus* Terence lists some of the crucial ingredients of the comic genre; the 'running slave' rubs shoulders with good matrons, bad prostitutes, the greedy parasite, and the boastful soldier. A list of typical comic actions includes 'a child substituted, the old man deceived by his slave, loving, hating, suspecting' (*qui magi licet currentem seruum scribere / bonas matronas facere, meretrices malas / parasitum edacem puerum supponi falli per seruum senem / amare odisse suspicari, Eun.* 36–40). But among these characters and actions the slave and his deceit hold a special place. Mercury, in Plautus' *Amphitryon*, makes a special association of comedy with the role of slaves when he announces to the audience that this will not be a tragedy, saying 'Since there's a slave part I'll make it a tragic-comedy' (*Amph.* 60–1).[1] Plautus was proud of his slaves; when Chrysalus, in *Bacchides*, boasts of having bamboozled his (senior) master he contrasts the paltry achievement in this area of the slaves of Greek New Comedy, the Parmenos and Syruses, who steal two or three *minae* from their masters; there is nothing worse, he adds, than a slave who lacks resourcefulness (*Bacch.* 649–52). That the plays of Menander featured deceiving slaves is attested by Ovid, who declares that Menander's plays will last as long 'as the deceiving slave, the hard father, the shameless bawd, the persuasive prostitute' (*Amores* 1.15.17–18).[2]

The slave and his trickery, then, are emblematic of comedy for the Romans, but it was Plautus who gave us the most exuberant examples of

---

[1] See also Plautus, *Mil.* 213 and Terence, *And.* 583–4 for slaves and comedy.

[2] However, among the plays of Menander of which substantial portions survive, only the *Aspis* contains a part for a scheming slave, but he is far from the mischievous Plautine type: 'A loyal slave working for the family, not what Plautus would have made him: a rogue challenging the family structure and supporting anarchy and dissipation' (Anderson (1993) 160 n. 7).

this type and featured them most prominently in their respective plays. Eight out of Plautus' twenty surviving plays feature intriguing clever slaves (*serui callidi*): *Pseudolus, Asinaria, Bacchides, Epidicus, Miles Gloriosus, Mostellaria, Persa, Poenulus*. Duckworth (1952, 106) calculates that 44 per cent of all monologue in Plautus belongs to slaves, while 25 per cent goes to the *senex*, the next character type in order of loquacity. Not surprisingly, male slaves are more prominent than female, though three slave girls in Plautus have important roles (Milphidippa in *Miles Gloriosus*, Pardalisca in *Casina*, and Astaphium in *Truculentus*). Terence's slaves make less of an impression, but he has prominent roles for slaves in *Andria, Heauton Timorumenos, Phormio*, and *Adelphoe*.[3]

If comedy celebrates the upturning of normal hierarchical relations, then Roman comedy situates this reversal primarily in the relation between slave and master. When the comic *adulescens* (young man) whose love has deprived him of his wits and his money, throws himself on the mercy of his resourceful slave, the reversal of social hierarchy is explicitly acknowledged by the characters themselves. The slave is hailed as the free man's *patronus* (roughly, patron), for instance,[4] or the reversal may be enacted on stage when the slave mounts his master and rides him like a beast of burden, as in the *Asinaria* (699–702).[5] Donatus, in his fourth century AD commentary, declared (*ad Eunuchum* 57) that it was permissible to present slaves more clever than their masters in comedies played in Greek dress (*palliata*), but generally not in comedies played in Roman dress (*togata*). The remains of *comoedia togata* are very scarce, but they suggest that Donatus may have been exaggerating.[6] Whatever the truth of his statement, it indicates that there was something subversive about these figures. But the subversive character of the clever slave is not confined within a single role; it acts as a lightning rod for other characters who may be dissatisfied with their position.

The slave also stands at a nodal point in comedy's characters and the power relations between the dramatis personae. Roman comedy is domestic comedy, its arena is the family, or rather the *familia* (a broader concept which includes, among others, the slaves). Within the *familia* there are inevitable tensions between members of the various hierarchies that govern it: fathers and sons, men and women, slave and free. As a servant of two masters, *adulescens* and *senex* (old man), the comic slave is the point where the tensions between father and son are played out.[7] It is the traditional role

---

[3] On Terence's slaves, see McCarthy (2004). See Wright (1974) 105–6 and 156–61 for *serui callidi* in the fragmentary remains of other Roman comic writers.
[4] *Asinaria*, 652–3 and 689.   [5] Segal (1987) 104–16 for the recognition of status reversal.
[6] Leigh (2004) 9.
[7] Dilemmas about which master to serve are expressed at *Ps.* 490–4 and *And.* 206–14.

of the *paterfamilias* to preserve the family fortune and of the young man to waste money in extravagant living. In some respects, as *paidagogos* (tutor) for instance, the slave might be a proxy of the father's authority, but the clever slave of comedy encourages and abets his young master's extravagant living without regard for the family's finances and his father's disapproval; in Holt Parker's ingenious pun, the clever slaves of Plautus act as *paidoparagogoi*, child *mis*leaders (Parker (1989/2001) 134). Son and slave are both in their different ways subject to the extraordinary powers of the *paterfamilias* and so they are natural allies and yet, of course, they are worlds apart. The *adulescens* must be distinguished from the slave because of the very possibility of confusion between their statuses. Terence has a slave contrast the *uerba* (words) that the son will incur for his transgressions against his father with the *uerbera* (blows) that will be undergone by the slave at the hand of his master (Terence *Haut.* 356). Only the extra syllable indicates how far the son is from the slave, the *dominus* from the *pater* (father). Does the absurd trickery of the slave distract us from the more disturbing rebellion of the son? Parker (1989/2001, 136) argues that 'It is the slave who acts, plans, intends, does and thereby takes on (and takes away) all the guilt that would have fallen to the son. To the son falls the important task of interceding for his alter ego with his father.' Whether or not we can see the slave as an alibi for the son's rebellion, it is clear that the comic slave is a character who allows the tensions written into the structure of the *familia* to be channelled and moved into the realm of the comically improbable.

Not only can slave and son find common cause in their subordinate relation to the *paterfamilias*, but so can slave and woman, subject to the *paterfamilias* along a different axis of power. Plautus' *Casina* explores this possibility when an alliance of women and slaves, the underlings of the *familia*, defeats the plan of the *senex* Lysidamus to possess his slave Casina by arranging a marriage of convenience between Casina and his bailiff Olympio.[8] Cleostrata, the *matrona* (married woman) of the play, identifies herself with the figure of the clever slave by adopting the language of slave trickery.[9] To make matters more complicated, the *paterfamilias* (head of the family) Lysidamus, who is also rebelling against his own familial role by usurping the son's role as lover, deploys military language to describe his

---

[8] The *Casina* exerted a powerful influence on Beaumarchais' (and Da Ponte/Mozart's) *Marriage of Figaro*, a play with the whiff of revolution about it (1784 Beaumarchais, 1786 Mozart).

[9] See Anderson (1993) 105 on Cleostrata's use of *ludus* and its compounds. But Rei (1998) 95 points out that Cleostrata is also differentiated from the slaves in that she does not don disguise or play a role.

plans much in the manner of the *seruus callidus*.[10] The *senex amator* (old man in love) acts as the rebellious slave when he seeks to fool a wife who wields power over him insofar as she holds the purse strings, a power which is compared to a master's dominance over his slave.[11] The slave role, then, has ramifications beyond the slaves in the dramatis personae, to become a mask that other characters can adopt when they 'play the slave' in the dramatic economy of the *familia*.

Another stock character with whom the slave has structural relations is the parasite.[12] As a trickster who has no ulterior motive for his trickeries, which he performs for the sheer joy of it, the slave is the mirror image of the parasite, who flatters and negotiates with his gulls for the sake of material rewards. By comparison, the slave is the more sympathetic character, exemplifying the comic value of pure anarchic fun, *ludus* in all its Latin senses of play, mockery, and deception. For Plautus' clever slaves *dolus* (deceit) is the essential action and *malitia* the essential source of pleasure, especially in those plays cast in what McCarthy (2000) has called the farcical mode, in which the slave's trickery is perpetrated for the sheer love of mischief and the provocation of a challenge.[13] In this respect, Terence is different from Plautus. Even where a Terentian slave perpetrates a *dolus* his motives are subordinated to the goals of the family in the more naturalistic mode of Terence's comedy.[14]

The Plautine slave's *malitia* puts him in danger of a *malum* (beating), but fortunately he is *callidus*, a word whose association of cunning with callouses is peculiarly appropriate to the comic slave. The slave's wit derives from his experience of punishment and from the need to avoid it, or perhaps from the fact that he is inured enough to beating that he is prepared to risk his back.[15] This is the story not only of the master fooled but also of the *malum* (beating) risked and avoided. It begins with someone in trouble. First of all, the *adulescens* and then, in a more physical way, his slave.

---

[10] *Cas.* 307–8, 344, and 352; cf. 953–9 and 1003 for the *senex* as slave threatened with a beating. Extended analyses of *Casina*'s complex dramatisation of the dynamics of power within the *familia* in McCarthy (2000) 77–121; Fitzgerald (2000) 81–6; Rei (1998) 99–104.

[11] *Cas.* 949–56. Cf. *As.* 87; *Men.* 766–7; Rei (1998) 95.

[12] In Terence's *Phormio* the slave Geta pays the parasite Phormio the compliment of calling him the cleverest (*callidiorem*, 591) man he has seen.

[13] On the Plautine slave's *malitia*, see Anderson (1993) 88–106.

[14] There is reason to believe that Terence shows himself conscious of this difference between his slaves and Plautus' when he has the *senex* Simo read Davos as a typical Plautine slave in *And.* 157–63; Simo's characterisation turns out to be completely false. See McCarthy (2004) 104 on the *Andria* passage and 100–5 on the difference between Terence's and Plautus' slaves more broadly.

[15] On the connection between *callidus* (clever) and the verb *calleo*, which can mean (of skin) to grow hard or (of people) to have experience, see Fitzgerald (2000) 41.

Just as it is the role of the *adulescens* to be in love because he is young, so it is the role of the slave to be bad because he is liable to be beaten. The relation between *adulescens* and slave, then, is both symbiotic and parodic. In one respect, slave and master form a continuous body, such that when the *adulescens* announces that he is head over heels in love (*Poen.* 153) his slave replies 'My shoulders feel it'. In *Epidicus* the eponymous slave is informed that his master is in love (*deperit, Ep.* 65) to which he replies that his back will be skinned (*deagetur corium de tergo meo*). The two verbs compounded with *de-* work in much the same way as the pun on *uerba* and *uerbera*, distinguishing the level of the master's concerns from that of the slave's. We are constantly reminded that within the symbiotic relation between master and slave distribution is unequal. 'What's the news?' asks the master and the slave replies 'you're in love and I'm hungry' (*Cas.* 704–5).[16] The woes of the lover are echoed in a more physical vein, by those of the slave. If the lover is miserable, the slave who is hung up for a beating is even more wretched, as Libanus reminds Leonida in *Asinaria*:

> LEO. o Libane, uti miser est homo qui amat.
> LIB. immo Hercle uero,
>   qui pendet multo est miserior.

> LEO: O Libanus, how wretched is the man who loves.
> LIB: Yes, by Hercules,
>   But he who is strung up is more wretched.   (Plautus, *As.* 616–17)

In these interchanges the slave provides an ironic echo of the free-born character's concerns, a perspective from which they seem unreal. Master and slave exchange troubles in the *Pseudolus*, when Calidorus tells his slave that he is 'flogged' by love (*uapulat, Ps.* 73), to which Pseudolus replies that he has a great treasure of *eheus* in the house, but of course they are not wrung out by anything as abstract as love, nor are the floggings that fall to the slave metaphorical. In this case, the slave's parodic relation to the master's 'sufferings' may have a subversive bite, and in general the servile version of the concerns of the free is a vision from below. There is a delicious scene in Terence's *Adelphoe* in which the slave Syrus applies Demea's self-satisfied exposition of his principles of teaching by example to his own efforts overseeing the preparations for a banquet (*Ad.* 412–32).

---

[16] Fitzgerald (2000) 84 argues that in *Casina*, Plautus expands the slave's 'You're in love and I'm hungry' into a nuanced exploration of relations of power and status within the household, cutting across the division of slave and free.

The comic slave represents an alternative humanity, parodic of the free citizen and released from the obligations that the demands of dignity impose on the free. Much of the verbal prestidigitation in Plautus and, to a lesser extent, Terence is assigned to the playful ingenuity with which slaves joke about punishment and claim respect for the beatings they have endured. One might compare the elegiac lover of a later period, whose ability to cast the life of love as a parodic shadow of the pursuits of more respectable citizens (*militat omnis amans*, i.e. all lovers are on military service) owes a good deal to the comic slave. The facetious use of mythical, and especially epic, precedent for less glorious activity is common to them both. In *Bacchides* 925–70, for instance, the slave Chrysalus delivers himself of a long comparison (to his advantage) between his tricking of the *senex* and the taking of Troy. The slave engaged on his *dolus* calls the senate in his breast, summons his troops, celebrates a victory, and relies on the virtue of his ancestors.[17] The emblems of citizenship are appropriated to the slave's achievements, creating a parallel world. One of the characteristics of his parallel world is that everything is made of leather, oxhide, elm or iron, the materials with which instruments of punishment are made.[18]

One can hardly exaggerate the extent to which the verbal texture of Plautine comedy is saturated with the language of punishment and torture. When one slave invites another to live it up while master is away the second slave replies 'My shoulders are already twitching as I hear you say that' (*iam scapulae pruriunt, quia te istaec audiui loqui*, *Persa* 36). Jokes about beatings seem to have been a comic cliché by the time of Aristophanes, but in Plautus they have become so ubiquitous and anticipated that the verbal ingenuity of the poet displays itself in a riddling allusiveness that can be very oblique. Asked how he is faring the Plautine slave has only to reply 'variously' (*uarie*, *Ep.* 17) to raise a laugh. The audience, primed to be on the lookout for whipping jokes, gets it immediately. But in case we don't, his interlocutor explains: 'I don't like that goaty, panthery type of man who fares variously.' We're talking about the mottled skin of the whipped slave. The slave's cunning, his improvisational versatility and shiftiness, have been inflicted on the slave himself as he comes to display his *uarius* nature on his own back. The devious versatility that is summed up in the metaphor *uorsipellem* (literally, skin-changing; *Bacch.* 658) is literalised on the slave's back. But within the special 'Saturnalian' time of comedy the slave will not actually be

[17] For instance, *As.* 545–7; *Persa* 753–7; *Ep.* 158–63.   [18] *Aul.* 601; *Persa* 23.

flogged.[19] Outside the play, of course, it's different, as the eponymous slave reminds his master at the end of *Pseudolus*: 'Why threaten me? I have a back' (*quid minitare? habeo tergum, Ps.* 1325).

What are we to make of this gruesome humour? For Parker (1989/2001) these jokes are a constant reminder of the ultimate power that the master wields. 'The crucifixion jokes, therefore, confirm the Roman audience in its sense of superiority and power. They serve to remind the audience of the servile nature of the characters, as well as the actors who perform them, and of the absolute mastery and everyday nature of the power they hold over them' (Parker 1989/2001, 132).[20] This certainly explains the ideological force of the jokes about punishment and torture, but other interpretations of the investments a free audience might have had in these jokes have been offered. McCarthy (2000, 26–7) alludes to the fact that, in the view of the masters, whipping defines the slave as the being without honour. The spectacle of slaves who are not only indifferent to this shame but who talk about their scars as a mark of honour is the spectacle of humans unburdened by the subjectivity of others in a way that was impossible for the masters. The slave who glories in his punishment offers to the free audience the fantasy of an existence that is freed from the demands of dignity. Fitzgerald (2000, 39) suggests that the fertile variety of Plautine language about torture and whipping can be illuminated by Bakhtin's concept of the grotesque body, a concept Bakhtin develops in his book on Rabelais (Bakhtin 1984). Rabelais' 'carnival text' features a vision of the body bursting its confines as it eats, excretes, and engages in sexual activity. This celebration of an overflowing body that is no longer individual but common to all represents the victory of a regenerative life over death. The swollen grotesque body of the tortured Plautine slave, copious in its variety and symbiotic with the Plautine text itself, transmutes the potentially disturbing reminder of the body's vulnerability provided by the beaten slave into a celebration of a regenerative life force.[21]

A very different, but equally striking, contribution of the slave characters to the distinctive nature of Plautine comedy is their metatheatricality.[22] English offers a convenient pun to point up the connection between the slave's plot to defraud his master and the plot of the play itself. Plautus makes much of the analogy between slave and playwright, producer and actor. The *locus classicus* is the scene in Plautus' *Pseudolus* in which the

---

[19] Segal (1987) 137–69.   [20] Crucifixion jokes: *As.* 548; *Most.* 56; *And.* 621; *Eun.* 544.
[21] See the reference to 'pregnant welts' in *As.* 276.
[22] On Plautine metatheatre, see Slater (1985) and Christenson in this volume.

eponymous slave ponders how he is going to make good on his promise to swindle the *senex* Simio out of the money needed by his young master. As yet, he has no plan, so, like a poet he must conjure something out of nothing (*Ps.* 401–5); later he will address the audience directly with the words:

> Suspicio est mi nunc uos suspicarier
> me idcirco haec tanta facinora promittere,
> qui uos oblectem, hanc fabulam dum transigam,
> neque sim facturus quod facturum dixeram.
> non demutabo. atque etiam certum, quod sciam,
> quo id sum facturus pacto nihil etiam scio,
> nisi quia futurumst. nam qui in scaenam prouenit,
> nouo modo nouom aliquid inuentum adferre addecet;
> si id facre nequeat, det locum illi qui queat.

I suspect that you suspect that I'm promising all these feats just to amuse you while I act out this play. And that I won't do what I have said I would do. I won't renege. Though as far as I know, I don't know how I am going to do it, only that I will. For anyone who comes on stage must bring on some new invention in some new style; if he can't do that, let him give way to someone who can.

(Plautus *Ps.* 562–70)

The slave is a liminal character, not quite socially integrated into the world of the free onstage, and so in a position to speak to the audience outside the fiction in a witty succession of asides. In this passage the emphasis on improvisation is particularly important: Pseudolus undertakes to work a deception without having first concocted a plan. The risky improvisation of the slave, who wavers between confidence in the resources of his *calliditas* and panic at the prospect of punishment, lends excitement to the unfolding of the plot: 'What will he do next?' is a question the audience might ask of Pseudolus or of Plautus. When, with typical swaggering confidence, Pseudolus announces to Simo, in the presence of his friend Callipho, that he will swindle Simo, Callipho says that he will postpone his planned visit to the country because he wants to watch Pseudolus' 'show' (*lubidost ludos tuos spectare, Pseudole, Ps.* 552), an interesting doubling of the theatrical event itself. Similarly, towards the beginning of *Miles Gloriosus* (145–55), the slave Palaestrio plays the role of the prologue explaining how he will engineer an optical illusion for his fellow slave; later, his deception requires him to stage a 'play' using two prostitutes as the actresses.

The metatheatricality of the plotting slave may have its roots in an association between actors and slaves at Rome, for the status of actors, subject to the disability of *infamia*, rendered them vulnerable to corporal punishment like slaves, and many of them were in fact slaves themselves.[23] At the end of *Asinaria* the *senex* Demaenetus has been caught by his wife with another woman (his son's girlfriend, but that is another story); he is dragged home by his wife, who will no doubt exact her revenge. The epilogue to this play suggests that what Demaenetus has done is nothing new or particularly heinous, and if the audience wants the old man to get off without a beating they only have to applaud (945). On one level, the rebellious slave role has been appropriated by the *senex*, who is subject to his rich wife, and the laws of comedy demand that he be excused. But if the *senex* really is a slave actor in disguise, and if he has performed his role well, he need fear no beating (cf. *Cist.* 684–5). The same words/rule? apply both to the role and to the actor.

It would be wrong to assimilate all comic slaves to the type of the *seruus callidus*. A popular Plautine set-piece is the slanging match between two slaves, sometimes contrasted as good and bad or urban and rustic.[24] The altercation between Grumio and Tranio at the beginning of *Mostellaria* (1–80) is the prime example. Grumio is the rustic slave who appears only in this scene to catch us up with the story thus far: the *senex* has been absent for a protracted period and in the meantime his son, under the influence of Tranio, has fallen into debauchery. Though it will be Tranio who will survive this interchange to become a protagonist of the comedy, it is Grumio who provides the point of view from which we first encounter him.

Duckworth (1952, 252) has aptly compared Grumio to the slave Eumaeus in the *Odyssey*, faithfully preserving the property of his master in the latter's absence, while Tranio, leading his young master into debauchery, destroys it. If Grumio reminds us of Eumaeus here, then the gradual shift of our sympathies over the course of this scene from Homer's 'good' slave (Grumio) to the 'bad' slave (Tranio) who articulates the values of comedy provides the perfect way in to the comic genre. Soon after this opening scene we are introduced to another slave, Scapha, who gives her mistress, the *meretrix* Philematium, some hard, realistic advice about prostitution and love (*Most.* 157–312) We can now site Tranio in relation both to the good slave Grumio and to Scapha who, from the point of view of the eavesdropping Philolaches, 'misleads' his beloved Philematium as Grumio does his master. Scapha, however, misleads her mistress not for the sheer pleasure of transgression, but rather from a knowledge of harsh realities derived from being at the bottom of the heap. So we are presented with two different kinds of bad servile advice – Tranio's is sheer *malitia*, whereas Scapha's is based on a cynical understanding of how the world works. The juxtaposition of

[23] Marshall (2006) 86–8.   [24] *Cas.* 89–143; *Truc.* 256–321; *Ep.* 1–28.

these scenes provides two different versions of the motivations that might underlie the slave's 'wickedness'.

When it comes to the question of what makes a good slave good, Plautus' Messenio in *Menaechmi* offers us a bottom line that is emphatically physical: Messenio considers part of the behaviour of the good slave that he has a proper regard for punishment and is able to prioritise the interests of his back over those of his belly, to prefer words (*uerba*) to blows (*uerbera*, *Men.* 977). Most of these moralising versions of the good slave are comic and not to be taken seriously. But in the *Captiui* the good slave/bad slave contrast is expanded from a scene into the fulcrum of a whole play, which mobilises and recasts some typical comic motifs to give us something like a problem play in which ideological questions are pointedly raised.[25] The protagonist of the *Captiui*, Tyndarus, is freeborn but was kidnapped as a boy and sold into slavery by a wicked slave of the household. The vicissitudes of war enslave Tyndarus together with his master (Philocrates), and they engage in a scheme to return home that involves deceiving their new master (Hegio) by exchanging roles. Philocrates, posing as the slave, is sent by Hegio to arrange for a ransom for 'himself', while Tyndarus remains behind, posing as Philocrates. Here we have a replay in a different mode of the typical Plautine plot in which the *senex* is deceived by the slave to further the interests of the son. A further twist is given to this model by the fact that Tyndarus' new master, on whom he is performing a 'noble' *dolus*, turns out to be his own father. Since Tyndarus, as the audience knows all along, will turn out to be of free birth, it is never quite clear whether we are to think of him as behaving as a faithful slave or as an honourable free person. If the latter, then the play anticipates the ancient novel, where freeborn characters are enslaved but retain their freeborn morality together with a beauty that marks them out from their fellow slaves.[26] If the former, then this element of the plot presents what Thalmann has called the 'benevolent' model of slavery, according to which the slave is potentially content with his lot and faithful, so that master–slave relations are assimilated to kinship. The deception wrought by Tyndarus and his original master means that they must trust each other; the slave (Tyndarus) remains faithful to his master, while the master, who returns to redeem his slave, is true to his paternal role. Thalmann argues that by playing off the faithful Tyndarus against the unrepentantly bad slave Stalagmus, who kidnapped and sold Tyndarus in the first place, Plautus balances the benevolent models of slavery with the suspicious model according to which the

---

[25] On slavery and the *Captiui*, see Thalmann (1996); McCarthy (2000) 167–209; Leigh (2004) 87–97.

[26] Compare Rei (1998) 95 on the *pseudomeretrices* of Plautus (women of free birth who have been enslaved and prostituted, portrayed as especially virtuous).

slave is inherently untrustworthy, and master–slave relations are based on force. Thalmann's view of the play is that it performs an ideological trick of reconciling the benevolent with the suspicious models of slavery, two incompatible attitudes to slaves that Roman masters held simultaneously, for the one justifies enslavement (of inherently base people), the other has persuasive, and self-congratulatory, force. But one might read the play as more problematic. McCarthy, for instance argues that it raises 'the essential problem that the honourable slave presents for his keepers: will his sense of honour require his obedience or his rebellion?' (187, comparing Seneca, *De Ira*, 3.29). The complexities of the play's reflection on slavery are considerable, and whatever its eventual ideological tendency (if indeed this can be established) it offers no support to those who believe there is such a thing as a slave by nature.

Tyndarus is the only slave who is actually punished in the course of a comedy, sent to the quarries by his master/father when the latter discovers that he has been duped. Returning from the quarries, Tyndarus seems to remind us of the difference between art and reality when he compares what he has experienced to paintings of Hades: 'I have seen many paintings depicting the torments of Hades but nothing is as like Hades as those quarries, where exhaustion must be driven from the body by toil' (*Capt.* 998–1000). Slavery in Roman comedy is no more an accurate portrayal of what happened to Roman slaves than the paintings of Hades are like Hades, and this is not the only time that we are reminded that behind the slaves of comedy, for whom punishment is no more than a threat, lie other slaves who are not protected by the conventions of this genre. When Artemona in Plautus' *Asinaria* realises that her husband has been stealing clothes from her and giving them to his mistress, she admits that she had blamed the slave girls for the thefts 'and used to torture the poor innocent things' (*atque insontis miseras cruciabam, Capt.* 888–9), a casual reference which has none of the usual jocular inventiveness in referring to the torture of slaves. With these anonymous slaves we reach the furthest point from the *serui callidi* who dominate the comedy of Plautus.

Further Reading

Stace (1968), Spranger (1984), and Duckworth (1952) contain some useful material on slaves in Roman comedy, though their approach is outdated. The most penetrating discussion of this topic is to be found in McCarthy (2000), which focuses on Plautus. Conveniently, McCarthy has followed this up with an excellent study of slaves in Terence (McCarthy 2004). Thalmann's (1997) study of the *Captiui* is challenging and theoretically sophisticated. Particular aspects of slaves in comedy are treated by Parker (1989/2001), Rei (1998), and Anderson (1993). Fitzgerald (2000) is a general study of slavery in Latin literature which deals with comedy in several places. More recently, Stewart (2012) has studied the plays of Plautus in relation to Roman slavery and Richlin (2014) the Plautine slaves in their contemporary context. Richlin (2017a) provides a challenging new account of Plautus as theatre by, through, and even for slaves. On the reception of the slave character, see Candiard (2017).

12

Mothers and Whores

Women's Studies and Gender Studies

Female characters have been taken into account in scholarship on the *comoedia palliata* since Donatus, yet the study of women in this genre has emerged as a topic in its own right only recently.[1] The first articles devoted exclusively to women in the *palliata* appeared in the 1970s; at the same time critics working on other aspects of comedy began offering insights into the theatrical functions of female characters.[2] However, it is only in the last fifteen years that feminist theory has been brought to bear on the study of comedy, and it has done so mostly in order to comment on linguistic strategies of characterisation.[3] The field is in fact so recent that the present collection of essays on the *palliata* was to be the first in English to include a chapter on gender (or, as a matter of fact, on women).[4]

The binary opposition evoked in the title of this essay is rooted in Freud's thesis that sons of distant mothers tend to treat wives as substitutes for mothers, and that they consequently separate objects of love ('mothers') from objects of sexual attraction ('whores').[5] This stereotypical assumption that a woman can only be either a 'mother' or a 'whore' is so deeply ingrained

---

[1] I am grateful to Amy Richlin for inspiring me to think of comedy in the context of women's lived experience, and to Martin Dinter, Sharon James, and David Konstan for helpful comments on earlier versions of this chapter.

[2] Among the earliest contributions were those by Fantham (1975) (see also (2000), (2004a), and (2004b); Schuhman (1977); Gilula (1980); Petrone (1989); see also Konstan (1983) *passim*; (1986); (1995) 120–40; Slater (1985)/(2000) 57–76; Moore (1998b) esp. 140–80.

[3] On gender in comedy, see Gold (1998) and James (1998a); on language, see Adams (1984); Dutsch (2004), (2005), and (2008); James (2005).

[4] That was the case when this chapter was first drafted in 2012. Since then, the Blackwell *Companion to Terence* was published, including Sharon James's excellent chapter on gender and sexuality (2013) 175–95; University of Wisconsin Press' *Women in Roman Republican Drama*, edited by Dutsch, James, and Konstan (2015), has also appeared in the meantime.

[5] Freud (1957); (1981) 165–75 and 179–90. These are, needless to say, illusory categories; see Janan (1994) especially 66–76 for perceptive comments on Catullus' fantasies of 'Woman'.

in today's popular culture that AIDS activists and WHO officials consider it a major obstacle to equal access to medical help.[6] Among the modern voices of protest against the reductionist vision of female sexuality represented by the 'mother/whore' dichotomy, one of the most poignant is that of French film-maker Jean Eustache, whose protagonist in *La maman et la putain* (*The Mother and the Whore* (1973)) is in love with two women: Marie who supports him financially and Veronika whom he picks up at a café. While the two seem at first to embody the 'mother/whore' dichotomy sig-nalled in the film's title, the protagonist quickly discovers that Marie really cares about sex while Veronika desires to have a baby and neither of them is willing to be reduced to one of the clichés. The film ends with an emotional monologue, in which Veronika claims that the category of *pute* (whore), a woman interested only in sex, does not correspond to any woman's lived experience, concluding that 'whores do not exist; (...) there is not one single whore on the planet'.

In this chapter I argue that the plots of Roman comedy testify to a similar interest in the limitations of sexual stereotypes, and that Plautus and Terence use their system of comic stock types and tension between the types and individual personae to explore interfaces between the roles of 'whore' and 'mother'.

According to Judith Butler, the act of performing one's gendered identity can be compared to the production of a linguistic utterance.[7] The *langue* (language) of gender, to use Saussurean terminology, is the set of social expectations, while the choices made with respect to these paradigms func-tion as its *parole* (utterances). Such utterances, thanks to their potential for both asserting and subverting the rules of gendered grammar, maintain and eventually modify the system of gendered roles. The process of creating gendered identities in the *palliata* depends on a very similar semantic rela-tionship between the taxonomy of stock types and the individual dramatis personae. With each character, the playwrights both reiterate and inflect the general rules of the system, suggesting new options.

Let us begin by positioning the figures of 'whore' and 'mother' against the typology of comic characters. The system of stock types in Roman comedy is built along the criteria of gender, social status, and age.[8] Within it, the prostitute (*meretrix*) can be of slave or free status, and either the property of the male pimp (*leno*) or the daughter of a female pimp (*lena*). Moreover, numerous plots (both Greek and Roman) also feature lost citizen girls temporarily cast as *meretrices*, traditionally termed

---

[6] So Booth (1998). [7] On gender as performance, see, for example, Butler (1999) 171–80.
[8] On designations of female dramatis personae in manuscripts, see Packman (1999).

pseudohetaerae. 'Whore' is, then, a role against which young female characters of all social classes (slaves, freedwomen, and even citizens) can be measured. Unlike the other stock types, which function in binary pairs (old man/old woman, young man/young woman, slave/maid, male pimp/female pimp), the *meretrix* has no direct male equivalent. Her closest match is the parasite, a young man ready to render all kinds of services in exchange for food. He might gratify his patron sexually, as the discreet double entendre in the *Menaechmi* 101–3 suggests. However, neither the parasites nor the *pueri delicati*, slaves with whom the male citizens occasionally have sex, play significant roles in the plots as objects of desire.[9] Although Plautus' prologues allude to male prostitution as an activity associated with the performance of comedy, the prostitute in the cast of characters is always female.[10]

In the cast of Roman comedy, the role of the mother is, as a rule, a luxury reserved for the citizen (*mulier*).[11] The plots make occasional concessions to the fact that biological motherhood transcends class divisions: in the *Poenulus* the nurse Giddenis finds her long-lost son, and in the *Truculentus* a prostitute pretends to have given birth. There is, however, a significant systemic exception in Plautine comedy: the female pimp (*lena*), who is always a freedwoman and former prostitute.[12] Unlike the male pimp who always owns slave *meretrices*, the *lena* acts as a procurer for her own daughter.[13] The role of parent-pimp, just like that of the prostitute, is reserved for women.[14] Both 'whore' and 'mother' are thus broader (if not universal) female roles that intersect with the traditional status-sensitive taxonomy of comic characters in ways that are bound to subvert, or at least nuance, sexual stereotyping.[15]

This essay falls into two parts, as Plautus and Terence work in somewhat different ways. I first offer a reading of two Plautine comedies that place the

---

[9] Lilja (1983) 15–46; Williams (1990) 34–7 collects most relevant passages; on *Menaechmi*, see Fontaine (2010) 236–7; on the interplay between the actors' and the characters' social status and gender, see Richlin (2015).

[10] On the attractiveness of the male actor in female clothing, see Dutsch (2008) 177–9.

[11] As Thais' story shows, emigrant women's daughters are likely candidates for prostitution; cf. *Eu.* 107: 'my mother was from Samos; she lived in Rhodos'.

[12] Although the *nutrix* is a mother figure, slaves are not represented as mothers of their own children; on Giddenis in the *Poenulus*, see Dutsch (2004). On the prostitute Phronesium posing as a *puerpera*, see Dutsch (2008) 112–16.

[13] One exception is the parasite Saturio who has his daughter pretend to be a captive sold to a male pimp.

[14] Saturio in the *Persa*, who forces his daughter to pretend to be a captive sold to a pimp, is the only male character whose behaviour verges on that of a pimp.

[15] The contrast between the two types was deeply ingrained in Roman law; cf. McGinn (1998) 152–3.

lena in the limelight: the *Asinaria* and the *Cistellaria*.[16] These plays offer an opportunity to examine the reasoning of both the typical pimp-mother (Cleareta in the *Asinaria* and the nameless *lena* in the *Cistellaria*) and that of one exceptional *lena* who acts against her type (Melaenis in the *Cistellaria*). The three pimps' daughters featured in both plots differ in their attitudes towards sex work, monogamy, and marriage; one of them (Gymnasium in the *Cistellaria*) seems reconciled with her occupation; two of them (Philaenium in the *Asinaria* and Selenium in the *Cistellaria*) are in love. More important, all the four women in the *Cistellaria*, far from being reduced to their dealings with clients, are shown to be capable of friendship and kindness. This type of *meretrix*, sometimes cast as protector of a young girl's innocence, is best known from Terence. I argue that Terence's predilection for the *bona meretrix* is a subtle way of interrogating these stereotypes. In foregrounding these diverse figures, I hope to draw attention to ways in which Roman comedy inflects and undermines contemporary sexual stereotypes.

Asinaria: It's My Job

From the perspective of the *lena* Cleareta, the plot of Plautus' *Asinaria* can be summarised as follows. One of the men pursuing her daughter Philaenium is Argyrippus, son of the wealthy Artemona and her hen-pecked husband Demaenetus. Argyrippus has no money of his own, but Philaenium is in love with him anyway. Philaenium's mother, however, remains steadfastly professional. She firmly demands payment, which the lad eventually delivers – just in time before his rival upsets the arrangement by contracting with Cleareta to secure Philaenium's services for the coming year. At Cleareta's house – her workplace as a *lena* – a party is held for Argyrippus and his father, who helped him obtain the money, and who now demands to sleep with Philaenium first. Argyrippus' mother, Artemona, however, warned by the rival's parasite, arrives to drag the father back home, leaving the son with Philaenium. Now there is a chance that the two rivals for Philaenium will agree to timeshare, thus doubling the *lena*'s income. It is the story of a tough bargain that turns out very well indeed – for Cleareta, the pimp.

The *lena* Cleareta appears on stage in two scenes that showcase the consummate professionalism of her behaviour. Cleareta's first appearance (*As.* 154–249) is in a scene in which Argyrippus delivers a long monologue

---

[16] I am grateful to one of CUP's anonymous readers for drawing my attention to the fact that both of these plays are adaptations of scripts by Menander; see Ludwig on Menander as the model for the nuanced portrayal of Thais in Terence's *Eunuchus* (1968) 173.

(*As.* 127–52) threatening to bring legal action (*As.* 131–2) against her. He threatens to reduce the pimp and her daughter to utter poverty (*As.* 139–45). Cleareta is undaunted by this violent speech (*As.* 162). She responds to the boy's pleading by reminding him that she is simply fulfilling her rôle as female pimp:

> ARG. male agis mecum.
> CL. quid me accusas, si facio officium meum?
>   nam neque fictum usquamst neque pictum neque scriptum in poematis
>   ubi lena bene agat cum quiquam amante quae frugi esse uolt.

> ARG: You are unfair to me.
>   CL: Why are you blaming me for doing my job? For there is no story
>   anywhere, no painting, nor any poem written, in which a lena who
>   wants to be thrifty treats her client well.   (Plautus, *As.* 173–5)

This *lena* tends to speak of herself in the first person plural, which stands sometimes for her entire household and sometimes for all the *lenae* as a group (*As.* 199–204).[17] She also easily slides into colourful parables that depict the generic *lena* in the third person, as a fisherman (*As.* 178–86) or bird-catcher (*As.* 215–26). From these adopted perspectives, she explains that her job description (*officium*) is part of a script that forces the female pimp to behave in a predetermined way. Cleareta's awareness of being manipulated like a puppet goes beyond the meta-theatrical: her references to various forms of artistic representation suggest that an imaginary cultural structure is determining her position. Her consciousness of this structure and of her place in it creates a quasi-Brechtian effect of distancing from a dominant ideology.[18]

In conversation with Philaenium (*As.* 504–44), Cleareta later forbids her daughter to see Argyrippus, for the sake of the livelihood of the entire household. Stressing the primacy of economic necessity, she forcefully denies her daughter the right to speak (*As.* 511, 516), acting, as Argyrippus has pointed out earlier (*As.* 247), 'like a slave owner *and* a mother':

> PH. sine me amare unum Argyrippum animi causa, quem uolo.
> CL. intro abi, nam te quidem edepol nihil est impudentius.

> PH: Please allow me to love only Argyrippus whom I desire for my own sake.
> CL: Go inside; I swear that there really is no creature more shameless than you.
>   (Plautus *As.* 542–3)

---

[17] See e.g., plural: *nos* (*As.* 155, 156); *percipimus* (*As.* 162); *quae uolumus* (*As.* 199); singular: *ego tibi misi mulierem* (*As.* 171); *facio officium meum* (*As.* 173).

[18] On alienation (*Verfremdungseffekt*) and the role of social awareness in Brecht's theatre, see Althusser (1962).

Concepts expected to guide exemplary relationships within a Roman family can be seen in Cleareta's demonstration of absolute power in this scene. As head of a Roman household, Cleareta is empowered to give orders to anyone (*imperium*). Absolute obedience, in the name of *pietas*, the love and respect that she owes her parent (*As.* 509) and *fas*, the quasi-religious duty to act accordingly, are also expected of her as a daughter (*As.* 514).[19] Plautus' use of this vocabulary of filial piety and good behaviour (*decorum*) in this scene transfers the ethical concepts that describe the relationships between citizen mothers and daughters into the context of prostitution, with its utmost financial insecurity. The resulting notion – that it is shameless for Philaenium to refuse to have many sexual partners – creates a humorous paradox that can be best appreciated against the background of the typical attitude of a comic mother towards an adult child's love interest.

Unlike the frigid mother of the aforementioned Freudian dichotomy, the mother of Roman comedy is an earthy figure who advocates healthy sex within the confines of marriage (including her own). Such mothers (Philippa in the Plautine *Epidicus*, Myrrina the mother-in-law in Terence's *Hecyra*) are particularly protective of their own daughters, granting sexual access to unmarried girls (*Cistellaria, Adelphoe*) only when they expect that it will lead to a secure monogamous relationship.[20] Sometimes mothers extend this protection to other female characters. The plot of the *Casina*, for instance, features a *materfamilias* shielding her ward against her own husband. To complete this picture of a mother's concern, we might add that mothers of sons in the *palliata* are also attuned to their children's needs. Eunomia in Plautus' *Aulularia* and Cleostrata in his *Casina* both help their sons obtain the girls they desire; Sostrata in Terence's *Hecyra* demonstrates a loving concern for her son's marriage, while Nausistrata in the *Phormio* insists that the family ought to foot the bill for the prostitute to whom her son is partial.

In the *Asinaria*, then, both Cleareta and the matron Artemona are atypical in their lack of concern for their children's happiness. In the final scene, when the matron reluctantly accepts that her son will stay with Philaenium – even if this is only to spite her husband – Artemona's attitude becomes closer to that of the typical comedic mother. The plot offers no similar opportunity to Cleareta, who as *lena* represents the very antithesis of citizen motherhood: a mother who instead of placing her daughter in a monogamous relationship forces her to have multiple partners. And yet, because of her concern with her

---

[19] Dixon (1992) 27–30 defines *pietas* as proper acknowledgement of family ties.

[20] If the mother is absent, the senior woman in the household takes over this responsibility (*Aulularia, Heauton, Phormio, Eunuchus*). See e.g., *Ph.* 113: 'so that she might grant me access'.

child's love life, typical of any mother's, this mother-procurer emerges as a perversely logical permutation of the mother figure. The mother-pimp simply interprets her maternal duties in the light of her harsh material circumstances.

Cleareta frequently, almost obsessively, draws attention to the material conditions that determine the actions of any *lena*. Fear of hunger dominates her discourse: she reminds Argyrippus that she needs to buy groceries (nothing extravagant, just the essential bread and wine *As.* 200). Her metaphors for the role of a *lena* (angling and bird hunting) have to do with finding food; she fears that if her daughter keeps rejecting lovers who can pay, the family will 'starve to death' (*As.* 530). These may be rhetorical clichés that invite the audience to dismiss the *lena*'s references to looming starvation as a mere excuse for her greed. Nevertheless the juxtaposition of penury and the Roman discourse of filial piety draws attention to the fact that Roman moral norms are meant to function under conditions of prosperity. Seen under conditions of penury, a reverse side of the Roman system emerges that is both shocking and logical: Philaenium's prostitution is in its own way an act of *pietas* and *decorum*. It does not matter whether we accept the *lena*'s arguments as her 'true' motivation, since, as she tells us herself, she is a construct. The juxtaposition of the prospect of hunger with the standards of chastity (*pudicitia*), love for parents (*pietas*), and decency (*decorum*) implies that such ethics are class-specific rather than universal. The representation of the demimonde in the *Asinaria*, with its loving girl and her hungry mother, leads to the conclusion that 'whores' (as Eustache's heroine suggested) do not in fact exist; there are only women who need grocery money.

Cistellaria: a Pimp With a Heart of Gold

In addition to the rhetoric of hunger, the *Cistellaria* uses another strategy for blurring the boundaries between 'whores' and 'mothers': it features a pimp who truly cares about her foster daughter.[21] The plot of this play is structured almost like a case study designed to illustrate the influence of nature versus nurture on women's ability to be mothers, wives, and friends. When the play begins, two former prostitutes, Melaenis and another unnamed *lena*, have each brought up a girl. The nameless *lena* has raised her own daughter, Gymnasium; Melaenis has raised Selenium, who, as a baby, was exposed by a citizen girl who fell victim to rape. While Gymnasium grows up to be

---

[21] See Konstan (1983) 94–114 for insightful comments on the relationships within the play (especially on Melaenis and Argyrippus); Fantham (2004a) for the literary context.

reconciled with prostitution, Selenium, the freeborn girl, falls in love and aspires to a monogamous relationship with her beloved. All this would suggest that the differences between the two classes are grounded in nature, were it not for the figure of Melaenis, who, although a former prostitute, is presented as a loving foster mother. Most important, however, is the play's presentation of the members of the 'meretricious profession' (*ordo meretricius*) as capable of affection and deserving of friendship.[22]

The opening scene shows Selenium and Gymnasium, the two young women, sharing a meal with the unnamed *lena* who is Gymnasium's mother. Melaenis, Selenium's mother, is absent.[23] There is humour in the contrast between the dialogue's leisurely, ladylike tone and the fact that the scene's protagonists are prostitutes, for whom time is money (cf. *Cist.* 106), and who would normally be competing for clients (cf. *Poen.* 36, 297–300). Selenium, the aspiring wife, has a favour to ask of her friend Gymnasium and her unnamed mother-pimp. Selenium wants Gymnasium to stay in the house in which she has been living for some time with her lover, Alcesimarchus. Selenium is obliged to leave that house, because Melaenis has ordered her to return home, since Alcesimarchus has been ordered by his father to marry a relative.

The dominant theme of this scene is women's capacity for love and friendship. The young women speak of their mutual love and devotion, while the older woman speaks of friendship and of the endless rivalry between matrons and the *ordo meretricius*. She calls for the *meretrices* to imitate the network of friendships that the topmost matrons foster among themselves, for matrons will never be friends of prostitutes. Such a network, she argues, would help her kind withstand the envy of legitimate wives. She adds that the *meretrices* do not deserve the wives' hostility, because prostitutes do not choose their profession but are compelled by hunger to practise it:

> Quia nos libertinae fuimus, ego et tua mater, ambae
> meretrices fuimus: illa te, ego hanc mihi educaui
> ex patribus conuenticiis. Neque ego hanc superbiae
> caussa pepuli ad meretricium questum, nisi ut ne essuriem.

Because we were freedwomen, your mother and I, we both became prostitutes. She brought you up and I brought up this girl here [Gymnasium], both children of fortuitous fathers. And I did not push her to prostitution out of arrogance but solely to avoid starvation.   (Plautus *Cist.* 38–41)

---

[22] On *ordo*, see Fantham (2004a) 234–5.
[23] For a comparison with Menander's *Synaristosai*, see Fantham (2004a) 224–6; see ibid. 229 on the possible origin of this motif in mime.

Her daughter, Gymnasium, not only has no objections, but is quite enthusiastic about her work (*addam operam sedulo, Cist.* 52), which she understands in terms of perverse *pietas*: 'Mother, it is seemly for me to aspire to be whatever you want me to be.' The *lena* Cleareta from the *Asinaria* would wholeheartedly agree.

Selenium, however, does not buy this argument: 'you could have given her to a husband,' she offers. This suggestion (which, of course, would make little sense given the girl's non-citizen status) initiates a series of jokes that explore the similarities between marrying off one's daughter and sending her to clients. The underlying concept is that like matrons, pimps must marry off their daughters, although unlike the upper-class women, they have to toil at doing so daily, or even more frequently. The prostitute must marry often; otherwise, her *familia* would starve (*Cist.* 42–5). Just as in the *Asinaria*, the vocabulary and imagery of citizen life, in this case to marry (*nubere*) and marry off (*nuptum dare*), are appropriated to describe mother–daughter relationships involving sex workers. Through this appropriation, Plautus cannily draws a parallel between mothers of citizen girls and pimps. The analogy works both ways: if female pimps act like matrons who marry off their daughters, then the matrons, in marrying off their daughters, likewise act as pimps.

The issue of frequency, as the ensuing exchange shows, is important. Selenium confesses that she suffers from heartache because of Alcesimarchus, and states the crux of the problem: 'I have wanted him all to myself to spend my life with' (*Cist.* 77). The unnamed *lena* finds this highly unprofessional. Her humorous comparison of marriage and prostitution notwithstanding, she draws the line at monogamous love, instructing Selenium that her ambition to love but one man and spend her whole life with him is fitting for a matron, but misplaced in a prostitute (*Cist.* 78–9). Love, she warns, should only be faked, as once a person truly loves, she begins to be more concerned with what is good for the loved one than what is good for herself (*Cist.* 95–7), and such an attitude cannot put food on the table. The *lena* is particularly shocked to discover that Selenium's mother has agreed to her daughter's request to remain faithful to one man (*Cist.* 86). As Selenium puts it, Melaenis 'complied with my wish, having proved as obliging to me as I am to her.' Although this is the demimonde, this mother–daughter relationship seems to be based on love and goodwill. And there is more: not only is Gymnasium willing to take some time off work and house-sit for Selenium, but her mother agrees to this – despite her misgivings and despite the lost income that will very likely result from Gymnasium's absence from home – all for the sake of friendship.

The opening scene of the *Cistellaria* highlights the differences and similarities between *mulieres* and *meretrices* in terms of their capacities for friendship and love. The prostitutes, as Gymnasium and her mother-*lena* demonstrate, are perfectly capable of friendly affection and loyalty. However, unlike matrons, who can love and marry only one man, they must be willing to 'marry' many times a day. That this practice should be the dictate of material circumstances is a motif we can recognise from the *Asinaria*. The *Cistellaria* further envisages two different reactions to these circumstances: while the *lena* and her daughter, Gymnasium, are perfectly happy with (or at least cynical about) the daughter's frequent nuptials, Melaenis and Selenium are willing to forgo potential profit and indulge the girl's desire to live the monogamous life of a matron, the Roman *uniuira*. And apparently they can afford to do so.

As soon as the audience/reader begins to wonder why the two mother–daughter pairs are so different, despite their similar background, it turns out that Selenium, the natural *uniuira*, is indeed a citizen. Although the play has hardly begun, Auxilium's speech (*Cist.* 149–202) offers a very clear indication of how it will end.[24] We hear that Selenium's mother married her father after all, and that both are now searching for their daughter. Since the slave who exposed Selenium as a baby also saw the unnamed *lena* pick her up, it is only a matter of time before he traces her and, through her, Melaenis and Selenium. The remaining scenes (over 500 lines) are largely devoted to developing the characters of Selenium and Melaenis. The younger woman demonstrates her wifely credentials, and the pimp mother acts like an upright citizen, forbidding her daughter to settle for anything less than a legitimate monogamous relationship.

Upon learning that Selenium's parents are looking for her and know of her whereabouts, Melaenis is distressed, but also quickly grasps the advantages of the new situation for both her daughter and herself (by revealing Selenium's identity, she will gain the friendship of Selenium's true parents). Her decision to bring Selenium back to her biological parents is motivated by a mixture of pragmatism and sentiment: she will have to do this good deed against her inclinations (*ingratiis*) in order to help her daughter achieve the status she longs for:

> Quamquam inuita te carebo, animum meum inducam tamen
> ut illud <quod minu' meam> quam tuam in rem bene conducat consulam.

---

[24] On suspense in comedy and in the *Cistellaria*, see Konstan (1983) 98–9; see also his comments on the damaged parts of the play, ibid.

Although I am unwilling to be separated from you, I will nevertheless persuade myself to be concerned more with what is advantageous to you than to me.

(Plautus *Cist.* 631–3)

This confession evokes the definition of love that the *lena* gives earlier, and would sound false if it were not for Melaenis' earlier testimonies of devotion to her foster daughter and anguish at losing her.[25] As it is, the reader/audience is encouraged to understand that while Melaenis is unhappy to lose her daughter (hence *ingratiis*), she is willing to let her go, both because this is better for Selenium and because the new relationship will be advantageous for herself.

Why, then, do the *lena* Melaenis and her foster-daughter Selenium have so much in common with respectable citizen mothers and daughters? In the case of Selenium, we may conclude that nurture has failed to transform a citizen girl into a 'whore'.[26] But Melaenis, the *lena* who acts like a citizen mother, is not revealed to be a citizen at the end of the play. Moreover, the *Cistellaria* also features Gymnasium, a *meretrix* acting like a solicitous friend (see especially *Cist.* 114–15), and even features a *lena* who is greedy, in keeping with her stock character, but who in the special instance of the play is uncharacteristically willing to forgo profit in order to do a favour for a friend.

Prostitutes, the play seems to say, although obliged to take many 'husbands', can be devoted mothers and loyal friends who cultivate relationships within their own community – and beyond it. The *lena*'s initial thesis, that friendship between matrons and prostitutes is impossible, is challenged when it turns out that the friendship between Gymnasium and Selenium transgresses class boundaries, as does Melaenis' kindness to her foster daughter. In the light of ancient theories, according to which friendship was conceivable only among equals, this possibility draws attention to personal qualities independent of social stereotypes, suggesting that the literary stock type (*meretrix, lena*) does not determine all aspects of a character's identity.[27] Thus, if the *Asinaria* stresses that roles of pimps and prostitutes are shaped by material conditions, the *Cistellaria* shows additionally that no one is *only* a 'whore'; sex workers are also daughters who try to please their mothers,

---

[25] Cf. *quae educauit eam sibi pro filia bene ac pudice* ('who brought her up as her own daughter well and in chastity', *Cist.* 172–3).

[26] A similarly radical distinction is suggested by Philippa in the *Epidicus*, who takes one glance at a flute player who has been mistaken for her lost daughter and indignantly exclaims: 'pigs don't smell like puppies!' (*Ep.* 579).

[27] On friendship and equality in the Hellenistic world, see Konstan (1997) 93–7.

friends willing to house-sit, and foster mothers who pick up and nurture babies abandoned by raped girls from good families. They do not live in a vacuum, but are part of social networks.

Among the Plautine plays, the *Cistellaria* is somewhat unusual in its focus on friendship between prostitutes, but it is not unique. The motif of mutual help also features prominently in the *Bacchides*, a play in which one twin sister helps the other. Other prostitutes, such as Philaenium in the *Asinaria* and Philematium in the *Mostellaria*, are represented as being devoted to their lovers – whenever the circumstances permit. Needless to say, such affectionate women must be contrasted with those, who, like Phronesium in the *Truculentus* (who adopts a child only to get more money from one of her lovers), embody the stereotype of the cynical and acquisitive *meretrix*. Nevertheless, the sheer variety of types of prostitutes, including maternal pimp and sisterly whore, underscores the potential of diverse responses to sexual stereotypes: a *lena* can act like Cleareta but she also can act like Melaenis; a prostitute can be ruthless, like Phronesium, but she can also be devoted, like Philaenium. Such portrayals of female pimps and prostitutes highlight the potential for subversive identities on stage and in everyday life.

Terence: For Such Is Human Nature

The plays of Terence evince an almost obsessive interest in the kind of plot that juxtaposes prostitutes and future wives. In fact, every single one of Terence's plots brings together a *meretrix* and a girl whose ability to become a wife and mother is temporarily thrown into question. *Heauton Timorumenos*, *Phormio*, *Eunuchus*, and *Adelphoe* feature double love affairs encouraging readers/audiences to compare the relative advantages of a young man being in love with a prostitute versus a modest young woman; the *Hecyra* shows a *meretrix* whose client falls in love with his own wife, while the *Andria* uses a narrative about a *meretrix* (*An.* 69–105) as a background for the young man's affair with her foster sister. Usually, the modest young woman is represented as the better choice, but the presence of the prostitute as a mirror for the citizen woman invites readers and audiences to envisage the heroine (that is, a future *materfamilias*) finding herself in a position comparable to that of a prostitute: she may pass for a sister of a *meretrix* (*Eunuchus*, *Andria*), be confused with one (*Heauton Timorumenos*), or be a prostitute's rival for her husband's affections (*Hecyra*).

The kindness of Terentian prostitutes has sparked a scholarly debate on whether the '*bona meretrix*' acts out of self-interest or disinterested goodwill.[28] This distinction, important as it may be to us, would not have been equally vital to the audiences and readers of ancient comedy. In fact, the mixture of self-interest and kindness professed by Melaenis in the *Cistellaria* and, as we will see, several of Terence's prostitutes, would have been perfectly honourable in the light of Aristotle's functional definition of virtue or the Stoic theory of *oikeiosis*.[29] For our purposes it is important to note that the three *bonae meretrices*, Thais in the *Eunuchus*, Bacchis in the *Hecyra*, and Chrysis in the *Andria*, do something that directly benefits a citizen girl.[30] Thus, Bacchis in the *Hecyra* identifies her client Pamphilus as the young man who had raped his present wife, Philumena, before they were married. In doing so, she gives Pamphilus a reason to recognise Philumena's child as his own and saves his marriage. In a soliloquy, Bacchis explains her action as part of an exchange: her relationship with Pamphilus has been beneficial to her, so it is now her turn to benefit him – and by the same token, his wife (*Hec.* 816–840). Thais in the *Eunuchus* claims to feel responsible for her foster sister after her mother's death (*Hec.* 146, 130) and acts as her guardian, trying to secure her freedom and locate her Athenian family.[31] Like Melaenis and Bacchis, Thais describes her motivation as both benevolent and calculated to secure the friendship of the girl's relatives (*Hec.* 145–9). Upon discovering that her foster sister has fallen victim to rape (*Hec.* 820–9), Thais expresses concern for the girl and her tears, not for her own lost prospects; she is later instrumental in negotiating her sister's marriage to Chaerea, the young man who raped her.

Especially revelatory of a prostitute's position within social networks is the story of Chrysis in the *Andria*, who manages to be a protective maternal presence even though she is a mere memory. The action of the play begins shortly after her death. Pamphilus' father Simo wants him to marry a suitable woman and leave Glycerium, a girl who passes for Chrysis' younger sister (but who will eventually prove to be a citizen). Pamphilus cannot bring himself to leave her, both because he loves Glycerium and because she is, in his eyes, his wife rather than his concubine. We learn that it was Chrysis who, on her deathbed, made sure that her foster sister was treated like a spouse. Tearfully, Pamphilus recalls Chrysis' last words in which, reminding him of

[28] On *bona meretrix*, see Gilula (1980) and Henry (1985); cf. also Knorr (1995) who argues that even Bacchis in *Heauton Timorumenos* should be considered 'good'. See also Traill's discussion of the stock type of hetaera in New Comedy (2008) 1–9.

[29] See for example, *Politics* 8.9 and the thesis that pursuit of self-interest, if properly understood, may be beneficial for the community. On *oikeiosis*, see e.g., Cicero *On Duties* 1.30 – with a reference to Terence.

[30] Bacchis in the *Heauton Timorumenos* does neither good nor harm; Bacchis in the *Adelphoe* and the flute player in the *Phormio* are silent characters.

[31] On the portrayal of Thais, see Konstan (1986).

Glycerium's vulnerability, she begged him not to abandon the girl and placed him under obligation to take care of her (*oro, obtestor*). Evoking her own sisterly love for him and the girl's devotion and obedience, Chrysis' dying wish made Pamphilus entirely responsible for her foster sister's fate: 'I give you to her, to be her husband, friend, guardian, and father.'[32]

Chrysis' aspirations for her foster sister (just like that of Thais for her own foster sister, and of Melaenis for her foster daughter) are nothing less than what citizen mothers want for their own daughters: a committed monogamous relationship that would provide the girl with material and emotional security. While Chrysis' kindness makes the happy resolution possible, Glycerium's citizen status is finally confirmed thanks to the intervention of Chrysis' male relative, Crito (*An.* 904–56). Crito comes to Athens looking for Chrysis' house. He pronounces strong disapproval for her lifestyle as 'the woman who preferred to enrich herself in improper ways rather than live in her home city in proper poverty' (*An.* 796–9), but he is eager to inherit her property. According to an Athenian law, Crito, as the closest living relative of Chrysis, was the person responsible for marrying her.[33] In the light of this law and of his interest in inheriting Chrysis' money, his characterisation of her lifestyle seems as hypocritical as it is harsh. In the end, however, he decides to become Glycerium's champion (*An.* 807–15) out of a mixture of kindness and self-interest (just like that professed by the *bonae meretrices*).

The responsibility of relatives for a young woman is emphasised in the account of Chrysis' life in Athens that Pamphilus' father Simo offers at the beginning of the play:

> Ex Andro commigrauit huc uiciniae,
> Inopia et cognatorum neglegentia
> Coacta egregia forma atque aetate integra.
> (...)
> Primo haec pudice uitam parce ac duriter
> Agebat, lana ac tela uictum quaeritans;
> Sed postquam amans accessit praetium policens
> Unus et item alter, ita ut ingeniumst omnium
> Hominum ab labore procliue ad lubidinem,
> Acceptit condicionem, dehinc quaestum occipit.

(...) she moved into this neighborhood from Andros forced by poverty and the indifference of her relatives. At first she lived in chastity, poverty and hardship, trying to earn her living by weaving wool. But after first one lover approached

---

[32] *Te isti uirum do, amicum tutorem patrem*; on characters of prostitutes with maternal disposition in Greek comedy, see Lape (2004b) 165–7.

[33] This law was crucial to the plot of Terence's *Phormio*. See also Bartholomä in this volume.

her, then another, promising a reward, she agreed on the condition – for all human nature leans away from hardship toward pleasure – and earned her living this way.   (Terence *An.* 70–9)

Granted, Simo's tone may be partially motivated by the principle *de mortuis nihil nisi bonum*, and Terence may be striving to present Chrysis in a good light because of her association with Glycerium. Yet it is nevertheless remarkable that Simo blames Chrysis' transformation from a hardworking girl into a *meretrix* on a series of circumstances rather than on some typically feminine weakness. She left her native Andros because she did not receive the help she should have had from her (male) relatives. Her community and extended family (including Crito) were thus responsible for her destitution. She did try to earn her living honestly, but was corrupted by the men who visited her, and finally succumbed to the generally human – not specifically female – tendency to choose an easy life over hardship.[34]

Despite his humane description of Chrysis' situation, Simo will become passionately opposed to Pamphilus' relationship with Glycerium, arguing that 'whorish love affairs' and marriage should be kept separate (*An.* 913). His professed compassion for Chrysis notwithstanding, he will later encourage his son to place Glycerium in a situation nearly identical to the one that led Chrysis to become a prostitute. Simo's attitude, like Crito's, is thus represented as hypocritical, and is possibly meant to come across as a critique of respectable citizens' disapproval of prostitution.[35] It is therefore tempting to see Simo's earlier comments on the shared human weakness (*omnium hominum procliue*) that moved Chrysis to choose easy pleasure (*lubido*) over hardship (*labor*) as applicable to his own motivations as well. Perhaps, then, we are invited to conclude that if orphaned girls become prostitutes, it is because good citizens like Crito and Simo find it convenient. Together with the other representations of the *meretrices*, the portrayal of Chrysis in the *Andria* suggests that it is within the bounds of human nature both to act like a 'whore', in order to make a living, and to place other people in situations that make them act like 'whores'. Here are, then, only human beings (*homines*) predisposed to choose comfort over hardship; 'whores' do not exist.

[34] The only prostitute whom Terence does not cast as benefactor of a citizen girl, Bacchis in the *Heauton Timorumenos*, develops this line of defence for the phenomenon of prostitution in a short monologue addressed to the virtuous Antiphila (*Haut.* 381–95): it is men, she explains, who divide women into wives and prostitutes, making fidelity profitable for the former, but not for the latter.
[35] Pamphilus' comment 'Isn't my father a nice man!' (*An.* 948) draws attention to Simo's sudden change of mind in the recognition scene.

Conclusion

The *palliata* thrives on tensions and paradoxes: prologues boast about the Hellenic pedigree of their 'barbarian' Latin plots; closing comments blend fiction and reality, reminding the audience that all the characters/actors can be flogged.[36] Gods come on stage to ask for applause (*Amphitruo*), men play women (*Casina*), slaves play masters (*Captiui*), whores act like citizens (*Cistellaria*); the taxonomy of stock types exists only to be questioned. The strategies for subverting the distinctions between 'mothers' and 'whores' are a part of these aesthetics. Plautus and Terence exploit the relationships between stock types and individual personae in different ways. Plautus makes the generic rules over-explicit: both Cleareta in his *Asinaria*, and the *lena* (Gymnasium's mother) in his *Cistellaria*, stress that they act in ways expected of typical mother-pimps. Moreover, in comparing their *modus operandi* to the Roman moral standards of *pietas*, these *lenae* present the mothering techniques of pimps as the reverse side of the moral system that encourages respectable mothers to marry off their daughters. This pastiche of the discourse of *pietas* draws attention to the material conditions necessary for conventional morality to work. Furthermore, the *Cistellaria* employs yet another strategy (which prefigures Terence's device of *bona meretrix*): both the *lena* Melaenis and her foster daughter Selenium act against their types, precisely in the ways expected of respectable citizen women, implying that morality need not be entirely determined by social class. The presentation of the women of the demimonde in the *Cistellaria* is remarkable for its inclusive perspective: instead of reducing the representations of prostitutes to their dealings with clients, it shows them as mothers, daughters, and friends, highlighting their desire to function within their communities.

This latter insight, that prostitutes do not exist in a void, also informs Terence's *Andria*, *Eunuchus*, and *Hecyra*, which present *meretrices* as women who desperately want to be integrated into their respective communities. Because of their non-citizen status, prostitutes cannot enter into legitimate relationships themselves, but they are eager to help younger women who are qualified to become lawful wives fulfil their ambitions and thus earn the goodwill of future citizen households. Terentian '*bonae*' *meretrices* are 'whores' by default. The *Andria* in particular draws attention to the social landscape within which prostitution exists: neglectful relatives (Crito), lovers eager to take advantage of destitute women, respectable neighbours who condone prostitution as long as it brings them no personal harm (Simo).

---

[36] See Sharrock's insightful comments on the importance of identity to the poetics of the *palliata* (2009) 86–101. On flogging, see *As.* 943–7 and Fitzgerald in this volume.

THE SOCIOLOGY OF ROMAN COMEDY

Plautus' and Terence's interest in the interface between the lives of citizen women and sex workers can be envisaged as a literary game in which the *parole* of nuanced personae is construed in an ongoing dialogue with the *langue* of the comic tradition. But performance cannot function in a social vacuum. Theatre is both a product of and a contributing factor to contemporary ideologies, and we must also consider representations of maternal pimps and protective prostitutes as a part of the larger social discourse of Republican Rome.[37] Plautus' exposure of the material conditions that shape the demimonde and its perverse discourse of family values, along with Terence's insistence on prostitutes' desire to earn a place within social networks, should therefore be considered as more than clever contributions to literary games. Through such literary devices, the Roman playwrights would have invited their audiences (and readers) to think beyond not only dramatic but also social stereotypes of 'mothers' and 'whores'.

Further Reading

There are several helpful studies of female stock types: on the wealthy matrons, see Schuhman (1977) and Stärk (1990); on the *meretrices*, see Henry (1985) and Fantham (2004a) and (2004b); on *bona meretrix*, see Gilula (1980). Among particularly useful analyses of individual plays are Gold (1998) on the *Casina*, Fantham (2004a) and (2004b) on the *Cistellaria* and *Poenulus*, Konstan (1986) on the *Eunuchus*, and Knorr on the *Self-tormentor* (1995). Several chapters on marriage and relationships in monographs on comedy offer useful insights: see especially Konstan (1983) *passim*; (1986); (1995) 120–40; Moore (1998b) esp. 140–80; cf. Slater on the *Casina* (1985) and (2000) 57–76. On the language of female characters, see Adams (1984). These works take the notion of 'female' or 'woman' as a given and explore how female personae function in the plots and performance of comedy. Conversely, studies of gender in comedy aim to find out what kinds of gendered identities (both female and male) comic plots and comic language construe. On gender in Latin comedy and elegy, see James (1998a); on language and gender, Dutsch (2004), (2005), and (2008), especially chs. 1, 2, and 3, and James (2005); on aspects of masculinity in comedy, see McDonnell (2006), ch. 1. See also James on gender and sexuality in Terence (2013). On the gendering of emotions in Greek and Roman comedy, see Dutsch and Konstan (2011). In general, see now Dutsch, James, and Konstan (2015).

---

[37] On drama as producer as well as product of ideology, see Lape (2004b) 11; cf. Dutsch (2008) 41–6 on comedy's participation in social discourse and Traill on the ideological engagement of works of fiction (2008) 13.

13

ANNA CLARK

Gods and Roman Comedy

Veneris causa adplaudite: eius haec in tutelast fabula

For Venus' sake applaud: this play is under her protection.

(*Truc.* 967)[1]

Gods and Comedies: Content *and* Context

The closing lines of Plautus' *Truculentus* highlight one of the many ways in which gods are integral to Roman comedy. They feature among the *dramatis personae* of individual plays, as both characters (the best-known being Jupiter and Mercury in Plautus' *Amphitruo*) and prologue-speakers (such as the Lar or household god in his *Aulularia* and the constellation Arcturus in his *Rudens*); they are drawn on by characters of both sexes and of every status; and they are presented as responsible in different ways for the plays themselves. When the courtesan Phronesium tells the audience at the end of the *Truculentus* to applaud 'for the sake of Venus', who has been guardian of the comedy, the sphere of Venus has been a focus throughout the play. Venus may even have been seen to watch over the performance in another way, for festivals framed the very staging of the comedies, which were put on at games in honour of a variety of gods. Although the precise festival setting is not always now visible to us as we read the text, the existence of this kind of frame is important. We do not know when or where the *Truculentus* was performed, but in some cases performance details are preserved in production notes to surviving texts: Plautus' *Stichus* was performed at the Plebeian Games (*ludi Plebeii*) of 200 BC, his *Pseudolus* at the opening of the temple of the Magna Mater in 191, while four of Terence's six extant comedies are known to have been performed in the 160s at the *Megalesia* in honour of the Magna Mater, and a fifth was staged at the Roman Games (*ludi Romani*). Comedies were staged at annual festivals, at the celebration of the dedication of some new temples, and sometimes at funerals. Rituals involving gods were

---

[1] All references to plays are those of Plautus unless otherwise specified.

in other words the means through which the comedies were made part of Roman society.

Roman comedy and the extant works of Plautus in particular are thus a rich resource for exploring engagements with gods in the third and second centuries BC, and to a lesser extent some of the practices through which humans sought to engage actively with gods or to understand their messages – practices such as sacrifice, divination, and the interpretation of dreams and portents.[2] Written during the years of the Romano-Carthaginian wars and the change-filled years of the second century, and performed in front of audiences of mixed gender and status, inhabitants and visitors, citizens and possibly even in practice slaves,[3] they provide us with an almost unrivalled opportunity to think about what people were laughing at during such festivals and about the role of gods on these occasions. We can discern within the details of even formulaic comedies some reactions to a changing society, and the plays are indeed themselves contemporary evidence of one practice within that society, one which brought together relatively large numbers of people.

Religion: the Right Approach?

The gods who were honoured in the festivals at which these plays were staged, the gods who appear on stage as characters or prologues in the comedies, and those who are invoked by a whole range of characters are all part of an interconnected picture. This picture is not, I would suggest, one in which engagements with gods should be isolated analytically into a separate category of 'religion'. The earliest examples of the Latin terms *religio* and *religiosus* in surviving texts do come from Plautus and Terence's plays (*Curc.* 350, *Merc.* 881, *As.* 782; Ter. *And.* 730, 941, Ter. *Haut.* 228, 650), but those terms do not map very easily onto what we understand by 'religion' and 'religious', meaning something closer to 'scruple' and '(over)scrupulous', sometimes with regard to gods. The picture we see is rather one in which gods were integral to nearly all aspects of life: living it, expressing one's understanding of it, and questioning aspects of it. Thus, although the plays clearly do not give us unmediated access to the full spectrum of engagements with gods in Roman contexts in the middle Republic, nor necessarily reflect accurately which gods were most frequently engaged with by the population at large or particular segments of the population, the myriad forms of

---

[2] See e.g. Plaut. *Ru.* 611–12 for an unsuccessful bid to understand a dream.
[3] Csapo and Slater (1994) 306–17 present the evidence for theatre audiences. Goldberg (1998) explores archaeological evidence for the size of audience at the Megalesia.

engagement that remain for us provide one interesting lens through which to view a society in a period of expansion and change.[4]

If we can accept without much difficulty that the view afforded by this lens is bound to be selective, we must also ask how distorting it is. It is hard to deny that the plays on the whole, performed as they were in the city as part of publicly funded entertainment celebrating the community and in honour of the city's gods, present a fairly safe picture in which piety is rewarded and impiety punished, albeit within a Saturnalian atmosphere in which many roles are reversed and clever slaves regularly triumph over their masters. The few characters who treat gods with real disrespect, as opposed to lively playfulness, do tend to be obviously negative individuals such as pimps (for example Ballio, who claims he would leave an offering to Jupiter half made if there were an opportunity for profit: *Ps.* 265–7) and to get their comeuppance. Two points need to be borne in mind here. First, although attitudes to gods portrayed in comedies may not reflect accurately attitudes outside the comic context, the gods of comedy and their portrayal were themselves part of and contributed to the complex amalgam of ideas about the divine in Rome.[5] Secondly, however, staging ideas about the rewards of piety in such dramatic contexts does more than simply replicate or reinforce a shared social assumption. To take one of the best-known and most discussed examples, when the piety of Hanno and other Carthaginians in Plautus' *Poenulus* is made very explicit throughout the play and is ultimately rewarded, questions are surely being raised about how gods were engaged with, and how successfully they might be approached, in different locations and by different people or peoples. Plautus' 'point' in presenting these characters in such a way in a comedy to be staged in a society that was fighting, or had more likely already defeated, Hannibal and the Carthaginians in the second Romano-Carthaginian War (218–201 BC) has been interpreted in diametrically opposed ways in modern scholarship. Rather than attempting to read beyond what the text can tell us and seeking answers to the question of what message Plautus was seeking to convey, we would do better to acknowledge that the plays raised questions about piety, and to note that they did so in a Rome in which Pietas (Piety or Duty) itself had received, or was shortly to receive, its own temple and its own place in the festival calendar.

The Variety of Roles Played by the Gods

Gods play a variety of roles in particular comedies. They are appealed to by characters on many occasions: in both Plautus and Terence's work, Hercules,

---

[4] Gruen (1992) explores that changing society from a variety of perspectives.
[5] Parker (1997) makes a complementary point about the gods of Greek tragedy.

the Dioscuri, and Jupiter are invoked very frequently indeed with words that may have been so ingrained in the vocabulary as to suggest little active decision on the part of the character to invoke a particular god – *pol, (me) hercle*, and *(me)castor* – while more specific appeals are made to Apollo, Jupiter, Spes (Hope), Salus (Salvation), Pietas (Piety/Duty), 'all the gods', Lares and Penates (household gods), Venus, Neptune, Hercules, the Tempestates (Storms), Mercury, Fortuna, and Juno Lucina (a goddess concerned with childbirth) by characters of each sex and every status. We shall return later to questions about the nature of the relationship with the divine suggested by these and other interactions. It is important first to emphasise other ways in which gods are shown to be integral to characters' lives. Gods in comedies can usefully be thought of as 'enablers' in a variety of senses. Perhaps the most obvious involves a god being responsible for a play, whether in the sense in which Venus in Plautus' *Truculentus* is given credit for the play and its plot at the end of the comedy, as discussed above, or in the way in which Jupiter's desire for the mortal Alcmena motivates the whole of the same playwright's *Amphitruo*, or in the way in which the domestic Lar's attitude sets up the plot of the *Aulularia*, because he chooses to reveal a hidden pot of gold to the miserly Euclio for the sake of Euclio's daughter, who is the first in generations to show the Lar veneration. 'Enabling' can also be understood in a variety of more subtle ways: gods are a means of allowing a character to explain or understand a particular situation.

Accordingly, individual characters on occasion claim that a god was responsible for or is driving their actions, whether in exculpatory terms, as when Lyconides' explains his rape of Phaedria at the festival in honour of Dionysus in the *Aulularia* by claiming that 'Some god incited me' (*Aul.* 737) or in Menaechmus' brother's more darkly comic attribution of a series of commands for unpleasant actions to be carried out against Menaechmus' wife to oracular instructions from Apollo (*Men.* 840–75). References by characters to particular gods and characters' interactions with respect to gods are also part of a wider set of mechanisms that allow the audience quickly to grasp the essential nature of particular, stock characters: Ballio's aforementioned claim that he would abandon a sacrifice to Jupiter for a chance at profit (*Ps.* 265–7) swiftly marks him out as the 'baddie', while Philocrates describes his fictional father's parsimony in terms of the latter's unwillingness to sacrifice even to his own genius (a man's guardian deity) with the best plate, lest it be stolen (*Capt.* 289–92). Cleomachus' calling on Bellona and Mars reinforces the costume and gestures of the swaggering soldier (*Bacch.* 847), while Curculio, the eponymous parasite, invokes Hercules as his foster nurse as one of many signals that make his large appetite clear both to the audience and to other characters (*Curc.* 358).

The boy who tells the braggart soldier Pyrgopolynices that he is especially favoured by Mars and Venus receives such a good reception that the soldier's pride in his martial exploits and his own perception of his success as a lover are made instantly clear (*Mil.* 1384). Well-known forms of engagement with gods such as the paying of a tithe to Hercules are also evoked to illustrate aspects of character. The default reaction of the parasite Gelasimus, for example, when believing that he is about to become rich, is to congratulate Hercules for the increase in tithe he will receive, and, when he is disappointed, to blame Hercules for his failure (*St.* 386, 395). Chrysalus also uses the practice of tithe-giving humorously to suggest that Mnesilochus should have given his father only one tenth of a sum of money and kept the rest for himself (*Bacch.* 665–6). All of this suggests that some prominent gods at least (as well as practices relating to gods, notably sacrifice) were well-known and resonant symbols. They allowed the characters and the audiences of the plays swiftly to understand what forms of behaviour were expected of those characters in a variety of social situations.

The close association of a god and his or her sphere also allowed a deity to serve as a reference point for that sphere, as well as to be seen controlling events relevant to it. A variety of characters in the *Rudens* and also in the *Mostellaria, Stichus*, and *Trinummus* understand Neptune to be responsible for shipwrecking storms and for saving people from them, while Lysidamus hopes that Mercury, god of trade, will harm the perfumer who sold him the perfume that his wife has scented on him (*Cas.* 238), and Therapontigonus interprets even the illness of the pimp who holds Planesium in terms of Aesculapius helping to keep Planesium safe (*Curc.* 699–700). In addition, Aesculapius' temple is even part of the play's fictional setting (the god had also had a temple on the Tiber Island in Rome since the early third century BC). Often the sphere and the name of the god become almost synonymous in characters' speech. We should not suggest that gods' names are mere shorthand for the realm or crop with which they are associated, as in the stock phrase 'without Ceres (=food) and Liber (=drink) Venus (=love) grows cold' (Ter. *Eun.* 733) or in Stichus' question to his fellow-slave at dinner, asking whether Sangarinus will take water or wine by asking which province he wants: 'Fons or Bacchus' (*St.* 699–700). Nor should we take simply as metaphor Toxilus describing being in love as having been 'wounded in Venus' battle' and 'transfixed by Cupid's arrow' (*Persa* 24–5). We should rather consider these examples as yet further illustrations of the frequency with which gods were evoked as part of the thought-world of characters in a whole range of situations, and the many ways in which divine names were part of a general linguistic repertoire. Furthermore, all the gods mentioned in these instances had temples and festivals in Rome, and it is only by understanding these evocations of them among other ways and forms in which they were present in civic life that we can gain a fuller appreciation of their overall role.

Festivals and shrines not only framed the plays physically, and formed an important and changing part of the wider civic context in which the comedies were performed: they also provided the setting for various actions within the plays. The *Poenulus* centres around the Aphrodisia (festival of Aphrodite), and although the play is set in Calydon, this might well have resonated with an audience in Rome where two shrines of Venus Erycina with different styles of cult were established within Plautus' lifetime (see further below). The shrine of Fides (the name has a variety of meanings, including Faith, Loyalty, and Credit) in the *Aulularia* also has resonance because a temple to Fides existed in Rome, irrespective of the identity of the putative shrine in the 'original' Greek version of the play.[6] Certain festivals are typically cited as the locale for the rape of a young girl that sets up a number of the plots: Phaedria is raped at the festival of Ceres (*Aul.* 36, 795), while the Dionysia is the site of the original seizure of the girl by the Lemnian merchant and where Alcesimarchus is said first to have spotted Selenium (*Cist.* 89–91, 156). The same festival features in the time set for payment to the pimp in the *Pseudolus* (59). That these examples are likely to have come straight from Athenian originals does not matter: they suggest temples and festivals as important physical and temporal markers and examples of times when large numbers of people came together. Such locations also play an enabling role for characters in negotiating topographies both fictional and semi-fictional: Daemones is referred to as a 'neighbour of Venus' (*Ru.* 849), while the well-known speech of the Choragus (Stage Manager) in the *Curculio* includes the shrine of Venus Cloacina and the temple of Castor mixed in among a whole series of monuments from the Roman forum that are used to identify the kinds of people who loiter there (*Curc.* 471, 481).[7] This seamless inclusion of temples among other buildings in the forum is both unsurprising and emblematic of the varying ways in which gods are made part of the framework, cast, and content of the comedies.

Before turning to two examples that will allow us to explore the comedies in the context of civic life in more detail, it is worth noting that gods' names evoke for characters not only the sphere of the god but also on occasion its appearance and stories associated with the deity in question. Much of the visual nature of the comedies is now lost or left to be inferred from the

[6] Clark (2007) 73–5 and 101–5 explores the resonance of Fides and the shrine of Fides in this play.
[7] Moore (1991) provides an excellent analysis of this well-known scene. See also Maltby (2004).

texts,[8] but Trachalio uses the shorthand 'an old Silenus' (where we might say 'an old goat'), with suitable elaboration of features, to describe the pimp Labrax, while Labrax himself expresses his fear of the men posted outside the temple of Venus by likening their clubs to that of Hercules (*Ru.* 317–20, 821–3).[9] Mythical stories associated with gods and their origins operate as enablers in the same way as those found in this example, and in other non-mythical instances already explored, although the gods who feature in these claims and comparisons are relatively few in number: Jupiter, Minerva, Venus, Vulcan, Saturn, Ops, Sol, and especially Hercules. Chaerea in Terence's *Eunuchus* takes inspiration from watching the girl he desires look at a picture of Jupiter disguising himself as a shower of gold to be with Danae, because he too is disguising himself (as a eunuch!) in order to be close to a girl (Ter. *Eun.* 583–91). Venus' birth from a shell provides Trachalio with a means of imploring her to grant Palaestra's request by punning on *conchas* ('shells' and 'genitalia', *Ru.* 704), while Jupiter's desire for Alcmena is not only the focus of Plautus' *Amphitruo*, but also a story used as a way of evoking female rivalry when Syra calls her mistress 'my Juno' and her mistress' rival 'Alcmena' (*Merc.* 689–90). Hercules is by some way the god most frequently drawn on by a wide range of characters, with his labours proving a fruitful form of comparison for the old gentleman Periphanes in terms of relations with women (*Ep.* 178–9), and for the slave Toxilus in describing the toils of a lover (*Persa* 1–5), while for Menaechmus the tale of Hercules stealing Hippolyta's girdle provides a resonant comparison for his own difficulties in stealing a garment from his wife to give to a courtesan (*Men.* 200–1).[10]

In many of these examples, and notably in the comparison with Hercules' labours, the characters describe themselves or others as gods. Their motivation does not appear primarily to be the arrogation of divinity to themselves, although as we shall see later the boundaries between human and divine are questioned in the comedies. Rather, the stories known about gods again enable the characters to make a point about their situation. This form of comparison is not limited to more elaborate mythical tales, and seems particularly useful to characters expressing flattery, appreciation of beauty, or great happiness. The parasite Saturio, for example, chooses to address the slave Toxilus as Jupiter in the hope of sharing a meal with him (*Persa* 100). Calidorus asks Pseudolus whether he should greet him as Spes (Hope) or as Salus (Salvation), both conveying a question as to whether his situation has been resolved or still has the potential to be resolved and thanking his slave

---

[8] Csapo and Slater (1994) give a full summary of other evidence.   [9] See also *Ru.* 420.
[10] Comparable examples may be found in *Bacch.* 152; Ter. *Eun.* 1027 and *Haut.* 1036–7.

for his work, all by comparing Pseudolus to deities that had long received cult in Rome (*Ps.* 709). A young man in love describes the joy he will experience if his problems are resolved with the words *deus sum* ('I am a god') (Ter. *Hec.* 843). Phaedromus expresses rapture at Planesium's beauty with the same exclamation (*Curc.* 167).[11] Ergasilus, parasite in the *Captiui*, trumpets the good news he has to report to Hegio by demanding sacrifice, and portraying himself as the deserving divine recipient of that sacrifice (with the emphasis on the food involved), claiming to be *for Hegio* Jupiter supreme, Salus (Salvation), Fortuna, Lux ('light'), Laetitia ('happiness'), and Gaudium ('joy') (*Capt.* 863–4; compare *Merc.* 867). The limiting *tibi* ('for you') modifies his claim, although it is clearly intended to be an extravagant celebration, with the express design of procuring him food. The mixing here of gods that received public cult in the city, like Jupiter, Salus, and various Fortunae, with other pleasant concepts is typical of Plautus. He may well be playing with the prominent introduction in the years in which he was writing of a variety of what I have elsewhere termed 'divine qualities'. When such divine qualities are called on by characters in the comedies, however, those with longer cult history in the city are most frequently chosen.[12]

The gods of comedy and especially those of Plautus appear very much part of the world of the comic (and the less comic) characters. If many gods appear familiar in the senses I have explored – of enabling of plots, characterisation, and a whole range of actions and forms of self-expression – they are also regarded warily as sources of power, with the ability to grant or reject appeals for help and to control lives through their power over the natural world and, especially in the case of Neptune, of storms at sea. The divine world is constantly talked of and made part of the characters' own, but it is neither a wholly comfortable world nor clearly bounded. Jests reveal play with boundaries, with who is and is not a god, and also over who knows and can decide who is and is not god. Mercury in the *Amphitruo* is at pains to emphasise his divinity because he appears on stage disguised as Sosia, mortal and slave of the great general Amphitruo, in order to help his father Jupiter (who is disguised as Amphitruo) to seduce Amphitruo's wife. As the audience watch one man play a god who is disguised as a slave and await the arrival of another man playing a god who is disguised as an eminent man, Mercury draws attention to the audience's difficulty in telling the difference between the god playing a mortal on stage and the mortal character they play. The problem is to be resolved visually for the spectators by Mercury wearing a small feather on his hat and Jupiter a tassel on his, but

---

[11] Further examples may be found at *Poen.* 277–8 and *Bacch.* 217.
[12] Clark (2007) ch. 3.

there is a deeper issue at stake, one concerning the relationship between mortal and divine, to which attention is also drawn here.[13] This tension is made particularly clear through Mercury's emphatic assertion *deus sum*: ('I am a god', *Amph.* 53) and his claim that he can change the genre of the play (*Amph.* 53–61), a play which ends with the offstage birth of the demigod Hercules and his mortal twin. The prologues Luxuria (Luxury) and Inopia (Want) in the *Trinummus* explicitly call attention to their creation by Plautus, and Plautus may deliberately draw attention to the ambiguous nature of Auxilium (Aid), a god named from a neuter noun, by delaying 'its' arrival as the prologue in the *Cistellaria* and having it draw attention to its divinity (*Cist.* 153–4).[14] Lydus further calls his tutor a 'barbarian' for questioning whether there is a god called Suavisaviatio ('Sweetkissmaking'; *Bacch.* 120–1). Although comic characters feel confident to engage with and play with these ideas, these jests are likely to reflect contemporary interest and possibly uncertainty about the introduction of new state deities and the range of deities receiving public cult, particularly those whose conceptual element was especially prominent in their names. Pyrgopolynices' boast that he is the grandson of Venus (*Mil.* 1265; a claim thrown back in his face by Periplectomenus and Cario once they have bested him: *Mil.* 1413, 1421) is effective in marking him out more strongly as the eponymous Braggart Soldier not only because of the extravagance of the claim on the part of a soldier but precisely because claims to special relationships with gods were another controversial aspect of the broader society in which the play was staged.[15]

Connections with Contemporary Society

This verbal, theological play serves as one set of examples of the broad topicality of Plautus' work. It is probable that we are now unable to recognise a number of more precise topical references, but rather than pursue fruitless attempts to locate these – attempts which have produced or which risk producing circular arguments and indefensible datings of specific plays[16] – it is more helpful to identify topical issues at a more general level. These issues give a good sense of ways in which engagements with gods not only, as

---

[13] See further below in Beard (2003) or as Henderson (2009) 115 puts it 'cult myth put before the people in carnival mode'.

[14] This point is attractively suggested by Feeney (1998) 90.

[15] See Hanson (1959) 51 and 69. Beard, North, and Price (1998) vol. 1, 84–7 discuss the evidence for Scipio Africanus' claimed connection with Jupiter and the extent to which claims in later writers may have been influenced by events of the late Republic.

[16] Leigh (2004) provides an incisive case against such attempts.

I have sought to emphasise in this chapter, permeate nearly all aspects of life portrayed in the comedies in enabling the characters to achieve many things – from seeking help from a god, to giving thanks, to displaying character traits, to explaining and understanding situations and people – but also reflect some of the social conditions and issues at stake during the years in which the playwrights were composing their work. Roman comedy, like Athenian New Comedy, was of course not satirical of contemporaneous events in the style of Aristophanic Comedy. It is nonetheless not difficult, without seeking prominent Romans of the day behind the depiction of particular characters, and without forgetting that the plays were primarily designed to entertain and to create laughter rather than to send the audience home pondering deep social and philosophical issues, to see that not all the laughter was comfortable and that some of the questions being raised were more specific than the universals of thwarted love.[17] The conflicts with the Carthaginians and the ensuing wars with Hellenistic kings raised questions about ways of fighting and interacting with other peoples, about just wars, and about the nature of a conquering people and its society, as well as ensuring that more Romans, including likely audience members, saw more parts and peoples of the Mediterranean world than had previously been the case. Even conflict between generations, itself a universal, gains extra resonance in a period of concern over rapid social change brought about by new practices, people (including slaves), and objects and materials from new forms of contact with different areas. One of the consequences of these concerns and these new contacts, as well as the number of opportunities created for generals to vow victory monuments, was the creation of new temples and cults in the city, from Mens (Mind), Venus Erycina (brought from Mount Eryx on Sicily after the defeat at Lake Trasimene), and Honos and Virtus (Honour and Virtue/ Courage) during the Hannibalic War to those of Juno Regina and others in the 170s.[18] Exploring one or two of these topicalities in Plautus will further illustrate that the integral role of gods in the plays was not limited to the comedies' content and frame, but extended to the context of city and empire in which the plays were staged. For while many of the often jocular and inverted forms of engagement with gods seen in Terence and especially in Plautus are unlikely to reflect with precision how audience members and other members of Roman society spoke to and of gods, being specific as they are to the genre of comedy, the underlying forms of engagement themselves

---

[17] See further Sharrock (2009).
[18] A full discussion of these temples and their introduction to Rome may conveniently be found in Orlin (1997) and Ziolkowski (1992).

do reflect or at least refract ideas and forms of address,[19] and also illuminate issues at stake elsewhere in society.

One of the most successful recent explorations of this kind of topicality is Mary Beard's analysis of Plautus' *Amphitruo* not in terms of a specific triumph and triumphing general but of the very idea of the triumph and the triumphing general.[20] She has argued persuasively for the play reversing the mimesis of the triumph itself, in which the victorious general 'acted' Jupiter for a day, by staging Jupiter acting the triumphant general Amphitruo for a day – or rather an extended night. Without forcing the possibility, she has further highlighted the extra layer of mimetic complexity that would have been present had *Amphitruo* been staged at the *ludi Romani*, at which the presiding magistrate wore triumphal dress. Another play whose date has been inferred from many different and usually misguided perspectives is Plautus' *Poenulus*. Galinsky has suggested that the probably interpolated scene I.2, in which Adelphasium and Anterastilis display very different attitudes towards the effort required to beautify them for the Aphrodisia, reflects debates surrounding the anticipated new shrine to Venus Erycina outside the Colline Gate that was dedicated in 181 and included temple prostitutes and forms of cult that were unlike those of the earlier temple to the same goddess that had been dedicated on the Capitol in 215 by order of the Sibylline Books after the defeat at Lake Trasimene (Livy 30.38, 40.34, 22. 9–10, 23.30–1).[21] Although the suggestion cannot be substantiated, given the degree of uncertainty over the play's date, the idea does summarise well one way in which discussion over new cults might be reflected in discussions within the comedies of suitable forms of behaviour in an ostensibly non-Roman location. In both these examples gods play very different roles: Jupiter and Mercury are protagonists in the *Amphitruo* and Venus a point of reference around which part of the plot turns in the *Poenulus* scene. What they share is their illustration of the interconnected nature of the social and civic fabric within which the plays were staged: in neither case are the issues on which they shed light particular to a separate 'religious' sphere. Rather, they each enable the airing in a public forum of issues of importance in the late third and early second centuries, such as (in these cases) increasing competition in the celebration of military success, and worries over new forms of behaviour, including those of women.

---

[19] Hanson (1959) is an excellent and detailed discussion of these forms of address and of much else of relevance to the topic of this chapter.

[20] Beard (2003) 41–3. See also O'Neill (2003). For the paragram A-m-ph-i-t-r-u-o / t-r-i-u-m-ph-o, see Henderson (2009) 116.

[21] Galinsky (1969).

Comparisons with New Comedy can be profitable, despite the importance of understanding Roman comedies as whole plays designed for performance. Plautus followed Menander in his use of divine prologues, though (with the probable exception of the *Rudens*) he employed the same creative adaptation in his choice of deity that we see in all aspects of his 'translations'. Although Terence, in contrast, did not put gods on the stage and emphasised divine agency less than did Plautus, we may nonetheless venture to generalise that both tend to allude to a greater variety of divine agents, perceived by both characters and audience, than we find in what survives of Menander and Diphilus.[22] This plurality and diversity of ways of understanding which gods were acting, and how, on the part of characters and also of individuals within the audience, may in fact tell us something interesting about what we usually call Roman religion. I have nonetheless deliberately not called this chapter 'Gods and Religion'. It is clear that among the many engagements outlined above it would be foolish to try to single out specific attitudes or deities as representative of religious attitudes or their foci. My aim has rather been to illustrate the wide range of ways in which gods are engaged with in the comedies, from being embedded in everyday vocabulary to specific appeals for divine aid, in order to emphasise the artificiality of separating their study from other aspects of the plays. Divinities and the divine were integral to the context and content of much of the work of Plautus in particular. Like other discourses in the comedies, they were one important means by which characters expressed themselves and explained their situations, and by which the comedies themselves made their audiences both laugh and reflect on some of the preoccupations of the age. It is in their illustration of such preoccupations, as performed in the contexts outlined above, that Roman comedies can be most revealing.

Further Reading

Hanson (1959) remains the most useful introduction to the topic, with Schilling (1979) offering a rather different approach. Fraenkel (2007), originally published in German in 1960, is an essential starting point for nearly all aspects of the study of Plautus, although his groundwork has now permitted further studies to consider the plays more organically. Studies that are not specifically concerned with gods but very important for considerations of how to relate the plays to society include McCarthy (2000) and Leigh (2004). Gruen (1990) and (1992) are important for the socio-political backdrop. Clark (2007) probes the issues surrounding a specific set of gods and their treatment by Plautus in more detail. All provide fuller bibliographies.

---

[22] See Zagagi (1994).

14

ANDREAS BARTHOLOMÄ*

Legal Laughter

Ius summum saepe summast malitia
('Utmost law is often utmost wickedness';
proverb quoted by the slave Syrus in Terence's *Self-Tormentor*)
(*Haut.* 796)[1]

Roman Comedy and the Law

Numerous titles of Greek New Comedy, such as Apollodorus' *Epidikazomene* ('The Woman adjudicated at Law')[2] or Menander's *Epitrepontes* ('The Arbitration'), indicate comic plots centred on legal matters. The fact that none of the extant comedies of Plautus and Terence bears a law-related title may lead to the assumption that the Roman playwrights left out any legal content in their adaptations. However, we frequently find legal plots and an abundance of parodies of and references to law in Roman comedies.

Most textbooks on Roman law include some, albeit brief, reference to the comedies of Plautus and Terence.[3] In addition, Watson's *Roman Private Law around 200 BC* (1971) relies heavily on Plautus' plays. Moreover, works on Ancient Greek law also draw on Roman comedy.[4] Passages alluding to law, however, occur in Horace, Ovid, and other poets as well.[5] But these authors have never attracted the attention of legal historians to the same extent. What makes Roman comedies so unique?

There are, in my opinion, two closely linked reasons: the Plautine and Terentian plays fall into a seminal phase of Roman private law that comprises ground-breaking developments for the evolution of one of the world's most influential legal traditions. In this period the law based on *leges* ('laws') and *mos maiorum* ('civilised customs'), the so-called *ius ciuile* ('civil law'), finds itself

---

* I would like to thank James Clackson, Cambridge, for his time and help with the English of this paper. All translations are my own unless otherwise stated.
[1] Cf. Cic. *Off.* 1.33: *summum ius summa iniuria* ('utmost law equals utmost injustice').
[2] Cf. Donat. Ter. *Ph.* 24–6.   [3] See Kaser (1971) to cite but one example.
[4] See Lipsius (1905–15), Pringsheim (1916), Pringsheim (1950), and Karabélias (2002).
[5] See Kenney (1969), Cloud (1989), and Hollis (1994).

next to the law based on the magistrates' edicts, the so-called *ius honorarium* ('magisterial law'). Referring to the most important branch of the latter, namely the law originating in the praetor's edict ('praetorian law'), the jurist Papinian (142–212 AD) has put the relation of these two layers of law in a nutshell: 'praetorian law (*ius praetorium*) is the law which the praetors introduced in order to support (*adiuuandi*), supplement (*supplendi*), or correct (*corrigendi*) the civil law (*ius ciuile*) for the sake of public interest (*propter utilitatem publicam*)'.[6] In addition, legal sources dating from the Republic are scarce. For whilst a great number of texts of the so-called 'time of classical jurisprudence' (*c.* mid-first century BC–mid-third century AD) has come down to us via the Digest, a compilation commissioned by the Byzantine emperor Justinian and published in 533 AD,[7] nothing comparable exists from our period.[8] Due to this lack of extant legal literature, legal historians are forced to rely on the few extant statutes such as the *Senatus Consultum de Bacchanalibus* of 186 BC (a decree by the Roman Senate forbidding the Bacchanalia, a mystery cult for the wine-god Bacchus in Italy), so that non-juristic texts of the same period such as Roman comedies have traditionally attracted much attention.

Therefore Roman comedy features heavily whenever we outline the development of Roman private law, and Plautus and Terence prove to be a veritable treasure trove for that purpose. In the same way, since the comedies abound in legal plots, parodies, and legal references, any interpretation of Roman comedy would be incomplete if we ignored the omnipresence of law in these plays.

To what extent, however, can works of literature serve as sources for the interpretation of law? And secondly, do the legal phenomena we find in the comedies relate to Roman or Greek law?

The discussion of the latter question has traditionally focused on Plautus. Whilst in the second half of the nineteenth century some scholars including Bekker, Pernard, and Costa were convinced that the Plautine comedies were reliable sources of Roman law,[9] the progress made by philologists by the end of the century prompted a 'Hellenic' counter-movement led by Dareste and Girard. They contested the relevance of the comedies for Roman law and emphasised their indebtedness to Greek New Comedy.[10]

In 1906, however, Fredershausen came up with a more nuanced approach: Passages for which no Greek original could be identified on the basis of

---

[6] Papin. (2 def.) dig. 1.1.7.1.
[7] See Kaiser (2015) for Justinian and the *Corpus Iuris Ciuilis*, esp. 127–33 for the Digest.
[8] Cf. Jolowicz & Nicholas (1972) 1–7; Riggsby (2010) 11–21.
[9] Costa (1890); Bekker (1892); Pernard (1900).
[10] Dareste (1892) and (1900); Girard (1893) 795–7.

external evidence were to be read against the background of (other) legal sources, both Roman and Greek. Those matching just one legal tradition were classed as either 'Roman' *or* 'Greek', and those compliant with both or corresponding to *neither* were placed in a third category.[11] In the first half of the twentieth century Kunkel suggested, against the background of Fraenkel's and Jachmann's philological works (1922; 1931) – as a rule of thumb – that law indispensable for the plot was most likely to be Greek, whilst legal metaphors, word-play, or mere references were most probably Plautine.[12]

The underlying idea of this approach is as follows: jokes based on unknown Greek law are bound to create little comic effect. If people are expected to laugh, they need to have at least a vague idea of the concept that is being played on. Hence playwrights avoid references to arcane Greek legal institutions as much as possible and substitute them with word-play and references related to Roman law. Nevertheless, employing well-known Greek legal concepts even if they were not part of the Greek original could add to Roman laughter. If, however, a play's plot was actually based on Greek law, the playwright had to stick to the original (or change the plot entirely). In such instances he needed to introduce the Roman audience to the relevant Greek law – often as early as in the exposition – or risk losing his audience.

Let us, however, also consider our initial question: what information can a fictional text provide on non-fictional matters such as law? This question arises not only in relation to ancient texts. Is it acceptable to infer anything about the law of homicide in the seventeenth century from Shakespeare's *Hamlet*, for instance? Can this play be seen as a critical contribution to a discourse on 'justice as vengeance' or even to the changes taking place in the law of homicide at that time?[13] In recent years, scholars have started to scrutinise legal phenomena in fictional texts and 'Law and Literature' has emerged as a new inter-disciplinary field of study. Broadly speaking, research concentrates on two complementary approaches. One analyses legal texts such as judgements, codes, and others by means of literary criticism and therefore treats legal texts as literature ('law *as* literature'). The other examines legal aspects in fictional texts ('law *in* literature').

As highlighted, one of the main objections to the latter approach is whether fictional texts can deliver any information about law at all. To focus on Roman comedy: can Plautus and Terence serve as serious and

---

[11] Fredershausen (1906) 15–19 and (1912) 199–200.
[12] Kunkel (1939) 6. Paoli followed this up in numerous essays, cf. Paoli (1976) and advocates analysis of each individual passage.
[13] Suggestions made by Posner (2009) 99–123 and Watkin (1984).

reliable sources of Roman or Greek law? This question is equally important for the scholar of Latin literature. Whenever we notice a legal reference, a parody, or even a legal plot, we must try to understand to what extent these verses relate to real and existing law since the playwright may, of course, have created his own fictional legal world to fit the plot.

Our framework for the interpretation of law in Roman comedy thus requires a further category to classify purely fictional law, which we may call 'stage law'. Whilst the line between stage law and parodies of existing law may be very narrow, this should not bar us from attempting to differentiate. The methodology for interpreting law in Roman comedy may thus be summed up as follows:

1 Law indispensable for the plot is most likely to be Greek.
2 Mere references, parodies, and law-related word-play are most likely to be Roman – unless they refer to well-known Greek legal phenomena.
3 Law possibly referring to both Greek *and* Roman law should be classified as such and not only as either Roman *or* Greek.
4 Law not referring to either of the two may be called stage law.

However, one caveat remains: every single passage needs to undergo an individual analysis as all four categories can appear within the same play.[14]

Roman Comedy and the 'Epiclerate'

The Roman playwrights' treatment of the so-called epiclerate, a peculiar element of the Greek law of intestate succession (i.e. inheritance in the absence of a will), may serve us as an example of law being indispensable for the plot. In fact, the epiclerate forms the basis of several plays of Greek Middle and New Comedy: not only do we know that Antiphanes, Alexis, Diphilus, and Menander amongst others wrote plays entitled *Epikleros* ('The Heiress');[15] the surviving verses of Menander's *Aspis* ('The Shield') showcase how much a play's storyline could depend on this legal institution.[16] We are thus led to expect finding its traces in Roman plays as well.

Whilst Roman law is essentially the law of *one* city, Rome, what we call 'Ancient Greek law' comprises the laws of *various* Greek *poleis* (cities).[17] However, one principle common to all Ancient Greek laws is the protection

---

[14] Cf. Paoli (1962) 68.
[15] Antiphanes fr. 94 K.-A.; Alexis fr. 78–80 K.-A.; Diphilos fr. 40 K.-A.; Menander fr. 129–136 K.-A.
[16] See Karabélias (1970); MacDowell (1982).
[17] For details, see Gagarin (2005); Thür (2006).

and preservation of the continuation of the *oikos* ('house/household'), endangered in cases of intestate succession. When the head of a family died, his sons became his heirs, whilst his daughters had no legal capacity to inherit; if there were no sons, the head of the family could adopt a male citizen and marry his own daughter off to him. However, when the deceased had not arranged such an adoption, the 'nearest male relative' (ὁ ἐγγύτατα γένους) on the father's side, in modern scholarship often called ὁ ἀγχιστεύς, was entitled to claim the inheritance (ὁ κλῆρος) before a magistrate by means of a 'process at law to adjudicate an inheritance' (ἐπιδικασία).[18]

A surviving daughter (ἐπίκληρος) was not so much an 'heiress' than a means of conferring the patrimony to the next generation. She met the same fate as the inheritance and was adjudicated to the 'claimant at law' (ἐπιδικαζόμενος). This man could now either marry her himself or marry her off with a dowry.[19] The issue resulting from this union then became legitimate heirs of the head of the family.[20] Understandably the woman's lot (and possibly also that of her true lover) made this law's application and misuse an inspiration for generations of comic writers.

The second century AD antiquarian Gellius quotes passages of both Menander's *Plokion* ('The Necklace') and Caecilius' adaptation *Plocium*.[21] As Paoli has pointed out, these lines shed some light on the treatment of the epiclerate in Roman comedy.[22] In Menander's play a husband complains about having been forced to sell a slave girl, whom his jealous wife considered a rival. The man describes the new situation at home as follows:

> ἐπ' ἀμφότερα νῦν ἡ 'πίκληρος ἡ κ‹αλὴ›
> μέλλει καθευδήσειν. κατείργασται μέγα
> καὶ περιβόητον ἔργον·

Now the pretty heiress [= jealous wife] can sleep on both ears.
She has accomplished her great and much talked of deed.
> (Gel. 2.23.9 = Men. fr. 296,1–3 K.-A. (*Plokion*))

Later on the husband refers to his wife as ἐπίκληρος a second time.[23] When adapting Menander's lines, Caecilius thus had to deal with the Greek epiclerate. However, instead of preserving this Greek legal institution in his Latin

---

[18] Cf. Harrison (1968) 9–12, 132–8; MacDowell (1978) 103.
[19] On the terminology, see Karabélias (2002) 85–7.
[20] Cf. Harrison (1968) 130–8; Lipsius (1905–15) 540–61; MacDowell (1978) 95; Wolff (1952) 17–21.
[21] Gel. 2.23.9–21 = Men. fr. 296–310 K.-A. & Caecil. com. 136–153 Guardì; see Riedweg (1993) for a discussion of these verses.
[22] Paoli (1943).   [23] Gel. 2.23.12 = Men. fr. 297 K.-A.

play and confronting his audience with it or cutting it out altogether, he has found a different solution:

> quae nisi dotem, omnia, quae nolis,
> habet:

She has everything you don't want except for her dowry.

(Gel. 2.23.10 = Caecil. com. 139–40 Guardì)

The Roman playwright has turned Menander's wife into an *uxor bene dotata* ('well-dowered bride'), a character we encounter several times in Roman comedy.[24] The epiclerate then with all its details as described above cannot have been indispensable for the plot since Caecilius did not keep it in his adaptation – at least in the extant verses. Otherwise the poet would have created unbearable inconsistencies in the plot. One way of dealing with the Greek ἐπίκληρος in Roman comedy was obviously to substitute her with a Roman figure, an *uxor bene dotata*.

Terence takes a different path. In the opening prologue of his *Phormio* he announces this play as a new comedy adapted from Apollodorus' *Epidikazomenos* ('The Claimant at Law').[25] We assume today that Apollodorus' original relied on the epiclerate.[26] Accordingly, if Terence wanted to stick to the plot, he needed to explain this Greek legal institution somehow and make it palatable to his audience. We must not forget that the plays were staged, and not printed for a reader who could pause and go back if a fact had escaped his notice. And even if the audience had seen plays featuring the Greek epiclerate before, the playwright could not rely on the audience to understand the complex law at once. Terence dealt with this problem in an elegant way: in the second scene of the *Phormio*, the slave Geta recounts to Davus his burdensome experience of taking care of the young man Antipho. Whilst Antipho's father Demipho was abroad, the youth fell in love with the girl Phanium, whom he wanted to marry in the absence of his father. In order to achieve this, the parasite Phormio had concocted a scheme, which Geta now reports to Davus as follows:

> hoc consilium quod dicam dedit:
> 'Lex est ut orbae, qui sint genere proxumi,
> is nubant, et illos ducere eadem haec lex iubet.'

---

[24] Cf. Schuhmann (1977) and Stärk (1990) 47–59.
[25] Ter. *Ph.* 24–8; but note Donat. Ter. *Ph.* 24–6 ('Epidikazomene').
[26] Collected fragments are Apollodorus Comicus fr. 16–28 K.-A.

He worked out a plan, which I'll explain. 'There is a law', he said 'that orphan girls shall marry their next-of-kin, and this same law compels the next-of-kin to marry them.'

(Transl. Barsby 2001)

(*Ph.* 124–6)

Geta begins his report with *lex est* ('there is a law'), which immediately creates a solemn, quasi nomothetic atmosphere. As the play that follows rests fundamentally on Phormio's plan, which again relies crucially on this law, Geta's explanation is not intended for Davus alone, but also for the theatre audience.[27] After all, his plan has already been carried out when the action begins and understanding this law is essential for the entire play.

Upon his return Demipho is not amused when he learns about his son Antipho's marriage with Phanium since Demipho had intended to marry his son off to his brother Chremes' daughter. In a dialogue Demipho complains to his slave Geta about what happened:

DE. an hoc dicet mihi:
      'inuitus feci. lex coegit'? audio, fateor. GE. places.

DE. uerum scientem, tacitum causam tradere aduorsariis,
      etiamne id lex coegit?

DE: Will he say: 'I did it against my will. The law compelled me'? All right. Granted.

GE: That's good of you.

DE: But to let the case go by default deliberately and without saying a word. Did the law compel that too? (Transl. Barsby (2001))

(*Ph.* 235–8)

Terence draws the image of the law defeating the young man Antipho in court. Such personification of law in general or of a specific law are common in ancient comedy. In Aristophanes' *Ecclesiazusae* for example an old hag tries to coerce a young man into sleeping with her. Eventually she draws upon a newly passed law, whereby the young man would be obliged to sleep with her. She proclaims: οὐκ ἐγώ, ἀλλ᾽ ὁ νόμος ἕλκει σ᾽ ('Not I, but the law it is who drags you').[28] In Terence's *Phormio*, however, Demipho criticises not the law itself or its application but rather his son's lack of effort in fighting it. Antipho could have easily provided the girl with a dowry and married her off to someone else, which is exactly what the cunning slave Phormio suggests in the second half of the play (*Ph.* 407–10). Terence's *Phormio* rests on the institution of the epiclerate. His approach, namely keeping the Greek law in

---

[27] For metatheatre, see the chapter of Christenson in this volume.

[28] See Sens (1991) 81–90 and Bartholomä (2018) for details.

the plot and explaining it to his audience, illustrates how a Roman playwright adapts a Greek play which relied heavily on legal technicalities.

Parody of Law: Plautus and *Mancipatio*

A passage from Plautus' *Truculentus* exemplifies the workings of legal parody unrelated to the plot. It is concerned with a peculiar Roman legal act of transferring ownership, the *mancipatio*.[29]

In Roman law *res* ('things/items') could be classified as 'corporeal vs. incorporeal', 'moveable vs. immoveable'. A further important differentiation, however, relates to the mode of transfer of (civic) ownership.[30] Items of minor importance and value for the family could be transferred by a mere handing over (*traditio*).[31] Civic ownership of more valuable *res*, however, such as slaves, oxen, horses, and Italic land, for example, had to be transferred by means of *mancipatio* (or *in iure cessio* – 'cession before the magistrate').

The *mancipatio* had already existed at the time of the XII Tables (*c.* 450 BC) and in Plautus' days this ritual was not only applied for the transfer of ownership, but also – with modifications – for the *coemptio* ('sale of a woman by which she passes into the *manus* ('a husband's power over his wife')), the *mancipatio familiae* ('mancipatory will, i.e. transfer of property to a trustee') or the *emancipatio* ('formal release from *patria potestas* (parental control)'). This multiplicity demonstrates that *mancipatio* must have been well-known to Roman audiences.[32] Nowadays the best source on the act of *mancipatio* is the elementary textbook ('*Institutiones*') of the second-century AD jurist Gaius, which was discovered only in 1816:

> It (i. e. *mancipatio*) is performed as follows: in the presence of no fewer than 5 Roman citizens of full age and also of a sixth person, having the same qualifications, known as the scale-holder (*libripens*), to hold a bronze scale, the party who is taking into full power (*is qui mancipio accipit*), holding a bronze ingot, says: 'I declare that this slave is mine by the *law of the Roman citizens* (*ex iure Quiritium*), and be he purchased to me with this bronze ingot (*hoc aere*) and bronze scale (*aeneaque libra*).' He then strikes the scale with the ingot and gives it as a symbolic price to him from whom he is receiving into full power.
>
> (Transl. adapted from de Zulueta 1946)
>
> (Gaius *Inst.* 1.119)

---

[29] Brophy (1974) 9 points out some twenty instances related to this family of words in Plautus.

[30] Gaius *Inst.* 2.18 (*magna differentia*); cf. Kaser (1971) 123–4; Nicholas (1962) 105–6; Riggsby (2010) 137.

[31] For further requirements, see Gaius *Inst.* 2.19–20; cf. Kaser (1971) 416–18.

[32] Cf. also the allusions in Lucr. 3.971 and Hor. *Ep.* 2.2.158–9.

In verses 209–255 of Plautus' *Truculentus* Astaphium, the maid of the courtesan Phronesium, goes to Strabax, an Athenian youth who is said to be very charming and generous (247: *nimi' pol mortalis lepidus nimi'que probu' dator*). However, Strabax' slave, Truculentus, after whom the play is named, is quite the opposite and well-known for his savage behaviour (250: *uiolentissumus*). And of course, it is not Strabax, but his unpleasant fellow who opens the door when Astaphium knocks. In the following dialogue Truculentus insults the slave girl and mocks her outward appearance, especially her bronze jewellery.

> TR.   ...
> aduenisti huc te ostentatum cum exornatis ossibus
> quia tibi suaso infecisti propudiosa pallulam?
> an eo bella es, quia accepisti tibi armillas aenas?
> AS.   nunc places, quom mi inclementer dicis. TR. quid hoc quod te rogo?
> mancupion qui accipias, gestas tecum ahenos anulos?

> TR: ... Have you come here to present yourself with your decorated bones,
> because you've dyed your little cloak with grey ink, you shameless creature?
> Are you pretty just because you've put on bronze bracelets?
> AS: Now that you speak roughly to me, I like you.
> TR: What about the question I am asking you? Are you carrying bronze rings
> with you so that you can make formal purchases?
> (Transl. adapted from de Melo 2013)
> (*Truc.* 270–4)

Here a dressed-up slave girl in a good mood encounters a truly ill-mannered and aggressive Truculentus who unleashes a cannonade of invectives. There is an obvious allusion to the rite of *mancipatio* since *aenos anulos* and *mancupio accipias* (274) must have reminded a Roman audience of the piece of bronze (*hoc aere*) and the scales (*aeneaque libra*) involved in the ritual mentioned above. The *mancipatio* pun arguably strikes a chord with a Roman audience; after all, *mancipatio* was omnipresent in Roman life, but it will only reveal itself to the modern reader or viewer after some laboured explanation or consultation of a commentary. Modern readers thus often face the risk of not realising the legal subtext. In addition, further legal subtexts are at show when Plautus' *Rudens* (956–86) plays with, contests, and interrogates the law on legal terms such as property when the slaves, who themselves are property, ponder that very category after pulling a trunk from the sea.[33]

---

[33] Henderson (2009) 103–5.

Beware of Legal References: *Scribam Dicam*

Let us return once more – briefly – to Geta's monologue in Terence's *Phormio*, which will show some of the potential pitfalls in applying the method formulated above too readily. Phormio not only told Geta about the epiclerate, but also suggested the following to the youth Antipho (*Ph.* 127):

> ego te cognatum dicam et tibi scribam dicam.

> I will say that you are related to her and have a claim written against you.
>
> (Transl. adapted from Barsby 2001)

We encounter the combination '*dicam scribere*' several times in Plautus and Terence, and indeed also in Cicero. All of them refer to first steps of legal procedure.[34] Here we are in the comfortable position to draw on the authority of the ancient grammarian Donatus (fourth century AD): in his commentary on Terence's *scriptam dicam* at *Ph.* 329 he explains that δίκη is the Greek word for Latin *causa* (i.e. 'legal claim'), which would in Latin turn out as *dica,* just like ἀκτή turned out as *acta* and Καλλιόπη as *Calliopa*.[35]

However, the mere fact that *dica* is a Latinisation of the Greek δίκη does not prove that the Greek equivalent of *scribam dicam*, δίκην γράφεσθαι (lit. 'to write a claim for oneself/to have a claim written'), was found in the Greek original that Terence was adapting for his *Phormio.* Therefore both Witt (1971a and 1971b) and Scafuro (1994) are cautious in their conclusions. Witt claims that Plautus and Terence did not use '*dicam scribere*' to denote 'to have a claim written' but merely in the more general sense of 'to sue/to prosecute'.[36] Scafuro suggests that some instances of the phrase '*dicam scribere*' might just be 'savvy Greek flavouring' added by the Latin authors.[37]

However, one one-verse fragment of Menander which has been transmitted by the fifth-century AD excerptist Stobaeus has so far not received its due attention.[38] It tells about a child bringing his parents to court, and uses the same Greek phrase but puts δίκην into the plural: δίκας γραφόμενος πρὸς γονεῖς μαίνηι, τάλαν. ('wretched one, you rage and have claims written against your parents'). Of course, the existence of this Menandrean line again cannot prove that all instances of '*dicam scribere*' in Plautus and Terence are mere translations from the Greek plays they are adapting. Nevertheless, it demonstrates that the phrase δίκην γράφεσθαι was part of the legal

---

[34] E.g. Pl. *Aul.* 759: *tibi scribam dicam; Poen.* 800: *susscribam ... dicam;* Ter. *Ph.* 329: *audisti mihi scriptam dicam?;* 439: *dicam ... inpingam grandem;* 668: *sescentas perinde scribito iam mihi dicas;* Cic. *Verr.* 2, 37: *scribitur Heraclio dica;* 2, 44: *ceteras dicas ... sortitus est.*

[35] Donat. Ter. *Ph.* 329.   [36] Witt (1971a) 8 and (1971b) 223.   [37] Scafuro (1997) 95–6.

[38] Menander fr. 824 K.-A.

terminology repertoire of Greek (New) Comedy.[39] Against the background of numerous plays of Greek New Comedy dealing with legal procedure, this Menandrean fragment should then allow us to be more confident that Plautus and Terence found the Greek phrase in the original lines they were adapting, and that these instances are not their own additions.

We have shown that mere legal references such as '*dicam scribere*' in Plautus and Terence may sometimes not allude to Roman, but to Greek law. This supports the caveat mentioned above: every passage has to undergo individual analysis. Otherwise the Greek law in Latin dress may escape our notice.

Law is – roughly speaking – a set of rules by which a society agrees to live and is thus predestined to play a role in all parts of life, even comedy. It is therefore hardly surprising that Roman comedy plays with it. As we have seen, understanding the law helps philologists to appreciate the plots and jokes of Roman comedy, whilst the comedies prove to be useful sources for the legal historian.

Further Reading

The following suggestions are necessarily selective; Ward (1995) and Posner (2009) provide a good starting point for 'Law and Literature' in general. See also Kenney (1969), Hollis (1994), and Cloud (1989). For a recent comprehensive bibliography on law and Plautus, see Gaertner (2011a) and (2011b) (in German). Most publications on Roman law and comedy include introductory sections that ease the reader into the matter, see Scafuro (1997) 1–21 and Gaertner (2011a). Paoli (1976) (in Italian) is an important collection of articles; Watson (1971) draws on comic passages in an attempt to reconstruct the law of 200 BC; Costa (1890) (for Plautus) and (1893) (for Terence) provide useful collections of assorted passages.

Stroux (1926), Kornhardt (1953), Büchner (1957), and Fuhrmann (1971) provide a lively discussion of the *sententia* 'summum ius summa iniuria'. Brown (2005) (Plautus' *Cistellaria*), Partsch (1910) (Plautus' *Persa*), Lallier (1878), and Lefèvre (1978b) 5–31 (both Terence's *Phormio*) discuss the legal framework of the respective plays. Gaertner (2011b) offers a line-by-line commentary on most Plautine passages referring to law. For Terence, see Schwind (1901). Aspects of legal language are also discussed by Dunn (1984) 5–66 and Karakasis (2003).

Procedural law: On settling disputes in general, see Scafuro (1997); on the usage of *arbiter* ('arbitrator') and *iudex* ('judge') in Plautus and Terence, see

---

[39] After all, Aristophanes had already played on having the δίκη written on a wax tablet. See Ar. *Nu.* 758–9; 770–2.

Ahrens (1970); on a *iudex'* social background, see Gagliardi (2007) or
(2008); on the *in ius uocatio* ('initiating procedure'), see Paoli (1952), Witt
(1971a) and (1971b), Scafuro (1997) 68–114; on *restitutio in integrum*
('reinstatement into the former legal position'), see Kornhardt (1954); on
interdicta ('interdicts'), see Falcone (1988).

Family law: In general, see Fredershausen (1912) and Watson (1967)
passim; legal information on the epiclerate may be found in Harrison (1968)
1–12, 122–38, and MacDowell (1978) 84–98; the most exhaustive treatment
is Karabélias (2002) for Athens and (2004) for other *poleis*; on the epiclerate
in New Comedy, see Paoli (1943), Scafuro (1997) 281–305, and Kuhn-
Treichel (2018); on fathers, sons, and daughters, see Bramante (2007); on
marriage, see Dees (1988) and Williams (1958); on divorce, see Rosenmeyer
(1995), Scafuro (1997) 306–26, Schuhmann (1976), and Nesselrath (2018).

Property & contracts: In general, see Watson (1965) (on obligations) and
(1968) (on property); on the stipulations in Plautus' *Pseudolus*, see Platschek
(2018); on *mancipatio*, see Brophy (1974), Tomulescu (1971), and Gaertner
(2018); on *pignus* ('pledge'), see Schanbacher (2006); on *depositum*
('deposit'), see Scheibelreiter (2012) and (2018); a contract for hiring
a prostitute is analysed by Scafuro (2003/2004); for private auctions, see
Donadio (2007); on sales in Plautus' *Curculio* and *Pseudolus*, see Pringsheim
(1916) 34–8; for a 'Romanistic approach' on the sale in Plautus' *Rudens*, see
Pennitz (2013); on arr(h)a in Plautus, see Pringsheim (1950) 415–29 and
MacCormack (1971).

15

ELAINE FANTHAM

Family Finances

While Roman versions of New Comedy offer far more variety of plot than the standard intrigues of the penniless young lover, there is one particular pattern that springs to mind first: the gratification of love requires money and the lover must find it at another's expense. Before exploring the various forms taken by this kind of trickery, it will be useful to recapitulate the resources and circumstances of the bourgeois Athenian household that typically features in New Comedy. Living on inherited property, the father will own his townhouse, and perhaps a plot of land up country, like the estate of Sostratos' father in Phyle in Menander's *Dyskolos*. This bi-location will be useful to the action when sons, and even occasionally fathers, need to misbehave unobserved – there are examples in *Mercator* and *Eunuchus* (629–34; 971–3). Other householders own estates away from Athens, and may travel to the islands still under Athenian control (Andros (*Andria*), Lemnos (*Ph.* 66)), or to trade abroad in Cilicia. Encouraged by a friend promising untold wealth (*Ph.* 67–8), one father is trading in Asia Minor while the other visits Lemnos to collect the rent or other proceeds from his wife's property. Such absences may last for months (unspecified in *Trinummus*, five months in *Hecyra*) or in extreme cases two to three years (*St.* 137; *Most.* 110 and 440 after a voyage to Egypt). In *Mostellaria* (206–7) Philolaches has not actually sold the house (though that will be a fiction of later acts) but has borrowed 40 *minae* at high interest to set free his girlfriend Philematium. The moneylender Misargurides (Money-hater) will come to bug him for the debt at the crucial moment when his father has just returned. Often, indeed, the crisis of the comedy is brought on by the father's return in the third or fourth act. So Theopropides in *Mostellaria* (599–607) when the moneylender Misargurides duns him in a formal demand, first for his principal, then at least his interest, is told a cock and bull story by his slave that his son owes 44 *minae* (*Most.* 652) because he borrowed it as a deposit on the new house he has bought next door. And if you doubt the exorbitance of these professional loan sharks, note that in *Epidicus* young Stratippocles has to pay a *nummus* per diem on each of the 40 *minae* he has borrowed.[1] But *Epidicus*, short as it is, demonstrates what amazing variety was available in the lover-*hetaera* plot. Stratippocles first browbeats his slave to purchase the lyre-player Acropolistis (*Ep.* 46–8), then falls in love with a beautiful Theban he has taken prisoner while campaigning, and tells Epidicus to dispose of Acropolistis. Unfortunately, Epidicus has set her up in the house of Stratippocles' father Periphanes by telling Periphanes that she is the long-lost daughter from Thebes whom he is expecting to come to Athens – and by training Acropolistis to call herself Telestis and act as his lost daughter. Now that Stratippocles has lost interest in her they have to find a way of selling her off. In fact three women are being juggled: the lyre-player Acropolistis, a nameless lyre-player hired for the day, and the long-lost daughter Telestis, who will not appear until Act v.

Luckily Periphanes thinks he has a customer – a Rhodian soldier who loves 'Acropolistis' – and tries to negotiate with him. He edges up her price, claims that she cost him 50 *minae* and asks for 60. But when the girl is brought on stage she is NOT the soldier's Acropolistis, but the nameless hired lyre-player, whom nobody wants: she is sent away. Next the Theban Philippa, the former lover of Periphanes, comes in quest of her daughter and Periphanes reassures her that he has her daughter at home. This time he brings out Acropolistis – that is a second, and equally wrong woman – who tells them that Stratippocles has used his father's money to set his mistress free. After three misidentifications the fourth time is lucky. It is the moneylender who comes from Thebes escorting Stratippocles' captive, Periphanes' real daughter Telestis, whom Epidicus recognizes (*Ep.* 636). But when Stratippocles discovers that the lovely captive is his own sister, he is frustrated (*Ep.* 648–50) and we never have the satisfaction of witnessing her happy reunion with either her mother or her father. The spectators must be content that Epidicus has earned forgiveness and the family has regained the missing child. And has father Periphanes lost his money? Certainly nobody buys the spare lyre-player Acropolistis during the play.

Another variant on the young man's purchase of his lover is offered by *Persa*, in which the freeborn Toxilus has no money to buy his girlfriend from the pimp Dordalus, but defrauds the pimp by selling him his friend Saturio's virgin daughter as an oriental captive – an illegal sale. The audience knows in

---

[1] *Ep.* 53–4: *argentum ab danista apud Thebas sumpsit faenore / in dies minasque argenti singulas nummis* ('He took that money from a moneylender in Thebes on interest, one coin for each mina per day'). Depending on the value of that daily coin – the word *nummus* is not only vague; it seems to fluctuate in comedy between a drachma and a didrachm – the annual interest rate on this loan might be as high as 91 per cent. On this kind of interest-bearing loan in ancient Athens, see Millett (1991) 160–78.

advance that her father will come to claim her free birth, leaving the pimp helpless to recover the money he has paid for fraudulent goods.

In *Trinummus* as opposed to *Mostellaria* the house sale is a real one. This play tends to be vague in its moralising, but we hear at *Trin.* 108–15 that Charmides was driven to go trading in Seleucia when his son smashed up his fortune (*rem confregit*, literally 'breaking it'), a relatively unusual metaphor for extravagance – usually we find *comedere* ('eating it up', cf. *Trin.* 405–6). Charmides left Callicles to watch over the son, and preserve something for his daughter's dowry, but while Callicles was away for six days the boy put up the house for sale, for 40 *minae* (the same price as many courtesans in comedy). Anxious about a treasure hidden in the house, Callicles has bought the house himself but left the son in possession of a rear apartment (*posticum*) while he has taken the kid sister into his own home as companion for his daughter. We learn later in the play that the young man has kept a plot of land to provide his sister with the dowry which is the mark of her respectable status and of his social obligation towards her intended husband, his thrifty friend Lysiteles ('the profitable man').

In fact the newly returned father happily promises Lysiteles a thousand Philippics (*mille auri Philippum dotis*, *Trin.* 1158). This is perhaps the best place to indicate the evidence of comedy for the size of such dowries, which will certainly have been an unexpected outlay for any father of a newly recovered daughter. Dowries account for as much as 10 talents (600 *minae*) from Chremes in Terence's *Andria* 951, or 2 talents from Chremes in *Heauton Timorumenos* (940).[2] If *Adelphoe* 915 alludes to the dowry the amount would be somewhat smaller (20 *minae*). Plautus is much less interested in dowries. Besides *Aulularia* in which the pot of gold was destined by the *Lar Familiaris* (spirit of the founder of the house) for Euclio's daughter's dowry, six plays survive in which a daughter is recognised: *Cistellaria, Curculio, Epidicus, Rudens, Trinummus,* and *Truculentus*. But Plautus usually leaves the recognition offstage in favour of scenes exacting vengeance on pimps. Apart from *Trinummus* only *Truculentus* mentions the dowry of Diniarchus' offstage wife, already the mother of his child: it must be imagined as large (about 10 talents?), since he reduces it by 6 talents (*Truc.* 845).

Young men in Athens usually had no money of their own, and Roman adolescents remained under their father's control as long as they lived.[3] If a young lover had to raise funds to buy his girl (and girls cost as much as

---

[2] As Casson (1976) 106 notes, the dowries of Roman comedy seem much higher than those mentioned in Menander (such as 2 talents in *Aspis*, 135–6 and 268–9). He suggests that this reflects increased levels of expenditure in second-century Rome.

[3] See Strauss (1993) 67–71 on the intricacies of a young Athenian's economic situation and Crook (1967) on *patria potestas*.

a Porsche or BMW) he just might be able to borrow a few *minae* interest free (*mutuom*) from a friend, but it is unlikely that he would be able to 'touch' his father (*tangere* is the metaphor in *Ps.* 120 *tuom tangam patrem*). When Calidorus comes begging the pimp Ballio for one more day while he tries to raise money to buy his girl, he is told:

> Si amabas, inuenires mutuom,
> Ad danistam deuenires, adderes faenusculum
> Surruperes patri [...]

> If you were in love you could have found a loan, resorted to the moneylender and added a little interest, or stolen from your father. (*Ps.* 286–8)

Calidorus' response is:

> Ego de patri surrupere possim quicquam, tam cauto seni?
> Atque adeo, si facere possim, pietas prohibet.

> Could I steal anything from my father, such a shrewd old man? And what's more, if I could have, piety forbids me. (*Ps.* 290–1)

Ballio even advises an advance purchase of futures in olive oil. Here, and only here in Plautus, the young man invokes the *lex quinauicenaria*, which prevents a son under the age of 25 from borrowing money to trade with (*Ps.* 301–3).

But money in *Pseudolus* is both restless and notional (that is, it changes hands through promises and bargains, not as physical coinage). We need to watch carefully how money changes hands to finance young Calidorus' purchase of his girl.

The play opens with Calidorus' receipt of the desperate letter from his girl. A soldier is buying her and the deal is set for this very day. The price is (only) 20 *minae*, and Pseudolus guarantees to provide it, making a public proclamation of his intent (*Ps.* 113, also 280).[4] But first master and slave try to bargain with the girl's owner Ballio – to no effect. Meanwhile Calidorus' father Simo has heard that his son is searching for money to buy and set free his girl (*Ps.* 415–20). He challenges Pseudolus; isn't it true that his son needs 20 *minae* (*Ps.* 484) to free her? Pseudolus agrees and issues his boast and his warning:

> SIMO   Ne quisquam credit nummum iam dico omnibus.
> PSEUD.   Tu mi hercle argentum dabis,
>   abs te equidem sumam [...] dabis.
>   Iam dico ut tu caueas.

---

[4] For these scenes' metapoetic significance, see Christenson in this volume.

SIMO	Si non abstuleris?
PSEUD.	Virgis caedito.
	Sed quid si abstulero?
SIMO	Do Iouem testem tibi
	te aetatem impune habiturum.

SIMO:	I'll warn the world not to trust you with any money.
PSEUD:	By Hercules you'll give me the money; I'll take it from you! […] You'll give it, and I'm telling you now to beware of me.

SIMO:	Supposing you don't get the girl?
PSEUD:	Then give me a beating. But supposing I do?
SIMO:	I give you Jupiter as my witness that you will enjoy your life unharmed.

(Ps. 508–15, excerpted)

We now have two intrigues; the internal plot of getting the girl, and a new meta-plot in which Pseudolus will get her price from his own master. In support of this secondary task Pseudolus and Simo have made a formal bargain or *stipulatio*. How will the slave do it? While Ballio is away from home Pseudolus is saved by the arrival of the soldier's batman Harpax with the soldier's token (*symbolus*) and the outstanding 5 *minae* due on the girl. He tells Harpax to wait nearby, and uses the time to borrow 5 *minae* from his master's friend Charinus, and equip an imported con-man, Simia, with a suitable disguise. Simia rehearses the abduction with Pseudolus, then uses the token and a letter to retrieve the girl.

This is the moment when Ballio is most deceived. He believes he has safely delivered the girl to the soldier's batman, and foiled Pseudolus. In his triumph he carries the *stipulatio* a step further, telling Simo to ask him for the 20 *minae*:

BALL.	Minae uiginti sanae et saluae sunt tibi,
	hodie quas aps te stipulatus est Pseudolus.
SIMO	Velim quidem hercle.
BALL.	Roga me uiginti minas […]
	roga obsecro hercle. Gestio promittere […]

BALL:	Your 20 *minae* are safe and sound, the ones Pseudolus bargained with you for.
SIMO:	I only wish […]
BALL:	Ask me for 20 *minae*, ask me please, I'm itching to promise them.

(Ps. 1068–72)

SIMO	Nullumst periclum quod sciam, stipularier.

SIMO:	As far as I know there's no risk in bargaining.

(Ps. 1076)

But then the real Harpax comes back, and they treat him as a trickster suborned by Pseudolus. It takes 100 lines for him to convince them that Pseudolus has beaten them to it. Ballio is doubly victimised; Harpax demands his 20 *minae*, and Simo another 20. Ballio leaves for the forum to raise the money for Harpax and postpones Simo's money until 'tomorrow' (*Ps.* 1231).

In the last act the drunken Pseudolus confronts Simo, who has brought him the 20 *minae*, then grudgingly agrees to forgive him half the 'debt'.

Plautus has turned the play about rescuing the girl into a different play about the circulation of money – a money-go-round of love. He will apply the same technique in his other great intrigue of fraud, *Bacchides*, adapted from Menander's *Disexapaton* or 'Double Deceiver'.[5] In this play Nicobulus, father of Mnesilochus, has sent his son to Ephesus to retrieve his money. So when Pistoclerus, a close friend of Mnesilochus, needs money to pay off the soldier Cleomachus who has purchased Mnesilochus' girl's twin sister Bacchis, Mnesilochus has it in his possession – in fact he has all of 1,200 gold Philippics, an enormous sum (*Bacch.* 230). He uses his slave Chrysalus to distract Nicobulus with a tall tale about pirates and leaving the money in safe deposit with Theotimus, priest of Ephesian Diana, guaranteed with his seal ring and publicly transferred (*populo praesente*). The old man Nicobulus will have to sail to Ephesus and fetch the money himself.

The plot would seem to be resolved before we reach act two. But no, Mnesilochus not knowing that there are two girls named Bacchis is led to believe his friend has deceived him in his absence with his own Bacchis and so confesses the fraud to his father and returns the money: *reddidi patri omne aurum* (I have paid back all the gold to my father, *Bacch.* 530 (see also 608, 681). It is perhaps odd, given the Roman obsession with money, that where Menander staged the son's return of the cash to his father at the end of act two (*Disexapaton* 18–63), Plautus omits the scene to focus instead on the friends' *reconciliation*. Now Chrysalus must come up with a second fraud, and he contrives through a false letter to convince old Nicobulus that the soldier, come to claim his purchase, Mnesilochus' Bacchis, is actually the woman's husband. So Mnesilochus risks the physical punishment meted out to adulterers – unless the old father bribes the soldier with the money. The soldier is paid off and all seems well: Chrysalus can utter his song of triumph like Agamemnon or Ulysses over Troy.

But is the play over? Well, not quite. Chrysalus has decided he needs 200 more gold Philippics to celebrate his victory. It takes another letter – apparently

---

[5] On the relationship between Menander's largely lost play and Plautus' comedy, see Handley (1968) and Barsby (1986).

another, third, deception – to bring out the old fathers, Nicobulus and Philoxenus (father of Pistoclerus).[6] Plautus crowns Chrysalus' victory when Nicobulus learns the truth from the soldier that Bacchis is not the soldier's wife but a *meretrix*. What is more, Chrysalus has also led Pistoclerus into woman-chasing extravagance. Disdaining to accept the money from his old master Nicobulus, in a ploy similar to that of *Pseudolus* 1061–6, Chrysalus even rejects a triumph: they are too common nowadays (*Bacch.* 1073). The two old men go to confront the Bacchis twins but end up seduced, and bribed with the return of half their outlay (*Bacch.* 1189) ensuring forgiveness for their sons on both erotic and financial grounds.[7]

Preoccupation with money and financial transactions may have increased with the development of the genre in both Greek New Comedy and Roman comedy. Perhaps we should return to the general question of how the bourgeois Athenian kept his inherited money, or made his own fortune. Assuming he had inherited a townhouse and a small estate in the hinterland from his father, he might simply sit back and live within the income, but more likely he would seek to make money from one of four sources: 1) rent or produce from the property itself; 2) rental income from investment property; single occupancy dwellings, workshops etc; 3) manufacture of goods; and 4) (overseas) trade. Comedy bears witness to 1) and 4) but the evidence for 2) and 3) is only to be found in oratory.

Thus although Athenian land was not fertile or lucrative, livestock – steers (*Persa* 259–60), donkeys, and pack animals (*Asinaria*) – could be sold, and the proceeds appropriated by or for the young lover. Income could be made from working slaves: for pimps from their *pornai* (prostitutes), as we witness in *Pseudolus*, but also from craftsmen slaves, who paid a proportion of their earnings to their masters. In *Adelphoe* we are told that the good slave Geta supports the widow and her daughter from his earnings.[8]

The fathers of comedy do not seem to go in for light industry but they do go in for trade.[9] Overseas voyages were not only a necessary plot ingredient, to allow the errant son to misbehave unperceived by his old father, but also a regular feature of Athenian business; compare the voyages of Theoropides

---

[6] Given Menander's title 'DOUBLE-deception', it is not surprising that Fraenkel (1922; 2007) saw the third deception and second letter as a Plautine addition to the Greek intrigue.
[7] On this scene, see also Dinter in this volume.
[8] Cf. Cohen (1992) 6: 'By the fourth century agricultural products were increasingly being raised for cash sale, consumer items were now often produced by commercial workshops...' A good accessible survey of sources of income, especially from slaves, craftsmen, rented or on contract, is Casson (1976) esp. 35–40.
[9] On Hellenistic business, see Calhoun (1968) and Casson (1984). Millett (1983) on maritime loans as well as Mossé (1983) on *Emporia* will be of particular interest among the other papers in Garnsey, Hopkins, and Whittaker (1983).

in *Mostellaria,* Charmides in *Trinummus,* the absentee brothers in *Stichus,* and as we shall see, the brothers of *Phormio.*

Casson (1976) helpfully distinguishes between the *naukleros* or ship owner – not usually a citizen but a metic or alien denied the right to purchase landed property – the *emporos,* or merchant, whether independent or agent, operating from Athens or abroad, and the banker/moneylender. The most explicit tale of trading is not surprisingly *Mercator* based on Philemon's *Emporos.* In the prologue Charinus provides two models of overseas trading: when his grandfather died his father Demipho sold up some land and bought a ship with a capacity of 300 *metretai* (roughly 500 gallons) and bought up goods from all sources until he had amassed his present wealth (*Merc.* 73–8). Now Charinus too has been trading, but instead of hiring a ship for him (*nauem conducere,* as in Ter. *Ad.* 225, and Caecilius *Adelphoe* fr. 6) Demipho built a light sloop (*cercurus*[10]) and loaded it with cargo, giving his son a further talent of silver in cash and an old trusted slave to guide him. They set out for Rhodes, where Charinus sold everything at a good price and made a huge profit (*lucrum ingens*) over and beyond the value at which his father assessed the goods – this would be his *peculium* (special fund for private use, *Merc.* 85–95). The two models differ in that Charinus' father built him a vessel so that he would continue as a small-scale *naukleros,* whereas older men who decided to make a single voyage would rent an existing ship (or space for their goods on deck or in the hold) from a ship-owner.

There are special circumstances attached to the maritime loans which financed such journeys. You clearly could not specify a duration for the journey or calculate the interest due on a maritime loan when voyages were so unpredictable and hazards somewhat greater than those for land-based loans. As Cohen explains, maritime loans were repayable with a pre-agreed interest equivalent not at a time but in a place – that is at the port of destination within X days of arrival.[11] The strangest aspect of the journey narratives in comedy, however, is that most merchants seem to have stayed away for two to three years: why so long?[12] The actual journeys between

---

[10] This is the only instance of Greek terminology in Plautus (apart from *lembus* (cutter), which was naturalised) and *stega,* ship's deck. According to Casson (1984) this *kerkyros* was well below average capacity, making it even more remarkable for Demipho to make a large profit.

[11] Cohen (1992) 134–50; but as Millett (1983) shows, there is continuing disagreement about the roles of maritime bankers. Casson (1976) notes that in the contract of Dem. 35.10, the rate of interest over four to five months up to September is 22.5% but thereafter varies from 67% to 90%.

[12] References for prolonged absence: two years *Bacch.* 388; *Most.* 79, 440; *St.* 40, 147, 214. See also Hindsholm (1990) and Knapp (1907).

248

Aegean ports would only last two to three weeks. Again Cohen (1992) draws on the scattered evidence of private lawsuits (such as Isocrates 17 and Demosthenes 32–5) to show that merchant voyages were a multiple activity; many merchants would travel in person with their commodities for export, each having paid for their share of the ship's cargo space: they would not all be aiming for the main destination, which would be intermediary to a further port for many of them; they would have to wait around in *emporia* consulting agents about the scheduled arrival of ships from the hinterland (carrying e.g. timber from the north coast of the Black Sea) and either themselves travelling beyond, or awaiting the arrival of ships bearing material they wished to purchase for importation. They would have agents, as would the major banks, through which to pay back maritime loans, which would eliminate the hazards of transporting actual coinage by sea. In addition, many trips may have involved time wasted waiting around in port for new cargo, or 'island hopping' side trips to make use of unoccupied space and time.

Thus Charinus' narrative suggests a simple model in which the merchant sets out from Athens' harbour at Piraeus with his commodities, sells them and purchases what he wants to import, turns the ship round and returns to Athens. But simplified as this is, the level of detail is exceptional in Roman comedy. There may have been far more incidental business details in the Greek originals, whose audience would understand the situation. *Mercator* seems to be an early play. Did Plautus actually suppress such details in later comedies in face of audience incomprehension or indifference?

One more example; the prologue of *Rudens* is circumstantial in explaining an attempted fraud forestalled by divine justice, when Jupiter through Arcturus his storm star and prologue speaker, causes the shipwreck of the absconding pimp Labrax, thus restoring the lost daughter to her virtuous and impoverished father, and making her eligible for marriage to her young lover. Apart from the price of 30 *minae* offered by her lover and its part payment, we get no financial information, only a morally satisfying tale. Imagine the same narrative in a courtroom speech: it would have been full of details of the cost of hiring the ship (cf. *Ru.* 57), the maritime insurance required, and the value of the pimp's possessions which perish in the shipwreck. But is this perhaps one more significant difference between Plautus' treatment of his Greek models, and Terence's more faithful adaptations?

Certainly, Terence's concern with the status of the head of the family, the *paterfamilias*, is reflected in all of his plays, and the family finances are protected. However, the most detailed and realistic seems to be his *Phormio*, not a Menandrian comedy but one adapted from the *Epidikazomenos* (or 'Litigator') of Menander's pupil Apollodorus of

Carystos.[13] *Phormio* is perhaps our best example of a play faithful to the intrigue of its (lost) Greek model and certainly the play most preoccupied with money.

The voyage from which the two brothers Demipho and Chremes are returning as the play opens seems to have produced neither profit nor loss, and its family problems have arisen simply because of their prolonged absence. In fact, the financial issues in *Phormio* are not related to trade, but to domestic law and the economy of marriage. In his father's absence, young Antipho has fallen in love with an orphan girl and married her. This will anger his father, since it was part of bourgeois family financial planning to get rich by marrying off the son to a wealthy girl with a large dowry. Since his father could nullify the marriage, Antipho's friend Phormio concocts a lawsuit that will oblige the young man to marry the girl as her next of kin. His father is angry that Antipho had acquiesced in the marriage instead of finding (as the law provided) a small dowry and a humbler man to serve as husband. In fact, Phormio's fiction will turn out to be most conveniently true, when the discovery of the girl's actual identity later in the play will make the marriage welcome to everyone concerned.

Antipho's father is so eager to make money that he reproaches his son with failing to borrow funds from a moneylender to pay off a putative husband for the girl. But scarcely a line passes in *Phormio* without reference to money, and petty household economies, from the opening soliloquy which approaches the central family through the modest finances of their slave Geta, to the imaginary household expenses of Phormio's fictitious future marriage.

Geta's friend Davos owes him the last instalment of a small debt and Davos has come to pay it out. He knows Geta needs it because he has to scrape together a wedding present for his young master. This leads to comment on the social injustice that poor men have to contribute to those who are richer; this bride will snatch everything he has scraped together; then Geta will be hit by another gift when the mistress gives birth, and yet another on the baby's birthday,[14] then another when the grown son is initiated: the ritual will just be the excuse for what gifts his mother takes. Davos gives the money to Geta and is duly thanked. But Geta protests that the friend who trusts him with his money hesitates to trust him with a family secret. What he has to tell begins with the voyages of the old master Demipho and his brother Chremes. Demipho went to Lemnos, and Chremes to Cilicia enticed by the financial

---

[13] Apollodorus's *Hecyra* ('Mother-in-Law') may have been written just as late in the history of the genre, but is not concerned with financial issues.

[14] Compare the birthday gifts, which the tyrannical Ballio expects from his women and his boy slave at *Ps.* 781.

incentives of an old family friend. Poor Geta has been left as the boys' guardian and has not been able to control them. Demipho's son Antipho has been relatively restrained, but his cousin Phaedria has fallen for a lyre-girl without having any money to buy her services. Meanwhile Antipho notices a lovely girl and approaches her old nurse and asks to court her; he is told he must either marry her or stay away.

It is at this point that the 'parasite' Phormio enters the story.[15] Geta quotes from Phormio the Athenian law about fatherless girls: their next of kin was obliged to marry them or provide a dowry and find them a husband.[16] For Phormio is not a conventional parasite, who earns his living or at least his dinners by providing flattery and entertainment such as Gelasimus and Ergasilus in *Stichus* and *Captiui*, or Gnatho in *Eunuchus*. Rather he is a *sycophantes*, a professional informer and litigator. Phormio has sued young Antipho alleging that he is the girl's next of kin and so obliged Antipho to marry her. What is more, Antipho's cousin Phaedria has no money with which to buy access to his girlfriend, a slave entertainer. Finally, a letter reports that Antipho's father and uncle are returning. The boys are full of self-pity and Geta considers running away. Antipho hides in his new home and Phaedria is left to defend his cousin.

Now at last Phormio enters the stage ready to challenge father Demipho. How come Demipho does not recall his cousin Stilpo? This is a name to remember for the plot. Demipho claims he had no such cousin and did not know anyone of that name. Instead he offers Phormio 5 *minae* as the girl's dowry (*Ph.* 410), and Phormio threatens him with a huge lawsuit.

This play, like four of Terence's five other plays, uses a double action, based on two young lovers, one aspiring to citizen marriage, the other infatuated with a professional, and therefore unmarriageable, non-citizen. So far the audience has been preoccupied with the unauthorised marriage of Antipho; but now the playwright switches attention to his cousin Phaedria. A soldier has made an offer for Phaedria's girl and her pimp owner does not want to wait for his 30 *minae* from Phaedria any longer. He will only switch the sale to Phaedria if he can bring the money before the soldier arrives (*Ph.* 531–3 and 557–8).

---

[15] On the *Phormio*, see Martin (1959); Arnott (1970); Konstan (1983); Goldberg (1986); Damon (2000) 89–100. Lefèvre (1978b) on the relationship of *Phormio* to *Epidikazomenos*, and Scafuro (1997) are carefully argued scholarship but not relevant to my financial approach.

[16] The legal situation of Athenian *epikleroi* (orphaned daughters) is spelled out for Terence's audience at *Ph.* 125–34. If the women were left wealthy by their fathers, the next of kin of these heiresses could choose to marry them and in both the fiction of comedy (Menander *Aspis*) and the fact of lawsuits the closest kinsman might divorce an unoffending wife in order to take over the heiress's estate. See also Bartholomä in this volume.

We still have not met Demipho's brother Chremes, whose arrival opens the fourth act. And the plot thickens when his brother asks him if he has brought back the daughter whom he went to fetch from Lemnos (*Ph.* 567–8). So he has a daughter in Lemnos! But he did not find her, because her mother had taken herself and the girl to Athens when she reached the age of marriage.

So who will the Lemnian daughter in *Phormio* marry? Chremes wants to find the girl a discreet husband so that he can conceal the relationship from his wife, who will otherwise throw him out of the house. Did wives really have such power? This one does, because she also has the family property; She is an *uxor dotata* (a rich wife, cf. glossary *dos*) though Terence never uses the term.[17]

Now Phormio comes up with a new story. It is not a commitment Phormio intends to keep, but he supposedly makes a new proposal; he claims that he wanted to marry his friend's daughter (young Phanium, the wife of Antipho) but could not afford it. But he is willing to marry her if Demipho will pay the equivalent of his betrothed's dowry. Once again we, the audience, are treated to a poor man's finances (but these are imaginary); Phormio has a mortgage of 10 *minae* on his plot of land, and another 10 on his cottage (*Ph.* 655–7). Then he needs to buy the new wife a maidservant and some furniture, and pay for the wedding feast. This will add up to another 10 *minae* (30 in all). Here Demipho jibs, but his brother urges him to accept and offers to foot the bill; let Phormio divorce his present wife and marry the girl (*Ph.* 677). Demipho has the money to pay from his wife's rentals in Lemnos and will tell her that his brother needed the money (*Ph.* 673–81). He does not care what happens to Antipho's wife. But he will find reason to care. As it is, he asks his wife Nausistrata to go and interview young Phanium and explain that they are giving her to Phormio as wife. In Attic law this was absolutely legitimate.

What a mess! In theory once Phormio has got the 30 *minae* to give to Phaedria to buy his girl, Phanium will have to leave the husband she loves. But coincidence steps in to save the intrigue; Chremes meets Phanium's old nurse Sophrona coming from Demipho's house: she has not been able to find the girl's father. When she sees Chremes she greets him as Stilpo (*Ph.* 740) and he pulls her away from the door and asks her not to use that name in earshot of his shrewish wife at home. Sophrona tells him his Lemnian 'wife' is dead and she has managed to marry off the girl 'to the young man Antipho'. Chremes does not understand. Has Antipho two wives? Phanium and his

---

[17] Any Roman wife allotted a large portion by her father qualified as an *uxor dotata*; but in Athens women ONLY inherited if their father died leaving them without brothers – the so-called *epikleroi*.

daughter? No, instead what he and his brother wanted has already happened and she is married to the husband her father desired.

Meanwhile Geta has been sent to tell Phanium that her husband's wife is coming. Phaedria has got the money he needs but Geta is still in trouble and will have to raise another loan to pay his debt.[18] It remains for the last main character to appear. This is Nausistrata, the betrayed wife of Chremes. And she too has her eye on family finances. Her father used to get 2 talents in rental (or produce?) from his estates in Lemnos and that was when the cost of living was much less (*Ph.* 790–2).[19]

Now comes the reckoning. As Chremes emerges from Phanium's house, his brother still does not realise she is Chremes' illegitimate daughter and will not take the hint that this girl is in fact a kinswoman (*cognata nobis, Ph.* 801). Nausistrata is happy with the marriage because she has found Phanium a real lady (*perliberalis*). But she will not be happy for long. Phormio meanwhile has discovered by eavesdropping that Chremes is Phanium's father by his mistress in Lemnos. Now he can relieve Phaedria of his financial troubles (*curam argentariam,* 886).

Phormio confronts the fathers and declares himself ready to marry Phanium. But now Demipho makes excuses and asks him to go to the forum and pay back the money. This will not do! Phormio is prepared to let the wife go, but not the dowry (*quom ego uostri honoris causa repudium alterae remiserim / quae dotis tantundem dabat,* 927–9) When Demipho summons him to court, Phormio denounces him for having a second wife:

> uos me indotatis modo
> patrocinari fortasse arbitramini?
> etiam dotatis soleo [...]
> hic quandam noram quoius uir uxorem [...]
> Lemni habuit aliam [...] ex qua filiam
> suscepit et eam clam educat.

You think I only play protector to unmarried women? I do it for dowered wives as well. I knew a woman here whose husband kept a second wife in Lemnos and reared her daughter and is bringing her up. (939–43)

Nausistrata went into her house at verse 795; now Phormio calls her out and tells her how her husband took a mistress and brought up her child. Now she understands all those trips to Lemnos and long stays there and the supposed low income from her produce:

---

[18] *Vorsuram solues,* 780, from *uertere* to convert: 'you'll pay the consolidated loan'.

[19] Casson (1976) 58 estimates that if revenues from the property in Lemnos were 2 *minae* a year its value would be 25 *minae*.

Haecin erat ea quae nostros minuit fructus uilitas?

Was this the slump in prices that reduced our income?   (1013)

We have come to the bottom line. Worse even than Chremes' infidelity is his financial cheating. From now on Nausistrata will let her son decide his father's fate, and revenges herself by inviting her new friend Phormio to dinner.

Conclusion

While younger spectators of New Comedy cheered on the adolescent lover, there must have been as many men in the audience who identified more closely with the *paterfamilias* whose money was needed to lubricate the intrigue. I started my survey of the economics of comedy by establishing the basis of the family resources, and then I examined the comic corpus of Plautus and Terence to determine the role this money plays. Approximately two-thirds of our plays are concerned with a young man's unauthorised love and the money it costs to hire or even buy and set free a courtesan (*meretrix*). But if the beloved girl is recognised as a citizen eligible for marriage to her lover, the only expense entailed will be providing her dowry. If she has been wrongly enslaved money spent by or for her lover can be recovered by suing her unlawful owner. The worst-case scenario is when the girl is a professional *meretrix* and in imminent danger of being bought and taken away – usually by a mercenary officer, since they were rich in cash; in that case, the lover has to raise her price within 24 hours – the maximum duration of the action. In these intrigues of fraud (*Bacchides, Pseudolus, Phormio*), the playwright's skill and audience's pleasure is to see how the lover gets his girl without expense to the father or legal consequences.

In addition, in the morality of comedy, adultery does not pay (i.e. intercourse with a respectable woman, though outside the comedies an hour of hanky-panky with a professional or slave was an acceptable prospect after the show, as in the finale of *Asinaria* or *Bacchides*). If it precedes the action it will be punished; if it is attempted during the action (*Casina, Menaechmi, Mercator*) it is not only frustrated but ends in the shaming of the offender. But a large part of the would-be adulterer's offence is financial, and a surprisingly large part of each denouement entails the restoration of misdirected moneys.

Further Reading

On lending and borrowing money (usually with outrageous interest rates) Millett (1991) is essential. Garnsey et al. (1983) contains many useful papers on ancient trade. Cohen (1992) provides an excellent introduction to ancient economic realities; Casson (1976) relates these to New Comedy. Skiles (1941) examines the vocabulary of commerce, Hindsholm (1990) the socio-economics of Roman comedy. Feeney (2010) elucidates the (financial) dynamics in *Pseudolus*. For the economics of Latin literature in general and Latin epic in particular, see Coffee (2009); on the finances in declamatory families, see Fantham (2004e).

Glossary of Financial and Commercial Terms in Comedy

Terms of accounting tend to cluster in a text. Thus Cicero *pro Q. Roscio Comoedo* 8–9 (For Quintus Roscius, the comic actor) reads:

> cum omnes qui <u>tabulas conficiant</u> menstruas paene <u>rationes in tabulas</u> trans-ferant, tu hoc <u>nomen</u> triennium amplius in aduersariis iacere pateris? <u>Utrum cetera nomina</u> in codicem <u>accepti et expensi</u> digesta habes an non?

> How come that while every one else who keeps account-books transfers his accounts almost every month into his books you allow this sum to remain among your memoranda for more than three years?

> Have you entered all other sums of money you received and expended regularly, or not?   (Transl. Fantham)

All underlined words are listed below. Because financial deception is a key element in Plautus I have singled out two symbolic sets of metaphors to illustrate the different analogies for financial deception by men and women, the direct attack (*tangere*) and the indirect wheedling of gifts and money by women. Thus images from hunting and fishing, warfare and gaming are appropriate to male deception. On this, see Fantham (1972). See also Skiles (1941) who complements some of the material below.

arrabo: deposit on a purchase; see *Most.* 918, 1013.

at/tondere AND **detondere**, 'to fleece': meretrices fleece their lovers of their renewable wealth as Italian shepherds shear their sheep of renewable wool. This motif is particularly well-developed in the last phase of *Bacchides*, the seduction of the old fathers (cf. Fantham (1972) 102–5 'deceit and intrigue').

auctio: auction: see *Men.* 1153 and compare the formal announcement (*praeconium*) of Menaechmus' auction: *auctio fiet Menaechmi mane sane septumi / uenibunt serui, supellex, fundi, aedes, omnia / uenibunt quiqui licebunt praesenti pecunia.* 'There will be an auction of Menaechmus' goods seven days from tomorrow; the slaves, furniture, farmstead, house and all; they will be for sale to whoever bids (*licere*) for ready cash.' (*Men.* 1157–9).

bolus: a cast of the dice or coup; see *Persa* 658, *Poen.* 101, *Truc.* 724, 844; oddly used in the mixed metaphor *tangere bolo* 'to make a haul' (i.e. to make a lot of money quickly, see *tangere* below).

bona: goods; cf. *me mea bona omnia doti dixisse illi.* (I have offered my whole estate as her dowry, *Haut.* 942).

circumducere: to cheat.

condicio: a bargain, especially an offer of marriage.

conducere: to hire, as in *nauem conducere* (to hire a ship); see *Ru.* 57, *Ad.* 225, Caecilius *Adelphoe* fr. 6. Note that the ships of *Rudens* and *Adelphoe* are hired by the itinerant pimps for a one-way journey like a moving van, and so for a finite time, whereas many of our merchants travel on hired ships for an unlimited time. How would this be worked financially?

conficere: to pay off a debt, and bring accounts up to date; see Cicero quotation above.

conlocare, locare: to invest money; also to place a girl as wife.

danista: a moneylender (Greek *daneizein*); see the Greek loan word *tarpezita*.

dissoluere: to pay off a debt.

dos: dowry; see *uxor dotata*, (a rich wife who controls her husband through her dowry) and contrast *indotata* (a dowerless girl).

faenus: interest; see *sumere faenore* (to borrow at interest) and the expressions *et sors et faenus* (both interest and principal) and *faenusculum* (a spot of interest).

fides: credit; see *res fidesque* (cash and credit); see e.g. Hor. *Epistles* 1.6.36–7.

flagitatio: public demand for return of money or property owed, which relied on naming and shaming; see *Most.* 575–608 as well as Catullus 45.

fructus: income, whether from rent or produce.

infitias ire: to renege or deny a debt; see *Most.* 1023.

lembus: Greek *lembos*, a swift launch; see e.g. *Bacch.* 279–86; also used as part of a metaphor for a predatory woman in *Men.* 442.

libella (argenti): the smallest coin, a tenth of an *as*; *Ps.* 97, 629, 1146.

lucrum: profit (loss is *damnum, iactura*).

mancipium: a slave seen as property.

mercatura: trade; see *in mercatura uorti* ('go in for trade' *Most.* 639).

merces: wages.

mercimonium: purchase; see *Most.* 904.

merx: wares, goods for sale; see *Men.* 25 cited below under **Onerare.**

minae: a large sum; 60 *minae* = one talent. Female companions cost from 20–60 *minae*.

mutuom, mutual: *pecunia*; an interest-free loan between friends.

nomen: an entry in a ledger, or named debtor (still uncommon in comedy); see Cicero above. The entry may refer primarily to the amount owed or to the debtor.

numerare: to pay out.

nummus: an unspecified coin, either a drachma = denarius, or 2 drachmas. But in *Bacchides* it is anomalously applied to the high denomination gold Philippic coins, presumably because no Roman could be expected to know the value of a Philippic?

onerare (*onus* 'load'): to load a ship; see *nauis oneraria* (a loaded ship) and *exonerare* (to unload); *onerauit nauem magnam multis mercibus* (he loaded the ship with many wares, *Men.* 25).

pignus: a pledge or security; see *opponere pignori* (to take a property as security or mortgage it).

portitor: customs inspector, harbour master.

praeconium: service as a herald or auctioneer; see *Men.* 1153.

praedium: a farmstead or estate.

praesenti: *pecunia*, **argento praesentario** cash down.

ratio: account: see *ratiuncula* (diminutive form, *Ph.* 36); *rationem putare* (to calculate a debt, *Most.* 299; see Cicero above.

ratio accepti et expensi: the balance of accounts; see *Most.* 147; see Cicero above.

repetere: to reclaim a debt.

res: profit, property, business; see *Metuas ne ab re sint tamen / omissiores paullo* ('you are afraid they will be a bit careless about money?', *Ad.* 830–1) contrasted with the preoccupation of the old with finance: *attentiores* *sumus ad rem omnes quam sat est* ('we pay too much attention to profit, business', *Ad.* 834) quoted back at Micio by his brother in *Ad.* 954.

res patria: patrimony; *res tua:* your property.

rescribere: to cancel or repay a debt; see *Ph.* 922.

sors: the principal or original sum borrowed.

stega: Greek; a ship's deck or covered cabin; see *Bacch.* 278.

stipulatio (verb **stipulare**): a formal promise to pay (often on certain conditions); see *Ps.* 511.

sumptus: expenses.

symbolus: a personal token, usually the imprint of a seal ring serving as a signature.

tabella, tabula: a notebook, record, account book.

tangere: unlike English 'to touch' which denotes only applying for a loan, Latin *tangere* is to deceive; cf. *Ps.* 120 *tuom tangam patrem* ('I will deceive your father') and *Ps.* 1308 *ut probe Ballio tactus est!* ('How rightly Ballio has been deceived!'); see Fantham (1972) 31 and 85.

trapezita: a moneylender (Greek *trapezites*); see *danista*.

uilitas: low price.

uorsuram soluere: 'consolidating(?)', to pay off a debt by taking out a new loan (as in *Ph.* 780); see Fantham (1972) 71 and Martin (1959) on this passage. But should this be ablative *uorsura soluere:* to pay off *by* a secondary loan, or *uorsuram:* to pay the secondary loan itself?

PART IV

The Reception of Roman Comedy

16

GESINE MANUWALD

The Reception of Republican Comedy in Antiquity

Introduction

Literary Roman dramas were originally produced for single performances at specific festivals (from about 240 BC); therefore reception initially did not extend beyond the immediate audiences. Hardly any information about reactions of spectators survives; it is likely that dramatic poets, producers, and organisers of festivals will have aimed at catering for the tastes of their audiences. Even though there was no entrance fee, presenting plays that went down well with the public was essential for poets and producers to further their careers and for organisers to make an impact. When, however, revival performances of existing plays began to emerge during the second century BC and dramatic scripts had become available as texts by the end of that century, dramas were gradually able to reach wider audiences.

From this period onwards there is increasing evidence for reactions to Republican *palliatae* (comedies in Greek dress) from a variety of people in different set-ups.[1] Over time these reactions vary in quantity and quality and illustrate different kinds of engagement with the plays: beyond watching plays, they include the reuse of motifs and phrases (by poets and other writers), commenting and editing (by scholars), or reading and assessment (by individual spectators or readers). This chapter reviews the extant information on the reception of Republican *palliatae* from the earliest available evidence in the Republican period until Late Antiquity (*c.* fifth century AD).

---

[1] On the reception of Plautus and Terence, cf. J. Blänsdorf and E. Lefèvre in Suerbaum (2002) §127, 222–7 and §129, 249–52; for an overview and brief discussion of *testimonia* on the reception of Plautus and Terence in antiquity, cf. Ronconi (1970) and (1972); of Terence, cf. Marti (1974).

Reception at Performances

Despite the almost complete absence of direct evidence on audience reactions in the early period, some comments and formal features in the dramatic texts as well as a few *testimonia* allow some conclusions.

For instance, Plautus' comedies in particular, but also Terence's prologues and epilogues, contain addresses to audiences. In addition to the conventional request for applause at the end (e.g. Plaut. *Bacch.* 1211; *Most.* 1181; *St.* 775), Plautus' characters appeal to the audience's experiences, invite their views or reactions, or share their plans with them (e.g. Plaut. *Most.* 354–61; 702–10; *Ps.* 584–5). Such passages reflect an effort to involve audiences and to present something they can relate to. In the early temporary performance spaces audiences were presumably closer to the stage in a less formal auditorium and therefore could engage closely with performances.[2]

On an intellectual level, the prologues to Plautus' and Terence's comedies reveal that by this time not only dramatic poets, but also audiences had an understanding of generic conventions and entertained corresponding expectations, for instance concerning the stock characters in *palliatae* as well as the appropriateness of certain figures and events in comedies (e.g. Plaut. *Amph.* 50–63; *Capt.* 55–62, 1029–36; Ter. *Haut.* 35–42; *Eun.* 35–41). Dramatic experience on the part of audiences is corroborated by numerous so-called metatheatrical references, especially in Plautus (cf. Christenson in this volume).

Obviously, dramatists only address audiences present in the theatre, and conclusions on the general attitude to dramatic performances cannot be drawn on this basis.[3] This is perhaps illustrated by the single Republican *palliata* for which some, albeit biased, information concerning the original performance survives, namely Terence's *Hecyra* (Ter. *Hec.* 1–57). According to the prologue speaker, this play only got a full staging at the third attempt, earlier performances having been disrupted. These disruptions were caused by rumours (presumably launched by Terence's opponents) about other spectacles to be given in the same venue, such as boxing or tightrope walking; therefore people who were keen on those rushed in and started to fight for places with those who were watching *Hecyra*. This means (at least according to Terence's presentation of the matter) that there was a proportion of the populace who had come to see *Hecyra*, while other groups were more interested in other entertainments.

---

[2] On the set-up for performances in front of the temple of Magna Mater on the Palatine, the original venue for dramatic productions at *Ludi Megalenses*, cf. Goldberg (1998) (with references).

[3] On the respective success of Plautus and Terence and on their popularity with audiences, cf. Parker (1996).

Still, what is regarded as the most successful drama during the Republican period proper on the basis of external criteria is a comedy by Terence: according to information in the ancient tradition, his *Eunuchus* earned the poet an unprecedented high sum in fees and was soon given a repeat performance (Suet./Donat. *Vita Ter.* 3; Donat. on Ter. *Eun., praef.* 1.6). That there was demand for additional performances of popular plays has also been inferred from the fact that the known instances of complete *instaurationes*, i.e. repetitions of entire festivals due to religious irregularities, fall within Plautus' lifetime. Hence these may have been arranged to give more people a chance to watch those plays.[4] This would mean that individual plays were clearly identifiable as favourites, and measures were taken to satisfy public demand.

From the second century B C onwards revivals of plays at different festivals became possible. The most obvious example is the surviving prologue to Plautus' *Casina*, which does not go back to Plautus himself, but was written for a revival, generally dated to about a generation after the original performance. In this prologue, the organisers claim that they offer a Plautine play to the audience, since there is demand for 'old' plays, particularly Plautine ones, as these are enjoyed by audiences in contrast to the worthless new ones (*Cas.* 5–20). Irrespective of the fact that the organisers are trying to advertise the play, this shows that Plautus' comedies were still in the public consciousness and audiences were assumed to be so educated that one could successfully argue with differences in quality.

In the argumentative context of the *Casina* prologue, a particular preference for Plautus' plays is alleged; but there is also talk of a general superiority of 'old' plays and a previous 'flower of poets'. Indeed, revivals in the middle of the second century B C included Terence's comedies. The information offered by the surviving so-called *didascaliae* to Terence's plays, which give 'technical' details about a play's performances, points to revivals of Terence's comedies in the 140s and early 130s B C.[5]

Since new dramas continued to be produced during this period, revivals of 'old' plays and performances of 'new' plays existed side by side from about the second half of the second century B C until the end of the Republic. The process of distinguishing between these two types of plays may have started even earlier; already in Terence's time there was an awareness that plays 'become old' (*inueterascere*) by repeated performances and that an 'old' play (*uetus fabula*) contrasts with a 'new' play (*noua fabula*), for

---

[4] Cf. Owens (2000) 386 and n. 7 (with further references).
[5] On the chronology of Terence's plays and their revivals (and the problems presented by the *didascaliae*), cf. the overview by Lefèvre in Suerbaum (2002) 236–7 (with bibliography).

which different rules of composition and perhaps different performance contexts apply (e.g. Ter. *Haut.* 7, 29, 43; *Hec.* 1–8, 12–13, 18–19).

A flourishing culture of revivals of earlier plays is attested for Cicero's time. A number of Cicero's frequent references to (serious and light) drama suggest implicitly or explicitly that he has recent performances in mind, for instance when he mentions audience reactions to particular scenes or performances or talks about details of actors' behaviour (e.g. Cic. *De Or.* 2.193; *Fin.* 5.63; *Tusc.* 1.106). However, the overwhelming majority of Cicero's statements refer to serious drama (mainly tragedy), and there are only a few comments that seem to point to revivals of *palliatae*, where actors are mentioned or stage characters are referred to as examples (Cic. *Q Rosc.* 20: Plaut. *Pseud.*; Cic. *Sen.* 65: Ter. *Ad.*; *Fam.* 9.22.1). It is uncertain whether this distribution reflects the actual situation or is due to Cicero's prejudices or argumentative aims; yet, since he quotes from comedies on a number of occasions (without specific reference to performances), it is clear that comedies were still vividly present in the public conscience.

It is obvious, merely on the basis of the prologue to Plautus' *Casina*, that revivals were not necessarily re-performances of the 'original' play, but could be adapted to the requirements of a new context; this was all the easier since no 'standard' versions of the texts existed in those times. The effects of subsequent generations of actors and directors modifying the texts are still noticeable in the surviving scripts (see below). It is also likely that *palliata* comedies, like tragedies, *praetextae* and *togatae* (e.g. Cic. *Sest.* 106–26), were interpreted according to the historical and political circumstances in the late Republic, i.e. that individual lines might be applied to particular topical issues. In those cases well-known plays are given a new level of meaning, which need not agree with the one originally intended, but makes the pieces more relevant to contemporary audiences.

After the end of the Republican period there is no clear evidence of performances of 'old' or 'new' *palliatae*, apart from a revival of a *togata*, a Roman comedy, in Nero's time (Suet. *Nero* 11.2: Afranius' *Incendium*). Apparently, reception of comedies via performances was coming to an end, presumably owing to changes in public taste and general developments in literary, historical, and social circumstances. However, the practice of revivals and the corresponding selection had already contributed to creating a 'canon of classics' among Republican comedies.

Reception within Dramatic Poetry

In addition to statements within dramatic scripts pointing to certain audience reactions, the earliest indications that dramatic performances in

Republican Rome were not one-off events but may have had a longer-lasting impact consist of reactions of the Republican playwrights to each other. Poets had obviously noticed that from the second Roman dramatist onwards there was a Roman dramatic tradition, in addition to the Greek tradition.

For instance, it is noteworthy that a few titles (and fragments) of *palliatae* are ascribed to both Naevius (*c.* 280/60–200 BC) and Plautus (*c.* 250–184 BC) in the textual transmission (e.g. *Carbonaria*; *Colax*). Although the relative chronology cannot be established beyond doubt and the relationship between the two versions is not known, the second-century writer Aulus Gellius (see below) records that Plautus revised and refined plays of 'old poets' in his own style, which therefore became attributed to him (Gell. *NA* 3.3.13). Such a procedure may apply to a comedy entitled *Colax* ('*Flatterer*'), based on a homonymous play by the Greek poet Menander, which is mentioned in the prologue to Terence's *Eunuchus* (Ter. *Eun.* 25–34). The precise interpretation of the Terentian passage is difficult; yet the likeliest reading is that Plautus had taken up a play by Naevius and adapted it, which therefore was an 'old play' according to Roman categories. This implies that at least Plautus regarded this 'old' play (like others) as so promising that he thought it worthwhile to adapt it and to present the revised version to contemporary audiences.

With reference to his own plays, Terence (*c.* 195/4–159 BC) discussed his methods of composition, justifying them against accusations raised by opponents. In this context he has the prologue speaker in his first play refer to Naevius, Plautus, and Ennius as paradigmatic predecessors and places himself in their tradition, which apparently contrasted with principles of some contemporary playwrights (Ter. *An.* 18–21). In a later play Terence has the prologue speaker allude to the fate of his immediate predecessor Caecilius Statius (*c.* 230/20–168/7 BC), who, like Terence, had problems obtaining a full staging of his plays at their first performances and was only eventually successful through the perseverance of their shared producer Ambivius Turpio (Ter. *Hec.* 14–27). While this is a different kind of relationship, it also shows that the first Roman comic poets remained in the public consciousness and could be used as authorities in an argument before contemporary audiences.

That later dramatists also took practical advantage of their predecessors' work is suggested by an author of the *Historia Augusta*, who records that comic writers liked to have some of their characters use established phrases and that a line in Terence's *Eunuchus* (Ter. *Eun.* 426) was coined by Livius Andronicus (Liv. Andr. *Pall.* 8 R.[3] = 6 W.), with a similar situation applying to Plautus and Caecilius (SHA 30, *Car.* 13.5).

On the other hand, Terence could apparently make the plausible claim that he had not known of earlier Latin plays, namely Naevius' and Plautus' versions of Menander's *Kolax*, but only of the Greek play (Ter. *Eun.* 25–34). In the same context it is reported that an opponent voiced criticism of Terence's play only after he had managed to sneak into a pre-performance (Ter. *Eun.* 19b–24). This invites the conclusion that there was an awareness of the existence of predecessors, but that their dramatic scripts were not yet generally available.

As a professional writer of *fabulae palliatae* Terence was followed only by Turpilius (d. 104/3 BC); and the fragments surviving from Turpilius' oeuvre do not mention Terence or obviously take up particular phrases from his works. Therefore one cannot establish Terence's ancient reception within his dramatic genre, but it is known that he was recognised across dramatic genres: Afranius, a writer of *fabulae togatae* and active in the second half of the second century BC, favoured Terence among all writers of light drama as an outstanding poet and a paradigmatic model (Suet./Donat. *Vita Ter.* 7). This comment, which is also the earliest known reference to Terence, shows the continuing influence of *palliatae* on subsequent dramas.

After the end of the Republican period no more *palliatae* were composed for full-scale production on stage, and what survives of dramatic texts written afterwards shows no signs of engagements with Republican *palliatae*. However, reception of these dramas in other forms continued (see below).

Reception via Texts and Early Scholarship

While initially the only way to get to know a play was by watching a performance, literary Roman drama was based on written scripts, provided by dramatic poets as the basis for producers. It is generally assumed that, originally, dramatic scripts remained in the possession of producers after the event; they might be used on other occasions or passed on to other producers, but were not made available to the general public.

At some point, however, dramatic scripts (of at least some plays) started to have a separate existence as 'texts': the second century BC saw the beginnings of scholarly criticism. Scholars started to gather texts, prepare editions and commentaries, discuss questions of authorship, assess playwrights, and assemble details of theatre history; a major stimulus seems to have been the fact that more and more comedies were ascribed to Plautus while it was known that not all of them could be genuine (cf. Gell. *NA* 3.3.11).

L. Aelius Stilo Praeconinus (*c.* 154–90 BC), a grammarian and a teacher of Varro and Cicero, as well as his son-in-law Servius Clodius, tried to separate genuine from spurious Plautine plays (cf. Cic. *Fam.* 9.16.4; Gell. *NA* 3.3.1, 3.3.11–12). Volcacius Sedigitus, Aurelius Opillus, and Manilius assembled catalogues of Plautus' plays; such catalogues are said to have attributed between 21 and 100 comedies to Plautus (cf. Gell. *NA* 3.3.1, 3.3.11–12; Serv. in Virg. *Aen.* 1, *praef.* [p. 4, ll. 87–9 edn Harv.]). The tragic poet Accius (170–*c.* 80 BC), who was also a scholar, compiled a list of Plautus' genuine plays (cf. Gell. *NA* 3.3.1, 3.3.9) and established a chronology of early dramatists (cf. Cic. *Brut.* 72–3). Volcacius Sedigitus drew up a canon of the ten best comic writers, in which Plautus comes second and Terence is sixth (fr. 1 *FPL*[3] = Gell. *NA* 15.24). All these activities contributed to establishing a 'canon' of Republican comic poets. Terence's works were studied by ancient grammarians since the second century BC; ancient sources name Porcius Licinus, Volcacius Sedigitus, Santra, Cosconius, Varro, Fenestella, Vallegius, Maecius Tarpa, and Verrius Flaccus.

A particularly influential person in the late Republic was Cicero's contemporary, the polymath Varro. Like Cicero's friend Atticus, Varro revised the chronology of early dramatists (cf. Cic. *Brut.* 71–3), and he wrote several treatises on the theatre. Thus Varro settled questions of biography and dating and identified a group of twenty-one Plautine plays (*fabulae Varronianae*), whose genuineness was accepted by 'the consensus of everyone' (according to Gellius), though he believed that other plays were also genuine due to their Plautine style (cf. Gell. *NA* 3.3.1–4, 3.3.10). Modern scholars assume that these twenty-one plays are the ones that have survived (almost) complete until the present day. Already in the second century CE Gellius thought that Varro's catalogue was more reliable than earlier lists of genuine works since it was based on internal criteria (*NA* 3.3.1–4). Cicero, influenced by Varro and Atticus, also discussed philological questions such as that of chronology (Cic. *Brut.* 71–3; *Tusc.* 1.3; *Sen.* 50).

That scholars in the first century BC studied early Roman drama so closely, apparently not regarding dramatic scripts as prompt books for performances, but as texts in their own right, helped drama to acquire a prestigious status and will have contributed to the preservation of texts. Because of the importance of this step it has been suggested that Roman drama as literature was not invented and created by dramatic poets active in the third and second centuries, but rather constructed by scholars in the first century BC, who endowed it with the corresponding status by exegetic activities.[6] Even though this theory has its problems as a single explanation, it is clear that the step from

---

[6] Cf. Goldberg (2005), with the review by Feeney (2006).

performances to reading and studying dramatic scripts cannot be underestimated as regards the assessment and approach to drama. From this period onwards, quotations and references to plays cluster around a select group of well-known dramas; obviously, a canon of works was being established.

Reception among Literary People

Apart from reception within the dramatic genre (see above), the earliest poetic reception of Roman comedy is found in the works of the satirist Lucilius, active in the second century B C. Lucilius critically confronted and discussed comedy, like other literary genres such as tragedy and epic; he seems to have found fault with comedy's overblown and unreal character. This is indicated by quotations of verses from various poets;[7] and apparently he even recreated stock comic features from a *palliata* by Caecilius entitled *Hymnis* in his satires, imitating and exaggerating typical elements of comedy.[8]

Later, comedy continued to have an influence on related literary genres, such as love poetry, in both form and motifs.[9] By such processes dramatic scripts acquired an additional role as sources and reference points; even though love poets of the first century B C and beyond reversed elements of Republican comedy, they seem not to have rejected the genre outright, but rather appropriated this model into their own poetry.[10] Even Horace, whose assessments of early comedy in his literary works are not entirely favourable (see below), seems to have modelled the role and function of his father in the *Satires* on fathers in Terentian comedy (Hor. *Sat.* 1.4).[11]

Another early sign of a poetic reaction to Plautus is a funeral epigram quoted in one of Varro's treatises and transmitted by Gellius (Gell. *NA* 1.24.3); while it is doubtful whether these lines were actually written by Plautus as recorded by Gellius, they illustrate that shortly after Plautus' time there was a feeling that he was an outstanding representative of comedy and its style.

By Cicero's time, reading plays had become an established form of reception besides watching performances. Cicero assumes that men of his background will have read plays as well as seen them on stage (esp. Cic. *Rab. Post.*

---

[7] Cf. Lucil. 736 M. = 747 W. vs. Plaut. *Merc.* 397.
[8] Cf. e.g. Lucil. 810, 815, 817, 878, 879–80, 881, 882–3, 888–9, 890, 891–3, 894 M. = 964, 965, 897, 900, 901–2, 903, 904–5, 887–8, 892, 893–5, 889 W.
[9] On comedy and love elegy, cf. e.g. Yardley (1972) (with further references).
[10] On the possible influence of comedy on Catullus, cf. e.g. Minarini (1987); Goldberg (2000).
[11] Cf. Leach (1972).

29; *Fin.* 1.4–5; *Acad.* 1.10; *Opt. gen.* 18). He presupposes that his various addressees are familiar with the main representatives of Republican drama; for instance, he frequently does not mention the names of playwrights or titles or only quotes the beginning of a line or passage, assuming (explicitly or implicitly) that people will recognise the quotation and know what follows (e.g. Cic. *Diu.* 2.104; *Planc.* 59; *Sest.* 126; *Tusc.* 2.44, 4.77; *Att.* 14.14.1; *Fam.* 9.22.1).

Cicero also voiced his assessment of poets (e.g. Cic. *Opt. gen.* 2) and discussed the contents of plays and their relevance to present-day audiences (e.g. Cic. *Rosc. Am.* 46–7; *Q Rosc.* 20; *Planc.* 59; *Caec.* 27; *Tusc.* 1.31; *Sen.* 24): referring to a comedy by Caecilius, Cicero stated that characters on stage are well known, not different from real individuals and thus prototypical representations of ways of behaviour (Cic. *Rosc. Am.* 46–7).[12] Cicero was aware of the fictitious character of stage drama (Cic. *De Or.* 2.193) and the poetic illusion in comedy (Cic. *Tusc.* 4.68); nevertheless, he believed that poets and actors empathised with their characters. Against this background he seems to have defined comedy as a 'mirror of life' (cf. Donat. *Com.* 5.1, 5.5) and regarded its language as close to everyday speaking (Cic. *Orat.* 184). Cicero took views and attitudes of dramatic characters seriously, reflected on their considerations and the structure of their argument and engaged with their views on cultural, religious, or philosophical issues.[13]

Furthermore, Cicero started a process of reflecting on the poetic quality and position of Roman dramatic texts in comparison with their Greek predecessors. Since he came back to this issue several times, discussed it in prefaces to his own works, and commented on possible objections by people with different views, it is likely that this question was considered among educated people in his time. In comparing Latin dramas with Greek models Cicero stressed (in line with his own argumentative goal) that Latin versions are literary products worth reading for Romans (Cic. *Fin.* 1.4–5; *Acad.* 1.10; *Opt. gen.* 18).

Concerning individual playwrights, Cicero noted the elegant wit of Plautus and the refined language of Terence (Cic. *Off.* 1.104; *Att.* 7.3.10; Suet./Donat. *Vita Ter.* 7 [Cic. fr. 2 *FPL³*]). Far more of Cicero's quotations from and references to *palliatae* are taken from Terence and Caecilius than from Plautus and Naevius. This probably indicates that

---

[12] Elsewhere Cicero claimed the same exemplarity for tragedy (Cic. *Planc.* 59; *Rab. Post.* 29; *Sest.* 102).
[13] For comments on drama in Cicero, cf. esp. Zillinger (1911); Wright (1931); Laidlaw (1960); on the attitude to comedy in the first century BC, particularly in Cicero, cf. Blänsdorf (1974).

Cicero found more material to illustrate his moral and philosophical arguments in their plays. This may be corroborated by the fact that Varro praised Terence for his character-drawing (Varro, *Men.* 399 B.; Charisius, *Ars Gram., Gramm. Lat.* 1.241.27–9 Keil). Caesar, on the other hand, agreed with Cicero in his praise for Terence's language, but he regretted the lack of 'comic force' and therefore regarded Terence as a 'halved Menander' (Suet./Donat. *Vita Ter.* 7 [Caes. fr. 1 *FPL³*]). In the late Republican period, there was obviously not only philological study, but also aesthetic criticism.

Reception of Comedy as a Benchmark of Roman Literary History

Restrained language and sober style were presumably among the reasons why Terence soon became a school author in contrast to Plautus (and other writers of Republican *palliatae*), which led to numerous copies of the text of his plays.

In the Augustan age with its specific poetic and aesthetic criteria, Horace regarded Plautus' metrics, jokes, and delineation of characters as sloppy and not sufficiently polished (Hor. *Epist.* 2.1.170b–6; *Ars P.* 270–4); he complained that Republican poets were highly regarded just because they were 'old' (Hor. *Epist.* 2.1.28–78). When it suited him, however, he adduced them as precedents: he pointed out that they were allowed to coin new words, and he demanded the same freedom for contemporary poets (Hor. *Ars P.* 53–5). He also recorded discussions about the relative merits of Republican poets and noted that Terence was regarded as outstanding in 'art' (Hor. *Epist.* 2.1.55–9).[14] Velleius Paterculus similarly saw Terence as a representative of a flourishing and more refined period of Roman drama (Vell. Pat. 1.17.1).

Later in the first century AD Plautus and Terence were still recognised as the main representatives of Roman comedy, but received mixed reception. In the overview of Roman literature within his treatise on the education of orators Quintilian voiced a general low opinion of Roman comedy, which was far behind Greek comedy, while he acknowledged that earlier generations had praised Plautus' language and ascribed Terence's writings to Scipio Africanus (Quint. *Inst.* 10.1.99–100). Quintilian's younger contemporary Pliny the Younger on the other hand regarded Plautus and Terence as such authorities in the field of Roman comedy that he compared good-quality writing of his own time to this paradigm (Plin. *Epist.* 1.16.6, 6.21.2–5).

---

[14] On Horace's debt to Terence, cf. di Benedetto (1962); Calboli (1997).

Republican comic writers, like all Republican poets, gained renewed appreciation in the second century A D, when the so-called archaists favoured the old (and by then old-fashioned) language of Republican times.[15] Besides comments in Fronto (Fronto, esp. pp. 56.18–57.4 v.d.H.), who considered the language of Plautus as a model, the testimony of Aulus Gellius is significant: Gellius not only expressed his admiration for Plautus' language (Gell. *NA* 1.7.17, 6.17.4, 19.8.6, 20.10.2), but, through his own scholarly activities, also transmitted a considerable amount of information on the work of earlier scholars (see above) and quotations of poetic texts. Gellius' admiration for Republican poets, however, did not make him uncritical; for when he compared extracts from Menander's *Plokion* with Caecilius' version (*Plocium*), he thought that the Latin comedy read well on its own; however, the juxtaposition with the Greek version revealed its inferiority, since Caecilius had worsened Menander's text by inserting mime-like elements, tragic bombast, and a less coherent style (Gell. *NA* 2.23). That Caecilius might have pursued particular aims by these changes is disregarded by Gellius; at any rate this discussion shows that the question of the respective quality of Greek and Roman comedies was still of interest in the second century A D.

Reception as Editorial Work

While dramatic texts started to be worked on almost as early as dramatic scripts lost their character as ephemeral pieces for single events, there were no autographs and no standard editions straightaway. Those poets and plays that had made it into the 'canon' later received scholarly editions and commentaries; yet quotations reveal that other plays were still known in antiquity.

In the second half of the first century A D M. Valerius Probus produced reading texts of Republican authors, including Terence, accompanied by notes. Eventually, perhaps at the end of the first century A D, an edition seems to have been produced on the basis of the work done in establishing the genuine plays, on which the entire transmission ultimately depends.[16] This edition reflected what was available at the time and was compiled according to the principle of preserving whatever was in circulation. It seems therefore to have included the genuine texts besides other versions, with the editor marking what he regarded as spurious: for instance, the text

---

[15] On Apuleius' debt to Plautus and his development of phrases in Plautine style, cf. e.g. Pasetti (2007).

[16] On the textual transmission of Plautus, cf. Tarrant (1983); also Deufert (2002); of Terence, cf. Reeve (1983) and Grant (1986); cf. also Radden Keefe's chapter in this volume.

contained so-called actors' interpolations, i.e. additions and changes made at later revivals; these are evident by several versions of endings (cf. Plautus' *Captiui, Poenulus*; Terence's *Andria*) and by doubling of passages (cf. Plaut. *Men.* 1037–44, repeated at 1028–9); in some plays sections are missing (cf. Plautus' *Amphitruo, Aulularia, Bacchides, Cistellaria*), while others clearly go back to revival performances (cf. Plautus' *Casina*). Hence, while ancient scholars debated which of the plays transmitted under Plautus' name were genuine, modern scholarly discussion has turned to the question of what constitutes the 'real Plautus', i.e. which sections of the transmitted dramatic scripts were written by Plautus.[17] On the other hand, this status of the text may provide glimpses into the performance history of the plays.

In the first decades of the second century AD Suetonius wrote a series of biographies including those of major Roman poets (*De uiris illustribus*). This work does not survive in full, but the life of Terence has been transmitted at the beginning of Donatus' fourth-century commentary (see below): this section includes details of Terence's life (some questionable) and a brief summary of views on Terence by early ancient writers.

The availability of editions for the main playwrights and the increasing distance from the time of composition in terms of language and cultural context presumably triggered the production of explanatory material on the works of those poets: a commentary on Plautus by Sisenna and comments by Q. Terentius Scaurus on Plautus' *Pseudolus*[18] as well as metrical plot summaries of the canonical plays are dated to the second century AD. Late Antiquity saw the emergence of manuscripts equipped with the names of poets and the titles of the dramas, plot summaries as well as lists of characters at the head of scenes.

Also in the second century AD the grammarian C. Sulpicius Apollinaris wrote plot summaries of twelve verses each for all of Terence's comedies (and perhaps more supportive material) for didactic purposes. At the turn of the century Helenius Acron and Arruntius Celsus each commented on some of Terence's plays. Aemilius Asper in the late second century, Euanthius and Aelius Donatus in the fourth century, as well as Eugraphius in the fifth/sixth centuries AD all compiled commentaries on the entire corpus.[19] The works of

---

[17] The theory that the amount of genuine text is limited and a substantial part of the material dates from later hands, put forward by Zwierlein (1990–2) and Deufert (2002), is stimulating, but has not won general agreement.

[18] Cf. Charisius, *Ars Gramm.*, *Gramm. Lat.* 1.198.24–6 Keil; Rufinus, *Comm. in metra Terent.*, *Gramm. Lat.* 6.560.28–61.10 Keil. On these writers, cf. Schmidt in Sallmann (1997a) §433 (Q. Terentius Scaurus); §445.1 (Sisenna).

[19] On these writers, cf. Schmidt in Sallmann (1997a) §436 (C. Sulpicius Apollinaris), §444 (Helenius Acron), §443 (Aemilius Asper); Schmidt in Herzog (1989) §526.2 (Euanthius), §527 (Aelius Donatus).

Donatus and Eugraphius survive; they seem to be compilations of material available in the grammatical tradition (with an emphasis on rhetoric in the case of Eugraphius), rearranged and supplemented by original comments, and also to have suffered in transmission.[20] There are also extant scholia on Terence, often covering the same ground as the commentaries, but frequently with a particular twist.[21] Besides, a manuscript of Terence's comedies dating back to the fourth/fifth centuries AD and fragments of three others survive. Hence Terence is one of the few ancient writers for whom an ancient biography, a variety of ancient explanatory material, and manuscripts pre-dating the Middle Ages are available. This is supplemented by numerous references and quotations in the secondary tradition.

Reception among Christian Writers

Republican comedy continued to be read until Late Antiquity (and beyond) as comments in a variety of late-antique writers demonstrate. Terence, along with Cicero, Sallust, and Virgil, was among the writers who were studied in school, often with the help of commentaries. In the fourth and early fifth centuries AD Lactantius, Ambrose, Jerome, and Augustine display a good knowledge of classical texts,[22] like the pagan writers Ausonius (Auson. *Epist.* 20 Green; *Protrepticus ad nepotem* 45–60) and Sidonius Apollinaris (Sid. *Ep.* 4.12.1–2). While Christian authors did not approve of the contents, they relied on writers such as Terence for linguistic and literary education, although occasionally fears were voiced that the contents might have a detrimental influence on readers (cf. August. *Conf.* 1.16.26; *De ciu. D.* 2.8). Theatrical performances of the classical type as well as the contents of the comedies were opposed by Christian writers since they regarded these events as pagan worship of the wrong divinities and the stories as offending Christian morality and setting negative examples (cf. e.g. August. *De ciu. D.* 2.7; *Ep.* 91.4). A good case in point is Tertullian's treatise *De spectaculis*, dating to around 200 AD: Tertullian reviews essential elements of performances at Roman festivals (alongside other spectacles) and criticises them from a Christian perspective, describing them as pagan worship and impure spectacles. As regards the stories and plots, Christians were upset especially

---

[20] For editions, cf. Wessner (1902/1905/1908); on Donatus' commentary, cf. Jakobi (1996).

[21] For editions, cf. Schlee (1893); Mountford (1934).

[22] On references of Christian writers to early Roman comedy, cf. Jürgens (1972) 88–145; cf. also Rapisarda (1987); on Augustine's knowledge of Republican comic writers (mainly Terence), cf. Hagendahl (1967) 219, 254–64, and 377–83; Rosa (1987); on Jerome's knowledge and use, cf. Adkin (1994) and López Fonseca (1998); on Ambrose's references, cf. Courcelle (1972).

by Plautus' *Amphitruo*, as they were enraged at this undignified presentation of gods (cf. Arn. *Adv. nat.* 4.35, 7.33; August. *De ciu. D.* 2.8).

However, the approach of Christian writers was not entirely dominated by ideological condemnation; at least some also engaged with the playwrights' literary techniques. According to his own admission, Jerome only turned from 'Ciceronianus' to 'Christianus' after a revelatory experience, whence he started to read Christian writings with great zeal (Hier. *Ep.* 22.30); and he was obviously familiar with early comic writers (Hier. *Apol. contra Rufin.* 1.13, 1.16). Importantly, Jerome, trained in exegetic and textual practices by his teacher Donatus (Hier. *Eccles.* 1.9), regarded Republican Roman writers, including comic poets, as models for his method of translating the Bible: to translate from the original text and not from an earlier translation into another language (in contrast to Augustine's view: cf. August. *Ep.* 28), and, particularly, into a readable style according to the requirements of the target language (Hier. *Ep.* 57.5, 106.3.2–4; *Comm. in Mich.* 2, *praef.*).

Conclusions

Palliata, comedy in Greek dress in Rome, seems to have made a noticeable impact from the start and to have retained this influential position throughout antiquity, with the reception taking different forms and being of different intensity over the centuries. Reactions to individual poets and works during the creative period of Republican drama, within dramatic poetry and then also outside it, were followed by the first scholarly endeavours concerning the playwrights and their writings after dramatic scripts had become available as texts in their own right. A period of revivals from the second century BC until the end of the Republic coincided with reading and assessing the texts as well as increasing influence on other literary genres. When there were no longer full-scale performances of traditional dramas in the imperial period, *palliatae* were mainly received as objects of study, as school texts, as items for commenting and editing and as topics for discussion. While Republican dramatists were highly regarded in the period of Cicero and Varro, they were largely disapproved of from the Augustan era onwards, until they met with renewed appreciation from 'archaists' in the second century AD, only to be opposed again by Christian writers in the third and fourth centuries AD, albeit for different reasons.

Terence and also Plautus were transmitted as ancient 'classics' beyond the fourth century AD; they are mentioned in this role in Macrobius (Macr. *Sat.* 2.1.10–11) and Sidonius Apollinaris (Sid. *Carm.* 2.182–92); yet these late-antique writers seem to have had hardly any direct knowledge of the dramatic texts. This agrees with the fact that Rufinus, a writer of metrical treatises in the fifth century A D, reported the view that the comedies were thought to be written without a metrical structure; to prove the contrary, he listed a number of authorities who stated that the works of Plautus and Terence as well as those by other comic and tragic writers were written in verse (Rufin. *Comm. in metra Terent., Gramm. Lat.* 6.564.20–5.5 Keil). The final item of (poetic) reception that could be classified as 'ancient' is the comedy *Querolus siue Aulularia*, written in Gaul in the fifth century A D, composed in prose and for recitation, based on Plautus and other ancient sources. Reception of Roman Republican comedy continued throughout the Middle Ages into the modern period (cf. the other chapters on reception in this volume).

Further Reading

Many books on Roman comedy, Plautus and/or Terence include some information on the reception of this dramatic genre and its poets; however, there is no comprehensive work on the reception of early Roman comedy, Plautus, or Terence in antiquity. The most useful overviews of the relevant passages illustrating the reception of Plautus and Terence, with brief discussion, are provided by J. Blänsdorf and E. Lefèvre at the relevant entries in Suerbaum (2002, in German), supplemented for Terence by Marti (1974, in German). Deufert (2002, in German) reviews the development of Plautus' comedies in antiquity from a textual perspective, with a view to separating the genuine from the spurious passages.

There are, at any rate, dedicated studies on various aspects of reception. The important period of the first century B C, represented particularly by the works of Cicero, is discussed by Zillinger (1911, in German), Wright (1931), Laidlaw (1960), and Blänsdorf (1974, in German).The textual transmission of the comedies by Plautus and Terence is summarised by Reeve (1983), Tarrant (1983), and Grant (1986). Information about the authors of late-antique commentaries can be found at the relevant entries in Sallmann (1997a and 1997b, in German) and Herzog (1989, in German). The extensive extant work of Donatus is analysed by Jakobi (1996, in German).

Reactions of Christian writers to Republican comedy are surveyed by Hagendahl (1967), Jürgens (1972, in German), and Rapisarda (1987, in Italian).

17

BEATRICE RADDEN KEEFE

The Manuscripts and Illustration of Plautus and Terence

This chapter surveys manuscripts and illustrations of the plays written by Plautus and Terence. There were other writers of *fabulae palliatae*, some of whom Terence mentions in his prologues, but no complete text of any of their plays has come down to us (cf. Manuwald 'Contexts' in this volume).[1] In contrast, twenty extant plays (and over 100 lines of a twenty-first) go under the name of Plautus (he is claimed to have written many more), and Terence is known to have composed six plays before he left Rome for Greece and never returned.[2]

The comedies of Plautus and Terence survive in a few late-antique manuscripts, most now in poor or fragmentary condition. The oldest extant Plautus manuscript is a fourth- or fifth-century palimpsest in a biblical text from the sixth century. (A palimpsest has an original, 'lower' text that has been erased and replaced with another, 'upper' text.) In this case, the Plautus comedies are the lower text, while the biblical text is the upper text. Now belonging to the Ambrosiana Library in Milan, this manuscript is known as the Ambrosian Palimpsest and by the siglum A.[3]

It was at the Ambrosiana Library, in the late eighteenth century, that Giovan Battista Branca first noticed a primary script beneath the upper biblical text, and

---

[1] On the carbonised papyrus roll from Herculaneum with sections of a comedy by the dramatist Caecilius Statius, see Kleve (1996).

[2] In *NA* 3.3, Gellius mentions that 130 plays were ascribed to Plautus, but also describes some disagreement over which were genuinely his. Plautus' twenty comedies are: *Amphitruo, Asinaria, Aulularia, Bacchides, Captiui, Casina, Cistellaria, Curculio, Epidicus, Menaechmi, Mercator, Miles Gloriosus, Mostellaria, Persa, Poenulus, Pseudolus, Rudens, Stichus, Trinummus, Truculentus*; the fragmentary twenty-first comedy is *Vidularia*. Additional fragments of Plautus are in Aragosti (2009). Terence's six comedies are: *Andria, Adelphoe, Eunuchus, Heauton Timorumenos, Hecyra, Phormio*. Suetonius' account of Terence's life is preserved in Aelius Donatus' commentary on the comedies: *Vita. Ter.* 4–5.

[3] This manuscript is G. 82 sup. = S.P. 9/13–20; reproductions are in Chatelain (1884) I: plate I; Lowe (1938) III: 23.

in 1815 Angelo Mai published readings from the Plautus text.[4] Chemicals used by Mai to recover this manuscript's lower text damaged the pages of parchment known as folios. The folios in the Ambrosian Palimpsest have since been described as like a 'sieve' or like 'Swiss cheese'; and in reproductions of the manuscript, one can see there are holes in the parchment in places where there was once ink – the chemicals Mai used reacted with the ink, making large portions of the Plautus text quite difficult (and often impossible) to read.[5] In 1889, Wilhelm Studemund produced a painstaking transcription of the palimpsest text, which continues to be relied upon by scholars.[6] More recently, the imaging techniques used by Walter Stockert on *Cistellaria*, once the sixth play in the manuscript, allow for the deciphering of some new readings.[7]

The manuscript itself is thought to have once included twenty-one Plautus comedies, but at some time in its history, perhaps when it was unbound and palimpsested in the sixth century, it lost several whole plays (*Amphitruo*, *Asinaria*, *Aulularia*, *Curculio*), nearly all of two more (*Captiui*, *Vidularia*), and large parts of others as well. The original Plautus manuscript is thought to have been made in Italy, and the palimpsest was later kept at the abbey of Bobbio, founded in the year 614.[8]

The better-preserved sections of the palimpsest show that it was copied in a script we term rustic capitals, within a single column of 19 lines on each page (the square text block measures about 175 by 175 mm). The comedy texts have been divided into scenes, with scene headings giving the names of characters in the following scene. For example, on fol. 210 v of the Ambrosian Palimpsest, in the comedy *Casina*, Studemund was able to read the names of the characters Alcesimus and Lysidamus written on a single, indented line, and the names of the characters Pardalisca and Lysidamus at the bottom of the next page (fol. 211 r), again written on a single, indented line. Given the spaces beneath such names in the manuscript, which always correspond to a single line of text, it is believed that the scene headings once included designations of the characters' roles written in now-lost red ink below their names; and that there were once single-letter speaker assignations (often called *sigla personarum*) within the comedy text that were also written in the lost red ink.[9] These scene headings and speaker assignations would have allowed the reader to know which characters are onstage in each scene and which character speaks each line. Further added material includes

[4] See Studemund (1889) v–vi; Mai (1815).
[5] Wattenbach (1875) 312; Lowe (1972) ii: 585.   [6] Studemund (1889).
[7] On the multispectral photography and computer imaging of *Cistellaria*, see Stockert (2008) and (2014).
[8] There is a description in Lowe (1938) iii: 23. See also Zironi (2004) 57–9.
[9] For these single-letter speaker assignations, see Jory (1963).

the production notices known as *didascaliae* (written in alternating lines of black and the lost red ink), metrical plot summaries known as *argumenta*, and running titles at the tops of pages giving the name of the author and of the comedy.

Three later Plautus manuscripts written in minuscule letters, the so-called Palatine manuscripts, are thought to descend not from the Ambrosian Palimpsest but from a now-lost manuscript containing twenty Plautus comedies; this manuscript is known as P.[10] The Ambrosian Palimpsest and P are thought to share a now-lost ancestor manuscript, possibly of the second century AD.[11] Like the Ambrosian Palimpsest, the Palatine manuscripts have scene headings and speaker assignations, or at least spaces left for them.[12] These organising elements are found most consistently in a tenth- or eleventh-century Plautus with twenty comedies, known variously as the Codex Camerarii, the Codex Vetus and by the siglum B. In a tenth-century manuscript with twelve of Plautus' comedies now kept in Heidelberg (known as the Codex Decurtatus and by the siglum C), scene headings and speaker assignations have not been consistently added; some parts of the manuscript are missing scene headings, other parts the speaker assigments, and some folios are missing both. In a tenth-century Plautus manuscript (known as the Codex Ursinianus and by the siglum D), this one with sixteen comedies, the scribes also did not consistently add scene headings and speaker assignations.[13] Without such organising and clarifying elements, the texts of the plays would have been difficult to read and fully understand. The scene headings were inserted as an aid to reading into both Plautus and Terence texts, perhaps as early as the second century AD; the speaker assignations are considered part of this second-century editing activity as well.[14]

---

[10] See Lindsay 1896 and 1904. These manuscripts are Vatican City, Pal. lat. 1615 (B); Heidelberg, UB, Pal. lat. 1613 (C); and Vatican City, BAV, Vat. lat. 3870 (D). There are digital facsimiles of D and B online at http://digi.vatlib.it; and there is a digital facsimile of C online at http://digi.ub.uni-heidelberg.de. It is generally believed that P was separated into two volumes, with the first eight plays in one and the remaining twelve in another. B is thought to have been copied both from P itself and from a lost descendant of the eight-play volume, which is known as P^{BD}. Four plays in D (these are: *Amphitruo*, *Asinia*, *Aulularia*, and part of *Captiui*) are thought to have been copied from P^{BD} as well. The rest of D, and C in its entirety, seems to have been copied from a lost descendant of the twelve-play volume, which is known as P^{CD}. For an overview of the textual tradition, see Tarrant (1983) 302–7. See also Chelius (1989).

[11] See Questa (1984) and (1985); Deufert (2002). For the lost sibling manuscript of P known as the Codex Turnebus (T), see Lindsay (1898) and Clementi (2009).

[12] On the scene headings in Plautus manuscripts, see Bader (1970) and Deufert (2002) ch. 6.

[13] The scene headings in the Palatine manuscripts frequently give just the role designations without character names.

[14] See Deufert (2002) ch. 6.

The earliest largely complete text of Terence's comedies is the Codex Bembinus, dating from the fifth or sixth century (and like the Ambrosian Palimpsest given the siglum A).[15] This manuscript's text is also structured with scene headings and speaker assignations. In a scene from the comedy *Adelphoe* on fol. 100 v of the Codex Bembinus, for instance, the names of four characters (Sannio, Bacchis, Aeschinus, and Parmeno) are written on a single line, with their role designations (*leno, meretrix, adulescens*, and *seruus*) added in red ink on the line just below. Greek letters in red ink written beside these names also serve as speaker assignations beside and within the main text, where they are written in red.[16]

The Codex Bembinus contains Terence's six plays (in the order *Andria, Eunuchus, Heauton Timorumenos, Phormio, Hecyra*, and *Adelphoe*), written in rustic capitals, with 25 lines of text on each page (the square text block measures about 123 by 123 mm). Each comedy begins with a *didascalia* (written in brown and red ink), a metrical summary of the play (called a *periocha* in this manuscript, but more often referred to as an *argumentum*) written in the second century AD by Sulpicius Apollinaris, as well as with a prologue written by Terence himself.[17] There are also running titles in red at the top of each page, giving the abbreviated name of the play and author. The scene headings, speaker attributions, and running titles would have allowed for a thorough and close reading of the comedies, which, from the manuscript's added scholia and corrections, we know did occur. These organising elements would have allowed the reader to easily dip into the comedy texts as well, to quickly locate a particular line or passage.

In addition to the Codex Bembinus, a manuscript that never seems to have left Italy, there is also a palimpsest manuscript of Terence kept in St Gall, with some lines from the play *Heauton Timorumenos* written in rustic capitals beneath an upper seventh- or eighth-century glossary.[18] And there are two papyrus fragments of the play *Andria*, one in Oxford, the other in Vienna.[19] Both of these papyrus fragments were found in Egypt, and both

---

[15] The Codex Bembinus is Vatican City, BAV, Vat. lat. 3226; there is a digital facsimile of the manuscript online at http://digi.vatlib.it. The standard study of the Codex Bembinus is Prete (1970). For the manuscript's history, see Ribuoli (1981b).

[16] Jory (1963).

[17] *Andria* does not begin in this way as much of this comedy is missing from the manuscript.

[18] The palimpsest is St Gall, Stiftsbibliothek, 912 (Sa); a description is in Lowe (1956) VII: no. 974.

[19] The Oxford papyrus of Terence is P.Oxy. 2401 (II^b), and the Vienna papyrus, Papyrussammlung der ÖNB, L 103 (II^a). See Lowe (1971) suppl.: no. 1717 (for the Oxford Papyrus) and Lowe (1963) X: no. 1537 (for the Vienna Papyrus). Further discussion of the Vienna papyrus is in Danese (1989). There is a digital facsimile of the palimpsest online at www.e-codices.unifr.ch; there are images of the Oxford fragment of

include explanatory, interlinear notes written in Greek.[20] The fourth-century Terence text written in half-uncial script on the Oxford fragment has both scene headings and speaker assignations. For instance, three character names (Pamphilus, Davus, and Charinus) are together on a line of text, with their roles (*adulescens, seruus, adulescens*) on the line below. The speaker assignations in this manuscript are two-letter abbreviations of character names: Pamphilus is *pa*, for instance, and Davus is *da*.

While both Plautus and Terence manuscripts include scene headings, speaker assignations, the production notices called *didascaliae*, and metrical summaries of the plays (*argumenta*) added to manuscripts of comedies perhaps in the same, second-century-AD milieu, the subsequent traditions of these works are quite distinct.[21] As the evidence of the Codex Bembinus and the palimpsest and papyrus fragments of Terence implies, far more Terence manuscripts survive than do those of Plautus. While Claudia Villa has catalogued 741 manuscripts of Terence's comedies, Alba Tontini has identified 177 surviving Plautus manuscripts.[22] Moreover, at least forty-eight Terence manuscripts received illustration, compared with the thirteen illustrated Plautus manuscripts that I know of. At least twenty-nine Terence manuscripts include author portraits (Figure 17.1), and six have cycles of more than 100 illustrations for scenes in the comedies.[23] In contrast, I have come across eight Plautus manuscripts with a portrait of the author, and none that have a large cycle of illustrations.[24] Plautus manuscripts often do include decorated borders and initials, as well as heraldic devices, typical ornament for luxury copies of the classics in humanist Italy; and the decorated border of one humanist Plautus manuscript in the British Library incorporates the figure of Mercury, who is not only the prologue speaker in the nearby prologue to the play *Amphitruo*, but also plays an important role in this comedy.[25]

    Andria at www.papyrology.ox.ac.uk; and there are images of the Vienna fragment of *Andria* on the ÖNB website (https://www.onb.ac.at).

[20] For an explanation of the interlinear notes in Greek, see McNamee (2007) 490–1.

[21] Deufert (2002) ch. 6.

[22] Villa (1984) and (2015); Tontini (2002b), (2010), and (2013). See also Munk Olsen (1996).

[23] These numbers are from Radden Keefe (2015). I count only those manuscripts as illustrated that have author portraits or illustrations that bear some relation to the comedy text; manuscripts with decorative elements or heraldic devices are not included.

[24] On Plautus illustrations, see Fachechi (1998) and (2002).

[25] The manuscript with Mercury in the margin is London, BL, MS Burney 228. Those manuscripts with portraits of Plautus are: Florence, BML, Plut. 36.40; London, BL, MS Burney 227; Milan, BA, H. 203 inf.; Paris, BnF, lat. 7888; Paris, BnF, lat. 7889; Vatican City, BAV, Pal. lat. 1616; Vatican City, BAV, Vat. lat. 3870; and Vienna, ÖNB, Cod. 111. There are reproductions of the British Library manuscripts at: www.bl.uk/catalogues/illuminatedmanu

Figure 17.1: Vatican City, BAV, Vat. lat. 3305, fol. 8v, a recitation by Calliopius and illustrations of the comedy *Andria*
© Vatican Library

scripts; there is a facsimile of BnF, lat. 7888 at https://gallica.bnf.fr (though it is in black and white and the author portrait is quite difficult to see); and there is a digital facsimile of Florence, BML, Plut. 36.40 online at http://mss.bmlonline.it/catalogo.aspx.

THE RECEPTION OF ROMAN COMEDY

Whilst illustrated Terence manuscripts survive from as early as the ninth century, the earliest illustrated Plautus manuscript seems to be a work produced in Paris around the year 1405.[26] Before this manuscript's first comedy, *Amphitruo*, one finds a miniature divided vertically into three parts: Amphitruo with his slave Sosia at war on Teleboa is in the left panel; Mercury, with the head of a dog, standing before a crowned and enthroned Alcumena is in the middle; and Jupiter in bed, embracing Alcumena while their child Hercules strangles two snakes, is in the right panel. The miniature has been attributed to a Paris-based illuminator known as the Virgil Master, also thought responsible for scenes in a number of classical texts, including a Virgil and a Vitruvius both now in Florence.[27] The Virgil Master creates a tripartite miniature showing three vignettes from different parts of *Amphitruo*, quite different from the opening miniatures showing a Roman theatrical performance of Terence found in near-contemporaneous manuscripts of Terence's comedies.[28]

Amphitruo is the Plautus comedy most often illustrated, as it is so often the first play in manuscripts of the comedies.[29] Beneath the prologue to *Amphitruo* in a northern Italian manuscript of around 1440 are two groups of figures flanking a heraldic device showing a gold eight-pointed star, possibly for the Stella family of Verona (Figure 17.2).[30] In the grouping on the left, Amphitruo, wearing armour, stands beside his wife Alcumena and before his slave Sosia; on the right, Jupiter (disguised as Amphitruo) touches Alcumena as Mercury (disguised as Sosia) looks on with arms crossed. The complex plot has been reduced to its most basic elements, and only a reading or prior knowledge of the comedy would allow the viewer to appreciate the illustration fully.

A third illustrated Plautus manuscript, made at Bourges in the year 1469, contains a large opening miniature before the beginning of the *argumenta* for *Amphitruo*, as well as four separate scenes on a single page at the beginning of the second play *Aulularia*.[31] Above the first *argumentum* for *Amphitruo* is

---

[26] This manuscript is Paris, BnF, lat. 7890. A digital facsimile of this manuscript is online at https://gallica.bnf.fr. For a description of the manuscript, see Fachechi (2002) 192–5.

[27] On this manuscript, see *Paris 1400* (ed. Taburet-Delahaye) (2004) 239–40, cat. no. 143 and Fachechi (2002) 192–5; for the Virgil Master, see Meiss (1974) 408–12. The Virgil is Florence, BML, Med. Pal. 69; the Vitruvius is Florence, BML, Plut. 30.10.

[28] These manuscripts are Paris, BnF, lat. 7907 A and Paris, Bibliothèque de l'Arsenal, 664 (the famous *Térence des ducs*). There are digital facsimiles of these manuscripts at https://gallica.bnf.fr. On these manuscripts, see *Paris 1400* (ed. Taburet-Delahaye) (2004) 241–4, cat. no. 145, and Meiss (1974) 41–54.

[29] Fachechi (1998).

[30] This manuscript is London, BL, Burney 227. For a description, see Fachechi (2002) 187–8.

[31] This manuscript is Paris, BnF, lat. 16234. There is a digital facsimile in black and white online at https://gallica.bnf.fr. For a description, see Fachechi (2002) 195–200.

E t enim ille annsʼ huc niſſii uꝼmio iupiter
N on minuſ q̃ ueſtrum quiuiſ formidat malum :
S umma matre natuſʼ humano patre .
M mm non eſt æquum ſibi ſi p̃mittẽt .
A t ego quoꝝ etiam qui iouiſ ſlm filuiſ
C ontagione mẽꝰ matiſ metuo malum :
P roptcrea pacem aducnio. et pacem ad uoſ affero :

Figure 17.2: London, BL, Burney 227, fol. 3r, illustration of the comedy *Amphitruo*
© British Library

a busy scene: Alcumena's twins are born (on the left, within a building in the foreground); Alcumena embraces a disguised Jupiter (also within this building) as Mercury confronts Sosia (on the right, outside the building); and in the background, Amphitruo sails home from war in Teleboa, shown on the top left. Several dramatic moments from the play are depicted here, but the illustration provides little sense of the overall narrative sequence. Once again, the viewer must know at least the outline of the plot, which is provided by the *argumenta* for the play (on this and the next page), in order to understand the image.

Although each of these depictions of *Amphitruo* is a distinct work, quite apparently unrelated to the others, in all three their fifteenth-century artists have chosen to provide a visual summary of the play, rather than focusing on individual scenes from the comedies or depicting performances of the plays. This is also true of a fifteenth-century Plautus manuscript with eight marginal illustrations now in the Vatican Library; here, the illuminator seems to have based at least some of his illustrations on the comedy titles:

there is, for instance, a miniature of two asses at the beginning of the comedy *Asinaria*, and a miniature of two men bound to a column before *Captiui*.[32] Another humanist Plautus manuscript, with miniatures attributed to the illuminator Guglielmo Giraldi (active 1445–90), provides an exception.[33] In this manuscript's opening miniature, which is placed above the beginning of the *argumentum* of *Amphitruo*, Hercules is in his crib in the foreground, strangling two snakes, as Alcumena sits in bed, attended by maids, and two men, possibly Amphitruo and Sosia, and a woman, possibly the maid Bromia, stand on the right. Here, the illuminator has chosen to illustrate the key scene of the birth of Alcumena's twins (described by Bromia at the very end of *Amphitruo*), albeit not entirely accurately. Bromia tells Amphitruo that his wife has just given birth to twin sons – one his and the other Jupiter's. Even though Bromia makes it clear that both sons are present when Jupiter's son Hercules kills the snakes, only Hercules can be found in the miniature.

A rather different kind of illustration is found in the aforementioned tenth-century Palatine manuscript known as the Codex Ursinianus (and by the siglum D). This was originally an unillustrated text of sixteen Plautus comedies, but the margins of its two opening pages were richly decorated in the sixteenth century with a flower border including cameo-like roundels, one representing Plautus (in the top margin of fol. 1 v), and the heraldic device of Pope Leo x.[34] The example of this refurbished Plautus demonstrates both the great revival of interest in this dramatist in the late Middle Ages, and the changes a manuscript could undergo after its text was first copied, especially if the author gained new popularity.[35]

A printed book of Plautus' comedies produced in 1511 goes some way to suggesting why a fully illustrated manuscript of Plautus (i.e. with an illustration for every scene) seems never to have been attempted. This book was illustrated with a cycle of 316 woodcut scenes for Lazzaro de'Soardi's edition produced in Venice – a formidable number of illustrations that may have been prohibitively large for earlier manuscript-makers often constrained by time, funds, or materials. Indeed, a good number of illustrated Terence manuscripts too were left unfinished, their

[32] This is the manuscript Vatican City, BAV, Ottob. lat. 2005. For a description of this manuscript, see Fachechi (2002) 180–4 and Tontini (2002b) 337–42.
[33] This manuscript is Madrid, BN, Vitr. 22.5. For a description of this manuscript, see Fachechi (2002) 188–91.
[34] For a description of the manuscript, see *Vedere i classici* (ed. Buonocore) 1996: 192–6, no. 16, fig. 107. See also Alexander (1998) 201 and 208 n. 36. There is a similar, cameo-like portrait of the author in Vienna, ÖNB, Cod. 111.
[35] Questa (1968).

illustrators – whatever their reasons – unable to complete such a large project.[36] Interestingly, in creating the cycle of woodcuts, the designer of the printed Plautus borrowed from the earlier tradition of illustrating Terence (even using the same full-page woodcut of a Roman theatre also used for de'Soardi's 1497 edition of Terence), thereby tying this new Plautus imagery to the much older tradition of Terence illustration.

The earliest illustrated manuscript of Terence's six comedies, and perhaps the best known – the cover of this publication shows its shelf of masks for the play *Andria* – dates from the first half of the ninth century.[37] Containing Terence's six comedies illustrated with 150 miniatures, this manuscript is known as the Vatican Terence, or as C.[38] Five of the comedies open with shelves holding masks for characters in the play, arranged in the order in which the characters appear onstage.[39] These shelves of masks are often referred to as *aediculae*. In the *aedicula* before the fourth play in the manuscript, *Adelphoe*, a *senex* ('old man') mask for Micio comes first on the top shelf, since he speaks alone in the opening scene (Figure 17.3). Beside this mask are those for his brother Demea (now somewhat defaced), the slave dealer Sannio (also damaged), and the young man Aeschinus, who are the next characters to appear onstage. On the page facing these masks is the *argumentum* of the play, written in rustic capitals in alternate lines of red and black above the masked prologue speaker, who makes a two-fingered speaking gesture in the direction of the *aedicula*. In a scene a few folios on in *Adelphoe* (Figure 17.4), Micio's nephew and beloved adopted son Aeschinus (mistakenly labelled Parmeno but corrected by a later hand), shown on the far right, rests a possessive hand on the shoulder of the music girl he abducted the night before, while on the far left his slave Parmeno (mistakenly labelled Sannio) is about to strike the girl's owner, Sannio (mistakenly labelled Aeschinus, then mistakenly corrected to Parmeno by a later hand).[40] Here, the masked figures stand much as they do in all the illustrations of scenes in the Vatican Terence, in frontal groupings, on an empty, unpainted background, in an unframed scene placed before the text it

---

[36] Terence manuscripts with unfinished cycles of illustration are: Leiden, UB, LIP 26, Leiden, UB, Voss. lat. Q. 38; Paris, BnF, lat. 7900; Paris, BnF, lat. 8193; Vatican City, BAV, Vat. lat. 3305; and Vatican City, BAV, Archivio di San Pietro, H 19.

[37] This manuscript is Vatican City, BAV, Vat. lat. 3868. For a description, see Wright (2006) 183–7. There is a digital facsimile of the manuscript online at http://digi.vatlib.it.

[38] Apart from the Codex Bembinus, manuscripts of Terence have been divided into three main groups: the δ-family (with the lost ancestor Δ), the γ-family (with the lost ancestor Γ), and so-called mixed texts (*codices mixti*) with readings from both families. For an overview of the textual tradition see Reeve (1983) 412–20 and Victor (2014). See also Grant (1986); Victor (1996) and (2003); Victor/Quesnel (1999).

[39] The second comedy in the Vatican Terence, *Eunuchus*, does not have an *aedicula*.

[40] This is an illustration before *Adelphoe* 155 (2.1).

Figure 17.3: Vatican City, BAV, Vat. lat. 3868, fol. 50v: masks for the comedy *Adelphoe*
© Vatican Library

illustrates. The scene headings found in unillustrated manuscripts of the comedies like the Codex Bembinus serve as figure labels in the illustrated Terence manuscripts. In fact, Günther Jachmann has argued that the creator of the cycle of illustrations found in the Vatican Terence and other manuscripts worked from the scene headings in an unillustrated manuscript of the comedies.[41]

The illustrations in another ninth-century Terence manuscript, known as the Paris Terence and by the siglum P, are so close to those in the Vatican Terence

[41] Jachmann (1924) 18–22.

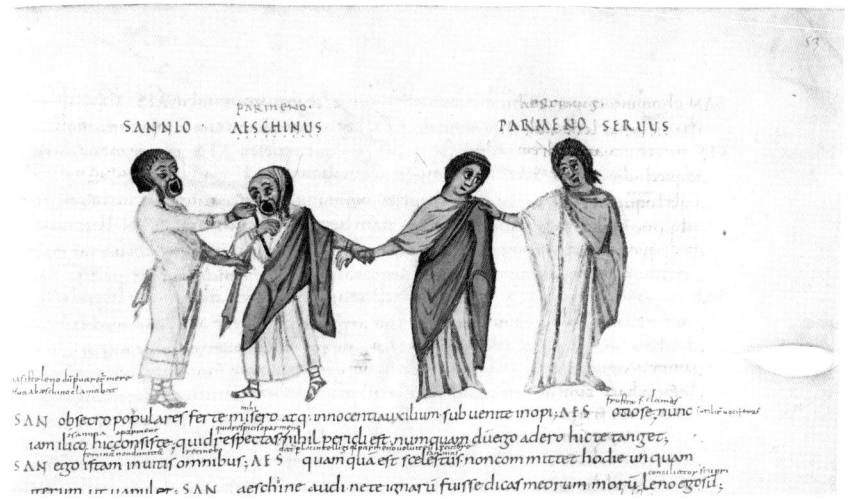

Figure 17.4: Vatican City, BAV, Vat. lat. 3868, fol. 53r, a scene from *Adelphoe* with Parmeno, Sannio, the nameless music girl, and Aeschinus (the figures have been mislabelled)
© Vatican Library

as to suggest they have a familial relationship; it has long been thought that these manuscripts are siblings, both carefully copied from the same exemplar that has been given various names, most recently U.[42] The play *Adelphoe* begins in the Paris Terence with shelves holding masks similar to those in the Vatican Terence miniature (Figure 17.5).[43] Differences, apart from those involving technique and materials (the Vatican Terence is painted in a range of colours, the Paris work is drawn in brown ink), include the representation of the *aedicula* structure, as well as the bird perched on the structure in the Paris drawing, which was added by a later hand. From their added scholia and corrections, and other additions such as the bird, it would seem both manuscripts have been carefully studied and much used.

A tenth-century Terence known as the Ambrosian Terence and by the siglum F is now considered to be a third copy of the lost model U used for the Vatican and Paris manuscripts.[44] This manuscript's cycle of brown ink drawings washed in a bluish colour is clearly tied to the earlier two. But important

[42] This manuscript is U in Wright (2006). Wright proposes that two other illustrated manuscripts, Paris, BnF, lat. 7900 and Milan, BA, H. 75 inf., are also copies of U. See also Jones and Morey (1930–1).

[43] This manuscript is Paris, BnF, lat. 7899; there is a digital facsmile of the manuscript online at https://gallica.bnf.fr. For a description of the manuscript, see Wright (2006) 192–7.

[44] This manuscript is Milan, BA, H. 75 inf. For a description of the manuscript, see Wright (2006) 197–201.

Figure 17.5: Paris, BnF, lat. 7899, fol. 96r, masks for the comedy *Adelphoe*
© Bibliothèque nationale de France

divergences must also be noted, including some in the manuscript's *aedicula* for *Adelphoe* (Figure 17.6). Not masks but instead masked busts of eight male characters have been drawn, arranged into four pairs over two rows. Notably, masks for the three female characters (shown in the second and third rows of shelves in the Vatican and Paris manuscripts) are not found in this illustration. Also, given how these masked busts are presented, the pairs of figures seem to be in dialogue. Here we get some idea of how the comedies were seen by this

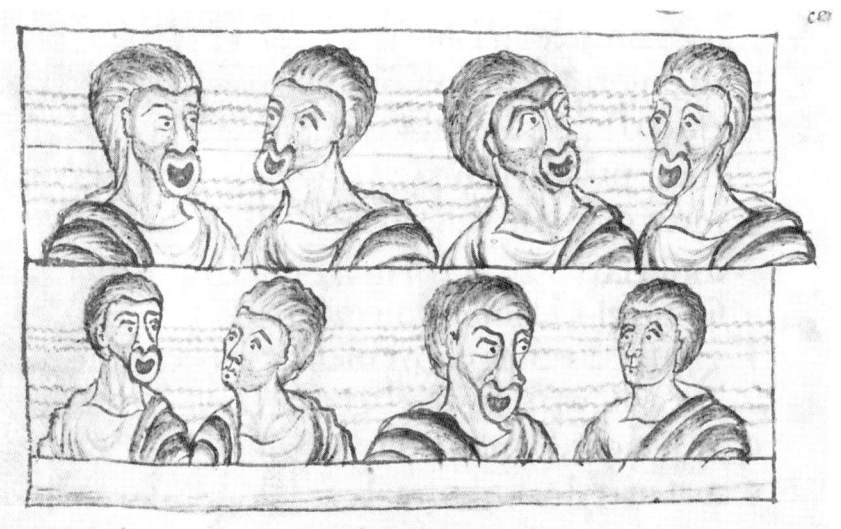

Figure 17.6: Milan, BA, H. 75 inf., fol. 53v, busts of characters in the comedy *Adelphoe*
© Veneranda Biblioteca Ambrosiana

illustrator, working in Rheims in the tenth century: as dialogues, and perhaps even as disputes or disagreements, between masters and slaves, fathers and sons, old men and adolescents.[45]

The illustrated Terence tradition includes manuscripts with scenes copied so faithfully that even the postures and gestures of the figures were closely replicated, as in a later, mid-twelfth-century manuscript known as the Oxford Terence (or as O).[46] In the third scene of *Adelphoe* in the Oxford Terence, the arrangement of figures as well as their poses and gestures are close to those in the Vatican and Paris works. Parmeno raises his right hand toward Sannio, who holds the right wrist of the music girl, her left shoulder clasped by the besotted Aeschinus (compare Figure 17.7 to Figure 17.4). Still, certain differences – including the more exaggerated masks with kidney-shaped mouths worn by Parmeno and Sannio, and the medieval clothing particularly noticeable on the figures of the music girl and Aeschinus – suggest the possibilities for artistic innovation, even when copying a model.

---

[45] For the fragment of a dispute between Terence and a young mocker, from a manuscript assigned to Rheims (Paris, BnF, lat. 8069), see Villa (1984) 67–98 and (2015); Giovini (2006a).

[46] This manuscript is Oxford, Bodl. Lib., Auct. F. 2. 13. A complete digital facsimile of the Oxford Terence is accessible at the Early Manuscripts at Oxford University website (http://image.ox.ac.uk). For a discussion of the manuscript, see Muir and Turner (2011).

Figure 17.7: Oxford, Bodl. Lib., Auct. F. 2. 13, fol. 100v, a scene from *Adelphoe* with Parmeno, Sannio, the nameless music girl, and Aeschinus
© Bodleian Library

In the case of other manuscripts, the aim was quite patently not to copy earlier scenes, even if the artists were familiar with them or had access to an illustrated model to work from. Instead, entirely new scenes were composed for the comedies, which include events that the text describes as happening offstage, as well as scenes illustrating Terence's prologues and recitations of the comedies. Examples of this different approach can be found in an eleventh-century Terence given the siglum N, where Glycerium's labour is not simply discussed but also shown in three miniatures (Figure 17.8).[47] In the first of three labour scenes, Glycerium lies on her side holding her head and belly in front of three women who sit attending her; Mysis, her maid, stands in the doorway on the left, about to go and fetch a midwife. None of the figures in this illustration, or in any other in N, is apparently masked as they are in the earlier manuscripts. These figures are not actors on a Roman stage making a formalised set of gestures, but more recognisably medieval characters, wearing medieval costumes, and in many illustrations making only simple pointing gestures at each other.[48]

Similar adaptations of Terence's comedies can be found in a twelfth-century illustrated Terence manuscript in Tours (known by the siglum Tur), with a large set of illustrations for all six plays. In this manuscript, Crito, described as

[47] This manuscript is Leiden, UB, Voss. lat. Q. 38. On how this manuscript's text was copied, see Victor (2003).
[48] For an overview of the gestures found in the Vatican Terence and the Paris Terence, see Wright (2006) 215–16.

Figure 17.8: Leiden University Library, VLQ 38, fol. 7r, a scene from *Andria* in which only Glycerium's maid Mysis speaks
© Leiden University Library

a *hospes* ('traveller') in *Andria*, wears a pilgrim's cap and scrip; the young man Chaerea, who disguises himself as a eunuch in *Eunuchus*, disguises himself in the long, hooded robes of a monk in three miniatures; and in the comedy *Phormio*, the parasite Gnatho sports the long hair and close-fitting robe of an early twelfth-century dandy.[49] Such alterations in N and Tur should be viewed in connection with medieval adaptations of the comedies, for instance Hrotsvit of Gandersheim's plays written in Lower Saxony in the tenth century, and the twelfth-century Latin comedies of the Loire valley (where at least two illustrated Terence manuscripts are thought to originate).[50] Terence illustrations, along with characters and plots, were clearly being adjusted to fit particular, changing medieval contexts.

Tur also does not feature the shelves of masks or prologue speakers found in the Vatican and Paris manuscripts. The play *Eunuchus* begins instead with an illustration of a figure reciting from a book as he sits on a carved bench on a raised and covered platform. Below are two groups of gesticulating men and women, perhaps representing the audience on the left and the actors on the right (Figure 17.9).[51] This is close to how medieval commentaries describe the

[49] For such fashionable dress, see Harris (1987).
[50] These are Tours, BM, 924 and Vatican City, BAV, Vat. lat. 3225.
[51] This manuscript is Tours, BM, 924. A full set of images is on the Enluminures website: www.enluminures.culture.fr.

Figure 17.9: Tours, BM, 924, fol. 13v, a performance of the comedy *Eunuchus*
© Bibliothèque municipale de Tours

plays as being performed in Terence's day.[52] At least by the ninth century, someone named Calliopius (whose name is mentioned in medieval copies of the comedies) was viewed as the *recitator* ('reciter') of the plays.[53]

We also find the figure of Calliopius seated beside Terence writing his comedies in the first miniature of the manuscript N, as well as in the frontispiece of an illustrated manuscript known as S, assigned to the Loire valley around the year 1100 (Figure 17.1).[54] In this full-page coloured drawing within a pedimented frame, Calliopius is seated in the topmost section above a group of gesticulating Romans, between the playwright himself (seated at left) and two of Terence's adversaries (standing at right). Beside Calliopius is a lectern on which is an open book, inscribed with the first words of the prologue to the play *Andria*, the text on the page facing this illustration. One of the two figures standing on the right has been labelled Luscius Lavinius. This is clearly meant to be Luscius Lanuvinus, Terence's second-century BC rival, whom Donatus identifies as the unnamed *maleuolus uetus poeta* ('malevolent old poet') against whom Terence defends himself in his prologues.

---

[52] For an overview of the medieval commentary tradition, see Riou (1997) and Villa (2007).
[53] On the mentions of Calliopius in medieval manuscripts, see Victor (2014).
[54] The manuscript is Vatican City, BAV, Vat. lat. 3305; for discussion of it, see Wright (1993) and Raffaelli (2002). There is a digital facsimile online at: http://digi.vatlib.it.

This illustrator seems to have known Terentian commentaries which mention Luscius Lanuvinus as Terence's rival, and which describe Calliopius as Terence's friend and the reciter of the comedies.[55]

Terence illustrations have largely been examined in terms of the relationships they imply between manuscripts, both surviving and hypothetical lost works. A potential flaw in this approach, however, is that it often presupposes that artists were solely interested in the faithful copying of earlier illustrations, and that variations between illustrations only occur when an artist has misunderstood or been unable to copy from an illustrated model.[56] Yet the Terence cycles seem to reveal something else entirely. They show the efforts of different artists to improve upon or update the illustrated model/s they knew of or worked from, selecting parts of the earlier illustrations they deemed crucial, useful or interesting, whilst at the same time introducing new figural arrangements or other elements, such as buildings and clothing, to clarify the action in scenes or highlight certain aspects of the plots.

Some lingering questions about the illustrated Terence tradition remain, including how many illustrated Terence manuscripts have been lost to us, and what the exact copying relationships between works like the Vatican Terence (C) and the Paris Terence (P), and between the Paris Terence and the Oxford Terence (O), really are. Whilst it is often repeated that the Vatican Terence and the Paris Terence were copied from the same lost late-antique illustrated Terence manuscript (U), and that the Paris Terence was in turn copied for the Oxford Terence, a number of textual scholars have raised doubts about these hypotheses.[57] Indeed, in a recent publication, Benjamin Victor has argued that the Vatican Terence, long held by art historians to be a near-facsimile copy of the lost late-antique archetypal manuscript U, was in fact copied from a medieval intermediary written in minuscules (which Victor calls ψ).[58]

What is clear is that the illustrators of the Vatican Terence (possibly via ψ) and the Paris Terence had access to illustrations of comedy from Late Antiquity. In a series of publications, T. B. L. Webster and others have gathered thousands of objects illustrating Greek New Comedy, the earliest dating from the late fourth century BC, with imagery related to that found in the Vatican and Paris manuscripts.[59] Perhaps the best comparison for the scene illustrations in these manuscripts are the mosaics unearthed at

---

[55] The Plautus manuscript Vatican City, BAV, Ottob. lat. 2005 also includes mention of Calliopius: Tontini (2002a) 338.
[56] Weitzmann (1970) 182–92; Lowden (1992) chs. 4–6; Dolezal (1996).
[57] Grant (1986) and Victor (2014).
[58] Victor (2014). The Paris Terence and Oxford Terence are now considered sibling manuscripts: Muir and Turner (2011) Introduction.
[59] Webster et al. (1995).

Figure 17.10: Lesbos, Archaeological Museum of Mytilene, mosaic panels with scenes from
Menander comedies
© Antike Kunst

Mytilene in the 1960s (Figure 17.10). Decorating the floors of a villa, the
mosaic panels show the Greek comic dramatist Menander, the muse of
comedy Thalia, and a scene from Plato's *Phaedo*, along with scenes from
several comedies by Menander.[60] In most of these scenes, masked figures
stand in frontal positions on groundlines and against a neutral background,
similar to how they appear in the Vatican and Paris Terence manuscripts.
These mosaics have been variously dated to the late third to early fourth

---

[60] The standard study is Charitonidis et al. (1970). See also Csapo (1999) and (2010) ch. 5.

centuries A D; but it is believed that these Menander scenes (as well as other Menander mosaics and artefacts illustrating his comedies) ultimately derive from a lost set of large-scale, publicly displayed paintings from the late fourth or early third centuries B C.[61] Showing key moments from Menander's comedies, these scenes are thought to have been copied into artists' copybooks and then reproduced in a range of media, over a long period of time.[62] From this, it is possible to imagine an enterprising designer/illustrator(s) using just such a copybook, with scenes from Menander's comedies, to create a new cycle of illustrations for Terence.[63]

Victor's recent appraisal of the copying relationships between the earliest illustrated manuscripts of Terence's comedies, including the Vatican Terence, the Paris Terence, and the Ambrosian Terence, calls for a re-examination of the cycles of illustration in these manuscripts. Fortunately, in the past few years, a great number of manuscripts of both Terence and Plautus have been taken from their shelves, digitised, and placed online. Since I began work on this article, the majority of the manuscripts I have discussed, as well as many I have not (including various illustrated Terence manuscripts of the fifteenth century), have been made freely available online. The resulting change in ease of access should not be underestimated: it will allow for easy study of heretofore entirely unknown or little-known works; and it will also enable comparisons between manuscripts. Until very recently, the simplest way to compare the cycles in the earliest illustrated Terence manuscripts has been to look at the plates in Leslie Webber Jones and Charles Rufus Morey's 1930 plate volume. This volume's halftone plates are all cropped to be roughly the same size, and are of the illustrations only. Now, it is possible to study and compare high-quality colour digital images of entire pages and of every folio of these manuscripts, not just those with illustration. I have no doubt we will learn a great deal more about the manuscripts and illustration of Plautus and Terence in the near future.

Further Reading

Plautus and Terence manuscripts produced before the year 1200 are catalogued in Munk Olsen (1982). Plautus manuscripts kept in the Vatican Library are described in Tontini (2002b); those in other Italian libraries are described in Tontini (2010); and Plautus manuscripts kept in non-Italian libraries are

---

[61] The mosaics and other artefacts illustrating Menander are discussed in Nervegna (2013).
[62] See Green (1985); Green (1994) 111–13 and 164–5; Webster et al. (1995) 1: 85.
[63] For the existence of such copybooks, see Donderer (2008).

listed in Tontini (2013). All extant medieval Terence manuscripts are listed and briefly described in Villa (1984) and (2015). The illustrated Plautus manuscripts are discussed in Fachechi (1998) and (2002); illustrated Terence manuscripts are discussed in Jones and Morey (1931), Meiss (1974), as well as Wright (2006), and are catalogued in Radden Keefe (2015).

18

MAREK THUE KRETSCHMER

The Anti-Terentian Dramas of Hrotsvit of Gandersheim

Given the insignificant influence of Hrotsvit (*c.* 935 – † after 973) in the Middle Ages, it was only after 1501, when the German humanist Conrad Celtis published the first printed edition of his 1494 'discovery' of the famous tenth-century St Emmeram manuscript (now known as Munich Clm 14485), that Hrotsvit became a more widely read author.[1] The manuscript was produced in Gandersheim, perhaps under the supervision of Hrotsvit herself, and contains all her works, except the *Primordia*: book 1, containing eight sacred legends (late 950s–962), one in elegiac couplets (the *Gongolfus*) and seven in leonine hexameters[2] (*Maria, Ascensio, Pelagius, Theophilus, Basilius, Dionysius*, and *Agnes*); book 11, containing six dramas (*c.* 962–5) in rhymed prose (*Gallicanus, Dulcitius, Calimachus, Abraham, Pafnutius*, and *Sapientia*); and what is usually referred to as book 111,[3] containing two historiographical poems (*c.* 968–early 970s) in leonine hexameters (*Gesta Ottonis* and *Primordia coenobii Gandeshemensis*).

In the preface to her anti-Terentian dramas Hrotsvit writes (*Praefatio* 1–3):[4]

> Plures inueniuntur catholici cuius nos penitus expurgare nequimus facti, qui pro cultioris facundia sermonis, gentilium uanitatem librorum utilitati praefer- unt sacrarum scripturarum. Sunt etiam alii sacris inherentes paginis, qui licet alia gentilium spernant, Terentii tamen fingmenta frequentius lectitant, et dum dulcedine sermonis delectantur, nefandarum notitia rerum maculantur. Unde ego Clamor Validus Gandeshemensis, non recusaui illum imitari dictando,

---

[1] For considerations of space I leave out this fascinating piece of reception history. For details, see Zeydel (1944) and (1945a); Grimm (1974); Wall (1987); Goullet (1993) 47–68; Cardelle de Hartmann (2003); Berschin (2005). For new evidence on the early reception, see Licht (2008).

[2] That is, with rhyme or assonance between the penthemimer and the end of the line.

[3] However, a third book does not correspond to any manuscript division. See Dronke (1984) 64 and Goullet (1999) xxxiv.

[4] Creizenach (1893) 18 invented the conventional epithet 'anti-Terentian'.

dum alii colunt legendo, quo eodem dictationis genere, quo turpia lasciuarum incesta feminarum recitabantur, laudabilis sacrarum castimonia uirginum iuxta mei facultatem ingenioli celebraretur.[5]

Many Catholics one may find, and we are also guilty of charges of this kind, who for the beauty of their eloquent style, prefer the uselessness of pagan guile to the usefulness of Sacred Scripture. There are also others, who, devoted to sacred reading and scorning the works of other pagans, yet frequently read Terence's fiction, and as they delight in the sweetness of his style and diction, they are stained by learning of wicked things in his depiction. Therefore I, the strong voice of Gandersheim, have not refused to imitate him in writing whom others laud in reading, so that in that selfsame form of composition in which the shameless acts of lascivious women were phrased the laudable chastity of sacred virgins may be praised within the limits of my little talent.[6]

Thus Hrotsvit presents six new Terentian dramas acceptable to a Catholic audience. Already in the preface Hrotsvit associates herself with John the Baptist: *ego Clamor Validus* is an allusion to the *ego uox clamantis* of John 1:23.[7] In addition, her first drama ends with the baptism of the pagan Terentianus. The lines from *Gallicanus* II 9.2, *parce, Terentiane, lacrimis et parce anxietati cordis* (Terentianus, let go of your tears, and let go of your heartfelt fears), supply the Christian answer to Terentianus' wish to be baptised, and through the word-play on the name (Terentianus/ Terentius) the lines are easily read as 'I, Hrotsvit, will baptise you, dear Terence'.[8]

Two questions in particular have dominated the scholarly discussions of these dramas: their 'theatricality', that is whether they were performed or not, and their indebtedness to Terence.[9] I will not discuss the problem of performance here and will instead explore the use of Terence in Hrotsvit's dramatic series. Before we approach this topic, however, I will, briefly present the historical context and Hrotsvit's cultural background.

---

[5] Berschin (2001) 132.

[6] Wilson (1989) 3. I have not attempted to replace Katharina Wilson's translation in rhymed prose. All translations of book 2 are from Wilson (1989). The translations of book 1 (without rhyme) are my own.

[7] Cf. Dronke (1984) 70.   [8] Cf. Talbot (2004) 156–7.

[9] The term 'theatricality' refers especially to Butler's monograph. Cf. Zeydel (1945b); Butler (1960); Nagel (1965) 65–75; Bertini (1980); Sticca (1985); Symes (2003); Snyder (2004); Mosetti Casaretto (2005). See also Giovini (2007) for the interesting case of the *Delusor*. For the question of indebtedness to Terence, see Roberts (1901); Coulter (1929); Homeyer (1968); de Luca (1974); Bertini (1980) 86ff.; Bean (1984); Newlands (1986); Giovini (2003).

Hrotsvit and the Ottonian Renaissance

It comes as no great surprise that the Munich manuscript was found at St Emmeram's Abbey in Regensburg, for it was in this Bavarian intellectual centre that Gerberga (940–1001), niece of Emperor Otto I and later on Hrotsvit's teacher, received her eminent schooling. St Emmeram boasted one of the finest scriptoria of the time, and when in 959 Gerberga became the seventh Abbess of Gandersheim, she did not come empty-handed. Her old bonds to the Bavarian monastery must have resulted in a lively exchange of books between St Emmeram and Gandersheim. Gerberga surely is responsible for the transfer of the Munich manuscript to St Emmeram, and we can easily imagine welcome additions to the Gandersheim library from which Hrotsvit would have benefited.[10] In the preface to her book of legends, Hrotsvit writes (*Praefatio* 6–7):

> ... satagebam iuxta meum posse licet minime necessarium aliquem tamen conficere textum ex sententiis scripturarum, quas intra aream nostri Gandeshemensis collegeram cęnobii. Primo sapientissime atque benignissimae Rikkardis magistrę aliarumque suae uicis instruente magisterio, deinde prona fauente clementia, regię indolis Gerbergae cuius nunc subdor dominio abbatisse, quę aetate minor, sed ut imperialem decebat neptem, scientia prouectior aliquot auctores quos ipsa prior a sapientissimis didicit me admodum pie erudiuit.[11]

> According to my abilities, however poor they may be, I have endeavoured to compose a text based on the content of the writings which I had collected within the space of our convent of Gandersheim, first under the tutelage of professor Rikkardis, a most learned and kind woman, and her colleagues, then under the auspicious protection of Gerberga, a lady of royal blood, to whose rule as abbess I am now submitted; who, younger than me but of much greater learning, as befits the imperial niece, has guided me, quite devotedly, in the study of authors whom she had read herself under the instruction of the best teachers.

Gerberga's teachings obviously yielded fruits, as both the legends and the *Gesta Ottonis* are dedicated to her. Their prefaces and dedications are in fact the only sources we have to the life of Hrotsvit, but they do not actually provide us with much biographical information. However, our knowledge of the Gandersheim convent and its connection to the imperial family dispels the enduring myth that Hrotsvit was an isolated figure in the Ottonian Renaissance.[12] Gandersheim

---

[10] Nagel (1965) 42 and 46. [11] Berschin (2001) 2.

[12] The collections of essays edited by Wilson (1987) and Brown, McMillin, and Wilson (2004) have been instrumental in contextualising the works of Hrotsvit. See also Hrotsvit's own encomium of Otto I and history of Gandersheim Abbey.

was no ordinary abbey; founded in 852 by the Saxon duke Liudolf (800–66) and his wife Oda (806–913), it subsequently obtained royal and imperial protection, becoming in many ways similar to an independent principality with daughters from the Saxon dynasty as ruling abbesses; the first three, Hathumod, Gerberga, and Christine, were daughters of Liudolf and Oda, and Hrotsvit may have been a relative of the abbess Hrotsvit who succeeded Christine.[13] Hence, it is reasonable to assume that Hrotsvit was descended from the Saxon aristocracy, and as a canoness she was not bound to a vow of poverty or *clausura*, that is, she could possess books and visit the court. Gerberga perhaps introduced her to members of the elite, thus nurturing Hrotsvit's genius. Hrotsvit's own words reveal something of these contacts, and in an explicative note inserted between the legends and the dramas she accounts for her sources:

> Huius omnem materiam sicut et prioris opusculi sumsi ab antiquis libris sub certis auctorum nominibus conscriptis, excepta superius scripta passione sancti Pelagii, cuius seriem martirii quidam eiusdem in qua passus est indigena ciuitatis mihi exposuit, qui ipsum pulcherrimum uirorum se uidisse et exitum rei attestatus est ueraciter agnouisse.[14]

> I took all the subject matter of this and the previous work from ancient books composed by certain named authors, except for the above written legend of St Pelagius. A native of the city where he suffered martyrdom told me the whole tale. He confirmed that he had seen this person, the fairest of men, and that he had certain knowledge of the result of the event.

We have good reason to believe that the source of Hrotsvit's legend of Cordoba's young martyr was a member of Caliph Abd al-Rahman III's embassy at the court of Otto I in 956.[15]

In addition Hrotsvit became acquainted with learned men at Otto's court who encouraged and supported her work, and she humbly thanks them in a letter preceding the dramas (*Epistola ad quosdam sapientes*, 2–3, 11):

> Vestrę igitur laudandę humilitatis magnitudinem satis admirari nequeo, mag-nificeque circa mei uilitatem benignitatis atque dilectionis plenitudinem, con-dignarum recompensatione gratiarum remetiri non sufficio, quia cum philosophicis adprime studiis enutriti, et scientia longe excellentius sitis per-fecti, mei opusculum uilis muliercule, uestra admiratione dignum duxistis, et largitorem in me operantis gratię fraterno affectu gratulantes laudastis (…) Quia enim attactu uestri fauoris atque petitionis harundineo more inclinata,

---

[13] We know that they were not one and the same woman; see, for instance, Butler (1960) 39. For a history of the convent, see Goetting (1950 and 1973) and Goullet (1993) 13–29.
[14] Berschin (2001) 131.   [15] See for instance Cerulli (1970) and McMillin (2004).

libellum quem tali intentione disposui, sed usque huc pro sui uilitate occultare, quam in palam proferre malui, uobis perscrutandum tradidi ...[16]

I cannot marvel enough at the extent of your laudable condescension and I cannot sufficiently requite your magnificent good will and your affection's generous magnitude in worthy attestations of gratitude on account of my own worthlessness, because you, who are profoundly nourished by the study of philosophy, and have long been the most outstanding among learned men, found the little work of a worthless woman worthy of your admiration, and encouraging me with fraternal affection you praised the Giver of the grace which is working in me (...) But touched by your good will and your encouragement, in the manner of the reed touched by the breeze, I was encouraged, I was put at ease to send you this little book for examination which I have written with such an intention but have preferred to keep hidden until now rather than show it openly because of its worthlessness ...[17]

As Hrotsvit mentions in her preface to the dramas, Terence was in vogue among the learned of her time, and Hrotsvit's own wish to rewrite his comedies may well have been prompted by the intellectual milieu at both the court and the convent.[18] What is more, she succeeded in finding patrons who must have not only taken pleasure in reading Roman comedy, but also had an opinion on *how* best to read it. Hrotsvit does not name her mentors, but we know of several learned individuals with both connections to the Ottonian court and a keen interest in Terence.[19]

In the period 952–62, two of the most distinguished prose writers of the age, Rather of Verona (887–974) and Liudprand of Cremona (920–72), were frequent guests at the court of Otto I. Leaving the difficult political climate in Italy, they had crossed the Alps as refugees and attached themselves to the German monarch. While in his service, they produced parts of their historical and autobiographical works that give us vivid insights into the political and intellectual scene of both sides of the Alps: Rather's *Phrenesis* (955–6) and Liudprand's *Antapodosis* (958–62). In fact, Liudprand wrote the *Antapodosis* at the request of Recemundus, bishop of Elvira and leader of Abd al-Rahman III's aforementioned embassy. Its many Terentian quotations and allusions indicate that Liudprand must have been a most fervent reader of the Roman comic playwright.[20]

---

[16] Berschin (2001) 134–5.   [17] Wilson (1989) 4–5.
[18] Munk Olsen (1991); Villa (1984); Reynolds (1983) 412–20.
[19] Plautus was almost unknown in the Middle Ages. See Reynolds (1983) 302–7 and Kenney (1982) 793. Two known readers of Plautus are Ratherius (*Sermo de Maria et Martha*) and Aimeric (*Ars lectoria*).
[20] Giovini (2001). With some 60 quotations, Liudprand is the most Terentian of the Ottonian authors. Rather's work contains *c.* 30 of them.

As Peter Dronke has suggested, Hrotsvit may have learned the technique of rhymed prose directly from Rather, who excelled in the art.[21] What I think may be an even more striking influence is the attitude towards Terence. Consider the following, which Rather wrote in his *Praeloquia* (935–7) 3.1:

> (...) nouimus ab ipsis quoque urbanae scientiae uiris hodie summa diligentia obseruari, quid cautius quam quid proferant uerius, utilius aestimari quod docet comicus quam quod interminatur Dominus, pluris pendi dictum: *Obsequium amicos, ueritas odium parit*, quam *Qui me erubuerit et meos sermones, et hunc Filius hominis erubescet, cum uenerit*; et forte illud, quia quasi disertius, ideo putetur utilius, quia pompaticum, ideo iudicatur saluberrimum; istud, quia foliorum uenustate, quin potius uanitatis opacissima densitate, nudatum, ideo a saeculi prudentibus ceu simplex atque, ut ita dicatur, rusticum uilipenso ducitur dignum, (...) Verum magistra eadem, quae et via est, Veritate, (...) satagamus hac arte sermonem moderari nostrum, (...) quo fit (ut ita loqui quanquam absurde liceat), ut nec Terentius alicuius minus prouide odium in nosmet exacuisse nec Christus alicuius amicitiam minus libere nos notet ueritati praetulisse.[22]

> (...) I know that men of sophistication today take great pains to find ways to say what is expedient rather than what is true. They find more advantageous what the comic poet encourages than what the Lord threatens. They value more highly the saying 'Flattery begets friends, the truth hatred' (Teren. *Andr.* 1.1) than 'Whoever is ashamed of me and my words, of him will the Son of Man be ashamed when he comes' (Luke 9:26); perhaps the former, as it is more rhetorical (as it were) is thought finer; because it is stylish, it is judged wholesome; whereas the latter, stripped as it is of charming style – or rather, stripped of the dark obscurities of vanity – is for that reason thought by the worldly-wise to be rather simple or rustic and worthy of little regard; (...) But let me strive that my words be controlled by the same master, Truth, which is also the Way (...) so that (if I may speak so, though absurdly) neither Terence may rebuke me for having thoughtlessly provoked anyone's hatred against me nor Christ for having preferred anyone's friendship to the truth.[23]

If such literature was delivered at court in Hrotsvit's presence, one could interpret her anti-Terentian project as a pious answer to Rather's indignation.[24]

Rather was summoned to Otto's court to instruct Otto's younger brother Bruno (925–65), the future archbishop of Cologne, and accordingly we find yet another eager Terentian in Bruno, for a passage from his biographer Ruotger indicates that he was one of those learned men who cultivated the Terentian style.[25] Finally, concrete evidence that Terence was read at Gandersheim comes from a Terence manuscript produced at Gandersheim

---

[21] Dronke (1984) 56. Otherwise, Goullet (1999) xxiii.   [22] *CCCM* 46A 77–8.
[23] Reid (1991) 94–5.   [24] See also Kretschmer (2014) 563–5.
[25] *Vita Brunonis* 8, *MGH SRG NS* 10 9. Cf. Dronke (1984) 57.

towards the end of the tenth century (Oxford, Bodleian Library, F. 6.27).[26] On the verso side of folio 112 we find the following note: *Adelheit, Hedwich, Matthilt, curiales adulescentulę unum par … amicitię* (the royal ladies Adelheit, Hedwig, and Mathilda, united by friendship). These royal readers of Terence were none other than Gerberga's sister Hedwig († 994), the erudite duchess of Swabia portrayed in the *Casus Sancti Galli* (ch. 90 and 94) and her two younger cousins, daughters of Otto II, Adelaide († 1043, Abbess of Gandersheim 1039–43) and Matilda († 1025). Hence, Terence was definitely well-liked by the Ottonian elite.

The Anti-Terentian Dramas

Conversion, martyrdom, and resurrection are the main topics of Hrotsvit's dramas, as the full titles of the Munich manuscript indicate.[27] Hrotsvit turns the Terentian plot upside down: the girl who resists all advances (or, in the case of *Abraham* and *Pafnutius*, the repenting prostitute who abandons her former life) replaces Terence's successful young suitor, and Christian nuptial imagery replaces the consummation of the young couple's marriage.[28]

Hrotsvit's indebtedness to Terence lies more in situations and subject matter than in style.[29] Hrotsvit imitates Terence's technique of rapid dialogues and expressions such as *hercle, edepol, euax, pro dolor, hem, non flocci facio*, and *di te perdant*, but on the level of plot we find that she develops a variety of subtle analogies, often of allusive character, with scenes of trickery, deception, disguise, and so forth. Following a presentation of each play's plot, I will offer examples of Terentian motifs in Hrotsvit.

Gallicanus

The emperor Constantine urges his general Gallicanus to wage war against the rebellious Scythians.[30] In return Gallicanus requests the hand of

---

[26] Villa (1984) 99–136.

[27] *Conuersio Gallicani principis milicie* (The Conversion of General Gallicanus); *Passio sanctarum uirginum Agapis, Chionie et Hirene* (The Martyrdom of the Holy Virgins Agape, Chionia, and Hirena); *Resuscitatio Drusiane et Calimachi* (The Resurrection of Drusiana and Calimachus); *Lapsus et conuersio Marie neptis Habrahe heremicole* (The Fall and Conversion of Mary, the Niece of the Hermit Abraham); *Conuersio Thaidis meretricis* (The Conversion of the Harlot Thais); and *Passio sanctarum uirginum Fidei, Spei et Karitatis* (The Martyrdom of the Holy Virgins Fides, Spes, and Karitas).

[28] See, for instance, Newlands (1986) 374, or Sticca (1971) 369–70.

[29] For an outline, see Giovini (2003) 57–64.

[30] Hrotsvit's first drama is based on the acts of the saints Gallicanus, John, and Paul. Cf. *AASS* 37–39 and 159–60.

Constantine's daughter Constance in marriage. Constance has taken a vow of chastity, however, and Constantine does not know how to resolve the problem. Constance advises him to pretend to agree to marriage on Gallicanus' successful return from the eastern campaign. As pledges of love Constance's chamberlains, John and Paul, join Gallicanus' retinue, and Gallicanus' daughters, Attica and Artemia, enter her court. Gallicanus' warfare turns out to be disastrous. He is about to surrender when John encourages him to become a Christian in order to obtain victory. Gallicanus assents and receives immediate military support from celestial armies. After victory and subsequent baptism, Gallicanus renounces his love for Constance and retires to a religious life at Ostia. In the second part of the drama the apostate emperor Julian is oppressing the Christians. Gallicanus goes into exile to Alexandria, where he dies as a martyr. John and Paul refuse to serve Julian, who orders his commander Terentianus to have them killed. The slaughter leads to a demonic possession of Terentianus' son; Terentianus repents and begs for baptism at the tomb of the martyrs John and Paul. Upon their receiving the holy water, Terentianus' son recovers.

Dulcitius

The three Christian sisters Agape, Chionia and Hirena are summoned to the court of the emperor Diocletian, who tries to force them to convert to the pagan gods and to marry dignitaries of his court. [31] The maidens refuse, and the emperor orders them to be incarcerated under the custody of the governor Dulcitius, who has them placed in a cell adjacent to the prison pantry where he can easily have his way with them. At night Dulcitius enters the prison with his soldiers and approaches the pantry determined to fulfil his desires, but struck by sudden madness, he mistakes the pots and pans for the virgins. After having passionately embraced the sooty kitchenware, Dulcitius comes out black as an Ethiopian, upon which his soldiers flee, believing he is the devil; even worse, the guards back at the palace fail to recognise him and beat him up. Wanting to avenge the humiliation, Dulcitius orders the girls to be exposed naked in public, but by miracle the clothes stick to their bodies and Dulcitius himself falls asleep. After the failure of Dulcitius, Diocletian entrusts Count Sissinus with the task of dealing with the Christian maidens. Agape and Chionia are condemned to the pyre, but they die with their bodies miraculously undamaged. Hirena is ordered to be taken to a brothel to become a harlot, but by divine intervention she is transported to

[31] The argument of the second play derives from the acts of the holy virgins Agape, Chionia, and Hirena. Cf. *AASS* 248–50. See also critical edition by Delehaye (1936).

a mountain top where Sissinus cannot reach her, before finally receiving the martyr's crown when killed by one of Sissinus' archers.

Calimachus

The pagan Calimachus reveals to his friends that he has fallen in love with a certain Drusiana, who lives in a chaste marriage with her Christian lord Andronicus.[32] In spite of his friends' dissuasions, Calimachus decides to seduce the Christian lady. Drusiana resists his advances and begs God for death in order to avoid a future scandal. After Drusiana's sudden death, Andronicus calls on St John; they bury her and entrust the procurator Fortunatus with guarding the tomb. Fortunatus talks Calimachus, still nursing a passion for Drusiana, into paying him to have access to her body. Just as Calimachus is about to defile the corpse, a snake inflicts a lethal bite on Fortunatus and scares Calimachus to death. Meanwhile, Andronicus and St John go to Drusiana's grave to pray for her soul. On their way a divine apparition announces the resurrection of Drusiana and Calimachus. At the tomb they discover the snake and the three dead bodies. Through the working of God, St John resurrects Calimachus, who, filled with remorse, confesses his sins and converts to a new life as a Christian. St John now restores Drusiana to life. She asks for the revival of Fortunatus, but Calimachus resents the idea of having mercy on the person who led him to sin. St John teaches him not to feel envy and grants to Drusiana the power of calling Fortunatus back to life. Fortunatus, however, rejects the divine grace and prefers a second death.

Abraham

The anchorite Abraham has just adopted his seven-year-old orphaned niece Mary and seeks advice from his fellow hermit Effrem about her upbringing. [33] Together they persuade her to embrace a virginal life. After twenty years as a recluse, Mary yields to the seduction of a lover who came to see her disguised as a monk. Despairing of forgiveness, she escapes her cell and settles in a nearby town where she lives as a prostitute. After consultation with Effrem, Abraham, ignorant of Mary's whereabouts, sends a friend to look for her. Two years later he brings news of the lost girl, and Abraham decides to recapture her *sub specie amatoris*, that is, disguised as a lover. On horseback in

---

[32] Hrotsvit has taken the plot from the apocryphal acts of St John the Apostle. Edition by Fabricius (1719²), vol. II, 542–57.

[33] The source of Hrotsvit's fourth drama derives from the *Vita Sanctae Mariae meretricis neptis Abrahae eremitae*. Cf. *PL* 73, cols. 651–60.

a soldier's garb, he arrives at the brothel and asks for a room. The keeper has dinner prepared, and on Abraham's request Mary joins the meal. The presence of Abraham at the table reminds Mary of her earlier life, and she suffers a moment of contrition. After supper the two retire to the bedroom. Abraham reveals his true identity and spends the rest of the night convincing her to resume her former life. At dawn Abraham accompanies Mary to her old cell and reports the good news to Effrem.

Pafnutius

In order to explain the cause of his sadness to his disciples, the hermit Pafnutius engages in an exposition of the theories of macrocosm and microcosm. [34] The sordid activity of the harlot Thais disturbs the cosmic harmony; her alluring beauty corrupts an ever-growing horde of men, which makes her an *iniuria factoris*, an insult to the Creator. Hence, Pafnutius, disguised as a lover, resolves to seek her out to change her ways. After finding and entering the prostitute's house, Pafnutius, by a series of vigorous admonitions, causes Thais to repent and abhor her sinful life. Heartened by Pafnutius' sincere solicitude, Thais determines to reconsider her existence. She calls together her host of lovers and publicly renounces the clients by burning all the possessions she earned from them. Pafnutius then takes Thais to a nearby convent, where she spends three years of severe penance immured in a narrow cell. At the end of this period, Pafnutius, anxious to know what has befallen Thais, seeks the counsel of his fellow hermit St Anthony, whose disciple Paul, through a divine vision, confirms that Thais has won God's mercy. Subsequently, Pafnutius pays a last visit to the convent to comfort and support the dying Thais.

Sapientia

Together with her daughters Fides, Spes, and Karitas, the foreign lady Sapientia has recently arrived in Rome, where she induces Romans to convert to Christianity.[35] The prefect Antiochus informs the emperor Hadrian about the new threat to the Roman Empire, upon which Sapientia and her girls are summoned to court to be interrogated by the emperor. After making an initial, unsuccessful exhortation to worship the pagan gods, Hadrian enquires about Sapientia's descent and the names and

---

[34] Hrotsvit's drama on the conversion of the harlot Thais is based on the *Vita sanctae Thaisis meretricis*. Cf. *PL* 73, cols. 661–2 (= *AASS* 225–6).

[35] The argument of Hrotsvit's last drama derives from the *passio* contained in the manuscript *Vindobonensis* 420 (159r – 165v), edited by Simonetti (1989) 681–95.

age of her daughters. Sapientia then teases the emperor with an intricate disquisition on the numbers 8, 10, and 12, the respective age of her three girls. Annoyed by Sapientia's bold and unwavering attitude, the emperor threatens torture and orders Sapientia and her children to be imprisoned, allowing them three days to reconsider. During the delay, Sapientia animates her children with her intent of marrying them to the Eternal King. At the second enquiry, Sapientia persists in refusing to observe the imperial will. Antiochus advises the emperor to have the girls pay homage to the goddess Diana. One by one they are interrogated, but they do not give in, prepared as they are to meet the celestial spouse. Thus, Sapientia is forced to witness the torture and ultimately the decapitation of her children. Followed by a group of matrons, Sapientia buries the remains of her daughters three miles outside Rome. At the tomb she prays to God to allow her to die and join her children in praising the Lord, upon which she passes away.

All of Hrotsvit's dramas are based on hagiographical sources, and certain similarities in argument between single plays are evident, notably between the *Dulcitius* and the *Sapientia* (the martyrdom of three sisters) and between the *Abraham* and the *Pafnutius* (the conversion of a harlot). However, Hrotsvit's pieces are anything but pale reworkings of saints' lives:[36] close readings reveal Terentian models neatly hidden behind holy masks.

Let us now turn to the Terentian motifs used by Hrotsvit. The initial situation of the *Gallicanus* (Act 1, scene 2) echoes the opening scene of the *Andria*.[37] In both plays a father feigns a future marriage in order to hinder his son's or would-be son-in-law's inopportune love. However, when juxtaposing the dialogues of the two plays, it becomes evident that the roles of conceiving and carrying out the stratagem are inverted. In the *Andria* the father thinks up the feigned marriage and asks his ex-slave Sosia to put it in practice.[38] By contrast,

[36] According to Giovini (2003), except for the *Sapientia*, which shows no trace of Terence, every drama evokes episodes from two or more Terentian comedies. Admittedly, the rudiments of some of the motifs may be latently present already in Hrotsvit's sources, but as Giovini's studies have shown, there can be no doubt that Hrotsvit's reworkings are original contributions that testify to a direct use of Terence. The presentation here relies partly on Giovini's results. To ensure the validity of my own examples, I have compared all the relevant passages of Hrotsvit with her sources.

[37] For a detailed analysis, see Giovini (2003) 79–103.

[38] Andria 157–8 + 168. Simo: *et nunc id operam do, ut per falsas nuptias / uera obiurgandi causa sit, si deneget (...) nunc tuomst officium has bene ut adsimules nuptias* ('Simo: And that's what I'm working on now: this fake marriage will provide real grounds for criticism, if he refuses it ... Now it's your job to make a good pretence of this wedding'). All quotations of Terence are from Kauer & Lindsay (1926). The translations are taken from Brown (2006).

in the *Gallicanus* it is the daughter Constantia who designs the plan and persuades her father to comply.[39]

The beginning of the *Dulcitius* resembles the opening of another Terentian play, the *Eunuchus*.[40] In the first scene of the *Eunuchus*, Phaedria has been rejected by his girl, the prostitute Thais, and complains about her insulting behaviour, but as soon as he catches sight of her in the second scene, the flames of love blaze up again; in the second scene of Hrotsvit's play, Dulcitius' corresponding fervour at the sight of the three girls is followed by a triple objection expressed by his soldiers (equivalent to Thais' locking out of Phaedria).[41] In both cases the rejection and unattainable love are followed by mental disturbance. Already in the first scene of the *Eunuchus*, Phaedria's slave Parmeno hints that his master's passion may turn into madness[42] and at the end of Act II, scene 1, this is what has happened: Parmeno hardly recognises the love-stricken Phaedria.[43] Similarly, Dulcitius, after leaving the pantry where he, out of his mind (*mente alienatus*), embraced the kitchenware, is no longer recognisable to his soldiers or to the guards of the palace. Interestingly, the guards' reaction lexically picks up

---

[39] Gallicanus 11.5–6. Constantia: *Simula prudenter, peracta expeditione ipsius uotis te satisfacturum esse, et, ut meum concordari credat uelle, suade, quo suas interim filias, Atticam ac Artemiam, uelut pro solidandi pignore amoris, mecum mansum ire meosque primicerios, Iohannem et Paulum, secum faciat iter arreptum ire. (...)* Constantinus: *Eam et Gallicanum laeta promissione circumueniam.* ('Constantia: Pretend prudently that you will fulfill his wish after he wins the war, and, so that he believes that I agreed to his plea, suggest to him that as pledges of his love, he let his two daughters Attica and Artemia live at court with me, while he accepts my chamberlains, John and Paul, in his retinue. ... Constantinus: I shall go and deceive Gallicanus with this joyful promise').

[40] For a detailed analysis, see Giovini (2003) 103–23.

[41] Compare *Eunuchus* 83–5 (Phaedria: ... *totus, Parmeno, / tremo horreoque, postquam aspexi hanc.* Parmeno: *bono animo es: / accede ad ignem hunc, iam calesces plus satis*; 'Phaedria: Parmeno, I'm all of a shiver, I tremble all over, now that I've caught sight of her! Parmeno: Cheer up! Draw nearer to this fire – you'll soon warm up more than enough!') and *Dulcitius* 1.1–2 (Dulcitius: *Captus sum illarum specie.* Milites: *Credibile.* Dulcitius: *Exaestuo illas ad mei amorem trahere.* Etc.; 'Dulcitius: I am captivated by their beauty. Soldiers: That is understandable. Dulcitius: To draw them to my love, I am eager. Etc').

[42] Cf. *Eunuchus* 59–63: Parmeno: *in amore haec omnia insunt uitia: iniuriae / suspiciones, inimicitiae, induatiae, / bellum, pax rursum: incerta haec si tu postules / ratione certa facere, nihilo plus agas / quam si des operam ut cum ratione insanias* ('Parmeno: Love contains all the following faults: wrongs, suspicions, enmities, truces, war, then peace again. These are uncertain things, and if you expected to make them certain by thinking about them you wouldn't get any further than if you worked on a method for being mad').

[43] Cf. *Eunuchus* 225–6: Parmeno: *di boni, quid hoc morbist? adeon homines inmutarier / ex amore ut non cognoscas eundem esse!* ('Parmeno: Ye gods, what sort of disease is this? To think that men can be so changed by love that you can't recognise them to be the same person!').

the parasite Gnatho's description of a fool from the scene that immediately follows in the *Eunuchus*.[44]

In the next scene (Act II, scene 3), Phaedria's younger brother Chaerea turns up all upset after having seen, followed, and lost track of the beautiful Pamphila on her way to Thais' house accompanied by Gnatho: Parmeno asks what troubles him, and Chaerea reveals his feelings. The efficient stichomythia *Eunuchus* 304–7 serves as a model for Hrotsvit's dramatisation of the enamoured Calimachus in sincere conversation with his friends (*Calimachus* II.1–2). In fact, both Chaerea and Calimachus declare their love by a straightforward *amo*.[45] What is more, the link between the two is strengthened by another analogy: they both resolve to rape their girl, the one inspired by an innocent joke (*Eunuchus* 369–78), the other by bribery (*Calimachus* VI.2).

Turning now to Hrotsvit's prostitutes Mary and Thais, it has been observed that in the *Adelphoe*, too, as in the *Abraham*, we find an indulgent uncle (Micio) who adopts his brother's child, and a girl (Bacchis) rescued from the brothel, and that both the *Eunuchus* and the *Pafnutius* open with a seemingly immoral harlot (both named Thais!) who turns out to be a good character.[46] But it is perhaps the disguise motif that constitutes the most obvious analogy of plot with a Terentian model.[47] Not unlike how Chaerea in the *Eunuchus* succeeds in raping Pamphila thanks to his disguise, the unnamed lover in the *Abraham* wins the favours of Mary owing to his monastic garb. In both cases the innocent appearance of a celibate man (a eunuch or a monk) allows the seduction to take place. Hrotsvit, however, has Mary rescued by the device of a sort of counter-disguise, or rather, a double disguise in the sense that it simulates a seduction: the second disguise annuls or reverses the first one. For when Hrotsvit has Abraham say that he will 'go to her, disguised as a lover' (*ipsam adeam sub specie amatoris*), she elaborates an antithetical play on sensual versus spiritual love and appearance versus intention: Abraham appears as a lover with the intention of rescuing Mary as opposed to the fraud who disguised himself as a monk in order to tempt her. The monk's disguise leads to perdition; Abraham's anti-disguise brings salvation. Similarly, in the *Pafnutius*, Thais' lovers bring damnation,

---

[44] Compare *Dulcitius* VI.1 (*quid hoc uile ac detestabile monstrum, scissis et nigellis panniculis obsitum?*; 'Who is this vile and detestable monster covered in torn and despicable rags?') with *Eunuchus* 236 (*uideo sentum squalidum aegrum, pannis annisque obsitum*; 'I saw that he was rough, filthy and seedy, overgrown with tatters and time'). Cf. Giovini (2003) 118–9.

[45] Coulter (1929) 523. For a detailed analysis, see Giovini (2003) 123–45.

[46] Dronke (1984) 72; Newlands (1986) 382ff.; Giovini (2003) 152ff.

[47] Coulter (1929) 524–7; de Luca (1974) 100–1; Bertini (1980) 87; Bean (1984) 388–9; Newlands (1986) 375ff.; Giovini (2003) 162ff.

as opposed to Pafnutius, Thais' true (i.e. spiritual) lover, who redeems the sinful prostitute (*Pafnutius* 1.25 + 28):

> PAF. Greges amatorum ad illam confluunt.
> DISC. Se ipsos perdunt. (...)
> PAF. Quid si illam adeam sub specie amatoris, si forte reuocari possit ab intentione nugacitatis?[48]

> PAF: Crowds of lovers flock to her, wishing to be near.
> DISC: Damning themselves in the process. (...)
> PAF: What if I visit her, disguised as a lover, to see if perchance she might be recovered from her worthless and frivolous life?[49]

Again, Hrotsvit uses the syntagma *adeam sub specie amatoris*, which both lexically and situationally picks up the Terentian *Hecyra* 716, where Phidippus persuades Laches to pay a visit to the prostitute Bacchis and persuade her to break off the affair she is having with his son.[50]

Towards the end of the *Abraham*, Hrotsvit elaborates a sort of biblical typology.[51] In scene 7, after the long and moving dialogue between Abraham and Mary in the bedroom, Abraham suggests that they begin their journey home, and Mary replies (*Abraham* VII.15): *Tuum est, pater amande, ut ad instar boni pastoris praecedas repertam ouem, et ego, paribus incedens uestigiis, subsequor praecedentem* (You, beloved father, must lead the way as the good shepherd leads the sheep gone astray; and I, advancing in your footsteps, will follow your lead). And the biblical imagery continues in Abraham's reply: *Haut ita; sed ego pedibus incedam, te autem equo superponam, ne itineris asperitas secet teneras plantas* (Not so; I will proceed on foot, but you will ride on my horse so that the sharp rocks of the road will not hurt your tender little feet). This allusion to the journey to Bethlehem[52] indicates that Hrotsvit associates the repentant Mary with Mary the mother of Jesus. Such an implicit association makes good sense in view of an earlier explicit association in scene 2, when Abraham and Effrem are convincing Mary to remain chaste (*Abraham* II.1–2):

---

[48] Berschin (2001) 226. [49] Wilson (1989) 103.

[50] *Hecyra* 716: *Quid agas? Meretricem hanc primum adeundam censeo* ('What are you to do? My proposal is that we should first approach this tart'). Cf. Giovini (2003) 165.

[51] For a discussion of typological elements in the *Abraham*, see Sticca (1971). For general discussions on typology in Hrotsvit's oeuvre, see Jennings (1998) and Talbot (2004).

[52] The image of Joseph letting Mary ride the donkey derives ultimately from the Protoevangelium of James 17:2.

ABRAHAM O adoptiua filia, o pars animę Maria, cede meis paternis mon-itionibus, meique comparis Effrem saluberrimis institucionibus et nitere, ut auctricem uirginitatis, quam ęquiuoco aequiperas nomine, imiteris et castitate.

EFFREM Multum disconuenit filia, ut quę cum dei genitrice Maria, per mysterium nominis praemines in axe inter sidera numquam casura, inferior meritis terrae uolutes in fimis.[53]

Abraham: Oh my adopted daughter, oh part of my soul, Mary, heed my fatherly admonitions and my companion Effrem's beneficial instructions. Strive to imitate in your chastity her who is the fount of virginity and whose name you bear.

Effrem: It would be most unfitting that you, daughter, who are joined to Mary, the mother of God, through your name's secret mystery and have been, thereby, raised to the axis of the sky among the stars that never set, should wish to debase yourself in your actions and sink to the lowest realms of the world.[54]

These lines prefigure the allusion of scene 7, and it is as if Hrotsvit is saying: 'Now, now is the time of Mary's true imitation of Mary!' In other words, this is when the whore becomes Madonna, and when Hrotsvit Christianises Terence.

Further Reading (* = in English)

Many good introductions to Hrotsvit exist, including Haight* (1965), Nagel (1965), Bertini (1980), Dronke* (1984), Wilson* (1984), and del Zotto (2009). Comprehensive analyses of Hrotsvit's oeuvre include Kuhn (1950), Michalka (1968), Wilson* (1988), Giovini (2003), and Wailes* (2006). There are also several articles on single dramas: Sticca* (1969, 1971, 1985), Beutner (1974), Chamberlain* (1980), Bertini (1985), Stura (1985), Robertini (1989), Simonetti (1989), Giovini (2001, 2006b), and Brown* (2004). Wilson* (ed., 1987) and Brown, McMillin, and Wilson* (eds., 2004) are fine contextual studies. Bisanti (2005) offers an outline of Hrotsvit studies from 1985 to 2005. After the completion of this chapter, two more titles have appeared: Augoustakis* (2013) and Brown and Wailes* (2012).

---

[53] Berschin (2001) 197.   [54] Wilson (1989) 72–3.

19

ROBERT S. MIOLA

Roman Comedy in Early Modern England

Plautus and Terence came to full and varied life in early modern England. In 1510–11 King's Hall, Cambridge, staged a production of Terence, the first known classical play performed at either Cambridge or Oxford. In 1522 Queens College, Cambridge, performed Plautus, perhaps *Miles Gloriosus*. The initial productions at Oxford came somewhat later: in 1559 Trinity College spent about twelve pounds 'for dresses and scenes in acting Terence's *Andria*, for the dinner of the Christmas Prince, and for the entertainment of the heads of the colleges and the most eminent doctors dining with the bursars or treasurers, at the time of acting the comedy'; in 1567–8, Merton College staged Plautus' *Menaechmi* with Richard Edwards' early tragicomedy *Damon and Pythias*. Before 1642 Cambridge staged thirty-three productions of Roman comedy (10 Terence, 23 Plautus) to Oxford's six (2 Terence, 4 Plautus).[1] Both ancient authors, however, occupied a central place in the grammar-school curriculum, though most schoolmasters, led by Erasmus, Scaliger, and Ascham, preferred Terence for the elegance of his Latin. 'I learned Terence i' the third form at Westminster' (Induction, 33–4), says a boy in Ben Jonson's *The Magnetic Lady* (1632); and Censure in the same playwright's *The Staple of News* (1626) crankily complains of student irresponsibility, 'We send them to learn their grammar and their Terence, and they learn their play-books' (3 Intermean, 37–8).[2]

Terence enjoyed a substantial head start on Plautus, of course, being the only Latin author besides Virgil whose complete surviving work appeared in a manuscript written before the sixth century. Some 650 manuscripts dating after 800 attest to Terence's enduring popularity from Late Antiquity into the Middle Ages. Plautus, by contrast, had to wait until 1429, when Nicolaus of Cusa discovered and put into circulation twelve previously unknown

---

[1] See Nelson (1989) II 963–76; Elliott (2004) II 846–55. The quotation is from Elliott I: 101.
[2] Quotations from Ben Jonson's works are cited to the new Cambridge edition (2012) and appear parenthetically in the text. On the grammar-school curriculum, see Baldwin (1944).

plays.³ Both Plautus and Terence supplied students in the early modern grammar school with complete dramas as well as discrete passages conveniently gathered in handbooks and florilegia. Nicholas Udall, for example, compiled for pupils at Eton *Flowers for Latin Speaking* (1533 often reprinted, and enlarged by John Higgins), which features conversational phrases culled line by line from Terence with some grammatical notes. The second scene of *Andria*, for example, furnishes everyday speech and the occasional reflection, for example, *Ades*, 'Come hither'; *Nunc non est narrandi locus*, 'It is no time nor place to show it or to tell it now'; *Spes mea me frustrata est*, 'My hope hath beguiled me' (1575, sigs. Aviir–v). In 1629 Joseph Webbe published editions of *Andria* and *Eunuchus* that present the Latin texts with full English translation on a grid of corresponding lines and columns for easier parsing and memorisation.

The classical playwrights who displayed so joyfully the workings of lust, avarice, and deceit on stage, of course, required careful handling for Christian students and audiences. Editors, teachers, compilers, translators, and adapters all practise elaborate strategies of containment and reformulation. The plays routinely appear with moralising commentary, and sometimes there is a prefatory word of caution. W. B.'s English version of *Menaechmi* (1595), for example, advertises itself on the title page, as 'Chosen purposely from out of the rest, as least harmful and most delightful.' In his *Defense of Poesy* (1595) Sir Philip Sidney articulates the standard argument that comedy serves a moral purpose by presenting vice in action:

> Now as in geometry the oblique must be known as well as the right, and in arithmetic the odd as well as the even, so in the actions of our life who seeth not the filthiness of evil wanteth a great foil to perceive the beauty of virtue. This doth the comedy handle so in our private and domestical matters as, with hearing it, we get as it were an experience, what is to be looked for of a niggardly Demea, of a crafty Davus, of a flattering Gnatho, of a vainglorious Thraso. (sig. F3v)

R. B.'s *Terence in English* (1598) similarly commends Terence,

> a comical poet, pithy, pleasant, and very profitable, as merry as Eutrapeles, as grave as Cato, as ethical as Plato; he can play craftily the cozener and cunningly the clown. He will tell you the nature of the fraudulent flatterer, the grim and greedy old sire, the roisting ruffian, the mincing minion and beastly bawd, that in telling the truth by these figments men might become wise to avoid such vices and learn to practice virtue. (sigs. ¶2r–v)

³ See Reynolds (1983); (1991).

Accordingly, R. B. glosses scenes with a moral exposition (*moralis expositio*) and a list of the moral lessons that can be found therein (*theses*). *Eunuchus* 4.5, for example, that wispy comic scene consisting of about a dozen lines from a drunk, flirtatious young Chremes, gives some serious moral instruction: *Ebrietas aufert memoriam, dissipat sensum, confundit intellectum, incitat libidinem, membraque debilitat omnia, atque uitam exterminat* (sig. L1v), 'drunkenness takes away the memory, dissipates the sense, confuses the intellect, arouses lust, weakens all the limbs, and extinguishes life'. Going a step further in his *Colloquia Plautina uiginti* (1646), Alexander Ross freely rearranges Plautine scenes and phrases into new creations for various didactic purposes. He also supplies commentary: one colloquy, for example, shows the uncertain condition of human life (*humanae uitae incerta conditio*), the exposure of youthful follies like drunkenness and lust, as well as the punishment of the pimp or *leno* (sig. *4).

So it is that Plautus and Terence first appear on the early modern popular stage sanitised and recontextualised for later (and Christian) audiences, as Bruce R. Smith has shown in some detail.[4] Alexander Nowell's prologues to performances of Terence at Westminster school in 1545 promise edification, as do the many adaptations of New Comedy, especially those in the movement that came to be known as 'Terence *moralisé*'. An early important illustration of this movement, running through some sixty editions in the sixteenth century, is Gulielmus Gnaphaeus' *Acolastus siue de filio prodigo* (1529). As its subtitle suggests, *Acolastus* recasts the New Comedic conflict between *senex* and *adulescens* as the biblical story of the Prodigal Son. The young man Acolastus falls prey to a New Comedic parasite and *meretrix* but finally repents and receives forgiveness from his father. In England, the New Comedic prodigal-son play takes the form of *Nice Wanton* (1560), *Misogonus* (1571), and George Gascoigne's *The Glass of Government* (1575). In Gascoigne's play, two fathers each send a pair of sons to study with Gnomaticus, a moral tutor. The younger sons in each pair – Philomusus ('Love-muse') and Philotimus ('Love-honour') – profit from the relentlessly moral regimen while the elder sons, Philautus ('Love-self') and Philosarchus ('Love-flesh'), rebel and come to bad ends. As in *Acolastus*, a New Comedic parasite (Echo) and *meretrix* (Lamia), here accompanied by a New Comedic *lena*, Pandarina, lead the youths to their eventual destruction.

Gascoigne invokes Terence directly three times in the play, beginning with the Prologue, which rejects the 'deformed shows' of classical times as morally inappropriate for the present:

---

[4] Smith (1988). On related conflicts and accommodations, see Beck (1973) and Hardin (2007).

I mean for to present
No Terence phrase; his time and mine are twain.
The verse that pleased a Roman rash intent
Might well offend the godly preacher's vein.
Deformed shows were then esteemed much.
Reformed speech doth now become us best. (sig. Aiiiv)

The tutor Gnomaticus, however, cautiously approves the ancient author: 'out of Terence may also be gathered many moral instructions amongst the rest of his wanton discourses, yet the true Christian must direct his steps by the infallible rule of God's word' (sig. Bi[v]). And the Chorus remembers that Terence, 'whose lore is not refused' (sig. Ciii), taught the difference between successful parents' care and masters' bodes ('instructions') abused. *The Glass of Government*, then, admits indebtedness to Roman comedy while proclaiming independence from it. At the end of this play some of the Terentian characters receive condign punishment: Echo receives a whipping; Lamia and Pandarina suffer the cucking stool in the market for three days before banishment. Gascoigne's paradoxical attitude of reliance and rejection is typical of the age and its appropriations. Thus the whirligig of time brings in its revenges.

The paradoxical mixture of reliance and rejection that characterises *The Glass of Government* appears as well in the anonymous *Jack Juggler* (1553–61). This play reworks an episode from Plautus' *Amphitryo*, wherein the servant Sosia returns home only to find a double in his place, the god Mercury in disguise. Similarly, Jack Juggler steals the identity of the servant Jenkin Caraway, takes his place in the master's home, and beats him as a madman. Both servants respond with protestation, frustration, and helpless bewilderment. Jenkin pleads, 'Or else tell me, if I be not he, / What my name from henceforth shall be?'[5] The remembrance of Plautus, however, is highly selective and adaptive. Perhaps mindful of the children first presenting the interlude, the anonymous author omits the main plot of *Amphitryo* – Jupiter's impersonation of the husband, his liaison with the wife, and the consequent birth of Hercules. He adds some English characters – a maid (Alison Trip-and-go), a gentlewoman (Dame Coy), and a gallant (Master Bongrace); invoking native medieval moral traditions, he identifies Jack Juggler on the title page (1565) as 'the Vice'. Citing Cicero, the Prologue defends comedy as 'very honest disport … replenished with precepts of philosophy' and 'much wisdom' (5). Moralising the entire action, the

---

[5] The text of *Jack Juggler* is based on that of Farmer (1906) 1–40 (22). Further references to this edition appear parenthetically in this chapter.

Epilogue laments the frequent deluding of innocents by the deceitful and powerful.

Beyond this general moral framing, the play engages contemporary theological controversy, specifically the doctrine of the Holy Eucharist. Rebuking Caraway for his incredible story, Master Bongrace says that Caraway has been deluded by a dream or a shadow (31) and threatens to rap him on his 'lying knave's snout' (32). He echoes contemporary attacks on the doctrine of transubstantiation and the very idea of discontinuous multilocation:

> Why, thou naughty villain, darest thou affirm to me
> That which was never seen nor hereafter shall be:
> That one man may have two bodies and two faces?
> And that one man at one time may be in two places? (30)

Summarising earlier critical observations, William N. West remarks that Protestants typically derided Catholic beliefs about the Eucharist as 'juggling':

> Nicholas Udall, a leading candidate for Jack Juggler's authorship, attacks 'the iuglyng sleyghtes of the Romish Babylon'; Thomas Cranmer, Archbishop of Canterbury, deviser of the *Book of Common Prayer*, and (eventually) Protestant martyr, protests that to follow 'the foolishness of the Papistes ... As that two bodies be in one place, and one body in many places at one tyme' is to treat Christ as 'a crafty iuglar, that made thinges to appere to mens sightes, that in dede were no suche thynges, but formes only'. Indeed, Cranmer refers specifically to the play that *Jack Juggler* calls its source text, Plautus's *Amphitruo*, as an analogue to the deception demanded by belief in transubstantiation.[6]

For a few remarkable moments *Jack Juggler* inflects Roman comedy into a theological satire that serves the regnant political power and the Church of England.

Adopting Roman comedies as their models, early modern playwrights sometimes attempted more complex accommodations. Both Shakespeare and Jonson look to Plautus for their early essays in dramatic comedy: *The Comedy of Errors* (1594) draws on *Amphitryo* and *Menaechmi*; *The Case Is Altered* (1597), on *Captiui* and *Aulularia*. George Chapman, however, looks to Terence: *All Fools* (1605) draws on *Heauton Timorumenos* and *Adelphoe*.

Shakespeare's *The Comedy of Errors* replays the lock-out scene in *Amphitryo*, when Antipholus of Ephesus and his servant return home to find the door shut and an insulting servant within (3.2). The identical twins in

---

[6] West (2009) 105. West cites Cranmer from *An Answer ... unto a crafty and sophistical cavillation devised by Stephen Gardiner* (1551) 299, 307, and 63–4.

Menaechmi get doubled in *Errors*, and the resulting confusions multiply exponentially. From 'Apollonius of Tyre' Shakespeare adds a frame plot that contributes missing parents, likewise split apart for many years. He transforms the *medicus* into Doctor Pinch, also a zany pedant who confidently pronounces one of the twins possessed and tries an exorcism, only to get slapped and later singed for his pains. Shakespeare transforms the female roles in Plautus' play to explore the mysteries and madness of love. He changes Erotium into the Courtesan, who provides some laughs and tells the only deliberate lie in the play. He greatly expands the nagging *matrona* into the complicated wife Adriana, who mistakes her husband for his twin, accuses him of infidelity, and receives finally a comic exposure for her jealousy ('She did betray me to my own reproof').[7] Shakespeare adds Luciana, Adriana's sister, to provide a love interest for the single twin, and also the spherical and sweating Nell, interested in love with the wrong Dromio. And, finally, he adds Emilia, certainly a surprise to the audience, the long-lost mother of the Antipholus twins, wife to the imprisoned Egeon, and now the Abbess who presides over the final reconciliations and reunions. In some views and productions (Tim Supple's 1996 Royal Shakespeare Company show, for example), the movement to the priory and to Abbess crowns scattered Christian resonances in the play (whose earliest recorded performances occurred on Holy Innocents' Day, December 28, during Christmas revels); the movement to the priory may also tilt the farce to a wondrous exploration of Providential care and kindness.

Two plays of Plautus likewise inspire Ben Jonson's earliest surviving comedy, *The Case Is Altered* (1597).[8] *Captiui* supplies the overplot featuring the wars between the French and the Milanese (originally the Aetolians and Elians) and also supplies the switch in identities between the captured master and servant (4.1). Plautus' slave (Tyndarus) is *callidus* (clever), hoping to receive for his pains, manumission, while Jonson's servant (Gaspar) is noble and self-sacrificing. The masters disguised as servants get released, while the servants disguised as masters remain imprisoned. After the ruse is revealed, the angry captors threaten torture but discover finally that the prisoners are long-lost sons. Plautus explores the social realities of slavery while Jonson co-opts the plot into a romantic comedy that includes some humorous characters, another lost child recovered (Isabel), as well as multiple marriages.

Plautus' *Aulularia*, specifically the characters of Euclio and Phaedria, supplies the scenes involving the miser Jaques and his daughter Rachel.

---

[7] 5.1.90. For all references to Shakespeare, I use Bevington's edition (2003), hereafter cited parenthetically in the text. For further discussion of *The Comedy of Errors*, see Miola (1994) 19–38.

[8] See Lumley (1901) 71–111.

In both plays the miser keeps his daughter in the house, receives suitors warily, hides his gold, examines a potential thief, and rages at the loss of his treasure. But Jonson practises an inventive *imitatio*. Characters play roles in both Plautine plots. The father-captor in the *Captiui* plot is also a suitor for the daughter in the *Aulularia* plot; Jaques is Euclio, the miser, but also Stalagmus, the former servant of the disguised master's father. The low comedy of Strobilius Jonson expands into the low comedy of Juniper and Onion. He also heightens the romance: unlike her prototype, Phaedria, Rachel has five suitors in love with her; Jonson adds other female characters to the action (Aurelia and Phoenixella). Multiple recognitions play in a grand sequence of reversals that prompts characters to declare 'the case is altered' no fewer than six times in the final act. In these early adaptations both Shakespeare and Jonson expand female roles, emphasise the love interest, combine, sophisticate, and multiply in unpredictable ways.

So too George Chapman, poet, playwright, and distinguished translator of Homer. Reconfiguring Terence's *Adelphoe* and *Heauton Timorumenos*, Chapman's festive comedy, *All Fools* (1605) provides a final example of creative *contaminatio*. The contrasting brothers of *Adelphoe* who exemplify different styles of fatherhood, one harsh, one mild, appear here as Gostanzo and Marc Antonio. As in Terence's play, the harsh brother, Gostanzo, gets tricked by a witty son and receives comedic exposure. *Heauton Timorumenos* supplies the two secret love affairs managed through various deceptions, as well as some characters. Bacchis the courtesan becomes Gratiana, Valerio's secret wife; Chremes' daughter Antiphila, exposed as an infant but finally restored to her parents by accident, becomes Bellanora, locked away from the world in her father's home; the tricky slave Syrus becomes Rinaldo, the quick-witted deceiving son. These changes enable a series of tricks and plot twists until the final sorting out and two weddings. Chapman adds a subplot starring the madly jealous Cornelio and his long-suffering wife Gazetta and some comic types, Pock the surgeon and a Notary. In accordance with the title, *All Fools*, he extends the indictment of folly to the audience itself. Quoting Persius, the Prologue asks, *Auriculas asini quis non habet?* (sig. A3v), 'Who does not have the ears of an ass?'. And the Epilogue leaves the audience with the unspoken word 'fools' ringing in their minds, if not their ears: 'We can but bring you meat, and set you stools, / And to our best cheer say, you are all—welcome' (sig. K1v). Chapman transforms Terence's thoughtful dramas into satirical city comedy.[9]

---

[9] So too the playwright Thomas Middleton, whose *Michaelmas Term* (1604) features a cynical reworking of the Terentian prodigal son; whose *No Wit, No Help Like a Woman's* (1611) features the enabling of marriages by the restoration of lost girls' identities.

The prolific Thomas Heywood, who claimed to have had 'an entire hand or at the least a main finger' in 220 plays ('To the Reader,' *The English Traveller*), also turned to Roman comedy for inspiration and imitation. *The Silver Age* (1613) combines *Amphitryo* with The Rape of Persephone, adding dumb shows, spectacles, and other myths.[10] In this play Juno and Iris descend from heaven, and Juno threatens retribution for her husband's dalliance with Alcmena. She attempts to hinder the birth of Hercules but fails. The infant Hercules then strangles the serpents Iris brings from Africa, grows up, and takes on other labours. *The Silver Age* is more pageant than drama, part of a five-play mythological sequence of classical themes and incidents, loosely organised according to the Four Ages, and introduced by the recurring figure of Homer. Heywood turns to Plautus again, this time to *Mostellaria*, for a diverting subplot in his domestic tragedy, *The English Traveller* (1633). As in Plautus' play, the son and tricky slave convince the returning father that the noisy revellers inside his house are actually haunting spirits. Again increasing the spectacle, Heywood presents on stage the rioters' escape from the house: with a key in hand, Reignald ushers Young Lionell, Blanda, Scapha, Rioter, and two Gallants out the back: 'Now is the gaol delivery. Through this back gate, / Shift for yourselves. I here unprison all' (71). Like his counterpart in Plautus, Tranio, the *callidus seruus*, Reignald, gets off without punishment.

Plautus supplies the main plot of Heywood's most complicated and thoroughgoing adaptation of Roman New Comedy, *The Captives, or The Lost Recovered* (1624). Modelled closely on *Rudens*, Heywood's play emphasises the beauty and moral character of the heroine: Palestra lives 'like to a rich and precious jewel lost' (1.1.34), replete with 'such sweet feature, goodness, modesty, / Such gentleness, such virtue' (42–3); 'She is that miracle, the only one' (111). Her companion, Scribonia (Plautus' Ampelisca), also receives more attention than the Plautine original: she turns out to be Palestra's long-lost cousin, Winifred, daughter to Thomas Ashburne, and the future wife of Treadway, a character apparently invented for her. Plautus' mute and off-stage *matrona* becomes the shrewish Isabel. As he heightens the romance, Heywood attempts to convert the Latin metrical music into new forms: Palestra and Scribonia sing a plea that finds answer in the cheerless, sung responses of Friar John offstage (2.1.88ff.); a monastic choir sings in Latin with music (2.1.189–90); Palestra and Mildew have an offstage duet at the time of the maidens' recapture (3.2.46ff.); Gripus sings in praise of poverty

---

[10] I cite *The English Traveller* from Heywood (1874), IV, and *The Captives* from Judson's edition (1921), hereafter parenthetically in the text. For discussion of Heywood's use of Roman comedy, see Gilbert (1913) and Rowland (1995).

a ballad, 'though set to a scurvy tune': 'Let each man speak as he's possessed; / I hold the poor man's state most blessed' (4.1.417ff.).

Heywood makes other changes to the Plautine original. The Temple of Venus becomes a monastery, the scene of a darkly comic subplot from Masuccio di Salerno. Friar John and Friar Richard hate each other and fight constantly, despite the pious Abbott's warnings and attempts at regulation. Lusting after Lady Averne, the founder of the monastery, Friar John attempts to arrange a tryst. Discovering his intentions, Lord Averne strangles the lecherous Friar John and dumps him in the monastery privy. Friar Richard finds him there, assaults the body, and then mistakenly thinks he has killed him. When Friar Richard faces punishment for the murder, Lord Averne confesses, but his good wife brings a pardon for him from the King. The main plot and subplot independently co-exist, intersecting briefly and inconsequentially when Palestra and Scribonia seek refuge in the monastery. Heywood departs finally from Plautus to resolve the *Rudens* action: there Labrax gets beaten but remains a mercenary pimp to the end, when he finally gets some money for the girls and an invitation to dinner. Heywood's *leno*, Mildew, however, confesses his theft of the girls, reveals Scribonia's true identity, and claims to have experienced a change of heart: 'I will resolve you like a convertite, / Not as the man I was' (5.3.183–4). Heywood, however, simply dismisses him from the story and focuses on the reunion of Lord Averne and his wife, and that of the two Ashburne families – brothers, fathers and daughters, cousins.

Such direct adaptation of specific Roman comedies constitutes only one kind of *imitatio* evident on the early modern English stage. Plautus and Terence defined comedy for later generations as domestic urban drama, containing a plot drawn from everyday circumstances, a conflict concerning love and money, and ending in restorations of identity and marriages. They set out a basic structure, capable of wide variation, consisting of a prologue, *protasis* (introduction), *epitasis* (complication), *catastrophe* (resolution) – complete with *anagnorisis* (recognition) and *peripeteia* (reversal) – and finally an epilogue. They contributed stock character types – the grasping pimp, braggart soldier, scheming courtesan, clever servant, love-struck youth, angry father, shrewish mother, and meek girl. Often these types appear in combination with non-classical figures drawn from poetry or prose fiction, as in Heywood's *The Captives*, in actions far removed from their origins. The classical plots and characters appear intermediated through other texts and mixed with other traditions.

One such figure who appears in various guises and situations is the *miles gloriosus*, or braggart soldier.[11] Plautus' *Miles Gloriosus* (based on the

---

[11] See Boughner (1954).

anonymous *Alazon*) and Terence's *Eunuchus*, both favourites among Renaissance translators and adapters, presented influential prototypes – Pyrgopolynices and Thraso. Typically the New Comedic *miles gloriosus* brags about his prowess in war and in love but proves to be embarrassingly inept in both. He generally suffers painful exposure: slaves thrash Pyrgoplynices, for example, and send him on his way; Thais's friends repel Thraso's assault on her house. The classical *miles gloriosus* generated many descendants who swaggered their way across the stages of Europe – Capitano Spavento of the Italian *commedia dell'arte*, the Spanish dandies, *bravi* (thugs), and captains of the Italian *commedia erudita*, the vaunting soldiers of the *comedias de capa y espada* (the cloak-and-sword plays) in Spain, the braggarts of the Pléiade and other French playwrights. Early on in England the blustering Thersites (*Thersites*, 1537) meets a real soldier who bashes and abashes him; the vainglorious suitor, Ralph Roister Doister, similarly meets his match in the virtuous Dame Christian Custance, who routs and beats him (*Ralph Roister Doister*, 1552). Other playwrights variously present the braggart soldier in their plays. Ben Jonson's Bobadilla affects expertise in the fashionable art of duelling in *Every Man In His Humour* (1598); Quintiliano dodges his creditors and schemes for money in Chapman's *May-Day* (1611); the cowardly boaster Bessus contrasts with the good soldier Mardonius and the reformed braggart Arbaces in Beaumont and Fletcher's *A King and No King* (1619).

Shakespeare provides variations of the *miles gloriosus* in Don Adriano de Armado (*Love's Labour's Lost*, 1588–97) and the noisy Pistol (*All's Well That Ends Well*, 1601–5), but his most complex and enduring braggart soldier is Falstaff, who appears in three plays, *1 Henry IV* (1596–7), *2 Henry IV* (1597–8), and *The Merry Wives of Windsor* (1597–1601). Part classical parasite, part medieval Vice, part folk Lord of Misrule, Falstaff blusters through the history plays. He invents a fantastic tale to cover his cowardice at Gadshill; he drinks sack and makes merry with the Hostess and others while distracting Prince Hal from the serious business of rule. He plays dead to avoid fighting. He misuses the king's press, collecting bribes for exemptions, and fielding finally an army of sick paupers: 'food for powder, food for powder. They'll fill a pit as well as better. Tush. Man, mortal men, mortal men' (*1HIV*, 4.2.64–6). He dies, we hear in *Henry V*, poor and alone. But Falstaff has a serious role to play in these plays, interrogating as he does the entire ethos of military honour that motivates the action and other characters. 'What is honour? A word. What is in that word, "honour"? What is that "honour"? Air' (*1HIV*, 5.1.133–5). This incarnation of the *miles gloriosus* raises searching questions about the nature of fame, heroism, and military action. And Falstaff does not remain dead for long. Shakespeare resurrects the medieval knight in *The Merry Wives of Windsor*, relocates him in Elizabethan England, and portrays him as a would-be lover, thus recuperating the amorous folly of the classical prototype. Falstaff suffers a series of exposures at the hands of the merry wives: hiding in a basket of dirty laundry he gets dumped in a river; he receives a beating while disguised as the fat woman of Brenford; dressed ridiculously as Herne the Hunter, he gets pinched and singed.

As the character of Falstaff suggests, early modern comedy frequently features fluent naturalisations of Plautus and Terence. Ben Jonson's *The Alchemist*, for another example, brilliantly adapts classical character and action to early Jacobean London.[12] The *meretrix* appears here as Doll Common, adept as her predecessors in disguise and trickery. 'A wench is a rare bait, with which a man / No sooner's taken, but he straight firks [runs] mad' (2.4.4–5). The *seruus callidus* becomes the servant Jeremy disguised as Face, relying on rhetoric, quick wit, and acting ability for his deceits. The victims are a group of contemporary gulls who parade on and off stage – Dapper, the lawyer's clerk, Drugger the tobacconist, Sir Epicure Mammon, the Anabaptists Ananias and Tribulation Wholesome. Along with the alchemist Subtle, Face fosters illusions and stokes desire for the philosopher's stone that can turn base metals to gold. Like Plautus' *Mostellaria*, with which it shares specific similarities, *The Alchemist* features the return of the absent master. In both plays the master knocks on the door and greets his surprised servant, who immediately invents a story to cover the noise and conceal the foolery going on in the house. At one point Face even echoes Tranio, the Plautine slave: 'Nothing's more wretched than a guilty conscience' (5.2.47); *Nihil est miserius quam animus hominis conscius / Sicut me habet* (*Most.* 544–5) The Plautine revelry within the house here yields to deceptions that cross and multiply in dazzling succession. Both Tranio and Face get discovered and deserve punishment, but they get off scot-free in the end. Plautine comedy thus serves Jonson in a glorious display of human wit and folly.

Early modern playwrights did not restrict so rich and potent a source as New Comedy to simple generic confines. Plautus and Terence inspire Renaissance tragicomedy as well as comedy, and even inspire tragedy. Nor should this surprise us. Shakespeare, Sidney, and Scaliger, Stephen Orgel observes, regard genre as a set of possibilities not as a set of rules.[13] Accordingly, early modern playwrights variously integrate New Comedic situations, characters, and motifs into tragedy. The New Comedic configuration featuring blocking fathers, young girls, and importunate lovers, for

---

[12] See Lumley (1901) 63–71.   [13] Orgel (1979).

example, richly supplies *Hamlet*. Polonius plays the blocking father (*senex iratus*), Ophelia the maiden (*uirgo*), and Hamlet the young man in love (*adulescens*). But Polonius completely misjudges both his daughter and her suitor, and his interference has tragic consequences for all. Ophelia may be a *uirgo*, but unlike those largely colourless and mute prototypes, her musical descent into madness suggests unprecedented depths of thwarted desire and suffering. And Hamlet both puts on and takes off the role of lover, the changes expressing both his cruelty and his anguish. The systematic deconstruction of the New Comedic configuration heightens audience perplexity and its sense of loss.

John Ford's *'Tis Pity She's a Whore* (1633) exhibits this configuration adapted (or perverted) almost beyond recognition. The blocking *senex* is a different kind of father, Friar Bonavantura, who begins the play by sternly warning the *adulescens* (Giovanni) to give up his amorous passion. Since this passion is an incestuous love for the youth's sister, the Friar's arguments are spiritual and moral, rather than pragmatic and financial. This blocking *senex* threatens damnation not disinheritance. Like his predecessors Giovanni energetically defends his passion, ignores the reasonable admonitions, and proceeds with courtship. Unlike them, he achieves an incestuous union. Like many of her predecessors, the sister, Annabella, has a number of suitors and gets pregnant; unlike them she passionately returns her brother's love, carries his child, and marries another to hide her deeds. The *seruus callidus* enters the action in the person of Vasquez, who pretends to help a jilted woman get revenge on his master, her former lover, but he treacherously poisons her instead. The New Comedic configuration comes to a similarly bloody conclusion that measures the great distance travelled from its origins: Annabella writes a warning letter in blood to her brother; he stabs her during a kiss and brings her skewered heart onstage. John Ford deploys the standard New Comedic configuration to explore the darkest potentialities of human passion.

Roman comedy flourished in early modern England, as it did in Italy, France, Spain, and Germany. Plautus and Terence bequeathed to later ages conventional situations and stock characters, a dense, expressive, and infinitely malleable set of dramatic codes. From the early efforts of schoolmasters, chrestomathers, and moralisers through to the first imitations, Gascoigne's *The Glass of Government* and the anonymous *Jack Juggler*, the appropriation is fervent and transformative. Later playwrights – William Shakespeare (*The Comedy of Errors*), Ben Jonson (*The Case is Altered*), and George Chapman (*All Fools*) – combine pairs of classical plays with native traditions. They emphasise the romantic interest and adapt ancient laughter to contemporary situations. The comedy of Plautus and Terence furnishes later ages with infinitely variable plots and characters: Plautus' *Mostellaria* inspires Heywood's *The English Traveller* as well as Jonson's comic masterpiece, *The Alchemist*. The *miles gloriosus*, 'the braggart soldier', swaggers on many stages in many forms before achieving apotheosis in Shakespeare's Falstaff. Roman comedy even furnishes early modern tragedy: the *senex-adulescens-uirgo* configuration controverted lends pathos to *Hamlet*; the configuration perverted supplies dark energy to *'Tis Pity She's a Whore*. The reception of Roman comedy, by any measure, constitutes a master narrative in the history of early modern drama.

Further Reading

T. W. Baldwin (1944) has written a foundational study on the educational curricula in England. Marvin Herrick (1960) and Louise George Clubb (1989) have explored the influence of Roman comedy in Italy. Bruce Smith (1988) reviews early modern adaptations and productions of Roman comedy. R. Hardin (2007) examines the critical controversy ignited by the discovery of Plautus regarding comic language and plots, audience response, and the nature of laughter. Some scholars have concentrated on Plautus and Terence in Shakespeare, among them Salingar (1974), Riehle (1990), and Miola (1994). Eleanor Lumley (1901) has done the same for Ben Jonson, George Rowe (1979) for Thomas Middleton. For work on other early modern playwrights and Roman comedy, one can consult the Modern Language Association bibliography, available online: https://www.mla.org/.

20

CÉLINE CANDIARD

Roman Comedy in Early Modern Italy and France

Much like today, at the end of the Middle Ages, Roman comedy was alive mostly in schools and universities. Several important discoveries, such as that of twelve Plautus comedies by Nicholas Cusanus in 1429 and that of Donatus' commentary on Terence by Giovanni Aurispa in 1433, fuelled the interest of scholars in Roman comedy.[1] In the Renaissance, European universities and schools provided the matrix for a new kind of theatre based on ancient models: ancient plays by Plautus and Terence were read, studied, translated, and performed there, so that scholars were progressively replacing the theatrical paradigm of medieval farce and morality plays with a new one and thus played a key role in the birth of modern comedy.

Plautus and Terence in Schools

In Italian universities and schools, from the fifteenth century onwards through the entire early modern period, the plays of Plautus and Terence were primarily valued for their linguistic benefit. Despite being in verse, they were seen as good examples of everyday conversation. Terence was particularly prized for the purity of his language and Plautus for his variety and inventiveness, which had already been praised by Cicero.[2] The fictional situations of Roman comedy, which stages young men facing their own passions against the opposition of their fathers, were also used for moral teaching, although often only after much expurgating and rearranging. Lastly, the performance of Roman comedies was, along with more edifying, religious texts, considered good training for diction, physical attitude, and public speech.

In Renaissance France, while Terence was prominent in the syllabus at the Université de Paris and its secondary-teaching *collèges*, Plautus was often

---

[1] On Donatus, see Manuwald in this volume.
[2] Cicero, *Off.* 1, 104. See Hurka in this volume.

kept for the more advanced classes or not taught at all. This may partly be due to Horace's harsh judgement of Plautus as crude and unsubtle, for his influence on French humanists was particularly strong.[3] Terence's texts were generally used for grammar teaching in the first years of secondary school. In the seventeenth century, he was the most frequently studied Latin author, along with Cicero, in the *Petites Ecoles* of Port-Royal (a prestigious, innovative teaching system set up by Jansenist intellectuals at Port-Royal-des-Champs, outside Paris), and the second author to be published in the collection of classical texts created for the education of the dauphin, the heir apparent to the French throne. The only exceptions are Jesuit schools, which accounted for one third of secondary schools in early modern France, for which Ignatius of Loyola expressly forbade the use of texts from Roman comedy, arguing that they could be morally disturbing for young souls; but the reluctance of Jesuit masters to comply with this ban led to its abolition in 1703, and shows the fundamental place Terence held in classical education. As late as 1775, Diderot emphasised the Latin playwright's importance in his own education, remembering how he was 'from a very young age raised on the milk of Homer, Virgil, Horace, Terence, Anacreon, Plato, Euripides, blended with that of Moses and the prophets'.[4]

In both Italy and France, the strong presence of Roman comedy in school syllabi played a significant role in the development of national comedy that contrasted with the medieval theatrical genres. Indeed, reading and commenting on ancient texts from a very young age allowed the cultivated public to be familiar with the domestic plots and characters in Roman comedy, which soon became the basis of most Italian and French comedies. During the whole early modern period, Roman comedy operated as a theatrical paradigm through the vehicle of secondary school, which most playwrights and even some actors attended, and was thus able to impose a set of standards and audience expectations which then served as a backdrop for innovation and experimentation.

In addition, the very first modern performances of ancient comedies occurred in schools and universities: the first we know of was a performance of Terence's *Andria* in Florence by the students of Giorgio Vespucci's school in 1476, which was followed by several similar events in Italy during the 1480s. In France, it seems that such performances were less frequent, although there are testimonies of a few performances of Roman comedies, such as an undetermined play by Terence that was performed by the students of the Verdun cathedral school in 1514. Such theatrical experiments had limited audiences, all the more since the plays were performed in

---

[3] Horace *Ars Poetica* 270–4.   [4] Diderot (1971) XI 797.

Latin by young amateurs in a pedagogical context. However their novelty made those events memorable enough to be recorded, and they did directly inspire the more lavish productions which took place in princely courts shortly afterwards, particularly in Italy, in cities such as Ferrara, Florence, Mantua, and Rome.

Printed Publications and Modern Translations

The spread of Roman comedy, fostered by schools and universities, really took a decisive turn with the first printed publications of Plautus' and Terence's plays. The very first edition of Terence's six comedies was printed in Strasbourg in 1470 (then a free imperial city of the Holy Roman Empire), and this was immediately followed by several publications in Italy – particularly in Venice – as early as 1471. Plautus' twenty comedies were then published soon afterwards in Venice, in 1472.

Terence's works were particularly popular in both Italy and Spain in the early modern period. Between 1470 and 1600 alone, they appeared in no fewer than 520 editions, two-thirds of which were printed in Italy and France. Although Italian publishers were a little ahead of their French counterparts, editions of Terence flourished in Lyon and Paris from the 1490s onwards. A French translation of his six comedies (*Therence en françoys*) was published in Paris in 1503, followed by several other scholarly publications such as the translation of Terence's *Andria* by Charles Estienne in 1542, which featured an explanatory introduction on the performance of comedies in antiquity.

Plautus, on the other hand, took longer to reach the French public. Although regularly published in Italy since the end of the fifteenth century, in France his works first appeared in print in Lyon in 1513, through a pirated version of an Italian edition, probably brought by Italian merchants and bankers who flocked to the city during the Renaissance. The first truly scholarly edition of Plautus' twenty comedies by Robert Estienne (Paris 1530) was reprinted less frequently than his edition of Terence published the year before. What is more, Plautus' complete works were not translated into French before Michel de Marolles' bilingual edition in 1658; until then, Plautus' plays were largely inaccessible to anyone who did not read Latin fluently. This French lack of interest in Plautus contrasts with the playwright's great popularity in Italy, where several translations in prose and in verse came out as early as the mid-1520s.

There are several explanations for this difference in reception. Readers' preferences for certain ancient authors, for example, might have been groomed by the school syllabi. The main reason, however, is probably the different status of comedy and of theatre in general in Italy and France.

In Renaissance Italy, ancient comedy (along with other forms) was soon considered to be a vehicle for princely families to display their power advantageously. Between 1486 and 1505, the Duke Ercole d'Este had no fewer than fourteen comedies by Plautus and Terence performed in Italian translation in front of his courtiers, enriched by musical interludes and ballets. Thus, at a very early date, Roman comedy was integrated into national and local cultural life, and this allowed Italian readers and spectators to appreciate fully the comic efficiency of Plautus' plays.

The situation was completely different in France, where comedy remained the domain of scholars and pedagogues until the end of the sixteenth century. French humanists, who leant on ancient texts in order to give their national literature more aesthetic poise and moral value, mostly approached the two Roman playwrights from a theoretical angle. On the whole, they deemed Terence to be more refined and morally edifying than Plautus. Montaigne considers him 'much more gentleman-like',[5] while Jacques Peletier du Mans criticises Plautus for 'carrying jokes to the point of scurrility'.[6] Even after the Renaissance this marked preference of French scholars for Terence remained, as is illustrated by d'Aubignac's *Pratique du Théâtre* (1657), which describes Terence as 'the better model'.[7] In Italy, however, both Plautus and Terence functioned as key models for writing comedy. Thus, in his *Mémoires*, Goldoni mentions reading 'Plautus, Terence, Aristophanes and Menander's fragments' eagerly in his youth, already planning to write for the theatre as an adult.[8]

A Model for Playwrights

Indeed, the general interest in Roman comedy during the Renaissance was not limited to reading plays and examining ancient theatrical practices. Soon after the first publications of Roman comedy, and much like the reception of other literary genres such as epic and lyric poetry, humanists adopted it as the new example to follow in order to give their national theatre more quality and prestige. French poet Joachim Du Bellay thus writes to his imaginary ideal disciple:

> As for comedies and tragedies, if kings and republics would restore them to their ancient dignity, which farces and morality plays have usurped, I would like you to work on them, and if you will do it to adorn your national language, you know where you must find their archetypes.[9]

---

[5] Montaigne, *Essays*, 2, 10. [6] Peletier du Mans (1555) II 7.
[7] D'Aubignac (2001) 333. [8] Carlo Goldoni (1787) part I.
[9] Joachim du Bellay (1549) I 4.

Although Du Bellay never wrote any drama, many Renaissance playwrights used the plays of Plautus and Terence as archetypes in order to reform contemporary theatre. The *palliata* was actually put forward as the chief model for the newly formed '*comédie régulière*' ('regular comedy', i.e. following ancient rules and models of composition, as opposed to medieval comic genres like farce).

This explains why, during the whole early modern period, Roman plays were often rewritten and adapted for modern audiences. In Florence, Machiavelli borrowed the plot from Plautus' *Casina* to write his *Clizia*, published in 1525 but probably performed ten years earlier. The Venetian playwright Ludovico Dolce produced a series of plays inspired by Plautus: *Il Ragazzo* (*The Boy*, 1541) also based on *Casina, Il Capitano* (*The Captain*, 1545) based on the *Miles Gloriosus, Il Marito* (*The Husband*, 1560) adapted from *Amphitruo*, and *Il Ruffiano* (*The Pimp*, 1560) adapted from *Rudens*. Even some cultivated political leaders, following Ercole d'Este in Ferrara, tried their hand at modernising ancient comedies, such as Lorenzino de' Medici whose *Aridiosa* (1536) is a contemporary version of Plautus' *Mostellaria*. Some of these adaptations are more complex, mixing elements from two or three Roman plays in one comedy in the same way that Roman comedy often 'contaminates' (brings together) several Greek models to create a single new play. This is the case with Ariosto's *Suppositi* (*The Changelings*, 1509), performed at the Este court in Ferrara, which borrows from both *Captiui* and *Eunuchus*. Although contemporary testimonies suggest that the Italian courtiers were more interested in the spectacular interludes featuring professional musicians, singers, and dancers than in the plays themselves that were performed by learned amateurs, these adaptations nevertheless represent a serious effort to update ancient material for the contemporary stage: plots are transposed to an urban Italian context with servants instead of slaves, and the text, generally in prose, is designed to recreate the natural tone of everyday conversation.

Frequently, French playwrights from the Renaissance followed the Italian example. When Jean-Antoine de Baïf adapted Plautus' *Miles Gloriosus* in *Le Brave* (*The Braggart*) in 1567, he set the play in Orléans, gave his characters French-sounding names like 'Taillebras' ('Arm-cutter') for the braggart soldier and 'Finet' ('Crafty') for the cunning servant, and wrote his play in octosyllables, which was the common verse for farce. Baïf's *L'Eunuque* (1573), based on Terence's *Eunuchus*, and Jacques de Cahaignes' *L'Avaricieux* (*The Curmudgeon*, 1580), which is a modern version of Plautus' *Aulularia*, both follow the same process. Such rewritings, however faithful to their Latin originals, should be carefully distinguished from scholarly translations: whereas the latter, published under the Latin author's name, were aiming to make ancient plays accessible to the literate public and to preserve their original significance, the former were usually written for the stage, presented under their modern author's name, and intended as new creations, not as reconstructions of ancient drama.

Even after the Renaissance, when Italian and French drama had developed their own original styles and repertoires, playwrights still occasionally revisited the ancient corpus. Jean de Rotrou explicitly proclaims his admiration for Plautus in the preface to his comedy *Clarice* (1643), and had previously already adapted three Plautine plays: *Menaechmi* with *Les Ménechmes* (1631), *Amphitruo* with *Les Sosies* (*The Sosias*, or *The Doubles*, 1636), and *Captiui* with *Les Captifs* (1638). Even Molière, in order to put an end to being despised as a mere popular farce writer, chose to link his work with that of his prestigious antecedents: in 1668, he produced two successive plays adapted from Plautus' corpus, *Amphitryon* and *L'Avare* (*The Miser*, based on *Aulularia*). Although Molière introduced several new elements, such as the character of Cleanthis, Sosie's wife, in *Amphitryon*, or Harpagon's love interest for Mariane in *L'Avare*, the Latin originals still shine through strongly. This is particularly so in some passages the details of which are very similar to the contemporary Plautus translation by Michel de Marolles.

The situation is somewhat different with Molière's 1671 play *Les Fourberies de Scapin* (*Scapin's Deceits*). The plot is based on Terence's *Phormio*: two young men, whose fathers are away travelling and have entrusted them to their servants' care, fall in love. One marries a poor orphan girl and the other tries to find money to free his beloved from the hands of her masters. When the fathers come back, both young men are in a predicament: one needs to make his father accept his marriage, and the other needs to obtain money from his parents. Their servants manage to trick the two old men and steal money from them, while – after a recognition scene – the marriage turns out to be fully legitimate. Not only the general plot, but also many scenes and even cues are directly borrowed from Terence's play, which Molière read in Michel de Marolles' 1647 translation. However, Molière also made several significant alterations, particularly regarding the main characters. Indeed, whereas in Terence's comedy the slave Geta and the parasite Phormio play all the tricks, the eponymous servant of Molière's *Scapin* is the true star of the comedy and the main trickster (although on occasion assisted by Sylvestre, another servant). By concentrating the tricks in one character, Molière adapts the play to the common practice of seventeenth-century French theatre, probably aiming to give himself star billing as *Scapin*. Moreover, the Neapolitan setting of the play, its three-act division, and its main character Scapin (inspired by Scappino from the *commedia dell'arte*) tend to eclipse its ancient origins to such an extent that this comedy was received more as an Italian-inspired farce than a respectable comedy based on Terence. In this way, Molière made sure to keep his audiences entertained despite his 'high-brow' classical model.

A century later, Beaumarchais' adaptation of *Casina* into his *Mariage de Figaro* (*The Marriage of Figaro*, 1784) goes even further. While clearly borrowing its general plot from Plautus (a married man trying to seduce his wife's maid and being fooled by his wife and servants), the Roman source is concealed by a very modern setting replete with many allusions to contemporary French society, which allows the play to be perceived as an innovative and subversive story.

Remarkably, when surveying early modern adaptations of Roman comedies both in Italy and France, one notices that a large majority of them are based on plays by Plautus. This clearly contrasts with the predominance of Terence in French syllabi and publications, and is not only caused by the greater number of plays in Plautus' corpus, but is also a symptom of the fact that theatre practitioners and scholarly theorists were holding very different views of Plautus. Indeed, whereas the latter generally praise Terence for his superior refinement and morality, the former value Plautus' inventiveness and efficacy on stage, particularly his *uis comica* (comic force). Even d'Aubignac, while asserting his preference for Terence, admits that Plautus' plays were generally better received:

> His plays, which were much more action-packed and less serious than Terence's, were always more successful in performance, although the others are more agreeable to the reader, having more honest characters, better conducted passions, and more elegant speeches.[10]

As professional playwrights for prominent theatre companies, Rotrou's and Molière's partiality for Plautus is understandable: concerned with the success of their plays, they appreciated his sense of fun and professional competence.

Influence on Farce and *Commedia Dell'Arte*

Furthermore, and despite the relatively small number of his published works compared with those of Terence, Plautus was particularly prized by '*irréguliers*' practitioners (i.e. not strictly following ancient rules and models of composition), whose ambitions were more practical than literary. The Paduan actor and playwright Ruzzante, considered one of the main forerunners of the *commedia dell'arte*, adapted *Rudens* into *La Piovana*

---

[10] D'Aubignac (2001) 333.

(*The Rain*, 1532) and *Asinaria* into *La Vaccaria* (*The Cows*, 1533).
Commedia dell'arte actors themselves, who were indeed much more erudite
than is usually thought, were often enthusiastic readers of Plautus, and even
borrowed his plots for their scenarios. Even French farce actors used Plautus
as one of their chief models. At a time when few of his comedies had been
translated into French, Gaultier-Garguille, a farce star from Paris, advised his
colleague Turlupin to read 'the French translations of Plautus' comedies,
along with a few Italian and Spanish authors' when searching for inspiration
for his own productions.[11]

Paradoxically, when comparing '*régulières*' comedies to contemporary
'*irrégulières*' productions, one finds the latter to be closer to the aesthetics of
Roman comedy, particularly regarding their dramaturgy and their systems of
characters. Indeed, while Italian *commedia erudita* ('learned comedy', written
and played by erudite amateurs) and French Renaissance playwrights tended
to compose unified plots in which every scene forms part of the general
narrative, the *commedia dell'arte* and the French farce showed a predilection
for one-off effects, which did not always fit within the general scheme of the
narrative. Such digressive passages were common enough in Roman comedy,
the best-known examples probably being the *seruus currens* scenes in which
the slave enters the stage running, offends everyone, and calls for his master
without realising that he is already on stage with him.[12] These scenes that only
delay the progress of the plot have no narrative function: the slave actually
holds up the plot by postponing his encounter with his master. They only serve
to create highly spectacular moments in which the slave occupies the stage with
virtuoso movements (probably carefully choreographed). The *commedia dell'-
arte* actors were particularly fond of such passages that gave them opportunity
to show off their skills and mastery. Each of them usually had a stock of
digressive scenes prepared in advance that they regularly inserted in their
shows. These intensely comic scenes called *lazzi*, which took place in a loose
narrative framework, formed the basis of *commedia dell'arte* plays and often
also of an actor's fame. It is quite significant that such passages cannot be
found in *commedia erudita* and French Renaissance comedy: usually staged by
amateurs, these genres are generally more literary and less influenced by
theatre practitioners; for passages of high entertainment value such as the
Roman *seruus currens* scenes or the *lazzi* from *commedia dell'arte* could
only be performed successfully by highly trained professional actors.

---

[11] *Testament de Gaultier-Garguille* (1634), included in Fournier (1858) 156.
[12] Examples of *seruus currens* scenes can be found in Plautus' *Asinaria* (267–95), *Mostellaria*
(348–65), *Trinummus* (1008–73), *Mercator* (111–34), and *Stichus* (274–314), and in
Terence's *Andria* (338–74), *Phormio* (178–230 and 841–83), and *Adelphoe* (299–354).
On slaves in comedy, see Fitzgerald in this volume.

Likewise, the *commedia dell'arte* and farce both gave much more prominence to the star characters of Roman comedy such as cunning slaves, miserly old men, and braggart soldiers, than learned comedy (*commedia erudita*) did. The *commedia dell'arte*'s structured system of *tipi fissi* ('fixed types', stock characters) adopted the typecasting of Roman comedy masks: an average Italian theatre company was usually composed of two lovers, one or two old men (e.g. the Venetian merchant Pantalone and the Bolognese Doctor), one or two *zanni* (servants from Bergama, one cunning and one clumsy), one *servetta* (young maid), and one *capitano* (braggart soldier), figures which roughly correspond to the Roman *adulescens* (young lover), *uirgo* (beloved), *senex* (old man), *seruus* (slave), *ancilla* (maid), and *miles* (soldier). While there is no real equivalent to the ancient comedy's *parasitus* (parasite) in Italian comedy, the figure of the glutton Pulcinella comes closest to fulfilling that function.

Commedia dell'arte developed the servant characters in particular, which played surprisingly insignificant roles in learned comedy despite their prominence in Plautine and Terentian plays. At an early date, the roles of the *Zanni* (originally a popular form of 'Giovanni') were moulded, along with that of the *Magnifico* (the old Venetian merchant who later became the Pantalone), forming the starring couple of Italian professional theatre: a farcical servant contrasting with a quick-tempered old man. The servant's role, which was later divided between a cunning and deceitful *zanni* (sometimes called Brighella or Scappino), and a second stupid and clumsy *zanni* (most of the time called Harlequin), remained prominent in more elaborate plays, performing scenes of jesting, buffoonery, and deception similar to that in the *seruus*' scenes in Plautus' and Terence's plays. In the same way, and probably under the influence of Italian companies that settled in Paris, the French farce started to employ similar characters from the beginning of the seventeenth century onwards: the star farce trio of the Hôtel de Bourgogne, the official Parisian company, consisted of Gaultier-Garguille, a French version of Pantalone, Gros-Guillaume, a fat, naïve servant with flour on his face, and Turlupin, a cunning, mischievous servant who enjoyed playing tricks on the other two.[13] Even in the streets, on the Pont-Neuf to be precise, a charlatan called Mondor sold his miracle cures with the help of Tabarin, a comedian who starred as the cunning servant in short farces he improvised with a small group of actors.[14]

---

[13] A rare published example of the trio's farces is the *Farce plaisante et récréative, tirée d'un des plus gentils esprits de ce temps* (Anonymous (1622) 28–33).
[14] Contemporary transcriptions of Tabarin's farces feature in the collection edited by Aventin (1858).

This remarkable development of servants' parts in professional productions contrasts with their limited prominence in learned comedies (*commedia erudita*) in both Italy and France. *Commedia erudita* playwrights preferred highlighting the lovers' parts, especially the one of the young *amorosa* ('girl in love'), who devises schemes and dresses up as a boy so as to follow the man she loves.[15] In French comedy, servant characters only developed in an important way in the middle of the seventeenth century, once '*comédie régulière*' started being played by professional actors. Significantly, the first French comedy actor to specialise in servants' roles was the former farce actor Jodelet. That actual ability of actors to perform virtuoso roles and scenes made a decisive impact on the way the Roman model was brought to Italian and French stages.

Indeed, the absence of professional actors capable of performing highly spectacular scenes accounts in part for the discrepancy between the claim of *commedia erudita* and French Renaissance comedy playwrights generally citing Roman comedy as their chief model and their actual plays, which hardly showcase anything ancient.[16] Although a few general characteristics from Roman comedy feature, such as domestic plots and love complications opposing younger and older generations but resulting in marriages, Plautine and Terentian models are often not recognisable. Besides *commedia erudita*'s non-professional contexts, which lead to the omission of demanding scenes, the use of other models contributes to explaining this fact. The very first Italian *commedie erudite* (excluding those that were translations of Roman plays) were already mixing several sources. Mantovano's *Formicone* (*The Ant*), performed in Ferrara in 1506 and generally considered to be the first original comedy written in Italian, partly based its plot on Apuleius' *Golden Ass*. Ariosto's *Cassaria* (*The Box*), performed in 1508, was derived partly from Roman comedy, partly from Italian novellas, like the ones collected by Boccaccio in his *Decameron*, and partly from contemporary everyday life, the elements of which were reinforced by the plays' realistic urban scenery. In France, similar reasons help to explain the inconsistency between the playwrights' claim to follow ancient models and their actual plays, which owe much more to the conventions of medieval drama than is usually admitted by the authors. Thus Etienne Jodelle's *Eugène* (1552), generally considered to be the first French '*comédie régulière*' ever

---

[15] See the Sienese comedies *Gl'Ingannati* (1532), *L'Ortensio* (1561), or Alessandro Piccolomini's *L'Alessandro* (1544).

[16] See for instance Jean de La Taille's 1562 prologue: 'A true comedy you shall see, and not a farce nor a morality play, for we do not fool about with such base and silly things, which only show the pure ignorance of our old Frenchmen. You shall see a comedy made on the pattern and the model of ancient Greeks, Latins and a few new Italians...'

performed, revolves around an adulterous plot involving a priest, which is typical of medieval farce. As a result, although early modern Italian and French comedy takes its name from the ancient dramatic genre, it is in fact a complex compound of several models and influences.

Competing Theoretical Texts

The main reason why Italian and French comedies were not just formed as modern avatars of Roman comedy is that the very idea and function of the theatre had undergone fundamental changes between antiquity and the early modern period. Whereas Roman drama was part of a religious ritual that gave it sense and form, early modern drama was a problematic practice that did not have a clear function and suffered the condemnation of parts of the Catholic Church. Accused of being misleading and morally corruptive, comedy needed to justify and to defend itself.

Indeed, whenever French and Italian playwrights and theorists claimed to imitate ancient models, they did not only mean ancient comedy, but also a whole theoretical corpus including Aristotle's *Poetics*, Horace's *Ars Poetica*, and Donatus' *De Comoedia* as well as his commentary on Terence. Handed down with much glossing and interpretative commentary, these texts provided early modern authors with a moral justification for writing comedy. The necessity to justify writing comedy had a major impact on theatrical production, particularly in France, where most new plays were performed in a scholarly context and accompanied by theoretical reflection. In Italy, however, where writing and performances of new comedies started half a century before the first theoretical publications and took place in the festive context of princely courts, the productions seem to be less directly linked to aesthetic doctrine.

One major principle to which most early modern theorists subscribe is the idea of theatre as imitation (Aristotle's famous concept of *mimesis*), which was corroborated by Euanthius' description of comedy (which became attached to Donatus' commentary) as 'an imitation of life, a mirror of habits, an image of truth'.[17] This concept allowed the defenders of drama to point to the instructive virtues of comedy: as an 'imitation of life', comedy was viewed as a pedagogical tool to describe human nature and the rules of society. This helps us understand that early modern comedy in both Italy and France tends to mix contemporary elements from daily life into its Roman models in order to produce an impression of reality. This also accounts for the near-disappearance of the ancient parasite character from the plays as it had no

---

[17] Aristotle, *Poetics*, 1, 1447a and Euanthius, *de fabula: excerpta de comoedia*, 5, 1.

direct counterpart in the early modern world, and in turn also explains the rise of the braggart soldier, who could easily be employed to parody the highly militarised societies of sixteenth- and seventeenth-century Italy and France.[18]

In addition, Roman comedy's depiction of slavery and its lack of respect for social hierarchies could prove problematic:

> Those ancient plays are usually based on the tricks of slaves only, and on the various devices they use to swindle old men and to find money for their young masters' debauchery: since we do not have slaves, and all their means to take money from fathers are not in use anymore, we do not relate to their way of living and thinking, and thus can neither approve them nor feel for them.[19]

D'Aubignac emphasises the dichotomy between the conventions of Roman comedy and the neo-Aristotelian demand for verisimilitude and blames the historical distance between ancient Rome and seventeenth-century France for this divergence. For this reason, as long as the production of French comedy was almost entirely dependent on pedagogical and scholarly circles, cunning servants remained non-existent.

Playwrights (and even actors) also cited comedy's purported purpose of moral edification in its defence: in order to justify its existence, comedy claimed to offer an equivalent to Aristotle's tragic *catharsis* (purgation) on the grounds of a rather vague link with a passage from Horace (*Ars Poetica* 343–4) that urges poets to 'mingle profit with pleasure, by delighting and instructing the reader at the same time'. For Molière and many *commedia dell'arte* artists, this meant that the function of comedy was to denounce and to ridicule human faults in order to correct them. For others, especially religious circles, it also implied that any actions and characters in comedy ought to be free from dishonesty. In both cases, the triumphing wily slaves, debauched young men, and frequent immorality in Roman comedy did not correspond to the theory's edifying ideal. In order to satisfy the demands of a Christian society, Roman plays needed to undergo a few adjustments such as the disappearance of their most infamous characters: pimps and prostitutes.

The drive towards a more realistic and moral type of comedy was all the more influential for playwrights since it was linked to good taste and literary poise. In order to assert their superiority over farce and medieval comic genres in general, writers of comedy and actors needed to avoid all coarseness and scurrility. This led many playwrights, such as Corneille and even

---

[18] Tristan L'Hermite's *Le Parasite* (1654) constitutes one notable exception. On the braggart soldier, see Boughner (1954).
[19] D'Aubignac (2001) 466.

Molière, to abstain from employing the traditional buffoons of comedy and write a number of plays that do not feature any braggart soldier or cunning servant. Corneille, in the '*Examen*' ('Foreword') of *Mélite*, his first play, prides himself on having written a comedy 'which made people laugh without any ridiculous characters, such as buffoon servants, parasites, braggarts, doctors, etc.'. More generally, writers tended to be less explicit than their Roman predecessors and avoided obscene gestures and formulations. In addition, ancient texts provided theorists with a series of formal principles, such as the unities of time, place, and action derived from Aristotle, and the division of plays into five acts, according to Horace, or three acts, according to Euanthius in Donatus' commentary.[20] The ancient model for comedy, from the Renaissance onwards, combined both the actual plays and these theoretical principles so that they came to be perceived as one homogeneous corpus.

In conclusion, although Roman plays inspired Italian and French comedy with their themes, plots, and system of characters, early modern sensibility in turn shaped the way in which Roman comedy reached the cultivated public. In both Italy and France comedy was accompanied by a theoretical arsenal that greatly influenced the way Roman comic texts were taught, translated, adapted, and imitated. The demand for verisimilitude and morality even occasionally eclipsed the original purpose of comedy: the pursuit of laughter.[21] Thankfully, drama theory did not completely submerge the original spirit of Roman comedy. For whenever comedy found a professional context that was commercially lucrative enough to resist the pressures of religious and learned circles, as it did in the Italian *commedia dell'arte* or the French seventeenth-century comedy, it revived the original brilliant cheerfulness of its ancient ancestor.

Further Reading

H. W. Lawton (1926) analyses the reception of Terence's plays in French Renaissance education, drama, and literary theory, while R. F. Hardin's article (2007) constitutes a recent comprehensive survey of Plautus'

---

[20] The five-act rule (taken from Horace, *AP*, 189–90) was generally adhered to in France, whereas Italian playwrights more often followed the three-act rule (derived from Donatus, *Exc. de Com.*, VII, 1). The division of Roman comedy into five acts that appears in medieval manuscripts does not go back to Plautus or Terence.

[21] The idea of laughter being only of secondary importance in comedy was developed by the Dutch scholar Daniel Heinsius in his *Ad Horatii de Plauto & Terentio Judicium Dissertatio* included in his edition of Terence's comedies (1618). Heinsius' idea was quite influential in France, where it was taken up by Corneille in the preface to his heroic comedy *Dom Sanche d'Aragon* (1650).

reception. M. T. Herrick (1960), L. G. Clubb (1989), and R. Andrews (1993) cover Italian Renaissance comedy, both scholarly and popular, and its reception of earlier writers. B. Jeffery (1969) and P. de Capitani (2005) handle French Renaissance and seventeenth-century comedy, demonstrating the influence of Italian drama on the evolution of French comedy during this period. A. Nicoll (1963) provides an illustrated history of Italian *commedia dell'arte*, both within Italy and outside, from the sixteenth to the eighteenth centuries. G. P. Shipp (1973) studies Molière's plays' relation to classical comedy, while D. C. Boughner (1954) concentrates on one specific type of character, the braggart soldier, from his first appearances in ancient comedy to medieval and Renaissance comedy. European comic theory in the Renaissance is thoroughly explored by M. T. Herrick (1950), and its French peculiarities are reviewed by H. W. Lawton (1949).

21

FLORIAN HURKA*

Roman Comedy in Germany
(from Humanism to Lessing)

The story of the impact of Roman comedy in Germany between the sixteenth and the eighteenth centuries falls under two headings. First there was an intensive effort, especially persistent during the period of Humanism, to arrive at an understanding of the surviving plays on an academic and intellectual level. This passive form of reception was seen as having moral and instructive value, as well as educational and linguistic utility. This explains why the *fabula palliata*, the genre of Roman plays in Greek dress, was given an important role in the education of the young. At the same time, just as in antiquity and the Middle Ages, a line was drawn between the perceived popular earthiness of Plautus and the more refined and elegant Terence, with greater value generally being attributed to the latter.

Second, the *palliata* also enjoyed a productive reception: from the time of the first German comedies, initially still composed in Latin, it served in varying degrees as a model and general reference point for German comic drama. It became a vehicle for intellectual debates and personal disputes, it served an admonitory purpose for religious conversion and edification, but it was also a medium for interpreting the ills of contemporary society, acquiring, especially in the Baroque period, a political dimension too.

1 Humanism and Reformation

German Humanism encountered the *palliata* on both these levels, in the passive intellectual form and in the productive literary form. The rediscovery of Donatus' *Commentary on Terence* in 1433 soon led, in Germany as elsewhere, to an intensification of academic interest in Roman comedy. This was exemplified by the steadily increasing number of university lectures, occasionally repeated in other cities because of their great success, or by the establishment of a professorship dedicated explicitly to Terence in 1502 by

* Both author and editor are grateful to Annemarie Künzl-Snodgrass for translating this contribution.

the Elector Frederick the Wise in the Academy of Wittenberg.[1] As a result of this intellectual engagement, authoritative studies on Plautus and Terence appeared over the next century or more: to some extent, their influence continues to this day. Besides Johannes Cosslinius (1646), Georg Fabricius (1553, 1555), Friedrich Taubmann (1605), Janus Gruter (1621), and Johann Philipp Pareus (1641), the long-running work on Plautus produced by Joachim Camerarius (1525–55), as well as the Terence editions of Philipp Melanchthon (1516, 1524) and Erasmus of Rotterdam (1532), are of outstanding importance.

This passive reception of comedy did not remain confined to academic circles: towards the end of the fifteenth century the first German translations appeared; by the end of the sixteenth, comedy had been taken on by more than a dozen writers, many of them prominent.[2] Earlier even than the German versions of Terence by Hans Nythart (beginning with the Eunuchus, Strasbourg 1486) are the translations of Plautus (*Bacchides, Menaechmi*) by Albrecht von Eyb (1420–75).[3] Von Eyb's prose translations, in contrast to later versions such as those of Joachim Greff (1535) and Christoph Freyßleben (1539), are to a large extent free of Latinisms.[4] Von Eyb also slips in German proverbs and phrases, as well as replacing 'kriechisch vn vngewonlich' (Greek and unusual) names with German ones, a practice comparable with that of the later sixteenth-century translators.[5]

In harmony with the ancient sources and with medieval thought, translators highlighted the moral didacticism of the plays.[6] Just as in the Middle Ages, Terence was given preference over Plautus in this regard.[7] Thus Peter

---

[1] On Peter Luder's Terence lecture in 1457, see Barner (1989) 246 and Bertalot (1915) 3. On the Terence chair in Wittenberg, see Reinhardstoettner (1886) 29.

[2] Reinhardstoettner (1886) 84–95.

[3] They were published posthumously in 1511 by von Eyb's nephew. On their dating, see Reinhardstoettner (1886) 87, Conrady (1954) 380, and generally Litwan (1984). These two earliest German translations of Plautus and Terence later develop a reception of their own with Hans Sachs. He makes significant use of Nythart's and von Eyb's work in writing *Ein comedi Plauti, heißt Monechmo* (1548) and *Von der bulerin Thais und ihren zweyen bulern, dem ritter Thraso und Phoedria* (1564). On the influence of von Eyb, cf. Günther (1886) 18–19; on that of Nythart (for Terence, Sachs also uses the 1540 translation by Valentin Boltz), see Riedel (2000) 55.

[4] Bernstein (1993) 106.

[5] Cited in Günther (1886) 11. It is true that van Eyb avoids Plautus's occasional use of descriptive names, but in the *Bacchides* he allows himself the joke of having all male names ending in –tz: Lentz, Götz, Pentz, Utz, Entz, Kuntz, Fritz (note also the monosyllabic nature of the names).

[6] This follows the idea, prevalent in antiquity, that comedy as *imitatio* or *speculum uitae* (imitation or mirror of life) allows insight into human characters and their emotions: Conrady (1954) 376.

[7] Cf. Reinhardstoettner (1886) 23, on the unequal reception of Plautus and Terence during the Middle Ages.

Luder (1415–72) in his 1456 inaugural lecture at the University of Heidelberg, a foundation text for the *studia humanitatis* (Humanism) in Germany, already points out the moral value of reading Terence.[8] This lack of qualms about the moral content of the plays was shared by other leading intellectuals of the time: Erasmus of Rotterdam (1465/69–1536) saw in Terence a suitable author for a young audience;[9] Philipp Melanchthon (1497–1560) showed a particular fondness for comedy when he focused on Terence in his Latin courses.[10] Martin Luther, too, had the audience's spiritual edification in mind when he voiced his approval of performing comedy steadily on the increase in number since the beginning of the sixteenth century.[11] In his Tischreden he defended the stage productions of Terence's comedies in schools: it served, so he said, not only the learning of the Latin language, but was also instructing the audience in social and moral views and duties. Luther dismissed the objection that the occasional coarse joke and amorous liaison ('bisweilen grobe(n) Zoten und Bühlerey') did not go well with Christian values, 'as by the same token you would not be allowed to read the Bible either'.[12]

The great success of Terence and (to a noticeably lesser degree) of Plautus in schools cannot be explained solely in terms of the value attributed to Roman comedy for the moral education of the young.[13] Reading comedy for linguistic instruction – as in antiquity and the Middle Ages – befitted the student.[14] Well aware of the differences between Plautus and Terence, the question, which of the two is to be preferred, was decided on grounds of stylistic *elegantia* (elegance) in favour of Terence.[15] But there were also some weighty voices on the opposing side: in the prologues to his editions of Plautus, Joachim Camerarius (1500–74) who was heavily involved in the Reformation, pondered at length the value of studying these comedies.[16] Camerarius, a close friend of Melanchthon, saw the benefit as lying mainly in the originality of Plautus' Latin. For the same reason Camerarius rejected

---

[8] Wattenbach (1869) 106.

[9] Erasmus gives a humorous interpretation of Terence's name: '*quod manibus esset terendus*' (to be torn apart by hands) according to Reinhardstoettner (1886) 33.

[10] Riedel (2000) 53.

[11] To cite but one example Terence's *Eunuchus* and Plautus's *Aulularia* were staged 1500/1502 by Laurentius Corvinus in Breslau and 1502/1503 by Konrad Celtis in Vienna.

[12] Luther (1883) 431–2.

[13] Plautus, with his *Miles Gloriosus*, also features in the curriculum. On the educational value of comedy, see Dinter in this volume.

[14] See Dittrich (1915) and Herrmann (1893).

[15] Reinhardstoetner (1886) 23. See also Manuwald's chapter on reception in antiquity in this volume.

[16] Schäfer (2004) 439–42. Georg Fabricius and Johannes Cosslinius also made use of Plautus in their teaching: Schäfer (2004) 449–53.

Terence, despite considering him morally less offensive. The latter's language, he claims, had become more literary, so that the real essence (*proprietas*) of the Latin language could only be found in Plautus. Camerarius saw this original state as indispensable for the true learning of Latin, as well as for the acquisition of an ethical and moral character.[17]

In the regions affected by the Reformation, this emphatic acceptance of comedy by leading Protestant intellectuals led to the establishment of dramas written and performed in schools, where Terence above all took precedence over Plautus, Aristophanes, Seneca, and the Greek tragedians.[18] This constituted the beginning of the modern, productive reception of the *fabula palliata* on German soil. Gulielmus Gnapheus (1493–1568), revered as *Terentius christianus*, composed the first Latin comedy for schools. He dramatised the parable of the prodigal son with recourse to motifs in Roman comedy, *Acolastus siue de filio prodigo* (Acolastus or 'of the prodigal son', 1529).[19] School plays in German, which followed soon after, adopted this approach of linking together ancient and Christian elements: Joachim Greff's (1510–52) translation of the *Aulularia* (1533) is followed by a Terence-influenced reworking of the Jacob story, *Spiel von dem Patriarchen Jakob und seinen zwelff Sönen* (Play about the Patriarch Jacob and his Twelve Sons, 1534).[20]

The beginning of comedy in Germany happened just a few decades earlier, at the end of the fifteenth century. Out of a jocular dialogue, originally an interlude in a celebratory lecture, Jakob Wimpheling from Schlettstadt (1450–1528) penned the *Stylpho* (1480/1496), the first neo-Latin comedy by a German author.[21] Wimpheling showed himself less influenced by the *palliata* in questions of dramatisation than Johannes Reuchlin (1455–1522) had been, in his *Sergius* of 1496 and his *Scaenica Progymnasmata* (1497).[22] The earliest German comedies are strikingly poor in action and seem more

---

[17] Stärk (2003) 246–8; Schäfer (2004) 437–42.

[18] Riedel (2000) 59–60. See Candiard's chapter in this volume on a similar development in the French reception of Roman comedy.

[19] Among others, the figure of the parasite appears on stage with great effect: Riedel (2000) 59. For earlier Christianisations of Roman comedy, see Kretschmer in this volume.

[20] Riedel (2000) 60.

[21] On the history of Stylpho's origins, see Dietl (2005) 149–50. The defective education of the eponymous hero, who had initially been able to obtain benefices from the Pope, is laid bare in six dialogues. His fall can be understood as a proud assertion of the *studia humanitatis* (Dietl (2005) 153–4).

[22] *Sergius*, composed in iambic trimeters, is a timely critique of the cult of relics, while the *Scaenica Progymnasmata* are dramatised exercises in rhetoric, apparently influenced in terms of content by the anonymous French farce *Maistre Pathelin*, and in terms of form by Seneca. Apart from the iambic trimeters, the choral odes at the end of the acts suggest a link with Seneca (Riedel (2000) 43).

like performed dialogues rather than actual plays.[23] Nor are these plays closely based on the *palliata* in formal terms. Nevertheless the first German comic playwrights, influenced by the high repute of the *palliata*, placed a high value on explicit references to Roman comedy. Thus Wimpheling, by using the title *Stylpho*, recalls a character in Terence's *Phormio*, while Reuchlin, in his prologue to *Sergius*, locates his play in between medieval comedy in prose and ancient comedy in verse.[24]

While there might also be references to the *palliata*, in terms of content in Reuchlin's *Scaenica Progymnasmata* references of this kind are more obvious in the work of Jakob Locher (1471–1528).[25] This humanist from Alsace shaped German theatre, not only with his political tragedies such as *Tragedia de Thurcis ac Suldano* (1497), but also with a dramatised sequel to the (morally particularly offensive) *Asinaria*, the *Ludicrum drama Plautino more fictum de sene amatore, filio corrupto et dotata muliere* (Hilarious drama in Plautine fashion about a lusting old man, his corrupt son, and his wealthy wife) of around 1503/5. This is a one-scene dialogue, which, in terms of dramatisation, is still reminiscent of the static technique of Wimpheling and Reuchlin. The play takes up the plot of Plautus' *Asinaria*, in the form of a quarrel between an old man who is led home by his wife, that same cuckolded wife, and a servant who acts as go-between.

Reuchlin had taken a stand against enemies of poetry as well as personal opponents in his *Sergius*.[26] Similarly Locher's prose work is meant as an attack on a personal enemy, the conservative professor of theology at Ingolstadt, Georg Zingel. In his 1503 *Apologia contra poetarum acerrimum hostem Georgium* (Defence against Georg, most fierce enemy of poets), Locher had previously sharply attacked Zingel for criticising the morals of Locher's own dramatic *oeuvre* to date. After comparing Zingel in his *Apologia* with the lecherous old man from the *Asinaria*, Locher assigns to Zingel this very role in the *Ludicrum drama* (see above), but without explicitly mentioning his name. In the argument between the old man, his wife, and the servant, all the moral depravity and patchy education of the *senex* (old man) is exposed: a clear attack on Zingel's reservations about the progressive endeavours of Humanism and on his moral criticism of Locher's dramatic works.[27] Locher's works constituted an independent if narrowly conceived reception of Plautus: they primarily served as an affirmation of his ideals, both personal and in terms of his general *Weltanschauung*.

---

[23] Riedel (2000) 25. [24] Dietl (2005) 152 and 166.
[25] Dietl (2005) 171. In any case, Wimpheling rates Reuchlin's play as equal in quality to the best comedies of Plautus (Dietl (2005) 173).
[26] Dietl (2005) 167. [27] Dietl (2005) 277–304.

Later sixteenth-century poets took up the dramatic technique of Roman comedy in a more refined manner.[28] The dramatic method of 'contamination', practised by Terence and, according to Terence's testimony, by Plautus too, reappears here: the Roman poets put together ('contaminated') scenes, roles, and plot lines from various Greek originals, and the German poets now used the same technique.[29]

The synthesis of ancient pagan with biblical elements, however, as found in the drama for schools persevered until late Humanism, fighting the cause of religious and moral edification, and even gained strength during the confessional age. Plautus' *Amphitruo* is linked with the birth of Jesus in Johannes Burmeister's *Sacri Mater Virgo* (1621): Alkmene is turned into Maria, Amphitryon into Joseph, Jupiter into the Holy Ghost. The role of Mercury is divided into two: an angel and the Devil, who tries through intrigues to prevent the birth of the Messiah.[30]

2 The Baroque Period

The main characteristic of Baroque literature, its typical vacillation between the two poles of mundane profanity and otherworldly spirituality, may explain the striking shift in the reception of the *palliata*, from Humanism to the age of the Baroque: 'Their experience of *vanitas* (futility) makes it almost impossible for a Baroque audience to relate to the attitude to life depicted in the events of the *palliata*.'[31]

Nevertheless Plautus and Terence certainly remained well-known names in the sevententh century. Both authors also received many plaudits from literary authors of this period.[32] Studying comedy for the sake of imbibing Latin form and style, however, was waning. While leading humanists had recommended the study of Plautus and Terence as particularly useful for acquiring the Latin language, statements to this effect were much rarer during the Baroque period, even if Roman comedy continued to be read and also, at times, performed in schools and universities.[33]

---

[28] Christoff Hegendorff, Petrus Dasypodius, or Georgius Macropedius amongst others (Riedel (2000) 57–61).

[29] On contamination in Roman comedy, see Manuwald and Telò in this volume. In the light of Hegendorff's close familiarity with Plautus and Terence (on which, see Riedel (2000) 25), it can be assumed that he uses the technique of 'contamination' in conscious imitation of ancient comedy.

[30] Reinhardstoettner (1886) 208–14 and Fontaine (2015).   [31] Conrady (1954) 386.

[32] Riedel (2000) 90.

[33] Reinhardstoettner (1886) 40–1. Even in the eighteenth century, Terence was still considered a morally edifying author fit for schools: Lefèvre (2008) 36–7.

In addition the number of new translations into German decreased: there were thus no translations of Plautus at all between 1608 and 1749.[34] Instead of the *palliata*, contemporary plays, mainly in German translation, found readers: Italian, French, and especially English comedies, which were made popular by professional English theatre groups touring Germany from the end of the sixteenth century onwards.[35]

The rise in interest in reading contemporary plays also found its reflection in the decreasing impact of the *palliata* on German theatre: during the Baroque period, moreover, tragedy in general, and Seneca in particular, became an all-powerful influence.[36] But all the same, certain motifs and roles from Roman comedy were taken up, either in combination with other material from antiquity, or as part of a comedy inspired by motifs from the *palliata*. As an example of the former, we may cite the *Irenaromachia* (1635) of Johann Rist (1607–67), a combination of Homer with Terence's *Andria*. For the latter type of reception, in European literature of the sixteenth and seventeenth centuries, the theme of the *Miles Gloriosus*, the bragging soldier, in particular is very popular, a role that appears in several *palliata* plays.[37] The most famous example is the *Horribilicribrifax Teutsch* (composed 1647–50; published only in 1663) by Andreas Gryphius (1616–64).[38]

In the play by Gryphius, with its convoluted love-plot where seven couples find each other at the end, the protagonists *Don Daradiridatumdarides Windbrecher von Tausend Mord* (Mr Windbreaker of Death City (lit.: of Thousand Murders) and *Don Horribilicribrifaz von Donnerkeil auf Wüsthausen* (Mr Thunderbolt of Havoc City) appear as recently reformed captains but also coarse braggarts. Their characteristics are shaped by correspondences with Roman comedies, and above all with Plautus' *Miles Gloriosus*, to which Gryphius himself draws attention through intertextual reference.[39] In addition, the Capitano figure of Italian comedy, which has his own roots in the *palliata*, is another model for these figures.[40] Gryphius'

---

[34] Conrady (1954) 386.   [35] Szyrocki (1979) 294–8.

[36] Overall, the Latin authors of the post-classical period acquired an exemplary character for Baroque authors both in terms of style and *Weltanschauung*. (Riedel (2000) 80).

[37] In Plautus' *Bacchides, Miles Gloriosus, Poenulus, Truculentus*, and the *Eunuchus* of Terence.

[38] In Germany the *Vincentio Ladislao* of Duke Heinrich Julius of Brunswick in 1594 preceded Gryphius' play (Conrady (1954) 386). In the Duke's play the eponymous hero is not only inclined to shameless bragging about his military deeds, but also knows how to present himself, in a bizarre and comical way, as outstanding in almost all important fields of knowledge (Reinhardstoettner (1886) 641).

[39] To cite but one example, in the play the schoolmaster Sempronius explicitly compares Horribilicribrifax with the soldier in Plautus' *Miles Gloriosus* Pyrgopolinices (Reinhardstoettner (1886) 646).

[40] Szyrocki (1979) 336–7.

'Jesting Play', written at the end of the Thirty Years' War and set in precisely that time, can be understood as a satire on contemporary reality, including its brutalised customs and degenerate language. Accordingly, in his play, Gryphius portrays a life devoid of consolation, in which deception and mistrust dominate.

3 The Enlightenment

Reception of antiquity in Germany reaches its high point in the eighteenth century. At the same time, a fundamental change in the perception of antiquity took place in the middle of that century: Latin literature had long been considered as authoritative and exemplary, but now ceded this role to Greek literature. Greek culture was recognised as superior to Roman in the aesthetic, moral, and also political spheres; correspondingly Latin literature is devalued. This shift of paradigm, initiated in Germany mainly by Johann Joachim Winckelmann (1717–68) and accepted by all the leading creative artists and intellectuals such as Herder, Goethe, Hegel, and Schiller, can be explained as the replacement of a courtly image of antiquity, appealing above all to the Roman Empire, by a citizen's perception of antiquity that is based on the ideals of the Greek *polis*.[41]

The focus on Greek models, so prevalent in the reception of antiquity during the Enlightenment, applied only with limitations to the reception of comic drama: while, during the Baroque, German comedy had had little recourse to the *palliata*, in the early Enlightenment Terence regained prominence.

The Leipzig professor Johann Christoph Gottsched (1700–66), author of the treatise *Versuch einer Critischen Dichtkunst* (The Art of Poetry, 1730), initiated a reform of the theatre that not only re-established the boundaries of genre between tragedy and comedy.[42] He also redefined the function of comedy, which in the form of a 'satirical comedy of ridicule' meant to educate the audience.[43] Gottsched generally prefererred Latin to Greek authors and included Terence, along with Virgil, Horace, and Ovid, among those (Roman) authors of classical antiquity who should be considered

---

[41] Riedel (1976) 21–2. The turn from Rome to Greece is particularly profound in Germany, in a way that differs from other European countries: while in France and England there is from the second half of the seventeenth century a continous reception of liberal Republican Rome, the German bourgeoisie, politically and economically less advanced, swoop on Hellas and its culture in the mid-eighteenth century, while largely neglecting the Latin world (Riedel (1976) 21).

[42] See Schulz (2007) 57.

[43] Riedel (1976) 33. Gottsched's reform generated comedy that is created by the bourgeoisie for the bourgeoisie, see Schulz (2007) 58.

exemplary. In his theatre reform, however, classical comedy gained its place only via classical French drama, taking the form of *Comédie larmoyante*, the serious and sentimental bourgeois comedy.[44]

At first, Gotthold Ephraim Lessing also shared the traditional admiration for Roman authors. But, Lessing recognised in Plautus the 'Father of all comic authors', a marked departure from the traditional preference for Terence over Plautus, as represented by German Humanism and also Gottsched. According to Lessing, Plautus had not only composed every type of comedy from farce to sentimental melodrama but, because of his common touch, should be preferred over Terence as a model for bourgeois comedy.

Lessing approached Plautus in three different ways. First, he wrote adaptations, a form of reception that had come to a complete standstill almost 150 years previously.[45] Second, Lessing created independent comedies such as *Die alte Jungfer* (The Spinster, 1749), where the influence of Plautus can be felt in the dramaturgy, occasional coarseness, literary resonances, and the prominent role of the servant.

Third came Lessing's theoretical examination of Plautus which is of particular importance for the history of literature: in Lessing's four essays in the *Beyträge zur Historie und Aufnahme des Theaters* (Papers on the History and Reception of Theatre) Plautus is portrayed as a particularly appropriate model for the 'tugendhafte Komödie' Lessing is promoting: 'virtuous comedy' that aims at educating and edifying the audience. In addition, Lessing addressed those coarse and graphic elements in Plautus which had featured so strongly in his earlier adaptations, but above all he reserved for fuller treatment those comedies that include both comic and sentimental elements and which are considered by no means typical of Plautus's fast-paced dramaturgy – that is, the *Captiui* and the *Trinummus*.[46] Lessing is adapting Plautus to fit his own concept of modern drama.

Lessing's theoretical engagement with Plautus goes hand in hand with a re-orientation in his own dramatic works: his adaptation of the *Pseudolus* (that remained a draft) demonstrated a reception influenced by his previously voiced views which he had developed based on the *Captiui* and *Trinummus*. Thus Lessing played down coarse and comical elements in

---

[44] Riedel (2000) 121. See also Candiard in this volume.
[45] See below p. 363. Lessing adapted *Stichus*, amongst other plays, in his fragmentary *Weiber sind Weiber* ('Women remain Women') where things become decidedly more obscene and morally depraved than in Plautus' original. With his adaptations of Plautus, Lessing was a forerunner of Jakob Reinhold Michael Lenz (1751–92), who wove ideas from the Enlightenment into his adaptations, such as social criticism and attacks on the aristocracy.
[46] Riedel (1976) 46–7.

Plautus that set him apart from Terence, and instead highlighted and added sentiment.[47]

In his *Hamburger Dramaturgie* (1767) Lessing reacted to the innovations in the field of comedy introduced by Denis Diderot (1713–84), who inserted the *genre sérieux* (bourgeois drama) into the traditional dichotomy of tragedy and comedy.[48] Again the contemporary discourse on drama influenced Lessing's engagement with ancient drama. Lessing showcased his approval of Diderot's theory of realistic theatre above all in his readings of Terence's *Adelphoe* and *Heauton Timorumenos*. Earlier Lessing had placed Terence second after Plautus, on the grounds of the latter's allegedly greater originality; but now Lessing dismissed the lively and bold elements in Terence's plays that are most reminiscent of Plautus' dramatic art, while simultaneously defending the plots' plausibility which Diderot had questioned.

The reason for the turn from Plautus to Terence, in Lessing's intellectual dissection of the *palliata*, lies in the importance of Terence for the contemporary discourse on the forms of domestic drama: Gottsched had brought Terence into play when discussing satirical comedy, a field actually rejected by Lessing primarily on the grounds of lack of realism. Diderot, however, pointed to Terence in a context welcomed by Lessing, that of the *genre sérieux*. As we can see, Terence constituted a point of reference for the general discourse on theatre in the eighteenth century.

We should also note that Lessing had meanwhile directed his interests in the direction of Greek literature, which he saw as more clearly apparent in Terence than in Plautus, whom he perceived as the more independent of the two. As isolated remarks in later works show, Lessing continued to engage with Plautus, though primarily with those plays that fitted his ideas of domestic comedy.

Lessing also adapted Plautus and Terence in his dramatic works later in his career. Some of the scenes and characters in *Minna von Barnhelm* (1767) are influenced by the *Trinummus* and the *Rudens*. Comedy's influence was particularly strong in his 'dramatic poem' *Nathan der Weise* (Nathan the Wise, 1779), where the recognition scene seems to be borrowed from the *Epidicus*, even if it is hewn into exemplifying Lessing's moral ideas of the general brotherhood of mankind. Some verbal echoes are reminiscent of, and some concepts are adopted from, Plautus' *Captiui* and Terence's *Heauton Timorumenos* – comedies with which Lessing engaged throughout his entire career.

---

[47] Riedel (1976) 45–6.   [48] On his method, see Korzeniewski (2003) 47.

With Lessing, the reception of the *palliata* reaches a high point, at which the two main strands of its reception in Germany come together. The fruits of Lessing's philological examination of Terence and, especially, of Plautus equal those of his dramatic engagement with Roman comedy. At the same time, Lessing's turn towards Greek literature, typical for the late Enlightenment and for German Classicism, brings to an end, at least in general terms, the heyday of the impact of Roman comedy in Germany.

Further Reading

Almost all literature on this topic is in German. Comprehensive collections covering the reception of comedy can be found in the works of Conrady (1954), Herrmann (1893), and above all Reinhardstoettner (1886) (available on Google Books), which are all still useful for their wealth of material. More recent publications, such as those of Dietl (2005), Korzeniewski (2003), and Riedel (1976), deliver a deeper analysis and an interpretation that meets modern demands. Riedel (2000) is to be especially commended for his breadth of horizons and comprehensiveness of themes. Kes (1988) presents the reception of the *palliata* in the late eighteenth and nineteenth centuries. Fontaine (2015) is an important publication in English.

22

CÉLINE CANDIARD

Roman Comedy on Stage and Screen in the Twentieth and Twenty-First Centuries

With the declining emphasis on Classics in secondary education, particularly after the Second World War, the general knowledge of Plautus' and Terence's drama amongst the Western population waned: as Latin progressively became a rare option, offered only in some schools to the best or most motivated students, the classical authors who had once dominated school culture were counted more and more as exotic curiosities that pupils rarely discovered before entering higher education. This progressive exclusion of classical comedy from the field of general culture during the course of the twentieth century was in part compensated for, although for a much more restricted public, by the development of scholarly interest in the subject, with numerous articles, studies, and critical editions and translations of Plautus' and Terence's plays in academic publications. Roman comedy is now, along with Greek bucolic or Etruscan archaeology, a specialised field in the academic discipline of Classics.

However, largely because of the decisive influence of Roman comedy on early modern European drama (particularly literary greats such as Shakespeare and Molière, see Candiard, Miola, and Hurka in this volume), Plautus' and Terence's plays occasionally capture the interest of professional stage directors, even though most Roman comedy productions are nowadays put on in academic contexts. In addition, Roman comedy still inspires playwrights, although less frequently than in the early modern period, to adaptations or rewriting: some base their work on one particular play, such as the authors of the many modern versions of Plautus' *Amphitruo*, whereas others combine several Roman plays and employ some typical plot pattern or conventional role types, as can be observed in original creations such as Burt Shevelove and Larry Gelbart's 1962 musical *A Funny Thing Happened on the Way to the Forum*. Lastly, a more furtive influence of Roman comic conventions and codes can be observed on various forms of comedy, often outside the sphere of theatre as such: disparate works such as P. G. Wodehouse's Jeeves stories or popular television comedy shows or movies offer excellent examples of the ongoing vitality of the Roman model.

Plautus and Terence on Stage

This vitality, however, is not obvious at first sight. Although twentieth-century theatre companies and stage directors have demonstrated clear interest in ancient drama and have integrated it into the general repertoire, their curiosity has almost exclusively benefited Greek tragedy, while comedy in general, and Roman comedy in particular, has often remained ignored. Such unequal treatment is easy to explain: not only has tragedy profited from strong positive prejudice since the early modern period, mainly due to the perceived nobility of its subject matter. For Greek literature and arts in general had been promoted, particularly in nineteenth- and early twentieth-century German historiography, by a mythological vision of Greece as the cradle of Western civilisation, which makes Roman culture appear, at best, a pale copy. As a result, whereas Aeschylus', Sophocles', and Euripides' tragedies are frequently translated and staged and perceived as carrying profound, universal messages, Plautus' and Terence's plays are rarely touched by theatre practitioners, and thus largely denied the prominence Greek tragedy enjoys in the Western cultural heritage.

Nevertheless, Roman comedy has not disappeared altogether from the modern stage. During the twentieth century, and still in the twenty-first century, teachers, academics, and even students have manifested their historical or textual approaches to the ancient material in various versions of Plautine or Terentian works. These range from reconstructions of the original stagings, modelled on archaeological and iconographical evidence, to modern translations, transpositions, and adaptations. The many and various scholarly productions of Roman comedy present such an overwhelming contrast with the relative disinterest of the professional scene that the phenomenon deserves to be noted. Indeed, the Oxford-based Archive of Performance of Greek and Roman Drama lists a large number of school or university productions or performances of Plautus' or Terence's plays between 1900 and 2011.[1] Most of them took place in universities with important Classics faculties, such as Oxford, Cambridge, Edinburgh, Glasgow, or Warwick in the United Kingdom; Harvard, Dartmouth, Wellesley, Bryn Mawr, St Olaf, or Michigan University in the United

---

[1] The APGRD database may be consulted online: www.apgrd.ox.ac.uk/asp/database.htm Although one could arguably point out that a university-based archive is particularly likely to record university-based performances, only Plautus and Terence feature such an overwhelming disproportion between professional and student productions.

States; and also Sydney (Australia), Munich (Germany), Neuchâtel (Switzerland), and the Sorbonne (France), to quote only the most frequent. While some of them are performed by student societies (such as the 'Groupe de Théâtre Antique' of the Université de Neuchâtel), they are generally supervised by an academic specialised in ancient drama. Many productions are staged in venues linked to research institutions, such as the Loeb Drama Center in Cambridge, Massachusetts, where a translation of Plautus' *Braggart Soldier* (*Miles Gloriosus*) by the scholar Erich Segal was put on in 1963, or the Malibu Getty Villa, for which Richard Beacham, from the University of California, advised on a production of Plautus' *Casina* in 1994.

Academic involvement in ancient comedy performances does not necessarily preclude professional production. The Getty Villa in particular invites stage directors and theatre companies every year to rehearse a production of classical theatre, offering them the expertise of academics. In 2007, award-winning director Meryl Friedman put on *Tug of War*; an adaptation of Plautus' *Rudens* translated by Amy Richlin, a professor in Classics at UCLA. Unlike most university productions, *Tug of War* presented the audience with an actual adaptation of the ancient play to a contemporary context: the setting was transferred from Cyrene to post-Katrina New Orleans, and the characters were turned into an all-African-American cast, dressed in modern American costumes and transposed into a modern world. In addition the cast was delivering the *cantica* (sung parts of the play) accompanied by gospel, blues, or rap music. Names used by Plautus were all translated so as to render the puns they contained, and thanks to a close collaboration between the director and the translator, the staging was able to convey much of what was implicit in the original Latin text. Below is a short excerpt from the translation, corresponding to lines 414–29 of Plautus' *Rudens*. In this scene the young prostitute Ampelisca (here translated as 'Vinita') knocks at the door of the house to ask for water and is flirtatiously welcomed by the slave Scaeparnio (here 'Shovelus'):

SHOVELUS: Who's that who's doing damage like that, getting violent with the front door?

VINITA: It's me.

SHOVELUS: Whoa, what good thing is this? Dang, a woman, and not bad looking.

VINITA: Hello, young man.

SHOVELUS: And a big hello to you, my dear young lady.

VINITA: I'm coming to see you.

SHOVELUS: I'll roll out the welcome, if you'll come back this evening,

so I can make my bid: now there's no way I can make you a little
        present this morning –
    but what do you say, pretty thing, sunshine?
VINITA: Hey, a little too friendly
    you got your hands there.
SHOVELUS: Lord God almighty, she is the image of Venus.
    Look at the joy in her little eyes; whoa, what kind of body is that –
    brown as a buzzard – I meant to say, brown as a berry.
    And what kind of tits are those – and what talent in that soul kiss.
VINITA: I'm not for sale to the neighbourhood; can you kindly keep your hands
    off me?
SHOVELUS: Ain't it okay to touch you, pretty thing, nice and pretty like this?
VINITA: When there's time, then I'll pay attention to foolin' around
        with you.
    Now, the business I got sent for, I wish you'd either say yes or no.
SHOVELUS: What you want now?
VINITA: A smart guy could tell what I want just from what I got.
SHOVELUS: Yeah, that smart guy could tell what *I* want from what *I* got.[2]

The general impression of the adaptation is extremely modern: it makes it
sound as if the action was taking place in a contemporary American setting.
In this respect, it does succeed in allowing today's audiences access to the play
in a very immediate way – even though, as was pointed out by some critics, it
is so precisely adapted to a particular type of audience and a particular period
that it would hardly be stageable in a non-US context for example.[3]

A comparable collaboration took place in France in 2001 and 2004, when
Classics professor Florence Dupont translated *Aulularia* and *Pseudolus* for
two productions directed by Brigitte Jaques-Wajeman, first performed in the
Louvre Museum in Paris, then at the Cartoucherie in Vincennes. While
backed by the expertise of Florence Dupont, Brigitte Jaques-Wajeman
declared her approach to be non-historical, giving a creative, contemporary
version of ancient texts. However, unlike *Tug of War*, her *La Marmite*
(*Aulularia*) and *Pseudolus* were not transposed into a specific contemporary
context but were instead set in a fantasy world that featured elements alluding both to ancient times and to more contemporary realities. This allowed
Jaques-Wajeman to adapt the play to modern performance conditions and
customs and still give the audience a sense of its perennial, universal values.

---

[2] As Amy Richlin's translation is unfortunately unpublished at present, this passage has
kindly been provided by the author for this volume.
[3] A point made by Vincent Hunink (2006) in his review of three Plautus translations by Amy
Richlin (2005).

Aside from universities and academic institutions, many ancient drama productions take place at archaeological sites, many of which organise specific festivals in the summer. The programmes of some festivals, however, showcase the general preference for Greek drama, particularly tragedies: understandably, this is the case in Greece, in the prestigious summer festival of Epidaurus to cite but one example. However, in the last few decades, Plautus' and, to a lesser extent, Terence's dramas have been regularly performed in the ancient theatres of Syracuse, Segesta, and Elea (Italy), Merida and Segobriga (Spain). Generally, translated versions were staged in order to make the shows as widely accessible as possible. But the one place where Plautus lovers are guaranteed to see his plays regularly performed is the North Italian town of Sarsina, which is known to be the Roman playwright's birthplace and has hosted an open-air theatre festival every July since 1956: although the programme usually consists of both ancient and modern plays, it contains at least a couple of Plautus' plays every season.[4]

Presently, Plautus and Terence do not fully belong to the 'classical' drama repertory, in the sense that they are not famous and respected enough by the general public to draw an audience automatically. Instead, their plays are generally performed to give audiences a better idea of what comedy was like in ancient times, or to allow them to discover important sources of inspiration for Shakespeare or Molière. These are generally the arguments put forward in the rare cases when professional institutions choose to put on plays by Plautus or Terence. In the BBC radio drama series that flourished from the late 1940s to the early 1980s, such a mass education purpose was clearly at stake. The BBC aired several English translations and adaptations of Roman comedies, such as *Pseudolus* in 1949, *Trinummus* in 1958, *Amphitryon* in 1961, *The Eunuch* in 1968, *Mostellaria* in 1969, and *The Pot of Gold* in 1980. This educational drive is even more obvious in the activities of companies like Theater Ludicrum (http://ludicrum .homestead.com). Director and Classics teacher George Bistransin has been regularly staging his own translations of Plautus' plays at the Strand Theater of Dorchester (Massachusetts) since 1985, for an audience consisting primarily of Latin students.

Noteworthy exceptions are Peter Oswald's translations of Plautus, particularly *The Haunted House*, staged by Polly Irvin at Bridge Lane Theatre, London, in 1994, and more recently *The Storm*, adapted from *Rudens* and performed at Shakespeare's Globe Theatre in 2005. Although the latter production, directed by Tim Carroll, was purposely programmed alongside Shakespeare's *Tempest* to emphasise the kinship of the two plays, it did not

---

[4] Information on the festival may be found online on www.plautusfestival.it/

aim at reconstructing ancient drama following historical principles. Peter Oswald and Tim Carroll chose to put the main focus of the play on the prostitutes, shown in a much trashier light than in Plautus' original version, and to introduce various anachronistic, deconstructionist elements but to keep the metatheatrical spirit of Roman plays. The scenery thus included photographic images of the Parthenon, while the main actor sometimes commented upon the writing, apologising for the feeble gags or the weak plot of the play. Instead of trying to bridge the distance between ancient comedy's codifications and the expectations of a contemporary audience, Oswald and Carroll chose to focus on this distance and play with it.

Roman Comedy Rewritten: Contemporary Versions of *Amphitruo*

Precisely because ancient comedy is composed in a way that does not necessarily correspond to the modern criteria of drama writing, it paradoxically appears easier to rewrite ancient plays altogether than to attempt translation or adaptation. Unlike the examples mentioned above, rewriting does not only consist of transposing the play to fit the taste of a modern audience: it involves changing the layout, and often part of the story, adding and taking out characters, and creating a new environment for interpretation. Reference to the original text and its author is then generally omitted and the new play is presented and perceived as a fully modern piece of work. Such rewrites are particularly abundant in the case of Plautus' *Amphitruo* which, after Rotrou, Molière, and Kleist in previous centuries, still proves a fruitful source of inspiration for playwrights and film-makers in modern times. Modern authors' strong interest in *Amphitruo* is relatively easy to explain: unlike other Roman comedies, *Amphitruo* is based on Greek mythology and presents famous mythological characters such as Jupiter, Mercury, Amphitryon, and Alcmene. In this, it is comparable to a tragedy and indeed the prologue of the play alerts us to the crossing of genres going on here (see Telò in this volume). In addition contemporary writers are much more inclined to rewrite a prominent myth than an unknown story. This is why *Amphitruo*, more than any other play by Plautus or Terence, inspired playwrights even after Roman comedy ceased to play a prominent part in general culture.

The most notable example of a twentieth-century rewriting of Plautus' *Amphitruo* is French playwright Jean Giraudoux's *Amphitryon 38*, first performed in 1929 at the Comédie des Champs-Elysées in a production by Louis Jouvet. The title of the play corresponds to Giraudoux's approximation of how many modern versions Plautus' comedy had inspired before his own. The first in a series of plays by Giraudoux based on characters and episodes of ancient mythology, such as *The Trojan War Will Not Take Place*

(1935), *Electra* (1937), and *The Apollo of Bellac* (1942), *Amphitryon 38* was translated into English in 1937 by Samuel Nathaniel Behrman for a production at the Shubert Theatre in New York. Like all of Giraudoux's mythology-inspired plays, *Amphitryon 38* presents itself as a mix between the ancient world and contemporary realities, as was highlighted in the first production of the play by Louis Jouvet's stage design, combining classical Greek architecture with Cubist art. Plautus' story and characters are preserved, along with their ancient setting. However, Giraudoux profoundly transforms the original play by turning it into a romantic comedy: Sosia's role is drastically reduced, while Alcmene becomes the true heroine of the play, embodying pure, absolute human love. Indeed, the main focus of the play is put on the couple Amphitryon and Alcmene who, presented in a noble and sympathetic light, are far from their humorous portrait in Plautus' play as a cuckold and a shrew. Through them, Giraudoux celebrates the greatness of human love, put forward as the only state of perfection humanity is able to achieve. In contrast, the gods' ideal existence appears as insipid and monotonous: despite his immortality and far-reaching powers, Jupiter is miserable because he cannot have Alcmene's true love for himself, and as a result he spends the entire play envying Amphitryon's lot.

Giraudoux' new interpretation of Amphitryon's story brings about some changes in the general layout of the play. Because the emphasis is put on romance rather than deception, the play begins with a quiet, amorous contemplation of Alcmene by Jupiter. Fascinated by the true perfection of her love for her husband, Jupiter decides to sideline Amphitryon with a war and steal his place. Jupiter's divine nature, however, turns out to be an obstacle to his happiness. Mercury needs to give him some advice: Jupiter must make himself seem more vulnerable and more human in order for his impersonation of Amphitryon to become credible (Act I, scene 5). Jupiter tries in vain to convince Alcmene to welcome him and love him for what he is, a god (Act II, scenes 2 and 5). When Mercury threatens her with severe punishments if she refuses to accept Jupiter as her lover, Alcmene manages to convince Leda, whom Jupiter had once ravished taking the shape of a swan, to swap places in the bedroom secretly (Act II, scenes 6 and 7). In this respect, unlike what is happening in Plautus' play, Giraudoux's Jupiter fails to obtain what he is really aiming for: although he manages in the end, through deception, to sleep with Alcmene, the triumph of his victory is spoilt by her constant reassertion of her love and faithfulness to her husband (Act II, scene 6). As a true Prometheus figure, Alcmene rebels against Jupiter's hegemonic love and firmly rejects him as she would a common suitor, refusing to be corrupted by her human nature in spite of her attraction for the god. When they finally part at the end of the play, Alcmene has clearly gained a position of control and offers Jupiter her friendship instead of the love he was begging for:

JUPITER: Here we are for the first time face to face, I know your virtue, and you know of my desire... Alone, at last! ...

ALCMENE: According to your reputation, you're often 'alone' this way, aren't you?

JUPITER: But rarely so in love, Alcmene, and never so weak. From no other woman would I have suffered this scorn. (...)

ALCMENE: O Jupiter, do you really fancy me?

JUPITER: If the word fancy is not only about fancies, but also about shy deer or flowering almond trees, then I fancy you, Alcmene.

ALCMENE: This is my luck. If you disliked me the slightest bit, you would not hesitate to make love to me by force so as to take your revenge.

JUPITER: And do you fancy me?

ALCMENE: How can you doubt it? Would it feel so much like cheating on my husband, with a god I loathe? Rape would be a disaster for my body, but I would preserve my honour.

JUPITER: Are you casting me aside because you love me? Are you resisting me because you are mine?

ALCMENE: That's love.

JUPITER: You make the Olympic gods speak very weighty words today.

ALCMENE: It won't harm them. People say that the most simple word from you, one single word, could destroy the world through its force.

JUPITER: Thebes doesn't risk anything today.

ALCMENE: Then why should Alcmene risk anything? Why do you need to torture me, to break up a perfect couple, to leave ruins behind you for a moment of bliss?

JUPITER: That's love...

ALCMENE: And what if I could offer you something better than love? You can make love to other women. But I would like to create a softer, but more powerful link between us: of all women I am the only one who can offer this to you. And I do offer it.

JUPITER: And what is this?

ALCMENE: Friendship!

Jean Giraudoux, *Amphitryon 38*, Act III, scene 6 (transl. the author)

While Plautus was emphasising the superiority of the gods, making Jupiter and Mercury appear as masterful deceivers, Giraudoux in contrast chooses to highlight the value and intensity of human love and provides a metaphysical background to Jupiter's amorous enterprise while creating a romantic, almost solemn atmosphere that contrasts with Plautus' farcical mood.[5]

Much lighter entertainment is Cole Porter's Broadway musical version of *Amphitruo* called *Out of This World*, which opened in New York at the New Century Theatre in December 1950. However, despite featuring Broadway performers popular at the time, such as George Gaynes as Jupiter, Charlotte Greenwood as Juno, or William Redfield as Mercury, the production was only moderately successful. The libretto, written by Dwight Taylor and Reginald Lawrence, offered a very free adaptation of Plautus' play: it tells the story of a young couple, Helen and Art O'Malley, a journalist, who travel to Greece in search of a news story about a gangster and attract the attention of Jupiter. Mercury is sent to separate the newlyweds and arrange a meeting between Helen and Jupiter, who has taken Art's appearance. In spite of Juno's attempts to counter her husband's plans, Jupiter's deception succeeds, but when he reveals the truth to Helen and offers to take her to Mount Olympus, she chooses her mortal husband, in a way falling in line with Giraudoux's Alcmene. The end of the play sees the two worlds of gods and humans separating again and re-establishes the couples of Art and Helen on earth and Jupiter and Juno in heaven.

This was not the first time Cole Porter had adapted a classic into a musical: two years earlier, in 1948, *Kiss Me Kate*, his version of Shakespeare's *Taming of the Shrew*, had been a major hit on Broadway defying all expectations, which allowed Porter to command a hefty advance of half a million US dollars for his next show. Doris Day and Jo Stafford who also later recorded some of the show's songs (as did Frank Sinatra) premiered Cole Porter's score for *Out of this World* nationwide on CBS radio the night before the show's Philadelphia opening. However, maybe due to the contrast between the mythological subject of *Amphitryon*, from which contemporary audiences tend to expect some kind of profundity, and the frivolous, almost camp spectacle that was presented in the fashion of 1920s musicals, the show was generally not judged well by the critics ('Ten years ago it would have been a crashing hit') and did have a relatively brief run of just 20 weeks on

---

[5] As the critics did not fail to notice, the play rather disappointed as comic entertainment and its Broadway premiere was only rescued by its leading couple Alfred Lunt and Lynn Fontanne: 'To provincial Lunt-Fontanne fans, Amphitryon 38 was pretty much what the doctor ordered. [....] What first-nighters found they had paid for was a comedy written with a stylish stylus, a sort of Jovian musing, some heavy-handed Olympian plotting—and the Lunts. Just as all but the extremely myopic soon discovered that the display of buttockry in the startling opening set was a plaster hoax, so none but the most zealous Lunt-Fontanne champions found Amphitryon 38 the perfect play.' (review in *Time* magazine, Monday November 8 1937, one week after the play's Broadway premiere at the Shubert Theatre).

Broadway with only 157 performances and had lost US $179 000 on a US $200 000 investment. Even a brief excerpt from the lyrics of the musical's first song, which follows the overture and the prologue, exemplifies this shift away from profundity:

> I Jupiter, I Rex,
> I Jupiter, am positively teeming with sex. . . .
> But I Jupiter, I Jove,
> I Jupiter, would like a brand new dish on my stove.
> I am tired of blasé goddesses
> With busting-out-all-over bodices.
> I crave a merry mortal with a sassy air
> And a baby blue, 32 brassiere.
> I Jupiter, I Rex,
> I Jupiter Rex,
> Am positively teeming, yes positively screaming for sex.
> I'm tired of blasé goddesses
> With busting-out-all-over bodices.
> I crave a sassy mortal with a merry air
> And a not-too-plump, bump-to-bump derriere.
> I Jupiter, I Rex,
> I Jupiter Rex,
> Am positively teeming, yes positively steaming with sex,
> Sex, sex, sex, sex, sex, sex, sex!

Porter showcases Jupiter's character as a sex-obsessed womaniser, which made him correspond to the conventions of vaudeville but may have seemed too daring to the audience at the time. Hasty reworking of the show – as well as occasional brushes with the censor's offices taking offence at the phrase 'goosing me' in Juno's song 'Nobody's Chasing Me' during the show's test run in the provincial theatres – did not help either. However, decades later in 1995 Porter's musical was produced again to great acclaim by Mark Brokaw at the New York City Center in concert performances highlighting Cole Porter's music rather than the dramaturgy and comic aspects of the show.

Not only has the story of Amphitryon inspired playwrights, but it also provided the subject for several films in the course of the twentieth century. As early as 1911, in the early times of cinema, French film director Etienne Arnaud produced *Amphitryon*, a silent short movie closely based on Plautus' comedy. In 1935, the same story was turned into a musical feature film directed by Reinhold Schünzel and Albert Valentin which was shot twice, successively with a German and then a French cast. Based on Plautus' play, the film also integrates elements from Molière and Kleist's adaptations (see the chapters on reception by Candiard and Hurka) such as the presence of an additional maidservant coupling up with Sosia. As a musical, it has some elements in common with Cole Porter's later adaptation, especially the musical style, but also a modern representation of the characters (Mercury, for example, wears roller skates) and its light, irreverent treatment of the original myth: the Amphitryon story is presented as a mere cuckold farce in which gods are not any different from men; one scene even shows the gods discovering statues of themselves and realising with great surprise how much men idealise them. The French and German titles of the movie, *Les Dieux s'amusent* (*Gods Having Fun*) and *Aus den Wolken kommt das Glück* (*Happiness Comes From The Sky*) aptly summarise the general effect of light amusement of this musical film.

A much more philosophical take, on the other hand, is Jean-Luc Godard's film version of Amphitryon's story, *Hélas pour moi* (*Alas For Me*), released in 1991. Clearly influenced by Giraudoux's *Amphitryon 38*, Godard's movie stars the same melancholic figure of a god falling in love with a woman who refuses the immortality he has to offer. However, the film transposes Jupiter into 'God' and, apart from the mysterious character called Max Mercure who accompanies him, Godard seems to drop mythological referencing altogether. Instead, Godard introduces some references to Christianity when he lets his main character say: 'I once had a little boy, he gave his life for you.' Transposing the story of Amphitryon into a contemporary context, in which God falls in love with a beautiful woman called Rachel and borrows the features of her husband Simon Donnadieu (literally, 'who gives to God') so as to spend a night with her, Godard's film presents itself as a philosophical meditation on the vulnerability of the Christian God in search of the love of humanity. Godard replaces the comic dimension of Plautus' original play with a more meditative tone and a metaphysical agenda that uses the mythological dimension of Plautus' *Amphitruo* as vehicle and leaves the story's comic potential unexplored.

Making New Things Out of Old: Modern 'Roman' Comedies

Paradoxically, much more faithful to the spirit of Roman comedy are musicals or sitcoms in which conventions, character types, and plot elements from Plautus and Terence's plays are recycled into contemporary formats. Although Roman plays are often not explicitly referenced in such productions, the inspiration they provide is still easily recognisable, all the more since the action of these musicals and sitcoms is normally situated in ancient Rome. They provide in a way an equivalent to Roman comedy's relation to Greek New Comedy as they recycle narrative patterns, roles, and settings, often of several plays at once, to create new stories situated in a fantastical

Rome, in the same way Plautus and Terence sometimes contaminated plays by Menander and set their storylines in Greece. In both cases, the setting of the plays obliges stereotyping and the author's imagination rather than historical reality and provides a pretext for presenting an imaginary world where anything can happen, without the constraints of realism.

The best-known and arguably the most successful example of this approach is that of Stephen Sondheim, Burt Shevelove, and Larry Gelbart in their musical *A Funny Thing Happened on the Way to the Forum*, first performed on Broadway in 1962 and turned into a musical film in 1966 which is still frequently staged all over the English-speaking world.[6] For the most part based on Plautus' *Pseudolus, Miles Gloriosus*, and *Mostellaria*, the play presents both plot and characters in perfect harmony with Plautine conventions. But the true genius of the show is to combine ancient comedy with references to popular American culture, particularly the humour of Jewish comedians starring in the show such as Zero Mostel, Phil Silvers, and Jack Gilford. Some critics even dubbed the show as taking place in 'Brooklyn-on-the-Tiber'.[7] In the musical and subsequently the film version, the actors resorted to the very acting skills and routines they were used to in their vaudevillian career.[8] Both faithful to the spirit of Plautine plays and consistent with the expectations the general public have of comedy, *A Funny Thing Happened on the Way to the Forum* successfully exemplifies the possible transposition of Roman drama into contemporary comic models.

In this respect, the opening song ('Comedy Tonight') of Richard Lester's 1966 movie is emblematic of the remainder of the musical: sung by the slave Pseudolus – just as the prologues of Roman comedy were sometimes recited by a play's main slave character[9] – it fits the principles of Roman comedy prologues as well as the customs of musical openings and of cinema theme songs. It mainly functions as an expository scene, presenting the streets of Rome as the general setting of the play, introducing the main characters plus offering a few taster images from the rest of the movie. In addition it provides a transition for the audience between their daily lives and the fictitious world they are about to enter: while the credits of the film are being displayed onscreen, Pseudolus is putting the audience into the right spirit for all the show's fun to come: '*Old situations, / New complications, / Nothing portentous or polite; / Tragedy tomorrow, / Comedy tonight!*' This emphasis on the

---

[6] Among the recent productions of this musical is the 1996 Broadway production directed by Jerry Zacks starring first Nathan Lane, and then Whoopi Goldberg as Pseudolus.

[7] See the title of Malamud (2001).   [8] See Malamud (2001) 198.

[9] Cf. the prologues of Plautus' *Mostellaria* presented by the slave Tranio, and of *Amphitruo*, presented by Mercury dressed up as the slave Sosia. On slaves in Roman comedy see Fitzgerald in this volume.

show's generic identity is comparable to Plautus' jokes in the prologue of *Amphitruo* (50–63), a play successively presented as a tragedy and as a comedy. This helps to focus the attention of the audience on the spectacle they are about to watch. In the same metatheatrical and self-ironic way the actor Zero Mostel switches back and forth between his slave role and his status as the star comedian playing the part.[10]

The characters of the show are on the whole faithful to the stereotypes of Roman comedy – some of them even bear names borrowed from across the Plautine corpus, such as Pseudolus, Lycus, or Gymnasia.[11] The *paterfamilias* (head of the family) bears the significant name of Senex ('old man') and is just as weak and lusty as some of the father figures in Roman comedy (Plautus' Demaenetus in *Asinaria* or Demipho in *Mercator*). His wife, Domina ('mistress') is dominant (who would have guessed) and sour-tempered and resembles Plautus' Cleostrata (*Casina*) or the unnamed wife of Menaechmus I (*Menaechmi*); and, as if to reinforce the stereotype, she is only surpassed in harshness by her own mother, who briefly appears armed with a whip. The two main slaves, Pseudolus and Hysterium, are both dressed in orange, which evokes slave uniforms and is reminiscent of the red wig conventionally worn by Roman actors playing slaves. As soon as the show starts, a mute dice-playing scene characterises Pseudolus immediately as the clever slave who swindles everyone, whereas Hysterium presents himself as *seruus bonus* (good slave) ready to beat up his own mate to please his demanding mistress. He will, however, transform in the run of the play into Pseudolus' (unwilling) partner in crime. As for the young man in love, tellingly called Hero so as to underline his function as the romantic male lead, he is as naïve and soppy as are his Roman counterparts such as Plautus' Calidorus in *Pseudolus* or Terence's Antipho in *Phormio*. In the film version he is played by a British actor, young Michael Crawford, whose plummy English accent not only marks his social standing above the slaves and the pimp, played by American comedians, but also helps to undermine comically the pathos in some of his scenes: when Hero threatens to stab himself out of amorous despair, the audience can hear a caricature of Shakespearian tragic lovers.

In addition to borrowing Roman comedy's comic stereotypes, several scenes appear to bear direct reference to passages from Roman plays. One scene in particular, in which the slave Hysterium makes the old neighbour

---

[10] As he puts it when interrupting the theme song: 'Pseudolus is probably my favourite character in the piece. A role of enormous variety and nuance, and played by an actor of such versatility, such magnificent range, such … Let me put it this way: I play the part.'

[11] Pseudolus is the name of the starring slave in Plautus' play *Pseudolus*. Lycus that of the pimp in *Poenulus*, and the name Gymnasia reminds us of Gymnasium, the young prostitute in *Cistellaria*.

Erronius believe that his house is haunted in order to keep him away, is directly borrowed from Plautus' *Mostellaria*, in which the slave Tranio tells his old master Theopropides that his son had to abandon their house because it was haunted by evil spirits (Plautus, *Most.* 446–531). Also, although in a less obvious way, the brothel scene in which the pimp introduces his prostitutes to Hero and Pseudolus is reminiscent of a passage of *Pseudolus* in which the *leno* Ballio reviews his troupe of girls and points out the talents of each one (Plautus, *Ps.* 185–229). The denouement of the show, with the recognition scene between Erronius and his long-lost children, Miles Gloriosus and Philia, who had been kidnapped by pirates in their infancy, copies similar conventional endings in a significant proportion of Roman plays. Plautus' *Captiui*, *Casina*, *Curculio*, *Epidicus*, *Poenulus*, and *Rudens*, as well as Terence's *Andria*, *Phormio*, and *Hecyra* all end with a recognition scene. And finally the songs of the musical fulfil a function similar to the *cantica* in Plautus' and Terence's plays, as they create a pause in the action and help to characterise the play's personae: the young lovers with the song 'Lovely' or the braggart soldier with his tune 'Bring Me My Bride'. They reveal a further similarity between Broadway musicals and Roman comedy, which both often prioritise putting on a spectacle over general plot design.

All those features tend to indicate a deep familiarity with Plautus' and Terence's works on the part of the writers of the show and the movie, and their concern to produce close equivalents to Roman comedy. This, however, does not prevent the show from altering some important details, in particular regarding the slave figures who, unlike their Roman models, actively pursue their freedom – probably so as to suit the modern disapproval of slavery. One might also point out that the *Miles Gloriosus* (literally 'braggart soldier') from the musical appears to be a truly strong, fearful, and even seductive soldier, much unlike Plautus' and Terence's *milites* (soldiers) who were mere pretenders. His triumphal entry with the song 'Bring Me My Bride', interpreted by the professional opera singer Leon Greene with his powerful baritone, produces a striking impression of military vigour. This choice may easily be explained by the producers' drive to highlight the parodic elements of the movie, above all parodies of the spectacular military scenes of epic historical drama films. The final chariot chase in particular clearly references William Wyler's famous *Ben Hur* movie, released just a few years earlier. In the same way as Roman comedy habitually refers to the related genre of tragedy (see Telò and Christenson in this volume) this movie adaptation makes fun of related movie genres and remains faithful to the spirit and entertainment purpose of Roman comedy.

The tremendous success of *A Funny Thing Happened on the Way to the Forum* soon inspired similar shows that looked back to ancient comedy – now back in fashion. The most famous of these is probably the British television comedy series *Up Pompeii* (1969–70) which itself gave rise to a film directed by Bob Kellett (1971), and more recently to a stage play produced by Bruce James (2011). In casting Frankie Howerd, who had been acclaimed as Pseudolus in the London production of *A Funny Thing Happened on the Way to the Forum* in 1963–5, in the main role of the slave Lurcio, the show clearly followed in the footsteps of the American musical.[12] Set in pre-eruption Pompeii, the *Up Pompeii* sitcom uses similar role types and plot patterns to the earlier musical/movie and added also a whiff of history with occasional references to the emperor Nero (AD 54–68). Each episode commenced with a metatheatrical prologue spoken into the camera by Frankie Howerd. Since the show was recorded in a studio in front of a live audience, the reactions of spectators were directly audible. These were also regularly solicited by frequent asides and off-the-cuff remarks from Frankie Howerd, who commented upon the sitcom's action with puns and anachronisms, systematising a theatrical device that could already be found in Plautus' and Terence's plays as well as in the Broadway musical. Nevertheless, the sitcom fails to reach the variety and richness of its musical counterpart: parodies seem less clever and the humour, largely influenced by the spirit and the gags of Gerald Thomas' *Carry On* movies, particularly *Carry On Cleo* (1964), a parody on Mankiewicz's movie *Cleopatra* (1963), focuses mostly on saucy situations. This results in a simplistic, occasionally even coarse adaptation of Roman comedy's stereotypes and conventions which propagates an image of ancient Rome as a culture of swindle and debauchery. While *A Funny Thing* could be considered a modern rewriting of Plautine drama, *Up Pompeii* is a sitcom for which Roman plays worked as a remote inspiration, even though the name of Plautus is regularly evoked by the main slave character.

These last few examples link easily with Roman plays thanks to their ancient setting and explicit allusions to ancient drama. Less clearly identifiable are the influences of Plautus and Terence on contemporary comedy or humour-writing, largely because they are generally mediated through several intermediaries such as early modern comedy or vaudeville. As we have seen in the chapters of Manuwald, Kretschmer, Candiard, and Hurka in this volume, over several centuries Roman comedy stood model for European

---

[12] Another link between these two shows is that Michael Horden, who played Hero's father Senex in *A Funny Thing Happened on the Way to the Forum*, also plays the father in the 1971 film *Up Pompeii*.

comedy, its character stereotypes and plot patterns, its prominent servants and preference for romance, and its use of metatheatricality. In this way, the influence of Roman comedy is continuing up to the present day in the performing arts and even more widely in literature, although not necessarily as clearly as in the examples discussed above. When P. G. Wodehouse, in his short stories and novels, gave Jeeves, the butler, playful superiority over his young master Bertie Wooster, he might not have been thinking directly of Plautus' cunning slaves, but their literary influence was still felt through more modern models such as Arlequin or Figaro.[13] Indeed, despite his matchless refinement which makes him a unique figure, Jeeves combines qualities already found in Plautus' and Terence's slaves: not only is he more intelligent than his master, but he also has expertise in the social codes of all circles of life, which allows him to take on all sorts of disguises comparable to those assumed by the slaves of ancient comedy. The repetitive plot patterns of the Jeeves novels and short stories – Bertie getting in trouble despite Jeeves' tactful warning, the predicament reaching a critical point, and Jeeves elegantly saving the day – are also comparable to the recurrent storylines of Roman plays. These recurrences were canonised, in accordance with the principles of sitcom, in the novels' television adaptation by Clive Exton (1990–3), with Stephen Fry as Jeeves and Hugh Laurie as Bertie.

In the same way that Roman audiences internalised the codes of comedy and were in all likelihood more sensitive towards code variations, rather than the ever so slightly repetitive standard plot and characters of the plays, viewers watching *Bugs Bunny* already know that Elmer will not succeed in killing Bugs and will have been mocked by him a thousand times by the end of each episode: they rather wonder how this repetitive pattern will give birth to new entertainment which happens mostly through inventive gags and the use of parody. In that way, rather than as a direct influence, Roman comedy constitutes a major archetype in the long tradition of Western comedy that contrasts with the neo-Aristotelian model that imposed unified plots and psychologised characters onto European drama in the early modern period.

In the twentieth and twenty-first centuries, Roman comedy ceased to be part of the common cultural knowledge of the educated public and became part of a specialised scholarly culture. This explains why Plautus and Terence are rarely staged outside academic contexts, or at least without academic initiative – though some companies are producing daring adaptations aiming to make the plays accessible to a wider public. From the corpus of Roman

---

[13] See for example *My Man Jeeves* (1919), *The Inimitable Jeeves* (1923), *Very Good, Jeeves!* (1930), or *The Mating Season* (1949). The writing of the Jeeves stories went on until the 1970s with *Much Obliged, Jeeves* (1971), published shortly before the author's death.

comedy, *Amphitruo* in particular seems to have been favoured. Benefiting from its mythological characters and setting, it tends to be ranked next to Greek tragedies and has inspired several adaptations into plays, musicals, and even films. The rest of the Plautine corpus profited from the initiative of Stephen Sondheim, Burt Shevelove, and Larry Gelbart to combine elements from several Roman plays to create a very Plautine Broadway musical. The huge success of *A Funny Thing Happened on the Way to the Forum* highlights the similarities between ancient comic conventions and modern practice, particularly in musical comedy, which presents the same alternation between spoken and sung passages as the *diuerbium* and *canticum* of Roman plays. More generally, although direct references to Plautus' and Terence's works are rare in today's shows, many a light comedy on stage, popular comedy in cinema or sitcom and cartoon on television regularly parade their ancient ancestors.

Further Reading

It could be stimulating for students and scholars to compare the academic editions and translations of Plautus and Terence available in university libraries to those adaptations intended for the stage, such as Amy Richlin's three Plautus plays (2005) and Peter Oswald's version of *Rudens, The Storm* (2006). Although several books survey the portrayal of ancient Greece and Rome in cinema, most of them remain focused on ancient history and only a few address the question of comedy. Among the latter are Jon Solomon's study (2001), particularly 283–305, which compares screen adaptations of other comic films on antiquity, and also Margaret Malamud's 2001 article on *A Funny Thing Happened on the Way to the Forum*. Among the several rewritings of Plautus' *Amphitruo* mentioned in this chapter, only Giraudoux's *Amphitryon 38* is available in print and English translation (1967). Cole Porter's *Out of This World* and Jean-Luc Godard's *Hélas pour moi* are analysed respectively in Ethan Mordden's study on Broadway musicals (2007) and in Richard Brody's study on Godard (2008), particularly 545–65. As for the similarities of Wodehouse's Jeeves and Tex Avery's cartoons with Plautus' and Terence's plays, they do not seem to have been investigated thoroughly in any printed work, but further details on their legacies, organisation, and use of parody can be found in the general studies by Richard Usbome (1981) and Floriane Place-Verghnes (2006).

BIBLIOGRAPHY

Abel, L. (1963) *Metatheatre: A New View of Dramatic Form*. New York.

Adams, J. N. (1984) 'Female Speech in Latin Comedy', *Antichthon* 18: 43–77.

Adams, J. N. (2003) *Bilingualism and the Latin Language*. Cambridge.

Adkin, N. (1994) 'Terence's *Eunuchus* and Jerome', *Rheinisches Museum* 137: 187–95.

Ahrens, H.-J. (1970) 'Arbiter und iudex in den plautinischen Komödien'. Diss. Kiel.

Alexander, J. (1998) 'Illumination for Cardinal Antoniottio Pallavicini (1442–1507)' in M. P. Brown and S. McKendrick (eds.) *Illuminating the Book: Makers and Interpreters: Essays in Honour of Janet Backhouse*. London: 191–208.

Allardice, J. T. (1929) *Syntax of Terence*. London.

Althusser, L. (1962) 'Le "Piccolo", Bertolazzi et Brecht (Notes sur un théatre matérialiste)', *Esprit* 30.12: 946–65.

Anderson, W. (1979) 'Plautus' *Trinummus*: The Absurdity of Officious Morality', *Traditio* 35: 333–45.

Anderson, W. (1993) *Barbarian Play: Plautus' Roman Comedy*. Toronto.

Andrews, R. (1993) *Scripts and Scenarios: The Performance of Comedy in Renaissance Italy*. Cambridge.

Anonymous (1622) 'Farce plaisante et récréative, tirée d'un des plus gentils esprits de ce temps' in *Tragédie nouvelle de la perfidie d'Aman, mignon et favori du roi Assuérus*. Paris: 28–33.

Apter, E. (2013) *Against World Literature: On the Politics of Untranslatability*. New York.

Aragosti, A. (2009) *Frammenti Plautini dalle commedie extravarroniane*. Bologna.

Arnott, W. G. (1963) 'The End of Terence's *Adelphoe*. A Postscript', *Greece and Rome* 10: 140–4.

Arnott, W. G. (1964a) 'The Confrontation of Sostratos and Gorgias', *Phoenix* 18: 110.

Arnott, W. G. (1964b) 'A Note on the Parallels between Menander's *Dyscolos* and Plautus' *Aulularia*', *Phoenix* 18: 232–7.

Arnott, W. G. (1970) 'Phormio parasitus*: A Study in Dramatic Methods of Characterisation', *Greece & Rome* 17: 32–57.

Arnott, W. G. (1972) 'Targets, Techniques and Traditions in Plautus' *Stichus*', *Bulletin of the Institute of Classical Studies* 19: 54–79.

Arnott, W. G. (1985) 'Terence's Prologues', *Papers of the Liverpool Latin Seminar* 5: 1–7.

Arnott, W. G. (1995) 'Menander's Manipulation of Language for the Individualization of Character' in F. de Martino and A. H. Sommerstein (eds.) *Lo spettacolo delle voci* 11. Bari: 147–64.

Arnott, W. G. (2001) 'Plautus' *Epidicus* and Greek Comedy' in U. Auhagen (ed.) *Studien zu Plautus' Epidicus*. Tübingen: 71–90.

Arnott, W. G. (2003) 'Diphilus' *KAHPOYMENOI* and Plautus' *Casina*' in R. Raffaelli and A. Tontini (eds.) *Lecturae Plautinae Sarsinates VI: Casina*. Urbino: 23–44.

Astin, A. E. (1967) *Scipio Aemilianus*. Oxford.

Astin, A. E. (1978) *Cato the Censor*. Oxford.

Aubignac, F. d' (2001) *La Pratique du Théâtre*, ed. Hélène Baby. Paris.

Augoustakis, A. (2007) '*Surus cor perfrigefacit*: Elephants in Plautus' *Pseudolus*', *Philologus* 151: 177–82.

Augoustakis, A. (2013) 'Hrotsvit of Gandersheim Christianizes Terence' in A. Augoustakis and A. Traill (eds.) *A Companion to Terence*. Malden, MA: 397–409.

Augoustakis, A., and A. Traill (eds.) (2013) *A Companion to Terence*. Malden, MA.

Auhagen, U. (2004) 'Das Hetärenfrühstück (*Cist.* I 1) – Griechisches und Römisches bei Plautus' in R. Hartkamp and F. Hurka (eds.) *Studien zu Plautus' Cistellaria*. Tübingen: 187–210.

Auhagen, U. (2009) *Die Hetäre in der griechischen und römischen Komödie*. München.

Aventin, G. (1858) *Œuvres complètes de Tabarin* (2 vols). Paris.

Bader, B. (1970) 'Szenentitel und Szeneneinteilung bei Plautus'. Diss. Tübingen.

Bagordo, A. (2001) *Beobachtungen zur Sprache des Terenz: mit besonderer Berücksichtigung der umgangssprachlichen Elemente*. Göttingen.

Bain, D. (1977) *Actors and Audience: A Study of Asides and Related Conventions in Greek Drama*. Oxford.

Bain, D. (1979) '*Plautus Vortit Barbare*: Plautus, *Bacchides* 526–61 and Menander, *Dis exapaton* 102–12' in D. West and T. Woodman (eds.) *Creative Imitation and Latin Literature*. Cambridge: 17–34.

Bain, D. (1984) 'Female Speech in Menander', *Antichthon* 18: 24–42.

Bakhtin, M. (1984) *Rabelais and His World*. Bloomington, IN.

Baldi, P. (2002) *The Foundations of Latin*. Berlin.

Baldwin, T. W. (1944) *William Shakspere's Small Latine and Lesse Greeke* (2 vols). Urbana, IL.

Barchiesi, A. (2002) 'Palingenre: Death, Rebirth and Horatian Iambos' in M. Paschalis (ed.) *Horace and Greek Lyric Poetry*. Rethymnon: 47–69.

Barchiesi, A. (2009) 'Roman Perspectives on the Greeks' in G. Boys-Stones, B. Graziosi and P. Vasunia (eds.) *The Oxford Handbook of Hellenic Studies*. Oxford: 98–113.

Barchiesi, M. (1970) 'Plauto e il "metateatro" antico', *Il Verri* 31: 113–30.

Barner, W. (1989) '*Studia toto amplectenda pectore*. Zu Peter Luders Programmrede vom Jahre 1546' in A. Buck and M. Bircher (eds.) *Respublica Guelpherbytana*. Amsterdam: 227–51.

Barsby, J. (1986) *Plautus*: Bacchides. Warminster.

Barsby, J. (1993) 'Problems of Adaptation in the *Eunuchus* of Terence' in N. W. Slater and B. Zimmermann (eds.) *Intertextualität in der griechisch-römischen Komödie*. Stuttgart: 160–79.

Barsby, J. (1999) *Terence:* Eunuchus. Cambridge.

Barsby, J. (2001) *Terence.* Phormio, *The Mother-in-Law, The Brothers.* Cambridge, MA.

Barsby, J. (2002) 'Terence and his Greek Models' in C. Questa and R. Raffaelli (eds.) *Due seminari plautini. La tradizione del testo. I modelli.* Urbino: 251–77.

Barsby, J. (2004a) 'Actors and Act-divisions in Poenulus and its Greek Original' in T. Baier (ed.) *Studien zu Plautus'* Poenulus. Tübingen: 93–111.

Barsby, J. (2004b) 'Some Aspects of the Language of *Cistellaria*' in R. Hartkamp and F. Hurka (eds.) *Studien zu Plautus'* Cistellaria. Tübingen: 335–45.

Barsby, J. (2007) 'Native Roman Rhetoric: Plautus and Terence' in W. Dominik and J. Hall (eds.) *A Companion to Roman Rhetoric.* Malden, MA and Oxford: 38–53.

Bartholomä, A. (2018) 'Epigenes' Kampf gegen das Gesetz (Ar. Eccl. 976–1111)' in H.-G. Nesselrath and J. Platschek (eds.), *Menschen und Recht. Fallstudien zu Rechtsfragen und ihrer Bedeutung in der griechischen und römischen Komödie.* Tübingen: 1–16.

Batstone, W. W. (2005) 'Plautine Farce and Plautine Freedom: An Essay on the Value of Metatheatre' in W. W. Batstone and G. Tissol (eds.) *Defining Genre and Gender in Latin Literature.* New York: 13–46.

Batstone, W. W. (2009) 'The Drama of Rhetoric at Rome' in E. Gunderson (ed.) *The Cambridge Companion to Ancient Rhetoric.* Cambridge: 212–37.

Beacham, R. C. (1991) *The Roman Theatre and its Audience.* London.

Beacham, R. C. (2nd edn 1995) *The Roman Theatre and its Audience.* London.

Beacham, R. C. (forthcoming) *Living Theatre: Roman Theatricalism in the Domestic Sphere.* New Haven.

Bean, J. R. (1984) 'Terence Chastened: Two Character Types from the Plays of Hrotsvitha of Gandersheim', *Michigan Academician* 16: 383–90.

Beard, M. (2003) 'The Triumph of the Absurd: Roman Street Theatre' in C. Edwards and G. Woolf (eds.) *Rome the Cosmopolis.* Cambridge: 21–43.

Beard, M., J. North, and S. Price (1998) *Religions of Rome* (2 vols). Cambridge.

Beare, W. (1930) 'Plautus and the *fabula Atellana*', *Classical Review* 44: 165–8.

Beare, W. (2nd edn 1955, 3rd edn 1964) *The Roman Stage: A Short History of Latin Drama in the Time of the Republic.* London.

Beaumarchais, P. A. C. de (2003) *The Figaro Trilogy,* ed. D. Coward. Oxford.

Beck, E. (1973) 'Terence Improved: the Paradigm of the Prodigal Son in English Renaissance Comedy', *Renaissance Drama* 6: 107–22.

Bekker, E. I. (1892) 'Die römischen Komiker als Rechtszeugen', *Zeitschrift der Savigny-Stiftung für Rechtsgeschichte (Romanistische Abteilung)* 13: 53–118.

Bellay, J. du (1549) *Défense et illustration de la langue française.* Paris.

Bennett, C. E. (1910–14) *Syntax of Early Latin.* Boston.

Benz, L. (1990) '*Megaronides Censorius* – Eine anticatonische Konzeption im plautinischen *Trinummus?*' in J. Blänsdorf (with J.-M. André and N. Frick) (eds.) *Theater und Gesellschaft im Imperium Romanum.* Tübingen: 55–68.

Benz, L. (1995) 'Die römisch-italische Stegreifspieltradition zur Zeit der Palliata' in L. Benz, E. Stärk, and G. Vogt-Spira (eds.) *Plautus und die Tradition des Stegreifspiels.* Tübingen: 139–54.

Benz, L. (2000) 'Ein Ausrufermimus im plautinischen *Stichus* (vv. 218–233)' in S. Gödde and T. Heinze (eds.) *Skenika: Beiträge zum antiken Theater und seiner Rezeption.* Darmstadt: 165–73.

Benz, L., E. Stärk, and G. Vogt-Spira (eds.) (1995) *Plautus und die Tradition des Stegreifspiels*. Tübingen.

Bernstein, E. (1993) 'Albrecht von Eyb' in S. Füssel (ed.) *Deutsche Dichter der frühen Neuzeit (1450–1600)*. Berlin: 96–110.

Bernstein, F. (1998) *Ludi publici. Untersuchungen zur Entstehung und Entwicklung der öffentlichen Spiele im republikanischen Rom*. Stuttgart.

Berschin, W. (2005) 'Tradition und Neubeginn bei Hrotsvit von Gandersheim († nach 968)' in W. Berschin (ed.) *Mittellateinische Studien*. Heidelberg: 237–48.

Berschin, W. (2001) *Hrotsvit – Opera Omnia*. Leipzig.

Bertalot, L. (1915) 'Humanistische Vorlesungsankündigungen in Deutschland im 15. Jahrhundert', *Zeitschrift für Geschichte der Erziehung und des Unterrichts* N.F. 5: 1–24.

Bertini, F. (1980) *Il 'Teatro' di Rosvita – con un saggio di traduzione e di interpretazione del Callimaco*. Genoa.

Bertini, F. (1985) 'Simbologia e struttura drammatica nel *Gallicanus* e nel *Pafnutius* di Rosvita' in H. Braet, J. Nowé and G. Tournoy (eds.) *The Theatre in the Middle Ages*. Leuven: 45–59.

Best, S. (2004) *The Fugitive's Properties: Law and the Poetics of Possession*. Chicago.

Bettini, M. (2002) 'I "Witz" di Gelasimus: clichés, modelli culturali, pragmatica dell'umorismo' in C. Questa and R. Raffaelli (eds.) *Due seminari plautini. La tradizione del testo. I modelli*. Urbino: 227–49.

Bettini, M. (2012) *Vertere: un'antropologia della traduzione nella cultura antica*. Turin.

Beutner, B. (1974) 'Der Traum des Abraham', *Mittellateinisches Jahrbuch* 9: 22–30.

Bexley, E. M. (2014) 'Plautus and Terence in Performance' in M. Fontaine and A. Scafuro (eds.) *The Oxford Handbook of Greek and Roman Comedy*. Oxford and New York: 462–76.

Bisanti, A. (2005) *Un ventennio di studi du Rosvita di Gandersheim*. Spoleto.

Blänsdorf, J. (1974) 'Das Bild der Komödie in der späten Republik' in U. Reinhardt, K. Sallmann, and H. Chelius (eds.) *Musa Iocosa. Arbeiten über Humor und Witz, Komik und Komödie der Antike*. Hildesheim and New York: 141–57.

Blänsdorf, J. (1996) 'Un trait original de la comédie de Plaute: le goût de la parodie', *Cahiers du groupe interdisciplinaire du théâtre antique* 9: 133–51.

Blänsdorf, J. (2003) '*Atellana fabula*' in H. Cancik and H. Schneider (eds.) *The New Pauly: Brill's Encyclopaedia of the Ancient World*. Leiden and Boston: vol. 2, cols. 224–6.

Bléry, H. (1965) *Syntaxe de la subordination dans Térence*. Rome.

Bloomer, W. M. (2011) *The School of Rome: Latin Studies and the Origins of Liberal Education*. Berkeley.

Boas, M. (1914) '*De librorum Catonianorum historia atque compositione*', *Mnemosyne* 42: 17–46.

Boas, M. (ed.) (1952) *Disticha Catonis. Opus post Marci Boas mortem edendum curavit Henricus Johannes Botschuyver*. Amsterdam.

Bonner, S. F. (1977) *Education in Ancient Rome: From the Elder Cato to the Younger Pliny*. Berkeley.

Booth, K. (1998) 'National Mother, Global Whore, and Transnational Femocrats: the Politics of AIDS and the Construction of Women at the World Health Organization', *Feminist Studies* 24.1: 115–39.

Boughner, D. C. (1954) *The Braggart in Renaissance Comedy. A Study in Comparative Drama from Aristophanes to Shakespeare*. Minneapolis.

Boyle, A. J. (2006) *An Introduction to Roman Tragedy*. London and New York.

Bramante, M. V. (2007) 'Patres, filii et filiae nelle commedie di Plauto. Note sul diritto nel teatro' in E. Cantarella and L. Gagliardi (eds.) *Diritto e teatro in Grecia e a Roma*. Milan: 95–116.

Branham, R. Bracht (ed.) (2005) *The Bakhtin Circle and Ancient Narrative*. Groningen.

Braun, L. (1970) *Die Cantica des Plautus*. Göttingen.

Braun, L. (1980) *Scenae suppositiciae, oder, Der falsche Plautus*. Göttingen.

Braun, M. (2000) 'Moribus vivitur antiquis – Bemerkungen zur Moral im *Trinummus*' in M. Braun, A. Haltenhoff and F. H. Mutschler (eds.) *Moribus antiquis res stat Romana. Römische Werte und römische Literatur im 3. und 2. Jh. v. Chr.* Munich and Leipzig: 185–204.

Brenk, F. E. (1987) '*Heteros tis eimi*: on the Language of Menander's Young Lovers', *Illinois Classical Studies* 12: 31–66.

Briguglio, F. (2010) 'Barthold Georg Niebuhr und die Entdeckung der Gaius-Institutionen – tatsächlich ein "Glückstern"?', *Zeitschrift der Savigny-Stiftung für Rechtsgeschichte (Romanistische Abteilung)* 128: 263–97.

Brody, R. (2008) *Everything Is Cinema: The Working Life of Jean-Luc Godard*. London.

Brophy, R. H. (1974) 'Mancupium and Mancipatio in Plautus: One Specimen of Plautine Legal Humor and Metaphor'. Diss. Univ. Michigan.

Brothers, A. J. (ed.) (2000) *Terence, The Eunuch*. Warminster.

Brotherton, B. (1926) *The Vocabulary of Intrigue in Roman Comedy*. Menasha, WI.

Brown, M. P. (1990, rev. edn 1993) *A Guide to Western Historical Scripts from Antiquity to 1600*. London and Toronto.

Brown, P. G. McC. (1995) 'Aeschinus at the Door: Terence, *Adelphoe* 623–43 and the Traditions of Greco-Roman Comedy' in R. Brock and A. J. Woodman (eds.) *Papers of the Leeds International Latin Seminar 8*. Leeds: 71–88.

Brown, P. G. McC. (2000) 'Knocking at the Door in Fifth-century Greek Tragedy' in S. Gödde and T. Heinze (eds.) *Skenika: Beiträge zum antiken Theater und seiner Rezeption*. Darmstadt: 1–16.

Brown, P. G. McC. (2005) 'The Legal and Social Framework of Plautus' *Cistellaria*', *PLLS* 12: 53–70.

Brown, P. G. McC. (2013) 'Greek Comedy and the *Atellana*' in R. Raffaelli and A. Tontini (eds.) *L'Atellana Preletteraria. Atti della seconda giornata di studi sull'Atellana*. Urbino: 7–27.

Brown, P. R. (2004) 'Hrotsvit's *Sapientia* as a Foreign Woman' in P. R. Brown, L. A. McMillin and K. Wilson (eds.) *Hrotsvit of Gandersheim – Contexts, Identities, Affinities, and Performances*. Toronto: 160–76.

Brown, P. R. (ed.) (2006) *Terence – The Comedies*. Oxford.

Brown, P. R., and S. L. Wailes (eds.) (2012) *A Companion to Hrotsvit of Gandersheim (fl. 960): Contextual and Interpretive Approaches*. Leiden.

Brown, P. R. (2013) 'Terence and Greek New Comedy' in A. Augoustakis and A. Traill (eds.) *A Companion to Terence*. Malden, MA: 17–32.

Brown, P. R. (2014) 'The Beginnings of Roman Comedy' in M. Fontaine and A. Scafuro (eds.) *The Oxford Handbook of Greek and Roman Comedy*. Oxford and New York: 401–8.

Büchner, K. (1957) '*Summum ius summa iniuria*' in K. Büchner (ed.) Humanitas Romana. *Studien über Werke und Wesen der Römer*. Heidelberg: 80–105.

Buck, C. H. (1940) *A Chronology of the Plays of Plautus*. Baltimore.

Buonocore, M. (ed.) (1996) *Vedere i classici: l'illustrazione libraria dei testi antichi dall'età romana al tardo Medioevo* (exhibition catalogue). Rome.

Burkert, W. (2000) '"Stumm wie ein Menander-Chor": Ein zusätzliches Testimonium', *Zeitschrift für Papyrologie und Epigraphik* 131: 23–4.

Butler, J. (1990, 1999 rev. repr.) *Gender Trouble: Feminism and the Subversion of Identity*. New York.

Butler, J. (1993) *Bodies That Matter: On the Discursive Limits of 'Sex'*. New York.

Butler, J. (1997) *Excitable Speech: A Politics of the Performative*. New York.

Butler, M. M. (1960) *Hrotsvitha – The Theatricality of Her Plays*. New York.

Cahn, W. (1996) *Romanesque Manuscripts: The Twelfth Century* (2 vols). London.

Cain, A. (2013) 'Terence in Late Antiquity' in A. Augoustakis and A. Traill (eds.) *A Companion to Terence*. Malden, MA and Oxford: 380–96.

Calboli, G. (1997) 'Zur Pindarode: Horaz und Terenz', *Philologus* 141: 86–113.

Calhoun, G. M. (1922, repr. 1968) *The Business Life of Ancient Greece*. New York.

Candiard, C. (2017) *Esclaves et valets vedettes dans les comédies de la Rome antique et de la France d'Ancien Régime*. Paris.

Cantarella, E., and L. Gagliardi (eds.) (2007) *Diritto e teatro a Grecia e a Roma*. Milan.

Capitani, P. de (2005) *Du spectaculaire à l'intime: un siècle de* commedia erudita *en Italie et en France, début du xvie siècle–milieu du xviie siècle*. Paris.

Cardelle de Hartmann, C. (2003) 'Die Roswitha-Edition des Humanisten Conrad Celtis' in C. Henkes, W. Hettche, G. Radecke, and E. Senne (eds.) *Schrift – Text – Edition*. Tübingen: 137–47.

Cardoso, I. T. (2001) '*Matronae virtuosae* no *Stichus* de Plauto', *Phaos* 1: 21–38.

Cardoso, I. T. (2005) '*Ars Plautina*: Metalinguagem em gestos e figurino'. Unpublished Diss. University of São Paulo (USP).

Cardoso, I. T. (2006) *Estico de Plauto*. Campinas.

Cardoso, I. T. (2009) '*Theatrum mundi*: Philologie und Nachahmung' in J. Schwindt (ed.) *Was ist eine philologische Frage?*. Frankfurt am Main: 82–111.

Cardoso, I. T. (2010) 'Ilusão e engano em Plauto' in Z. A. Cardoso and A. S. Duarte (eds.) *Estudos sobre o teatro antigo*. São Paulo: 95–126.

Cardoso, I. T. (2011) *Trompe l'oeil: Philologie und Illusion*. Göttingen.

Carney, T. F. (1964) 'The Words *sodes* and *quaeso* in Terentian Usage', *Acta Classica* 7: 57–63.

Casson, L. (1976) 'The Athenian Upper Class and New Comedy', *Transactions and Proceedings of the American Philological Association* 106: 29–59.

Casson, L. (1984) *Ancient Trade and Society*. Detroit.

Caston, R. R. (2014) 'Reinvention in Terence's *Eunuchus*', *Transactions and Proceedings of the American Philological Association* 144: 41–70.

Cavarero, A. (2016) *Inclinations: A Critique of Rectitude*, transl. A. S. Sitze and A. Minervini. Stanford.

Cerulli, E. (1970) 'Le calife 'Abd ar-Rahmān III de Cordove et le martyr Pélage dans un poème de Hrotsvitha', *Studia Islamica* 32: 69–76.

Chamberlain, D. (1980) 'Musical Learning and Dramatic Action in Hrotsvit's *Pafnutius*', *Studies in Philology* 77: 319–43.

Chambers, E. K. (1903) *The Medieval Stage* (2 vols). London.

Charitonidis, S., L. Kahil, and R. Ginouvès (1970) *Les Mosaïques de la Maison du Ménandre à Mytilène*. Bern.

Chatelain, E. (1884–1900) *Paléographie des classiques latins* (2 vols). Paris.

Chelius, K. H. (1989) *Die Codices minores des Plautus: Forschungen zur Geschichte und Kritik*. Baden-Baden.

Chiarini, G. (ed.) (1992) *Tito Maccio Plauto, Casina*. Rome.

Christenson, D. M. (2000) *Plautus:* Amphitruo. Cambridge.

Christenson, D. M. (2008) *Plautus: Four Plays* (Casina, Amphitryon, Captiui, Pseudolus). Newburyport, MA.

Christenson, D. M. (2010) *Roman Comedy: Five Plays by Plautus and Terence*. Newburyport, MA.

Christenson, D. M. (2013) '*Eunuchus*' in A. Augoustakis and A. Traill (eds.) *A Companion to Terence*. Malden, MA: 262–80.

Cicu, L. (1988) *Problemi e strutture del mimo a Roma*. Sassari.

Clackson, J., and G. Horrocks (2007) *The Blackwell History of the Latin Language*. Oxford.

Clark, A. J. (2007) *Divine Qualities: Cult and Community in Republican Rome*. Oxford.

Clementi, G. (2009) *La filologia plautina negli Adversaria di Adrien Turnèbe*. Alessandria.

Cloud, J. D. (1989) 'Satirists and the Law' in S. H. Braund (ed.) *Satire and Society in Ancient Rome*. Exeter: 49–67.

Clubb, L. G. (1989) *Italian Drama in Shakespeare's Time*. New Haven and London.

Coffee, N. (2009) *The Commerce of War: Exchange and Social Order in Latin Epic*. Chicago.

Cohen, E. (1992) *Athenian Economy and Society*. Princeton.

Cohen, K. (1977) 'Eisenstein's Subversive Adaptation' in G. Peary and R. Shatzkin (eds.) *The Classic American Novel and the Movies*. New York: 245–56.

Collart, J. (1979) *Plaute: Curculio*. Paris.

Comerci, G. (1994) '*Humanitas, liberalitas, aequitas*: Nuova paideia e mediazione sociale negli *Adelphoe* di Terenzio', *Bollettino di studi latini* 24: 3–44.

Connolly, J. (2007) *The State of Speech: Rhetoric and Political Thought in Ancient Rome*. Princeton, NJ.

Connors, C. (2004) 'Monkey Business: Imitation, Authenticity and Identity from Pithekoussai to Plautus', *Classical Antiquity* 23: 179–207.

Conrady, K. O. (1954) 'Zu den deutschen Plautusübertragungen. Ein Überblick von Albrecht von Eyb bis zu J. M. R. Lenz', *Euphorion* 48: 373–96.

Cooper, L. (1922) *An Aristotelian Theory of Comedy: With an Adaptation of* The Poetics, *and a Translation of the* Tractatus Coislinianus. New York.

Corno, D. del. (1975) 'Alcuni aspetti del linguaggio di Menandro', *Studi classici e orientali* 23: 13–48.

Costa, E. (1890) *Il diritto privato romano nelle commedie di Plauto*. Turin. (Reprint Rome 1968).

Costa, E. (1893) *Il diritto privato nelle commedie di Terenzio*. Bologna. (Reprint Rome 1970.)

Costa, L. N. (2013) *Plauto,* Anfitrião. Campinas.

Coulter, C. C. (1929) 'The "Terentian" Comedies of a Tenth-Century Nun', *Classical Journal* 24: 515–29.

Courcelle, P. (1972) 'Ambroise de Milan face aux comiques latins', *Revue des études latines* 50: 223–31.

Creizenach, W. (1893) *Geschichte des neuren Dramas I (Mittelalter und Frührenaissance)*. Halle.

Crook, J. A. (1967) '*Patria Potestas*', *Classical Quarterly* 17: 113–22.

Csapo, E. (1999) 'Performance and Iconographic Tradition in the Illustrations of Menander' in J. Porter (ed.) *Crossing the Stages: The Production, Performance and Reception of Ancient Theater*. Iowa City: 154–77.

Csapo, E. (2000) 'From Aristophanes to Menander? Genre Transformation in Greek Comedy' in M. Depew and D. Obbink (eds.) *Matrices of Genre: Authors, Canons, and Society*. Cambridge, MA: 115–34.

Csapo, E. (2010) 'Cooking with Menander: Slices from the Ancient Home Entertainment Industry?' in E. Csapo (ed.) *Actors and Ancient Theater*. Malden, MA: 140–67.

Csapo, E., and W. J. Slater (eds.) (1994) *The Context of Ancient Drama*. Ann Arbor.

Dahlheim, A. W. (1968) *Struktur und Entwicklung des römischen Völkerrechts im 3. und 2. Jahrhundert v. Chr.* Munich.

Damen, M. L. (1990) 'Structure and Symmetry in Terence's *Adelphoe*', *Illinois Classical Studies* 15: 85–106.

Damen, M. L. (1992) 'Translating Scenes: Plautus' Adaptation of Menander's *Dis Exapaton*', *Phoenix* 46: 205–31.

Damen, M. L. (1995) '"By the Gods, Boy ... Stop Bothering Me! Can't You Tell Menander from Plautus?" Or How *Dis Exapaton* Does Not Help Us Understand *Bacchides*', *Antichthon* 29: 15–29.

Damon, C. (4th edn 2000) *The Mask of the Parasite*. Ann Arbor.

Danese, R. M. (1985) 'Plauto, *Pseud.* 702–705a: la "costruzione stilistica" di un eroe perfetto', *Materiali e discussioni* 14: 101–12.

Danese, R. M. (1989) 'Revisione del P. Vindob. L 103 (Terenzio)', *SCO* 39: 133–57.

Danese, R. M. (2006) 'Plauto e l'*urbanitas* del dialetto', *Linguistica e Letteratura* 31: 37–66.

Danese, R. M. (2002) 'Modelli letterari e modelli culturali del teatro plautino' in C. Questa and R. Raffaelli (eds.) *Due seminari plautini. La tradizione del testo. I modelli*. Urbino: 133–53.

Dareste, R. (1892) 'Review of Costa 1890', *Journal de Savants* 1892: 145–54, reprinted with slight modifications in R. Dareste (1902) *Nouvelles études d'histoire du droit*, as part of 'Le droit romain et le droit grec dans Plaute'. Paris: 149–63.

Dareste, R. (1900) 'Review of Costa 1890, Becker 1892, Pernard 1900 et al.', *Nouvelle revue historique de droit français et étranger* 24: 677–87, reprinted with slight modifications in R. Dareste (1902) *Nouvelles études d'histoire du droit*, as part of 'Le droit romain et le droit grec dans Plaute'. Paris: 163–75.

Daviault, A. (1981) Comoedia Togata. *Fragments*. Paris.

De Certeau, M. (1984) *The Practice of Everyday Life*. Berkeley, Los Angeles and London.

De Luca, K. (1974) 'Hrotsvit's "Imitation" of Terence', *Classical Folia* 28: 89–102.

De Man, P. (1985) '"Conclusions", Walter Benjamin's "The Task of the Translator" Messenger Lecture, Cornell University, March 4, 1983', *Yale French Studies* 69: 25–46.

374

De Melo, W. D. C. (2007) *The Early Latin Verbal System: Archaic Forms in Plautus, Terence, and Beyond*. Oxford.

De Melo, W. D. C. (2010) 'The Language of Atellan Farce' in R. Raffaelli and A. Tontini (eds.) *L'Atellana letteraria: Atti della prima giornata di studi sull'Atellana: Succivo (CE) 30 Ottobre 2009*. Urbino: 121–55.

De Melo, W. D. C. (2011a) 'The Language of Roman Comedy' in J. Clackson (ed.) *A Companion to the Latin Language*. Malden, MA: 321–43.

De Melo, W. D. C. (2011b) *Plautus*: Amphitryon; The Comedy of Asses; The Pot of Gold; The Two Bacchises; The Captives. Cambridge, MA.

De Melo, W. D. C. (2011c) *Plautus*: Casina; The Casket Comedy; Curculio; Epidicus; The Two Menaechmuses. Cambridge, MA.

De Melo, W. D. C. (2013) *Plautus*: Stichus; Three-Dollar Day; Truculentus; The Tale of a Travelling-Bag; Fragments. Cambridge, MA.

De Zulueta, F. (1946) *The Institutes of Gaius. Part 1. Text with Critical Notes and Translation*. Oxford.

Debouy, E. (2010) 'The Titles of the *Atellanae*: an Attempt at a Typology' in R. Raffaelli and A. Tontini (eds.) *L'Atellana letteraria: Atti della prima giornata di studi sull'Atellana: Succivo (CE) 30 Ottobre 2009*. Urbino: 157–68.

Dees, R. L. (1988) 'Aspects of the Roman Law of Marriage in Plautus' *Casina*', *Iura* 39: 107–20.

Del Zotto, C. (2009) *Rosvita – La poetessa degli imperatori sassoni* (Donne d'Oriente e d'Occidente 22). Milan.

Delehaye, H. (1936) *Étude sur le légendier romain – Les saints de novembre et de décembre*. Brussels: 227–35.

Deleuze, G., and F. Guattari (1986) *Kafka: Toward a Minor Literature*, transl. D. Polan and R. Bensmaïa. Minneapolis.

Denard, H. (2007) 'Lost Theatre and Performance Traditions in Greece and Italy' in M. McDonald and M. Walton (eds.) *The Cambridge Companion to Greek and Roman Theatre*. Cambridge: 139–60.

Derrida, J. (1985) 'Deconstruction in America: An Interview with Jacques Derrida', *Critical Exchange* 17: 1–33.

Derrida, J. (1996) *Archive Fever: A Freudian Impression*, transl. E. Prenowitz. Chicago.

Dessen, C. S. (1977) 'Plautus' Satiric Comedy: the *Truculentus*', *Philological Quarterly* 56: 145–68.

Dessen, C. S. (1995) 'The Figure of the Eunuch in Terence's *Eunuchus*', *Helios* 22: 123–39.

Detienne, M., and J.-P. Vernant (1991) *Cunning Intelligence in Greek Culture and Society*, transl. J. Lloyd. Chicago.

Deufert, M. (2002) *Textgeschichte und Rezeption der plautinischen Komödien im Altertum*. Berlin.

Di Benedetto, A. (1962) 'Echi terenziani in Orazio', *Rendiconti della Accademia di Archeologia, Lettere e Belle Arti di Napoli*, N.S. 37: 35–57.

Dickey, E., and A. Chahoud (2010) *Colloquial and Literary Latin*. Cambridge.

Dickie, M. W. (1981) 'The Disavowal of *Invidia* in Roman Iamb and Satire', *Papers of the Leeds International Latin Seminar* 3: 183–208.

Diderot, D. (1971) *Œuvres complètes*, ed. Roger Lewinter (15 vols). Paris.

Dietl, C. (2005) *Die Dramen Jacob Lochers und die frühe Humanistenbühne im süddeutschen Raum*. Berlin and New York.

Dittrich, P. (1915) 'Plautus und Terenz in Pädagogik und Schulwesen der deutschen Humanisten'. Diss. Leipzig.

Dixon, S. (1992) *Roman Family*. Baltimore.

Dixon, S. (2001) *Childhood, Class and Kin in the Roman World*. London.

Dobrov, G. W. (2001) *Figures of Play: Greek Drama and Metafictional Poetics*. Oxford.

Dolezal, M. L. (1996) 'The Elusive Quest for the "Real Thing": The Chicago Lectionary Project Thirty Years On', *Gesta* 35: 128–41.

Donadio, N. (2007) 'Le auctiones private all'epoca di Plauto' in E. Cantarella and L. Gagliardi (eds.) *Diritto e teatro in Grecia e a Roma*'. Milan: 117–97.

Donderer, M. (2008) 'Antike Musterbücher und (k)ein Ende: Ein neuer Papyrus und die Aussage der Mosaiken', *Musiva et Sectilia* 2–3: 81–113.

Douglas, M. (1999) *Implicit Meanings: Selected Essays in Anthropology*. London and Boston.

Dover, K. J. (1972) *Aristophanic Comedy*. Berkeley, CA.

Dressler, A. (2016) 'Plautus and the Politics of Property: Reification, Recognition, and Utopia', *MD* 77: 9–56.

Dronke, P. (1984) 'Hrotsvitha' in P. Dronke (ed.) *Women Writers of the Middle Ages – A Critical Study of Texts from Perpetua († 203) to Marguerite Porete († 1310)*. Cambridge: 55–83.

Duckworth, G. E. (1952/1994) *The Nature of Roman Comedy. A Study in Popular Entertainment*, Princeton, NJ. Second edition (1994) with a foreword and bibliographical appendix by R. Hunter, Norman, OK, and Bristol.

Dunn, W. R. (1984) 'Formal Language in Plautus'. Diss. Harvard.

Dutsch, D. (2002) 'Towards a Grammar of Gesture. A Comparison Between Types of Hand Movements of the Actor and the Orator in Quintilian's *Institutio oratoria* 11.3.85–184', *Gesture* 2.2: 259–81.

Dutsch, D. (2004) 'Female Furniture: a Reading of Plautus' *Poenulus* 1141–6', *Classical Quarterly* 54.2: 625–30.

Dutsch, D. (2005) 'Roman Pharmacology: Plautus' *blanda venena*', *Greece and Rome* 52.2: 205–20.

Dutsch, D. (2008) *Feminine Discourse in Roman Comedy: On Echoes and Voices*. Oxford.

Dutsch, D., and D. Konstan (2011) 'Women's Emotions in New Comedy' in D. Munteanu (ed.) *Emotion, Genre, Gender in Antiquity*. London: 57–88.

Dutsch, D., S. James, and D. Konstan (2015) *Women in Republican Roman Drama*. Madison, WI.

Eagleton, T. (1981) *Walter Benjamin, or Towards a Revolutionary Criticism*. London.

Easterling, P., and E. Hall (eds.) (2002) *Greek and Roman Actors: Aspects of an Ancient Profession*. Cambridge.

Edwards, C. (1993) *The Politics of Immorality in Ancient Rome*. Cambridge.

Ehrman, R. K. (1985) 'Terentian Prologues and the Parabases of Old Comedy', *Latomus* 44: 370–6.

Elliott, J. R., et al. (eds.) (2004) *Records of Early English Drama* (2 vols). Oxford and Toronto.

Ernout, A. (2nd edn 1957) *Plautus, Titus Maccius:* Pseudolus. Rudens. Stichus. Paris.

Ernout, A., and F. Thomas (1972) *Syntaxe latine.* Paris.

Fabricius, J. A. (2nd edn 1719) *Codex apocryphus Novi Testamenti*, II. Hamburg.

Fachechi, G. M. (1998) 'Amphitruo Illustrato' in R. Raffaelli and A. Tontini (ed.) *Lecturae Plautinae Sarsinates I Amphitruo.* Urbino: 89–96.

Fachechi, G. M. (2002) 'Plauto illustrato fra Medioevo e Umanesimo', *Rendiconti dell'Accademia dei Lincei* 13: 177–242.

Falcone, G. (1988) 'Testimonianze Plautine in tema di interdicta', *Annali del Seminario Giuridico dell'Univ. di Palermo* 40: 175–213.

Fantham, E. (1965) 'The *Curculio* of Plautus: An Illustration of Plautine Methods in Adaptation', *Classical Quarterly* 59: 84–100.

Fantham, E. (1968a) 'Terence, Diphilus and Menander: A Reexamination of Terence *Adelphoe* Act II', *Philologus* 112: 196–216.

Fantham, E. (1968b) 'Act IV of the *Menaechmi*: Plautus and His Greek Original', *Classical Philology* 63: 175–83.

Fantham, E. (1972) *Comparative Studies in Republican Latin Imagery.* Toronto.

Fantham, E. (1975) 'Sex, Status, and Survival in Hellenistic Athens: a Study of Women in New Comedy', *Phoenix* 29: 44–74.

Fantham, E. (1978) 'Adaptation and Survival: A Genre Study of Roman Comedy in Relation to Its Greek Sources' in P. G. Ruggiers (ed.) *Versions of Medieval Comedy.* Norman, OK: 297–317.

Fantham, E. (1988) 'Mime: The Missing Link in Roman Literary History', *The Classical World* 82: 153–63.

Fantham, E. (1993) 'The Growth of Literature and Criticism at Rome' in G. A. Kennedy (ed.) *The Cambridge History of Literary Criticism, I: Classical Criticism.* Cambridge.

Fantham, E. (2000) 'DOMINA-tricks' in E. Stärk and G. Vogt-Spira (eds.) *Dramatische Wäldchen.* Hildesheim, Zurich and New York: 287–99.

Fantham, E. (2002) 'Orator and/et Actor' in P. Easterling and E. Hall (eds.) *Greek and Roman Actors: Aspects of an Ancient Profession.* Cambridge: 362–76.

Fantham, E. (2004a) 'Women of the Demi-monde and Sisterly Solidarity in the *Cistellaria*' in R. Hartkamp and F. Hurka (eds.) *Studien zu Plautus'* Cistellaria. Tübingen: 221–38.

Fantham, E. (2004b) 'Maiden in Other-land or Broads Abroad: Plautus' *Poenulae*' in T. Baier (ed.) *Studien zu Plautus'* Poenulus. Tübingen: 235–51.

Fantham, E. (2004c) 'Literature of the Roman Republic' in H. I. Flower (ed.) *The Cambridge Companion to the Roman Republic.* Cambridge: 271–93.

Fantham, E. (2004d) 'Terence and the Familiarisation of Comedy' in A. J. Boyle (ed.) *Rethinking Terence. Ramus* 33: 20–34.

Fantham, E. (2004e) 'Disowning and Dysfunction in the Declamatory Family', *Materiali e discussioni per l'analisi dei testi classici* 53: 65–82.

Farmer, J. (ed.) (1906) *Early English Dramatists. Anonymous Plays, Third Series.* London.

Feeney, D. (1998) *Literature and Religion at Rome: Cultures, Contexts, and Beliefs.* Cambridge.

Feeney, D. (2006) 'Review of Goldberg 2005', *Bryn Mawr Classical Review* 2006.08.45.

Feeney, D. (2010) 'Crediting Pseudolus: Trust, Belief, and the Credit Crunch in Plautus' *Pseudolus*', *Classical Philology* 105: 281–300.

Feeney, D. (2016) *Beyond Greek: The Beginnings of Latin Literature*. Cambridge, MA.

Fitzgerald, W. (2000) *Slavery and the Roman Literary Imagination*. Cambridge.

Flamerie de Lachapelle, G. (2011) *Publius Syrus. Sentences*. Paris.

Flower, H. I. (ed.) (2004) *The Cambridge Companion to the Roman Republic*. Cambridge.

Fögen, T. (2009) '*Sermo corporis*: Ancient Reflections on *gestus*, *vultus* and *vox*' in T. Fögen (ed.) *Bodies and Boundaries in Graeco-Roman Antiquity*. Berlin and New York: 15–43.

Fontaine, M. (2010) *Funny Words in Plautine Comedy*. New York and Oxford.

Fontaine, M. (2014a) 'Between Two Paradigms: Plautus' in M. Fontaine and A. Scafuro (eds.) *The Oxford Handbook of Greek and Roman Comedy*. Oxford and New York: 516–37.

Fontaine, M. (2014b) 'The Terentian Reformation: From Menander to Alexandria' in M. Fontaine and A. Scafuro (eds.) *The Oxford Handbook of Greek and Roman Comedy*. Oxford and New York: 538–54.

Fontaine, M. (2014c) 'Dynamic of Appropriation in Roman Comedy: Menander's *Kolax* in Three Roman Receptions (Naevius, Plautus, and Terence's *Eunuchus*)' in S. D. Olson (ed.) *Ancient Comedy and Reception: Essays in Honor of Jeffrey Henderson*. Berlin and Boston: 180–202.

Fontaine, M. (2014d) 'The Reception of Greek Comedy in Rome' in M. Revermann (ed.) *The Cambridge Companion to Greek Comedy*. Cambridge: 404–23.

Fontaine, M. (2015) *Joannes Burmeister: Aulularia and other Inversions of Plautus*. Leuven.

Fontaine, M., and A. Scafuro (eds.) (2014) *The Oxford Handbook of Greek and Roman Comedy*. Oxford and New York.

Forehand, W. E. (1973) 'The Use of Imagery in Plautus' *Miles Gloriosus*', *Rivista di studi classici* 21: 5–16.

Fortier, M. (2002) *Theory/Theatre: An Introduction*. London.

Fortson, IV, B. W. (2008) *Language and Rhythm in Plautus*. Berlin.

Fournier, E. (ed.) (1858) *Chansons de Gaultier-Garguille*. Paris.

Fraenkel, E. (1922) *Plautinisches im Plautus*. Berlin. (Translated into Italian (1960) *Elementi Plautini* and into English (2007) *Plautine Elements*.)

Fraenkel, E. (1935) 'Naevius', *Paulys Realencyclopädie* Suppl. 6: 622–40.

Fraenkel, E. (1960) *Elementi Plautini in Plauto*. Florence. (Translation with addenda of *Plautinisches im Plautus*, Berlin (1922).)

Fraenkel, E. (2007) *Plautine Elements in Plautus*, Oxford. (Translation by Tomas Drevikovsky and Frances Muecke of *Plautinisches im Plautus*, Berlin (1922).)

Frangoulidis, S. (1994) 'Palaestrio as Playwright: Plautus, *Miles Gloriosus* 209–212' in C. Deroux (ed.) *Studies in Latin Literature and Roman History VII*. Brussels: 72–86.

Frangoulidis, S. (1995) 'The Parasite as Poet-playwright and the Slave as Parasite in Terence's *Phormio*', *Bollettino di studi latini* 25.2: 397–425.

Frangoulidis, S. (1996) '(Meta)theatre as Therapy in Terence's *Phormio*', *Classica et Mediaevalia* 47: 169–206.

Frangoulidis, S. (2013) '*Phormio*' in A. Augoustakis and A. Traill (eds.), *A Companion to Terence*. Malden, MA: 281–94.

Franko, G. F. (1999) 'Imagery and Names in Plautus' *Casina*', *Classical Journal* 95: 1–17.

Franko, G. F. (2013) 'Terence and the Traditions of Roman New Comedy' in A. Augoustakis and A. Traill (eds.) *A Companion to Terence*. Malden, MA and Oxford: 33–51.

Franko, G. F. (2014) 'Festivals, Producers, Theatrical Spaces, and Records' in M. Fontaine and A. Scafuro (eds.) *The Oxford Handbook of Greek and Roman Comedy*. Oxford and New York.

Frassinetti, P. (1953) Fabula Atellana. *Saggio sul teatro popolare latino*. Genoa.

Frauenfelder, D. W. (1996) 'Respecting Terence, *Adelphoe* 155–75', *Classical World* 90: 23–32.

Fredershausen, O. (1906) 'De iure Plautino et Terentiano'. Diss. Göttingen.

Fredershausen, O. (1912) 'Weitere Studien über das Recht bei Plautus und Terenz', *Hermes* 47: 199–249.

Freud, S. (1957–81) *The Standard Edition of the Complete Psychological Works of Sigmund Freud XI*. London.

Fuhrmann, M. (1971) 'Philologische Bemerkungen zur Sentenz "*Summum ius summa iniuria*"' in *Studi in onore di Edoardo Volterra II*. Milan: 53–81.

Gaertner, J. F. (2011a) *Das antike Recht und die griechisch-römische Neue Komödie: Untersuchungen zu Plautus und seinen griechischen Vorbildern I* (2 vols). Habil. Leipzig.

Gaertner, J. F. (2011b) *Das antike Recht und die griechisch-römische Neue Komödie: Untersuchungen zu Plautus und seinen griechischen Vorbildern II* (2 vols). Habil. Leipzig.

Gaertner, J. F. (2018) 'Die Funktion des *mancipium* in der römischen Komödie' in H.-G. Nesselrath and J. Platschek (eds.), *Menschen und Recht. Fallstudien zu Rechtsfragen und ihrer Bedeutung in der griechischen und römischen Komödie*. Tübingen: 137–61.

Gagarin, M. (2005) 'The Unity of Greek Law' in M. Gagarin and D. Cohen (eds.) *The Cambridge Companion to Ancient Greek Law*. Cambridge: 29–40.

Gagliardi, L. (2007) 'La figura del giudice privato del processo civile romano. Per un'analisi storico-sociologica sulla base delle fonti letterarie (da Plauto a Macrobio)' in E. Cantarella and L. Gagliardi (eds.) *Diritto e teatro in Grecia e a Roma*. Milan: 199–217. (Reprinted in German with slight modifications as Gagliardi (2008)).

Gagliardi, L. (2008) 'Zur Figur des iudex privatus im römischen Zivilprozess. Eine historisch-soziologische Untersuchung auf der Grundlage literarischer Quellen', *Revue internationale des droits de l'antiquité* 55: 241–66. (= German version of Gagliardi (2007) with slight modifications.)

Gaiser, K. (1972) 'Zur Eigenart der römischen Komödie: Plautus und Terenz gegenüber ihren griechischen Vorbildern', *Aufstieg und Niedergang der römischen Welt* I.2. Berlin and New York: 1027–113.

Galinsky, G. K. (1966) 'Scipionic Themes in Plautus' *Amphitruo*', *Transactions and Proceedings of the American Philological Association* 97: 203–35.

Galinsky, G. K. (1969) 'Plautus' *Poenulus* and the Cult of Venus Erycina' in J. Bibauw (ed.) *Hommages à Marcel Renard I*. Brussels: 358–64.

Galinsky, G. K. (1996) *Augustan Culture: An Interpretive Introduction*. Princeton, NJ.
K. Hopkins, and R. Whittaker (eds.) (1983) *Trade in the Ancient Economy*. Berkeley.
Germany, R. (2013) 'Andria' in A. Augoustakis and A. Traill (eds.) *A Companion to Terence*. Malden, MA: 225–42.
Gerschner, R. (2002) *Die Deklination der Nomina bei Plautus*. Heidelberg.
Gigante, M. (1971) *Rintone e il teatro in Magna Grecia*. Naples.
Gilbert, A. H. (1913) 'Thomas Heywood's Debt to Plautus', *Journal of English and Germanic Philology* 12: 593–611.
Gildenhard, I. (2007) *Paideia Romana. Cicero's Tusculan Disputations*. Cambridge.
Gilleland, M. E. (1979) 'Linguistic Differentiation of Character Type and Sex in the Comedies of Plautus and Terence'. Diss. Charlottesville.
Gilula, D. (1978) 'Where Did the Audience Go?', *Scripta Classica Israelica* 4: 45–9.
Gilula, D. (1980) 'The Concept of *bona meretrix*: A Study of Terence's Courtesans', *Rivista di filologia e di istruzione classica* 108: 142–65.
Gilula, D. (1981) 'Who's Afraid of Rope-walkers and Gladiators? (Ter. *Hec.* 1–57)', *Athenaeum* 59: 29–37.
Gilula, D. (1989) 'Greek Drama in Rome: Some Aspects of Cultural Transposition' in H. Scolnicov and P. Holland (eds.) *The Play Out of Context. Transferring Plays from Culture to Culture*. Cambridge: 99–109.
Giovini, M. (2001) 'Riscritture Terenziane – il motivo delle "nozze simulate" nel *Gallicanus*', *Maia* 53: 649–73.
Giovini, M. (2003) *Rosvita e l'imitari dictando terenziano*. Genoa.
Giovini, M. (2006a) 'Elementi poetici e drammatici nel Delusor (X sec.)', *Studi umanistici piceni* 26: 126–47.
Giovini, M. (2006b) 'La cucina infernale e la mirabile illusione: Il *Dulcitius* di Rosvita fra drammaturgia e innografia', *Mediaevalia* 27: 155–83.
Giovini, M. (2007) *Un conflictus terenziano del X secolo: il Delusor*. Milan.
Girard, P. F. (1893) 'Review of Costa 1890, Bekker 1892 et al.', *Nouvelle revue historique de droit français et étranger* 17: 789–97.
Giraudoux, J. (1967) *Three Plays, Volume 2* – Siegfried; Amphitryon 38; Electra, transl. Phyllis La Farge and Peter Judd. London.
Goddard Elliott, A. (1984) *Seven Medieval Latin Comedies*. New York.
Goetting, H. (1950) 'Die Anfänge des Reichsstifts Gandersheim', *Braunschweigisches Jahrbuch* 31: 5–52.
Goetting, H. (1973) *Die Bistümer der Kirchenprovinz Mainz – Das Bistum Hildesheim I: Das Reichsunmittelbare Kanonissenstift Gandersheim*. Berlin.
Gold, B. (1998) '"Vested Interests" in Plautus' *Casina*: Cross-Dressing in Roman Comedy', *Helios* 25: 17–29.
Goldberg, S. (1983) 'Terence, Cato, and the Rhetorical Prologue', *Classical Philology* 78: 198–211.
Goldberg, S. (1986) *Understanding Terence*. Princeton, NJ.
Goldberg, S. (1989) 'Poetry, Politics, and Ennius', *Transactions and Proceedings of the American Philological Association* 119: 247–61.
Goldberg, S. (1990) 'Act to Action in Plautus' *Bacchides*', *Classical Philology* 85: 191–201.
Goldberg, S. (1995) 'Improvisation, Plot, and Plautus' *Curculio*' in L. Benz, E. Stärk, and G. Vogt-Spira (eds.) *Plautus und die Tradition des Stegreifspiels*. Tübingen: 33–41.

Goldberg, S. (1998) 'Plautus on the Palatine', *Journal of Roman Studies* 88: 1–20.

Goldberg, S. (2000) 'Catullus 42 and the Comic Legacy' in E. Stärk and G. Vogt-Spira (eds.) *Dramatische Wäldchen.* Hildesheim, Zurich and New York: 475–89.

Goldberg, S. (2004) 'Plautus and his Alternatives. Textual Doublets in *Cistellaria*' in R. Hartkamp and F. Hurka (eds.) *Studien zu Plautus' Cistellaria.* Tübingen: 385–98.

Goldberg, S. (2005) *Constructing Literature in the Roman Republic. Poetry and its Reception.* Cambridge.

Goldberg, S. (2007a) 'Comedy and society from Menander to Terence' in M. McDonald and M. Walton (eds.) *The Cambridge Companion to Greek and Roman Theatre.* Cambridge: 124–38.

Goldberg, S. (2007b) 'Reading Roman Tragedy', *International Journal of the Classical Tradition* 13.4: 571–84.

Goldberg, S. (2007c) 'The Early Republic: the Beginnings to 90 BC' in S. Harrison (ed.) *A Companion to Latin Literature.* Oxford: 15–30.

Goldberg, S. (ed.) (2013) *Terence,* Hecyra. Cambridge and New York.

Goldberg, S. (2018) 'Theater without Theaters: Seeing Plays the Roman Way', *TAPA* 148: 139–72.

Goldoni, C. (1787) *Mémoires de Goldoni, pour servir à l'histoire de ma vie et à celle du théâtre.* Paris.

Gordan, P. W. G. (1974) *Two Renaissance Book Hunters: The Letters of Poggius Bracciolini to Nicholaus de Niccolis.* New York and London.

Gotter, U. (2008) 'Cultural Differences and Cross-Cultural Contact: Greek and Roman Concepts of Power', *Harvard Studies in Classical Philology* 104: 179–230.

Goullet, M. (1993) 'Les drames de Hrotsvita de Gandersheim, édition critique avec introduction, traduction, et notes.' Diss. Metz.

Goullet, M. (ed.) (1999) *Hrotsvita – Théâtre.* Paris.

Gowers, E. (1993) *The Loaded Table: Representations of Food in Roman Literature.* Oxford.

Gowers, E. (2004) 'The Plot Thickens: Hidden Outlines in Terence's Prologues' in A. J. Boyle (ed.) *Rethinking Terence. Ramus* 33: 150–66.

Graf, F. (1992) 'Gestures and Conventions: the Gestures of Roman Actors and Orators' in J. Bremmer and H. Roodenburg (eds.) *A Cultural History of Gesture.* Ithaca, NY: 36–58.

Grant, J. N. (1975) 'The Ending of Terence's *Adelphoe* and the Menandrian original', *American Journal of Philology* 96: 42–60.

Grant, J. N. (1986) *Studies in the Textual Tradition of Terence.* Toronto, Buffalo, NY, and London.

Gratwick, A. S. (1973) 'Titus Maccius Plautus', *Classical Quarterly* 23: 78–84.

Gratwick, A. S. (1982a) 'Drama' in E. J. Kenney and W. V. Clausen (eds.) *The Cambridge History of Classical Literature II: Latin Literature.* Cambridge: 77–137.

Gratwick, A. S. (1982b) 'Light Drama' in E. J. Kenney and W. V. Clausen (eds.) *The Cambridge History of Classical Literature II: Latin Literature.* Cambridge: 93–127. (= Subsection of Gratwick (1982a).)

Gratwick, A. S. (1987) *Terence: The Brothers.* Warminster.

Gratwick, A. S. (ed.) (1993) *Plautus: Menaechmi.* Cambridge.

Gratwick, A. S. (1995) 'The Schizophrenic Lover and the Logic of Farce: Plautus, *Bacchides* 500–511' in L. Benz, E. Stärk, and G. Vogt-Spira (eds.) *Plautus und die Tradition des Stegreifspiels*. Tübingen: 97–106.

Gratwick, A. S. (ed.) (2nd edn 1999) *Terence: The Brothers*. Warminster.

Green, J. R. (1985) 'Drunk Again: A Study in the Iconography of the Comic Theater', *American Journal of Archeology* 89: 465–72.

Green, J. R. (1994) *Theatre in Ancient Greek Society*. London.

Green, P. (1993) *Alexander to Actium: The Historical Evolution of the Hellenistic Age*. Berkeley.

Greenberg, N. A. (1979–80) 'Success and Failure in the *Adelphoe*', *CW* 73: 221–36.

Griffith, M. (2007) '"Telling the Tale": A Performing Tradition from Homer to Pantomime' in M. McDonald and M. Walton (eds.) *The Cambridge Companion to Greek and Roman Theatre*. Cambridge: 13–35.

Grilli, A. (1979) 'Educazione urbana ed educazione rustica in Terenzio' in *La città antica come fatto di cultura: Atti del convegno di Como e Bellagio, 16–19 giugno 1979*. Como: 23–34.

Grimal, P. (1986) 'Analyse du *Trinummus* et les débuts de la philosophie à Rome' in P. Grimal (ed.) *Rome. La literature et l'histoire I*. Rome: 363–75.

Grimm, H. (1974) 'Des Conradus Celtis Editio Princeps der Opera Hrotsvite von 1501 und Albrecht Dürers Anteil daran', *Philobiblon* 18: 3–25.

Grube, G. M. A. (1965) *The Greek and Roman Critics*. Indianapolis.

Gruen, E. S. (1990) *Studies in Greek Culture and Roman Policy*. Leiden, New York, Copenhagen and Cologne. (Paperback edition: Berkeley and London (1996)).

Gruen, E. S. (1992) *Culture and National Identity in Republican Rome*. Ithaca, NY.

Guardì, T. (1974) *Cecilio Stazio. I frammenti*. Palermo.

Guardì, T. (1981) 'Note sulla lingua di Titinio', *Pan* 7: 145–65.

Guardì, T. (1985) *Titinio e Atta. Fabula togata. I frammenti*. Milan.

Guastella, G. (1988) *La contaminazione e il parassita. Due studi su teatro e cultura romana*. Pisa.

Guastella, G. (2002) 'I monologhi di ingresso dei parassiti: Plauto e i modeli' in C. Questa and R. Raffaelli (eds.) *Due seminari plautini. La tradizione del testo. I modelli*. Urbino: 155–98.

Gunderson, E. (2000) *Staging Masculinity: The Rhetoric of Performance in the Roman World*. Ann Arbor.

Gunderson, E. (2009) *Nox Philologiae. Aulus Gellius and the Fantasy of the Roman Library*. Madison, WI.

Gunderson, E. (2015) *Laughing Awry: Plautus and Tragicomedy*. Oxford.

Gunderson, E. (2017) 'Rhetoric and Declamation' in M. J. MacDonald (ed.) *The Oxford Handbook of Rhetorical Studies*. Oxford: 267–78.

Günther, O. (1886) *Plautuserneuerungen in der deutschen Literatur des XV.–XVII. Jahrhunderts und ihre Verfasser*. Diss. Leipzig.

Habinek, T. (1998) *The Politics of Latin Literature: Writing, Identity and Empire in Ancient Rome*. Princeton, NJ.

Hadot, I. (1997) 'Geschichte der Bildung: *Artes liberales*' in F. Graf (ed.) *Einleitung in die lateinische Philologie*. Stuttgart and Leipzig: 17–34.

Haffter, H. (1934) *Untersuchungen zur altlateinischen Dichtersprache*. Berlin.

Hagendahl, H. (1967) *Augustine and the Latin Classics* (2 vols). Gothenburg.

Haight, A. L. (ed.) (1965) *Hroswitha of Gandersheim – Her Life, Times, and Works, and a Comprehensive Bibliography*. New York.

Hall, E. (2002) 'The Singing Actors of Antiquity' in P. Easterling and E. Hall (eds.) *Greek and Roman Actors: Aspects of an Ancient Profession*. Cambridge: 3–38.

Hallett, J. P. (1993) 'Plautine Ingredients in the Performance of the *Pseudolus*', *Classical World* 87: 21–6.

Halliwell, S. (2008) *Greek Laughter: A Study of Cultural Psychology from Homer to Early Christianity*. Cambridge.

Halporn, J. (1993) 'Roman Comedy and Greek Models' in R. Scodel (ed.)*Theatre and Society in the Classical World*. Ann Arbor: 191–213.

Hammer, D. (2009) 'What is Politics in the Ancient World?' in R. K. Balot (ed.) *A Companion to Greek and Roman Political Thought*. Malden, MA: 20–36.

Hammond, M., A. M. Mack, and W. Moskalew (eds.) (1963) *Plautus*, Miles Gloriosus. Cambridge, MA.

Handley, E. W. (1968) *Menander and Plautus. A Study in Comparison*. London.

Handley, E. W. (1997) 'Menander, *Dis Exapaton*' in *The Oxyrhynchus Papyri* 64: 14–42.

Handley, E. W. (2001) '*Actoris opera*: Words, Action and Acting in *Dis Exapaton* and *Bacchides*' in R. Raffaelli and A. Tontini (eds.) *Lecturae Plautinae Sarsinates IV: Bacchides*. Urbino: 13–36.

Handley, E. W. (2002a) 'Acting, Action and Words in New Comedy' in P. Easterling and E. Hall (eds.) *Greek and Roman Actors: Aspects of an Ancient Profession*. Cambridge and New York: 165–88.

Handley, E. W. (2002b) 'Theme and Variations. A Comparative Study in Plautine Comedy' in C. Questa and R. Raffaelli (eds.) *Due seminari plautini. La tradizione del testo. I modelli*. Urbino: 105–20.

Handley, E. W. (2011) 'The Rediscovery of Menander' in D. Obbink and R. Rutherford (eds.) *Culture in Pieces: Essays on Ancient Texts in Honour of Peter Parsons*. Oxford: 138–59.

Hanson, J. A. (1959) 'Plautus as a Source Book for Roman Religion', *Transactions and Proceedings of the American Philological Association* 90: 48–101.

Hanson, J. A. (1965) 'The Glorious Military' in T. A. Dorey and D. R. Dudley (eds.) *Roman Drama*. London: 51–85.

Happ, H. (1967) 'Die lateinische Umgangssprache und die Kunstsprache des Plautus', *Glotta* 45: 60–104.

Hardin, R. F. (2007) 'Encountering Plautus in the Renaissance: A Humanist Debate on Comedy', *Renaissance Quarterly* 60.3: 789–818.

Hardy, C. S. (2005) 'The Parasite's Daughter: Metatheatrical Costuming in Plautus' *Persa*', *Classical World* 99: 25–33.

Harries, B. (2007) 'Acting the Part: Techniques of the Comic Stage in Cicero's Early Speeches' in J. Booth (ed.) *Cicero on the Attack: Invective and Subversion in the Orations and Beyond*. Swansea: 129–47.

Harris, J. (1987) '"Thieves, Harlots and Stinking Goats": Fashionable Dress and Aesthetic Attitudes in Romanesque Art', *Costume* 21: 4–15.

Harrison, A. R. W. (1968) *The Law of Athens I. The Family and Property*. Oxford.

Harrsen, M. (1965) 'The Manuscripts' in A. L. Haight (ed.) *Hroswitha of Gandersheim*. New York: 42–53.

Harsh, P. W. (1940) 'The Position of Archaic Forms in the Verse of Plautus', *Classical Philology* 35: 126–42.

Hartkamp, R. F. (2004) *Von 'leno' zu 'ruffiano': die Darstellung, Entwicklung und Funktion der Figur des Kupplers in der römischen Palliata und in der italienischen Renaissancekomödie.* Tübingen.

Harvey, P. B. (1986) 'Historical Topicality in Plautus', *The Classical Word* 79: 297–304.

Haury, A. (1976) 'Une "Année de la femme" à Rome, 195 avant J.-C.?', *L'Italie préromaine et la Rome républicaine.* Paris: 427–36.

Hellegouarc'h, J. (1963) *Le vocabulaire latin des relations et des partis politiques sous la République.* Paris.

Henderson, J. (1999) 'Entertaining Arguments: Terence, *Adelphoe*' in J. Henderson (ed.) *Writing Down Rome. Satire, Comedy, and Other Offences in Latin Poetry.* Oxford: 38–68.

Henderson, J. (2004) 'Terence's Selbstaussöhnung: Payback Time of the Self (*Heautontimorumenus*)' in A. J. Boyle (ed.) *Rethinking Terence. Ramus* 33: 53–81.

Henderson, J. (2006) (ed.) *Plautus: The One about the Asses.* Madison, WI.

Henderson, J. (2009) (ed.) *A Plautus Reader: Selections from Eleven Plays.* Mundelein, IL.

Henry, M. M. (1985) *Menander's Courtesans and the Greek Comic Tradition.* Frankfurt am Main.

Hermand, L. (2011) '*Homo sum*: l'usage cicéronien des maximes de Térence' in Ch. Mauduit and P. Paré-Rey (eds.) *Les Maximes théâtrales en Grèce et à Rome: transferts, réécritures, remplois.* Lyon: 295–304.

Herrick, M. T. (1950) *Comic Theory in the Sixteenth Century.* Urbana, IL.

Herrick, M. T. (1960) *Italian Comedy in the Renaissance.* Urbana, IL.

Herrmann, M. (1893) 'Terenz in Deutschland bis zum Ausgang des 16. Jahrhunderts', *Mitteilungen der Gesellschaft für deutsche Erziehungs- und Schulgeschichte* 3: 1–28.

Herzog, R. (ed.) (1989) *Restauration und Erneuerung. Die lateinische Literatur von 284 bis 374 n. Chr.* Munich.

Heywood, T. (1874) *The Dramatic Works of Thomas Heywood*, ed. R. H. Shepherd (6 vols). London.

Heywood, T. (1921) *The Captives, or The Lost Recovered*, ed. A. C. Judson. New Haven.

Heywood, T. (1996) *Three Marriage Plays*, ed. P. Merchant. Manchester.

Hinds, S. (1998) *Allusion and Intertext.* Cambridge.

Hindsholm, S. C. (1990) *Plautus' verden: økonomiske og sociale relationer i komedierne.* Copenhagen.

Hoffmann, Z. (1980–1) 'Gebetsparodien in Plautus' *Komödien*', *Helikon* 20–1: 207–18.

Hofmann, J. B. (1951) *Lateinische Umgangssprache.* Heidelberg.

Hofmann, J. B. and Szantyr, A. (1965) *Lateinische Syntax und Stilistik.* Munich.

Hofmann, W. (1995) 'Die Körpersprache der Schauspieler als Mittel des Komischen bei Plautus' in L. Benz, E. Stärk and G. Vogt-Spira (eds.) *Plautus und die Tradition des Stegreifspiels.* Tübingen: 205–18.

Hokenson, J. (2006) *The Idea of Comedy: History, Theory, Critique.* Madison, NJ.

Holford-Strevens, L. (2003) *Aulus Gellius. An Antonine Scholar and his Achievement.* Oxford.

Hollis, A. S. (1994) 'Rights of Way in Ovid (*Heroides* 20.146) and Plautus (*Curculio* 36)', *Classical Quarterly* 44: 545–9.

Homeyer, H. (1968) '"Imitatio" and "aemulatio" im Werk der Hrotsvitha von Gandersheim', *Studi Medievali* 9, 966–79.

Hordern, J. H. (2004) *Sophron's Mimes. Text, Translation, and Commentary.* Oxford.

Hornby, R. (1986) *Drama, Metadrama, and Perception.* Lewisburg, PA.

Hosley, R. (1967) 'The Formal Influence of Plautus and Terence' in J. R. Brown and B. Harris (ed.) *Elizabethan Theatre.* New York: 130–45.

Höttemann, B. (1993) 'Phlyakenposse und Atellane' in G. Vogt-Spira (ed.) *Beiträge zur mündlichen Kultur der Römer.* Tübingen: 89–112.

Hough, J. N. (1947) 'Terence's Use of Greek Words', *The Classical World* 41: 18–21.

Hough, J. N. (1970) 'Rapid Repartee in Roman Comedy', *Classical Journal* 65: 162–7.

Hunink, V. (2006) 'Review of Richlin, A. (2005)', *Rome and the Mysterious Orient: Three Plays by Plautus, translated with introductions and notes.* Berkeley, *Bryn Mawr Classical Review*, 2006.05.35. Accessed on 18 September 2017 at: http://bmcr.brynmawr.edu/2006/2006-05-35.html

Hunter, R. L. (1980) 'Philemon, Plautus, and the *Trinummus*', *Museum Helveticum* 37: 216–30.

Hunter, R. L. (1981) 'The *Aulularia* of Plautus and its Greek Original', *Proceedings of the Cambridge Philological Society* 27: 37–49.

Hunter, R. L. (1985) *The New Comedy of Greece and Rome.* Cambridge.

Hunter, R. L (1987) 'Middle Comedy and the *Amphitruo* of Plautus', *Dioniso* 57: 281–98.

Hunter, R. L. (2002) 'Acting Down: the Ideology of Hellenistic Performance' in P. Easterling and E. Hall (eds.) *Greek and Roman Actors. Aspects of an Ancient Profession.* Cambridge: 189–206.

Hunter, R. L. (2006) *The Shadow of Callimachus. Studies in the Reception of Poetry at Rome.* Cambridge.

Hunter, R. L. (2009) *Critical Moments in Classical Literature.* Cambridge.

Hutcheon, L. (2006) *A Theory of Adaptation.* New York and London.

Jachmann, G. (1924) *Die Geschichte des Terenztextes im Altertum.* Basle.

Jachmann, G. (1931) *Plautinisches und Attisches.* Berlin.

Jacques, J.-M. (2004) 'Le *Disexapaton* de Ménandre, modèle des *Bacchides* de Plaute', *Revue des études anciennes* 106: 23–47.

Jaeger, W. (1945) *Paideia: The Ideals of Greek Culture* (3 vols), transl. Gilbert Highet. Oxford.

Jakobi, R. (1996) *Die Kunst der Exegese im Terenzkommentar des Donat.* Berlin and New York.

James, S. L. (1998a) 'Introduction: Constructions of Gender and Genre in Roman Comedy and Elegy', *Helios* 25: 3–16.

James, S. L. (1998b) 'From Boys to Men: Rape and Developing Masculinity in Terence's *Hecyra* and *Eunuchus*', *Helios* 25: 31–47.

James, S. L. (2005) 'Effeminate Elegy, Comic Women and the Gender of Language: Recovering a Female Voice in Latin', paper for the January 2005 APA Seminar 'The Gender of Latin'. Boston.

James, S. L. (2010) 'Trafficking Pasicompsa: A Courtesan's Travels and Travails in Plautus' *Mercator*', *New England Classical Journal* 37: 39–50.

James, S. L. (2013) 'Gender and Sexuality in Terence', in A. Augoustakis and A. Traill (eds.) *A Companion to Terence*. Malden, MA: 175–94.

Janan, M. (1994) *When the Lamp is Shattered: Desire and Narrative in Catullus*. Carbondale, IL.

Janko, R. (1984) *Aristotle on Comedy: Towards a Reconstruction of Poetics II*. London.

Jeffery, B. (1969) *French Renaissance Comedy, 1552–1630*. Oxford.

Jenkins, T. E. (2005) 'At Play with Writing: Letters and Readers in Plautus', *Transactions and Proceedings of the American Philological Association* 135: 359–92.

Jennings, M. (1998) '"Like Shining from Shook Foil": Liturgical Typology in Hrotsvit's Legends and Dramas', *Mittellateinisches Jahrbuch* 33: 37–52.

Jenson, J. (1997) 'Aulus Gellius als Literaturkritiker: Impressionist oder Systematiker? Versuch einer Aufstellung seiner literaturkritischen Werttypologie', *Classica et Mediaevalia* 48: 359–88.

Jocelyn, H. D. (1967) *The Tragedies of Ennius: The Fragments*. Cambridge.

Jocelyn, H. D. (1969) 'The Poet Cn. Naevius, P. Cornelius Scipio and Q. Caecilius Metellus', *Antichthon* 3: 32–47.

Jocelyn, H. D. (1973) '*Homo sum: humani nil a me alienum puto* (Terence, *Heauton timorumenos* 77)', *Antichthon* 7: 14–46.

Jocelyn, H. D. (1995) 'Horace and the Reputation of Plautus in the Late First Century BC' in S. J. Harrison (ed.) *Homage to Horace. A Bimillenary Celebration*. Oxford: 228–47.

Jocelyn, H. D. (2000) 'The Unpretty Boy of Plautus' *Pseudolus* (767–789)' in E. Stärk and G. Vogt-Spira (eds.) *Dramatische Wäldchen*. Hildesheim, Zurich, and New York: 431–60.

Johnson, W. R. (1968) 'Micio and the Perils of Perfection', *CSCA* 1: 171–86.

Johnson Chase, W. (1922) *The Distichs of Cato, A Famous Medieval Textbook*. Madison, WI.

Jolowicz, H. F., and B. Nicholas (3rd edn 1972) *Historical Introduction to the Study of Roman Law*. Cambridge.

Jones, L. W., and C. R. Morey (1930–1) *The Miniatures of the Manuscripts of Terence prior to the Thirteenth Century* (2 vols). Princeton, NJ.

Jonson, B. (2012) *Works*, eds. D. Bevington, M. Butler and I. Donaldson (7 vols). Cambridge.

Jory, E. J. (1963) '"Algebraic" Notation in Dramatic Texts', *Bulletin of the Institute of Classical Studies* 10: 65–78.

Jürgens, H. (1972) *Pompa diaboli. Die lateinischen Kirchenväter und das antike Theater*. Stuttgart, Berlin, Cologne and Mainz.

Kaiser, W. (2015) 'Justinian and the *Corpus Iuris Civilis*' in D. Johnston (ed.) *The Cambridge Companion to Roman Law*. Cambridge: 119–48.

Karabélias, E. (1970) 'Une nouvelle source pour l'étude du droit attique: Le "Bouclier" de Ménandre (P. Bodmer XXVI)', *Revue internationale de droit français et étranger* 48: 357–89.

Karabélias, E. (2002) *L' épiclérat attique: Recherches sur la condition juridique de la fille épiclère athénienne*. Athens.

Karabélias, E. (2004) *Recherches sur la condition juridique et sociale de la fille unique dans le monde grec ancien excepté Athènes*. Athens.

Karakasis, E. (2003) 'Legal Language in Plautus with Special Reference to "*Trinummus*"', *Mnemosyne* 56: 194–209.

Karakasis, E. (2005) *Terence and the Language of Roman Comedy*. Cambridge.

Karakasis, E. (2014) 'The Language of the *Palliata*' in M. Fontaine and A. Scafuro (eds.) *The Oxford Handbook of Greek and Roman Comedy*. Oxford and New York: 555–79.

Kaser, M. (2nd edn 1971) *Das Römische Privatrecht. Erster Abschnitt. Das altrömische, das vorklassische und klassische Recht*. Munich.

Katsouris, A. G. (1975) *Linguistic and Stylistic Characterisation: Tragedy and Menander*. Ioannina.

Kauer, R., and W. M. Lindsay (1926) *Comoediae*: Andria, Heauton Timorumenos, Eunuchus, Phormio, Hecyra, Adelphoe. Oxford.

Kauer, R., and W. M. Lindsay (1958 and 1961) *P. Terenti Afri Comoediae*. Oxford. (Reprint of 1926 edn with additions by O. Skutsch.)

Kenney, E. J. (1969) 'Ovid and the Law', *Yale Classical Studies* 21: 243–63.

Kenney, E. J. (ed.) (1982) *The Cambridge History of Classical Literature II: Latin Literature*. Cambridge.

Kes, B. R. (1988) *Die Rezeption der Komödien des Plautus und Terenz im 19. Jahrhundert: Theorie – Bearbeitung – Bühne*. Amsterdam.

Killeen, J. F. (1973) 'Plautus *Miles Gloriosus* 211', *Classical Philology* 68: 53–4.

Kleve, K. (1996) 'How to Read an Illegible Papyrus. Towards an Edition of *PHerc*. 78, Caecilius Statius, *Obolostates sive Faenerator*', *Cronache Ercolanesi* 26: 5–14.

Knapp, C. (1907) 'Travels in Ancient Times as Seen in Plautus and Terence', *Classical Philology* 2: 1–24 and 281–304.

Knecht, T. (1986) 'Das römische Sprichwort – Abgrenzungen, Formen, Anwendung' in Neukam, P. (ed.) *Reflexionen antiker Kulturen*. Munich: 47–59.

Knorr, O. (1995) 'The Character of Bacchis in *Heautontimoroumenos*', *American Journal of Philology* 116.2: 221–35.

Knorr, O. (2007) 'Metatheatrical Humor in the Comedies of Terence' in P. Kruschwitz, W. W. Ehlers, and F. Felgentreu (eds.) *Terentius Poeta*. Munich: 167–74.

Konstan, D. (1983) *Roman Comedy*. Ithaca, NY and London.

Konstan, D. (1986) 'Love in Terence's *Eunuch*: The Origins of Erotic Subjectivity', *American Journal of Philology* 107.3: 369–493.

Konstan, D. (1995) *Greek Comedy and Ideology*. New York and Oxford.

Konstan, D. (1997) *Friendship in the Classical World*. Cambridge.

Konstan, D., and S. Raval (2018) 'Comic Violence and the Citizen Body' in M. Gale and D. Scourfield (eds.) *Texts and Violence in the Roman World*. Cambridge and New York: 44–62.

Kornhardt, H. (1953) '*Summum ius*', *Hermes* 81: 77–85.

Kornhardt, H. (1954) '*Restitutio in integrum* bei Terenz' in O. Hiltbrunner (ed.) *Thesaurismata*. Munich: 65–78.

Korzeniewski, U. (2003) *Sophokles! Die Alten! Philoktet! Lessing und die antiken Dramatiker*. Konstanz.

Kretschmer, M. T. (2014) 'Autorità e no: Alcune considerazioni sul progetto anti-terenziano di Rosvita di Gandersheim' in E. D'Angelo and J. Ziolkowski (eds.)

Auctor et Auctoritas in Latinis medii aevi litteris: Author and Authorship in Medieval Latin Literature. Florence: 555–65.

Krieter Spiro, M. (1997) *Sklaven, Köche und Hetären: das Dienstpersonal bei Menander: Stellung, Rolle, Komik und Sprache*. Stuttgart.

Kroll, W. (1910–12) 'Der lateinische Relativsatz', *Glotta* 3: 1–18.

Kruschwitz, P. (2002) 'Ist Geld die "Wurzel allen Übels"? Zur Interpretation von Plautus' *Aulularia*', *Hermes* 130: 146–63.

Kuhn, H. (1950) 'Hrotsviths von Gandersheim dichterisches Programm', *Deutsche Vierteljahrsschrift für Literaturwissenschaft und Geistesgeschichte* 24: 181–96.

Kuhn-Treichel, T. (2018) 'Das Epiklerat im *Phormio* des Terenz und im Ἐπιδικαζόμενος des Apollodor von Karystos' in H.-G. Nesselrath and J. Platschek (eds.), *Menschen und Recht. Fallstudien zu Rechtsfragen und ihrer Bedeutung in der griechischen und römischen Komödie*. Tübingen: 111–35.

Kunkel, W. (1939) 'Fides als schöpferisches Element im römischen Schuldrecht' in M. Kaser, H. Kreller and W. Kunkel (eds.) *Festschrift Paul Koschaker II* (3 vols). Weimar: 1–15.

La Taille, J. de (1562) *Les Corrivaux*. Paris.

Lada-Richards, I. (2004) 'Authorial Voice and Theatrical Self-definition in Terence and Beyond: The "Hecyra" Prologues in Ancient and Modern Contexts', *Greece and Rome* (Ser. 2) 51.1: 55–82.

Laidlaw, W. A. (1960) 'Cicero and the Stage', *Hermathena* 94: 56–66.

Lallier, R. (1878) 'Le procès du Phormion. Etude sur les moeurs judiciaires d'Athènes', *Annuaire de l'association des études grecques en France* 12: 48–62.

Lape, S. (2004a) 'The Terentian Marriage-Plot: Reproducing Fathers and Sons' in A. Boyle (ed.) *Rethinking Terence. Ramus* 33: 35–52.

Lape, S. (2004b) *Reproducing Athens: Menander's Comedy, Democratic Culture, and the Hellenistic City*. Princeton, NJ.

Lawton, H. W. (1926) *Contribution à l'histoire de l'humanisme: Térence en France au xvie siècle*. Paris.

Lawton, H. W. (1949) *Handbook of French Renaissance Dramatic Theory*. Manchester.

Le Guen, B. (2014) 'The Diffusion of Comedy from the Age of Alexander to the Beginning of the Roman Empire' in M. Fontaine and A. Scafuro (eds.) *The Oxford Handbook of Greek and Roman Comedy*. Oxford and New York: 359–77.

Leach, E. W. (1969) '*Meam quom formam noscito*. Language and Characterization in *Menaechmi*', *Arethusa* 2: 30–45.

Leach, E. W. (1971) 'Horace's *pater optimus* and Terence's *Demea*: Autobiographical Fiction and Comedy in *sermo* I. 4', *American Journal of Philology* 92: 616–32.

Leach, E. W. (1974) 'Plautus' *Rudens*: Venus Born from a Shell', *Texas Studies in Literature and Language* 15: 915–32.

Lefèvre, E. (1978a) 'Plautus-Studien II: die Brief-Intrige in Menanders *Dis exapaton* und ihre Verdoppelung in den *Bacchides*', *Hermes* 106: 518–38.

Lefèvre, E. (1978b) *Der Phormio des Terenz und der Epidikazomenos des Apollodor von Karystos*. Munich.

Lefèvre, E. (1982) *Maccus vortit barbare. Vom tragischen Amphitryon zum tragiko-mischen Amphitruo*. Mainz and Wiesbaden.

Lefèvre, E. (1990) 'Politik und Gesellschaft in Plautus' *Trinummus*' in J. Blänsdorf (with J.-M. André and N. Frick) (eds.) *Theater und Gesellschaft im Imperium Romanum*. Tübingen: 45–54. (Reprinted in English in R. Scodel (ed.) (1993) *Theatre and Society in the Classical World*. Ann Arbor: 177–90.)

Lefèvre, E. (1995) *Plautus und Philemon*. Tübingen.

Lefèvre, E. (1998) 'Plautus' *Captiui* oder die *Palliata* als Prätexta' in L. Benz and E. Lefèvre (eds.) *Maccus barbarus. Sechs Kapitel zur Originalität der Captivi des Plautus*. Tübingen: 9–50.

Lefèvre, E. (1999) *Terenz' und Apollodors* Hecyra. Munich.

Lefèvre, E. (2001) 'Menander, *Dis Exapaton* 6–113 und Plautus, *Bacchides* 500–561' in L. Benz (ed.) *Scriptoralia Romana. Die Römische Literatur zwischen Mündlichkeit und Schriftlichkeit*. Tübingen: 141–68.

Lefèvre, E. (2008) *Terenz' und Menanders* Andria. Munich.

Lefèvre, E. (2010) '*Atellana e palliata*: gli influssi reciproci' in R. Raffaelli and A. Tontini (eds.) *L'Atellana Letteraria. Atti della Prima Giornata di Studi sull'Atellana. Succivo (CE) 30 ottobre 2009*. Urbino: 89–123.

Lefèvre, E., E. Stärk, and G. Vogt-Spira (eds.) (1991) Plautus barbarus: *sechs Kapitel zur Originalität des Plautus*. Tübingen.

Leigh, M. (2004) *Comedy and the Rise of Rome*. Oxford.

Leitao, D. (2012) *The Pregnant Male as Myth and Metaphor in Classical Greek Literature*. Cambridge.

Lentano, M. (1993) '*Parce ac duriter*, Catone, Plauto e una formula felice', *Maia* n.s. 45: 11–16.

Leo, F. (1895) *Plautinische Forschungen zur Kritik und Geschichte der Komödie*. Berlin.

Leo, F. (1895–6). *Plauti comoediae*. Berlin.

Leo, F. (1912) *Plautinische Forschungen zur Kritik und Geschichte der Komödie*, 2nd edn. Berlin.

Licht, T. (2008) 'Hrotsvitspuren in ottonischer Dichtung (nebst einem neuen Hrotsvitgedicht)', *Mittellateinisches Jahrbuch* 43: 347–53.

Lilja, S. (1965) *Terms of Abuse in Roman Comedy*. Helsinki.

Lilja, S. (1983) *Homosexuality in Republican and Augustan Rome*. Helsinki.

Lindsay, W. M. (1896) *The Palatine Text of Plautus*. Oxford.

Lindsay, W. M. (1898) *The Codex Turnebi of Plautus*. Oxford.

Lindsay, W. M. (1900) *The* Captiui *of Plautus*. London.

Lindsay, W. M. (1904) *The Ancient Editions of Plautus*. Oxford.

Lindsay, W. M. (1904–5) *T. Macci Plauti Comoediae* (2 vols). Oxford.

Lindsay, W. M. (1907) *Syntax of Plautus*. Oxford.

Lindsay, W. M. (1922) *Early Latin Verse*. Oxford.

Lindsay, W. M. (1955–6, reprint) *Plautus, Titus Maccius, Comoediae* (2 vols). Oxford.

Lipsius, J. H. (1905–15) *Das attische Recht und Rechtsverfahren* (3 vols). Leipzig.

Little, A. McN. G. (1938) 'Plautus and Popular Drama', *Harvard Studies in Classical Philology* 49: 205–28.

Litwan, P. A. (1984) 'Die Plautus-Übersetzungen des Albrecht von Eyb: Lateinisch-deutsche Textausgabe'. Diss. Basle, Bern, Frankfurt am Main, and New York.

Livan, G. (2005) *Appunti sulla lingua e lo stile di Cecilio Stazio*. Bologna.

Livingstone, I. (2004) *A Linguistic Commentary on Livius Andronicus*. New York and London.

Löfstedt, E. (1911) *Philologischer Kommentar zur* Peregrinatio Aetheriae: *Untersuchungen zur Geschichte der lateinischen Sprache.* Uppsala.

López Fonseca, A. (1998) 'San Jerónimo, lector de los cómicos latinos: cristianos y paganos', *Cuadernos de filología clásica. Estudios latinos* 15: 333–52.

Lowden, J. (1992) *The Octateuchs: A Study in Byzantine Manuscript Illustration.* University Park, PA.

Lowe, E. A. (1934–71) *Codices latini antiquiores.* Oxford.

Lowe, E. A. (1972) *Palaeographical Papers, 1907–1965.* Oxford.

Lowe, J. C. (1989) 'Plautus' Parasites and the *Atellana'* in G. Vogt-Spira (ed.) *Studien zur vorliterarischen Periode im frühen Rom.* Tübingen: 161–9.

Lowe, J. C. (1992) 'Aspects of Plautus' Originality in the *Asinaria'*, *Classical Quarterly* 42: 152–75.

Lowe, J. C. (2001) 'Greek and Roman Elements in Epidicus' Intrigue' in U. Auhagen (ed.) *Studien zu Plautus' Epidicus.* Tübingen: 57–70.

Lowe, J. C. (2003) 'The Lot-drawing Scene in Plautus' *Casina'*, *Classical Quarterly* 53: 175–83.

Lowe, J. C. (2007) 'Some Problems of Dramatic Space in Plautus', *Classical Quarterly* 57: 109–16.

Lowe, N. J. (2006) 'Aristophanic Spacecraft' in L. Kozak and J. Rich (eds.) *Playing Around Aristophanes.* Oxford: 48–64.

Lowe, N. J. (2008) *Comedy.* Cambridge.

Lowrie, M. (2005) 'Slander and Horse Law in Horace, *Sermones* 2.1', *Law and Literature* 17: 405–31.

Ludwig, W. (1968) 'The Originality of Terence and His Greek Models', *Greek, Roman and Byzantine Studies* 9: 169–82.

Lumley, E. P. (1901) *The Influence of Plautus on the Comedies of Ben Jonson.* New York.

Luther, M. (1883) *Werke: Kritische Gesamtausgabe II.1.* Weimar.

MacCary, W. T., and M. M. Willcock (eds.) (1976) Plautus, *Casina.* Cambridge.

MacCormack, G. (1971) 'A Note on *arra* in Plautus', *The Irish Jurist* 6: 360–6.

MacDowell, D. M. (1978) *The Law in Classical Athens.* London.

MacDowell, D. M. (1982) 'Love Versus the Law: An Essay on Menander's *Aspis'*, *Greece and Rome* 29: 42–52.

MacKendrick, P. (1954) 'Demetrius of Phalerum, Cato and the *Adelphoe'*, *Rivista di Filologia e Istruzione Classica* 32: 18–35.

Mai, A. (1815) *Macci Plauti fragmenta inedita.* Milan.

Maidment, K. J. (1935) 'The Later Comic Chorus', *Classical Quarterly* 29:1–24.

Major, W. E. (1997) 'Menander in a Macedonian World', *Greek, Roman and Byzantine Studies* 38: 41–73.

Malamud, M. (2001) 'Brooklyn-on-the-Tiber: Roman Comedy on Broadway and in Film' in S. R. Joshel, M. Malamud, and D. T. McGuire, Jr. (eds.) *Imperial Projections. Ancient Rome in Modern Popular Culture.* Baltimore and London: 191–208.

Maland, C. J. (2007) *City Lights.* London.

Malcovati, E. (1953) *Oratorum Romanorum Fragmenta Liberae Rei Publicae.* Turin.

Mal-Maeder, D. van (2007) *La fiction des déclamations.* Leiden and Boston.

Maltby, R. (1976) 'A Comparative Study of the Language of Plautus and Terence', Diss. Cambridge.

Maltby, R. (1979) 'Linguistic Characterisation of Old Men in Terence', *Classical Philology* 74: 136–47.

Maltby, R. (1983) 'The Last Act of Terence's *Heautontimoroumenos*', *Papers of the Leeds International Latin Seminar* 4: 27–41.

Maltby, R. (1985) 'The Distribution of Greek Loan-words in Terence', *Classical Quarterly* 35: 110–23.

Maltby, R. (1995) 'The Distribution of Greek Loan-words in Plautus', *Papers of the Leeds International Latin Seminar* 8: 31–69.

Maltby, R. (2004) 'The Love Gods in Plautus', *Paideia* 59: 255–70.

Maltby, R. (2007) 'The Distribution of Imagery by Plays and Characters in Terence' in P. Kruschwitz, W. W. Ehlers, and F. Felgentreu (eds.) *Terentius Poeta*. Munich: 143–65.

Mandolfo, C. (2004) 'La lingua di Nevio comico', *Sileno* 30: 143–62.

Manuwald, G. (2001) *Fabulae praetextae. Spuren einer literarischen Gattung der Römer*. Munich.

Manuwald, G. (2011) *Roman Republican Theatre*. Cambridge.

Maquerlot, J.-P. (1992) 'Playing Within the Play. Towards a Semiotics of Metadrama and Metatheatre' in F. Laroque (ed.) *The Show Within: Dramatic and Other Insets; English Renaissance Drama (1550–1642)*. Montpellier: 39–49.

Mariotti, S. (2nd edn 1986) *Livio Andronico e la traduzione artistica*. Urbino.

Marmorale, E. V. (2nd edn 1950) *Naevius Poeta*. Florence.

Marouzeau, J. (1947) *Térence I: Andrienne, Eunuque*. Paris.

Marrou, H. I. (7th edn 1975) *Histoire de l'education dans l'antiquité*. Paris.

Marshall, C.W. (1999) '*Quis Hic Loquitur?*: Plautine Delivery and the 'Double Aside', *Syllecta Classica* 10: 105–31.

Marshall, C. W. (2006) *The Stagecraft and Performance of Roman Comedy*. Cambridge and New York.

Marshall, C. W. (2010) 'Living Next Door to a Roman Comedy: Structure in Plautus' *Mercator*', *New England Classical Journal* 37: 65–78.

Marti, H. (1959) *Untersuchungen zur dramatischen Technik bei Plautus und Terenz*. Winterthur.

Marti, H. (1974) *Zeugnisse zur Nachwirkung des Dichters Terenz im Altertum*. Hildesheim.

Martin, R.H. (ed.) (1959) *Terence:* Phormio. London.

Martin, R. H. (ed.) (1976) *Terence:* Adelphoe. Cambridge.

Martin, R. H. (1995) 'A Not-so-minor Character in Terence's *Eunuchus*', *Classical Philology* 90: 139–51.

Marx, F. (1928) *Plautus:* Rudens. Leipzig.

Mastronarde, D. J. (2002) *Euripides:* Medea. Cambridge.

Mattingly, H. B. (1960) 'Naevius and the Metelli', *Historia* 9: 414–39.

Matzner, S., and S. Harrison (2018) *Complex Inferiorities: The Politics of the Weaker Voice in Latin Literature*. Oxford.

Mauduit, Ch., and P. Paré-Rey (eds.) (2011) *Les Maximes théâtrales en Grèce et à Rome: transferts, réécritures, remplois*. Lyon.

Maurice, L. (2007) 'Structure and Stagecraft in Plautus' *Miles Gloriosus*', *Mnemosyne* 60: 407–26.

McCarthy, K. (2000) *Slaves, Masters and the Art of Authority in Plautine Comedy*. Princeton, NJ.

McCarthy, K. (2004) 'The Joker in the Pack: Slaves in Terence', *Helios* 33: 100–19.

McDonald, M., and M. Walton (eds.) (2007) *The Cambridge Companion to Greek and Roman Theatre*. Cambridge.

McDonnell, M. (2006) *Roman Manliness: 'Virtus' and the Roman Republic*. Cambridge.

McElduff, S. (2004) 'More than Menander's Acolyte: Terence on Translation' in A. J. Boyle (ed.) *Rethinking Terence*. *Ramus* 33: 120–9.

McGinn, T. (1998) *Prostitution, Sexuality, and Law in Ancient Rome*. Oxford.

McMillin, L. A. (2004) '"Weighed Down with a Thousand Evils": Images of Muslims in Hrotsvit's *Pelagius*' in P. R. Brown, L. A. McMillin, and K. Wilson (eds.) *Hrotsvit of Gandersheim: Contexts, Identities, Affinities, and Performances*. Toronto, Buffalo, NY and London: 40–55.

McNamee, K. (2007) *Annotations in Greek and Latin Texts from Egypt*. New Haven, CT.

Meiss, M. (1974) *French Painting in the Time of Jean de Berry. The Limbourgs and Their Contemporaries* (2 vols). New York.

Michalka, E. (1968) 'Studien über Intention und Gestaltung in den dramatischen Werken Hrotsvits von Gandersheim'. Diss. Heidelberg. Clausthal-Zellerfeld.

Millar, F. (1984) 'The Political Character of the Roman Republic, 200–151 B.C.', *Journal of Roman Studies* 74: 1–19.

Millett, P. (1983) 'Maritime Loans and the Structure of Credit in Fourth-Century Athens' in P. Garnsey, K. Hopkins, and R. Whittaker (eds.) *Trade in the Ancient Economy*. Berkeley: 36–52.

Millett, P. (1991) *Lending and Borrowing in Ancient Athens*. Cambridge.

Minarini, A. (1987) 'Conflitto d'amore: Terenzio in Catullo' in A. Minarini, *Studi Terenziani*. Bologna: 59–79.

Miniconi, P. J. (1958) 'Les termes d'injure dans le théâtre comique', *Revue des études latines* 36: 159–75.

Miola, R. S. (1994) *Shakespeare and Classical Comedy*. Oxford.

Molière (2010) *Œuvres complètes*, ed. G. Forestier and C. Bourqui (2 vols). Paris.

Monda, S. (2013) 'La preistoria dell'Atellana nelle fonti storiche e letterarie' in R. Raffaelli and A. Tontini (eds.) *L'Atellana preletteraria. Atti sella seconda giornata di studi sull'Atellana*. Urbino: 95–124.

Montaigne, M. de (2006) *Essays* (3 vols), transl. John Florio. London.

Moodie, E. (2009) 'Old Men and Metatheatre in Terence: Terence's Dramatic Competition', *Ramus* 38: 145–73.

Moore, T. J. (1991) '*Palliata Togata*: Plautus, *Curculio* 462–86', *American Journal of Philology* 112: 343–62.

Moore, T. J. (1998a) 'Music and Structure in Roman Comedy', *American Journal of Philology* 119: 245–73.

Moore, T. J. (1998b) *The Theater of Plautus: Playing to the Audience*. Austin, TX.

Moore, T. J. (1999) 'Facing the Music: Character and Musical Accompaniment in Roman Comedy', *Syllecta classica* 19: 130–53.

Moore, T. J. (2007) 'Terence as Musical Innovator' in P. Kruschwitz, W. W. Ehlers, and F. Felgentreu (eds.) *Terentius Poeta*. Munich: 93–109.

Moore, T. J. (2008) 'When Did the Tibicen Play? Meter and Musical Accompaniment in Roman Comedy', *Transactions and Proceedings of the American Philological Association* 138: 3–46.

Moore, T. J. (2012) *Music in Roman Comedy*. Cambridge.

Moore, T. J. (2016) 'The Meters of Roman Comedy', Washington University in St. Louis Libraries: http://romancomedy.wulib.wustl.edu/

Mordden, E. (2007) *All That Glittered: The Golden Age of Drama on Broadway, 1919–1959*. New York.

Morstein-Marx, R. (2004) *Mass Oratory and Political Power in the Late Roman Republic*. Cambridge.

Mosetti Casaretto, F. (2005) 'Rosvita, l'osceno e la rinascita della commedia', *L'immagine riflessa* N. S. 14: 71–85.

Mossé, C. (1983) 'The "World of the Emporium" in the Private Speeches of Demosthenes' in P. Garnsey, K. Hopkins and R. Whittaker (eds.) *Trade in the Ancient Economy*. Berkeley: 53–63.

Mountford, J. F. (1934) *The Scholia Bembina. Edited with Annotations*. Liverpool.

Muecke, F. (1986) 'Plautus and the Theater of Disguise', *Classical Antiquity* 5: 216–29.

Müller, A. (1913) 'Die Schimpfwörter in der römischen Komödie', *Philologus* 72: 492–502.

Müller, R. (1997) *Sprechen und Sprache: dialoglinguistische Studien zu Terenz*. Heidelberg.

Müller, R. (2013) 'Terence in Latin Literature from the Second Century BCE to the Second Century CE' in A. Augoustakis and A. Traill (eds.), *A Companion to Terence*. Chichester: 363–79.

Muir, B. J., and A. J. Turner (eds.) (2011) *Terence's Comedies*. Oxford.

Munk Olsen, B. (1982–9) *L'étude des auteurs classiques latins aux XIe et XIIe siècles* (3 vols). Paris.

Munk Olsen, B. (1991) *I classici nel canone scolastico altomedievale*. Spoleto.

Munk Olsen, B. (1996) 'The Production of Classics in the Eleventh and Twelfth Centuries' in C. A. Chavannes-Mazel and M. M. Smith (eds.) *Medieval Manuscripts of the Latin Classics: Production and Use*. Los Altos Hills: 1–17.

Nagel, B. (1965) *Hrotsvit von Gandersheim*. Stuttgart.

Neiiendam, K. (1969) 'Le théâtre de la Renaissance à Rome (1480 environ à 1530)', *Analecta Romana Instituti Danici* 5: 103–97.

Nellhaus, T. (2000) 'Social Ontology and (Meta)theatricality: Reflexions on Performance and Communication in History', *Journal of Dramatic Theory and Criticism* 14: 3–39.

Nelson, A. (ed.) (1989) *Records of Early English Drama*. Cambridge (2 vols). Toronto.

Nervegna, S. (2013) *Menander in Antiquity: The Contexts of Reception*. Cambridge.

Nesselrath, H.-G. (2018) 'Ehescheidungen bei Plautus' in H.-G. Nesselrath and J. Platschek (eds.), *Menschen und Recht. Fallstudien zu Rechtsfragen und ihrer Bedeutung in der griechischen und römischen Komödie*. Tübingen: 53–73.

Neue, F., and C. Wagener (1892–1905) *Formenlehre der lateinischen Sprache*. Leipzig.

Newlands, C. E. (1986) 'Hrotswitha's Debt to Terence', *Transactions of the American Philological Association* 116: 369–91.

Nicholas, B. (1962) *An Introduction to Roman Law*. Oxford. (Reprinted (2010) with a foreword, revised bibliography, and glossary of Latin terms by E. Metzger.)

Nicoll, A. (1963) *The World of Harlequin: A Critical Study of the Commedia dell'Arte*. Cambridge.

Nicolson, F. W. (1893) 'The Use of *hercle (mehercle), edepol (pol)* and *ecastor (mecastor)* by Plautus and Terence', *Harvard Studies in Classical Philology* 4: 99–103.

Nixon, R. (1997) *Plautus:* Amphitryon. The Comedy of Asses. The Pot of Gold. The Two Bacchises. The Captives. Repr. London.

Nuñez, S. (1995) 'Materiales para una sociología de la lengua latina: Terencio y los modificadores de imperativo', *Florentia Iliberritana* 6: 347–66.

Nünlist, R. (1998) *Poetologische Bildersprache in der frühgriechischen Dichtung*. Stuttgart and Leipzig.

O' Bryhim, S. (1989) 'The Originality of Plautus' *Casina*', *American Journal of Philology* 110: 81–103.

O'Neill, P. (2003) 'Triumph Songs, Reversal and Plautus' *Amphitruo*', *Ramus* 32: 1–38.

Oakley, S. P. (1998) *A Commentary on Livy Books VI–X*. Oxford.

Oliensis, E. (1998) *Horace and the Rhetoric of Authority*. Cambridge.

Olivieri, A. (ed.) (1946) *Frammenti della commedia greca e del mimo nella Sicilia e nella Magna Grecia* (2 vols). Naples.

Olson, E. (1968) *The Theory of Comedy*. Bloomington, IN.

Olson, S. D. (ed.) (2007) *Broken Laughter. Select Fragments of Greek Comedy*. Oxford.

Oniga, R. (2002) 'I modelli dell'*Anfitrione* di Plauto' in C. Questa and R. Raffaelli *Due seminari plautini. La tradizione del testo. I modelli*. Urbino: 199–225.

Orgel, S. (1979) 'Shakespeare and the Kinds of Drama', *Critical Inquiry* 6: 107–23.

Orlin, E. M. (1997) *Temples, Religion and Politics in the Roman Republic*. Leiden and Cologne.

Oswald, P. (2006) *The Storm, or The Howler*. London.

Owens, W. M. (1994) 'The Third Deception in *Bacchides: Fides* and Plautus' Originality', *American Journal of Philology* 115: 381–407.

Owens, W. M. (2000) 'Plautus' *Stichus* and the Political Crisis of 200 B.C.', *American Journal of Philology* 121: 385–407.

Packman, Z. (1999) 'Feminine Role Designations in the Comedies of Plautus', *American Journal of Philology* 120.2: 245–58.

Pailler, J.-M., and Payen, P. (eds.) (2004) *Que reste-t-il de l'éducation classique? Relire le Marrou, Histoire de l'éducation dans l'antiquité*. Toulouse.

Palmer, L. R. (1954) *The Latin Language*. London.

Panayotakis, C. (2005) 'Non-verbal Behaviour on the Roman Comic Stage' in D. Cairns (ed.) *Body Language in the Greek and Roman Worlds*. Swansea: 175–93.

Panayotakis, C. (2010) *Decimus Laberius: The Fragments*. Cambridge.

Paoli, U. E. (1943) 'L'ΕΠΙΚΛΗΡΟΣ attica nella "palliata" romana', *Atene e Roma* 11: 19–29. (Reprinted in Paoli (1976) 103–12.)

Paoli, U. E. (1952) 'La *in ius vocatio* dans les comédies de Plaute', *Studi Senesi* 63: 283–304. (Reprinted in Paoli (1976) 113–27.)

Paoli, U. E. (1962) *Comici latini e diritto attico*. Milan. (Reprinted in Paoli, U. E. (1976) 31–78.)

Paoli, U. E. (1976) *Altri studi di diritto greco e romano*. Milan.

Papadimitriou, M. (1998) Στοιχεία της ομιλούμενης Λατινικής στον Τερέντιο και η χρήση τους στη διαφοροποίηση του λόγου των χαρακτήρων του. Ioannina.

Paponi, S. (2005) *Per una nuova edizione di Nevio comico*. Pisa.

Parker, H. N. (1989/2001) 'Crucially Funny or Tranio on the Couch: The *Servus Callidus* and Jokes about Torture', *Transactions and Proceedings of the American Philological Association* 119: 233–46. (Reprinted in E. Segal (ed.) (2001) *Oxford Readings in Menander, Plautus and Terence*. Oxford: 127–37.)

Parker, H. N. (1996) 'Plautus vs. Terence: Audience and Popularity Re-examined', *American Journal of Philology* 117: 585–617.

Parker, R. (1997) 'Gods Cruel and Kind: Tragic and Civic Theology' in C. Pelling (ed.) *Greek Tragedy and the Historian*. Oxford: 143–60.

Partsch, J. (1910) 'Römisches und griechisches Recht in Plautus' Persa', *Hermes* 45: 595–614.

Pasetti, L. (2007) *Plauto in Apuleio*. Bologna.

Pasquazi-Bagnolini, A. (1977) *Note sulla lingua di Afranio*. Florence.

Patterson, C. B. (1998) *The Family in Greek History*. Cambridge, MA.

Pauly, A. F., Wissowa, G., Kroll, W., Mittelhaus, K., and Ziegler, K. J. F. (eds.) (1893–1980) *Paulys Realencyclopädie der classischen Altertumswissenschaft*. Stuttgart.

Peletier du Mans, J. (1555) *Art Poétique*. Lyon.

Pennitz, M. (2013) 'Zum Prozess wegen des Kaufs einer vermeintlichen Sklavin. Plautus' Rudens als römischrechtliche Quelle?' in P. Mauritsch and C. Ulf (eds.) *Kultur(en). Formen des Alltäglichen in der Antike. Festschrift für Ingomar Weiler zum 75. Geburtstag*. Graz: 567–84.

Pernard, L. (1900) *Le droit romain et le droit grec dans le théatre de Plaute et de Térence*. Lyon.

Petersmann, H. (1973) T. Maccius Plautus, *Stichus*. Heidelberg.

Petersmann, H. (1989) 'Mündlichkeit und Schriftlichkeit in der Atellane' in G. Vogt-Spira (ed.) *Studien zur vorliterarischen Periode im frühen Rom*. Tübingen: 137–59.

Petersmann, H. (1996–7) 'Die Nachahmung des *sermo rusticus* auf der Bühne des Plautus und Terenz', *Acta Antiqua Academiae Scientiarum Hungaricae* 37.3–4: 199–211.

Petrides, A. K. (2014). 'Plautus between Greek Comedy and Atellan Farce: Assessments and Reassessments' in M. Fontaine and A. Scafuro (eds.) *The Oxford Handbook of Greek and Roman Comedy*. Oxford and New York: 424–43.

Petrone, G. (1983) *Teatro antico e inganno: finzioni plautine*. Palermo.

Petrone, G. (1989) 'Tradizione misogina e trionfo dell' intelligenza femminile nella commedia plautina' in R. Uglione (ed.) *Atti del ii convegno nazionale di studi su La donna nel mondo antico, Torino 18–20 aprile 1988*. Turin: 87–103.

Petrone, G. (1995) 'Scene mimiche in Plauto' in L. Benz, E. Stärk, and G. Vogt-Spira (eds.) *Plautus und die Tradition des Stegreifspiels*. Tübingen: 171–83.

Piccaluga, G. (1991) '*At ego aiio id fieri in Graecia et Carthagini / Et hic…* (Plaut. *Cas.*71 sg.): il linguaggio 'religioso' in Plauto', *Rivista storica dell'Antichità* 21: 9–22.

Place-Verghnes, F. (2006) *Tex Avery: A Unique Legacy, 1942–1955*. Eastleigh.

Platschek, J. (2018) 'Die Stipulationen in Plautus' *Pseudolus*' in H.-G. Nesselrath and J. Platschek (eds.), *Menschen und Recht. Fallstudien zu Rechtsfragen und ihrer Bedeutung in der griechischen und römischen Komödie*. Tübingen: 31–52.

Platter, C. (1993) 'The Uninvited Guest: Aristophanes in Bakhtin's "History of Laughter"', *Arethusa* 26: 201–16.

Platter, C. (2007) *Aristophanes and the Carnival of Genres*. Baltimore.

Ploen, H. (1882) *De copiae verborum differentiis inter varia poesis Romanae antiquioris genera intercedentibus*. Strasbourg.

Porter, J. I. (2010) *The Origins of Aesthetic Thought in Ancient Greece. Matter, Sensation and Experience*. Cambridge.

Posner, R. A. (3rd edn 2009) *Law and Literature*. Cambridge, MA, and London.

Prete, S. (1970) *Il Codice di Terenzio, Vaticano Latino 3226: saggio critico e riproduzioni del manoscritto*. Vatican City.

Pringsheim, F. (1916) *Der Kauf mit fremdem Geld: Studien über die Bedeutung der Preiszahlung für den Eigentumserwerb nach griechischem und römischem Recht*. Leipzig.

Pringsheim, F. (1950) *The Greek Law of Sale*. Weimar.

Pucci, P. (1982) 'The Proem of the *Odyssey*', *Arethusa* 15: 39–62.

Purdie, S. (1993) *Comedy: The Mastery of Discourse*. Hemel Hempstead.

Purves, A. (2011) 'Homer and the Art of Overtaking', *American Journal of Philology* 132: 523–51.

Questa, C. (1968) *Per la storia del testo di Plauto nel rinascimento: I, La recensione di Poggio Bracciolini*. Rome.

Questa, C. (1984) *Numeri innumeri: ricerche sui cantica e la tradizione manoscritta di Plauto*. Rome.

Questa, C. (1985) *Parerga Plautina: struttura e tradizione manoscritta delle commedie*. Urbino.

Questa, C. (1995) *Titi Macci Plauti Cantica*. Urbino.

Questa, C. (2001) 'Per un'edizione di Plauto', *Giornate Filologiche 'Francesco Della Corte'* 2: 61–83.

Questa, C. (2007) *La metrica di Plauto e di Terenzio*. Urbino.

Radden Keefe, B. (2015) 'Illustrating the Manuscripts of Terence' in A. J. Turner and G. Torello-Hill (eds.) *Terence between Late Antiquity and the Age of Printing*. Leiden.

Raffaelli, R. (2002) 'Un prologo medievale di Terenzio' in C. Questa and R. Raffaelli (eds.) *Due seminari plautini. La tradizione del testo. I modelli*. Urbino: 89–101.

Raffaelli, R., and A. Tontini (eds.) (2010) *L'Atellana Letteraria. Atti della prima giornata di studi sull'Atellana. Succivo (CE) 30 ottobre 2009*. Urbino.

Raffaelli, R., and A. Tontini (eds.) (2013) *L'Atellana Preletteraria. Atti sella seconda giornata di studi sull'Atellana*. Urbino.

Raios, D. (1998) *Ρωμαϊκή κωμωδία: Πλαύτου Μέναιχμοι*. Ioannina.

Rapisarda, C. A. (1987) 'Il teatro classico nel pensiero cristiano antico' in L. de Finis (ed.) *Teatro e pubblico nell'antichità. Atti del Convegno Nazionale, Trento – 25/27 Aprile 1986*. Trento: 94–113.

Rawson, E. (1991) 'Theatrical Life in Republican Rome' in F. Millar (ed.) *Roman Culture and Society. Collected Papers*. Oxford: 468–87. (Originally published in *Papers of the British School at Rome* 53 (1985) 97–113.)

Reeve, M. D. (1983) 'Terence' in L. D. Reynolds (ed.) *Texts and Transmission. A Survey of the Latin Classics*. Oxford: 412–20. (Repr. with corr. 1986; repr. 1990.)

Rei, A. (1998) 'Villains, Wives and Slaves in the Comedies of Plautus' in S. Joshel and S. Murnaghan (eds.) *Women and Slaves in Greco-Roman Culture: Differential Equations*. London: 92–108.

Reich, V. (1933) 'Sprachliche Characteristik bei Terenz (Studien zum Kommentar des Donat)', *Wiener Studien* 51: 72–94.

Reid, P. L. D. (1991) *The Complete Works of Rather of Verona*. Binghamton.

Reinhardstoettner, K. von (1886) *Plautus: Spätere Bearbeitungen plautinischer Lustspiele. Leipzig.*

Revermann, M. (2006). *Comic Business: Theatricality, Dramatic Technique, and Performance Contexts of Aristophanic Comedy*. Oxford.

Reynolds, L. D. (ed.) (1983) *Texts and Transmission: A Survey of the Latin Classics.* Oxford.

Reynolds, L. D., and N. G. Wilson (3rd edn 1991) *Scribes and Scholars: A Guide to the Transmission of Greek and Latin Literature*. Oxford.

Ribbeck, O. (2nd edn 1871, 3rd edn 1897) *Scaenicae Romanorum poesis fragmenta I: Tragicorum Romanorum fragmenta*. Leipzig. (Repr. of 2nd edn. Hildesheim (1962).)

Ribbeck, O. (2nd edn 1873, 3rd edn 1898) *Scaenicae Romanorum poesis fragmenta II. Comicorum Romanorum praeter Plautum et Terentium fragmenta.* Leipzig.

Ribuoli, R. (1981a) *La collazione polizianea del codice Bembino di Terenzio*. Rome.

Ribuoli, R. (1981b) 'Per la storia del codice Bembino di Terenzio', *Rivista di filologia e di istruzione classica* 109: 163–77.

Richlin, A. (2nd edn 1992) *The Garden of Priapus. Sexuality and Aggression in Roman Humor*. New York and Oxford.

Richlin, A. (1993) 'Not Before Homosexuality: The Materiality of the *cinaedus* and the Roman Law against Love between Men', *Journal of the History of Sexuality* 3.4: 523–73.

Richlin, A. (2005) *Rome and the Mysterious Orient: Three Plays by Plautus.* Berkeley.

Richlin, A. (2014) 'Talking to Slaves in the Plautine Audience', *Classical Antiquity* 33: 174–226.

Richlin, A. (2015) 'Slave-Woman Drag' in D. Dutsch, S. James, and D. Konstan (eds.) *Women in Republican Roman Drama*. Madison: 37–68.

Richlin, A. (2017a) *Slave Theatre in the Roman Republic: Plautus and Popular Comedy*. Cambridge.

Richlin, A. (2017b) 'The Traffic in Shtick' in M. P. Loar, C. MacDonald, D. Padilla Peralta (eds.), *Rome, Empire of Plunder: The Dynamics of Cultural Appropriation*, 169-93. Cambridge.

Riedel, V. (1976) *Lessing und die römische Literatur*. Weimar.

Riedel, V. (2000) *Antikerezeption in der deutschen Literatur vom Renaissance-Humanismus bis zur Gegenwart*. Stuttgart and Weimar.

Riedweg, C. (1993) 'Menander in Rom – Beobachtungen zu Caecilius Statius Plocium fr. I (136–153 Guardi)' in N. W. Slater and B. Zimmermann (eds.) *Intertextualität in der griechisch-römischen Komödie*. Stuttgart: 133–59.

Riehle, W. (1990) *Shakespeare, Plautus, and the Humanist Tradition*. Cambridge.

Riggsby, A. M. (2010) *Roman Law and the Legal World of the Romans.* Cambridge.

Riou, Y.-F. (1997) 'Les commentaires médiévaux de Térence' in N. Mann and B. Munk Olsen (eds.), *Medieval and Renaissance Scholarship. Proceedings of the Second European Science Foundation Workshop on the Classical Tradition of the Middle Ages and the Renaissance*. Leiden.

Robertini, L. (1989) 'Il *Sapientia* di Rosvita e le fonti agiografiche', *Studi Medievali* 30: 649–59.

Roberts, A. J. (1901) 'Did Hrotswitha Imitate Terence?', *Modern Language Notes* 16: 239–41.

Robinson, L. (1946–7) 'Censorship in Republican Drama', *Classical Journal* 42: 147–50.

Rocha, C. M. da (2013) *Plautus*, Cásina. Campinas.

Rochette, B. (1998) '*Poeta barbarus* (Plaute, *Miles Gloriosus* 211)', *Latomus* 57: 414–16.

Ronconi, A. ([1970] 1972) 'Sulla fortuna di Plauto e di Terenzio nel mondo romano', *Maia* 22 (1970): 19–37. Repr. as 'La critica plautina e terenziana nel mondo romano' in A. Ronconi, *Interpretazioni letterarie nei classici*. Florence: 142–68.

Rosa, F. (1987) 'Appunti sulla presenza di Terenzio nell'opera di S. Agostino' in L. de Finis (ed.) *Teatro e pubblico nell'antichità. Atti del Convegno Nazionale, Trento – 25/27 Aprile 1986*. Trento: 114–31.

Rosén, H. (1999) Latine loqui: *Trends and Directions in the Crystallisation of Classical Latin*. Munich.

Rosen, R. M. (1990) 'Hipponax and the Homeric Odysseus', *Eikasmos* 1: 11–25.

Rosen, R. M. (2007) *Making Mockery*. Oxford.

Rosenmeyer, P. A. (1995) 'Enacting the Law: Plautus' Use of the Divorce Formula on Stage', *Phoenix* 49: 201–17.

Rosenmeyer, T. G. (2002) '"Metatheater": An Essay on Overload', *Arion* 10: 87–119.

Rosenstein, N., and R. Morstein-Marx (eds.) (2006) *A Companion to the Roman Republic*. Oxford.

Rostagni, A. (1944) (ed.) *Suetonio:* De Poetis. Turin.

Rotrou, J. de (1998–2007) *Théâtre complet*, ed. G. Forestier (9 vols). Paris.

Rowe, G. E. (1979) *Thomas Middleton and the New Comedy Tradition*. Lincoln.

Rowland, R. (1995) '"The Captives": Thomas Heywood's "Whole Monopoly off Mischeiff"', *Modern Language Review* 90: 585–602.

Ruffell, I. A. (2003) 'Beyond Satire: Horace, Popular Invective and the Segregation of Literature', *Journal of Roman Studies* 93: 35–65.

Russo, J. (1997) 'Prose Genres for the Performance of Traditional Wisdom in Ancient Greece: Proverb, Maxim, Apophthegm' in L. Edmunds and R. W. Wallace (eds.) *Poet, Public, and Performance in Ancient Greece*. Baltimore: 49–64.

Rychlewska, L. (1971) *Turpilii comici fragmenta*. Leipzig.

Sabbadini, S. (1935) *Poeti Latini: Nevio*. Udine.

Salat, P. (1967) 'L'adjectif *miser*, ses synonymes et ses antonymes chez Plaute et chez Térence', *Revue des études latines* 45: 252–75.

Salingar, L. (1974) *Shakespeare and the Traditions of Comedy*. Cambridge.

Saller, R. P. (1986) '*Patria Potestas* and the Stereotype of the Roman Family', *Continuity and Change* 1: 7–22.

Saller, R. P. (1991) 'Corporeal Punishment, Authority and Obedience in the Roman Household' in B. Rawson (ed.) *Marriage, Divorce and Children in the Roman World*. Oxford: 144–65.

Saller, R. P. (1999) '*Pater Familias, Mater Familias* and the Gendered Semantics of the Roman Household', *Classical Philology* 94: 182–97.

Sallmann, K. (ed.) (1997a) *Die Literatur des Umbruchs. Von der römischen zur christlichen Literatur. 117 bis 284 n. Chr.* Munich.

Sallmann, K. (1997b) 'Moralistische Spruchdichtung' in K. Sallmann et al. (eds.) *Die Literatur des Umbruchs. Von der römischen zur christlichen Literatur. 117–284 n. Chr.* Munich: 606–12.

Sánchez Vendramini, D. N. (2009) 'Naevius' Fehde mit Q. Caecilius Metellus', *Mnemosyne* 62: 471–6.

Sandbach, F. H. (1970) 'Menander's Manipulation of Language for Dramatic Purposes' in E. G. Turner (ed.) *Ménandre Fondation Hardt Entretiens XVI.* Vandœuvres-Geneva: 111–43.

Sandbach, F. H. (1977) *The Comic Theatre of Greece and Rome*. New York.

Sandbach, F. H. (1982) 'How Terence's *Hecyra* failed', *Classical Quarterly* 32: 134–5.

Saussure, F. de (2002) *Écrits de linguistique générale*, eds. S. Bouquet and R. Engler. Paris.

Scafolgio, G. (2005) 'Plautus and Ennius: A Note on Plautus, *Bacchides* 962–5', *Classical Quarterly* 55: 632–8.

Scafuro, A. (1994) 'Witnessing and False Witnessing: Proving Citizenship and Kin Identity in Fourth-Century Athens' in A. Boeghold and A. Scafuro (eds.) *Athenian Identity and Civic Ideology*. Baltimore: 156–98.

Scafuro, A. (1997) *The Forensic Stage. Settling Disputes in Graeco-Roman New Comedy*. Cambridge.

Scafuro, A. (2003/04) 'The Rigmarole of the Parasite's Contract for a Prostitute in *Asinaria*: Legal Documents in Plautus and his Predecessors', *Leeds International Classical Studies* 3.4.

Schäfer, E. (2004) 'Plautus-Philologie im Zeichen des Camerarius' in R. Hartkamp and F. Hurka (eds.) *Studien zu Plautus' Cistellaria*. Tübingen: 437–76.

Schanbacher, D. (2006) 'Zu Ursprung und Entwicklung des römischen Pfandrechts', *Zeitschrift der Savigny-Stiftung für Rechtsgeschichte (Romanistische Abteilung)* 123: 49–70.

Schauer, M. (2012) *Tragicorum Romanorum Fragmenta I.* Göttingen.

Schauwecker, Y. (2002) 'Zum Sprechverhalten der Frauentypen bei Plautus', *Gymnasium* 109: 191–211.

Scheibelreiter, P. (2012) 'Das depositum in Plautus' *Bacchides*: Zu einer frühen Quelle für die offene Verwahrung', *Zeitschrift der Savigny-Stiftung für Rechtsgeschichte (Romanistische Abteilung)* 129: 206–44.

Scheibelreiter, P. (2018) '*Ut id servarem rem sibi*. Zu den rechtlichen Grundlagen des Sujets der Geldverwahrung in der plautinischen Komödie' in H.-G. Nesselrath and J. Platschek (eds.), *Menschen und Recht. Fallstudien zu Rechtsfragen und ihrer Bedeutung in der griechischen und römischen Komödie*. Tübingen: 75–110.

Schilling, R. (1979) 'Les dieux dans le théâtre de Plaute' in R. Schilling, *Rites, cultes, dieux de Rome*. Paris: 389–400.

Schlee, F. (1893) *Scholia Terentiana. Collegit et disposuit.* Leipzig.

Schmidt, E. (ed.) (2001) *L'Histoire littéraire immanente dans la poésie latine.* Geneva.

Schuhmann, E. (1976) 'Ehescheidungen in den Komödien des Plautus', *Zeitschrift der Savigny-Stiftung für Rechtsgeschichte (Romanistische Abteilung)* 93: 19–32.

Schuhmann, E. (1977) 'Der Typ der *uxor dotata* in den Komödien des Plautus', *Philologus* 121.1: 45–65.

Schulz, G.-M. (2007) *Einführung in die deutsche Komödie.* Darmstadt.

Schutter, K. H. E. (1952) *Quibus annis comoediae Plautinae primum actae sint quaeritur.* Groningen.

Schwind, A. (1901) *Über das Recht bei Terenz. Programm des k. neuen Gymnasiums zu Würzburg.* Würzburg.

Sear, F. (2006) *Roman Theatres. An Architectural Study.* Oxford.

Segal, E. (1968) *Roman Laughter: The Comedy of Plautus.* Cambridge, MA.

Segal, E. (2nd edn 1987) *Roman Laughter: The Comedy of Plautus.* Oxford.

Sens, A. (1991) 'Not I, but the Law: Juridical and Legislative Language in Aristophanes' *Ecclesiazusae*'. Diss. Harvard.

Shakespeare, W. (5th edn 2003) *Complete Works,* ed. D. Bevington. New York.

Sharrock, A. (1996) 'The Art of Deceit: *Pseudolus* and the Nature of Reading', *Classical Quarterly* 46: 152–74.

Sharrock, A. (2009) *Reading Roman Comedy: Poetics and Playfulness in Plautus and Terence.* Cambridge and New York.

Sharrock, A. (2013) 'Terence and Non-comic Intertexts' in A. Augoustakis and A. Traill (eds.) *A Companion to Terence.* Malden, MA: 52–68.

Sharrock, A. (2014) 'Terence as Reader and Innovator' in S. Papaioannou (ed.) *Reading Terence, Terence Reading.* Newcastle-upon-Tyne: 119–42.

Sheets, G. A. (1983) 'Plautus and Early Roman Tragedy', *Illinois Classical Studies* 8: 195–209.

Shipp, G. P. (1953) 'Greek in Plautus', *Wiener Studien* 66: 105–12.

Shipp, G. P. (1960) *P. Terenti Afri* Andria. Melbourne.

Shipp, G. P. (1973) 'A Classicist Looks at Molière', *Journal of the Australasian Universities Language and Literature Association* 39: 51–60.

Simonetti, A. (1989) 'Le fonti agiografiche di due drammi di Rosvita', *Studi Medievali* 30: 661–95.

Sinclair, P. (1995) *Tacitus the Sententious Historian: A Sociology of Rhetoric in Annales 1–6.* University Park, PA.

Skemer, D. C. et al. (2013) *Medieval and Renaissance Manuscripts in the Princeton University Library* (2 vols). Princeton, NJ.

Skiles, J. W. D. (1941) 'The Commercial Vocabulary of Early Latin as Shown in the Comedies of Plautus', *Classical Journal* 69: 519–36.

Skutsch, O. (1951) 'Review of Marmorale, *Naevius Poeta*', *Classical Review* N.S. 1: 174–7.

Skutsch, O. (1968) *Studia Enniana.* London.

Slater, N. W. (1985) *Plautus in Performance. The Theatre of the Mind.* Princeton, NJ.

Slater, N. W. (1990) '*Amphitruo, Bacchae,* and Metatheatre', *Lexis* 5–6: 101–25.

Slater, N. W. (1992) 'Two Republican Poets on Drama, Terence and Accius' in B. Zimmermann (ed.) *Antike Dramentheorien und ihre Rezeption.* Stuttgart: 85–103.

Slater, N. W. (2000) *Plautus in Performance: The Theatre of the Mind*, 2nd edn. Amsterdam.

Slater, N. W. (2001) 'Appearance, Reality, and the Spectre of Incest in Epidicus' in U. Auhagen (ed.) *Studien zu Plautus' Epidicus*. Tübingen: 191–203.

Slater, N. W. (2004) 'Slavery, Authority, and Loyalty: The Case of Syncerastus' in T. Baier (ed.) *Studien zu Plautus' Poenulus*. Tübingen: 291–8.

Slater, N. W. (2011) 'Plautus the Theologian' in A. P. M. H. Lardinois, J. H. Blok and M. G. M. van der Poel (eds.) *Sacred Words: Orality, Literacy, and Religion, Orality and Literacy in the Ancient World VIII*. Leiden and Boston.

Smith, B. R. (1988) *Ancient Scripts and Modern Experience on the English Stage, 1500–1700*. Princeton, NJ.

Smith, J. A. (2004) 'Buy Young, Sell Old: Playing the Market Economies of Phormio and Terence' in A. J. Boyle (ed.) *Rethinking Terence*. *Ramus* 33: 82–99.

Smith, K. W. (1890). *Archaisms of Terence Mentioned in the Commentary of Donatus*. Baltimore.

Snyder, J. (2004) '"Bring Me a Soldier's Garb and a Good Horse": Embedded Stage Directions in the Dramas of Hrotsvit of Gandersheim' in P. R. Brown, L. A. McMillin, and K. Wilson (eds.) *Hrotsvit of Gandersheim: Contexts, Identities, Affinities, and Performances*. Toronto, Buffalo, NY and London: 235–50.

Solomon, J. (2001) *The Ancient World in the Cinema*. New Haven and London.

Spaltenstein, F. (2008) *Commentaire des fragments dramatiques de Livius Andronicus*. Brussels.

Spranger, P. (2nd edn 1984) *Historische Untersuchungen zu den Sklavenfiguren des Plautus und Terenz*. Stuttgart.

Squintu, C. (2003) 'Note sulla lingua di Pomponio', *Annali della Facoltà di Lettere e Filosofia della Università di Cagliari* 21: 69–87.

Stace, C. (1968) 'The Slaves of Plautus', *Greece and Rome* 15: 64–77.

Staden, H. von (1996) 'Liminal Perils: Early Roman Receptions of Greek Medicine' in F. J. Ragep, S. P. Ragep and S. Livesey (eds.) *Tradition, Transmission, Transformation: Proceedings of Two Conferences on Pre-modern Science Held at the University of Oklahoma*. Amsterdam: 369–418.

Stadter, P. (1968) 'Special Effects in Plautine Dialogue: *Miles Gloriosus* III, ii', *Classical Philology* 63: 146–7.

Stambusky, A. A. (1977) 'Roman Comedy on Trial in the Republic: The Case of Censorship against Gnaeus Naevius the Playwright', *Educational Theatre Journal* 29.1: 29–36.

Stärk, E. (1989) *Die* Menaechmi *des Plautus und kein griechisches Original*. Tübingen.

Stärk, E. (1990) 'Plautus' *uxores dotatae* im Spannungsfeld literarischer Fiktion und gesellschaftlicher Realität' in J. Blänsdorf (ed.) *Theater und Gesellschaft*. Tübingen: 69–79.

Stärk, E. (2003) 'Camerarius' Plautus' in R. Kößling and G. Wartenberg (eds.) *Joachim Camerarius*. Tübingen: 235–48.

Stärk, E., and Vogt-Spira, G. (eds.) (2000) *Dramatische Wäldchen*. Hildesheim, Zurich and New York.

Starks, J. H., Jr. (2013) '*Opera in bello, in otio, in negotio*: Terence and Rome in the 160s BCE' in A. Augoustakis and A. Traill (eds.) *A Companion to Terence*. Malden, MA and Oxford: 132–55.

Stehle, E. (1984) 'Pseudolus as Socrates, Poet and Trickster' in D. F. Bright and E. S. Ramage (eds.) *Classical Texts and Their Traditions: Studies in Honor of C. R. Trahman*. Chico, CA: 239–51.

Stein, J. P. (1970) Morality in Plautus' *Trinummus*', *Classical Bulletin* 47: 7–13.

Steiner, D. (2001) 'Slander's Bite: *Nemean* 7. 102–5 and the Language of Invective', *Journal of Hellenic Studies* 120: 154–8.

Steiner, D. (2009) 'Diverting Demons: Ritual, Poetic Mockery and the Odysseus-Iros Encounter', *Classical Antiquity* 28: 71–100.

Stewart, R. (2012) *Plautus and Roman Slavery*. Malden, MA and Oxford.

Sticca, S. (1969) 'Hrotswitha's *Dulcitius* and its *spiritualis significatio*' in J. Bibauw (ed.) *Hommages à Marcel Renard*. Brussels: 700–6.

Sticca, S. (1971) 'Hrotswitha's *Abraham* and exegetical tradition' in *Fons Perennis – Saggi critici di Filologia Classica raccolti in onore del Prof. Vittorio D'Agostino*. Turin.

Sticca, S. (1979) 'Sacred Drama and Comic Realism in the Plays of Hrotswitha of Gandersheim', *Acta* 6: 117–43.

Sticca, S. (1985) 'Sacred Drama and Tragic Realism in Hrotswitha's *Paphnutius*' in H. Braet, J. Nowé and G. Tournoy (eds.) *The Theatre in the Middle Ages*. Leuven: 12–44.

Sticca, S. (1987) 'The Hagiographical and Monastic Context of Hrotswitha's Plays' in K. M. Wilson (ed.) *Hrotsvit of Gandersheim – Rara avis in Saxonia?* Ann Arbor: 1–34.

Stockert, W. (1982) 'Zur sprachlichen Charakterisierung der Personen in Plautus' *Aulularia*', *Gymnasium* 89: 4–14.

Stockert, W. (2004) 'Schworen auch Frauen bei Herkules? Bemerkungen zu *Cist.* 52 und anderen Plautus-Stellen' in R. Hartkamp and F. Hurka (eds.) *Studien zu Plautus' Cistellaria*. Tübingen: 363–9.

Stockert, W. (2008) 'Die Wiedererweckung eines Codex. Virtuelle Arbeit am Codex Ambrosianus des Plautus', *Rendiconti della Classe di Scienze morali, storiche e filologiche dell'Accademia dei Lincei* 19: 407–34.

Stockert, W. (2014) 'The Rebirth of a Codex: Virtual Work on the Ambrosian Palimpsest of Plautus' in M. Fontaine and A. Scafuro (eds.) *The Oxford Handbook of Greek and Roman Comedy*. Oxford and New York.

Strasburger, H. (1966). 'Der Scipionenkreis', *Hermes* 94: 60–72.

Strauss, B. S. (1993). *Fathers and Sons in Athens: Ideology and Society in the Era of the Peloponnesian War*. London: 67–71.

Strecker, K. (ed.) (2nd edn 1930) *Hrotsvithae Opera*. Leipzig.

Stroup, S. C. (2007) 'Greek Rhetoric Meets Rome: Expansion, Resistance, and Acculturation' in W. J. Dominik and J. Hall (eds.) *A Companion to Roman Rhetoric*. Malden, MA: 23–37.

Stroux, J. (1926) *Summum ius summa iniuria: Ein Kapitel aus der Geschichte der interpretatio iuris*. Leipzig.

Studemund, W. (1889) *Fabularum reliquiae Ambrosianae: codicis rescripti Ambrosiani apographum*. Berlin.

Stura, R. (1985) 'La I scena del *Pafnutius* di Rosvita', *Sandalion* 8–9: 269–84.

Styan, J. L. (1975) *Drama, Stage and Audience*. London.

Suerbaum, W. (ed.) (2002) *Handbuch der Lateinischen Literatur der Antike. Erster Band. Die Archaische Literatur. Von den Anfängen bis Sullas Tod. Die vorliterarische Periode und die Zeit von 240 bis 78 v. Chr.* Munich.

Sussman, L. (1994) *The Declamations of Calpurnius Flaccus: Text, Translation, and Commentary.* Leiden, New York and Cologne.

Syme, R. (1939) *The Roman Revolution.* Oxford.

Symes, C. (2003) 'The Performance and Preservation of Medieval Latin Comedy', *European Medieval Drama* 7: 29–50.

Szyrocki, M. (1979) *Die deutsche Literatur des Barock.* Stuttgart.

Taburet-Delahaye (ed.) (2004) *Paris 1400. Les arts sous Charles VI (exhibition catalogue Musée du Louvre).* Paris.

Taladoire, B. A. (1951) *Commentaires sur la mimique et l'expression corporelle du comédien romain.* Montpellier.

Taladoire, B. A. (1956) *Essai sur le comique de Plaute.* Monaco.

Talbot, R. (2004) 'Hrotsvit's Dramas: Is There a Roman in These Texts?' in P. R. Brown, L. A. McMillin, and K. Wilson (eds.) *Hrotsvit of Gandersheim: Contexts, Identities, Affinities, and Performances.* Toronto, Buffalo, NY and London: 147–59.

Tarrant, R. J. (1983) 'Plautus' in L. D. Reynolds (ed.) *Texts and Transmission. A Survey of the Latin Classics.* Oxford: 302–7. (Repr. with corr. 1986; repr. 1990.)

Telò, M. (2010) 'Embodying the Tragic Father(s): Autobiography and Intertextuality in Aristophanes', *Classical Antiquity* 29: 278–326.

Telò, M. (2014) 'On the Sauce: Cratinus, Cyclopean Poetics and the Roiling Sea of Epic', *Arethusa* 47: 303–20.

Telò, M. (2016) *Aristophanes and The Cloak of Comedy: Affect, Aesthetics, and the Canon.* Chicago and London.

Thalmann, W. (1996) 'Versions of Slavery in the *Captiui* of Plautus', *Ramus* 25.2: 112–45.

Thierfelder, A. (1939) 'Plautus und römische Tragödie', *Hermes* 74: 155–66.

Thumiger, C. (2009) 'On Ancient and Modern (Meta)theatres: Definitions and Practices', *Materiali e Discussioni* 63: 9–58.

Thür, G. (2006) 'Die Einheit des "Griechischen Rechts". Gedanken zum Prozessrecht in den griechischen Poleis', *Dike* 9: 23–62.

Tomulescu, C. S. (1971) 'La *mancipatio* nelle commedie di Plauto', *Labeo* 17: 284–302.

Tontini, A. (2002a) 'La tradizione manoscritta umanistica di Plauto' in C. Questa and R. Raffaelli (eds.) *Due seminari plautini. La tradizione del testo. I modelli.* Urbino: 57–88.

Tontini, A. (2002b) *Censimento critico dei manoscritti plautini I. Biblioteca Apostolica Vaticana.* Rome.

Tontini, A. (2010) *Censimento critico dei manoscritti plautini II. Le biblioteche italiane.* Rome.

Too, Y. L (ed.) (2001) *Education in Greek and Roman Antiquity.* Leiden.

Traill, A. (2001) 'Knocking on Knemon's door: Stagecraft and Symbolism in the *Dyskolos*', *Transactions and Proceedings of the American Philological Association* 131: 87–108.

Traill, A. (2008) *Women and the Comic Plot in Menander.* Cambridge.

Traill, A. (2013) '*Adelphoe*' in A. Augoustakis and A. Traill (eds.) *A Companion to Terence.* Malden, MA: 318–39.

Traina, A. (1974) Vortit barbare. *Le traduzioni poetiche da Livio Andronico a Cicerone.* Rome.

Tschernjaew, P. (1900) *Terentiana*. Kasan.

Usbome, R. (1981) *A Wodehouse Companion*. London.

Vardi, A. (1996) '*Diiudicatio Locorum*: Gellius and the History of a Mode in Ancient Comparative Criticism', *Classical Quarterly* 46: 492–514.

Vasaly, A. (1993) *Representations: Images of the World in Ciceronian Oratory*. Berkeley.

Vereecke, E. (1971) 'Titinius, Plaute et les origines de la *fabula togata*', *L'Antiquité classique* 40: 156–85.

Victor, B. (1989) 'The *alter exitus Andriae*', *Latomus* 48: 63–74.

Victor, B. (1996) 'A Problem of Method in the History of Texts and Its Implications for the Manuscript Tradition of Terence', *Revue d'histoire des textes* 26: 269–87.

Victor, B. (2003) 'Simultaneous Copying of Classical Texts, 800–1100: Techniques and their Consequences' in H. Spilling (ed.) *La collaboration dans la production de l'écrit médiéval*. Paris: 347–58.

Victor, B. (2013) 'History of the Text and Scholia' in A. Augoustakis and A. Traill (eds.) *A Companion to Terence*. Malden, MA: 343–62.

Victor, B. (2014) 'The Transmission of Terence' in M. Fontaine and A. C. Scafuro (eds.) *The Oxford Handbook of Greek and Roman Comedy*. Oxford and New York: 699–716.

Victor, B., and B. Quesnel (1999) 'The Colometric Evidence for the History of the Terence-Text in the Early Middle Ages', *Revue d'histoire des textes* 29: 141–68.

Villa, C. (1984) *La 'Lectura Terentii' – Volume primo: Da Ildemaro a Francesco Petrarca*. Padua.

Villa, C. (2007) 'Commenti medioevali alle commedie di Terenzio' in P. Kruschwitz, W.-W. Ehlers and F. Felgentreu (eds.), *Terentius Poeta*. Munich: 29–35.

Villa, C. (2015) 'Terence's Audience and Readership in the Ninth to Eleventh Centuries' in A. J. Turner and G. Torello-Hill (eds.) *Terence Between Late Antiquity and the Age of Printing*. Leiden.

Vincent, H. (2013) 'Language and Humour in Terence' in A. Augoustakis and A. Traill (eds.) *A Companion to Terence*. Malden, MA: 69–88.

Vogt-Spira, G. (1991) '*Stichus* oder Ein Parasit wird Hauptperson' in E. Lefèvre, E. Stärk, and G. Vogt-Spira (eds.) *Plautus barbarus: sechs Kapitel zur Originalität des Plautus*. Tübingen: 163–74.

Vogt-Spira, G. (ed.) (1993) *Beiträge zur mündlichen Kultur der Römer*. Tübingen.

Vogt-Spira, G. (1998) 'Plauto fra teatro greco e superamento della farsa italica. Proposta di un modello triadico', *Quaderni Urbinati di Cultura Classica* 58: 111–35.

Wahrmann, P. (1908) 'Vulgärlateinisches bei Terenz', *Wiener Studien* 30: 75–103.

Wailes, S. L. (2006) *Spirituality and Politics in the Works of Hrotsvit of Gandersheim*. Selinsgrove.

Wall, G. (1987) 'Hrotsvit and the German Humanists' in K. M. Wilson (ed.) *Hrotsvit of Gandersheim – Rara avis in Saxonia?* Ann Arbor: 253–61.

Wallace-Hadrill, A. (2008) *Rome's Cultural Revolution*. Cambridge.

Ward, I. (1995) *Law and Literature. Possibilities and Perspectives*. Cambridge.

Warmington, E. H. (1935) *Remains of Old Latin I. Ennius and Caecilius*. London and Cambridge, MA. (Rev. and repr. 1967; several repr.)

Warmington, E. H. (1936) *Remains of Old Latin II. Livius Andronicus, Naevius, Pacuvius and Accius*. London and Cambridge, MA. (Repr. 1957, with minor bibliographical additions; several repr.)

Warnecke, B. (1910) 'Gebärdenspiel und Mimik der römischen Schauspieler', *Neue Jahrbücher für das klassische Altertum* 25: 580–94.

Watkin, T. G. (1984) 'Hamlet and the Law of Homicide', *The Law Quarterly Review* 100: 282–310.

Watson, A. (1965) *The Law of Obligations in the Later Roman Republic*. Oxford.

Watson, A. (1967) *The Law of Persons in the Later Roman Republic*. Oxford.

Watson, A. (1968) *The Law of Property in the Later Roman Republic*. Oxford.

Watson, A. (1970) 'The Development of the Praetor's Edict', *The Journal of Roman Studies* 60: 105–119.

Watson, A. (1971) *Roman Private Law Around 200 BC*. Edinburgh.

Watson, W. (2012) *The Lost Second Book of Aristotle's Poetics*. Chicago.

Wattenbach, W. (1869) 'Peter Luder, der erste humanistische Lehrer in Heidelberg', *Zeitschrift für die Geschichte des Oberrheins* 22: 33–127.

Wattenbach, W. (1875) *Das Schriftwesen im Mittelalter*, 2nd edn. Leipzig.

Webster, T. B. L. (1974) *An Introduction to Menander*. Manchester.

Webster, T. B. L. et al. (1995) *Monuments Illustrating New Comedy* (2 vols). London.

Weitzmann, K. (1970) *Illustrations in Roll and Codex: A Study of the Origin and Method of Text Illustration*. Princeton, NJ.

Wessner, P. (ed.) (1902/1905/1908) *Aeli Donati quod fertur commentum Terenti. Accedunt Eugraphi commentum et scholia Bembina* (3 vols). Leipzig.

Wessner, P. (1963) *Donatus, Aeli Donati commentum Terenti* (2 vols). Stuttgart.

West, A. F. (1887) 'On a Patriotic Passage in the *Miles Gloriosus* of Plautus', *American Journal of Philology* 8: 15–33.

West, W. (2009) 'What's the Matter with Shakespeare? Physics, Identity, Playing', *South Central Review* 26: 103–26.

Wight Duff, J., and Duff, A. M. (1961) '*Dicta Catonis*' in *Minor Latin Poets*. London and Cambridge, MA: 583–639.

Wille, G. (1967) Musica Romana: *Die Bedeutung der Musik im Leben der Römer*. Amsterdam.

Williams, C. A. (1990) *Roman Homosexuality: Ideologies of Masculinity in Classical Antiquity*. Oxford.

Williams, G. (1958) 'Some Aspects of Roman Marriage Ceremonies and Ideals', *Journal of Roman Studies* 48: 16–29.

Wilson, K. M. (ed.) (1984) *Medieval Women Writers*. Manchester.

Wilson, K. M. (ed.) (1987) *Hrotsvit of Gandersheim – Rara avis in Saxonia?* Ann Arbor.

Wilson, K. M. (1988) *Hrotsvit of Gandersheim – The Ethics of Authorial Stance*. Leiden.

Wilson, K. M. (1989) *The Plays of Hrotsvit of Gandersheim*. New York.

Winterfeld, P. von (1902) *Hrotsvithae opera*. Berlin.

Wiseman, T. P. (1999) 'The Games of Flora' in B. Bergmann and C. Kondoleon (eds.) *The Art of Ancient Spectacle*. New Haven and London: 195–203.

Witt, P. (1971a) '*In ius vocare* bei Plautus und Terenz. Zur Interpretation römischen Rechts in klassischen Übersetzungen'. Diss. Freiburg.

Witt, P. (1971b) 'Die Übersetzung von Rechtsbegriffen dargestellt am Beispiel der "*in ius vocatio*" bei Plautus und Terenz', *Studia et Documenta Historiae et Iuris* 37: 217–60.

Wlosok, A. (1990) 'Vater und Vatervorstellungen in der römischen Kultur' in E. Heck and E. A. Schmidt (eds.) *Res humanae–res divinae*. Heidelberg: 35–83.

Wolff, H. J. (1952) 'Die Grundlagen des griechischen Eherechts', *Revue d'histoire du droit* 20: 1–29.

Woolf, V. (1926) 'The Movies and Reality', *New Republic* 47: 308–10.

Worman, N. (2008) *Abusive Mouths in Classical Athens*. Cambridge.

Wray, D. (2001) *Catullus and the Poetics of Roman Manhood*. Cambridge.

Wright, D. H. (1993) 'The Forgotten Early Romanesque Illustrations of Terence in Vat. Lat. 3305', *Zeitschrift für Kunstgeschichte* 56: 183–206.

Wright, D. H. (2006) *The Lost Late Antique Illustrated Terence*. Vatican City.

Wright, F. W. (1931) *Cicero and the Theater*. Northampton, MA.

Wright, J. (1974) *Dancing in Chains: The Stylistic Unity of the Comoedia Palliata*. Rome.

Wright, J. (1975) 'The Transformations of Pseudolus', *Transactions and Proceedings of the American Philological Association* 105: 403–16.

Wright, M. (2013) 'Comedy Versus Tragedy in *Wasps*' in E. Bakola, L. Prauscello, and M. Telò (eds.) *Greek Comedy and the Discourse of Genres*. Cambridge: 205–25.

Wüst, E. (1932) 'Mimos', *Paulys Realencyclopädie* 15: 1727–64.

Yardley, J. C. (1972) 'Comic Influences in Propertius', *Phoenix* 26: 134–9.

Young, N. H. (1987) '*Paidagogos*: The Social Setting of a Pauline Metaphor', *Novum Testamentum* 29: 150–76.

Zagagi, N. (1994) *The Comedy of Menander: Convention, Variation and Originality*. London.

Zetzel, J. E. G. (1972) 'Cicero and the Scipionic Circle', *Harvard Studies in Classical Philology* 76, 173–80.

Zeydel, E. H. (1944) 'Knowledge of Hrotsvitha's Works Prior to 1500', *Modern Language Notes* 59: 382–5.

Zeydel, E. H. (1945a) 'The Reception of Hrotsvitha by the German Humanists after 1493', *The Journal of English and Germanic Philology* 44: 239–49.

Zeydel, E. H. (1945b) 'Were Hrotsvitha's Dramas Performed during Her Lifetime?', *Speculum* 20: 443–56.

Zillinger, W. (1911) *Cicero und die altrömischen Dichter*. Würzburg.

Zimmermann, B. (1995) 'Pantomimische Elemente in den Komödien des Plautus' in L. Benz, E. Stärk, and G. Vogt-Spira (eds.) *Plautus und die Tradition des Stegreifspiels*. Tübingen: 193–204.

Zini, S. (1938) *Il linguaggio dei personaggi nelle commedie di Menandro*. Florence.

Ziolkowski, A. (1992) *The Temples of Mid-Republican Rome and Their Historical and Topographical Context*. Rome.

Ziolkowski, J. M. (2007) Nota Bene: *Reading Classics and Writing Melodies in the Early Middle Ages*. Turnhout.

Zironi, A. (2004) *Il monastero longobardo di Bobbio: crocevia di codici, uomini, culture*. Spoleto.

Zwierlein, O. (1990–2) *Zur Kritik und Exegese des Plautus* (4 vols). Stuttgart.

INDEX RERUM
Compiled by Astrid Khoo

INDEX LOCORUM
Compiled by Astrid Khoo

341–95, 127
Asinaria
10–12, 41, 49
119, 49
173–5, 204
255, 49
542–3, 204
616–17, 192
945, 196
Aulularia
167–9, 75
475–535, 75
Bacchae
641, 57
649–61, 51
692–711, 57
940, 51
948–52, 51
Bacchides
649–52, 188
925–70, 193
1088, 42
Captiui
888–9, 198
998–1000, 198
Casina
31–4, 54
64, 10
64–6, 54
320, 54
621–29a, 115
630–40, 117
641–7, 118
969–70, 54
Cistellaria
38–41, 207
42–5, 208
52, 208
631–3, 210
Epidicus
17, 193
65, 192
257–62, 53
371, 52
Eunuchus
383–7, 146
925–33, 147
1084–5, 148
Mercator
364–7, 90
379–84, 90
426–8, 91
429–47, 91

448–65, 91
466–8, 91
468–73, 91
830–63, 93
873–80, 93
910–12, 93
921–7, 93
931–47, 94
Miles Gloriosus
209–12, 71
210–16, 132
218–30, 73
901, 9
Mostellaria
1–80, 196
157–312, 196
Pseudolus
286–8, 244
290–1, 244
399–405, 138
401–4, 138
401–5, 1
508–15, 245
552, 138
562–70, 195
562–73a, 139
601–3, 139
720–1, 139
724–6, 139
924–30, 140
1017–22, 140
1076, 245
1243–4, 52
Rudens
85–8, 142
268, 143
332–3, 143
513, 144
523–4, 144
535–6, 41
593, 143
1212–17, 4
1235–48, 145
1249–52, 145
Stichus
155–273, 124
755–75, 102
Truculentus
209–55, 237
270–4, 237

Quintilian
Institutio Oratoria, 20

Cambridge Companions to . . .

AUTHORS

Tennessee Williams edited by Matthew C. Roudané

August Wilson edited by Christopher Bigsby

Mary Wollstonecraft edited by Claudia L. Johnson

Virginia Woolf edited by Susan Sellers (second edition)

Wordsworth edited by Stephen Gill

W. B. Yeats edited by Marjorie Howes and John Kelly

Xenophon edited by Michael A. Flower

Zola edited by Brian Nelson

TOPICS

The Actress edited by Maggie B. Gale and John Stokes

The African American Novel edited by Maryemma Graham

The African American Slave Narrative edited by Audrey A. Fisch

Theatre History by David Wiles and Christine Dymkowski

African American Theatre by Harvey Young

Allegory edited by Rita Copeland and Peter Struck

American Crime Fiction edited by Catherine Ross Nickerson

American Gothic edited by Jeffrey Andrew Weinstock

American Literature of the 1930s edited by William Solomon

American Modernism edited by Walter Kalaidjian

American Poetry Since 1945 edited by Jennifer Ashton

American Realism and Naturalism edited by Donald Pizer

American Travel Writing edited by Alfred Bendixen and Judith Hamera

American Women Playwrights edited by Brenda Murphy

Ancient Rhetoric edited by Erik Gunderson

Arthurian Legend edited by Elizabeth Archibald and Ad Putter

Australian Literature edited by Elizabeth Webby

The Beats edited by Stephen Belletto

British Black and Asian Literature (1945–2010) edited by Deirdre Osborne

British Literature of the French Revolution edited by Pamela Clemit

British Romanticism edited by Stuart Curran (second edition)

British Romantic Poetry edited by James Chandler and Maureen N. McLane

British Theatre, 1730–1830, edited by Jane Moody and Daniel O'Quinn

Canadian Literature edited by Eva-Marie Kröller (second edition)

Children's Literature edited by M. O. Grenby and Andrea Immel

The Classic Russian Novel edited by Malcolm V. Jones and Robin Feuer Miller

Contemporary Irish Poetry edited by Matthew Campbell

Creative Writing edited by David Morley and Philip Neilsen

Crime Fiction edited by Martin Priestman

Dracula edited by Roger Luckhurst

Early Modern Women's Writing edited by Laura Lunger Knoppers

The Eighteenth-Century Novel edited by John Richetti

Eighteenth-Century Poetry edited by John Sitter

Emma edited by Peter Sabor

English Literature, 1500–1600 edited by Arthur F. Kinney

English Literature, 1650–1740 edited by Steven N. Zwicker

English Literature, 1740–1830 edited by Thomas Keymer and Jon Mee

English Literature, 1830–1914 edited by Joanne Shattock

English Melodrama edited by Carolyn Williams

English Novelists edited by Adrian Poole

English Poetry, Donne to Marvell edited by Thomas N. Corns

English Poets edited by Claude Rawson

English Renaissance Drama, second edition edited by A. R. Braunmuller and Michael Hattaway

English Renaissance Tragedy edited by Emma Smith and Garrett A. Sullivan Jr.

English Restoration Theatre edited by Deborah C. Payne Fisk